The
ILLUSTRATED
ENCYCLOPEDIA OF
AUTOMOBILES

The
ILLUSTRATED
ENCYCLOPEDIA OF
AUTOMOBILES

Edited by David Burgess Wise

CHARTWELL
BOOKS, INC.

Title page illustration: 1936 Triumph Dolomite roadster

A QUARTO BOOK

Published by Chartwell Books Inc.,
A Division of Book Sales Inc.,
110 Enterprise Avenue, Secausus,
New Jersey 07094

ISBN 0-89009-772-0
First Published in 1979
Reprinted 1988
Reprinted 1989
Reprinted 1991

This book was designed and produced by Quarto
Publishing Limited, 6 Blundell St, London N7
Designers: Roger Daniels, Marian Sanders,
Nick Clark
Editor: Richard Crossman

Phototypeset in England by Filmtype Services
Limited, Scarborough
Colour separation by Sakai Lithocolour Company
Limited, Hong Kong
Printed by Leefung-Asco Printers Limited,
Hong Kong

1936 Auburn 852 supercharged cabriolet

Contents

Introduction

OVER THE PAST CENTURY, the motor car industry has probably attracted more visionaries and charlatans, optimists and rogues than any other commercial activity. Today, the industry is essential to the commercial well-being of many industrialized countries—indeed, major companies can dispose of budgets far greater than those of many perfectly healthy nations.

But for every one of the few great motor companies active today, hundreds of marques

1975 Ferrari 308 GTB coupé

have run their course. For every Henry Ford and William Morris, there has been a legion of hopefuls who have formed a company, marketed perhaps a few dozen cars and then vanished into limbo, perhaps springing up with a new factory or a new marque name at another point in motoring history, their failures running a necessary counterpoint to the great success stories.

The promise of riches has attracted men of amazingly diverse backgrounds to found motor companies—hat-makers, pork-butchers,

mouth-organ salesmen and voting-machine manufacturers are some of the less likely candidates.

Out of this rich field, this book covers the most significant and entertaining marques sold—or intended to be sold—for use on the road. Cars built specifically for racing are omitted, as are specialized off-road vehicles like dune-buggies.

My team of contributors—each man an acknowledged specialist in his field—has made this book possible, bringing a breadth and depth

of knowledge unrivalled in the field of motoring history.

Illustrations have been carefully chosen to show—wherever possible—vehicles in their contemporary setting. Many rare cars are illustrated for the first time in print.

Having owned a Clyno—one of the great lost causes of the British motor industry—for almost 20 entertaining years, I have long realized that the companies which have failed often made better products than those which survived.

This book is, in part, a tribute to the many cheerful optimists whose products, of whatever merit, have remained up to now largely unrecorded. For my part, I have found the hunt for these obscure marques an exciting one; it has involved many hours of research, both in my own collection of automotive literature and in the unparalleled library of the Veteran Car Club of Great Britain, which, as befits the world's first old car club, has a rich collection of source material from all over the world. My visits there have garnered hundreds of obscure marques,

recorded in the pages of magazines—*Automotor Journal, Horseless Age, La Vie Automobile*—as long-dead as the cars they chronicle.

This book, I hope, will bring their histories to life again.

David Burgess Wise

DAVID BURGESS WISE 1979

Prehistory

MAN'S SEARCH FOR some form of motive power to replace the horse goes back over 300 years; clockwork, wind power and elaborate clockwork gearing were all tried before the power of steam became tractable enough to be used to drive a vehicle. Not that it was initially too successful: the oldest surviving self-propelled vehicle, Cugnot's 1770 *fardier*, owes its preservation to the fact that on its trial runs it ran amok and knocked down a wall! Put into store, it survived the French Revolution, was acquired by the Conservatoire des Arts et Métiers in Paris in 1799, and has been a major exhibit there ever since.

It was followed by a number of even less practical designs from optimistic French, English and American engineers, and it was not until 1801 that the first successful road carriage appeared. This was the work of the Cornish mining engineer Richard Trevithick and led to his London Carriage of 1803, which made a number of successful runs in the capital before it was dismantled to power a hoop rolling mill. Trevithick lacked the staying power to perfect either this or his other great invention, the railway carriage. He was succeeded by a lunatic gaggle of inventors who proposed machines driven by articulated legs, tiny railway engines running inside a drum like squirrels, compressed air, gunpowder and 'vanes, or fliers, like the sails of a windmill'.

Then, between 1820 and 1840, came a golden age of steam, with skilled engineers devising and operating steam carriages of advanced and ingenious design; men like Gurney, Hancock and Macerone all produced designs which were practicable, capable of achieving quite lengthy journeys and operating with a relatively high degree of reliability. Walter Hancock, a better mechanic than businessman, operated his steam coaches on regular scheduled services in London in the 1830s, but was rooked by his associates, and eventually called it a day after 12 years of experiment had brought him little more than unpaid debts and the hostility of those with vested interests, who, fearing that the steam carriage would prove a threat to the thousands whose livelihood depended on the horse, promoted swingeing tolls on the turnpike roads; an 1831 Parliamentary Commission, though largely favourable to the steam carriage, failed to prevent such injustices, and the final blow to the builders of steam carriages came with the advent of the railway age. Railway engines, running on smooth, level rails, had none of the problems experienced by steam carriages running on uneven, badly maintained roads, and this newer form of locomotion soon eclipsed the steam carriage, even though legislation restricting the speed and operation of steam carriages was not enacted until 1863, when it was decreed that all 'road locomotives' should have a man with a red flag walking ahead.

It was the advent of the bicycle in the 1860s which revived touring by road.

Some of the successes and failures of the prehistory of motoring: James's steam carriage (**1**) was one of the better road carriages of the early 1830s, while Dr Church's Birmingham Road Carriage (**2**) was never completed in this baroque style. The 1770 Cugnot (**3**) is the world's oldest self-propelled vehicle to survive, though it is possible that it never ran. Johann Hautsch of Nürnberg devised this curious clockwork carriage (**4**) in the seventeenth century, while the Hancock steam drag of c.1830 (**5**) represents the high point of early British steam carriages.

Radiators

The earliest cars, which, if they even had radiators to cool their engines, had them slung at the rear of the chassis or some other anatomically improbable position, lacked a certain amount of character. When, however, Mercedes developed the honeycomb radiator into a recognizable marque symbol, cars began to acquire personality. And, despite the hiding of the radiator behind a grille, it is still front end treatment that gives a car its character.

When Ettore Bugatti originally adopted a shape for the radiators of his cars (1), he apparently followed the outline of a chairback designed by his furniture-designer father, Carlo. The 1949 Bristol 400 (2) took its functional radiator openings from the BMW with which it was closely connected. Typical of its era, the 1913 Unic radiator (3) reflects honest craftsmanship, while the flamboyant frontal treatment of the 1959 Ford Fairlane Skyliner (4) is a product of a time when the stylist was king. On the other hand, the 1936 Railton (5) cloaked its American origins behind a very English radiator.

6

7

NH 3610

8

JTR 867

10

Like an Art Deco fencer's mask, the radiator grill of the 1936 Triumph Dolomite (**6**) is one of the more extreme designs of a decade when styling began to influence sales. But the crude front end of the 1921 Carden cyclecar (**7**) is purely a dummy, aping larger cars. The 'dollar grin' of the 1947 Buick Eight (**8**) celebrates an age of promise (of increased sales!) after World War Two; over 20 years on, a new era of restraint is marked by the bland front end of the 1970 Monteverdi 375L (**9**). The Rolls-Royce radiator (**10**) has remained true to its original design concept for over 75 years.

1880 to 1900

THE INTERNAL COMBUSTION engine appeared early in the history of the motor vehicle, but took over three-quarters of a century to be perfected to the level where it could be used in a vehicle capable of running on the roads—the 1805 powered cart of the Swiss Isaac de Rivaz was no more than an elaborate toy, only capable of crawling from one side of a room to another, and the 1863 car built in Paris by J-J. Etienne Lenoir took three hours to cover six miles. It was not until the mid-1880s that the first successful petrol cars appeared, developed independently by two German engineers, Gottlieb Daimler and Karl Benz.

Of the two vehicles, that of Benz was incontestably superior, for it was designed as an entity, using the new technology of the cycle industry, while Daimler's carriage was no more than an adapted horse vehicle. Benz went into limited production of his three-wheeled carriages (described in his catalogue as 'an agreeable vehicle, as well as a mountain-climbing apparatus') in 1888; Daimler was more interested in selling his engines as a universal power source.

Neither man found immediate success, but neither had the great geniuses of the steam vehicle who were their contemporaries. The Bollée family of Le Mans built some truly advanced steam carriages between 1873 and the mid-1880s, vehicles which pioneered independent front suspension, while blacksmith's son Léon Serpollet conceived the 'flash boiler' for instantaneous generation of steam and held the first driving licence issued in Paris. And while the Comte De Dion and his engineers Bouton and Trépardoux built some excellent steam vehicles during the 1880s and early 1890s, they were to achieve their greatest fame as manufacturers of light petrol vehicles, from 1895 on.

The crucial event in the story of the motor car was the 1889 Paris World Exhibition, for it was there that the French engineers Panhard and Levassor saw the Daimler 'Steelwheeler' car powered by the Daimler vee-twin engine. Levassor's lady friend, an astute widow named Louise Sarazin, held the French rights to the Daimler engine in succession to her late husband, and Panhard and Levassor began manufacturing these power units in 1890. They could, however, see no future for the motor car, and so granted the right to use Daimler engines in self-propelled vehicles to the ironmongery and cycle firm of Peugeot (who had just decided not to go ahead with the planned production of Serpollet steamers).

It was in France, too, that Benz enjoyed his first limited success, for his Paris agent, Emile Roger, managed to sell one or two Benz cars in Paris (and, coincidentally, garaged his first Benz in Panhard and Levassor's workshop). But it was not until his first four-wheeler, the 1893 Viktoria, that Benz began series production.

Peugeot were already established as motor manufacturers by that date, for in 1891 they had

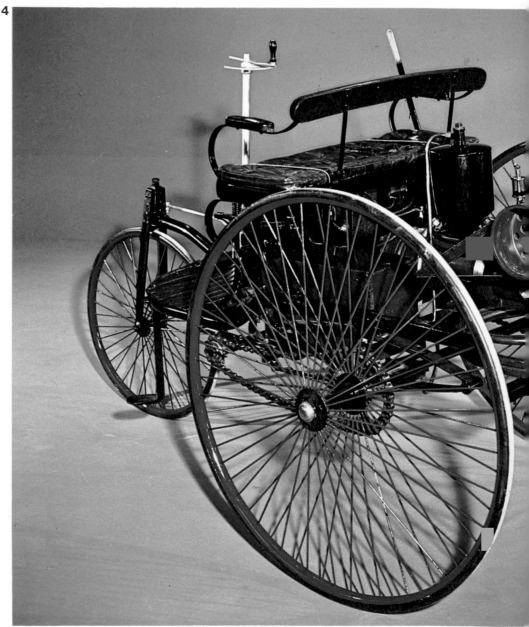

2

3

5

6

De Dion, Bouton and Trépardoux built this neat little steam car in 1885 (**1**); the lordly Bollée *Mancelle* steam carriage of 1873 (**2**) was a precursor of petrol car design, with the engine under a frontal bonnet driving the rear wheels, and independent front suspension. Indeed, the 1899 Fiat 3½hp (**3**) and its contemporaries were far more primitive in concept. The first petrol car conceived as an entity was the 1885–86 Benz three-wheeler (**4**). Serpollet's 1888 three-wheeler (**5**) used his high-speed flash boiler. The 1895 tricar (**6**) utilized the power unit from a Leyland steam lawnmower.

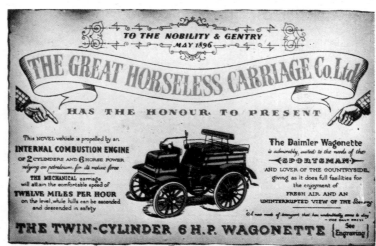

TO THE NOBILITY & GENTRY
MAY 1896

THE GREAT HORSELESS CARRIAGE Co. Ltd.

HAS THE HONOUR TO PRESENT

This NOVEL vehicle is propelled by an
INTERNAL COMBUSTION ENGINE
OF 2 CYLINDERS AND 6 HORSE POWER
relying on petroleum for its motive force
THE MECHANICAL carriage
will attain the comfortable speed of
TWELVE MILES PER HOUR
on the level, while hills can be ascended
and descended in safety

The Daimler Wagonette
is admirably suited to the needs of the
SPORTSMAN
AND LOVER OF THE COUNTRYSIDE,
giving as it does full facilities for
the enjoyment of
FRESH AIR AND AN
UNINTERRUPTED VIEW OF THE Scenery

THE TWIN-CYLINDER 6 H.P. WAGONETTE {See Engraving}

Couched in glowing Victorian prose, this advertisement (**left**) is, in fact, a pastiche conceived for Daimler's 40th anniversary in 1936! Built by a firm once famed for sewing machines and cycles, the 1898 Hurtu (**below**) (whose name did nothing to recommend the marque to timorous English motorists!) is a typical horseless carriage.

actually sold 5 cars, boosting production to a dizzy 29 the following year.

The success of the Peugeot cars inspired Panhard and Levassor to reconsider their early opinion of the horseless carriage, and, after building a couple of crude dogcarts with the engine at the rear, Levassor devised the famous *Système Panhard*, with the engine at the front driving the rear wheels via a sliding pinion gearbox inspired by the mechanism of a lathe, a layout which, however '*brusque et brutale*' its inventor thought it, has been used on the majority of motor cars built since.

In America, the motor car was evolving along different lines from Europe and, in January-February 1891, the New World's first petrol vehicle, a friction-driven three-wheeler built by John W. Lambert of Ohio City, made its first tentative runs. In 1895, America's first motor manufacturing company was founded by the Duryea brothers, Charles and Frank (whose prototype dated from 1893); the following year they exported a couple of vehicles to Britain. However, anti-motoring prejudice in that country was running high, and there was little encouragement for motor vehicles, either home-grown or imported (though the company promotions of the so-called 'father of the British motor industry', H. J. Lawson, succeeded in parting a good many credulous investors from a large amount of cash).

Lawson had influential friends and in 1896 succeeded in getting the ridiculous requirement for motor cars to be preceded by a man on foot (a legacy of the old Locomotives on Highways Acts of 1865 and 1878) to be repealed, and held a commemorative run to Brighton on November 14, 1896 to celebrate the raising of the speed limit to 12 mph. Some of the participating machines, though, covered the distance by train and were cosmetically muddied after they had been unloaded, and the first machine home, a Duryea, was not one of the marques under Lawson's aegis (he had expensively purchased a great number of motor car patents in a forlorn effort to monopolize the nascent British car industry).

Demand for motor cars was growing steadily during the latter part of the 1890s, and by now the Benz had become the world's most popular car, with the 2000th production vehicle being delivered in 1899. Motoring was still the sport of a few rich eccentrics, however, and many people had never seen a car.

It was to remedy this defect that, in 1900, the Automobile Club of Great Britain and Ireland held its famous 1000 Miles Trial, which took in most of the major cities of England and Scotland. A total of 65 cars, many English Daimler and MMC models built by Lawson's empire, set out from Hyde Park Corner, London, in April; the major part of this entry finished the run without major mishap, proving that the motor car had at last become a reliable—or relatively so — touring vehicle after a century's gestation.

Badges and mascots

Radiator badges were the heraldry of the early motor car. Starting as simply makers' plates fixed to the radiator, badges quickly developed into a minor art form. Some badges, indeed, were masterpieces of the enameller's craft; the Invicta was endowed with a polychromatic butterfly badge delicate enough for jewellery. As for mascots, they began as good luck charms like teddy bears tied to the radiator, but soon the techniques of statuary were being employed to produce mascots of real beauty. The Hispano stork and the Rolls-Royce 'Spirit of Ecstasy' became marque symbols, though owners also commissioned individual mascots, like the Wagnerian soprano whose Métallurgique was endowed with a sterling silver Seigfried clad in chain mail.

(1) The Calometer temperature gauge, a popular 1920s accessory, on a 1927 Morris-Cowley. (2) Packard's emblem – 'a pelican in her piety'. (3) A one-off mascot on a Cadillac V-8. (4) The Hotchkiss badge recalls the firm's origin. (5) A 1914 Star 15.9hp. (6) Jaguar's mascot, derived from a sculpture by motoring artist Gordon Crosby. (7) The Armstrong Siddeley sphinx.

1901 to 1914

THE NEW CENTURY was spectacularly ushered in by 'the car of the day after tomorrow', the Mercedes, designed by Daimler's engineer, Wilhelm Maybach. The contract to produce the first batch of 30 cars had been signed within a month of Gottlieb Daimler's death in March 1900. They had been ordered by the wealthy Austro-Hungarian Consul at Nice, Emil Jellinek, who insisted that they be christened after his daughter Mercédès, a name which found such favour with the wealthy car-buying public that all German Daimler cars were soon known as 'Mercedes', too.

The advanced design of the Mercedes, which combined in one harmonious whole elements such as the honeycomb radiator, pressed steel chassis and gear-lever moving in a gate rather than a quadrant, 'set the fashion to the world' and soon many high-priced cars were copying its layout; even comparatively small cars like the Peugeot were built on Mercedes lines.

These cars did not, however, represent the 'popular motoring' of the early 1900s; this was the province of single-cylinder runabouts like the De Dion and the Renault—again, these well-built cars were widely imitated—and, in America, first by light and temperamental steam cars like the Locomobile and then by gas buggies, of which the most famous was the Curved-Dash Oldsmobile.

But the development of the motor industry in America was being hampered—as it had in Britain a few years earlier—by the shadow of monopoly. A patent lawyer named George Baldwin Selden had drawn up a 'master patent' for the motor vehicle in 1879, published it in 1895 and claimed that all gasoline-driven vehicles were infringements of that patent. His claims were eventually given commercial teeth by the Association of Licenced Automobile Manufacturers, established to administer the Selden Patent in 1902, to which most major American car firms were persuaded to belong.

However, Henry Ford, who founded his Ford Motor Company in June 1903, decided to stand against the ALAM, who began proceedings against him in 1904. After lengthy litigation, which resulted in the ALAM building a car to Selden's 1879 design and Ford building a car with an engine based on that of the 1863 Lenoir, Ford won the day in 1911—not long before the Selden Patent would have expired anyway—but the victory established him as a folk hero.

Ford's great achievement, after five years' work, was to introduce in October 1908 the immortal Model T, which became so popular that he was forced to introduce the car industry's first moving production line in order to build enough cars to satisfy demand. His 'Universal Car' changed the face of motoring; over 16·5 million were built before production ended in 1927, truly 'putting the world on wheels' and transforming the face of society.

A 1901 Curved-Dash Oldsmobile

Though the Edwardian era saw motoring become more popular, on the other hand it also saw the finest and most elegant cars of all time, built to a standard of craftsmanship which could never be repeated. After World War One, many of the great marques faded away in a genteel decline: Delaunay-Belleville, 'the Car Magnificent', the favourite marque of the Tsar of Russia and one of the very best of the French cars of the pre-1914 era, became just a *petit bourgeois* in the 1920s.

Napier, the British company which popularized the six-cylinder engine, enjoyed perhaps even greater acclaim than its rival, Rolls-Royce, while its sales were controlled by that bombastic character Selwyn Francis Edge; when Napier gave him a £160,000 'golden handshake' after a dispute over policy in 1912, however, the company's fortunes seemed to leave with him. Edge, having agreed to leave the motor industry for seven years, became a successful Sussex pig-farmer; Napier built very few cars after the war, concentrating instead on its aero engines.

Such ostentatious machinery relied for its existence on a pool of highly skilled, lowly paid craftsmen with a surpassing pride in their work; against the onslaught of cheap machines produced in America by unskilled labour using production techniques which eliminated most of the human factor, the big luxury cars stood little chance. They represented only a tiny fraction of the potential market for the motor vehicle and, even if their production had not been decimated by the drying up of the car market as a result of the war, they would inevitably have died out as a result of the social changes in the post-war world.

Europe, indeed, experienced an outburst of popular motoring in the 1910–14 period which owed nothing to American concepts of mass production; instead, it grew out of the motor-cycle industry, whose engines, single-cylinder or vee-twin, offered lightness and power. Optimistic enthusiasts installed these engines in chassis of often suicidal crudeness, with cart-type centre-pivot steering in many cases, as well as other unmechanical devices such as wire cables coiled round the steering column instead of a conventional steering box and drag link, belt and pulley transmission and tandem-seat layouts with the driver in the second row of the stalls. These crude devices, known as cyclecars, flourished especially in England and France; attempts to transplant them to America failed because they were simply unsuited to the very different motoring environment there.

The worst of the cyclecars were short-lived, however; the designs of the late Edwardian period which promised perhaps the most for the future were the new light cars like the Morris-Oxford, the Standard and the Hillman, all 'big cars in miniature' of around 1100cc, with four cylinders and built on proper engineering lines. These admirable machines were to be the pattern for the popular family cars of the 1920s.

One of the great names of motoring in the Edwardian era was Napier: this 1907 60hp six-cylinder (**1**) has been constructed as a replica of the car on which S. F. Edge averaged over 60mph for 24 hours to inaugurate the Brooklands race track. This 1903 Fiat 16/20hp (**2**) was shown at the Agricultural Hall Exhibition in London: its Grosvenor tonneau body is English-built. The popular impression that motor cars were 'engines of death' is illustrated by this 1904 cartoon (**3**); a more idealized concept of motoring is shown in the 1908 Argyll advertisement (**4**).

Another, if humbler, 'immortal' of the period was the twin-cylinder Renault AX (**5**), for this chassis was used on the taxis which ferried troops to the Battle of the Marne and saved Paris in 1914. Some of the ignorant fear of motoring may have been caused by the strange garb affected by early motorists, like these sinister anti-dust masks (**6**), from 1907.

5

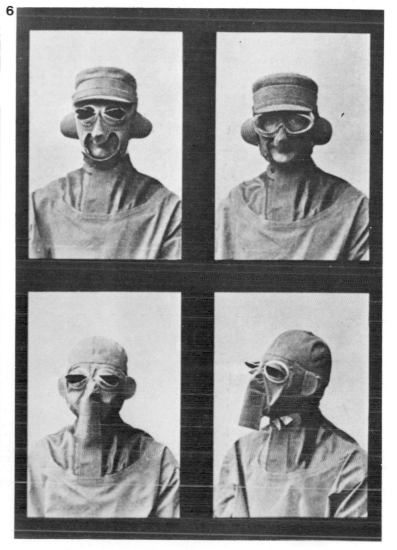

'The ARGYLL"

OUR LEADING LINES FOR 1908
4 16 H.P (Model de Luxe) £375 & 40 H.P £650.
STAND N° 36.

4

6

Wheels

The wheel is one of man's most fundamental inventions, as it has no parallel in nature. The earliest cars rolled into the world on wire wheels derived from cycle practice, or on wooden wheels developed from those used on carriages. These basic types have been followed by many different patterns of wheel: only the roundness has remained constant.

The wire wheels of the 1898 Hurtu (**1**) are typical of those used on many early light cars. Their spindly construction makes them unsuitable for high speed. One of the odder inventions of Edwardian times was this hub-mounted tyre pump (**2**), here fitted to a wooden-wheeled Gladiator. Wooden artillery wheels (**3**) were common on most pre-World War One European cars, and were still being used in America throughout the 1920s. Bugatti's famous spoked aluminium wheels (**4**) were developed for racing use. Cheap to make and light in weight, they could be changed complete with brake drum.

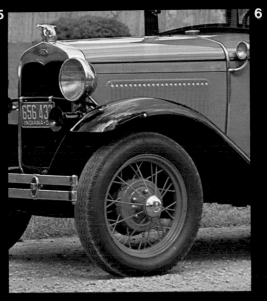

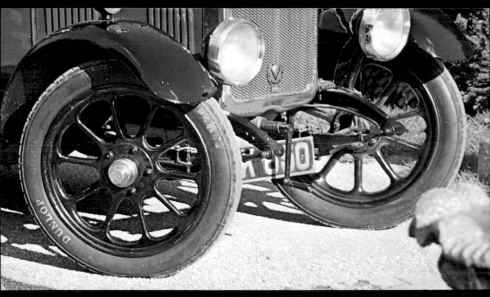

The spokes on the wheels of this Model A Ford (5) are electrically welded to the rim, not located by adjustable nipples as on conventional wire wheels. The wheels on this 1923 Calcott (6) are pressed steel simulating wooden artillery wheels, a popular fashion on British light cars of the 1920s. Wheeltrims have ranged from vulgar (7) to the elegantly practical (8), the latter being used to protect a wire-spoked wheel and make it easier to clean. Styling of wheels is nothing new – compare the Bugatti of the 1930s (9) with the Alfasud (10)

1915 to 1930

THE TECHNOLOGY of the motor age revolutionized the way that World War One was fought. The internal combustion engine gave new mobility to the infantry who, before hostilities in Europe came to a standstill in the trenches, could be rushed to reinforce weak points in the front line (most notably when the French General Gallieni sent 6000 reinforcements to repel Von Kluck's attack on Paris in 1914); it also provided motorcycles for despatch riders, permitted H. G. Wells's forecast of 'land ironclads' to be fulfilled in the angular shapes of the first armoured cars and tanks and, perhaps most significantly, gave warfare a new dimension by taking it into the air.

One way and another, most of those who fought in the war were given an insight into the utility of the motor vehicle, and when peace came many returning soldiers were only too anxious to spend their demobilization pay on a car of their own. The result was a boom such as the motor industry had never known. Especially in Britain and France, the established manufacturers found themselves contending for the favours of the car-buying public with a whole new sub-industry of optimists who, working from inadequate back-street premises, assembled light cars and cyclecars from proprietary components in the hope that they might make their fortunes. Most found only commercial failure, like the British firm who, with the bailiffs mounting a 24-hour watch outside the doors of their London factory, broke an exit through the unguarded rear wall, loaded as much of their machinery as possible on to the finished chassis and drove off to seek new (but unforthcoming) fortune in the Midlands.

If the American industry had already developed to the extent where success in popular car sales would inevitably go to the established big battalions (even Chrysler, founded in 1924, sprang from the established Maxwell-Briscoe grouping), there was still room in Europe for new mass-producers. Most spectacular of these was André Citroën, a former gear manufacturer, who, with the aim of bringing Ford-style mass-production to France, enjoyed an immediate success with his 10 hp launched in 1919. However, the rise of Citroën spelt doom for the dozens of optimistic assemblers who clustered most thickly in the north-western suburbs of Paris.

The boom collapsed in 1920–21, speeded on its way by strikes, hold-ups, shortages, loss of stock market confidence in the car industry, restrictions on hire-purchase sales, costlier raw materials, and the introduction of a swingeing horsepower tax in Britain.

Only the fittest survived: Ford, whose example was followed by a number of American and European makers, cut prices in order to boost falling sales (though he compensated for

The Blackhawk of 1929 was a short-lived attempt by Stutz to build a lower-priced car.

the loss on the cars by compelling the dealers to take $40-worth of spare parts on which there had been no reduction) and gained a brief respite, though even he had to close down for some months to clear unsold stocks. It was not until 1922 that the motor industry was back on course and a second generation of post-war popular cars began to emerge, most notably the Austin Seven.

Many of the cars of the 1920s profited from the technology of the aero engines developed during the war, most notably the overhead camshaft Hispano-Suiza V-8. Wolseley built this engine under licence and used an overhead camshaft on their post-war cars, but it was not until after the 1927 takeover by Morris that this Wolseley design realized its full potential, especially in MG sports cars.

Hispano-Suiza put their aero engine expertise to full account in the 1919 32cv of 6·6 litres, a splendid machine with servo-assisted four-wheel brakes and delightful handling characteristics, whose overall conception was several years ahead of any of its rivals.

Bentley, who had built rotary aero engines during the war, brought out an in-line four with an overhead camshaft in 1919 (though it was not put into production until 1921); this 3-litre was to become one of the immortal sporting cars.

Many leading manufacturers adopted the overhead camshaft layout during this period, but Rolls-Royce, whose aero engines had used this layout, stuck resolutely to side valves on their cars until the advent of the 20 in 1922; this had pushrod ohv, a configuration followed on the 1925 Phantom which was to supplant the Silver Ghost, which had side valves till the end.

Oddly enough, apart from honourable exceptions like the Hispano, it was the cheaper cars which pioneered the use of brakes on all four wheels, one of the most positive advances in car equipment in the early 1920s. Possibly it was felt

that luxury cars would be handled by professional drivers, who would be less likely to indulge in the kind of reckless driving that would require powerful brakes! Moreover, some American popular car makers, appalled at the cost of retooling their cars to accept brakes on the front wheels, actually campaigned against their introduction on the grounds that they were dangerous.

As the decade wore on, more features designed to make motoring more comfortable and safer became commonplace—windscreen wipers, electric starters, safety glass (first standardized on the 1928 Model A Ford), all-steel coachwork, saloon bodies, low-pressure tyres, cellulose paint and chromium plating all became available on popular cars. Styling and the annual model change became an accepted part of the selling of motor cars, bringing with them huge tooling costs which could only be borne by the biggest companies. Many old-established firms just could not keep up and were swept away by the onslaught of the depression in 1929.

Typical of American quality car design in the late 1920s is this 1929 Packard 640 six-cylinder phaeton (**1**). The Hispano H6B (**2**) was one of the great designs of the 1920s. A 1925 aluminium-bodied sports version of the 10.8hp Riley (**3**), normally known as the 'Redwinger'. Two of the most famous popular cars of the era were the Morris-Cowley 'Bullnose' (**4**) and the Model T Ford (**5**). Their very different designs reflect popular taste in Britain and America.

Body styles

Since the dawn of motoring, a bewildering lexicon of words has been used to describe automobile bodywork, many descending from horse-carriage practice, others coined by car manufacturers. Some became standard practice, like the use of the word 'torpedo' to describe an open four-seater touring car; others, like the similar 'gunboat roadster', vanished into limbo. Fashion, too, has played its part in determining names: in America, 'touring' was superseded by 'phaeton' in an attempt to standardize coachwork nomenclature. And, of course, there are the national differences in usage – a 'saloon' is a closed car in England, a public bar in America, where the car becomes a 'sedan'. Henry Ford devised the names 'Tudor' (two-door) and 'Fordor' (four-door) to describe the Model T sedan; after more than 50 years these names are still in use internally in the Ford Motor Company. Today, there is little variation in body styles – most cars are saloons, though 'hatchback' and 'notchback' are specialized subdivisions of the type. Legislation has all but killed off the convertible, save for specialist sports cars, and the word coupé – once used for two-seaters with a folding hood that was normally kept erected – now means any sporting saloon that is lower than average!

The pane of glass ahead of the folding rear roof section of this Fiat Tipo 4 (1) of c. 1914 vintage identifies it as a three-quarter landaulette; a landaulette has the rear roof folding from immediately behind the door pillar. A sedan (2) of the traditional pattern is mounted on this 1931 Chevrolet. Chrysler, however, created a new name when they applied wood to the metal panelling of their Town and Country range: this 1949 two-seater (3) emphasizes the 'sporty-formal' ethos of that model. Designed to eliminate body rattles, the Weymann saloon (4), here mounted on a Peugeot, had lightweight wood framing with a leathercloth covering.

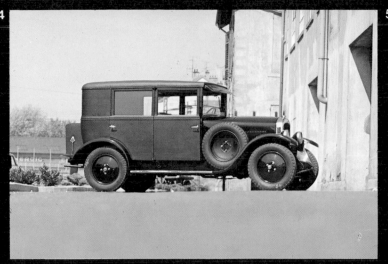

Two-seaters of a semi-sporting nature, like this 1938 Citroën 7cv (**5**), are often known as roadsters. The 1975 Lotus Elite (**6**) and the wicker-bodied Bugatti (**7**) show how specialist manufacturers are free of the styling constraints imposed on mass-producers. John Tjaarda styled the 1937 Lincoln-Zephyr V12 (**8**), one of the pioneering aerodynamic cars.

1931 to 1945

PERHAPS THE MOST significant pointer to the changing status of the motor car can be gauged from the fact that, at the beginning of the 1920s, the majority of cars were open tourers; by 1931, saloon bodies were fitted to 90 per cent of the cars produced. A contemporary editorial sums up the more functional, utilitarian role of the typical 1930s motor car: 'Today there is no room for the cheap and shoddy, or for immature design. The day has passed when unmechanical contraptions can claim the serious attention of the public... manufacturers no longer expect the public to carry out the testing of new productions for them'.

However, the public was also calling for smaller engines, more suited to the economic climate of the times. To cope with the weight of saloon bodywork and all the popular accessories, these little engines had to be geared low. Consequently they revved high and hard, and their bores wore alarmingly. The days when durability was a feature taken for granted on all but the shoddiest of cars seemed long past.

The design of cars now began to change radically as well. The demand for more capacious bodywork on small chassis led to the engine being pushed forward over the front axle. The radiator became a functional unit concealed behind a decorative grille which became more elaborate and exaggerated as the decade wore on until on some cars it resembled a chromium-plated waterfall or fencer's mask.

During the 1930–35 period, there was a vogue for streamlining which found its full flower in devices like the Chrysler Airflow, the Singer Airstream and the Fitzmaurice-bodied Ford V-8. Even on more staid cars, the angularity of line that had characterized the models of the late 1920s gave way to more flowing contours. Though most cars still retained running boards, the separate side valances were eliminated by bringing the lower door edges down to give a lower, more bulbous look, accentuated by the adoption of wings with side panels, often blended into the radiator and bonnet.

The swept tails of the new-style coachwork now usually concealed some kind of luggage accommodation as well, a feature sadly lacking on most 1920s models, which usually boasted a luggage grid and nothing more.

'Well-rounded and commodious', the cars of the 1930s offered greater comfort and convenience than their forebears. The stylist, however, had taken over from the engineer and the craftsman bodybuilder and, as a result, the new cars were often deficient in handling as the main masses were now concentrated at either end, like a dumb-bell. New suspension systems—especially independent front springing—also brought their handling problems, and some cars had to be fitted with bumpers incorporating a harmonic damping device to prevent them from

Henry Ford's 'last mechanical triumph' was his 1932 V8, seen here with phaeton bodywork.

shimmying right off the road on their supersoft springing.

Not that all was gloom and despondency in the 1930s: some manufacturers produced excellent cars during the decade. Morris and Austin continued to build soundly engineered small cars (though Herbert Austin was distinctly upset when his designers insisted on moving the radiator behind a dummy grille, as he felt that it was a kind of heresy), while the last two new models in which Henry Ford was personally involved, the 8hp Model 19Y and the V-8 (both appeared in 1932), were instantly and deservedly successful.

And, of course, there was the famous front-wheel-drive Citroën, which made its debut in 1934. Though its development costs had all but bankrupted André Citroën—who was forced to sell out to Michelin—this was one of the truly great cars.

A lesser, though no less significant, happening was the metamorphosis of the SS marque from a merely meretricious styling exercise into a modestly priced, excellently finished, well-equipped saloon—the first Jaguar.

The same year that the SS Jaguar was launched—1936—Dr Porsche built the prototype Volkswagens, the 'Strength through Joy' cars sponsored by the Nazi Party and intended to be sold to the German public at £50–£55 to keep them from buying imported models—the first of over 20 million of this most popular car of all time. Few Volkswagens, however, were built before the war (though the design was readily adapted for military purposes).

In many ways the 1930s were a watershed—they saw the last of the big luxury cars from makers such as Hispano-Suiza, Duesenberg and Minerva, as well as the end of many small, independent manufacturers and coachbuilders (victims of the swing to mass-produced cars with pressed-steel bodies). The motor industry had reached the point where it had become vital to the economic well-being of the major industrialized countries. Now it was to prove just as vital in providing weapons of war.

In Britain, five of the largest motor manufacturers set up 'shadow factories' in the late 1930s which could be used to produce aero engine parts in the event of war—they were to produce many thousands of aero engines and complete aircraft during the hostilities. Ford joined the five soon after the outbreak of war and was soon building Rolls-Royce Merlin engines on a moving production line in Manchester, while in the USA Ford mass-production expertise was given its greatest test in manufacturing Liberator bombers on a gigantic production line at Willow Run, Michigan.

From the ubiquitous Jeep, through staff cars, trucks, tanks and powerboats to the biggest bomber aircraft, the motor industry played a crucial role in World War Two. Re-adapting to peacetime production was, however, to prove almost as big a test of the industry's abilities.

The 1930s saw a rapid evolution in body design, from traditional shapes like the Zagato-bodied 2.3-litre Alfa Romeo (6) – which nevertheless influenced the styling of many lesser breeds of sports car – to the avant-garde Cord (1) designed by Ray Dietrich and deemed worthy to be shown in New York's Museum of Modern Art. The Type 57 Bugatti (2) has saloon coachwork far more restrained than some of Jean Bugatti's creations on this chassis, while patrician marques like Packard (3) and Rolls-Royce (4) made some concessions to fashion while retaining their innate dignity. So, too, at a more humble level, did the Austin Seven (5).

Engines

Sophisticated and powerful though the engine of a modern car may be, nevertheless it operates on principles first successfully applied over a century ago. The first car engines were simple affairs, usually with one or two cylinders, though since the turn of the century multi-cylinder power units have predominated, normally with four, six or eight cylinders, though non-conformist configurations with three, five, twelve or sixteen cylinders have been tried. Rotary engines have also made sporadic appearances, too. But the main changes in the power unit have been technical improvements: the replacement of the atmospherically operated automatic inlet valve by mechanical inlet valves in the early 1900s, the adoption of monobloc cylinder castings instead of cylinders cast singly or in pairs, the general use of detachable cylinder heads, and the change from side to overhead valves. Today, the overhead camshaft, once the premise of high-powered sports and racing cars, is a common feature of family cars, thanks to the invention of the cogged driving belt, which replaces the complex gear trains of earlier designs and is cheap to install and silent in operation.

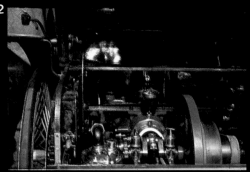

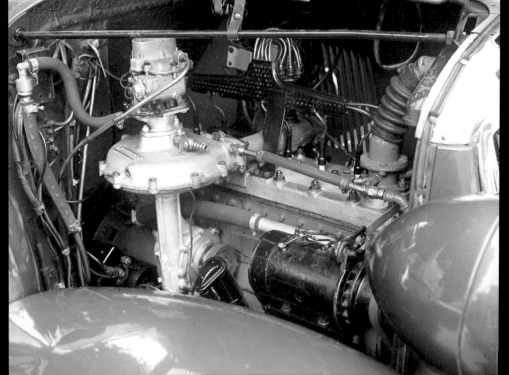

Engines developed rapidly: compare the 1908 Hutton (**1**) with its electrolytically-deposited copper water-jackets and dual ignition (the twin carburettors are an anachronism) with the primitive 1900 Benz (**2**) which has an exposed, grease-lubricated crankshaft like its 1885 forebear. The Jaguar XK120 engine, with its twin ohc (**3**) was a classic 1940s design capable of great development, while the 1934 Graham straight-eight, with its centrifugal supercharger (**4**), was a more short-lived way of obtaining increased performance.

5

6

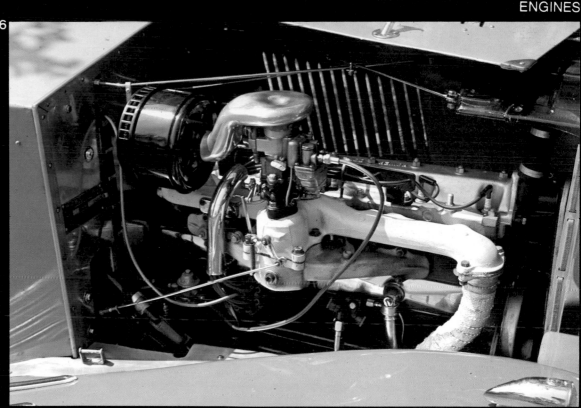

7

8

9

A more modestly priced dohc power unit was the Lotus Twin Cam, here seen in a 1971 Lotus Super Seven (5), while the Oldsmobile six in this 1936 Railton (6) was a simple side-valve unit relying on good power/weight ratio for performance. In more Wagnerian vein is the 1908 Grand Prix Benz unit (7) which promised plenty of 'sturm und drang' with pushrod ohv and drainpipe exhaust. Measure it against the tiny sv engine of the 1936 Morris Eight (8) and the powerful American Ford V-8 of the 1970 AC Cobra (9).

1946 to 1960

BESET BY POST-WAR materials shortages and government interference, motor manufacturers nevertheless soon returned to production, inevitably with slightly modernized pre-war models in most cases though some manufacturers did actually manage to produce all-new cars, notably Armstrong-Siddeley in Britain.

Despite shortages of fuel and tyres, there was a vast demand in Britain for cars, but the government forced manufacturers to export half their output, even though these cars had been designed mostly for the very insular requirements of pre-war Britain. To curb the speculators who had been buying new cars and selling them at an inflated profit, purchasers had to sign a 'covenant' guaranteeing that they would not resell for initially one year, later two.

There was much talk of technical developments arising from wartime projects, but devices such as automatic transmission were only generally adopted in America, and reports that hydraulic suspension, or springing by rubber or torsion bars, were about to be adopted on British cars proved to be more than a little premature. Indeed, some makers seemed unready to come to terms with the future, as one report noted: 'Since wind resistance is an important factor in brake performance, streamlining may lead to braking difficulties, as was shown in experiments carried out in France'.

European manufacturers had also the problem of rebuilding war-shattered plant; in France, the industry had lost machine tools, equipment and labour to Germany and suffered much bomb damage. A shortage of sheet steel and tyres also helped to keep production to about a sixth of the 1938 level in 1946–48, though some recovery was apparent by 1949 when the first post-war Salon de l'Automobile was held in Paris and production had risen to about four times the 1938 monthly level.

Other manufacturing countries had similar difficulties, those of Germany being compounded by the division of the country and the replacement of the Reichsmark (£1 = RM24) by the Deutschmark (£1 = DM11.75), an effective devaluation of around 100 per cent. Nevertheless, the country's most prolific manufacturer, Volkswagen, continued to make progress despite opinions from British experts—and from Henry Ford II—that the VW was too noisy and uncomfortable to be competitive. And though the BMW factory had ended up in the Russian Zone, the first—and only—'war reparation' design to come out of Germany became the BMW-based Bristol 400.

That was only one of the classic sports cars to appear after the war; more famous still was the Jaguar XK 120, with a twin-cam engine reportedly developed during wartime firewatching duty. It made its debut in 1948 along with two, more utilitarian, designs — the Morris Minor and the Citroën 2cv.

A classic post-war sports car, the Jaguar XK 120

Built by the most traditionally minded motor company of all, the Morgan 4/4 (**1**) of the 1950s was little changed in appearance from its ancestor of the mid-1930s. Like all Morgans built since 1910, it had sliding-pillar independent front suspension. The advanced and complex Citroën DS (**2**) supplanted the immortal *traction avant* in 1955. The 1946 Lincoln (**3**) shows how even quality post-war American cars adopted extreme styling for their radiator grilles.

The 1950s saw the motor industry entering a period of traumatic change. Those brave attempts by independent companies like Kaiser and Crosley to carve a foothold in the American market against the corporate giants of the Big Three—Ford, GM and Chrysler—came to nothing, and the most respected of the old-established independents like Packard, Nash and Studebaker were in decline and would soon vanish, either by attrition or by merger. The American car industry had become stereotyped. Its typical product—generally superlatively hideous—had either a six-cylinder engine (often of fairly antique provenance) or a V-8, and boasted excruciatingly named accessories and components like Hi-Fyre or Firedome engines, HydraMatic or UltraMatic transmissions, even FlightSweep styling. This was the era of the exaggerated tailfin and the grinning chrome grille, and the 'performance car' that could only go fast in a straight line. The announcement of small 'compact' cars in 1959 brought, as well as the Ford Falcon and Chrysler Valiant of conventional design, the unorthodox rear-engined Chevrolet Corvair whose unAmerican handling activities ensured that the US industry went straight from nadir to Nader.

There were mergers in Europe, too, like the shotgun wedding between Austin and Morris, a union born out of strife which would lay the seeds of trouble for that British Motor Corporation's ultimate descendant, British Leyland. But, at that time, their products—small family cars—were just what the public wanted. Fuel economy became even more significant after the 1956 Suez War, when petrol was rationed, and the event created a new race of cyclecars, only now they called them 'bubblecars', and many of them came from German firms grounded in the aircraft industry like Heinkel and Messerschmitt.

In the main, these bubblecars were beastly machines whose only merit lay in their economy; their death-knell was tolled by the advent of an epochal design by Alec Issigonis—the 1959 Mini Minor, which gave a new word to the popular vocabulary and heralded a new race of decently engineered small cars with sports car-like handling. Its layout of front-wheel drive and transverse engine was to set the pattern for the coming 20 years and more.

But the 1950s had their glamour cars, too: Britain produced the big Healeys, the Triumph TRs and the first MG to abandon the perpendicular lines of the 1930s, the slippery profiled MGA, even available with a temperamental twin-cam engine; Italy built big, powerful sports cars like the Ferrari America and Super America; France, which had taxed the *grand'routiers* like Delahaye out of existence, introduced the avant-garde Citroën DS; and Germany, once again *persona grata* after its post-war isolation, brought out the unique and distinctive Mercedes 300SL coupé, with its stylish, if not entirely practical, gull-wing doors.

One of the most sought-after sports cars of the 1950s, both then and now, was the 300SL Mercedes (**4**), with its unorthodox gull-wing doors. Cadillac set the fashion for fins in the 1950s: by the 1954 models (**5**) this vulgar trend had reached its peak.

Dashboards

Though the very first cars were devoid of instruments, by 1899 enterprising accessory manufacturers had begun to offer speedometers: 'motor timepieces' soon followed, along with voltmeters, gradient meters, odometers and petrol gauges. The first 'idiot lights' appeared in 1908 in the shape of a patent oil indicating device which glowed white when there was sufficient oil, red when the level was too low. The invention of the dipstick soon rendered this 'Lubrimeter' superfluous. By 1910, there was even an instrument to measure petrol consumption. Some of these ingenious devices, too far ahead of their time to be commercially viable, have been 're-invented' and, in modern form, appear on some of the latest cars.

Compare the traditional approach of the instrument panel on the 1959 R-type Continental Bentley (1) with the modern approach (2) of the 1979 Saab 900 saloon, with padded steering wheel for safety. The 1951 Porsche 356 Speedster's instrument panel (3) reflects the character both of the car and of the era in which it was built.

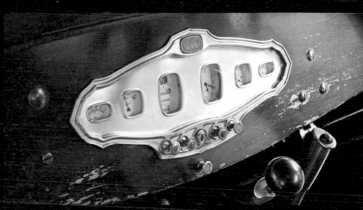

The complex instrumentation of the 1929 Mercedes 38/250 SS (**4**) is appropriate to a high-performance supercharged car, yet its racing ancestor, the 1908 Benz (**5**) has a bare minimum of instruments, most importantly the drip indicator which shows that oil is going to the engine bearings in sufficient quantity. The 1979 Panther J72 (**6**) represents an attempt to blend traditional dash layout with modern safety requirements. In late-1920s American cars, like the 1929 Stutz Blackhawk (**7**), the hand of the stylist appeared to be set against easy interpretation of the instrument readings, a defect shared by the 1958 Chevrolet dash (**8**). The 1979 Aston Martin (**9**), however, represents a return to classicism (though its stablemate, the Lagonda, made extensive use of digital readouts).

1961 to 1979

THE VERY SUCCESS of the American compact cars brought new problems to their makers in the early 1960s. For, instead of capturing a whole new market, they encroached into established sales areas, and American dealers began the decade with upwards of a million unsold 'full-size' cars on their hands. Not only that, but the compacts also hit exports of European cars to the USA, and many dealers just stopped selling foreign cars. The only two makes which really managed to hang on to their American sales were Volkswagen and Renault; interestingly enough, in the late 1970s these two firms were to remain most heavily committed to the USA market, VW opening a plant in Pennsylvania in 1978 which gave them third place in sales in a remarkably short space of time, and Renault tying up a sales deal with AMC (which VW had pushed into fourth place).

America was making its presence felt in Europe, too. Ford of America took control of its English affiliate for a record sum of money, and Chrysler began a step-by-step takeover of the Rootes Group with governmental blessing, the task of sorting out the company's financial problems having been judged beyond the powers of mere government officials.

Mergers were the order of the day, for Standard-Triumph joined up with the Leyland Group in 1960, and the same year Jaguar and Daimler combined. Jaguar-Daimler was itself absorbed by the BMC in 1966, while Leyland took over Rover (which had acquired Alvis). Finally, Leyland and the BMC merged early in 1967, after much hard bargaining (though as a prime reason for the merger had been political rather than commercial, the huge and complex group faced extraordinary difficulties right from the start). The result was British Leyland, which later became BL. The problems it inherited included model lines which competed with one another, thus reducing group efficiency, and the fact that their most outstanding popular model, the Mini, was being produced at a loss—indeed, it was to reach its twentieth birthday before it showed a profit.

German manufacturers were uniting, too: Mercedes had already linked with Auto-Union-DKW, and Volkswagen and NSU also became part of the same grouping during the decade, while the old two-stroke DKW was succeeded by a revived Audi marque. In France, Citroën took over Panhard, one of the industry's oldest marques, in 1965, but ended car production there two years later.

There were many reasons why Europe's manufacturers were joining together—as well as direct mergers, the decade also saw the start of programmes of cooperation jointly to develop components such as engines for the benefit of several makers, who perhaps could

Named after Enzo Ferrari's dead son, the Dino brought Ferrari-style motoring to a wider circle. This is a 1972 model.

not stand the ever-increasing cost of developing new power plants on their own.

And there was a new source of competition as well, for the Japanese were beginning to send their cars to Europe in small numbers. It was the start of an onslaught which was to become such a torrent that, in little over a decade, manufacturers from some European countries—especially Britain—had to strike a 'gentleman's agreement' with the Japanese manufacturers that the latter would hold down exports to a 'prudent' level, since it was felt that their products were placing too much stress on the indigenous manufacturers. Just how good the Japanese products had become was to be emphasized in 1979, when BL announced that it was to build a Honda model as a stopgap.

A crucial turning point in the history of the automobile came with the Arab embargo on oil exports following the Arab-Israeli War of late 1973. Though supplies were gradually restored to something approaching normality, the system had suffered a shock from which it would perhaps never fully recover, for the era of cheap oil was over.

For America, the experience was particularly traumatic, for the public had become accustomed to unlimited use of big, 'gas-guzzling' cars. Shortages in petrol supply gave Americans a chilling reminder of what life without cars could mean. The eventual result, once panic measures like the virtually overnight switching of production from large models to compacts had subsided, was an almost nationwide blanket speed limit of 55 mph and government insistence on the production of more fuel-efficient cars for the 1980s. There was even, following post-revolutionary cuts in petrol supplies from Iran, the introduction in 1979 of rationing in California, where three-car families were common. This represented a dramatic turnabout in future model policies, and involved vast expenditure. For Ford in 1978, the outlay needed to develop new, more economical cars for the early 1980s fuel consumption limits was greater than the total sum of investment over the company's previous 75 years. For General Motors, it represented an annual bill of $3·2 billion from 1975 on to revise its model range, an increase of 135 per cent on previous years. And for Chrysler, finance had to be found by selling off most of its foreign holdings, notably Chrysler Europe, acquired by Peugeot-Citroën.

In fact, Europe was now the focus of the world car industry. The European manufacturers had overtaken the output of American firms in the late 1960s, and, by the end of the 1970s, were building about 20 per cent more. Long conditioned by higher petrol prices and fiscal restrictions on engine size, Europe had developed smaller, more efficient cars.

In less than a century, the motor car has totally changed society, and become vital to the economic life of many nations. But what does the next century hold for the motor car?

A group of cars which epitomizes the face of motoring in the 1970s. The 1978 Chrysler (now Talbot) Sunbeam (1) is typical of the modern breed of small hatchback cars. Porsche's 928 (2) is one of the ultimate sporting cars, while the Range Rover (3), with its go-anywhere four-wheel drive, is a practical workhorse as well as a status symbol leisure vehicle. Oldsmobile's Omega (4) is one of their 1980 'X-cars', designed to incorporate more 'European' characteristics than earlier American models. Aston Martin's 1979 V8 (5) and the Bertone-styled Fiat X1/9 (6) show opposite ends of the sporting scale.

Art and the automobile

Since automobile art first arose in Paris at the turn of the century, mainly taking the form of caricatures and allegorical posters, it has embraced many forms and schools of art, being particularly evident in the contemporary Pop Art and Photo Realism movements in the USA. Popular items for collectors of 'automobiliana' include posters, sculptures, mascots, ornaments, glassware, even 'polychrome sculptural masses' formed from car components fed into a hydraulic press.

An 1898 poster (**1**) by Belgian racing cyclist Georges Gaudy, this was one of the first posters to advertise a motor race; the car is probably a Benz, and the driver, Old Father Time. More serious artists are painting car subjects today than at any time in the past, and nowhere is this more evident than in the Pop Art and Photo Realism movements; this example of the Photo Realism school is *Wrecking Yard III* (**2**) by the American Don Eddy. (**3**) A squared-up drawing and water-colour by Geo Ham (Georges Hamel), a famous French illustrator most active in the 1930s and 1940s.

4

GRAND-PRIX Dieppe
de l'A·C·F·1907
NAZZARO
sur F·I·A·T·

5

6

7

8

The Michelin Tyre Company's building in Fulham
Road, London, was the work of architect François
Espinasse. Dating from 1910, it is decorated with
coloured tiles depicting contemporary racing
successes; this scene (**4**) is of the 1907 French
Grand Prix. The Hispano-Suiza catalogue (**5**) was
illustrated by René Vincent, a leading motoring
artist from before World War One to the 1930s.
(**6**) Motoring ornaments are widely collected items
of 'automobiliana'; this is a porcelain Art Deco
example. *Automobilia* (**7**) is a 1960s Pop Art
composition by Peter Philips. (**8**) A 3.5-litre BMW
decorated by American sculptor Alexander
Calder, inventor of the 'mobile'.

The evolution of mass production

THE PHENOMENAL GROWTH of the car industry would not have been possible without the introduction of mass-production methods. It is generally thought that mass production was invented by Henry Ford, and introduced in his Highland Park, Detroit, factory in 1913. Yet Ford was only applying the lessons of over 100 years' progress in large-scale manufacturing.

As far back as 1798, Eli Whitney, given a rush order for 10,000 muskets by the United States Government, built machines that duplicated gun parts so accurately that they could quickly be assembled into finished muskets without hand fitting. He demonstrated this by scrambling the parts of 10 muskets and then assembling a musket from parts taken at random.

Contemporaneously, Marc Brunel (father of Isambard Kingdom Brunel) was supplying the British Navy with rigging blocks produced on automatic machines at Portsmouth Dockyard—'machinery so perfect appears to act with the happy certainty of instinct, and the foresight of reason combined', wrote one visitor. The machines were produced in association with Henry Maudslay, whose standardization of screw threads and accurate lathes and planing machinery brought the standards of precision that would make mass production truly feasible.

Another vital feature of mass production, the moving conveyor belt, had appeared in 1783 in an automatic grain mill devised by Oliver Evans, who later built one of America's first

Today, mass-production car factories are making increasing use of computers to control production processes, as in the Fiat works (**below**). However, there has also been a revival in 'traditional' hand production methods for limited-production cars, as in the Panther factory (**bottom and below right**).

steam carriages. Evans's mill used belt, bucket and screw conveyors, and could be operated by only two men, one pouring grain into a hopper at one end of the mill, the other putting flour into sacks at the other end.

The technique was carried a stage further in the Chicago meat factories from the 1860s, when the meat packers adopted the method of hanging pigs from an overhead conveyor, so that all the operations from slaughtering to jointing were carried out by a series of workers, each carrying out a single operation on the carcass. It took just four minutes from catching a pig in the stock pen until its carcass arrived in the cooling room to be turned into hams, sausages and pork chops. Output was more than doubled.

The idea that output could be multiplied by dividing work had been given impetus by Elihu Root, who joined Samuel Colt's armament factory in 1849 and boosted production of Colt Six Shooters by dividing and simplifying the steps in their manufacture and inventing new machinery to fill the gaps in the sequence.

Frederick Winslow Taylor, a contemporary of Henry Ford, was the original 'efficiency expert', who devised time and motion studies based on the theory that production was fastest when worker efficiency was highest.

Such ideas were more likely to find a receptive audience in America, where skilled labour was scarce and expensive, and American metal-working machinery had become the best in the world by the dawn of the motor age. The Lanchester brothers in Britain were thought remarkable for insisting on rigorous interchangeability of parts; in America, interchangeability was a necessity, though men like Henry Leland, schooled in the high standards of

the arms industry, did bring it to a high pitch.

But all the early American mass-production motor manufacturers worked in similar ways: chassis were erected where they stood, parts being brought to them. It worked well enough in industries like the manufacture of sewing machines or typewriters (where America also excelled) but was clumsy where cars were being made in great numbers.

Progress towards more effective production was rapid. White, for example, had an overhead craneway running the full 600ft length of their Cleveland plant, feeding the buildings branching off on either side (though a similar scheme had been used by J. G. Bodmer in England in 1839). Chalmers-Detroit had a chassis assembly room by 1909 in which frames were ranged in two parallel rows, with overhead tracks bringing in motors and other heavy parts at the appropriate moment.

But mass production as we know it today resulted from Henry Ford's combining all the best features of these pioneering ventures in his newly completed Highland Park plant in Detroit in 1913. Ford constantly experimented with gravity slides, conveyors, and the placement of men and tools for maximum efficiency. Breaking each manufacturing operation into its constituent parts, he multiplied the production of anything from flywheel magnetos to complete engines, often by a factor of four.

Department by department he established sub-assembly lines until, in his own words, 'everything in the plant moved'.

The ultimate step was the creation of the moving final assembly line, where the chassis itself moved, starting without wheels at one end of the line and emerging at the other end as a completed car, driven off under its own power.

One of the first Ford components to be mass produced was the flywheel magneto (**right**). This remarkable series of photographs was taken in the Ford Highland Park plant in 1915 to illustrate the first-ever book on mass-production of motor vehicles. Carefully synchronized feeder lines supplied components to the final assembly line, and the mass-production thus made possible enabled prices to be cut and, simultaneously, the minimum daily wage at Ford to be raised to $5. Model Ts came forth in ever-increasing numbers at ever-docreasing prices until a car was leaving the production lines every 10 seconds, at prices as low as $260 (around £50), and an annual production figure of 2,000,000 was achieved.

How cars are made

THE BUILDING OF A CAR begins with the manufacture of its individual components—up to 15,000 of them. Some of the steel components are forged or cast, but most are made from sheet steel pressed into hundreds of different shapes by huge presses capable of exerting pressures of up to 2000 tons per square inch.

The pressings are carried by fork-lift trucks to the pre-production line workshops, and in separate processes the building of the superstructure and underbody begins. First, small sub-assemblies are put together by spot welding. Then these are fitted into jigs, which hold the pieces in place as they are joined by automatic welders; from these the major superstructure and underbody emerge complete. Modern body

weld units can complete up to 1000 welds simultaneously with absolute accuracy.

Now the doors, plus bonnet and boot lid—all arriving ready-made by overhead monorail conveyor—are fitted. Major panel joints have been gas-welded to give greater strength and flexibility when the car is under stress from cornering or rough roads. Finally the bodywork is prepared for painting; each body shell will be finished in plain or metallic colours to an individual order tapped out by teleprinter.

The car is degreased by high-pressure sprays and phosphated to provide a good anti-corrosion and paint adhesion surface; the body is then stoved. Now the car is totally immersed in an electrocoat primer paint process. This

provides a paint film on all areas of the body, including those box sections which are inaccessible under normal processes. The surplus paint is rinsed off and the body is stoved in a gas-fired oven. All outer joints are sealed before the body passes through electrostatic paint spraying equipment. This automatically applies a grey primer sealing coat, which is then stoved. A protective material is applied to the underbody. Each body is wet sanded, rinsed with de-mineralized water and finally dried. The car is then ready to receive three top coats of enamel paint which is applied manually and stoved in a steam-heated oven.

The cars now move on to the trim shop; each has already acquired an individual identity, and

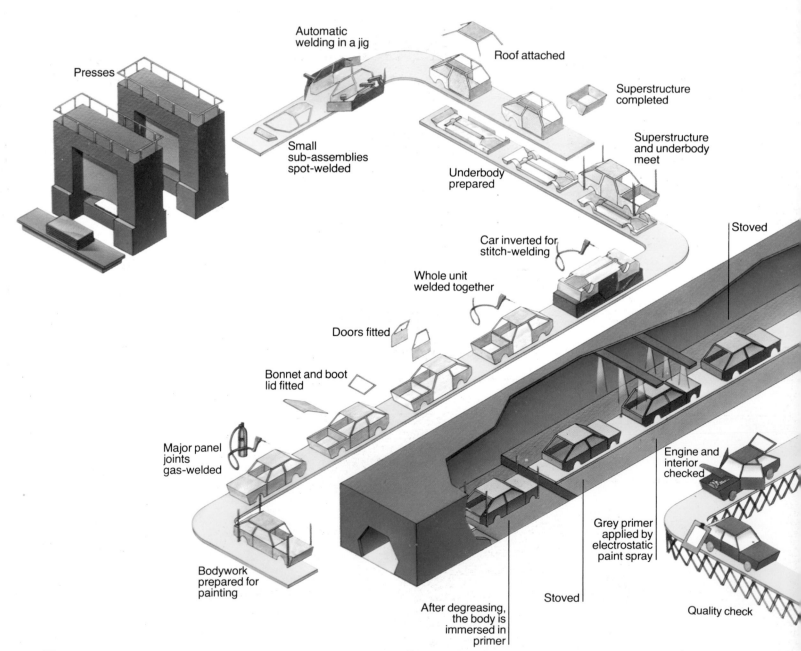

Presses

Automatic welding in a jig

Small sub-assemblies spot-welded

Roof attached

Superstructure completed

Underbody prepared

Superstructure and underbody meet

Car inverted for stitch-welding

Whole unit welded together

Stoved

Doors fitted

Bonnet and boot lid fitted

Major panel joints gas-welded

Bodywork prepared for painting

After degreasing, the body is immersed in primer

Stoved

Grey primer applied by electrostatic paint spray

Engine and interior checked

Quality check

details of its trim specification are transferred from a teleprinter to a card on the bonnet. The build-up starts as components stockpiled beside the production line are fitted—the grille, electrical wiring, lights, head lining, door windows, windscreen.

Then come the under-bonnet parts like horns, battery, brake fluid reservoirs, steering column, radiator and pipes, as well as the instrument panel. Nowadays, much of the complex wiring loom has been eliminated by printed circuits and plug-in modules.

The engine, having been given a 'hot' running test, arrives at the production line complete with carburettors, exhaust manifold, alternator and fan. The clutch/gearbox unit, drive shaft, rear axle, front and rear suspensions—including hubs and brakes—are fitted in a special jig and everything is bolted together. The engine/transmission/suspension assembly moves forward to meet the line from the body shops; the correct body unit is lowered to meet it. The nearly completed car now moves along a raised line. The wipers and interior trim are fitted; the radiator is filled and hydraulic fluid fed into the brake system.

Wheels, made in a separate plant and already fitted with tyres, arrive on a gravity conveyor and are bolted on, and the car rolls forward on its own for the first time. Fuel is added to the tank.

Seats are the last item to be added to the interior. The engine idles as it is checked; then suspension and steering settings are adjusted and checked.

After a final examination of the trim the car undergoes a quality check before it goes on to the roller testing station to test the engine, transmission, steering, brakes and lights. A diagnostic unit checks that the electrical circuit is fully functional. The car is driven on to a conveyorized water test where jets of water at 20 psi are directed on to the cars for four minutes as they pass through the tunnel.

Dried down, it has its final check, then it is parked in the trade compound to await the dealer's delivery conveyor lorries to take it to the showroom.

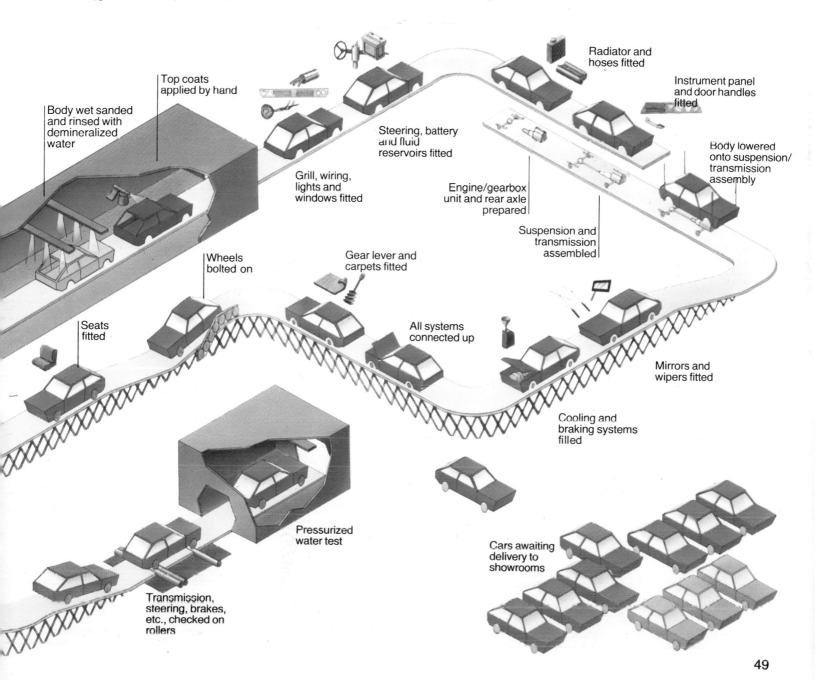

Body wet sanded and rinsed with demineralized water

Top coats applied by hand

Grill, wiring, lights and windows fitted

Steering, battery and fluid reservoirs fitted

Radiator and hoses fitted

Instrument panel and door handles fitted

Engine/gearbox unit and rear axle prepared

Suspension and transmission assembled

Body lowered onto suspension/transmission assembly

Wheels bolted on

Gear lever and carpets fitted

All systems connected up

Mirrors and wipers fitted

Seats fitted

Cooling and braking systems filled

Pressurized water test

Cars awaiting delivery to showrooms

Transmission, steering, brakes, etc., checked on rollers

Developing a new car

A NEW CAR USUALLY starts as a designer's concept, based on a number of assumptions, known as the 'package', which specify the broad outlines of the vehicle—how many passengers the vehicle must accommodate, the layout of engine, transmission and suspension, and the luggage space. Length, width, height, wheelbase and passenger compartment dimensions are also laid down—the cost of developing a new car these days is so great that it must be designed to fill a perceived gap in the market or to succeed a well-established success. Cars are no longer launched in the fond belief that merit alone will sell them.

Each new programme results in a number of sketches for further development, and the best of these are developed into more detailed illustrations—'renderings'—to evaluate the design's potential.

A wheeled 'armature'—a wood and foam plastic skeleton slightly smaller than the finished vehicle—is covered in a special modelling clay, applied warm and shaped to the contours of the design rendering by highly skilled clay modellers. Frequently referring to full-scale brush renderings or fullsize line drawings, the modellers scrape and form the clay using a wide variety of special tools, many of their own manufacture. Because the clay is so malleable, it can be reshaped easily until the designer is satisfied with the appearance of the model.

Now the clay can be 'finished' to give it a realistic appearance. A glossy skin of thin plastic sheet can be applied to simulate paintwork, a similar material gives the impression of windows, and metal foil represents the brightwork.

If the finished clay is approved, a glass-fibre moulding can be taken. This can be fitted with seats, trim and instrument panel (which have already been developed by a separate design team) to give a very good idea of the final form

the car will take. Usually, a number of models is made for assessment.

These days, the techniques of the market researcher are often called in to ensure that the production vehicle will appeal to the motoring public. Before one popular model was put into production, the various prototypes were assembled in secret in a hall in Switzerland, and potential buyers flown in from Britain, Germany, Italy, France and Spain to assess these designs and compare them with competitive vehicles. Similar 'clinics' were held in the USA, South America, Spain and Germany. Additionally, surveys questioned over 5000 members of the public on what they expected in terms of engine size, options, specifications and serviceability in such a vehicle. The answers, surprisingly uniform, showed that the designers were on the right track.

During the development stages, a design changes continually, especially now that the

A draughtsman makes a full-size drawing of a proposed new model so that critical dimensions can be evaluated (**left**). Because of the cost of building full-size prototypes, fifth-scale models of a new car are made so that wind-tunnel tests can be carried out to 'fine-tune' the aerodynamics before a project is committed to sheet metal (**above**). Using modelling clay, highly skilled modellers create not only full-size mockups of a new design, but also interior features like the facia panel (**right**).

wind-tunnel is an indispensable part of the design equipment. One family car went through over 250 detail body changes as a result of wind-tunnel testing.

Wind-tunnel testing has produced such features of modern car design as front-end air dams and rear-end spoilers; it has contributed to more economical engines and improved roadholding at speed.

Computers are playing an increased role in car body development, too: the principle is to analyze half of the complete body, which, as the vehicle is virtually symmetrical about a longitudinal centre line, gives information for the whole car.

The input of loads on a vehicle can be computer-simulated, and the computer then calulates the resultant stress distribution throughout the structure. Individual panels can be studied under tension and compression, torsion and bending. Redundant members can be eliminated and panel strengths maximized while still reducing overall weight.

The computer can go beyond designing the basic structure and showing how it will perform in normal service: it can also run crash tests on the theoretical structure. By simulating barrier crash tests on a 'hybrid-analogue' computer, effective 'management' of the energy absorbed in a crash can be arranged. One computer-designed body shell was given an actual crash test when it was found it performed exactly as

Crash behaviour of new models is assessed in controlled tests (**above**), though today much of the information that used to be gained by destroying expensive prototypes can be gained from computer programmes. Unwanted noises can be detected and eliminated by running tests in an anechoic chamber (**left**), a totally soundless environment. Wind-tunnel tests on the completed prototype (**right**) produce much valuable information.

forecast—the displacement of the steering column into the driving compartment was accurately predicted, and the doors still opened after the impact.

However, computer analysis is only part of the body design process, and must be verified by accelerated tests on the track and in the laboratory. Much valuable time can be saved by simulating the effect of rough roads on a test rig which feeds shock loads into a prototype metal body shell by means of hydraulic rams attached to the suspension pickup points. Tape recordings taken from a test car running across a proving track feed in 'real-life' torsion and bending loads. Finally, prototypes are given extended tests on the manufacturer's proving grounds, where all types of road surface are reproduced and where years of normal use can be condensed into a few weeks.

In fact, before any modern car is put on sale, every component will have been subjected to thousands of test cycles, prototypes will have been deliberately destroyed to prove the protection given by the passenger compartment in accidents, and cost of servicing and maintenance will have been exhaustively analyzed.

The manufacturer will have spent anything up to a billion dollars to develop this new model, and in the end its commercial success or failure still rely on whether the motorist finds it attractive and sound value for money. That is the most crucial test of all.

A global industry

TRADITIONALLY, CAR PRODUCTION has been mainly centred in the northern United States and north-western Europe, with Japan playing an increasingly important role since the 1950s. But now other countries are important car producers. For example, when production of VW's Beetle was phased out in Germany, this robust design continued to be built in Brazil and Nigeria, where its relative simplicity of design made it more suitable for local conditions than more modern and sophisticated designs. And the so-called 'Third World' countries, where labour costs are low, may soon move into world markets as inexorably as the Japanese have done. Already the first South Korean cars have reached Europe, establishing a 'beach-head' for imports from this Asian country whose motor industry is only a few years old (even though, as far back as 1912, it was claimed that the Koreans called all cars 'Ford' because there were so many Model Ts on their roads).

Conversely, the major European and American manufacturers are actively moving into new manufacturing markets, like Egypt, Morocco or Kenya, competing for market supremacy in Mexico, Argentina or Venezuela, and expanding into new European markets like Spain and Portugal.

In the case of the two American giants (Ford and GM), these overseas markets were vital to their continued success in the USA, where a slaving domestic market and the vast expense of meeting the Government's corporate average fuel economy (CAFE) limits meant that, to finance the cars of the 1980s, manufacturers needed the volume that only the world market could supply.

For the third-biggest US company, Chrysler, the cost of meeting CAFE and of developing new models for the 1980s prompted entrenchment and the selling-off of most of its overseas subsidiaries to raise revenue.

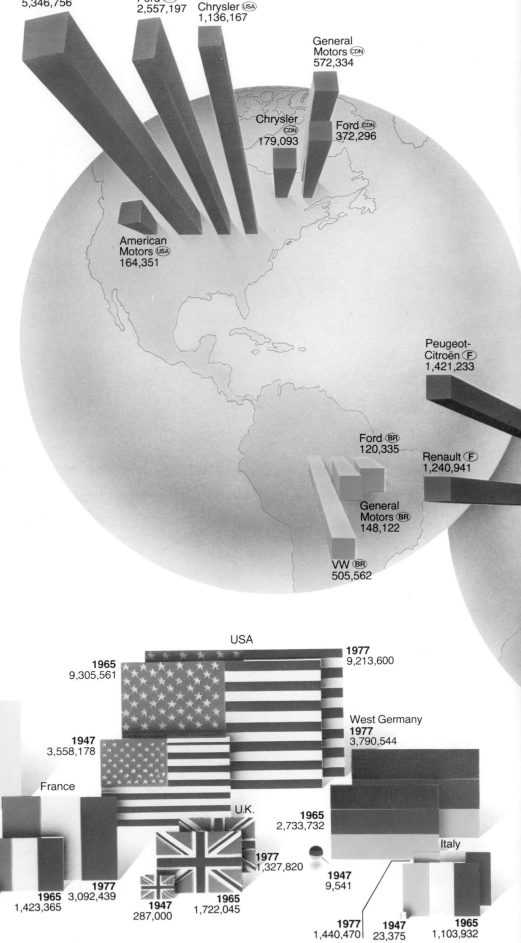

General Motors (USA)
5,346,756

Ford (USA)
2,557,197

Chrysler (USA)
1,136,167

General Motors (CDN)
572,334

Chrysler (CDN)
179,093

Ford (CDN)
372,296

American Motors (USA)
164,351

Peugeot-Citroën (F)
1,421,233

Ford (BR)
120,335

Renault (F)
1,240,941

General Motors (BR)
148,122

VW (BR)
505,562

Production figures for the principal car manufacturing countries for the years 1947, 1965 and 1977

Japan
1977 5,431,045
1965 696,176
1947 110

USA
1965 9,305,561
1977 9,213,600
1947 3,558,178

West Germany
1977 3,790,544
1965 2,733,732

France
1977 3,092,439
1965 1,423,365
1947 66,277

U.K.
1977 1,327,820
1965 1,722,045
1947 287,000

Sweden
1947 2,545
1965 181,755
1977 235,383

Canada
1977 1,161,314
1965 710,711
1947 167,257

Italy
1947 9,541
1977 1,440,470
1947 23,375
1965 1,103,932

**The World's Leading Car
Manufacturers (1978 figures)**

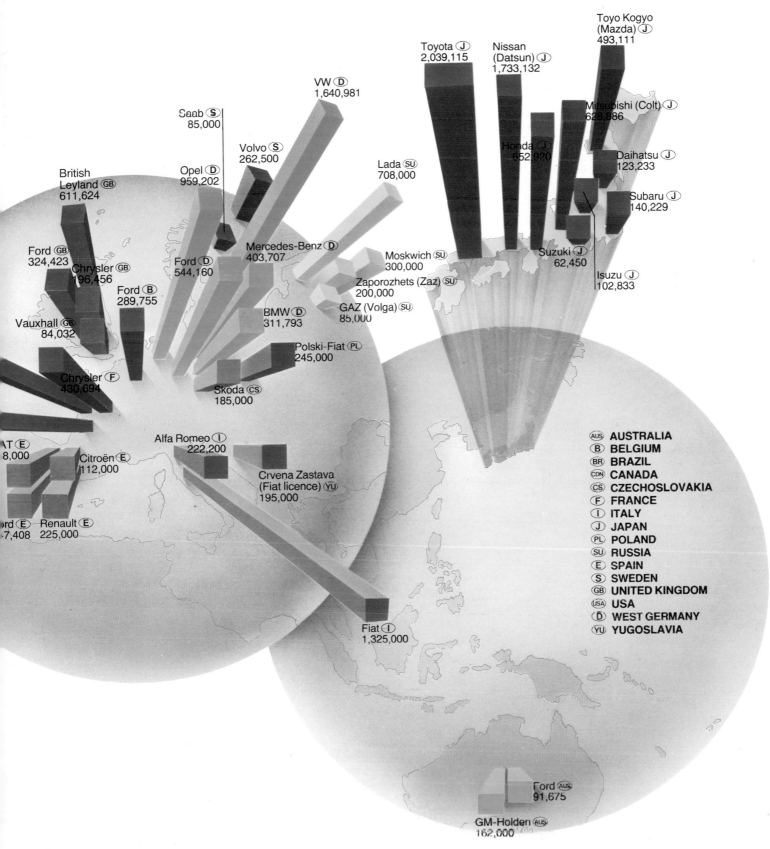

Toyota Ⓙ
2,039,115

Nissan
(Datsun) Ⓙ
1,733,132

Toyo Kogyo
(Mazda) Ⓙ
493,111

VW Ⓓ
1,640,981

Mitsubishi (Colt) Ⓙ
628,886

Saab Ⓢ
85,000

Volvo Ⓢ
262,500

Honda Ⓙ
652,920

Daihatsu Ⓙ
123,233

Opel Ⓓ
959,202

Lada ⓈⓊ
708,000

British
Leyland ⒼⒷ
611,624

Subaru Ⓙ
140,229

Ford ⒼⒷ
324,423

Mercedes-Benz Ⓓ
403,707

Moskwich ⓈⓊ
300,000

Ford Ⓓ
544,160

Chrysler ⒼⒷ
196,456

Suzuki Ⓙ
62,450

Zaporozhets (Zaz) ⓈⓊ
200,000

Ford Ⓑ
289,755

BMW Ⓓ
311,793

GAZ (Volga) ⓈⓊ
85,000

Isuzu Ⓙ
102,833

Vauxhall ⒼⒷ
84,032

Polski-Fiat ⓅⓁ
245,000

Chrysler Ⓕ
430,694

Skoda ⒸⓈ
185,000

AT Ⓔ
8,000

Alfa Romeo Ⓘ
222,200

Citroën Ⓔ
112,000

Crvena Zastava
(Fiat licence) ⓎⓊ
195,000

ord Ⓔ
7,408

Renault Ⓔ
225,000

Ⓐ ᵁˢ	**AUSTRALIA**
Ⓑ	**BELGIUM**
Ⓑ ᴿ	**BRAZIL**
Ⓒ ᴰ ᴺ	**CANADA**
Ⓒ ˢ	**CZECHOSLOVAKIA**
Ⓕ	**FRANCE**
Ⓘ	**ITALY**
Ⓙ	**JAPAN**
Ⓟ ᴸ	**POLAND**
ⓈⓊ	**RUSSIA**
Ⓔ	**SPAIN**
Ⓢ	**SWEDEN**
Ⓖ Ⓑ	**UNITED KINGDOM**
Ⓤ ˢᴬ	**USA**
Ⓓ	**WEST GERMANY**
Ⓨ Ⓤ	**YUGOSLAVIA**

Fiat Ⓘ
1,325,000

Ford Ⓐ ᵁˢ
91,675

GM-Holden Ⓐ ᵁˢ
162,000

55

Alternative power sources

THOUGH THE FOUR-STROKE internal combustion engine has been around for over a century, it has had remarkably few challengers to its supremacy.

In the early days of motoring, steam and electricity both had their advocates, but their shortcomings led to their general demise. Steam—external combustion—needed a boiler and water tank, and was complex to operate and maintain, while the electric car needed heavy accumulators to give even the most modest of ranges; it enjoyed something of a vogue in America as a town car, however, up to the 1920s.

Once the electric starter was a commonplace item of equipment, the supremacy of the petrol engine was assured, until, that is, fuel shortages inspired manufacturers to search for viable alternatives. During World War One, cars had been run on coal gas carried in bags like embryo Zeppelins, either on the roof or in trailers; during World War Two, private cars were fitted with gas producers generating combustible gas from carbon, usually in the form of charcoal.

Serious development of alternative power sources did not begin, however, until the 1950s. Rover in Britain led the way with production of gas turbine prototypes, and both General Motors and Ford began experiments along these lines. The major American manufacturers also began looking anew at steam and electric vehicles.

Turbines failed to meet the requirements of the car industry, though they had some attraction to truck builders. Their main fault was a 'time-lag' when accelerating; also, their application to mass-produced cars depends on the development of low-cost, high-temperature components designed for satisfactory engine efficiency and performance.

Another candidate which was tried and found wanting was the Stirling 'hot-air' engine, appropriately designed by a preacher in the early 1800s. Powered by a closed-circuit system utilizing heat expansion of an inert gas, the external-combustion Stirling was at one time seriously considered by Ford as a possibility for the production cars of the late 1980s, but the programme got no further than the building of mobile test beds.

Rotary piston engines, long a fruitful field for hopeful inventors, came to the fore with the Wankel trochoidal engine pioneered by NSU in 1963, but failed to stay the course. Though rotaries are more compact than conventional reciprocating engines, they are costlier to produce and maintain, and are not so fuel-efficient.

Even the 'pollution-free' and noiseless electric car has not solved the problems which bedevilled it at the turn of the century. It still relies on heavy storage batteries with limited range, and needs to be recharged at frequent intervals. And, if its batteries are recharged from a conventional oil-fired generating station, the source of the atmospheric pollution is only

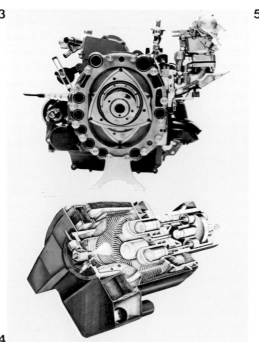

Some modern sports cars, like this 1979 Ford Mustang (1), use an exhaust-driven turbocharger for forced induction to obtain greater efficiency from a conventional petrol engine. In the mid-1960s, Ford of Britain developed a small urban electric car prototype, the Comuta (2), but shelved the project in 1967. The most commercially successful 'alternative' engine is the Wankel rotary-piston unit. This is a Citroën-built example (3). The closed-cycle Ford-Philips Stirling 'hot-air' engine (4) was tested in a Pinto car but apparently did not live up to its early promise. In Brazil in 1979, Fiat introduced the 147 saloon running on locally produced sugar cane alcohol (5), promoted by an all-girl rally team. In the summer of 1979, Californian Ken Eacrett drove his solar-powered three-wheeler (6) across the USA. Taking its power from a solar panel on the roof, the car had a 25mph top speed.

transferred from the car to the power station.

One of the more promising alternative power sources is the stratified-charge engine—basically a more efficient variant of the conventional petrol engine. There are two main types, the divided chamber engine and the fuel-injected stratified-charge engine.

The first type is typified by Honda's CVCC engine, which features a dual carburettor and a precombustion chamber, while Ford's PROCO ('programmed combustion') engine represents the second type. This has a special cylinder and piston head design, and uses fuel injectors to deliver a finely atomized spray of fuel directly into the combustion chamber.

But perhaps the most successful 'alternative engine' is also one of the oldest, the diesel, first devised in the 1890s. Long proven in trucks, by the late 1970s diesels were appearing in a small VW family car, the Golf. Able to run on cheaper, less volatile oil fuel than the petrol engine, and of proven longevity, the compression ignition diesel engine only suffered by comparison, as it tended to be harsher-running and less lively. However, it holds great hope for the future.

Cars of the future

WHAT SHAPE WILL TOMORROW'S car take? One thing is certain: it will not be a science-fiction fantasy vehicle powered by some revolutionary new power plant. Tomorrow's car will, in fact, be very much like today's, except that it will be far more efficient—'socially responsible' is the current in-phrase.

So far, the various alternative power sources that have been tried have all been found wanting: nothing works as well as the internal combustion engine, despite the fact that it has been around for almost a century in production cars. However, it may need to change its diet: petrol is getting scarcer and more expensive, and the prophets of doom say it may run out early in the twenty-first century. Already, new fuels are being investigated. In 1979, Saab-Finland laun-

ched a multifuel engine capable of running on fuel distilled from timber, so that the nation could aim at self-sufficiency.

The US Transportation Secretary Brock Adams called for 'the re-invention of the car', with a target of around 50 miles to the gallon for an American family car of the mid-1980s.

In Sweden, the Royal Academy of Engineering Science forecast that cars of the year 2000, despite the expected stricter anti-pollution and safety requirements, would be as roomy and comfortable as present-day models.

Their equipment, however, will be vastly more sophisticated. Volkswagen—which has declared itself committed to a piston engine for tomorrow's cars—foresees an increased use of electronic aids to driving. In-car computers,

VW predicts, will handle engine management, anti-lock braking, fault diagnosis and crash sensor equipment. By the end of the 1980s, digital displays could have replaced conventional instrument dials, and aircraft-style 'head-up read-outs' will give traffic and weather information from roadside computer links.

More efficient aerodynamics will provide dramatic fuel savings—up to 30 per cent in some cases—and both petrol and diesel engines may be turbocharged for increased efficiency. Low-weight materials will also help fuel economy—Ford-US was already testing carbon-fibre wheels in 1978.

Lighter, quieter, more fuel-efficient, more spacious—these will be the main attributes of tomorrow's car.

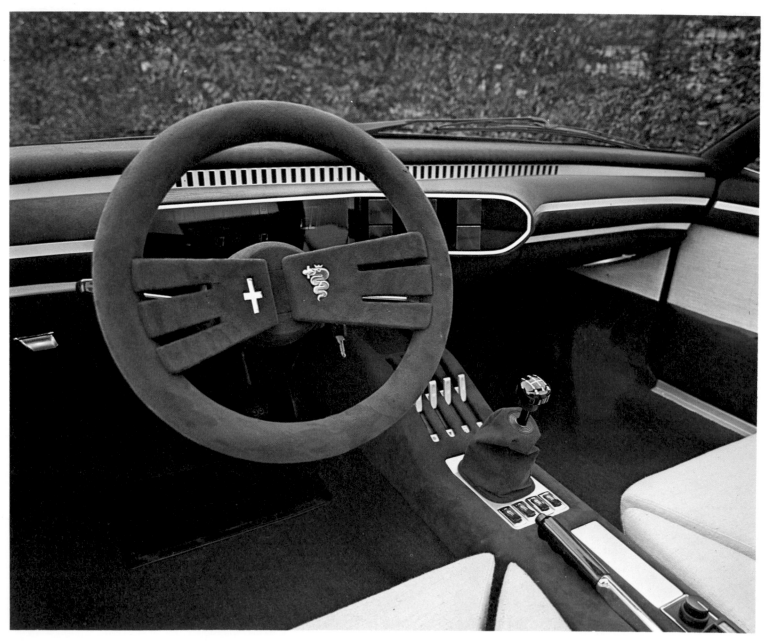

The 'dream cars' of the 1970s take a more thoughtful look into the future than their often bizarre predecessors of the 1950s and 1960s. Aerodynamics play a vital part in their design for an increasingly fuel-conscious world – the Ghia-styled 'Coins' of 1974 (**right**) forecast what shape the Ford sports coupé of the future might take, while the same studio's Corrida (**below**) showed how one car, in this case the Ford Fiesta, could fulfil several functions. Alfa Romeo's Eagle (**opposite**) made interesting use of digital displays instead of conventional instrumentation.

Founders of the motor industry

APPERSON, Edgar *(1870–1959)* **and Elmer** *(1861–1920)*
Collaborated with Elwood Haynes to build one of America's first cars in 1894, later forming Haynes-Apperson. After they broke with Haynes, they founded the Apperson Brothers Motor Car Company.

Herbert Austin

AUSTIN, Herbert *(1866–1941)*
Briton who worked for the Wolseley Sheep Shearing Company in Australia, then returned to England to build the first Wolseley car (1895). Left Wolseley to found Austin (1906), where landmark designs included the Seven and the 12/4. He was knighted in 1917 and became Lord Austin in 1936.

BENTLEY, Walter Owen *(1888–1971)*
Trained as a railway engineer, fitted some of the first aluminium pistons to DFP cars in 1914. After building aeroengines during World War One, he launched the Bentley car in 1919. He later worked for Lagonda.

Karl Benz

BENZ, Karl *(1844–1929)*
Began development of a petrol engine in 1878, founding Benz & Co. in 1883. Built his first motor car in 1885–86, the first petrol car conceived as a unity and owing nothing to horse-drawn carriages.

BIRKIGT, Marc *(1878–1953)*
Swiss engineer who moved to Spain, and became designer of Hispano-Suiza cars and aeroengines.

BOLLEE, Amédée *père (1844–1916)*
French bell-founder and designer of steam carriages which pioneered independent front suspension and other technical features well ahead of their time.

BOLLEE, Amédée *fils (1867–1926)*
Began with steam carriages, but turned to petrol cars in 1896, building a streamlined racer in 1899 with underslung chassis, rear-mounted twin carburettor, and four-cylinder engine with hemispherical combustion chambers.

BOLLEE, Léon *(1870–1913)*
First achieved fame with the invention of a calculating machine, then, in 1895, devised a sporting tandem-seat voiturette. In contrast, from 1903 he built refined and silent quality cars of advanced design.

BRISCOE, Benjamin *(1869–1945)*
Founded, with Jonathan Maxwell, the Maxwell-Briscoe Motor Company in 1903, and in 1910 organized the United States Motor Company, a combine of some 130 firms, which folded in 1912. In 1913 Briscoe began building cars under his own name. A visit to the 1912 London Motorcycle Show introduced him to cyclecars, which he built in France and America in conjunction with his brother Frank (1875–1954).

BUGATTI, Ettore *(1881–1947)*
Born in Milan, he was designing for De Dietrich before he was 21, moved to Mathis, and in 1910 built the first Bugatti car at Molsheim (Alsace). 'Le Patron', rarely seen without his bowler hat, also affected digitated shoes.

BUICK, David Dunbar *(1855–1929)*
Applied the money he made from the invention of the enamelled bathtub to the development of a car engine with ohv. He then, in 1903, organized the Buick Motor Car Company with backing from the Briscoe brothers, but was bought out by Billy Durant late in 1904.

David Buick

CHADWICK, Lee Sherman *(1875–1958)*
Built his first car in 1899, joining Searchmont in 1900. His Chadwick company lasted from 1903 to 1911, and his racing cars pioneered the use of superchargers. His latter years were spent as the head of a stove company.

CHAPIN, Roy *(1880–1936)*
Started with Olds, then, in 1906, helped found Thomas-Detroit (later Chalmers). In 1909 he organized, along with Howard Coffin, the Hudson Motor Car Company. He was an active crusader for better roads for America.

CHAPMAN, Colin *(born 1928)*
English designer/constructor of Lotus sports and racing cars.

CHARRON, Fernand *(1866–1928)*
French cycle and car racer who collaborated (with Girardot and Voigt) in the CGV car, having made a 'killing' from holding the sole agency for Panhard-Levassor at a time of great demand. Sold his share of Charron Ltd. (as CGV became) to work for his father-in-law, Adolphe Clément, but they split up and Charron eventually built the 'Alda' car. Though he was very bald, the fashionable M. Charron rarely wore a hat, a matter for some comment at the time.

Louis Chevrolet

CHEVROLET, Louis *(1878–1941)*
Swiss racing driver who arrived in the USA in 1900 to sell a wine pump he had invented. He became a team driver for Buick and, with Etienne Planche, designed the first Chevrolet Six in 1911. He left Chevrolet to found the Frontenac Motor Company, building racing cars and 'go-faster' equipment for Model T Fords.

CHRISTIE, John Walter *(1886–1944)*
Pioneered front-wheel drive in the USA, even competing in the French Grand Prix with huge, if not particularly reliable, fwd racers. He also produced fwd tractor units for fire appliances and built an advanced tank in the 1930s.

CHRYSLER, Walter Percy *(1875–1940)*
A locomotive engineer who joined Buick in 1911, rising to become President – as well as first Vice-President of General Motors. Moved to Willys in 1920, saving this company – and Maxwell-Chalmers – from bankruptcy. He converted Maxwell into the Chrysler Corporation, acquiring Dodge in 1928.

CITROEN, André *(1878–1935)*
Frenchman who worked with Mors pre-World War One, and devised a double chevron gear which was used as the emblem of the car-producing company he founded in 1919. Development of a magnificent new factory and of the classic fwd Citroën car caused his death.

CLEMENT, Adolphe *(1855–1928)*
French cycle manufacturer who made a fortune from the French rights for the Dunlop pneumatic tyre and his exceedingly complex business dealings when he entered the motor car industry. As a result of selling the manufacturing rights to the 'Clément' car, he changed his name to 'Clément-Bayard'. His company also pioneered aeroplanes and airships.

COATALEN, Louis *(1879–1962)*
Breton engineer who came to England in 1900, working for Crowden, Humber and Hillman. His greatest designs were for Sunbeam, where he became Managing Director and built the first V-12 racing car in 1913.

CORD, Erret Lobban *(1894–1974)*
Dynamic entrepreneur who created the Auburn-Duesenberg-Cord empire, and also owned Lycoming engines, American Airlines, Stinson Aircraft and New York Shipbuilding before he was 35.

Gottlieb Daimler

DAIMLER, Gottlieb *(1834–1900)*
Born in Württemberg and trained as an engineer; becoming interested in gas engines in the 1860s, he helped develop the Otto gas engine. During the 1880s he set up on his own to develop a 'universal power source' in the shape of a light petrol engine, in collaboration with Wilhelm Maybach. This engine was fitted into a carriage in 1886, creating the first Daimler car.

DARRACQ, Alexandre *(1855–1931)*
Born in Bordeaux, Darracq entered the cycle industry in 1891, building 'Gladiator' cycles; selling out in 1896, he moved first into components, then into motor vehicles. Darracq voiturettes were particularly famous. He retired in 1912 to take a financial interest in the Deauville casino. Though Darracq built many thousands of cars, he never drove and disliked riding in them.

Georges Bouton (*left*) and Albert De Dion

DE DION, Albert *(1856–1946)*
Famous as a duellist and gambler, Comte De Dion sponsored two brothers-in-law, Bouton and Trépardoux, in the construction of steam carriages. The first practicable De Dion Bouton petrol engines appeared in 1894 and were fitted to tricycles, voiturettes (for which the marque became renowned) appearing in 1899. De Dion also founded the motoring daily *L'Auto*. He became a Marquis in 1901.

DELAGE, Louis *(1877–1947)*
French builder who supplied components to marques such as Helbe, then made complete Delage light cars from 1906. After 1919, Delage also built luxury cars.

DOBLE, Abner *(1890–1961)*
Built his first steam car in 1906, and drove a prototype to Detroit in 1914 to seek backing. Began production in San Francisco in 1920. Output was always limited, but he gained great acclaim. He later acted as a steam power consultant for overseas firms, including Sentinel steam waggons in England.

DODGE, John *(1864–1920)* **and Horace** *(1868–1920)*
Machinists and cycle makers, the Dodges built transmissions for Olds (1901–02), then made chassis and engines for Henry Ford in return for a tenth of his company. They sold their Ford shares for $25,000,000 and founded the Dodge Brothers company, coining the word 'dependable' to describe their products.

DUESENBERG, Frederick *(1877–1932)*
Designed his first car in 1904, and by 1913 had organized the Duesenberg Motor Company to build engines. During the 1930s Fred and his brother August built the Duesenberg luxury cars, though E. L. Cord took control of the company in 1927. Fred Duesenberg died in a car crash.

DURANT, William Crapo *(1860–1947)*
Having become a major force in the carriage industry, Billy Durant took over Buick in 1904, then, in 1908, founded the General Motors group. Ousted in 1910, by 1915 he was ready to take over again via his Chevrolet company. However, a share crash in 1920 put him out of GM again, so he established a 'Second Empire' which survived until the Depression.

DURYEA, Charles *(1861–1939)* **and Frank** *(1870–1967)*
In 1893 built the first practicable American car to lead to a production company, the Duryea Motor Power Wagon Company (1896).

EARL, Harley *(1893–1969)*
In the early 1920s was a director of Don Lee Corporation, which built custom coachwork for the wealthy. Became director of 'art and color' at GM in 1927, and is recognized as the first mass-production stylist. Among his styling innovations were tailfins.

S. F. Edge on a 1903 Napier

EDGE, Selwyn Francis *(1868–1940)*
Born in Sydney, New South Wales, came to England and became known as a racing cyclist. Promoted the Napier car and achieving some notable racing victories, including the only British victory in the Gordon Bennett Cup series (1902). In the 1920s, backed AC and Cubitt cars.

FLANDERS, Walter *(1871–1923)*
One of the US car industry's first mass-production experts. He was hired by Ford as production manager in 1908, but left in 1909 to found EMF. Later, he founded the United States Motor Company group.

FORD, Henry *(1863–1947)*
Son of an immigrant Irish farmer, Henry Ford wanted to lift the drudgery off farm life, and became an engineer in Detroit. In 1896 he built his first car. After two unsuccessful attempts to found manufacturing companies, he established the Ford Motor Company on June 16, 1903. He successfully defied the ALAM monopoly group.

FRANKLIN, Herbert *(1867–1956)*
Newspaper proprietor who became a pioneer of die casting, then in 1902 put the first air-cooled Franklin car on the market.

FRAZER, Joseph W. *(1894–1973)*
Having worked for Packard, GM and Pierce-Arrow, Frazer became President of Willys-Overland in 1939 and, with Henry Kaiser, founded Kaiser-Frazer in 1946 in an attempt to break the monopoly of the 'Big Three' in the popular car market.

HAYNES, Elwood G. *(1857–1925)*
Built his first car in 1894 with the help of the Apperson Brothers, and started the Haynes Automobile Company in 1898. He was also a pioneering metallurgist.

ISSIGONIS, Sir Alec *(born 1906)*
Designer of Morris Minor (1948), Mini-Minor (1959) and other fwd British Motor Corporation family cars.

JANO, Vittorio *(1891–1965)*
Italian designer for Fiat, Alfa Romeo and Lancia, for whom he created some of the finest sports and racing cars of all time.

JEFFERY, Thomas B. *(1845–1910)*
An Englishman who emigrated to the USA in 1863, and in 1879 began manufacturing 'Rambler' bicycles. He invented a 'clincher' tyre in 1891, and built his first successful car in 1900. Production of Rambler cars started in 1902.

JOHNSON, Claude *(1864–1926)*
First Secretary of the ACGBI (later the Royal Automobile Club). Introduced Rolls to Royce, and was first Managing Director of Rolls-Royce.

JORDAN, Edward *(1882–1958)*
A journalist who became Advertising Manager of the Thomas B. Jeffery Company, leaving to found the Jordan Motor Car Company in 1916. He became better known for his evocative advertising copy than for his cars.

KELSEY, Cadwallader *(1880–1970)*
Having built an experimental car in 1897, began production of Auto-Tri three-wheelers. Worked for Maxwell as Sales Manager 1905–09, then produced the Motorette car (1910–1912) and the Kelsey car (1921–1924).

KETTERING, Charles F. *(1876–1958)*
'Boss Ket' organized Delco laboratories to develop an electrical ignition system, and subsequently perfected the electric self-starter for the 1911 Cadillac. In 1920 he became head of the GM research laboratories.

KING, Charles Brady *(1868–1957)*
Built Detroit's first motor vehicle in 1896, and later designed the 'Silent Northern' and 'King 8' cars, turning to aeroengines in 1916.

LANCHESTER, Frederick *(1868–1946)*
British pioneer who built an advanced car in 1895. Apart from his contributions to automobile engineering, was one of the great pioneers of aeronautics.

LAWSON, Harry J. *(1852–1925)*
Company promotor, nicknamed 'Father of the British Motor Industry'. Attempted, from 1896, to form a patent monopoly to control the industry, and floated a number of overcapitalized companies, notably Daimler of Coventry (which survived the collapse of his empire in the early 1900s).

LEDWINKA, Hans *(1878–1967)*
Austrian designer who worked for Nesselsdorf, Steyr and Tatra, where he devised backbone chassis, all-independent suspension and air-cooled engines, latterly rear-mounted.

Hans Ledwinka

LELAND, Henry M. *(1843–1932)*
'The Master of Precision' learned his art in the arms industry. He also invented the mechanical hair-clipper and began building engines. He reorganized the Henry Ford Company as Cadillac after Ford resigned in 1902, later founding Lincoln.

LENOIR, J-J. Etienne *(1822–1900)*
A Belgian, he invented a successful method of enamelling clock faces in 1847, and in the late 1850s devised a gas engine. He built his first horseless carriage in Paris in 1862, later selling it to the Czar of Russia.

LEVASSOR, Emile *(1844–1897)*
Co-founder of Panhard-Levassor and inventor of the *Système Panhard*, in which the engine was at the front, under a bonnet, driving the rear wheels via a sliding-pinion gearbox. Died as a delayed effect of a racing accident.

MARKUS, Seigfried *(1831–1898)*
Austrian inventor who built a number of experimental internal combustion-engined test-benches from 1868. His first true car, long claimed to have been built in 1875, is now known to date from the late 1880s.

MAXWELL, Jonathan Dixon *(1864–1968)*
Starting in the cycle industry with Elmer Apperson, he worked on the 1894 Haynes-Apperson. In 1903, he joined Ben Briscoe to found the Maxwell-Briscoe company.

METZ, Charles *(1864–1937)*
Famed for his Orient cycles, Metz began production of the crude Orient Buckboard. In 1909 he introduced the low-priced friction-drive Metz 22, sold initially for home assembly.

MORRIS, William *(1877–1963)*
Starting as an Oxford cycle agent, Morris (who became Lord Nuffield) built his first Morris-Oxford light car in 1912, and came to dominate the British motor industry in the 1920s. He was renowned for his philanthropy.

NASH, Charles W. *(1864–1948)*
An itinerant farm worker, Charles Nash joined the Durant-Dort carriage company, then moved to Buick with Billy Durant, becoming President of that company in 1910 and of the whole GM group in 1912. He left to take over Jeffery and transform it into the Nash Motor Company.

OLDS, Ransom Eli *(1864–1950)*
Claimed to have built his first steam car in 1896, and his first petrol car in 1894. Success came with the 1901 Curved-Dash Oldsmobile. He later founded Reo, and also invented an early motor mower.

PENNINGTON, Edmund Joel *(1858–1911)*
American 'mechanical charlatan', who 'invented' an airship in 1885, and produced a number of eccentric motor vehicles which defied normal mechanical laws.

PEUGEOT, Armand *(1849–1915)*
Son of one of France's leading ironmongers, Peugeot translated his firm's expertise in making steel rods to replace whalebone in crinoline skirts into the manufacture of cycles. In 1889 the Peugeot company built a steam car designed by Serpollet, but then constructed tubular-framed Daimler-engined cars, France's first production cars.

POPE, Albert Augustus *(1843–1909)*
Colonel Pope founded a successful cycle manufacturing group in 1879, and moved into the motor industry via electric vehicles as early as 1896. Pope's motor group was dragged down by the decline of the cycle business.

PORSCHE, Ferdinand *(1875–1952)*
Austrian designer for Steyr, Austro-Daimler, Mercedes, Auto-Union, Cisitalia and Porsche, he created the original Volkswagen in the 1930s.

Ferdinand Porsche

PORTER, Finley Robertson *(1872–1964)*
Designed the classic Mercer Raceabout, as well as FRP and Porter cars, becoming Chief Engineer of Curtiss Aircraft in 1919.

RENAULT, Louis *(1877–1944)*
Son of a rich Parisian button maker, Louis Renault rebuilt his De Dion tricycle into a shaft-driven voiturette in 1898, and received so many orders that he began production of similar vehicles. By 1900, Renault was building 350 cars a year and was established as one of France's leading makes. Louis Renault died in prison during World War Two, having been accused of collaborating with the Germans during the Occupation of France.

RIKER, Andrew L. *(1868–1930)*
Built his first electric tricycle in 1884, but did not begin production until 1899. In 1902 joined Locomobile to design their first petrol cars.

ROESCH, Georges *(1891–1969)*
Brilliant Swiss engineer who became Chief Engineer of Clement Talbot of London at 25, designing high speed tourers of great refinement.

ROLLS, The Hon. Charles Stuart
(1877–1910)
Interested in machinery from an early age, Lord Llangottock's youngest son was a pioneer motorist and racing driver who entered the motor trade. Anxious to sell a car bearing his own name, he joined with the engineer Royce. Rolls died in a flying accident at Bournemouth, having been the first man to fly the English Channel both ways.

The Hon. C. S. Rolls (*left*) and Henry Royce

ROYCE, Henry *(1863–1933)*
Electrical engineer who built a twin-cylinder car in 1903, and went on to construct the 'best car in the world' as well as some remarkable aeroengines.

SELDEN, George Baldwin *(1846–1932)*
A patent attorney who experimented with engines from 1873 to 1875, and designed a self-propelled vehicle on which he filed a patent in 1879, the patent being granted in 1895. He sold the patent to Columbia Electric on a royalty basis in 1899, when it was used to try and create a monopoly group (Association of Licenced Automobile Manufacturers).

SERPOLLET, Léon *(1858–1907)*
Frenchman who devised the flash boiler for rapid production of steam, and built a steam tricycle in 1887. He built a number of steam three-wheelers in the 1890s, but did not seriously begin car production until the turn of the century. His sprint racers broke many speed records. His aim was to build a steamer that was as simple to control as a petrol vehicle, but his death from consumption ended the Serpollet company.

Frederick Simms

SIMMS, Frederick R. *(1863–1944)*
Brought the first Daimler engines into Britain in 1891, and fitted these power units into motor launches on the Thames. Formed the Daimler Motor Syndicate in 1893, which was taken over by Lawson interests in 1896. He invented the name 'motor-car', and helped to found the Automobile Club of Great Britain and Ireland (later the Royal Automobile Club) and the Society of Motor Manufacturers and Traders. He also built Simms cars.

SLOAN, Alfred P. *(1875–1966)*
At Durant's behest, formed the United Motors Corporation of accessory manufacturers, which was later absorbed by GM. An administrative genius, Sloan reorganized the corporate structure of GM, becoming its President from 1923–1936.

STANLEY, Francis E. *(1849–1918)* **and**
Freelan O. *(1849–1940)*
The Stanley twins used the proceeds from the sale of their photographic dry-plate business to develop a steam car, the rights to which were bought for $250,000 to create Locomobile. The Stanleys came up with an improved design, Stanley steamers being built into the 1920s.

STUTZ, Harry *(1871–1930)*
Designed an improved rear axle, then became Sales Manager for Schebler carburettors, engineer for Marion and designer of the American Underslung. Manufacture of Stutz cars began in 1911; Harry Stutz resigned in 1919, later founding HCS. He was also a talented saxophonist.

THOMAS, Edwin Ross *(1850–1936)*
Though he founded the E. R. Thomas Motor Company in Buffalo, NY, in 1900 (it built the Thomas Flyer which won the round-the-world New York-Paris Race of 1908), Edwin Thomas never learned to drive.

VOISIN, Gabriel *(1880–1973)*
French aviation pioneer who went into car production between the wars with advanced and unorthodox sleeve-valve cars.

WHITE, Windsor *(1866–1958)*, **Rollin**
(1872–1968) **and Walter** *(1876–1929)*
Rollin and Windsor built the first White Steamer in 1900, and Walter was sent to London the next year to develop the European market. Rollin left the White Company (Windsor was its President) in 1914 to build Cleveland tractors, and launched the Rollin car in 1923.

WILLS, Childe Harold *(1878–1940)*
A brilliant metallurgist who helped Henry Ford develop his first cars (and also designed the famous 'Ford' script logo) and became Chief Engineer of the Ford Motor Company. He developed vanadium and molybdenum steel alloys for the motor industry. With his severance pay from Ford he founded Wills Ste Claire. In 1933 he became Chrysler's chief metallurgist.

Childe Harold Wills

WILLYS, John North *(1873–1933)*
In 1906 undertook to sell the entire output of Overland, then mounted an effort to save the company when it got into difficulties in 1907, moving production to Toledo. He built Overland production up to 95,000 units – second only to Ford – in 1915.

WINTON, Alexander *(1860–1932)*
Scots marine engineer who jumped ship in America in 1880, starting bicycle production in 1896. Built his first car in 1896, founding the Winton Motor Carriage Company next year. In 1903, he launched an eight-cylinder 'Bullet' racer. His designs featured pneumatic controls. When car production was suspended in 1924, he began manufacture of diesel engines.

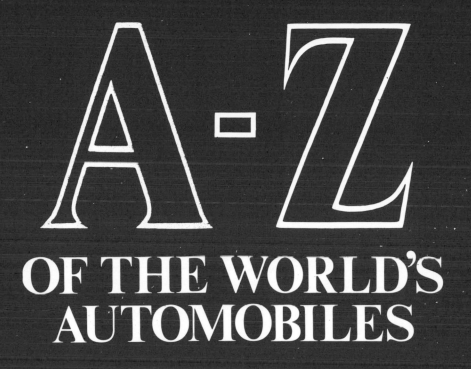

A-Z

OF THE WORLD'S
AUTOMOBILES

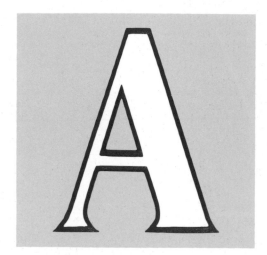

A

AAA/*France 1919–1920*
The Ateliers d'Automobiles et d'Aviation, of Paris, offered electric 'voitures de luxe' on petrol car lines.

AAA electric 'voiture de luxe', 1919

AACHENER/*Germany 1902*
The Aix-la-Chapelle Steel Works made engines of 1¾ hp to 11 hp and components, as well as complete cars, later marketed as 'Fafnir'.

AAG/*Germany 1900–1901*
Produced 5 hp voiturettes to the design of Professor Klingenberg. A leading politician and head of the AEG group, Emil Rathenau, bought the AAG factory and founded the 'Neue Automobil Gesellschaft', which built NAG cars until 1934.

AAG/*Germany 1906–1907*
A four-cylinder, four-speed, shaft-drive car designed by an engineer named Burchardt.

ABADAL/*Spain 1912–1923*
Francisco Abadal was a forceful Hispano-Suiza salesman who began building fast luxury cars in Barcelona in 1912. These had 3104cc four-cylinder and 4521cc six-cylinder engines closely patterned on the Hispano. Abadals were soon being built under licence by Impéria of Belgium as Impéria-Abadals. Abadal acquired the Buick agency in 1916, and Barcelona Abadals after that date had Buick power units and custom coachwork. In Belgium M. A. Van Roggen, formerly of Springuel, took over Impéria, and built about 170 more Impéria-Abadals, including a 2992cc 16-valve four-cylinder ohc sports model and three prototype 5630cc straight-eights.

ABARTH/*Italy 1950–1971*
Founded by former racing motorcyclist Carlo Abarth in Turin, this factory concentrated on sports and racing cars. It also produced a wide range of tuning equipment for various Fiat models from the 500cc upwards. There were also Abarth sports-racing cars with own make dohc engines of 1098cc, 1496cc and 1966cc, as well as very fast Fiat-Abarths of 598 to 2323cc. In 1964, there was a 695cc, 66 bhp model and a 982cc 'Bialbero' dohc model with 114 bhp. There were numerous prototypes, which included a dohc V-12 5980cc racer, and a 2986cc V-8 with dohc and 310 bhp. Abarth also co-operated with Simca and created some fast Simca-Abarth cars, too. In 1971 Abarth, whose pre-war home was at Vienna, decided to 'slow down' and Fiat took over his works.

ABBEY/*England 1922*
The short-lived friction-drive Abbey was an assembled car with a 10·8 hp Coventry-Climax engine.

Autobianchi A 112 Abarth

ABBOTT-DETROIT/*USA 1909–1919*
The Abbott-Detroit was a powerful, well-designed luxury car with a Continental engine. By 1913, electric lighting and starting had been standardized, and the cars were guaranteed for life. The 1913 range cost from $1700 for the 34/40 hp Foredoor Roadster, to $3050 for the seven-passenger Limousine, and included a 44/50 hp Battleship Roadster at $2150. In 1914 three models were offered: the 34 hp Model F, the 32 hp Model L, and the 27 hp Model K.

ABC/*USA 1906–1910*
'The cheapest high-grade car in America', the St Louis-built ABC was available with 18 hp twin- and 30 hp four-cylinder engines, solid or pneumatic tyres, and friction drive.

ABC/*England 1920–1929*
The ABC was a light car powered by a 1203cc flat-twin air-cooled engine designed by Granville Bradshaw, who was also responsible for the ABC motor cycle. The company was based in Hersham, Surrey, and during the earliest years of its existence was part of the Harper Bean combine. The car was not cheap, selling for £414 in 1920. Although initially unreliable, later examples were more refined, having enclosed pushrods, stronger valve gear and a better lubrication system. Surprisingly, the 'radiator' cap was the petrol tank filler! A Super Sports version with twin carburettors appeared in 1925, and was the only model available in the last four years of the car's production.

1923 ABC four-seater chummy

ABC/*USA 1922*
Although planned and advertised by the Arthur-Boynton Co. of Albany, New York, this light car (which would have sold for $300) never materialized.

ABERDONIA/*England 1911–1915*
The 20 hp Aberdonia, built in Park Royal, London, cost £500 with seven-seated touring coachwork, £700 with 'special landau body'. This was a weird mid-engined forward-control device.

ABINGDON/*England 1902–1903*
The Abingdon range for 1903 consisted of a 6½ hp De Dion-engined two-seater, tonneau-bodied 12 hp and 16 hp twins and a 24 hp four-cylinder.

ABINGDON/*England 1922–1923*
An assembled car, powered by an 11·9 hp Dorman engine, the Abingdon was only built in small numbers. Motor cycles were produced until 1925. In 1905–06, the company had built the 5 hp AKD tricar.

ABLE/*USA 1917–1919*
Featuring its own engines, but otherwise proprietary components, the Able was a small production car built at Mount Vernon, New York. It became the Vernon in 1920.

ABLE/*France 1920–1927*
A small cyclecar made at Avignon by Paul Toulouse, with proprietary engines like SCAP, Chapuis-Dornier and CIME, from 1100cc to 1500cc. Some of them were sold under the 'Toulouse' name.

AC
England 1908 to date
The original AC was the 5/6 hp Sociable, evolved from the company's commercial three-wheeler, the Autocarrier, with a passenger chair replacing the box body. The single rear wheel was driven by a one-cylinder air-cooled engine with two-speed epicyclic gearbox in the hub of the back wheel. These durable little three-wheelers were made up until 1914. However, in the previous year AC announced their four-wheeler, having an 1100cc Fivet engine with gearbox fashionably placed in the rear axle. This reappeared after the First World War, though by this time powered by a 1½-litre Anzani engine, which remained in production until 1927. At the 1919 Motor Show, AC displayed John Weller's remarkable 1991cc overhead camshaft wet liner six-cylinder engine, though it did not go into production until 1922. Nevertheless the engine was produced up until 1963, by which time output had been boosted threefold, from 35 to 103 bhp. In 1921 S. F. Edge became chairman and governing director and his influence was no doubt responsible for the company's active participation in long-distance record work. Unfortunately all was not well with the company's finances and it went into voluntary liquidation, no cars being built between 1929 and 1931. In 1930 William and Charles Hurlock bought the company and production restarted with

1914 AC 10hp four-cylinder

1934 AC March Special

AC 3000 ME coupé, 1972

the faithful Weller 2-litre six continuing to give sterling service. The designs were intelligently updated, the rear-mounted gearbox being replaced by a Moss 'box in unit with the engine, while underslung chassis frames were introduced. These good-looking sports cars attained some popularity in the 1930s, the handsome coachwork originating from the company's Thames Ditton factory. After the Second World War an AC saloon appeared, though rather surprisingly it retained a leaf-sprung front suspension until it ceased production in 1957. Much more significant was the Ace of 1954, having an all independent tubular framed Tojeiro designed chassis. Initially the famous 2-litre six was pressed into service, though this was replaced by 2- and 2·2-litre Bristol and 2·6-litre British Ford power units. In 1963 the car received an even more significant transplant, an American Ford 4·2- (and later 4·7-)litre V-8; the Cobra had arrived! The model's sporting pedigree was amply reflected by Cobras being placed 4th at Le Mans in 1964 and 1966. Yet another variation on the theme came with the Cobra 427 it being fitted with a 7-litre Ford engine with handsome bodywork by Frua. Later, in 1967, a slightly larger V-8 — also by Ford — of 7016cc was fitted, the model being designated the 428, available until 1973. Latest AC offering is a sports car powered by a 3-litre Ford V-6 engine mounted transversely behind the driver.

1910 AC three-wheeler

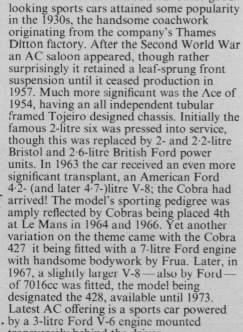
AC Cobra in racing trim

ACADEMY/*England 1906–1908*
A dual-control 14 hp model built by West of Coventry, mainly for Motor Schools, London, (who offered a course of 12 lessons for £3.3s), but also shown at the 1906 Olympia Show.

ACADIAN/*Canada 1962 to date*
Chevrolets built in the Oshawa, Ontario, plant of General Motors, differing in styling details from their USA counterparts.

ACCLES-TURRELL/*England 1899–1902*
Accles-Turrell began in 1899 with a two-seater 3 hp light carriage, equipped with an engine of their own make (fitted with the 'A-T Sponge Carburettor'). In 1901 the rights to the 'New Turrell' car ('vibrationless, very simple, quiet and efficient'), which had a 10/15 hp engine designed by F. H. De Veuille under the front seat, were acquired by Pollock Ltd, of Ashton-under-Lyne, who soon joined forces with Accles to form the famous tube-making company Accles & Pollock.

ACE/*England 1913*
An 8 hp, £125, four-cylinder chain-driven light car from the same manufacturer as the Salmon and Baguley.

ACE/*USA 1920–1922*
This assembled car emphasized 'square' coachwork lines which set it apart from its contemporaries. Both Continental and Herschell-Spillman six-cylinder engines were used, as well as a Gray four. The Ace was taken over by the American Motor Truck Co.

ACHILLES/*England 1904–1908*
Built in Frome, Somerset, the Achilles was a shaft-drive voiturette of 8 hp or 9 hp.

ACME/*USA 1903–1909*
Acme, of Reading, Pa., built powerful chain-driven touring cars, culminating in the 1909 Vanderbilt Six of 9653cc, with overdrive fourth speed.

ADAMS/*England 1905–1914*
American-born Edward R. Hewitt had assisted Sir Hiram Maxim to build a gigantic steam aeroplane in 1894; he subsequently designed a 'gas-buggy' on Oldsmobile lines which was built in England by the Adams Manufacturing Company of Bedford. With a 10 hp single-cylinder horizontal engine, the Adams had a supposedly foolproof epicyclic transmission: 'Pedals to push, that's all' was the marque's slogan. Following Hewitt's return to America, where he built similar cars under his own name, more conventional shaft-driven cars with vertical engines were introduced in 1906. These included two- and four-cylinder models and one of the earliest British V-8s, with a 35/40 hp engine based on the French Antoinette aeroengine, for which Adams were agents. Crankshaft breakages plagued the V-8 Adams. The year 1910 saw an advanced 16 hp with front-wheel brakes, and compressed-air starting, jacking and tyre-inflating equipment. The 'pedals-to-push' gear was still offered, alongside a conventional four-speed transmission and an odd three-speed planetary gearchange operated by a pedal moving in a gate.

ADAMS-FARWELL/*USA 1904–1913*
The Adams Company, of East Dubuque, Iowa, built their first experimental car in 1899. In 1904 they went into production with a car with a rear-mounted three-cylinder rotary air-cooled engine. By 1906 this had become a 40/45 hp five-cylinder, an unusual choice of power unit for a high-priced luxury car.

ADAMSON/*England 1914–1925*
R. Barton Adamson's little bullnosed cyclecar had a 9 hp 1075cc twin-cylinder engine and an underslung chassis.

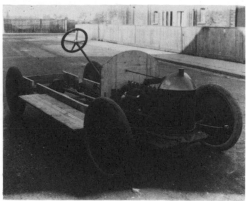
Adamson cyclecar chassis, 1914

ADD/*England 1971 to date*
Automotive Design and Development Ltd were responsible for the birth of the futuristic Nova, arguably one of the best-looking cars ever, with its shades of Ford GT40 and Lamborghini Muira. A glass-fibre shell, married to VW Beetle chassis and mechanicals, the Nova won worldwide acclaim. Nowadays it is marketed by Nova Cars Ltd, Brighouse, Yorkshire.

ADDISON/*England 1906*
'The Mercedes of the Tri-Car World', the Liverpool-built Addison had a 6½ hp two-cylinder engine controlled by variable-lift inlet valves.

ADELPHIA/*USA 1920*
This was a car planned for export and equipped with right-hand drive. It was powered by a four-cylinder Herschell-Spillman engine. Pilot models only were built.

ADER/*France 1896–1907*
Clément Ader, who left the ground in his steam aeroplane 'Eole' in 1890, was also a pioneer of the telephone: his 'Société Industrielle des Téléphones' of Paris built a range of vee-engined cars, including an early V-8 which ran in the 1903 Paris-Madrid. In 1903 Ader listed twin-cylinder cars of 904cc and 1571cc, and fours of 1810cc and 3142cc, available with a wide range of coachwork. A 24 hp vertical four was introduced at the December 1903 Paris Salon.

ADK/*Belgium 1923–1930*
Automobiles de Kuyper SA of Anderlecht, Brussels, announced a 1594cc pushrod ohv six-cylinder with twin carburettors and unit engine/gearbox construction at the 1927 Brussels Show.

c.1908 Adams 40/50hp V-8 phaeton

ADLER / *Germany 1900–1940*

This famous factory produced bicycles, typewriters, motorcycles and excellent cars. In pre-Great War days, Adler built cars from 1032cc to 9081cc with De Dion and—from 1902 onwards—own-make two- and four-cylinder sv engines. Driven by Erwin and Otto Kleyer, sons of Heinrich Kleyer, founder of Adler, and by Alfred Theves (founder of the ATE piston-ring works), these cars won many sporting events. Popular models of the 1920s, when Karl Irion drove many Adlers in races, were 2298cc, 1550cc and 4700cc four-cylinder and 2580cc six-cylinder cars. Gropius and Neuss coachwork was seen on many 'Standard' models, built between 1927 and 1934. They had 2916cc six-cylinder and 3887cc eight-cylinder engines. The front-wheel-drive Trumpf models of the 1930s with 995cc (Trumpf-Junior), 1494cc and 1645cc four-cylinder sv engines, gained many successes in races, including the Le Mans 24 hours. Among rear-driven Adler cars were the 1943cc 'Favorit', the 2916cc six-cylinder 'Diplomat' (with 65 hp at 3800 rpm) and the 1910cc four-cylinder and 2494cc six-cylinder models with neat, partially-streamlined bodywork by Ambi-Budd and Karmann, built until the Second World War. Adler employed some superb designers including Rumpler and Röhr, but only built motorcycles after World War Two.

ADRIA / *USA 1921–1922*

The Adria was an assembled car with a four-cylinder Supreme engine. Promotion was unsuccessful, although prototypes were built.

ADVANCE / *England 1906–1908*

Northampton motorcycle makers who also offered a 6 hp tricar.

AEM / *France 1924–1927*

Electric cars made in Neuilly, near Paris, by the Société d'Application Electro-Mécanique. Most of them were used as delivery vans. Top speed was 25–30 km/h (15–19 mph) and range around 80–100 km (50–60 miles). Some light cars were made and sold under the name of Electrocyclette.

AER / *France 1930*

A one-time subsidiary of BNC, the AER marque offered two cars in the American idiom, a sv 1991cc six-cylinder with CIME engine and an American sv straight-eight of 4241cc. Breaking with tradition, suspension was by a pneumatic device which quickly proved unreliable. These cars were later reissued with conventional suspension, under the name 'Aigle'.

AERO / *Czechoslovakia 1929–1939*

Designed by Břetislav Novotný, the Aero was made by a well-known aircraft and car-body factory, owned by Dr Kabeš. It originally had a 499cc single-cylinder two-stroke engine with water cooling. The next model was a 660cc vertical twin, followed by a 998cc twin-cylinder version. Designed by Ing. Bašek, the 1934 Aero was a front-wheel-drive design with a similar engine and a very sporting and comfortable four-seater body. The last model—also fwd—had a 1997cc four-cylinder 50 PS two-stroke engine. Famous drivers like Turek, Formanek,

1909 Adler landaulette

Hodač, Pohl, Michl, Holoubek, and Uher won many events in Aero cars.

AEROCAR / *USA 1905–1908*

Henry Ford's former backer, coal merchant Alexander Malcomson, was behind this short-lived air-cooled 24 hp four-cylinder luxury car which sold for $2800.

AERO CAR / *England 1919–1920*

A 5/7 hp Blackburne flat-twin engine powered this cyclecar with a Sturmey Archer gearbox.

AERO CAR / *USA 1921*

Using a two-cycle engine to drive a propeller, this tiny car of only 60 inches wheelbase was to have sold for $160. One prototype was made.

AEROCAR / *USA 1948 to date*

Moulton P. Taylor's four-passenger Aerocar can be converted into a light aeroplane in five minutes by attaching wings and a pusher propeller. So far, seven Aerocars have been built.

AEROFORD / *England 1920–1925*

The Aeroford was one of many attempts to disguise the ubiquitous Ford Model T, a special bonnet and different grille being the main ingredients of the deception.

AERTS / *Holland 1899*

Built a handful of cars at Dongen.

AFA / *Spain 1943–1944*

A 5 cv cabriolet built in Barcelona.

AGA / *Germany 1919–1929*

Once a very big manufacturer, who by 1922 was building 1000 cars a month. Aga was then part of the Stinnes group of companies, making a

1420cc four-cylinder car, which was also used as a taxicab. Via Stinnes, the factory was also connected with Dinos and even Rabag (licence-built Bugatti), but when Stinnes died in 1924, all these factories ran into difficulties. After 1926, production was on a limited scale. A sports-racing version driven by Willy Loge had a 1490cc engine and won many races. Scholl, Phillip and Pagani drove Aga cars in the 1924 Targa-Florio in Sicily, Scholl finishing 14th, behind Alfred Neubauer in a Mercedes.

1925 AGA saloon

AGERON / *France 1910–1914*

Ageron of Lyon built friction-drive one-, two- and four-cylinder light cars of 6, 8 and 10hp.

AGR / *England 1911–1915*

Ariel & General Repairs (the London branch of Ariel Cars) of Brixton, offered a 10/12 hp four-cylinder model apparently based on the French Hurtu, for which they were agents — in 1913, at a chassis price of £255.

AILLOUD / *France 1898*

Claudius Ailloud, of St Foy-les-Lyon, built this twin-cylinder air-cooled voiturette.

AIREDALE/*England 1919–1925*
Successor to the 'Tiny', this was a 14hp Dorman-engined car.

AIRPHIBIAN/*USA 1946*
A six-cylinder 165hp engine powered this aluminium-bodied car with independent suspension and aircraft-sized wheels. Fabric wings and fuselage could be easily attached to convert it into an aeroplane.

AIRWAY/*USA 1949–1950*
T. P. Hall made this two-seat minicar with an all-aluminium body/chassis and rear-mounted 10hp Onan engine. Only one fluid-drive speed was normally used (plus an emergency low).

1948 Airway sedan

AJAMS/*France 1920*
A light cyclecar made in Neuilly by M. Ajams, with a tubular frame in the 'birdcage' style. The engine was a 1093cc water-cooled twin-cylinder 9hp unit, with a three-speed gearbox. Too advanced in design, the Ajams soon died.

AJAX/*Switzerland 1906–1910*
A chain-driven monobloc 20/27cv four, the Ajax first appeared in 1906, the company failing soon after. Reformed in 1907, Ajax introduced four new models, a 2270cc 16cv and a 3267cc 24cv, both fours, and bi-bloc sixes of 3405cc and 4900cc. A curious feature was a mechanical starter which operated as soon as anyone stood on the running board! A misguided venture into taxi operation forced Ajax out of business in February 1910.

AJAX/*France 1913–1919*
The American Briscoe brothers promoted this 12hp cyclecar from Neuilly. Production continued after they had returned to the USA.

AJAX/*USA 1921*
Built in Hyde Park, Massachusetts, this was an assembled car which reached the prototype stage only. The Ajax had a Continental 7-R six-cylinder engine and a 116 inch wheelbase.

AJAX/*USA 1926*
This light six of advanced specification was introduced by Nash in 1926, and built in the former Mitchell factory in Racine, Wisconsin. It had a seven-bearing engine with full pressure lubrication and four-wheel-braking. However, the Ajax name was dropped in mid-1926, and the car became the Nash Light Six.

AJS/*England 1930–1933*
Motorcycle manufacturers A. J. Stevens Ltd briefly turned to the light car field with a 1018cc Coventry-Climax-engined model. Few were sold and the designs were taken over by Crossley; a 1½-litre model failed to materialize except for an appearance at the Motor Show of 1932.

AL/*France 1907*
A 24hp petrol-electric car built by L'Energie Electro-Mécanique, of Suresnes (Seine).

ALAN/*Germany 1923–1925*
Built in limited numbers, the Alan was an 'inflation period car' of simple design. The 30hp engine, a four-cylinder with overhead valves, was made by Siemens in Berlin.

ALAND/*USA 1916–1917*
An advanced 2·5-litre 16-valve ohc car with aluminium pistons and four-wheel brakes.

ALBA/*Austria 1907–1908*
Alba of Trieste (then part of Austria) began production in 1907 in a purpose-built 20,000m² factory. Their first cars had pair-cast 40/45hp engines of 6872cc.

ALBA/*France 1913–1920*
Made in Suresnes, a Paris suburb, the Alba lasted for seven years of constant mediocrity. Three engines were fitted — an ohv 8hp of 1172cc, a 10hp of 2001cc, offered first with side-valves then, towards the end of production, with overhead valves. In advance of their time, Albas were fitted with front-wheel brakes. They entered for Le Mans in 1924, but without success.

ALBANY/*England 1971 to date*
The product of a slack period in the construction industry, the Albany successfully evokes Edwardian engineering without being a replica of any specific marque. Nowadays for export only, the open-top Albany is powered by the 1500cc Triumph Spitfire engine.

ALBANY RUNABOUT
USA 1907–1908
A short-lived high-wheeler from Albany, Indiana, marketed as 'the Busy Man's Car'.

ALBATROS/*England 1923–1924*
The unfortunately named Albatros used Coventry-Climax engines of 8 and 10hp. Only a few examples of this Coventry-built light car were made.

ALBATROSS/*USA 1939*
This was a sports car venture with plans to market an ultra-streamlined four-seater tourer body on a standard Mercury chassis, based on a custom-built car which was made in Europe for famed cartoonist Peter Arno. Although the proposed car was advertised in at least one periodical, it is doubtful whether any Albatross cars were made.

ALBERFORD/*England 1922*
'The ideal owner-driver car' was based on a lengthened, underslung Model T Ford chassis with wire wheels and Rolls-Royce-type radiator. Prices ranged from £253 (two-seater) to £333 (saloon).

ALBERT/*England 1920–1924*
A proprietary 1½-litre ohv engine powered this well-made car, which boasted a Rolls-Royce-like radiator. In 1920, the manufacturers, Adam Grimaldi & Co. of Vauxhall, were taken over by Gwynne of Chiswick, later cars being called Gwynne-Alberts. By this time a 14hp engine had been fitted.

ALBION/*Scotland 1900–1913*
The first Abions were varnished-wood dog-carts of rustic appearance with a flat-twin 8hp engine and gear-change by 'Patent Combination Clutches'. A 16hp vertical-twin appeared in 1903, joined by a 24hp four in 1906. Solid-tyred shooting-brakes were a speciality. A 15hp monobloc four powered the last private Albions: from 1913 the firm concentrated on its excellent commercial vehicles.

ALC/*England 1913*
An 8hp twin-cylinder cyclecar selling for £100 complete.

ALCO/*USA 1905–1913*
One of the great names of the Edwardian era in America, Alco were twice winners of the Vanderbilt Cup. Their first products were licence-built French Berliets (coincidentally, both the American Locomotive Company and Berliet were famous steam locomotive builders) chain-drive 24hp and 40hp cars. Shaft-drive appeared in 1907, while the most famous Alco, the 60hp six, came two years later. The 1912 60hp Alco Berline, with Pullman ventilators in a clerestory roof, sold for a colossal $7250.

ALCYON/*France 1906–1928*
A well-established pushbike and motorcycle manufacturer, Alcyon of Courbevoie built voiturettes pre-1914, and in the 1920s produced cyclecars, which were actually two-stroke flat-twins made under the Alcyon name. Later, Alcyon also made a cyclecar of similar design, the main difference being the single-cylinder engine; this proved a complete flop.

ALDA/*France 1912–1922*
'Ah-La Délicieuse Automobile!'—the name invented for this marque created by Fernand Charron (late of CGV) by the readers of *l'Auto*. With a dashboard radiator and a 3187cc four-cylinder engine, capable, it was claimed, 'of 6 to

1913 Alda Coupe de l'Auto racer

47 mph in top gear', the 1912 Alda sold for £395 as a chassis in England. The cars were available

with the Henriod rotary valve system; a six-cylinder version was also listed. Post-war, only the four was offered, rebored to 3563cc.

ALDO/*USA 1910–1911*
A twin-cylinder buggy built in Chicago.

ALENA STEAM CAR/*USA 1922*
Only two Alena cars, both touring models, were built by a company which specialized in commercial vehicles and tractors. The wheelbase was 126 inches.

ALESBURY/*Ireland 1907–1908*
Powered by an 8/10 hp Stevens engine, the solid-tyred Alesbury was exhibited in Dublin in 1907.

1929 Alfa Romeo Spider AR 1750 SS

1938–39 Alfa Romeo 6C 2300 Berlinetta

Alfa Romeo Alfetta 2000 L, 1977

ALFA ROMEO
Italy 1910 to date
Originally founded in 1906 as a branch factory of the French Darracq, the works were sold in 1909 to an Italian group (Anonima Lombardo Fabbrica Automobili) led by Ugo Stella, which produced 2400cc and 4100cc four-cylinder models with sv engines. Another pre-1914 Alfa was the big 6100cc ohv version, built in very limited numbers only. In 1915, Nicola Romeo took over and added his name to the 'Alfa'. A superb engineer and a racing enthusiast, his cars became known all over the world. Famous models of the early 1920s were the Merosi-designed 2916cc and 2994cc ohv six-cylinder models, followed by Vittorio Jano's 1991cc six-cylinder and 1987cc eight-cylinder cars with superchargers, which won many big races. Other Jano-designed sports cars had 1487cc, 1752cc and 1920cc sohc and dohc engines. The 2236cc, 2632cc and 2905cc Tipo 'B' eight-cylinder dohc racers, including some monopostos, were among the

greatest in the world. Later some were built with 3160cc and even 3822cc engines and all were supercharged. Larger cars, including a 4492cc V-12 and the Bimotore with two eight-cylinder engines, were built and also raced. Until 1938 Enzo Ferrari headed the racing department, 'Alfa Corse', run directly by the works. It was then headed by the Spanish designer Wilfredo Ricart, but it was Gioachino Colombo who created, together with Ferrari, the superb Tipo 158 racing 1·5-litre car, which also won many races after World War Two. Among touring and sporting Alfa power units were dohc 2309cc and 2443cc sixes and also 'detuned' 2905cc Tipo 'B' racing engines. Well known after the war were 1997cc, 2995cc and 3576cc 'Disco Volante' models and the Alessio-designed 1884cc and 1975cc four-cylinder sohc cars as well as—from 1955 onwards—the fast 1290cc Giuliettas which eventually grew into the 1570cc 'Giulias'. The 1962 season saw the birth of the 2595cc dohc six-cylinder 2600: other models at that date were

four-cylinders of 845cc, 1290cc, 1570cc and 1975cc. Afterwards some models—like the 845cc—were dropped, while the six-cylinder versions were given 2584cc engines. Like all models, they were supplied with a wide range of bodywork. In 1970, the 200 bhp, 2593cc V-8 'Montreal' with a coupé body by Bertone was introduced. Alfa-Romeo, owned since 1934 by the Italian Government, built a big new factory in the impoverished south of Italy in the early 1970s for the manufacture of small cars. The result was the first 'Alfasud' of 1971, with an ohc 1186cc flat-four and front-wheel-drive. The latest Alfasud range contains 1186cc, 1286cc, 1337cc and 1490cc models designed by Rudolf Hruska. Other Alfa-Romeo models include the 1290cc Giulia Super, which is also available with a 1570cc or a 1760cc diesel engine. There is also the open Spider, the 1350cc and 1570cc Giulietta and the Alfettas with 1570cc, 1779cc and 1962cc dohc four-cylinder engines and De Dion rear-axles.

ALFGANG/*Denmark 1912–1914*
Only two cars were built by M. Alfgang, Silkeborg, before World War One stopped further production. The cars used French engines of unknown make.

ALFI/*Germany 1921–1924*
Product of an electrical company, the first Alfi had a sv 940cc four-cylinder engine, made by Steudel at Kamenz in Saxony. The second version had an Atos (Berlin) 1320cc four-cylinder motor.

L'ALKOLUMINE/*France 1899*
M. Martha, the inventor of this alcohol-powered car from Amiens, said it gave 'very little odour and vibration'.

ALLARD/*England 1899–1902*
Allard & Co. of Coventry, started production with motor tricycles, a four-seater 4½ hp car based on the Benz, and a 3 hp air-cooled car with an engine said to be of their own make. In 1902 they offered a 9 hp light car, merging with Rex later that year.

ALLARD/*England 1936–c1962*
Winner of the Monte Carlo Rally and the first-ever British Hillclimb Championship in cars bearing his own name, the ever-enthusiastic Sydney Allard became a legend in his own time. The first Allard special was completed in 1936 and was based on a 1934 TT Ford V-8 – not surprising, perhaps, as the Allards were much in the same mould, being strong, powerful cars built with competition very much in mind. A few production cars were built from 1937, basically two-seat Ford V-8s, but from 1945 came the first true Allards, the K1, the L and the J1, still Ford-based but with long-nosed bodies designed by Godfrey Imhof. The J-type could also be specified with a 3917cc Mercury V-8. A drophead coupé version of the L, the M-type, appeared in 1947. In 1949 came the immortal J2 Allard, with coil spring ifs, de Dion rear axle and a 4375cc Mercury. With Ardun ohv conversion, the stark J2 could top 110 mph. Production of Allard cars ceased in the 1960s with the Ford Zephyr-engined Palm Beach model.

ALL-BRITISH/*Scotland 1906–1908*
George Johnston, formerly of Arrol-Johnston, set up this company at Bridgeton, Glasgow, to build a 54 hp eight-cylinder car of curious design, with the cylinders arranged as two parallel fours, the pistons being actuated by rocking beams driven by connecting rods from a conventional four-throw crank. This unit was needlessly complex, and only a dozen All-British cars saw the light of day.

ALLDAYS & ONIONS/*England 1898–1918*
Founded in the mid-1800s, the Alldays & Onions Pneumatic Engineering Co. of Birmingham, entered the car field with the Traveller quadricycle. In 1900 Alldays showed a rear-engined flat-twin 7 hp four-seater of 'novel construction' at the National Show. It combined shaft, belt and gear transmission with great inefficiency. A shaft-drive single appeared in 1903, followed in 1905 by a twin-cylinder 10/12 hp which lasted until 1913. A 20/25 hp

1912 Alldays and Onions 10hp

four followed, joined in 1908 by a 14/18 hp. A 30/35 six of 4891cc was introduced for 1911, and a vee-twin light car, the Midget, appeared in 1913. There was a neat bullnosed 9 hp four in 1914. In 1918 Alldays merged with Enfield (which they had owned since 1907).

1902 Alldays Traveller Voiturette

ALLEN/*USA 1913–1914*
Friction-drive two- and four-cylinders from a Philadelphia manufacturer.

ALLEN/*USA 1913–1921*
Built at Fostoria, Ohio, the Allen used Sommers four-cylinder engines, acquiring this power unit manufacturer in 1915. The 1920 Allen 43, with bevel-sided touring coachwork and a high-shouldered radiator, was a handsome car which nevertheless failed to avert the company's bankruptcy. Willys acquired the remnants.

ALLEN KINGSTON/*USA 1907–1909*
Designed on European lines to avoid the 45 per cent duty on imported cars, these 45 hp 7400cc four-cylinder cars were built by the New York Car & Truck Company for motor agent Walter C. Allen of New York. The Allen Kingston

combined 'the best features of the Fiat, the Renault and the Mercedes in a harmonious new construction of the highest quality'.

ALLIANCE/*Germany 1903–1905*
A supplier of components for car production, Alliance of Berlin also built complete cars with two- and four-cylinder engines. Early versions had De Dion motors.

ALLIANCE/*France 1905–1908*
With a similar radiator to the Mass, this Parisian marque was also known as 'Aiglon'. In 1908 an 18 hp four with Tony Huber engine was listed: it sold in England for £450.

ALLRIGHT/*Germany 1908–1913*
Known in Germany as 'Allreit', this Cologne-Lindenthal factory also built Allright, Tiger, Roland and Vindec-Special motorcycles and bicycles. The Allright-Mobil had 5 hp or 7 hp vee-twin engines; the last ones had sv 960cc engines with air-cooling.

ALLSTATE/*USA 1952–1953*
'The lowest-priced full-sized sedan on the US market' claimed Sears Roebuck's Allstate auto accessory chain (though it was similar to the

Allen Classic phaeton from Ohio

even cheaper Henry J). Offered with either a four-cylinder 68hp or an L-head six 80hp engine, only 2363 were sold in 12 months and the line was discontinued after the second model year.

ALL-VELO/*Sweden 1904–1906*
Starting with importing bicycles, the Allmanna Velociped-Aktiebolaget, of Landskrona, decided to buy unassembled Waltham Orient Buckboards from the USA. They were sold as All-Velos; possibly around 50 were assembled. Most parts except engine, axles and steering were wood, and the car had a single-cylinder air-cooled engine at the rear, with friction drive. Brakes were fitted only on the right rear wheel and there was tiller steering.

ALMA 6/*France 1926–1929*
Very few cars were made by this Courbevoie factory. This marque made its own engines instead of using proprietary units. The Alma engine, developed by aircraft engineer Vaslin, was a 1643cc with three valves per cylinder.

ALP/*Belgium 1920*.
Designed by the former chief engineer of Métallurgique, this 2121cc light car was built by Automobiles Leroux-Pisart of Brussels.

ALPENA/*USA 1910–1914*
Designed for speed, the Alpena Flyer featured unit engine/gearbox construction with three-point suspension (and the Alpena Company was fined $400,000 in a court case brought against them by the patentee of this design, one Emile Huber).

ALPINE/*France 1952 to date*
Jean Rédelé founded this well-known marque of rear-engined sports cars in Dieppe in 1952. Having built some prototypes for racing, he started production in 1956 with the 4cv Renault-based Alpine A106, followed by the 'Mille Miles'. Two new models were presented in 1958—the A108 roadster and the 'Tour de France' with a top speed of 112 mph. From 1959 the Alpine was built under licence in Brazil by Interlagos. At the beginning of the 1960s Rédelé presented a new car, the long-lived Alpine A110, which began with Dauphine or Dauphine-Gordini engines, and was then R8 and R8-Gordini engined. With the latter engine, the car could reach 130 mph. The car was later equipped with Renault engines such as the 1108cc and 1296cc Renault-Gordini, R16 TS and R12-Gordini. Alpine had many victories in rallies, as well as in road racing, and was a regular entrant at Le Mans for many years. The R16 TS-engined Alpine A310 presented in 1971 eventually supplanted the A110. A 2664cc A310 V6 subsequently became available. In 1976 Alpine and Renault jointly presented the Renault 5 'Alpine' ('Gordini' in the UK), a hotted-up version of the standard Renault 5.

ALSACE/*USA 1920–1921*
Built by Piedmont for export, the Alsace was equipped with a right-hand drive and differed from other Piedmont products in its Rolls-Royce-shaped radiator. The wheelbase was 116 inches and a four-cylinder Herschell-Spillman engine was employed.

ALTA/*England 1931–1954*
Geoffrey Taylor's Altas were initially powered by an 1100cc engine of his own design, having an aluminium block, wet liners and shaft-driven twin overhead camshafts. This was mounted in a low-slung chassis frame and in 1935 1496cc and 1961cc engines became available. From these sports cars, racing machines naturally evolved, 1937 seeing an all independent suspension 1½-litre supercharged car offered for sale.

After the war Taylor built a car for the current Formula 1 and later supplied engines for HWM and Connaught racing cars.

ALTENA/*Holland 1900–1906*
Altena of Haarlem-Heemstede built between 40 and 50 cars, initially using De Dion engines.

ALTER/*USA 1914–1917*
A four-cylinder from Plymouth, Michigan.

ALTHAM/*USA 1896–1899*
George J. Altham, of Fall River, Massachusetts, was a pioneer manufacturer of 'hydrocarbon carriages'. The company collapsed at the end of 1899 when the treasurer absconded with most of the stock and real estate deeds.

ALUMINUM/*USA 1920–1922*
The Aluminum was built by the Aluminum Manufacturers, Inc, of Cleveland, Ohio, in a research attempt to emphasize and prove the advantages of this metal in automobile construction. In all, six were built, five-passenger touring cars weighing 2400lb, with a 126-inch wheelbase and four-cylinder Alcoa engines. In 1922 Pierce-Arrow interests entered the picture and the cars built after that point were under Pierce-Arrow direction and known as Pomeroy cars.

ALVAREZ/*Spain 1921–c1923*
Also known as 'MA', this was a sporting cyclecar with brakes on all four wheels built by Jesus Battlo of Barcelona.

ALVA SPORT/*France 1913–1921*
The Alva Sport made in Courbevoie used two different four-cylinder engines, an ohc 1496cc and an ohv 2651cc unit. Even when fitted with Perrot front-wheel brakes, Alvas suffered from archaic features such as a cone clutch.

Alpine Sports

Alvis 12/50 'ducksback', c.1925, at Brooklands

1928 Alvis fwd team at Le Mans

1961/62 Alvis TD21 drophead coupé

ALVIS
England 1920–1967

The Alvis took its name from an aluminium piston designed by G. P. H. de Freville, who was responsible, along with T. G. John, for the design of the first model, the 10/30. Then in 1922 Captain T. G. Smith-Clarke joined the company as chief engineer and he created the famous 12/50 of 1923, along with W. M. Dunn who was chief designer. The uncertainty of the company's financial state was reflected by the appointment of a receiver in 1924, though once production of the 12/50 got under way prospects brightened considerably. This pushrod-engined car was available with long-stroke (1598cc) touring or short-stroke (1486cc) sports form being replaced by the similar 12/60. In its turn the four-cylinder theme was continued by the 1½-litre Firefly. Alvis played a progressive role in the development of front-wheel-drive in Europe. In 1925 they produced a low-slung sprint car, powered by a 12/50 engine mounted back to front, and

in the following year a 1½-litre supercharged dohc straight-eight grand prix car. In 1928 came the Front Wheel Drive production car using an ohc four-cylinder 1482cc engine, with the option of an Alvis designed and built supercharger and all-independent suspension. Although it only remained in production for two years a few straight-eight examples were also built. A six-cylinder Alvis of 1870cc appeared in 1928, though the following year the capacity was upped to 2148cc, the model being named the Silver Eagle. From this power unit sprang the successful six-cylinder Alvises of the 1930s: the Speed 20 (2·5- and 2·7-litres), Speed 25 (3·5-litres) and the 4·3-litre, plus the touring Crested Eagle and Silver Crest. These well-engineered cars were among the handsomest thoroughbreds of their day and also some of the fastest. At one time the 4·3 model was one of the quickest saloons on the British market, being capable of over 100 mph. In 1933 the company's progressive technical outlook was reflected by the last-named

model, which had independent front suspension and an all-synchromesh gearbox. Not that four-cylinder models were neglected. George Lanchester was responsible for the design of the 12/70 which replaced the Firebird of 1935 in 1938. After the Second World War, Alvis adopted a one-model policy, the TA 14 appearing in 1946, having evolved from the pre-war 12/70. Its four-cylinder pushrod engine was of 1892cc. This cart-sprung model survived until 1950, when it was replaced by the six-cylinder TA 21, with a 3-litre engine which produced 90 bhp. This in its turn was succeeded by the TC 21/100 with a guaranteed 100 mph, though this was dropped in 1956. That year the gracious Graber-designed saloon appeared on what was basically a TC 21/100 chassis and in 1959 it was named the TD 21, evolving into the TE 21 in 1964. The following year the company was acquired by Rover, private car production ceasing in the summer of 1967, though military vehicles are still being manufactured.

AMAZON/*England 1921–1922*
A light car with a rear-mounted 6/9 hp Coventry-Victor power unit.

AMBASSADOR/*USA 1921–1926*
The Ambassador had been known as the Shaw before Yellow Cab bought the business. A few large cars were sold under the name before the Model D-1 was introduced as a 'drive yourself' car in 1924. The car became the Hertz in 1926.

AMC/*England 1900*
The Automobile Manufacturing Company of London offered this 10 hp steam car with flash boiler, 'absolutely safe in the hands of a novice'. Top speed was said to be 40 mph.

AMC BORGWARD ISABELLA
Mexico 1979
A sedan with Mexican Borgward engine and AMC coachwork.

AMCO/*USA 1919–1920*
The Amco was an export automobile with left- or right-hand steering optional. Amco cars were marketed in a single colour — beige — and carried a radiator especially designed for tropical climates. A GB & S four-cylinder engine was used and the cars had a wheelbase of 114 inches.

AMERICA/*Spain 1917–1922*
The four-cylinder 'valveless' Tipo A America of 1917 had a primitive form of synchromesh gearbox and worm final drive, but this Barcelona firm's main product was the Tipo B of 1097cc; Tipo C was an ohv racing model.

AMERICAN/*USA 1899*
The American Automobile Company of New York offered 'hydro-carbon carriages' which could be started from the seat by chain-and-sprocket gearing.

AMERICAN/*USA 1902–1903*
A wheel-steered gas buggy from Cleveland, Ohio.

AMERICAN/*USA 1916–1924*
The American was one of many assembled cars built during its time and Amco, Rutenber and Herschell-Spillman engines were employed over the years. For a time, racing driver Louis Chevrolet served as head of American's engineering department. Never a large producer, peak year was 1920 when some 1500 units left the factory at Plainfield, NJ. In 1923 the American car became connected with the Bessemer Truck Corporation, and that October, the new combine became Amalgamated Motors, which also included the Northway and Winther companies.

AMERICAN AUSTIN, AMERICAN BANTAM/*USA 1930–1941*
This was America's version of the Austin Seven, introduced with the hope of creating a large market of small-car enthusiasts and users in the United States. The cars with their four-cylinder engines rather resembled miniature Chevrolets with horizontal hood louvres *à la* Stutz or Marmon. The coupé at $445 was billed as a sedan and at that price should have appealed to more buyers than it did. But the Depression and the appeal of known secondhand cars at a lower price did not help Austin sales. Slightly more than 8000 units were sold during the car's first year of sales — subsequently sales fell off to the point that production was suspended in 1934 until 1937. In 1937, the car was redesigned by Alexis de Sakhnoffski and the name was changed to Bantam. The facelift and new name helped a little, as did a new line of body styles, including light trucks and a station waggon. The Bantam pioneered the design for the first Jeep. These first Jeeps were built by Bantam for the US Army, by which time passenger car production had ended.

AMERICAN CHOCOLATE/*USA 1903–1906*
Well known as makers of coin-in-the-slot confectionery dispensers, American Chocolate of New York began assembling 30, 40 and 50 hp cars from imported components, under the supervision of the Swiss engineer William Walter, who had built his first car in 1898. From 1906, when the company relocated in Trenton, New Jersey, cars were built under the name Walter.

AMERICAN ELECTRIC/*USA 1899–1902*
Based in New York, this company built a wide range of electric carriages capable, it was claimed, of running 35 to 50 miles — 'very few private carriages would ever be subjected to such a test,' claimed this optimistic manufacturer.

AMERICAN ELECTRIC/*USA 1913–1915*
An amalgamation of three electric car companies: Argo, Borland and Broc.

1900 American Electric Golf Trap

AMC

AMERICAN MOTORS/*USA 1954 to date*
Financial difficulties forced Nash and Hudson to merge under the presidency of George Romney, who concentrated on the 1950-introduced Rambler, largely to the exclusion of the two older marques which vanished in 1957. That year, the Rambler range was expanded to 20 models, including the new 5359cc Rebel V-8. Rambler was still marketing the Metropolitan sub-compact built by Austin, a legacy of Nash days. In 1959 AMC revived the six-cylinder Rambler as the American, and brought back the Nash Ambassador with the 5359cc V-8 as a top of the range model. There was now a complete line of Rebels. Unable to match the competition from the 'Big Three' compacts, the Metropolitan ceased production in 1960, but unsold stocks were still being cleared in 1962. Sleek new styling earned Rambler and Ambassador *Motor Trend*'s 'Car of the Year' award in 1963, while the little American was remodelled in 1964, offering superior specification to its rivals. AMC's entry in the 'musclecar' stakes was the four-seater Javelin Sports coupé of 1968, with 4752cc, 5621cc or 6391cc V-8s, or a 3802cc six. Front disc brakes were optional on the V-8s. The Javelin was followed in mid-season by the AMX two-seater with the 6391cc V-8, featuring disc brakes and sports suspension. The Rambler name was dropped in 1970, when a famous name, the Hornet, was revived for a 3261cc six (three V-8 engines were optional). In mid-March that year, AMC announced the Gremlin sub-compact, little bigger than a VW, with lift-up rear window and 3621cc or 3802cc six-cylinder engine. An intermediate model, the Matador, was built in 1971, available as sedan, wagon or sport coupé. Ambassador production ended in 1974, and a new model 'designed around the passenger compartment', the Pacer, appeared. Just 171 inches long, it was 6 inches wider than the Cadillac Seville and boasted windows covering a third of its exterior. The 3802cc six was standard until 1978, when a 4982cc V-8 was offered. Hornet production ceased in 1978, 400,000 units having been sold. It was then replaced by the Concord luxury compact, while for 1979, the Gremlin (dropped a year earlier) was replaced by the Spirit, available as hatchback or sedan, while a 'Limited' edition of the Concord boasted a high level of specification including leather trim. There were also a 'Limited' Pacer and a new sporty AMX with four-speed manual gearbox. AMC's fortunes were aided by a 1970 merger with Kaiser Jeep, while in 1979 an agreement with Renault provided for the production and sale of the Renault R18 by an AMC factory in the USA.

AMC Rambler Classic Wagon, 1965

1968 AMC Javelin

AMC Pacer De Luxe Hatchback, 1978

1958 Ambassador

AMERICAN SIMPLEX, AMPLEX
USA 1906–1915
A four-cylinder 50 hp two-stroke engine powered the American Simplex — 'A motor car symphony' — from Mishawaka, Indiana. From 1910, the name was shortened to 'Amplex'. The 1911 30/50 hp toy tonneau sold for $4300.

AMERICAN STEAM CAR / *USA 1924–1931*
This car, produced by Thomas Derr, catered largely for former Stanley owners and most of the company's operations were limited to conversions. Most used Hudson chassis and bodies.

AMERICAN STEAMER / *USA 1922–1924*
Not to be confused with Thomas Derr's American Steam Car, the American Steamer was a product of the American Steam Truck Co. of Elgin, Ill., and was typical of the renaissance of steam cars which tried to get on the American automobile market in the early 1920s. Featuring a twin-cylinder compound double-acting motor, the American Steamer line offered a touring car, roadster, coupé and sedan. At least 16 cars are known to have been built and possibly as many as 20 may have left the factory.

1924 American Steamer

AMERICAN UNDERSLUNG
USA 1905–1914
One of the classic marques of its day, the American Underslung from Indianapolis was the brainchild of Harry Stutz. An underslung chassis and big 41 × 4½in wheels gave the American Underslung its distinctive appearance. Prices ranged from $1250 to $4500, and Teetor-Harley engines of 40 hp and 50 hp were used. From 1905 to 1908 the car was also available with a conventional chassis as the 'American Tourist'.

AMES / *USA 1910–1915*
A beetle-backed 'gentleman's roadster' and a five-passenger tourer were the initial products of this Owensboro, Kentucky company.

AMG / *Sweden 1903–1905*
From 1897 the AB Motorfabriken i Göteborg built stationary engines. In the first years of the century they imported French Richard-Brasier cars; Swedish production of cars based on this marque was proposed, but the plans failed. In 1903 a new model was shown, using twin-cylinder air-cooled engines bought from the German Fafnir company. These tended to overheat and were soon changed to water-cooling. Only engines were imported, the rest of the car being manufactured in Sweden. About 10 cars were built.

AMHERST / *Canada 1912*
The 'Two-in-One' Amherst 40 could be converted into a truck by removing the rear seats. Only nine were completed.

Amilcar Pegase sports, 1937 Le Mans

AMILCAR / *France 1921–1939*
This well-known French marque started in 1921 as a small cyclecar, designed by Jules Salomon and Edmond Moyet, and bore a close resemblance to the pre-war Le Zèbre. The first model was the 903cc CC, available in a sport version, the CS, and the family C4. The sv engine had splash lubrication, and there was a three-speed gearbox. But the most famous of all was the CGS 'Grand Sport' of 1924 with a sv engine of 1074cc and four-wheel brakes; it evolved into the more sporty CGSS 'Grand Sport Surbaissé'. These were made under licence as Pluto in Germany and Grofri in Austria. In the mid-1920s, the marque entered proper motor racing, building a batch of supercharged dohc 1100cc six-cylinder cars that used a roller bearing crankshaft in the full racing version, but were also available with plain bearings. Amilcar also built a light touring car, the M-type, with a sv 1200cc engine, launched in 1928, followed by M2, M3 and M4 versions. They also made a straight-eight in 1928, with an ohc 2-litre engine. This C8 proved unreliable and expensive and disappeared very quickly. In the late 1930s, Amilcar introduced two new models, the 14 cv with a four-cylinder Delahaye engine and the Compound. The latter was made when Amilcar was taken over by Hotchkiss. Very advanced in design, the front-wheel-drive Compound featured a monocoque frame made out of light alloy and independent suspension all round. The engine was an ohv four-cylinder of 1185cc. Production was not resumed after World War Two.

AMIOT (AMIOT-PENEAU)
France 1897–1902
A front-wheel-drive power-pack for converting horse-carriages into motor cars, the Amiot, from Asnières, originally had a 6 hp Cyclope engine: an electric version was also available.

AMITRON / *USA 1967*
Powered by two lithium-nickel fluoride batteries, the Amitron was a three-passenger vehicle produced by American Motors and Gulton Industries. Capable of travelling 150 miles at 50 mph on a single charge, the Energy Re-generation Brake system automatically switched the motors to generators, which recharged the batteries and increased the range.

AMOR / *Germany 1924–1925*
Another small car built in limited numbers. It had a 16 hp four-cylinder proprietary engine.

AMPERE / *France 1906–1909*
The Ampère, built at Billancourt (Seine), had a 10/16 hp four-cylinder engine driving through an electric clutch ('variation of speed by electric transmission, with neither dynamo nor accumulators').

AMPHICAR / *Germany 1961–1965*
Designed by Hans Trippel, who had produced amphibian cars at the Bugatti factory at Molsheim during the War, the Amphicar — built by the Quandt Group at Lübeck but mainly at Berlin-Borsigwalde — had an English 1147cc Triumph four-cylinder engine with 38 hp at 4750 rpm. Most cars were sold in the USA. Total production was about 2800 units.

AMX / *Italy 1969–1972*
Made at the former Bizzarini factory at Turin, the Italian-built AMX was another Bizzarini design and contained many parts made by the American Motor Corporation, which had taken over the small Bizzarini works. Ital Design supplied the bodywork for the mid-engined car, which had a 6383cc AMV V-8 engine developing 345 PS (SAE) at 5100 rpm.

ANADOL / *Turkey 1966 to date*
Turkey's first production car, the Reliant/Ogle styled Anadol is built in Istanbul, and powered by Ford — currently 1300cc and 1600cc.

ANAHUAC / *USA 1922*
Patterned on a contemporary Polish car, the Anahuac was to have been marketed in Mexico by a Mexican concern. Wheelbase was 115 inches and only four units were completed by the builder, Frontenac Motor Corp. of Indianapolis, Indiana.

ANASAGASTI / *Argentina 1912–1914*
Horacio Anasagasti of Buenos Aires is credited with building the first Argentinian car, a 15 hp Ballot-engined vehicle. In 1912–13 he came to Europe to prove his designs in competition, entering a team for the 1912 Tour de France and a Picker-engined racer for the 1913 Coupe de l'Auto. He returned to Argentina and is said to have built about 50 touring Anasagastis.

1913 Coupe de l'Auto Anasagasti

ANCHOR BUGGY/*USA 1910–1911*
A high-wheeler from Cincinnati, Ohio.

ANDERHEGGEN/*Holland 1901–1902*
A light 4 hp four-seater *vis-à-vis* built in Amsterdam. Total production was under ten.

ANDERSON/*USA 1916–1925*
Anderson, the most successful of all American cars built in the southern states, was the outgrowth of a South Carolina carriage works. Andersons were sold throughout the country by an active dealership. Using Continental six-cylinder engines, the make was noted for its attractive body styles and colour combinations, production reaching nearly 2000 units in 1923.

Anderson Sport roadster, 1921

ANDERSON ELECTRIC/*France 1912*
A costly electric car with five speeds and Edison batteries shown at the 1912 Paris Salon. The 3/9 hp cost Fr 13,500 and the 4/12 hp, Fr 18,500.

ANDRE/*England 1933–1934*
This lightweight two-seater sports car used a vee-twin ohv JAP engine of 728cc; only half-a-dozen were made.

ANGLADA/*Spain 1902–1908*
Angladas were built in Puerto de Santa Maria (Andalucia), as one- or four-cylinder cars of 6 to 36 cv. A 24 hp four was the first Spanish car bought by Alfonso XIII, in 1904.

ANGLIAN/*England 1905–1907*
Tricars built in Beccles, Suffolk, with either 3½ hp single-cylinder De Dion or 5 hp 'twin coupled' power units.

ANGLO-AMERICAN
England 1899–1900
This York company claimed these 'exceptionally powerful motors were manufactured throughout in our own works,' but they were probably Continental imports. Motor tricycles with 2 hp engines were also offered.

ANGLO-DANE/*Denmark 1902–1917*
H. C. Fredriksen of Copenhagen was building bicycles in the 1890s using British parts — hence the name. The first cars were light trucks with single-cylinder Kelecom engines. Later cars had single-cylinder 4·5 hp engines and friction drive, and a few passenger cars were also built with twin-cylinder engines.

ANGLO-FRENCH/*England 1896–1897*
Leon l'Hollier's Anglo-French Motor Carriage Company of Birmingham modified Roger-Benz cars for the British market.

1921 Angus-Sanderson

ANGUS-SANDERSON/*England 1919–1927*
The Angus-Sanderson was, in concept, rather like the Bean and Cubitt. The intention was to mass produce one model following the successful Ford practice. An assembly of proprietary parts, the Angus-Sanderson had a 2·3-litre engine by Tylor, a Wrigley gearbox and rear axle, springs by Woodhead and wheels by courtesy of Goodyear. Unfortunately all the brave words of the day failed to produce many cars. Production moved from County Durham to Hendon, Middlesex in 1921 and a smaller 8 hp car was toyed with in 1925, but production finally ceased two years later.

ANHUT/*USA 1909–1910*
Open two- and four-seat 3785cc ohv sixes built in Detroit; taken over in 1910 by Barnes.

ANKER/*Germany 1919–1920*
This small company based at Berlin built cars up from war-surplus car components, mainly of the 1145cc four-cylinder Wanderer.

ANSALDO/*Italy 1921–1931*
Ansaldo was a leading armaments concern which entered car manufacture with an ohc 1847cc four-cylinder model. It developed 36 bhp at 3600 rpm. A sports version had a 1981cc engine, and there was also a six-cylinder version of 1991cc. Later six-cylinder models had engines of 2179cc. Among the last cars made by Ansaldo was an ohv straight-eight of 3532cc. The Ansaldos were cars of good quality and modern design. They competed in many races. When Wikov in Czechoslovakia began manufacture in 1928, they built the 1453cc Ansaldo Tipo 10.

ANSBACH/*Germany 1910–1913*
Forerunner of Faun, Ansbach was famous for lorries and buses. Their 1559cc four-cylinder 14 hp touring car was known as the Kautz.

ANSTED/*USA 1922*
The Ansted or Ansted-Lexington was actually a custom-designed Lexington roadster which was marketed under the Ansted emblem, the engine being an Ansted six. Luxuriously appointed, this sporty car cost $4500.

ANSTED/*USA 1926–1927*
Following the sale of Lexington's plant in Connersville, Indiana, to Auburn, the Lexington-Ansted interests marketed their last cars as Ansteds. These differed from the Lexington only in the radiators, emblems and hubcaps.

ANTOINE/*Belgium 1900–1905*
V. Antoine of Liège was an engine manufacturer who also offered a 4 hp voiturette and, in 1905, a 15/25 hp car.

ANTOINETTE/*France 1906–1908*
Better known as builders of aeroplanes and aeroengines, Antoinette of Puteaux showed a car with a 32 hp V-8 engine and hydraulic clutches instead of a gearbox and differential at the 1906 Paris Salon. The following year, a 16 hp four and 30 hp V-8 were available.

ANZANI/*Italy 1923–1924*
Famous as producers of proprietary engines for motorcycles, cars, aeroplanes, and boats, Anzani also built a number of 1098cc cyclecars.

APOLLO/*Germany 1910–1927*
Ruppe & Son of Apolda (Thuringia) produced first Piccolo, then, from 1910, Apollo cars. The first Apollo, the 'Mobbel', had an air-cooled 624cc single-cylinder ioe engine. There were also

10/30 Apollo chassis

air-cooled 1608cc in-line fours and a 1575cc V-4. Four separate cylinders in line powered the 1770cc model 'E'. Designed by racing driver Karl Slevogt, the model 'B' had an ohv 960cc four-cylinder engine: another of his superb creations had an ohv 2040cc engine. Other Apollos had sv four-cylinder engines of up to 3440cc. Some models after 1920 had wishbone suspension; the last Apollo cars had ohv 1200cc four-cylinder engines or sv 1551cc Steudel four-cylinder power units. Hugo Ruppe, son of the factory founder, was a famous two-stroke engine designer; he built the air-cooled MAF cars, which in 1920 became part of Apollo. Slevogt raced Apollo cars with streamlined Jaray bodies during the mid-1920s.

APOLLO / USA 1962–1964
The Apollo was a well-engineered, fast sports/personal car with Italian hand-made two-seater aluminium convertible or fastback bodywork and a V-6 or V-8 Buick engine. Ninety were produced before it was renamed the Vetta Ventura.

APOLLO / England 1971–1972
The Can-Am racer-inspired Apollo was the brainchild of Allen Pearce. Originally intended purely for his own use, this dramatic-looking VW-based glass-fibre sports car very nearly entered serious production in 1972.

APPERSON / USA 1902–1926
After the Apperson brothers broke away from Haynes-Apperson (q.v.) they continued for a while with a front-mounted flat-twin engine, then used a horizontal four. Vertical fours were the order of the day by 1904, when 24hp and 40hp models were offered. In 1906 a 95hp four was catalogued at $10,500, and a year later came the first of the famous Jackrabbit speedsters, a 60hp selling at $5000. For a time, the entire range was known as the 'Jack Rabbit': a 32·4hp four and a 33·7hp six were listed in 1913; a 33·8hp 90 degree V-8 of 5502cc appeared during 1914. In 1916, the 'Roadaplane' six and eights were announced. A sporty tourer designed by Conover T. Silver, the 'Silver-Apperson', was launched in 1917: after 1919 it was known as the 'Anniversary'. In 1923 a proprietary six of 3243cc appeared, and a Lycoming eight was also available from 1924. By now, both Apperson and Haynes were losing sales, but a rumoured re-marriage came to nothing, and the introduction of four-wheel brakes on the 1926 Appersons failed to halt the company's end.

APPLE / USA 1917–1918
The $1150 Apple 8 from Dayton, Ohio, was, agents were assured, 'a car which you can sell!!!' Unfortunately, the public did not buy!

1917/18 Apple 8

1913 Arden four-seater tourer

AQUILA-ITALIANA / Italy 1906–1914
Designed by Guilio Cesare Cappa, these were big four- and six-cylinder cars with ioe engines of advanced design. After 1908 there was an interruption in manufacture, but new models appeared late in 1911. These had 4192cc six-cylinder engines and proved successful in many races. Among their drivers were Meo Costantini, who afterwards joined Bugatti at Molsheim, where he became a racing driver and eventually Chef d'Equipe, and Carlo Masetti, elder brother of Count Giulio Masetti.

ARAB / England 1926–1928
That enigmatic genius Reid Railton was responsible for the design of the Arab, a sporting 2-litre which appeared in 1926. The engine was an ohc four-cylinder, with leaf-valve springs as

on Parry Thomas's Leyland Eight, a reminder that Railton had worked for Thomas. But after the Welshman's death attempting to break the World Land Speed Record in 1927, Railton lost heart in the Arab project. A pity, for the two-seater was good for 80mph while the more potent Super Sports was able to touch 90mph.

ARBEE / England 1904
A 6hp two-speeded car with 'slow running engine' — hardly a compelling sales gimmick!

ARDEN / England 1912–1916
Starting life as a crudely finished vee-twin JAP-engined cyclecar with wooden chassis, the Arden grew up into a well-built four-cylinder 1096cc Alpha-engined light car, eventually with full four-seater coachwork.

L'ARDENNAIS / France 1901–c1903
This voiturette, from Rethel (Ardennes) came with interchangeable water- and air-cooled cylinders, for summer and winter use.

ARDSLEY / USA 1905–1906
W. S. Howard, who had built cars under his own name, designed this 30/35hp four.

1916 Argo

ARGO / USA 1915–1916
A short-lived attempt to rival Ford at producing 'a motor car for the millions' the 1916 Argo, from Jackson, Michigan, sold for $405 in two-seater form. The firm originally made a cyclecar—the four–cylinder 'Motorvique'—based on the Briscoes' French-built Ajax.

ARGONAUT / USA 1959–1963
The first name applied to this proposed behemoth was the 'Argonaut State Limousine', but the name was soon changed to the 'Argonaut Motor Machine', the car being planned to be the finest and most luxurious in the world. The prototype of the Argonaut was mounted on a Chrysler chassis. Prices quoted ranged from $26,800 to $36,000 and a variety of stainless and special steels were planned for the car's manufacture. A 12-cylinder ohc aluminium air-cooled engine developing some 1010bhp was designed and all Argonauts were to have carried a four-year guarantee. In its catalogue, Argonaut claimed two of its models, the 'Smoke' and the 'Raceway', had a maximum speed of 240 miles per hour. One Argonaut is known to have reached private hands.

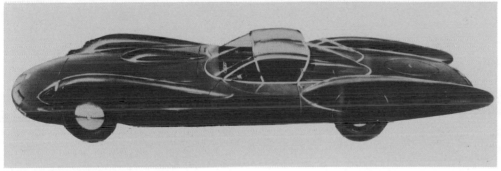
Argonaut State Limousine

ARGONNE/USA 1919–1920

The Argonne—24 of which constituted the firm's entire output—was a sports roadster with a 118–128-inch wheelbase and a four-cylinder Buda engine, although a Rochester-Duesenberg power plant could be had as an option. The radiator of the Argonne was sharply pointed, similar to that of the Austro-Daimler.

ARGUS/Germany 1901–1909

Founded by Paul Jeannin, Argus originally built copies of the Panhard & Levassor cars. They also had P & L engines and most other components came from France. Engines of Argus's own design and manufacture appeared in 1903; Argus cars had now 2380cc two-cylinder and 4960cc and 9240cc four-cylinder engines. They were luxurious and expensive cars.

1976 Argyl coupé

ARGYL/Scotland 1976 to date

Ex-Mini racer and supercharger expert Bob Henderson is also builder of Scotland's only sports car. Based on a sturdy tubular chassis the striking mid-engined Caledonian is powered by a variety of engines including a supercharged version of the Rover V-8.

1923 Ariel 10hp tourer

ARIEL/England 1900–1915, 1922–1925

Ariel of Birmingham began with motor tricycles and quadricycles, but by 1902 a 10 hp twin-cylinder car was being built. In 1903 came the company's first four-cylinder, the 16 hp. A design peculiarity of these cars was a leather cone clutch entirely separate from the flywheel. A six-cylinder model, whose tubular chassis seemed totally inadequate, appeared early in 1904. A 16 hp Ariel was the first car up Snowdon, in 1904. A completely new range was announced at the end of 1905 under the name 'Ariel-Simplex': these were Mercedes-inspired fours of 15 hp and 25/30 hp and a 35/40 hp six. In 1907–08 came the monstrous 50/60 hp six, which offered 15·9 litres for a chassis price of £950. In 1907 Ariel sold their Bournbrook, Birmingham, factory to British Lorraine-Dietrich, and Ariel cars were thereafter assembled at the Coventry Ordnance Works. The outbreak of World War One put paid to a 1·3-litre light car. After 1918 the Ariel Nine with a flat-twin air-cooled engine (and made by A. Harper Sons and Bean) was an abortive attempt to cash in on the small car market.

ARIES/France 1903–1938

Ariès began building two- and four-cylinder cars in a big factory at Asnières (Seine), building 20 chassis at a time. These shaft-drive cars used a curious double rear axle, and the engines were

1924 1.5-litre Ariès at Le Mans

made by Aster. In 1907, Ariès made a V-4 engine with desmodromic valves, as well as six-cylinder cars. In 1910 Ariès entered the field of commercial vehicles, mainly supplying the French army: during the war, the works built many military lorries, and also Hispano-Suiza aero-engines. After the war Ariès presented a 7 cv ohc 1085cc four-cylinder and a 15cv 3-litre offered in two versions. The first had a sv Aster unit, and the second a sporty ohc engine—some of these Ariès with the ohc 3-litre engine were successful in racing events. During the financial crisis of the 1930s Ariès stopped production of the 1100cc and the 3-litre cars, which had become outdated. They were replaced by new 1500cc

ARGYLL
Scotland 1899–1932

Alex Govan's first voiturette was copied from the contemporary Renault and had a 2¾ hp De Dion engine and shaft-drive: 1901 models had a 5 hp engine, 1902 cars an 8 hp unit. A 10 hp twin with radiator tubes forming the bonnet sides soon appeared, and in 1904 there was a range of front-radiatored Aster-engined cars—a 10 hp of 1985cc, and

fours of 3054cc, 3686cc and 4849cc. All had Govan's awkward gearbox with T-shaped gate and separate change-speed and reverse levers. Argyll was now Scotland's biggest make, and moved from Bridgeton, Glasgow, into a grandiose terracotta factory at Alexandria, on the outskirts of the city. It was never used to capacity and with Govan's death in 1907, Argyll began a gentle decline. The famous 'Flying Fifteen' joined the range

in 1910, as did a six-cylinder; Rubury four-wheel brakes were available in 1911, and in 1912 the single sleeve-valve engine designed by J. P. McCollum and Argyll director Baillie P. Burt made its debut: by 1914 all the range had Burt-McCollum engines. Argyll changed hands in 1914, and 1920s production, starting in 1920 with the revived pre-war 15·9 hp (joined in 1922 by a 1½-litre), was on a small scale.

c.1906 Argyll 15hp landaulette

1908 Argyll 14hp tourer

and 2-litre models with a curious arrangement of a three-speed gearbox augmented by two-speed gears in the back axle, giving six speeds forward. Very few were made. At the outbreak of the war production of both touring cars and lorries was suspended. After the war, Ariès briefly made moped engines under the ABG name.

ARIMOFA/*Germany 1921–1922*
Starting with a small cyclecar with a 12 hp Steudel twin-cylinder engine built in limited numbers, Arimofa continued in 1923–25 with the Ari two-stroke motorcycle.

ARISTA/*France 1912 1915*
Taking its name from its founder, P. Arista-Ruffier, the Arista marque was built in Paris. There were eight models in its natal year: a 720cc single and fours of 1460cc, 1726cc and 1847cc, all with friction drive and sold complete with bodywork and tyres, and fours of 1460cc, 1593cc, 1847cc and 2001cc with conventional gearboxes, all sold as untyred chassis.

ARISTA/*France 1956–1963*
A garage in Paris made these glass-fibre-bodied cars with Panhard engine and components.

ARKLEY/*England 1971 to date*
A bug-eyed, glass-fibre panelled sports car, the Arkley SS kit was designed by Morgan man John Britten to allow rusted Sprites and Midgets to live another day. Several hundred have been sold since the car was introduced in 1971.

1971 Arkley sports two-seater

ARKON/*England 1971–1972*
Strictly a one-off, the 33-inch high Arkon was the product of a year's devotion by students Richard Moon and Neil Morgan. The exotic-looking GT is powered by a rear-mounted Imp engine set on a Triumph Spitfire chassis.

ARMADALE/*England 1906–1907*
This 'perfect little three-wheeler' was built by Toboggan Motors of London, and featured infinitely variable friction drive and a pressed steel chassis, an unusual feature on a tricar.

ARMSTRONG/*England 1902–1904*
'Claimed to be the best hill-climber extant', the Armstrong had an 8 hp International engine.

ARMSTRONG SIDDELEY

ARMSTRONG SIDDELEY
England 1919–1960
Armstrong Siddeley was created by an amalgamation of Armstrong-Whitworth and Siddeley-Deasy of Coventry. The outcome of this union was a fairly massive first car, a 5-litre 30 hp, though a smaller 18 appeared in 1922 and a 2-litre 14 hp came in 1923. The year 1928 saw the introduction of a 15 hp six while the following year a 12 hp car joined the range. It was also a pioneering year for the marque with the Wilson preselector gearbox being offered, originally as an optional extra, though it became standard equipment on Armstrongs from 1933. In 1930 four models were being marketed, of 12, 15, 20 and 30 hp, the latter costing £1450. Armstrong Siddeley's rather staid image was endorsed during the 1930s by a range of six-cylinder cars with ohv engines though a four-cylinder 12 hp was produced up until 1936. A reminder that Armstrong Siddeley was one of the country's largest manufacturers of aeroengines came in 1933 when the 5-litre six-cylinder Siddeley Special was announced with Hiduminium aluminium alloy engine. The model cost £950. The very week the war in Europe ended, Armstrong Siddeley announced their first post-war models: the Lancaster four-door saloon and the Hurricane drophead coupé, echoing the names of aircraft built by the Hawker Siddeley Group (as it had become in 1935) during the war. These cars were powered by 2-litre six-cylinder engines though the capacity was increased to 2·3-litres in 1949. From 1953 the company announced the Sapphire, with a six-cylinder engine of 3435cc, and in 1956 the number of models was increased: these were the 234, a 2·3-litre four, and the 236, with the older 2·3-litre six-cylinder engine. Armstrong Siddeley's last model was the Star Sapphire of 1958, with a 4-litre engine and automatic transmission. In 1959, however, Bristol Aero Engines merged with Hawker Siddeley to form Bristol Siddeley. A casualty of this union was Armstrong Siddeley cars: the last one left the Coventry works in 1960.

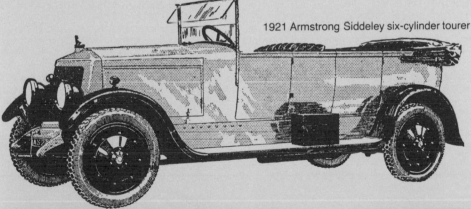

1921 Armstrong Siddeley six-cylinder tourer

1956 Armstrong Siddeley 346 saloon

ARMSTRONG-WHITWORTH
England 1904–1919

The famous Tyneside engineering and ship-building company began by taking over construction of the flat-four Wilson-Pilcher, with its preselective transmission, which had first appeared in 1901. From 1906 they were increasingly preoccupied with the Armstrong-Whitworth, a handsome machine on Mercedes lines, with engines from 12/14 hp to 40 hp, mostly fours, though a 30/50 hp six appeared in 1912.

1913 Armstrong-Whitworth 17/25hp tourer

ARNO / *England 1908*
Introduced at the 1908 Stanley Show, the Coventry-built Arno had a 25 hp White & Poppe engine and shaft drive.

ARNOLD / *England 1896*
Arnold's were agricultural engineers at East Peckham, Kent, who built a dozen cars based on the Benz. One survives.

ARNOLT / *USA 1953–1964*
S. H. Arnolt Inc. of Chicago combined an MG chassis and engine with Italian Bertone coachwork of steel and aluminium to produce four-passenger coupés and convertibles. British Bristol 404 chassis with six-cylinder 130hp engines were later used to produce Arnolt Bristols.

ARROL-JOHNSTON (ARROL-ASTER)
Scotland 1895–1929

When his experimental steam tram went up in flames in 1894, locomotive engineer George Johnston turned to internal combustion, building a heavy dog-cart with an opposed-twin engine with four pistons. A syndicate formed to produce this 'Mo-Car' was headed by Sir William Arrol, engineer of the Forth Bridge. High, slow, and started by pulling on a rope through the floorboards, the dog-cart was built until 1906. In 1905 it was joined by a 3023cc 12/15 hp model of more modern appearance, but still with an opposed-piston engine. There was also a three-cylinder version of the dog-cart, an uncouth 16 hp with the centre cylinder of greater bore than the outer pair. In 1906 came a 24/30 hp vertical four of 4654cc, followed in 1907 by a 38/45 hp of 8832cc. The 12/15 hp twin survived until 1909, in which year T. C. Pullinger, ex-Darracq and Humber, joined Arrol-Johnston, sweeping away the old range in favour of a new 15·9 hp of 2835cc, with a dashboard radiator and four-wheel brakes (dropped in 1911). An 11·9 hp was introduced for 1912, and in 1913 production shifted from Paisley to Dumfries, where 50 electric cars were built for Edison. Arrol-Johnston's 1919 'Victory' model, designed by G. W. A. Brown, had an ohc 2651cc engine but proved 'unsellable and unreliable', and was replaced by a modernized 15·9 hp. A short-lived 14 hp appeared in 1924, replaced in 1925 by a 12·3 hp—there was also a 3290cc 'Empire' model for the Colonies. In 1927 Arrol-Johnston merged with Aster: alongside sleeve-valve Arrol-Asters there were pushrod Arrol-Johnstons of 15/40 and 17/50 hp. Final folly was the straight-eight sleeve-valve Arrol-Aster 23/70 hp of 3292cc.

ARSENAL / *England 1898–1899*
A Bollée-like 'reputed 3½ hp' tricycle built at St Albans, Hertfordshire, by a company boasting 'practically the control of one of the largest and best-equipped plants of American Automatic Machinery'. Costing £59, the tiller-steered Arsenal could carry 'two or three persons, or four children'.

ARZAC / *France 1926–1927*
A small cyclecar made in Paris with front-wheel drive, independent suspension on all four wheels, and a two-stroke engine available in 483cc and 500cc forms.

AS / *France 1924–1928*
The AS made by Automobiles Serrano was a small car from la Garenne-Colombes with such proprietary engines as Chapuis-Dornier, Ruby and CIME.

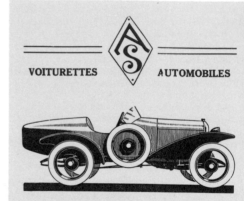

AS Type A2S 7/30cv sports

1907 Arrol-Johnston used on Shackleton's South Pole expedition

ASA/*Italy 1962–1969*
A small, high-efficiency 'dream car', created by
Bizzarini and — as far as the ohc 1032cc four-
cylinder engine was concerned — by Enzo Ferrari. It was built in a small factory at Milan,
owned by the De Nora Electrochemical Group
of companies. A racing version of the 1000 GT
Coupé had 1092cc and 95 bhp, later even
105 bhp. Only a few ASA cars were made, but
they gained successes in Italian sporting events.
A few larger four- and six-cylinder cars, mainly
prototypes, were also individually built to
order. All had glass-fibre bodywork.

ASARDO/*USA 1959–1960*
The American Special Automotive Research
and Design Organisation of Bergen, NJ, built
this sport coupé with an Alfa Romeo four-
cylinder engine and four-speed gearbox. A
glass-fibre body was mounted on a lightweight
tubular space frame.

ASCORT/*Australia 1958–1960*
Though unrecognizable as such, this four-seater
grand touring coupé was basically a Volkswagen Beetle. The locally-made, roomy,
double-skinned glass-fibre body was remarkably well conceived and appointed. The 1·2-litre
Beetle engine was modified with an Okrasa kit
to produce 54 bhp. Total vehicle weight was 33
per cent less than a standard sedan, giving brisk
acceleration. More than a dozen were built
before the project collapsed.

ASCOT/*England 1904*
The 3½ hp engine of the Ascot Forecar was
equipped with a 'patented method for
mechanically-controlling valves, doing away
with useless pinions and cams'.

ASCOT/*England 1928–1930*
Cyril Pullin was responsible for the Ascot and
he also produced the Ascot-Pullin motorcycle at
the same time. The Ascot was largely based on
the Hungarian Fejes, being assembled from
welded steel pressings, but it never went into
production. A larger 2¼-litre six did become a
reality, however.

ASHLEY/*England 1954–1962*
The Ashley name was first attached to sports
bodies for Austin Sevens, and over 500 were
built during the 1950s. Ford-powered Ashleys
followed, first with proprietary chassis and then
with their own. The Sportiva was their final car,
special bonnets and hardtops for Sprites their
last commercial projects.

ASHTON-EVANS/*England 1919–1928*
The first of this Birmingham marque had a rear
track of only 8 inches, but from 1920 a normal
rear-axle was used. All had 1½-litre Coventry-
Climax engines and constant-mesh gearboxes.

ASPA/*Czechoslovakia 1924–1925*
Made by a small machine factory at Příbram,
the Aspa, successor to the Stelka, had a Ford
Model T engine and many other Ford parts.
Only a few were built.

ASQUITH/*England 1901–1902*
Built by a Halifax machine tool works, the

The Ascort coupé

Asquith had a front-mounted De Dion engine
and, originally, belt-drive, replaced by a two-
speed gearbox because the belts slipped disas-
trously. Probably only one car was built, as the
firm decided to concentrate on building boring
machinery.

ASS/*France 1919–1920*
'L'automobile pour tous', the ASS was powered
by a 12 hp two-stroke Thomas engine: ambitious plans for mass production were
unrealized.

ASTATIC/*France 1920–1922*
Made at Saint-Ouen, the Astatic was another
attempt to market a car with independent
suspension all round, by means of leaf-springs.
The engine was an 1100cc SCAP.

Ashton-Evans two-seater, c.1922

= **A.S.S.** =
L'AUTOMOBILE POUR TOUS

1920 ASS four-seater

ASTER/*France 1900–1910*
Best known as suppliers of power units to
manufacturers such as Gladiator, Ariès, West,
Argyll, Whitlock and Dennis, this firm from St
Denis (Seine) also built chassis. It seems unlikely
that a complete car was marketed by the Aster
company, though a four-cylinder chassis was
exhibited at the 1907 Paris Salon.

ASTER/*England 1922–1930*
Aster only made six-cylinder cars; the first, the
18/50, had a 2618cc engine, being enlarged to 3
litres in 1926. Later examples of this marque
had Burt-McCollum single sleeve-valve engines.

1959 Aston Martin DB4

Aston Martin 1486cc sports at Brooklands, 1925

Aston Martin DB4 GT

1973 Aston Martin V-8

ASTON MARTIN
England 1922 to date

The original Aston Martin was built in 1914 by Lionel Martin and Robert Bamford, the Aston prefix deriving from the Aston Clinton hillclimb where the car had successfully competed. This first car used an Isotta-Fraschini voiturette chassis, powered by a 1·4-litre Coventry-Simplex engine. Car production proper started in 1921, the cars having sv 1½-litre engines. More exciting developments came in 1922 when a four-cylinder 16-valve car was designed for Count Zborowski, who held the company's purse strings. Unfortunately it failed to live up to expectations on the race tracks, but became available to private customers the following year. Single cam variants were also available. After Zborowski's death at Monza in 1924 the company struggled on until the 1925 Motor Show, but was wound up a few weeks later. At the end of 1925 Bamford and Martin Ltd. was purchased by W. S. Renwick for £6000. He had met a fellow engineer, A. C. Bertelli, at Armstrong Siddeley and they had gone on to form an engineering concern which produced just one car, the R and B. It had an ohc 1½-litre four-cylinder engine and formed the basis of the Bertelli-designed Aston Martins up until

1936. This 1½-litre model established a good competition record at Brooklands, Le Mans and the Mille Miglia, thus perpetuating the marque's sporting pedigree. Finance was also a problem and after a brief flirtation with Frazer Nash in 1931 and later with L. Prideaux Brune, the company came under the control of R. G. Sutherland in 1933. A new 2-litre model succeeded the 1½-litre series for 1937 and although superficially resembling the smaller capacity car, it lacked the commercial and competition success. The first Aston Martin of the post-war years had a Claude Hill-designed pushrod 2-litre engine and independent front suspension, but only a few were made before the company was taken over by the David Brown group in 1947. Experiments continued in 1948–49, the resultant cars being dubbed DB1s. Meanwhile David Brown had also acquired Lagonda and the outcome of this liaison was that the dohc 2·6-litre six-cylinder engine which W. O. Bentley had designed for the post-war Lagonda was fitted in a square-tube space frame and entered in the 1949 Le Mans, emerging the following year as the DB2. The DB3 of 1954 was a sports-racer actively campaigned by the factory, while the Eberan von Eberhorst-designed DB3S maintained

the company's sporting activities. The DBR that followed gave Aston Martin a car with which to win Le Mans (in 1959) along with the Sports Car Constructors' Championship. However, the DB4 which appeared for the 1960 season was a completely new car, having a Tadec Marek-designed all-aluminium dohc 3·7-litre engine and a platform-frame chassis, trailing link and coil rear suspension and handsome coachwork constructed on the Superleggera principle (a tubular metal cage clad in hand-fashioned aluminium). The DB5 announced in 1963 offered a 4-litre engine with many of the troubles that had plagued the earlier DB4s ironed out, while the 1966 DB6 offered true four-seater motoring coupled with sensational performance. The following year saw the DBS 6 and DBS Vantage, a more expensive and powerful variant that remained in production until 1973. A new 5·4-litre all-aluminium V-8 appeared in the DBS V-8 of 1970, being renamed the V-8 in 1972. It was also used to power the Lagonda model which reached full production status in 1978. David Brown sold out to Company Developments Ltd in 1972 and in 1975 the company was again reconstructed by a new consortium who have succeeded in making Aston Martin profitable once again.

ASTRA/*USA 1920*
Built by a subsidiary concern of the Dorris, the 108-inch wheelbase Astra was shown in its native St Louis in 1920. It used a Leroi four-cylinder engine and featured a slightly pointed radiator. An estimated five to ten units were made before the company failed in June 1920.

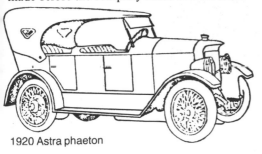
1920 Astra phaeton

ASTRA/*France 1922*
A small cyclecar with a twin-cylinder two-stroke engine of 496cc which featured independent suspension on all four wheels plus friction drive.

ASTRA/*England 1956–1959*
Claimed to be the smallest and cheapest four-wheeler on the British market, the utility Astra had a rear-mounted 322cc engine and all-round independent suspension. It was built by British Anzani of Hampton Hill, Middlesex.

ASTRESSE/*France 1898*
Using engines built under Grivel licence, this Levallois-Perret manufacturer claimed to build two to three cars monthly.

ASTRO-GNOME/*USA 1956*
Built by the Richard Arbib Co., NY, the Astro-Gnome looked like something from a Flash Gordon film, with its fluted aluminium side panels anodized in different blending hues. A bubble canopy, giving unobstructed vision all round, covered the passengers, but could be raised to allow walk-in entry and exit. Only one prototype was made.

ATALANTA/*England 1915–1916*
Built in Staines, this was a £195 light car with an own-make four-cylinder 1097cc engine.

ATALANTA/*England 1937–1939*
The Atalanta sports car, which featured all-independent suspension, used Albert Gough's

slightly erratic 1½- and 2-litre engines, previously fitted to some Frazer Nashes. More popular was the 4·3-litre V-12 Lincoln-Zephyr option. After the war Richard Gaylard Shattock revived the name with the RGS Atalanta, offering complete cars with glass-fibre bodywork or kits of parts until 1958

ATHMAC/*England 1913*
A friction-drive 1110cc cyclecar from Leyton, Essex.

ATLA/*France 1957–1959*
Another small car using small Renault 4cv engines and glass-fibre body. Made by Jacques Durand (who later made CG and Jidé sports cars), the Atla boasted 'gull-wing' doors.

ATLAS/*USA 1907–1913*
The 'two-cycle' Atlas, built in Springfield, Mass., was available with 22hp twin-cylinder and 34hp three-cylinder engines. Knight sleeve-valve engines were used from 1911.

ATS/*Italy 1963–1964*
Connected with Count Volpi's 'Scuderia Serenissima' Formula One racing team, only a very few of these V-8 sports coupés with engines up to 245bhp were built. Like the 'Serenissima' which followed them, they were never fully developed.

ATTILA/*England 1903–1906*
The Hunslet Engine Company, of Leeds, could not resist calling these three-cylinder 20hp vehicles after the most famous Hun of all.

ATVIDABERG/*Sweden 1910–1911*
A Holsman high-wheeler was imported from the USA in 1910 by Åtvidabergs Vagnfabrik AB, and used as a pattern. The engine was a flat-twin and top speed was about 45 km/h (28 mph). Some of the later engines had four cylinders. There was a two-speed gearbox, and to engage reverse, the whole engine was slid backwards under the frame: 35 cars were planned, 12 were built and the rest converted for railway inspection use.

AUBURN/*USA 1900–1936*
Frank and Morris Eckhart's Auburn (Indiana) Carriage Company, dating from 1874, built its first car in 1900 and went into production with a 'one-lunger' two-seater in 1903. It was followed

1955–36 Auburn model 862 sedan

in 1905 by a twin-cylinder and in 1909 with a 25/30 hp Rutenber-engined four. A Rutenber-engined six appeared in 1912. A range of proprietary-engined sixes took Auburn through to a change of ownership in 1919, followed by the launch of the Continental-engined 26 hp 'Beauty-Six'. Its lack of sales success brought in the dynamic Errett Lobban Cord as first general manager, then as President. Early in 1925 came the 'Eight-in-Line', developed into the 4523cc '8-88' with a range of striking body styles. In 1928 the first of the boat-tailed Auburn Speedsters appeared, capable of over 108 mph with its 115 hp engine. In 1929, over 22,000 Auburns were sold, falling to under 14,000 the next year, but boosted to a record 28,000 in 1931 by restyled coachwork on the new 8-98 model. The 6407cc Lycoming-engined V-12 of 1932–33 proved a near-flop; however, Gordon Buehrig's blown outside-exhaust 851/852 Speedsters of 1935–36 were an all-time classic — but they sold at a loss.

AUBURN/*USA 1966 to date*
Three companies currently offer glass-fibre replicas of the 1935–37 Auburn Speedster, with power ranging from Ford Galaxie to Jaguar XJ6 engines. Glenn Pray's Auburn Replicar appeared in 1966, with a 7-litre Ford V-8, while Elegant Motors of Indianapolis launched their version in 1974; the 1979 range consisted of the 856 Speedster, 898 2+2 Phaeton and 898 Phaeton Elegante, all using Chevrolet Corvette frame and running gear. In 1976, the Custom Coach Company of Pasadena launched their 876 Speedster in kit form, followed by a phaeton in 1978. Kits are now being phased out in favour of complete cars.

Elegant Motors' 1979 Auburn replica

AUDI/*Germany 1909 to date*
Founded by the creator of Horch cars, August Horch, at Zwickau in East Germany, Audi became part of the Auto-Union in 1932, was nationalized in 1945, and became defunct until 1965, when the name 'Audi' was resumed at the 'new' Auto-Union works at Ingolstadt in Western Germany. The Audi of today is one of Germany's leading cars, now part of the great VW Group, following Audi's merger with NSU's car side. Horch's first Audi was a 2612cc car; other superb quality four-cylinder models of 3564cc, 4680cc and 5720cc followed. Driven in major sporting events, they proved very successful. Pre-war models had ioe engines; after the war, new sv engines of 2071cc were introduced: there was also an ohv 3500cc 50 hp. The first six-cylinder motor, an ohc 4655cc unit, appeared in 1924, the first straight-eight sv 4872cc appeared in 1928 after J. S. Ras-

1930 Audi Zwickau eight-cylinder limousine

1978 Audi 100 5S five-cylinder

mussen—then head of DKW—had bought the remains of the American Rickenbacker car works and began building the Rickenbacker eight-cylinder engines in Germany. At about the same time he also bought Audi (Horch had left the works in 1920). 1929 saw the

introduction of the Audi Zwickau 4371cc and 5130cc eights, followed in 1931 by a 3838cc six-cylinder and a small 1·1-litre four with a Peugeot motor. Most Audis were luxurious cars with special coachwork. Audi joined Wanderer, DKW and Horch in the newly formed Auto-Union in 1932, and the 1933-built front-engined 1963cc Audi got a Wanderer six-cylinder ohv engine. It was followed by a similar 2255cc model and a 3281cc car with an ohc Horch six-cylinder motor. Mercedes controlled the destiny of Audi in the mid-1960s and also designed the first post-war Audi 1·7-litre four-cylinder engine . . . and before the first new Audi was on the market, they had sold Auto-Union to VW. The new range consisted of cars from 1496cc to 1871cc and, with the Audi 50 of 1974, also 1093cc and 1272cc cars of first-class design and workmanship. There is also a 1984cc 100 GL. All these new Audis are front-wheel-drive cars.

AUDIBERT & LAVIROTTE
France 1894–1901
The oldest makers of motor cars in Lyon, Audibert & Lavirotte built Benz-like cars of up to 6 hp, with rear-mounted engines and belt drive. In 1900, they built three 36 hp racers. They built an interior drive 'Berline de Voyage' – the first saloon car? – as early as 1898.

AULTMAN/*USA 1901*
A light steam carriage built in Canton, Ohio. Its makers also built a four-wheel-drive steam truck.

AUREA/*Italy 1921–1930*
A small producer, whose ohv four-cylinder cars had initially 1460cc, later 1497cc, engines. They were well-made but heavy. Production ceased around 1926, but a few more cars were assembled from existing parts.

AURORA/*England 1904*
The Aurora Tri-Motor was a $3\frac{1}{2}$ hp tricar on motorcycle lines.

AURORA/*USA 1957–1958*
Father Alfred A. Juliano, a Catholic Priest, built this safety-inspired car of extraordinary appearance on a Buick chassis with a choice of Chrysler, Cadillac or Lincoln engine.

AUSTIN/*USA 1901–1921*
Big, powerful touring cars from Grand Rapids, Michigan: the 1907 60 hp Austin was an eight-seater tourer, while the 1908 90 hp six was, according to Walter S. Austin, the 'sportiest kind of car it is possible to get'. A V-12 appeared in 1917.

1979 Audi 80

1908 Austin Grand Prix in road-going guise
(boxer Jack Johnson at the wheel)

AUSTIN/*England 1906 to date*

Herbert Austin started his motoring career as Wolseley's general manager, leaving in 1905 to set up his own company in an old printing works at Longbridge, seven miles south of Birmingham. He began production the following year. His cars were conventional but well made, having T-head engines with separate cylinders. His first was a 25/30 hp model, but three years after its formation the company was able to offer a range of three four-cylinder models (15, 18/24 and 40 hp) and a 60 hp six-cylinder. This last-named model formed the basis of a racing variant that Austin entered for the 1908 French Grand Prix, finishing in 18th and 19th places. The year 1910 saw the appearance of a 1·6-litre four-cylinder car, initially for export: it became available for home consumption 12 months later, together with a single-cylinder 1100cc car (in effect a re-radiatored Swift) which appeared in 1909. At the outbreak of the First World War Austin was offering three four-cylinder models, the largest being close on 6-litres capacity. Austin's marketing philosophy experienced a marked change after the First World War, for he offered just one model: the 3·6-litre 20 of 1919. Unfortunately, this big car failed to sell in sufficient numbers, and it was not long before the company was placed under a receivership and a new model, virtually a scaled-down 20, the famous 1·6-litre Twelve, was rushed into production in 1921. This solid and reliable car remained in production until 1936,

though the car was slightly scaled-up and the engine capacity increased to 1861cc in 1927. The famous Austin Seven was announced in 1922. When it appeared, the Seven was the smallest British four-cylinder car, being initially of 696cc, though this was soon increased to 747cc. Inspired by the Peugeot Quadrilette, its tiny splash-lubricated engine was designed by an 18-year-old draughtsman, Stanley Edge. This four-wheel brake car, with transverse suspension at the front and quarter elliptics at the rear, remained in production until 1939, by which time 290,000 had been made: it was also manufactured under licence in France, Germany, Japan and America. Its sporting successes included a third place in the 1929 TT and a win in the 1930 500 Miles Race at Brooklands. A fashionable 3·4-litre six-cylinder 20 went on

sale in 1927, the older four-cylinder model remaining in production until the following year. The six was scaled down to produce the 2·3-litre Sixteen of 1928, but a less happy variation was the 12·6 of 1931. The successful Ten (1125cc) was introduced the following year, a Ten remaining a feature of the Austin range until 1947. The Light 12/4 (1535cc) appeared in 1932 sharing a similar production run. The famous Seven was replaced in 1939 by the 900cc Eight, this again being phased out in 1947. Austin's first overhead valve engine, the 2199cc Sixteen, was fitted in the 1940 12 body and chassis in 1945, though independent front suspension had to wait for the 1948 Princess and Sheerline and the 1·2-litre A40. Austin and Morris merged in 1952 to form the British Motor Corporation and that year saw the →

c. 1926 Austin Heavy 12/4 two-seater

continued from previous page

Austin Seven tourer, *c*.1926

appearance of the A30 with 803cc ohv engine; it was also Longbridge's first unitary construction car. The quaintly styled Metropolitan, made initially for Nash, appeared in 1954, powered by an A40 engine. New models in 1955 included the Cambridge, with A40 or A50 power units, together with the Westminster, which was fitted with a 2·6-litre six. Farina styling was a feature of the 1959 range, which saw further rationalization with MG, Morris, Wolseley and Riley offering badge-engineered versions of the Austin Cambridge theme. Britain's most revolutionary car appeared in 1959. Alec Issigonis's fwd Mini was initially sold as the Austin Seven and powered by an A series 848cc transversely-mounted engine with four-speed gearbox mounted beneath. Rubber suspension by Alex Moulton, 10-inch wheels and a distinctive box-like shape were unconventional features of the design that has since altered small-car technology throughout the world. It was followed in 1964 by the 1100 with Hydrolastic suspension (also appearing under the Morris trade mark) and the 1800 two years later. Rear-wheel drive lingered on until the short-lived 3-litre was phased out in 1971. The year 1968 saw the engulfment of BMC by Leyland to form British Leyland and the following year came the Maxi, powered by an ohc 1485cc engine, and utilizing a fashionable tailgate. A more powerful 1748cc engine became available for the 1971 season. The fwd Allegro of 1973 was offered with a range of 1100, 1300, 1500 and 1750cc power units.

1979 Austin Maxi 1750 HLS

AUSTIN-HEALEY / *England 1953–1971*

The Healey 100 was the undisputed star of the London Motor Show in 1952. Graceful but sturdy and very competitively priced, it caused an immediate sensation, as did the ensuing announcement that production was going to be on a very large scale and undertaken not by the Donald Healey Motor Co., but by Austin at Longbridge — enter the Austin-Healey. When production of the 'Big Healey' finally ceased in December 1967, nearly 74,000 cars had been completed. Of course the Austin-Healey name was also carried on 'Frog-Eye' Sprites, 48,999 of which were made, as well as the thousands of the subsequent Sprites, Mks II–IV, which were mechanically identical and bodily similar to the equivalent MG Midgets.

1955 Austin-Healey

Austin-Healey 'Frog-Eye' Sprite with Donald Healey

AUSTRAL / *France 1907*

'Touring tricars' and motorized delivery tricycles were offered by this Parisian company.

AUSTRALIAN SIX / *Australia 1919–1930*

This grandiose attempt to compete against imported US cars consisted of a mixture of local and imported parts, with a conventional chassis layout and a choice of five locally-made bodies. Most Australian Sixes were fitted with Rutenber six-cylinder engines and Muncie or Grand Lees gearboxes, but some had an imported ohv Anstead engine. High local production costs forced the company to close after 900 cars had been built. Several survive.

Australian Six tourer, 1922

AUSTRALIS / *Australia 1897–1907*

The company commenced with a quadricycle, and then produced a 7hp twin-cylinder light buggy, selling for $270.

AUSTRO-DAIMLER
Austria 1899–1934

Originally a branch of the German Daimler factory, the works at Wiener-Neustadt became independent in 1906, and built some excellent cars. The firm's first designer was Paul Daimler — son of the great Gottlieb Daimler — followed by Ferdinand Porsche — who was responsible for the Mercédès-Electrique-Mixte of 1902–07 — Karl Rabe, Oskar Hacker and others. The factory also competed successfully in sporting events. Among A-D cars, the 'Prince Heinrich' model of 1911 with an ohc 5714cc four-cylinder engine became famous. It developed 95 bhp at 2100 rpm, while a less potent version had side-valves and a 6900cc engine developing 60 hp at only 1200 rpm. Both were Porsche designs. The smallest model was a 2212cc four-cylinder. In the early 1920s Porsche also created the 1·3-litre 'Sascha' racing cars, financed by Count 'Sascha' Kolowrat and built at the A-D works. The outstanding production car of that era was the ADM with ohc six-cylinder engines of 2540cc, 2650cc and 2994cc. The last model — ADM III — developed 110 hp at 4000 rpm and was one of the great cars of the late 1920s. The 100hp ADR was a luxurious, less sporting version. The year 1931 saw the introduction of a 4624cc eight-cylinder A-D, a superb, very expensive luxury motor car. The last great car built at Wiener-Neustadt was the six-cylinder 'Bergmeister' with an ohc 3614cc engine developing 120 hp at 3600 rpm and a top speed of 90 mph. In 1928 Austro-Daimler amalgamated with Puch and in 1930 with Steyr. Porsche, who had left in 1923 for Daimler-Benz at Stuttgart, later designed a big car for Steyr: Steyr soon afterwards joined Austro-Daimler.

Austrian (Austro) Daimler touring car, 1913

1907 Austro-Daimler Mercedes Electrique driven by Porsche

c.1930 Austro-Daimler ADR 6 saloon

AUSTRO-FIAT/*Austria 1912–1936*
Originally a branch factory of Fiat (Turin), Fiat at Vienna became independent after the First World War and built touring cars with 2072cc and, later, 1300cc sv four-cylinder engines. The factory eventually became part of the Austro-Daimler, Steyr, Puch combine, and after 1936 built commercial vehicles only.

AUSTRO-GRADE/*Austria 1923–1925*
The Grade was an 808cc two-stroke twin-cylinder car, designed by the German aircraft and two-stroke engine pioneer Hans Grade. In the design, Grade incorporated many aircraft principles, especially in the 'streamlined' body. The Austrian branch was at Klosterneuburg, near Vienna.

AUSTRO-RUMPLER/*Austria 1920–1922*
Edmund Rumpler was a famous aircraft- and car-designer. In 1921 he created rear-engined streamlined cars, and in 1922 designed the Benz 'Teardrop' racing car with the engine in the back. In Austria he tried to build 10 hp cyclecars with a newly formed company, but few were made before the factory ran out of funds.

AUSTRO-TATRA/*Austria 1932–1948*
There was always a close connection between the Czechoslovakian Tatra works and their Austrian branch at Vienna. For many years they assembled cars in Vienna, especially the models 11 and 12, and afterwards built the Tatra 57—a 1260cc four-cylinder with the transverse-mounted flat air-cooled engine in front—under licence.

AUTOBIANCHI/*Italy 1955 to date*
These excellent small cars are built in the old Bianchi works. Autobianchi, controlled by Fiat since 1967, concentrated for many years on the Fiat-based two-cylinder 499cc Bianchina, which was available in various forms, mostly with 17·5 bhp and 21 bhp engines. Subsequently, 792cc and 1221cc four-cylinder models were added. From 1969 onwards, Autobianchi also built 903cc and 1403cc Fiat-based four-cylinder cars. In 1975 Autobianchi merged with Lancia, another Fiat-controlled car factory. They still produce the 499cc two-cylinder Giardiniera, the A112 four-cylinder transverse-engined model, and the A112 Abarth with 1049cc 70 bhp engine and a 100 mph top speed.

AUTO-BOB/*USA 1914*
'My Boy's Delight', this $150 3–5 hp cyclecar was intended for 10- to 15-year-olds.

AUTO-BUGGY/*USA 1906–1911*
A high-wheeler with a 1647cc two-cylinder engine, built by International Harvester.

AUTOCAR/*USA 1899–1911*
The first Autocar was built at Swissvale, Pa., in 1899 — it was a single-seat 4 hp buggy with tiller steering. In January 1900 the 'high-powered touring carriage' was announced: 1901 saw a 'high-powered touring carriage' with a front engine of 18 hp and left-hand-drive. Big two- and four-cylinder cars appeared in 1907; only trucks were built after 1911.

AUTOCAR/*England 1903*
A 20 hp model from Manchester.

AUTOCRAT/*England 1911–1926*
A Birmingham-built light car, originally available with 1088cc or 1300cc four-cylinder engines. By 1921 the 11·9 hp Autocrat had a Lucas dyno-start as standard.

AUTOETTE/*USA 1952–1957*
The Autoette Electric Car Co. of Long Beach, California, built this three-wheeled electric car for town use.

AUTO LEGER/*France c1906–1910*
This light car from Lyon had 'a bonnet in the form of a flying dragon, whose head and wings were shaped into radiator and mudguards'.

AUTOLETTE/*Holland 1905–1906*
A three-wheeler built in Rotterdam.

AUTOMATIC ELECTRIC/*USA 1921–1922*
Very few of these cars were manufactured, production being confined to a two-passenger roadster at $1200.

L'AUTO-MIXTE/*Belgium 1905–1912*
Petrol-electric cars built in Liège: a Knight-engined model appeared in 1912.

AUTOMOBILE COMPANY OF AMERICA/*USA 1899*
Originally known as the 'American Motor', the power units built by this company were built in single- and twin-cylinder form. A complete car, the Stanhope—'one of the newest and most approved styles on the market'—was made.

AUTOMOBILE CONSTRUCTION *USA 1914*
An assemble-it-yourself chassis for the trade from Philadelphia, with a 1557cc Continental.

AUTOMOBILETTE/*France 1911–1924*
Starting before World War One with a small cyclecar with vee-twin engines and belt drive, Automobilette resumed after the war with a more conventional four-cylinder car. Some were sold under the name of CAB ('Construction Automobile de Bellevue') from the name of the town where the works were situated. Some time after the closure, the constructor, M. Coignet, started again with the Coignet-Delaage.

AUTOMOTETTE/*France 1898*
A light tiller-steered three-wheeled carriage with a 3 hp horizontal single-cylinder engine and dual-ratio belt-drive.

AUTOMOTO/*France 1901–1907*
Also sold in England as the Automotor, this make was originally known as the Chavanet (1898–1900). Automotos were available either as complete cars, from a 4 hp single-cylinder voiturette to a 24/30 hp four, or as a kit of parts for home assembly.

AUTOMOTOR/*USA 1900–1904*
Designed by Hinsdale Smith, this car originally appeared as the Meteor. It was a light runabout powered by a De Dion engine: 3½ hp and 5 hp models were offered.

AUTOMOTRICE/*France 1901–1907*
Henri Popp began production of these cars in Bergerac, though it later shifted to Paris. It is thought that l'Automotrice was the successor to the Cyrano. By 1903 the company had become known as the Société Française d'Automobiles,

Autobianchi A112 Elegant saloon

and offered a 6/9 hp single, 9/12 hp twin and fours of 12, 16 and 24 hp. What is thought to be an early six-cylinder appeared in the touring car class at the November 1903 Dourdan hillclimb, driven by Gasté.

AUTO PARTS/*USA 1909*
Like the Metz, this 23 hp shaft-drive car from Chicago was sold in 'instalments' for home assembly: $450 got 'ten outfits of our $600 car'.

AUTO-PRATIQUE/*France 1912–1913*
A single-cylinder 601cc shaft-drive voiturette from Paris.

AUTO-TRI/*USA 1898–1900*
The Auto-Tri was a three-wheeled car built by C. W. Kelsey, who would later build the Motorette and Kelsey automobiles. The one-cylinder Auto-Tri existed as a prototype only, although the Auto-Tri Company was formally set up at Chestnut Hill, Pennsylvania, and maintained its existence, despite its lack of output, until 1900.

AUTOTRIX/*England 1913*
A three-wheeled cyclecar with a choice of 6 hp or 8 hp twin-cylinder power units.

AUTO UNION/*Germany 1932 to date*
The Auto Union was the result of the merger in 1932 of DKW, Horch, Wanderer and Audi for financial reasons. Only DKW, thanks to big motorcycle sales, was really financially sound. There was at that time no real car bearing the Auto Union sign only . . . with the exception of the Porsche designed rear-engined racing cars. A DKW became an Auto Union-DKW and that was also the case with the three other factories. Everything finished after World War Two when these factories—now in East Germany—were nationalized. It was not until the 1950s, when Auto Union was established in the western part of Germany at Ingolstadt and Düsseldorf, that the Auto Union insignia appeared once more on DKW cars. Years later, the name was changed to Audi NSU Auto Union AG, with the old NSU works as the HQ. The great VW group is now the 'parent' of all cars built under the Auto Union banner.

1959/60 Auto Union

AUTOVIA/*England 1937–1938*
A Riley subsidiary, the V-8 Autovia was of 2·8 litres capacity and no doubt inspired by the Ford V-8. A preselector gearbox was fitted and also, surprisingly, a worm driven rear-axle. The project died with the Riley collapse in 1938.

*c.*1914 Averies chassis

AV/*England 1919–1926*
This cyclecar was initially a single-seater, but later two passengers were catered for. Engines were vee-twin, either by JAP or Blackburne, mounted at the rear.

AVALLONE/*Brazil c1976 to date*
A GM Chevette engine powers this replica MG-TF from Sao Paulo.

AVANTI II/*USA 1965 to date*
Two businessmen acquired part of the defunct Studebaker factory, as well as all rights, parts, drawings and equipment, and, employing ex-Studebaker personnel, formed the Avanti Motor Corporation. Produced in limited numbers, the Avanti II is indistinguishable externally from the original.

AVERIES/*England 1913–1915*
Marketed by John Averies, who imported La Ponette cars, this 1094cc light car was based on the Dupressoir 'Rolling'.

AVIETTE/*England 1914–1916*
A gawky belt-driven cyclecar sold by Hurlin, with 4 hp and 8 hp JAP or Blumfield power.

AVIS/*Austria 1925–1928*
Made in limited numbers by an aircraft firm at Wiener-Neustadt, the Avis had sv 798cc two- and 1096cc four-cylinder engines.

AVON/*England 1902*
Built in Bristol, the Avon was a wheel-steered three-wheeler with car-type bodywork with a 3¾ hp engine and twin radiators, one each side of the seat. Its three-speed gearbox was controlled by Bowden cable.

Another Avro venture, the 1924 two-wheel Monocar

AVRO/*England 1919–1920*
Built by the aircraft manufacturer A. V. Roe, the Avro was a short-lived affair, powered by a 1300cc four-cylinder engine though a two-stroke and five-cylinder radial were options.

AWS-SHOPPER/*Germany 1973–1974*
A small, simple shopping car built mainly from Goggomobil parts, with a 248cc two-stroke engine. It was expensive and of limited appeal.

![B]

BABCOCK/*USA 1906–1912*
'A contented woman is she who operates a Babcock Electric — she knows there is nothing to fear', boasted the Buffalo, NY, makers of this marque.

9·5 hp Peters engine and gearbox, and had some sporting pretensions.

BACHTOLD/*Switzerland 1898–1899*
A motor tricycle from Steckborn shown at the 1899 National Show in London, based on the Egg. Only six were made.

BACON/*USA 1920–1921*
The Bacon was built in prototype form only as a two-passenger roadster featuring wire wheels and a four-cylinder Herschell-Spillman engine.

BACS/*England 1906*
This 18/24 hp model was sold by the British Automobile Commercial Syndicate of London.

BADENIA/*Germany 1925*
Ex-Benz employees built this 2860cc car, which had a modified six-cylinder sv Benz engine.

BADGER/*USA 1908–c1910*
An early four-wheel-drive car with a 55/60 hp four-cylinder engine.

BADGER/*USA 1910–1912*
A 30 hp four built in Columbus, Wisconsin.

stroke double-piston engines. His power units were also used in BF racing cars.

1923 Baer 4/18 PS Cabriolet

BAGULEY/*England 1911–1914*
The 15/20 hp Baguley was a well-designed, conventional car, available with either plate or cone clutch and worm or bevel final drive. The standard model (chassis £360) had semi-elliptic rear springs, the de luxe (chassis £370) had three-quarter elliptics.

BAILEY/*USA 1907–1915*
Electric runabouts and victorias from Amesbury, Mass.

BAILLEAU/*France 1901–1914*
M. Bailleau's 1902 light motor car was 'specially built to meet demand for a popular-priced two-seater vehicle'. A 16 hp four was listed in 1906.

BAJA/*Austria 1921–1924*
The Baja cyclecar was driven by 490cc single-cylinder or 678cc vee-twin JAP engines.

BAJA GT/*England 1969 to date*
A survivor of the 'Buggy' era, the Baja has rakish glass-fibre bodywork adorning the inevitable VW chassis. Engine choices have varied from 'Beetle' 1200 to Chevrolet Corvair.

BAKER/*USA 1899–1914*
Most Baker Electrics were little more than wheeled battery boxes, but in 1902 Walter Baker unveiled his super-streamlined electric 'Torpedo' land speed contender, the first car to have seat-belts fitted and capable of over 75 mph. He also built an electric brougham for the King of Siam in 1909. In 1914, Baker merged with Rauch & Lang.

1908 Babcock Electric Victoria, Model 6

BABY BLAKE/*England 1922*
The unusual thing about the Baby Blake was that it was fitted with two engines, both two-strokes. An ingenious friction drive was employed.

BABY-RHONE/*France 1941*
A single-seat electric voiturette.

BAC/*England 1921–1923*
The BAC, with its handsome radiator, used a

BADMINTON/*France/England 1907–1908*
An early 'joint venture', the round-radiatored Badminton had a French chassis and English coachwork; it was built by Teste & Lassen, and was available with 20 hp and 25 hp fours.

BAER/*Germany 1921–1924*
Paul Baer was a two-stroke enthusiast, like many others in the Berlin of the 1920s. He built a 770cc two-cylinder car with a double-diameter piston and also produced proprietary two-

1923 Baker steam car

BAKER STEAM CAR/*USA 1920–1924*
Probably no more than half-a-dozen Baker Steamers were built, although the 1921 calendar year saw a touring car, roadster and a 2½-ton truck completed, all disc-wheeled of conventional appearance. Boilers designed by the company's head, Dr. H. O. Baker, were however used as replacements for Stanley boilers.

1930 Ballot RH-3 3-litre tourer

BALBOA/*USA 1924–1925*
The Balboa was a California-built car with a factory in Fullerton which never went into actual production. Three prototype models were made: the 1924 pilot model featured a Kessler eight-cylinder engine, this being supplanted by another power plant, probably of Balboa design, a year later. The cars were disc-wheeled and had 127–131-inch wheelbases. Balboas had distinctive lines and were ahead of their time in general appearance.

1925 Balboa five-passenger phaeton

BALDWIN/*USA 1896–1899*
Based in Providence, Rhode Island, Baldwin built chain-drive steamers, with either surrey or *dos-à-dos* coachwork. Unlike other light American steamers, the Baldwin had a condenser so that the exhaust steam could be recycled.

BALDWIN/*USA 1900–1901*
Baldwin, of Connellsville, Pa., claimed to have materials on hand for the manufacture of 180 steam cars, but went bankrupt amid accusations of fraud.

BALLOT/*France 1919–1932*
Ballot really started as far back as 1905, when the brothers Edouard and Maurice Ballot started manufacturing marine engines and proprietary power units. After the war, they entered motor racing when ex-Peugeot engineer Henry designed a straight-eight 4·9-litre car for the 1921 French Grand Prix. They later evolved a 2-litre racing car from which was developed a touring version, the 2 LS. This was a dohc 1944cc four which stayed in production until 1924. In 1923, Ballot presented the ohc 2 LT with three-bearing crankshaft; a sport version, the 2 LTS, was soon evolved with bigger valves. In 1926 a six-cylinder was presented at the Paris Show but never went into production: it was replaced the following year by the ohc 2·8-litre type RH straight-eight. The engine was then enlarged to 3 litres, but the car was too heavy to enjoy success. In 1931 the Ballot factory was taken over by Hispano-Suiza. The Ballot HS 26, which had been launched at the Paris Show in 1930, was renamed Hispano 'Junior'. The six-cylinder engine of 4580cc was designed by Birkigt and made at the Hispano Works: Ballot provided only the chassis. Nevertheless, the Ballot factory closed its doors in 1932.

BALZER/*USA 1894–1901*
Steven Balzer of New York was a pioneer builder of motor carriages. In 1899 he received an order for ten cars from 'Paris, France'. His 1901 8 hp had a three-cylinder 2500cc rotary.

BAMBER & LEWIS/*England 1898*
A two-seater 'oil motor car' from Meopham, Kent, said to be of the company's own manufacture. May also have been known as the 'Vesta'.

BANDINI/*Italy 1948–1956*
Four-cylinder 746cc sports-cars with Fiat-based engines, built in limited numbers. The highly tuned engines had ohv and also ohc cylinder-heads and proved fast in many races, but failed as far as consistent reliability was concerned.

BARAUF/*USA 1920*
Probably only one Barauf car was built. This was exhibited in February 1920. The car was a five-passenger touring model featuring a 108-inch wheelbase and a four-cylinder Leroi engine. It could be converted into a utility.

BARBARINO/*America 1924–1925*
Salvatore Barbarino was an automobile engineer and designer who took over the assets of the defunct Richelieu automobile and announced a new Barbarino car late in 1924. Only ten were completed. The cars featured a Leroi four-cylinder engine, disc wheels and a high rounded radiator reminiscent of Fiat or Kissel. All bodies for this 110-inch wheelbase car were supplied by Chupurdy & Co. of New York City.

BARCLAY/*England 1933*
The Birmingham-built Barclay was an assembled family saloon, having a 10 hp Coventry-Climax engine, Moss gearbox and ENV rear-axle.

BARD/*England 1899–1900*
Forerunner of Calthorpe, George Hands's Bard Cycle Company showed Grappler-tyred motor tricycles and quadricycles at the 1899 Stanley Show.

BARDON/*France 1898–1906*
Like the Gobron-Brillié, the Bardon used an opposed-piston engine, but in this case there were two pistons and four flywheels. Engines of 5 hp to 12 hp were offered.

1903 Bardon 12hp

BARIMAR/*France 1913*
Barimar of London were welding engineers who could carry out spectacular repairs on broken or cracked castings: the 8 hp Barimar car seemed out of character for this company, as it was a spindly single-cylinder model imported from France.

1913 Barimar 8hp cyclecar

BARLEY/*USA 1922–1925*
The Barley was named after Albert Barley and built by the Barley Motor Car Co. of Kalamazoo, Michigan, as a companion car to the Roamer which had been made by Barley since 1916. Strictly an assembled car, Barleys featured both Continental and Herschell-Spillman engines, a wheelbase of 118 inches and prices starting at $1395. In 1925, the name was dropped and the Barley became the Roamer 6-50 — with the exception of the taxicab line, which was continued under its old name of Pennant.

BARLOW STEAM CAR/*USA 1923*
This 130-inch wheelbase $3000 touring car appeared in a single pilot model only. The company's plan to manufacture buses also failed to materialize.

BARNARD/*England 1921–1922*
An American Henderson four-cylinder motor-cycle engine powered this chain-driven device, which was built in East London.

BARNES/*England 1905–1906*
Tricars from Deptford, Kent, with own-make 6/8 hp and 12 hp twin-cylinder engines..

BARNES/*USA 1907–1912*
Builders of an air-cooled four-cylinder, who acquired Anhut in 1910.

BARRE/*France 1902–1930*
Barré, of Niort (Deux-Sèvres) began production with light cars powered by De Dion, Aster or Buchet engines flexibly mounted on springs. In 1908 Barré added a Ballot-engined car. In 1920 came a car with a SCAP 1600cc engine. The company changed its name to Barré & Lamberthon in 1923, but never re-attained its pre-war success, as sales were confined to local customers.

BARRELLIER/*France 1919*
This three-wheeler was a 'Voiturette for war-wounded', powered by an air-cooled horizontal twin.

BARRIERE/*France 1898–1900*
Barrière of Paris built a 'Sociable Tricycle' seating two side-by-side as well as a 2 hp tricycle of more conventional layout.

BARRINGTON/*England 1932–1936*
A project that never reached production status; Barrington Budd hoped to market a car powered by a two-stroke three-cylinder engine of his own design. A 782cc version mounted in a two-seater body was built, but further ideas came to nothing.

BARRON-VIALLE/*France 1909–1929*
The founders of this firm, Barron and Vialle, joined forces at Lyon in 1912 when the coachbuilder Vialle (established in 1909) decided to build lorries. After the war Barron and Vialle acquired the manufacturing rights of the Automobiles Six of Strasbourg. They presented their car in 1924. This was an ohc six-cylinder of 2078cc ('Super Six'). The same year the firm also presented a straight-eight ('Super Huit') of 2771cc. They also made another version with the eight-cylinder engine in the six-cylinder chassis. Until 1924, the name of Barron-Vialle was never featured on the radiator. The firm enjoyed steady local sales but nevertheless closed its doors in 1929: Vialle continued lorry production in another works at Arandon.

1913 Barré 3-litre sports in the Tour de France

BARROWS/*USA 1896–1899*
A front-wheel-drive electric tricycle built in New York. The makers planned to offer these machines for hire rather than for sale.

BARTLETT/*Canada 1913–1917*
With air suspension and solid tyres, the Bartlett appeared in prototype form with independent front suspension and four-wheel brakes augmented by retractable spikes which dug into the road through the tyres (which caused a 26-car pile-up when they were tested). The ifs and spike braking were omitted from the 600 Bartlett cars and trucks produced in the firm's Toronto works. Production was halted when Bartlett's USA suppliers went over to war work.

BASSETT/*England 1899–1901*
A two-speed light car with 4 hp Schwanemeyer twin-cylinder engine.

BASSON'S STAR/*USA 1956*
Basson's Industries, of New York, offered a

glass-fibre single-cylinder two-stroke three-wheeler for $999. It was no more successful than their previous attempt—the Martin Stationette of 1954.

BASTAERT/*France 1907–1908*
A Parisian voiturette manufacturer who exhibited at the 1907 Paris Salon.

BASTIN/*Belgium 1908–1909*
A round-radiatored light four-cylinder from Liège.

BAT/*England 1904–1909*
The 6 hp twin-cylinder Bat-Kar was a three-seater, three-wheeled voiturette from a well-known Penge motorcycle maker. In 1909 came a curious four-wheeler, the Carcycle (with a 7/9 hp JAP twin) which incorporated a detachable belt-driven cycle.

BATES/*USA 1903–1905*
'Buy a Bates and keep your dates' was the slogan of this unsuccessful venture by gas engine manufacturers Madison F. Bates and J. P. Edmonds, of Lansing, Michigan.

BATTEN/*England 1935–1938*
Batten-Specials were based on the Ford V-8 chassis, with stark open two- and four-seat bodies.

BAUGHAN/*England 1922–1929*
The 1922 Baughan, from Stroud, Gloucestershire, was a 998cc twin-cylinder cyclecar with chain-drive.

BAYLEY/*England 1905–1907*
This 18/20 hp four-cylinder worm-drive model was made by the English Motor-Car Company of London, who also made the Lipscomb car.

The 1936 Batten-Special range

BAYLISS-THOMAS/*England 1922–1929*
From the Birmingham-based manufacturer of Excelsior motorcycles, this was an assembled car, which started with a 1½-litre Coventry-Climax engine, an 1100cc ohv Meadows four being added in 1923. Sports two-seaters were available: production was on a limited scale after 1925.

1924 Bean 14hp and 10ft Eccles caravan

9/19hp Bayliss-Thomas Popular, 1923

BAY STATE/*USA 1906–1907*
Rossell Drisko's Bay State Forty, from Boston, was powered by a 5·8-litre four-cylinder engine.

BAY STATE/*USA 1922–1924*
A successful small-production car, the Bay State was manufactured by R. H. Long in Framingham, Mass., and in its three years of production, some 2500 were sold. The car featured a Continental six-cylinder engine and proven standard components, on a 121-inch wheelbase. The cars were designed by a former Winton designer, which probably explains the similarity of the radiator shape. A complete line of body styles was offered in both open and closed models, including a sport phaeton. Prices ranged from $1800 to $2850.

BEACON/*England 1912–1914*
A vee-twin cyclecar available with woven cane bodywork.

BEAN/*England 1919–1929*
A. Harper, Sons & Bean was a well-established Dudley engineering firm which wished to emulate Henry Ford by mass-producing its first car, the 11·9 of 1920. As time was of the essence, they updated the pre-war 1174cc Perry, producing it in a specially acquired factory with moving

assembly line in nearby Tipton. After getting off to a good start in 1920, they were soon placed under a receivership, due to the collapse of their holding company, which included ABC, Swift and Vulcan, plus a host of component manufacturers. By the time production re-started in 1922 they had lost out to William Morris's Cowley. In 1923 the overweight 14 hp was announced, having unit-construction engine and gearbox and detachable cylinder head, something that the Edwardian-inspired 11·9 had not offered. A scaled down 14, the 12 with the same engine capacity as the old 11·9, appeared in 1924. Hadfields, a Sheffield steel company, who had been associated with Bean's since 1919, took over the company in 1926 — ironically their centenary year — and production later moved exclusively to Tipton. A six-cylinder model, the 18/50, with Meadows engine and gearbox appeared in 1927, though the Imperial Six with a 3·8-litre Bean engine and aimed at the colonial market only reached the prototype stage. In 1928 the 14/40 Hadfield Bean appeared with separate gearbox and worm-driven rear-axle. The car was hopelessly unreliable and pro-

1923 Bean 11.9hp tourer

duction ceased in 1929, but not before a sporting version, the 14/70, put in a fleeting appearance. Commercial vehicle production, which had begun in 1924, continued until 1931.

BEARDMORE/*Scotland 1920–1928*
The first three Beardmore models were built in three separate plants at Glasgow, Coatbridge and Paisley: these were a 10 hp (1486cc), a 15 hp (2413cc) and a 20 hp (4071cc). The 10 hp was developed into the ohc Eleven 1860cc of 1922, which in turn produced the 2-litre Sports, with aluminium pistons and a 70 mph top speed, which took the Shelsley Walsh record in 1925. A side-valve 16 hp followed, but after 1928 Beardmore concentrated on taxicab construction.

BEATRIX/*France 1907–1908*
Monobloc six-cylinders of 46 hp (5184cc) and 58 hp (6574cc) built by Tisserand of Paris.

BEAUFORT/*England/Germany 1902–1910*
The Beaufort was built in Germany with English capital, solely for the British market. The 1902 range consisted of 6 hp and 8 hp singles and 12 hp and 16 hp twins. A 20 hp four was introduced for 1903. A Beaufort was the first car to climb the Round Tower, a notable Copenhagen landmark, in 1902.

1903 Beaufort 6hp single-cylinder

BEAUJANGLE CAN-AM
England 1972–1974
Supposedly inspired by the great Can-Am racers, the Beaujangle was a sports two-seater based on VW chassis and running gear. Changes to the suspension gave the Beaujangle superior handling to the more conventional 'Buggies'.

BEAUMONT / *USA 1966–1969*
The Beaumont was GM's Canadian Chevelle, having only minor alterations from the American version. Phased out in 1969, it was replaced by Canadian-built Pontiac Tempests and Le Mans.

BEAVER / *USA 1916–1923*
One of the very few cars to have been built in the state of Oregon, the Beaver, made in Gresham, was an assembled six-cylinder car with wormdrive. Only a few were built in the company's eight years of business.

BECHEREAU / *France 1924–1925*
Coming from the aeronautics industry (he had made record breaking aeroplanes), Louis Béchereau started in Paris making cars based on the Salmson cyclecar, but with independent suspension on all four wheels by means of coil springs and swinging arms. With an aerodynamic body, the Béchereau was too advanced for the public.

BECK / *France 1920–1922*
This Lyon marque presented its first car at the 1920 Brussels Show. The car had coil spring independent suspension all round. A second car was presented at the Paris Show the following year. The ohc four-cylinder engine had a swept volume of 1500cc.

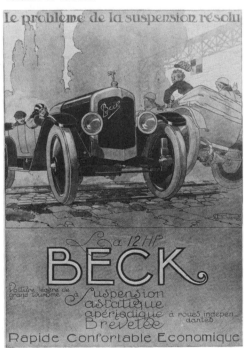

1922 Beck 12hp

BECKMANN / *Germany 1900–1926*
Early Beckmann cars had much in common with Panhard designs; afterwards the company built good cars with engines ranging from 1768cc to 7320cc. After the Great War, models with 2072cc and 2583cc four-cylinder engines were built in limited numbers. The last version had a 2015cc four-cylinder Selve sv engine. Opel bought Beckmann's Breslau factory in 1927.

BEDELIA / *France 1909–1925*
Certainly one of the very first cyclecars in the world, the Bédélia was built in Paris by Bourbeau & Devaux. It was noteworthy for having the pilot seated at the rear and the passenger at the front. The car was made of wood and plywood, and used first single-cylinder Aster engines, then their own 1056cc vee-twin. The car was belt driven. Bédélias sold very well until the war, and in 1920 the firm sold the manufacturing rights to M. Mahieux, who made modifications, including seating the passengers side-by-side. The marque collapsed in 1925.

Family outing in a 1913 Bedelia

The Bedelia range – 'tourisme', 'sport' and 'livraison' – in 1913

BEESTON / *England 1899*
This well-known Coventry cycle and motorcycle maker built a number of 3½ hp single-cylinder tricycles, quadricycles and voiturettes.

BEECHCRAFT / *USA 1948*
Built by the Beechcraft Aeroplane Company, the Beechcraft could have revolutionized the industry had production not been prevented by development costs! Advanced features included independent air-bag suspension, air shock absorbers and unitized aluminium body. Power was to be by a four-cylinder Franklin air-cooled engine driving an electric generator, which in turn powered electric motors, one for each wheel.

BEGBIE / *England 1903–1904*
A wood-framed 6½ hp Aster-engined voiturette built at Willesden Junction, London. The company also offered 'chassis for coachbuilders'.

BEGGS / *USA 1918–1923*
The Beggs was a typical assembled car, the Continental engine being used exclusively throughout its existence. Successor to a flourishing line of buggies and farm waggons, it had a 120-inch wheelbase and could be had in both open and closed models priced at $1495 to $2150, the prices being lower in its last years of production. Several hundred were made.

BEGOT ET MAZURIE / *France 1900–1902*
Known to a disgruntled latterday British owner as the 'Bag o' Misery', this 750cc voiturette from Reims was notable chiefly for the tasteful arabesques cast into its gearbox casing.

BELCAR / *Switzerland 1955*
A three-wheeled 197cc minicar produced in limited numbers.

BELGA / *Belgium 1920–1921*
The Belga, from Marchienne-Zone, was a 10/12 hp Ballot-engined light car with a Domecq-Cazaux eight-speed friction transmission incorporated in the cone clutch assembly.

BELGICA / *Belgium 1902–1909*
Built by a cycle company established in Brussels in 1885, Belgica cars initially consisted of an 8 hp single, a 12 hp twin and a 20 hp four. In 1905 came a 24/30 hp four, joined in 1907 by a 60 hp six. The company's latter cars were known as Saventhem-Belgicas. At the 1908 Agricultural Hall Show in London 24 hp and 30 hp fours and a 58 hp six with pair-cast cylinders — 'a very fine piece of work' — were exhibited. Excelsior subsequently acquired the company.

BELGRAVE
England 1904–1905
This 16/24 hp double-phaeton was sold by Donne & Willans, who imported the Rochet-Schneider into England.

BELL / *England 1905–1914*
Bell Brothers of Ravensthorpe, Yorkshire, began with an 8/10 hp twin, followed by fours of 16, 20, 24 and 30 hp. After World War One the Co-operative Wholesale Society took over the company and built CWS lorries to Bell design in Manchester, though the cars were theoretically available until 1926.

BELL/ *USA 1915–1922*
'The sensation of the year 1915', the four-cylinder Bell Model 16 from York, Pa., sold for only $775. Between 1916–18, Bells were also licence-built in Barrie, Ontario.

BELL/ *France 1923–1925*
Built in Paris by M. Bellois, this was a cyclecar with independent suspension and brakes on all four wheels. The engine was a 1308cc flat-four.

BELLAMY/ *France 1904*
Bellamy, who enlivened the early days at Brooklands with a hilariously unsuccessful flying machine (and who eventually vanished in a balloon race), built this monstrous 38,507cc eight-cylinder for a young American lady.

BELLANGER/ *France 1912–1925*
Most Bellanger cars were used as Paris taxis. The first models made at Neuilly from 1912–14 were fitted with Daimler-Knight engines of 9/13 hp (2001cc), 15 hp (2548cc), 20 hp (3308cc) and 38 hp (6280cc). After the war, Bellanger used American Briscoe sv engines from 1920 to

Post World War One advertising for the Bellanger

1914 Bellanger 15hp chassis

1923 for the 15 hp 'Tourisme' and 'Sport' (3231cc), and the 24 hp Sport (4253cc). In 1921 they launched a luxury car, the 50 hp V-8 of 6361cc. Bellanger halted car production in 1923, continuing only with aeroengines. They started to sell De Dion Bouton cars under the name of 'Bellanger' in 1928, but closed down soon after.

BELLE/ *England 1901–1903*
Ex-Hewetson engineer E. J. Coles, of Holloway, London, claimed to have built this car himself, though it was probably based on an imported chassis. It had an inclined 7 hp engine and belt drive, and was normally fitted with solid tyres.

BELMONT/ *USA 1909–1910*
'Possessed of snap, style and finish,' the four-cylinder $1650 Belmont 30 from New Haven, Conn., had overhead exhaust valves.

1923 Belsize Bradshaw two-seater

BELSIZE/ *England 1896–1925*
Marshall & Company, of Manchester, fore-runners of Belsize, began work in 1896 on a Benz-like car based on the French Hurtu, initially with tiller steering. The name 'Belsize' was first used in 1901. Cars of up to 40 hp were produced, but in 1911 a 10/12 hp of advanced design, with unit engine/gearbox made its bow. This was built up to the outbreak of the war, along with a 15·9 hp; Belsize were then building 50 cars and lorries a week. HE shells and aero engines were built during the war, and production resumed with a four-cylinder '15 hp' of 2799cc. In 1921 came the Belsize-Bradshaw, with a twin-cylinder 'oil-boiler' engine. Dying flings were a 1696cc six (1924) and a 2·5-litre straight-eight (1925).

BENHAM/ *USA 1914–1917*
Designed by Skelton and Goodwin, the Benham successor to S. & M. was a left-hand-drive luxury six-cylinder which sold for $2585.

BEN HUR/ *USA 1916–1918*
An assembled car produced in limited numbers at Willoughby, Ohio, the Ben Hur was powered by a six-cylinder Buda engine.

Benjamin 'Bagatelle' sports, 1924

BENJAMIN/ *France 1921–1931*
Benjamin made light cars and cyclecars at Asnières. Production started with a cyclecar in 1921 with a 751cc four-cylinder engine which proved to be a great commercial success. In 1924, Benjamin presented a very interesting new model with a 547cc twin-cylinder two-stroke engine with pumping piston. They also made a three-cylinder car based on the same design. They quickly came back to more conventional cars with a voiturette with sv or ohv Chapuis-Dornier engines, but in 1924 presented another original car with a rear-mounted twin-cylinder four-stroke of 636cc, later of 616cc. The car was a complete failure. Following financial difficulties in 1927, the marque turned back to Chapuis-Dornier-engined cars, but went into liquidation until production was resumed under the name of 'Benova'. The revived company built cars with various proprietary engines, including a straight-eight SCAP of 1502cc. The last cars were Ruby engined. The final closure occurred in 1931.

BENNER SIX/ *USA 1908–c1909*
An ohv pair-cast six of 3784cc, in unit with a two-speed gearbox, powered this $1750 roadster from New York.

BENNET/ *England 1904*
A 12 hp four-cylinder model shown at the 1904 Cordingly Exhibition in London.

BENTALL/ *England 1906–1913*
Agricultural engineers since 1792, Bentall of Maldon, Essex, offered round-radiatored cars of 8 and 11 hp (two-cylinder), 16 hp (four-cylinder) and an over-square 16/20 hp four. A former employee claimed production ceased because Bentalls only paid their engineers 'farm wages', being in a mainly agricultural area.

BENTLEY
England 1920 to date

One of the truly great British sports cars, the first Bentley appeared at the 1919 Motor Show but did not reach the public until 1921. This car was a long-stroke ohc 3-litre model, having a fixed head and four valves per cylinder. Although this remained in production until 1929, the next model was a more sophisticated six-cylinder 6½-litre car which appeared in 1926. W. O. Bentley reverted to his four-cylinder theme with the 4½-litre of 1927 (and supercharged by Sir Henry Birkin for 1930) though the mighty 8-litre of 1930 was a further development of the 6½-litre layout. Although today the Bentley represents to most of us the personification of the Vintage sports car,

many were fitted with stately and elegant saloon bodywork. However, the open four-seater cars are forever associated with the Le Mans 24 hour race. The Cricklewood company chalked up no less than five wins in 1924, 1927, 1928, 1929 and 1930, the last three victories going to a car driven by Woolf Barnato, who had taken the company under his financial wing in 1927. The results of the depression of 1929 were the last straw as far as the company's finances were concerned, and in 1931 they were bought by Rolls-Royce for £125,265, pipping Napier to the post. In 1933, when the first Rolls-Royce-built Bentley appeared, it was based on the Derby company's 3·7-litre 20/25 model: 1936 saw this capacity increased to 4½ litres. Independent front suspension put

in a brief appearance in 1940 on the Mark V car. The first post-war model, the Mark VI, was the same capacity (4257cc) as its pre-war counterpart, though the engine featured an overhead inlet/side exhaust layout. It was offered with a standard steel body by Pressed Steel, the first Rolls-Royce product to be so equipped. Although 1952 saw the announcement of the 4566cc Mulliner-bodied Continental, the marque's identity became more closely allied to Rolls-Royce and 1960 saw the disappearance of the faithful six, this being replaced by a 6·2-litre V-8. The current models use a 6750cc V-8 engine; the Corniche is available in saloon and convertible form, and the T series car shares the same monocoque body as the Rolls-Royce Silver Shadow.

1927 'works' 3-litre Bentley with Le Mans trim at Brooklands

1929 Speed Six Bentley

1933/34 3½-litre Derby Bentley

c.1968 Bentley T Series 2-door saloon

BENZ SOHNE/*Germany 1905–1926*
After Karl Benz left Mannheim, he headed, with his sons Eugen and — later — Richard, this new Ladenburg-based car factory. Karl Benz retired in 1912. They built some excellent cars with engines from 2608cc to 3565cc and also sleeve-valve models under Henriod-Licence. Production after the war was on a small scale. The range included sv 1638cc and 3560cc fours.

BERG/*USA 1902–1905*
Panhard-like four-cylinder chain-drive cars of 15/20 and 24hp from New York: in 1905 Berg merged with the Worthington Automobile Company, who modified Leon Bollées for the US market and also sold an 18hp five-seater called the Meteor.

BERGANTIN/*Argentina 1960–1962*
A forerunner of IKA-Renault, with a Willys-Jeep engine in an Alfa Romeo 1900 bodyshell.

BERGDOLL/*USA 1908–1913*
Louis J. Bergdoll, from a well-known Philadelphia society family, boasted that the Bergdoll 30 was 'backed by millions'. It was assembled from proprietary components, including a Westinghouse engine and Driggs-Seabury chassis, and sold at prices ranging from $1500 to $2500.

BERGE/*France 1922–1923*
R. Caillat of Le Pré-St-Gervais offered 7 and 10hp voiturettes, a 10/14hp light car and an 11/35hp sports model.

1922 Berge 10/14hp cabriolet

BERG ELECTRIC /*USA 1921–1922*
Few Berg Electric cars were ever completed, those units known to have been made being sold as town cars and limousines for private use as well as for hire. Artillery-wheeled, the 126-inch wheelbase Bergs had a General Motors 60 volt, 28 amp motor. The limousine cost $2650.

BERGEON/*France 1897 c1898*
Using 5hp Landry & Beyroux engines, this Bordelais manufacturer constructed four-seated victorias with the advanced feature of a vee-windscreen.

BERGMANN/*Germany 1909–1922*
This electricity company built a 50hp car and soon afterwards took over the licence for Belgian Métallurgique cars. On the payroll was Ernst Lehmann, one of Germany's leading car designers, also connected with Métallurgique. Among his designs were 1560cc and 1728cc twin-cylinder and 2800cc to 6320cc four-cylinder Bergmann-Métallurgique cars. Other four-cylinder models included 9880cc, 7320cc, 3365cc and 1560cc sv-engined versions. The last Bergmann designs had 55hp four-cylinder and 45hp six-cylinder side-valve engines.

BENZ
Germany 1885–1926
Karl Benz of Mannheim built his first motor car in 1885–86. Three-wheelers of similar design followed, but proved more popular in France than Germany. The 1893 'Viktoria' had a 2000cc water-cooled single-cylinder engine, but there were also 1730cc and even 2900cc versions. Another model, built until 1902, was the 3hp 'Comfortable' with a 1045cc single-cylinder engine: 1902 saw the introduction of the 'Parsifal' with 10, 12 and 14hp two-cylinder and 20 and 30hp four-cylinder engines. It was this design which created much trouble in the factory, because both Benz and Marius Barbarou claimed responsibility: Benz resigned in a huff. Barbarou became chief designer, followed in this capacity by Fritz Erle and Hans Nibel. Many superb cars, from 1950cc to a big 10,080cc developing 105 bhp (at 1400 rpm!), left the Mannheim factory, which after the war built a sporting ohc 1570cc car, the popular 6/18. Less sporting was the sv 2080cc 8/20 hp. In 1923 a sv 2860cc six-cylinder appeared and also a sporting 4130cc six-cylinder, built until 1926, when Benz merged with Daimler (Mercedes). There was also a 7025cc six-cylinder. Benz also built many racing cars, including in 1909 the 200hp 'Blitzen'-Benz and in 1922–24 the rear-engined, Edmund Rumpler-designed, 1980cc Benz 'Teardrop' racing car.

1887–88 Benz three-wheeler

BENZ CARS.
4½ H.P.,   6 H.P.,   7 H.P.,   10 H.P.,   16 H.P.,   20 H.P.
Ideals.   Phaetons.   Tonneaux.
Reliable.   Fast.   Durable.   Elegant.
1902 front-engined 10hp Benz

A modified Benz Viktoria, c.1898

1921 Benz Sportwagen

BERKELEY / *England 1913*
A low-priced (£120) 14/18 hp four-cylinder.

BERKELEY / *England 1956–1962*
Small, glass-fibre-bodied, motorcycle-engined sports cars. Performance of the later versions was very good, thanks to more powerful engines and a weight of around 7 cwt (785 lb). Designed by Laurence Bond at the request of Charles Panter of Berkeley Caravans, the cars sold in steady numbers until the company's demise.

BERKSHIRE / *USA 1905–1913*
The first production Berkshires used Herschell-Spillman engines: from 1907 they used 6211cc fours of their own make.

BERLIET / *France 1895–1936*
Marius Berliet started building single-cylinder cars in a small shed, in 1895: in 1900 he offered twin-cylinder cars also. After taking over Audibert & Lavirotte in 1901, M. Berliet built two- and four-cylinder cars, and a year later he introduced a completely new design with a honeycomb radiator and steel chassis frame instead of wood. In 1906 Berliet sold the US licence for his design to the American Locomotive Co. From 1907 to the outbreak of war, Berliet production was mainly centred on three models: fours of 2412cc and 4398cc and a six of 9500cc. A 1539cc model was current from 1910–12. Berliet made cars until 1917, but developed their lorry department during the war for the needs of the French Army. After the war they resumed production of cars with a 12 hp (2613cc), 15 hp (3308cc) and 22 hp (4398cc), plus other minor models. The sv engines were all of pre-war design. In 1924 Berliet presented new ohv engines: a 7 hp (1159cc) would-be popular car, a 12 hp (2484cc) and an 18 hp (3969cc), these models co-existing with the old side-valves. With the growth of lorry sales, Berliet had less and less interest in making cars. Nevertheless they launched two

1923 Berliet 12cv tourer

new six-cylinders of 1800cc and 4000cc in 1927. In 1933, only two car models were listed: a 1600cc and a 2000cc, available in side-valve as well as ohv form. The last model, presented in 1936, was the Dauphine, a modern-looking car similar to the Chrysler Airflow, with independent front suspension. Marius Berliet died shortly after the war; a change of policy had already suppressed cars in favour of lorries. Berliet, which was taken over by Citroën in 1967, still make lorries.

BERNA / *Switzerland 1902–1907*
One of the great Swiss truck firms, Berna — of Berne — began with a rear-engined car on De Dion lines and curious three-seater coachwork in which the front-seat passenger sat sideways. A front-engined 8 cv appeared in 1903, joined by a 5 cv the following year. The last Berna touring cars were six monobloc fours built in 1907.

BERNARDET / *France 1946–1950*
A well-known builder, Bernardet started to build economy cars with 750cc and 800cc two-stroke engines just after World War Two. They had no great success so Bernardet returned to sidecars and also made scooters.

BERSEY / *England 1894–1899*
Walter C. Bersey's first experimental electric vehicle, an omnibus, appeared in 1888, but it was not until he and Desmond FitzGerald had developed a suitable dry cell for propulsion purposes that he began to promote his designs commercially, starting with a parcels van, which ran 1000 miles in London during 1894. Bersey concentrated on vans, formal landaus and cabs (he built London's first taxi fleet in 1897, and also supplied electric cabs to Paris) because he felt that no form of pleasure car could ever replace the horse.

1896 Bersey Cab undergoing Scotland Yard testing

1901 Bertrand

BERTRAND / *France 1901–1902*
Two-speed voiturettes from Paris with Clément, De Dion, Buchet or Aster engines.

BESSEYRE & RAYNE / *France 1908*
Remarkable for what it omitted from the expected specification, this was a two-stroke four 'without gearchange or water circulation'.

BEVERLEY-BARNES
England 1924–1931
The straight-eight ohc Beverley-Barnes was made in small numbers by Lenaerts and Dolphens and varied in engine capacity from 2¼ to 5 litres; at least one was Bean-engined! These luxury cars were only made in small numbers and did not survive the Depression.

BF / *Germany 1922–1926*
A small factory, concentrating on fast two-stroke cars. Bolle-Fiedler of Berlin also built 1096cc and 1496cc racing cars, with three- and four-cylinder engines, which were driven by the designer Max Fiedler. Production versions had 1026cc motors.

1913 Bianchi 25/30hp Prince Henry Torpedo

BIANCHI / *Italy 1898–1938*
Founded in 1885 by Edoardo Bianchi, this Milan factory, still well known for bicycles, commenced manufacture of motorcycles and cars in 1898. They built many touring car models over the years. Some had ohv 8-litre in-line engines, but most were of 1460cc, 2690cc or 2890cc; there was also a popular ohv 1287cc four-cylinder. Bianchi cars were of sound, sturdy design. Attempts to revive production with new designs after World War Two failed, partly as a result of the great demand for bicycles and motorcycles, partly because of the high costs of developing the new cars.

BIDDLE / *USA 1915–1923*
A highly regarded small luxury automobile, distinguished by a pointed radiator similar to the Mercedes or American Singer. With prices ranging from $2950 to over $5000 for custom-bodied models, Biddle cars were known for their

A 40hp Berliet in the 1905 Coupe des Pyrenees

exquisite individually designed coachwork. Although a Buda engine was standard equipment, the Rochester-Duesenberg engine was used on 1918 models and available as an option after.

BIFORT/*England 1914–1920*
A 10 hp light car built in Fareham, Hants.

BIGNAN/*France 1918–1931*
In 1920, Bignan (who had made proprietary engines before World War One) started to build the Bignan Sport in the Grégoire factory at Poissy. There were two models, of 2951cc and 3457cc, with fixed-head sv engines. Bignan also made a real sports-racing car whose Causan-designed ohc 2959cc engine had four valves per cylinder. In 1922, Bignan made another, very raceworthy sports car, the famous 2-litre with desmodromic valves, replaced in 1924 by another 2-litre, with four valves per cylinder. On the touring side, Jacques Bignan presented in 1922 an ohc 1693cc 10 hp, followed with an 11 hp in 1923. After a first failure in 1926, Bignan quickly resumed production with a new management and launched a car with two valves per cylinder. Of minor interest, for they were not true Bignan cars, the marque also made 8 hp 1200cc and 10 hp 1500cc SCAP-engined cars and a 10 hp with 1600cc Ballot engine. It also turned to badge-engineering with Salmson cyclecars bearing Bignan radiators. Forced to meet more and more financial demands, Bignan started to run his business under the new name of 'La Cigogne' and built a new six-cylinder 2·5-litre and an eight-cylinder SCAP-engined car in 1929. Between 1930 and 1931, Bignan only repaired cars, and then closed.

A Bignan Sport in the 1925 Le Mans Race

1920 Bignan Sport 3-litre

BIJOU/*England 1901–1904*
The Protector Lamp and Lighting Company of Eccles, near Manchester, built a tiny motor fire engine in 1901. Their Bijou light cars had 5 hp water-cooled engines and were capable of 20 mph.

1904 Bijou 5hp voiturette

BIJ'T VUUR/*Holland 1902–1906*
Aster-engined cars from Arnhem. Only a few were built.

BILLINGS-BURNS/*England 1900*
Designed by F. D. Billings of Coventry, this voiturette was powered by a 2¼ hp De Dion engine.

BINGHAMTON ELECTRIC/*USA 1920*
Only two or three of these two-passenger electric coupés were made by the Binghamton Electric Truck Co., of Binghamton, NY.

BINNEY & BURNHAM/*USA 1901–1902*
An ineptly named twin-cylinder steamer from Boston.

BIOTA/*England 1969–1976*
The Biota was a striking, open-topped two-seater with a Mini engine mounted in the nose of a light tubular chassis clothed in a neat fibreglass body. About 31 Biotas were built for road and track, one winning the 1972 Castrol BARC Hillclimb Championship driven by Chris Seaman. Weighing a mere 8 cwt, all Biotas enjoyed lively performance.

BIRCH/*USA 1916–1923*
Like the Bush, the Chicago-based Birch was strictly a mail-order car. A complete line of four- and six-cylinder models featured Leroi, Lycoming, Beaver and Herschell-Spillman engines. Production was limited to open models until 1921, when a sedan augmented the line. Wheelbases ranged from 108 to 117 inches and the car's main appeal was probably its low price. From the aesthetic point of view, little could be said for the Birch.

BIRD/*USA 1897–1898*
A rear-engined friction-drive *dos-à-dos*, built by Henry Bird of Buffalo, NY.

BIRMINGHAM
USA 1921–1922
The Birmingham of Jamestown, NY, featured independent suspension by transverse semi-elliptic springs and a fabric-covered body, a novelty in America. Powered by a Continental six-cylinder engine and other proven components, about 20 units were produced. The design, without the independent suspension or fabric body, was used later on the Canadian Parker car.

BISCUTER/*Spain 1953–1958*
Gabriel Voisin's last production vehicle was unlike anything he had done before, save in the

originality of its conception: it was a tiny two-seater, with duralumin monocoque body and a 197cc Spanish-built Villiers engine driving the front wheels. Built in Barcelona, it proved a popular solution to the problem of providing basic transport for the car-hungry Spaniards during the 1950s.

BITTER/*Germany 1973 to date*
Produces luxurious 5354cc V-8 230 HP coupés with ohc Opel 'Diplomat' engines and body-work by Baur of Stuttgart. The production of Bitter cars at Gevelsberg is on a small scale.

BIZZARINI/*Italy 1965–1969*
Giotto Bizzarini, who mainly built prototypes at Livorno, first created the Iso-Grifo, then a couple of cars bearing his own name. They were of advanced design, although his very sporting cars had front engines, when other designers were already switching to rear engines. Best known were his GT Strada 5300, a high-efficiency coupé with Type 327 Chevrolet Corvette engine and the GT Europa 1900 with an 1897cc ohv four-cylinder Opel motor. The engine used in the Strada was a 5359cc ohv V-8 developing 355 bhp at 5800 rpm. Its top speed was 172 mph. All Bizzarini cars were hand-made.

BJERING/*Norway 1919–1920*
A great problem in Norway was the narrow roads, especially in winter when ordinary cars were too wide for the narrow track the snow plough left for them. The Bjering car from Gjovik was designed for this, with tandem seating, the driver in the rear seat to obtain better traction. Engine was an air-cooled V-4 of Norwegian design placed in the middle of the car. Four cars were built before it was re-designed, with a four-cylinder engine at the rear. Only two of these were built.

BLACK/*USA 1899*
Phaetons, *dos-à-dos* and 'business waggons' of 2½ hp to 8 hp were offered by this Indianapolis manufacturer.

BLACK/*USA 1903–1909*
'Speed! I guess yes!' was the optimistic slogan used to advertise this 10 hp, twin-cylinder high-wheeler from Chicago, with a maximum velocity of 25 mph.

BLACKBURN/*England 1919–1925*
Built by the well-known aircraft company, the Blackburn was a conventional enough car with a 3160cc Coventry-Simplex engine.

BLACKHAWK/*USA 1929–1931*
The Blackhawk initially appeared as the Stutz Model B-B in 1928, but a year later it was given marque status. Both an own-make six and a Continental eight were featured. Despite certain efforts to give the Blackhawk an image of its own, it was almost always regarded as just another model of Stutz.

BLACK PRINCE/*England 1920*
The short-lived Black Prince was a belt-driven cyclecar, largely made of wood and driven by a 2¾ hp Union air-cooled engine.

BLAKE/*England 1899–1904*
Blake's first car, built in 1899, was a Benz-like vehicle with a 3 hp horizontal Blake engine, which he planned to fit with a Dawson dynamo/starter unit. The 1902 4 hp voiturette had a twin-cylinder horizontal engine, of Blake's own construction. The company sub-sequently concentrated on building engines for motor launches.

1922 Blériot 739cc *'conduite interieure'*

BLERIOT/*France 1921–1922*
Made by Blériot Aéronautique at Suresnes, the Blériot cyclecar had a small twin-cylinder two-stroke engine of 739cc, and a chassis made of wood. Only a few were made by the firm, who were also making motorcycles at this time.

BLERIOT-WHIPPET/*England 1920–1927*
Infinitely variable transmission by pulley and belt was an unconventional feature of this cyclecar. The engine was a centrally mounted Blackburne vee-twin. Later variants were shaft- and chain-driven.

BLM/*USA 1906–1908*
A sporting four-cylinder built in New York by Breese, Lawrence and Moulton. Engines of up to 11,120cc were used.

BLODGETT/*USA 1922*
Only one prototype was built, a five-passenger touring car featuring disc wheels and a six-cylinder Continental engine. Manufacturer was the Blodgett Engineering & Tool Co., of Detroit.

BLOMSTROM/*USA 1906*
Blomstrom of Detroit built the Gyroscope, a friction-drive flat-twin model with vertical crankshaft and fore-and-aft cylinders for 'gyro-scopic stability in running—no skidding!' The company later merged with De Luxe.

LE BLON/*France 1898*
Benz-like voiturettes with 4 hp twin cylinder engines, sold in England as the 'Lynx'.

BLUMBERG/*USA 1920*
A handful of four- and eight-cylinder auto-mobiles were built by this manufacturer of tractors. A V-8 was offered, with a wheelbase of 124 inches and an asking price of $3000.

BMF/*Germany 1904–1907*
This Berlin-based factory was the predecessor of Oryx, which in 1909 merged with Dürkopp. BMF built 22 hp Fafnir-engined cars and sup-plied many Berlin taxicabs. Some models had friction drive.

1922 Black Prince 2¾hp cyclecar

BMW/*Germany 1928 to date*
When BMW bought the Dixi car works at Eisenach (now East Germany), they also acquired the licence for the Austin Seven. They were soon building the 'Wartburg'; this sports car had a two-seater body and an 18 hp engine, which gained the first racing successes on four wheels for this Munich-based company. The first true BMW design was an ohv 788cc four-cylinder in 1931. Other versions with 845cc and, in 1933, the first six-cylinder BMW— an 1173cc Fritz Feidler design followed. The 1490cc six-cylinder developing 34 bhp was built also as a two-seater 40 bhp sports car and, from 1936 onwards, a 1911cc six-cylinder was made. Most famous version was the 328, developing 80 bhp at 4500 rpm, which won many races with drivers including Prince Bira and Dick

Seaman. The last pre-war model was a 3485cc six-cylinder touring car with 90 bhp at 3500 rpm. In England BMW cars were sold by Frazer Nash and also raced under the Frazer Nash name. As a result of the war BMW lost the Eisenach works, but bought the Glas car works at Dingolfing in 1966; they also built a new factory there. The first post-war car was the 501 with a 1971cc six-cylinder engine, built from 1952 onwards. Improved versions—and also a 2077cc model—followed. A V-8 appeared in 1954; first with 2580cc, later with 3168cc and up to 160 bhp at 5600 rpm. Using modified 246cc single-cylinder ohv motorcycle engines, from 1955, BMW built the Italian Isetta bubble cars under licence. There was also a 298cc model and a 582cc BMW-Isetta, which used an ohv flat-twin of BMW's own manufacture. New small

cars with 697cc flat-twin engines appeared on the market in 1959. They saved BMW during a depression, when even motorcycle sales slumped. New, bigger car models came into production in 1962 with four-cylinder ohc engines of 1499cc, 1573cc, 1773cc and 1990cc capacity and subsequently ohc six-cylinder engines of 2494cc to 3295cc. All these engines came in a variety of models. Among later models were the 316, 318, 320 and 320i with 1573cc, 1766cc, 1990cc and 2315cc ohc engines and the 518, 520, 520i, 525, 528/530i range which also included six-cylinder ohc in-line engines of 1990cc, 2494cc and 2788cc. The 630 and 633 CSi cars use 2986cc and 3210cc engines developing up to 200 bhp, while the 728, 730 and 733i are powered by 2799cc, 2986cc and 3210cc six-cylinder ohc engines

1929 BMW Wartburg sports

BMW 327 Cabriolet, 1938

1968/70 BMW 1800

1978 BMW 630 coupé

1926 BNC 1100cc sports

BNC/*France 1923–1950*

Bollack, Netter et Cie built many excellent sports cars, initially evolved from the Jack Muller cyclecar. The first models used SCAP and Ruby engines from 900cc to 1100cc in sv or ohv form. They started with true sports cars in 1927 with the 'Montlhéry', 'Monza' and 'Miramas' models with Ruby and SCAP engines. Some of these—mainly the SCAP-engined models—were supercharged. They sold very well; under the management of M. de Ricoux, they entered the field of larger cars with the ill-fated AER in 1930. BNC took over Lombard in 1929. Some BNC racing cars used 1500cc Meadows engines. The firm closed its doors in the late 1930s: the BNC marque was taken over by their agent, M. Sirejols, who continued to assemble cars from parts until 1950, some of them using BMW 328 and Ford Ten engines.

BOB/*Germany 1920–1925*

A small producer who fitted 990cc and 1268cc Siemens & Halske four-cylinder engines into own-make frames. Bob cars had a 'sporting touch' and competed in many German races. The last 1268cc versions had own-make engines.

BOBBI-KAR/*USA 1945–1948*

Produced by the Bobbi Motor Car Corp., first in California and then in Birmingham, Alabama, the Bobbi-Kar had Torsilastic independent suspension consisting of rubber welded to steel, combined with torsional rigidity. Rear-mounted water- or air-cooled engines ranged from one to four cylinders. Some bodies were of plastic but a coupé with removable steel top and a wood-panelled sedan almost went into production.

BOBBY-ALBA/*France 1920–1924*

Made by Lucien Bollack (later of BNC), these light cars had sv Ballot engines of 1131cc.

BOCAR/*USA 1958–1960*

Bob Carnes designed and built a high performance two-seater sports car with a plastic body and tubular frame. Powered by a supercharged

Bock & Hollender sporting two-seater, 1907

BOLLEE/*France 1873–1924*

The Bollées, a gifted family of bellfounders from Le Mans, sired three marques: the steam carriages of Amédée Bollée *père*, built between 1873–81 (his *Mancelle* of 1878, with independent front suspension, set the style for cars to come, and was built in a small series); the advanced petrol cars of Amédée Bollée *fils* (1896–1913); the fiery three-wheeled Léon Bollée (1896), first vehicle to bear the name 'voiturette'. The 1896 Amédée Bollée car was the first shaft-driven car with spiral bevel gearing: Amédée *fils* subsequently built the streamlined racing *torpilleurs*, the 1899 model featuring a 20 hp monobloc four, with twin carburettors, a chassis independently sprung at the front, underslung at the rear. But their disappointing performance inspired Amédée

1900 Amédée Bollée 6hp phaeton

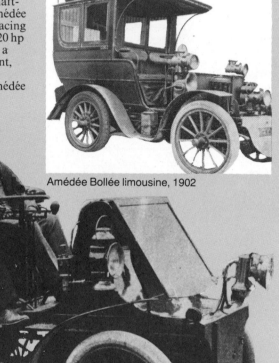

Amédée Bollée limousine, 1902

to concentrate on refined limited production cars, his 1907 Type E, the first ergonomically designed car, featuring hydraulic tappets. The last Amédée Bollée cars left the works in 1913—but some were assembled from spares until 1919. Léon Bollée's factory built large, conventional cars from 1903 to 1924, when it was taken over by Morris.

or fuel-injected Corvette engine with Volkswagen suspension, Buick brakes and Jaguar wire wheels, this limited production car was priced at $4146.

BOCK & HOLLENDER/*Austria 1899–1910*

Bock & Hollender built cars—known also as the 'Regent'—and motorcycles. The cars mainly had four-cylinder engines of 16 hp, 24 hp and—eventually—40 hp. Early models had chain drive. Works-driver Karl Trummer won many hillclimbs in these cars.

BOES/*Germany 1903–1906*

Like other early German producers, Boes built cars with vee-twins and also with in-line four-cylinder proprietary engines.

BOISSAYE/*France 1901*

A 'real racing carriage so dear to quick speeds amateurs', the Boissaye was a 24 hp four.

BOITEL/*France 1946–1949*

The small Boitel used 400cc and 589cc two-stroke engines, but few were sold.

BOLIDE/*France 1899–1908*
Léon Lefèvbre started production with a range of high-built belt-drive racing cars with horizontal engines with one, two and four cylinders, the biggest being 11,699cc. Chain-drive came in 1901, and by 1902 Bolides were of conventional design, with vertical engines of various proprietary makes. Lefèvbre left around 1906 to make the Prima car, and the last new Bolide design was a six-cylinder shown at the December 1906 Paris Salon.

BOLIDE/*USA 1969 to date*
The Bolide prototype Can-Am I, designed by Andrew J. Griffith, was immediately followed by Can-Am II with a 5752cc Ford V-8 engine. A four-wheel-drive ORV Bolide using the 3687cc Jeep 160 hp V-6 engine is also produced.

BOLSOVER/*England 1907–1909*
A three-cylinder steamer from Durham.

BOLWELL/*Australia 1963–1974*
The Bolwell brothers started in business building glass-fibre kit cars, and by 1970 had graduated to the factory-built Nagari sports coupé. This beautiful and exciting machine was powered by a Ford V-8 302 engine. The Lotus-type backbone chassis incorporated four-wheel independent suspension of Bolwell design. The firm had planned to export to the US market but tough safety and emission regulations made this impracticable. Nearly 100 Nagaris (and hundreds of the earlier Mark 7 models) were sold in Australia. Many still survive.

BOND/*England 1922–1928*
Powered by a six-cylinder American Continental engine, the Bond also appeared as a sports car in 1925 with a 1496cc four-cylinder Meadows engine.

Bolwell Nagari sports

Borgward Isabella coupé

Bond Equipe GT, 1962

BOND/*England 1949–1976*
Now part of Reliant, the Bond started life as a basic three-wheeler with a 122cc (later 197cc) Villiers two-stroke driving the front wheel by chain (and only with a kick-starter until 1952). The Minicar lasted into the mid-1960s, by which time Bond also offered the Triumph-Herald-based Equipe, with glass-fibre bodywork. The Bond Bug was a sporty three-wheeler of idiosyncratic design.

BONDIS/*France 1910–1911*
Showed a range of cars with 8, 12, 16 and 20 hp engines at the 1910 Paris Salon.

BONNEVILLE/*France 1898*
A 'train-cycle' consisting of a quadricycle with trailer attachment.

BONSTETTIN/*France 1897*
The weird transmission of this voiturette consisted of a pyramidal flywheel with surface teeth engaged by a movable crown wheel linked to a complex belt and edge-bevel final-drive.

BORBEIN/*USA 1903–1909*
Component manufacturers from St Louis who sold cars complete, except for engine and tyres: the 1909 four-passenger roadster cost $598.

BORDEREL-CAIL/*France 1905–c1908*
Ironmaster Borderel was, it seems, the keeper of Meg Steinheil, the *grande cocotte* who caused the embarrassing death of French President Félix Faure in 1899; La Société Cail was one of France's oldest locomotive builders. F. Gros was the designer of this curious four-cylinder six-wheeler on which the centre axle drove and the front and back axles steered.

BORGWARD/*Germany 1939–1961*
Carl F. Borgward was 73 when he died in 1963; his large car works had closed down two years earlier. Forerunners of his Borgward cars were the Hansa, Hansa-Lloyd and some other makes, which he either founded or bought when the former manufacturer of car radiators was on the way up. The first model bearing the Borgward name had an ohv four-cylinder 1498cc engine; the next cars were of 1758cc and there was also a diesel-engined model. The popular Borgward 'Isabella' was built from 1954 in various models with ohv 1493cc four-cylinder engines. Borgward also competed in sports car events with 1493cc ohc cars. The small-car ranges were built under the Lloyd and Goliath trade marks and when the Bremen works disappeared, these makes also became victims of the collapse.

BORLAND/*USA 1913–1914*
A six-speed, shaft-drive electric built by Borland-Grannis of Chicago.

BORO GT/*England 1971*
A very professional one-off on the lines of the Unipower. Designed and built by Eric Lacey, the alloy-bodied, two-seater Boro featured its own tubular chassis and was powered by a rear-mounted Mini engine.

BOSS/*USA 1903–1907*
Boss Knitting Machines, of Reading, Pa., built this 8 hp twin-cylinder steam car designed by one James L. Eck.

BOTYS/*France 1907*
A single-cylinder voiturette of 942cc: one competed in the 1907 Coupe des Voiturettes.

BOUDREUX/*France 1907–1908*
This Parisian voiturette maker offered the 'simplified' Boudreux-Verdet engines in 'mono-duplex, biduplex, tetraduplex and quadruplex' forms.

BOULET/*France 1903*
A 'suspended quadri-voiturette' with 4 hp, 6 hp and 9 hp rear-mounted Aster engines; one entered for the Paris-Madrid race.

BOULT/*France 1898*
A three-wheeler voiturette on similar lines to the Bollée.

BOUND/*England 1920*
The friction-drive Bound monocar, built in Southampton, used a 3½ hp Precision engine.

BOUQUET, GARCIN & SCHIVRE
France 1899–1906
The 1899 BGS electric was 'an elegant and, stately design for a private pleasure carriage', which could cover 60 miles on one charge of its 770 lb battery pack, at speeds up to 15 mph.

BOURASSA/*Canada 1899–1932*
Henri-Emile Bourassa of Montreal built one-off cars to special order: he tried for six years to raise finance for his 1926 Bourassa Six design, then broke up the prototype in despair.

BOUR DAVIS/*USA 1915–1922*
The Bour Davis was a conventionally assembled car, featuring a Continental six-cylinder engine and other well-known components, initially produced at Detroit. The company failed in 1917, but within two years operations were re-established in Shreveport, Louisiana, where cars were built with prices starting at $1650. In 1922 the name was changed to Ponder and one final car, essentially a Bour Davis, was produced with a Ponder emblem on its radiator.

BOURGUIGNONNE
France 1899–early 1900s
Chesnay de Falletane & Cie, of Dijon, invented a curious 'sprinkling' cooling system for the 3 hp single-cylinder power unit of their voiturette. Nominally air-cooled, the cylinder barrel was sprayed with water from a tank pressurized by the heat of the exhaust, which was also utilized to vaporize the fuel.

BOUVIER-DREUX/*France 1897*
A light-weight voiturette powered by an opposed-twin air-cooled engine, the Bouvier-Dreux sold for Fr 3000 in two-seater form.

BOVY/*Belgium c1908–c1914*
A Brussels truck builder offering a limited number of cars, mostly twin-cylinder landaulettes.

BOWEN/*England 1906–c1908*
A 1305cc two-cylinder car built in London by Bowen & Co., of the Phoenix Brass Foundry, Mount Pleasant.

1907 Brasier 30/40hp limousine

BOWMAN/*USA 1921–1922*
Bowman of Covington, Kentucky, produced a handful of roadsters and touring cars in its short lifespan. Powered by a four-cylinder engine of its own manufacture, the 108-inch wheelbase Bowman sold in a price range of around $1000.

BOW-V-CAR/*England 1922–1923*
The integral chassis/body Bow-V-Car was a brief essay on the cyclecar theme using a 10 hp vee-twin Precision engine.

BOYER/*France 1901–1907*
A light car which made its name by being driven without a breakdown from Paris to Barcelona, no mean feat in that era. The Boyer had a tubular chassis and final drive by side chains, and was available with De Dion, Aster, Buchet or Meteor power units of 7½/12 hp. It was built at Neuilly-sur-Seine. In 1905 a 16 cv Boyer won a gold medal for easy starting, springing into life (on the handle) in 0·8 second. The firm's last offering was a six-cylinder, shown at the 1906 Paris Salon.

BOZIER/*France 1901–1920*
Starting as makers of motor tricycles and a gear-change system, used, among others, by Dennis, Bozier were building tricars under Austral

1914 Brasier 30hp chassis

licence by 1905, as well as a 4½ hp De Dion-engined voiturette. Single, twins and fours of up to 24 hp were listed up to 1914, when production almost certainly ceased.

BPD/*England 1913*
An 8 hp cyclecar from Shoreham, Sussex.

BRADBURY/*England 1905*
Better known as motorcycle manufacturers, Bradbury of Manchester also built a range of 'Peerless' forecars with 4½ hp water-cooled engines.

BRADLEY/*USA 1920–1921*
An undistinguished assembled car, the Bradley featured both four- and six-cylinder Lycoming-engined touring cars.

BRAMWELL-ROBINSON/*USA 1899–1901*
A 'very natty little three-wheeled sociable' built by a firm of paper box machinery manufacturers from Hyde Park, Mass. Bramwell built cars under his own name to 1904.

BRASIER/*France 1905–1930*
After Georges Richard left to found Unic, Richard-Brasier became simply 'Brasier', offering reliable cars such as the 10 hp twin of 1526cc and the 1847cc four. The 1551cc 11 hp introduced in 1909 lasted until 1915. A new range was launched in 1911, with a pair-cast six-cylinder of 4766cc and a four-cylinder derivative of 3177cc, plus other models including a 24 hp four of 3562cc. In 1914, the flat radiator gave way to a round one and four new cars were introduced—a 9 hp, a 12 hp, a 16 hp and a 22 hp. After World War One, the Brasier factory resumed production in 1919 with a 3404cc 18 hp which had an electric starter: this only remained in production until the end of 1920. The year after, a new car appeared, the 2120cc 12 hp, current until 1926. A 9 hp of 1452cc was introduced in 1924. In 1926 the marque name was changed to Chaigneau-Brasier, presenting a fwd straight-eight of 3078cc, which in the late 1920s proved too much in advance of its time.

BRAUN/*Austria 1899–1908*
Designed by August Braun, the Austrian Braun cars had no connection with the German car of the same name. August Braun built cars with one, two, and four cylinders, of 5 hp, 9 hp, 15 hp and 20 hp. They were of good quality; by 1902 magneto ignition was standard.

BRAUN/*Germany 1910–1913*
A fire-fighting equipment factory, Justus Christian Braun of Nuremberg was connected with Premier of Coventry and built not only Premier motorcycles, but also four-cylinder Kaiser cars in limited quantities, with, among others, Fafnir engines from 18 hp to 70 hp.

BRAVO/*Germany 1921–1922*
Built a small 10 hp two-cylinder car, but was soon taken over for the production of the Mannheim-built Rabag-Bugatti (licence-built Bugatti Type 22 and 23).

BRECHT/*USA 1901–1903*
Built three styles of steam car, three of electric.

BREESE-PARIS/*USA/France 1921–1925*
Built to special order only, the Breese-Paris was a sports roadster designed by the American Robert Breese, whose brother had built the BLM. An ohc 1390cc four was used on some cars; others had side-valve Ballot fours.

BREEZE/*USA 1909–1910*
A range of 14 hp high-wheelers priced from $425 to $850, built in Cincinnati.

BREGUET/*France 1942–1944*
During the German Occupation, the Ateliers d'Aviation Louis Bréguet built some electric cars in their Toulouse works.

BREMS/*Denmark 1900–1907*
The first of the Brems cars from Viborg was clearly inspired by the German Wartburg car (two members of the family had been working at the Wartburg works in Eisenach!). Six single-cylinder cars were built and sold, and finally another twin-cylinder 9 hp car with a three-speed gearbox was built.

Brennabor Juwel 3147cc eight-cylinder, 1930

BRENNABOR/*Germany 1908–1934*
Brennabor built prams, bicycles, motorcycles, three-wheelers and cars, and was for some time the biggest car manufacturer in Germany. The firm used initially Fafnir two- and four-cylinder engines, afterwards units of their own make. They produced in pre-Great War days cars from 904cc to 3800cc, which in England and other export markets were known as 'Brenna'. Most models were designed by Carl Reichstein, one of the founders of Brennabor at Brandenburg/Havel, now in East Germany. They were of good quality and advanced design. In the early 1920s, daily production was around 120 cars, many of them the 1569cc with ohv and ioe engines of 20 hp and 25 hp. In 1927 a new sv 2090cc four-cylinder and a sv 3080cc six-cylinder appeared. Another six-cylinder, the Juwel, had a 2460cc engine. Added to this model in 1930 was the 3417cc eight-cylinder Juwel and also a fwd version of the Juwel 6. The last Brennabor range consisted of the rear-wheel-driven 995cc Model D and two (1950cc and 2500cc) six-cylinder models. The factory also built low and fast racing cars in the 1920s which were driven by Reichstein, Mitzlaff, Bakasch, Neidlich and other works drivers. Brennabor also competed successfully in big trials, such as the Alpine trial and the Europa-Fahrt 10,000 km. The racing cars had dohc 1499cc four-cylinder engines.

BREW-HATCHER/*USA 1904–1905*
A five-passenger 16 hp tourer from Cleveland.

BREWSTER/*USA 1915–1925, 1934–1936*
The original Brewster automobile was manufactured by the carriage firm of Brewster & Co., at Long Island City, NY. The Brewsters were powered by a four-cylinder Knight engine and distinguished by an oval radiator, an option of either left- or right-hand steering, and a complete line of exquisite open and closed coachwork. Brewster cars were quite popular in New York City and its environs, selling at prices in the $10,000 range. Very little change marked the outward appearance of these Brewsters from the first car built to the last models before the company suspended production. Roughly 300 cars were built between 1915 and 1925. In 1934, the late John S. Inskip, who had been president of Rolls-Royce of America, Inc., set up the Springfield Manufacturing Company in the former Rolls-Royce works and began production of a second Brewster automobile, American Rolls-Royce having bought out Brewster & Company in 1926. The new line of cars were essentially examples of Brewster bodies mounted on lengthened Ford V-8 chassis, although in a few cases, Buick, Oldsmobile — and even one Rolls-Royce — chassis were used. The chassis featured heart-shaped

1936 Brewster station wagon

1936 Brewster Town Car

1901 Brennabor 1-litre saloon

grilles, flared fenders and split bumpers and most of them were town-cars listed at $3500. A few convertible-sedans and convertible-coupés were also produced. Approximately 300 of these latter-day Brewsters were completed and sold before production was phased out and Springfield Manufacturing closed its doors. Mr. Inskip became US distributor for Rolls-Royce.

BRICKLIN/*USA 1974–1976*
Malcolm Bricklin hoped to break into the Corvette market with his SV-1 sports car, but never remotely approached his planned output of 12,000 units a year. The Bricklin bristled with unusual features—colour-impregnated acrylic outer skin bonded to a glass-fibre body, gull-wing doors and 12 mph crash-resistant bumpers were some of them. The steel perimeter frame encircled the passenger compartment at bumper height, and AMC suspension, brakes and 5899cc V-8 were used (though a change was made to a 5161cc Ford unit in 1975).

BRIERRE/*France 1900–1905*
Brierre of Paris started with a 3½cv voiturette, then built Cottereau cars under licence.

BRILLIE/*France 1904–1908*
Eugène Brillié left Gobron-Brillié in 1903 to produce a range of four-cylinder cars with conventional ioe engines and shaft-drive, built by the Schneider armaments company. His Brillié-Schneider buses and trucks enjoyed greater success.

BRISCOE/*USA 1914–1921*
The car with the 'half-million-dollar motor' was originally designed in France by Benjamin Briscoe, who built the Ajax cyclecar at Neuilly (Seine) in 1913–19. Early examples of this 2514cc four-cylinder car had a 'cyclops' headlamp incorporated in the radiator header tank; later models had conventional lighting. A few V-8s were built in 1916; from 1921 to 1923 the four-cylinder Briscoe was produced under the name 'Earl'. Total Briscoe and Earl production was in the region of 75,000.

BRISTOL/*England 1902–1907*
Motor agent Arthur Johnson built his first car—a 10 hp twin—in 1902. At first, cars were built solely for hire, but from 1902 cars were sold on a limited basis: about six 10 hp and 18 of the four-cylinder 16/20 model of 1905–07.

BRISTOL/*England 1945 to date*
The car division of the Bristol Aeroplane Company was formed in 1945 with the intention of building high performance cars of quality— a maxim that is as applicable today as it was then. The aeronautical ancestry of the early 400 Series was very evident in the unusual styling, but the marque soon found success. Bristol's 2-litre engine powered many racing as well as road cars to success in the 1950s, not least the Formula 2 Cooper-Bristols. Nowadays, though production still continues at Filton, Bristol Cars Ltd—as the company is now known—has no direct links with the aircraft industry and is owned and run by former racing driver and business wizard Anthony Crook. Fast and very luxurious, today's Bristols use American V-8s.

1914 Briscoe 2514cc tourer with cyclops headlamp

BRIT/*England 1914*
The two Brit cyclecars (8 hp and 9·5 hp) built by the Britannia Engineering Company of Nottingham both sold for £100.

BRITANNIA/*England 1896–1899*
Electrics designed by Vaughan-Sherrin, whose first car dated from 1897.

BRITANNIA/*England 1899, 1906–1908*
Britannia Lathes of Colchester first catalogued the 'Facile' heavy oil cars in 1899: in 1906 they announced fours of 12/18 hp and 24/40 hp and a 30/45 hp six, all with round copper radiators.

BRITISH/*England 1905–1907*
The 6½ hp twin-cylinder and 10/12 hp four-cylinder cars from this maker had 'tilting steering wheel, dashboard starting, patent change speed gear'.

BRITISH DUPLEX/*England 1906–c1909*
Built in Clerkenwell, the British Duplex had a curious two-stroke 'air scavenging' engine ('no crankcase as pump, no outside moving parts').

BRITISH SALMSON/*England 1934–1939*
The dohc 1½-litre British Salmson was an Anglicized version of the French Salmson S4C model, though the 20-90 of 1936 was an entirely British

confection, having a dohc 2·6-litre engine. Less lively was the 14 hp model of 1937–38. French four-cylinder Salmsons were also sold.

BRITANNIA/*England 1957–1961*
Limited production GT cars with glass-fibre bodywork, Ford engine and all-round independent suspension.

BRITON/*England 1908–1929*
In 1909 the Star Cycle Company, Wolverhampton, which had been building the 10 hp 'Little Briton' semi-racer since 1908, changed its name to the Briton Motor Company and moved into a new factory. The intention was to build a lower-priced running mate for the Star. A 14 hp four-cylinder model, with either tourer, landaulette or 'racer' bodywork, was added to the range. In 1913, the marque acquired a handsome 'bull-nose' radiator like the Star. A 10/12 hp Briton was introduced in 1914, and formed the basis of post-Armistice production. However, the original company went into liquidation in 1922, when it was purchased by C. A. Weight, who resumed production with a 1372cc side-valve four. About 1000 were built before production ceased, the last four being shipped to Australia. By that time Mr. Weight was making spares for Caterpillar tractors, in which direction the company's future lay.

1977 Bristol 412

BROADSPEED GT/*England 1966–1968*
A luxury fastback Mini, the Broadspeed GT was the brainchild of ex-Mini racer and eminent tuner, Ralph Broad. Some 28 GTs were built, plus one 140 hp version known as the GTS.

BROC/*USA 1909–1916*
Typical electrics, the Broc cars from Cleveland, Ohio, came in a range of closed styles: the 1914 Brougham cost $3100 and was said to be capable of 24 mph.

BROCK/*USA/Canada 1921*
The Brock was to have been a six-cylindered assembled car, its factory being in Amherstburg, Ontario, Canada. Allegedly designed by the brother of noted American author Booth Tarkington, the prototype car, a 118-inch wheelbase touring model with a Continental engine, was eventually assembled at Detroit. Unfortunately the plans for Canadian production failed to materialize.

BROCKLEBANK/*England 1927–1929*
An attempt by a Birmingham steel company to emulate the contemporary American cars, this was a 2-litre six with Lockheed hydraulic brakes.

BROCKVILLE ATLAS/*Canada 1912–1914*
The first 80 Brockvilles were assembled from Everitt parts bought from Tudhope: thereafter US Atlas fours of 30 hp and 40 hp were used. A Rutenber six appeared in 1914. The plant later assembled Briscoes for Canada.

BROGAN/*USA 1946–1948*
A small three-wheeler powered by a 10 hp air-cooled rear-mounted engine. Built by the B & B Specialty Co., in Rossmoyne, Ohio, the Brogan had clutchless gears.

BRONS/*Holland 1899*
A prototype light omnibus from Delfzijl.

BROOKE/*England 1900–1913*
'Quite notorious for the excellence of its motorboats', the marine engineering firm of J. W. Brooke & Company of Lowestoft had a six-cylinder engine running in a motor launch in 1903, before the first Napier six took to the roads. Their early cars were three-cylinder horizontal-engine models with all-chain transmissions, distinguished by a steering wheel whose deeply dished centre could be used as a repository for gloves, maps or tools. The first six-cylinder Brooke car also appeared late in 1903, and was closely followed by a vertical-engine 15/20 hp four-cylinder. In 1906, however, a one-model policy was followed, and a 25/30 hp six was standardized. A similar 40/60 hp model appeared in 1907, but Brooke production was gradually run down, ceasing altogether in 1913. Before that, Brooke had built a curious car for a resident of Calcutta; it had an elaborate bonnet in the shape of a swan, whose eyes lit up at night, and whose exhaust could be directed through a whistle in the beak!

BROOKE-SPACKE/*USA 1920–1921*
An air-cooled vee-twin powered this cyclecar from Indianapolis.

BROOKS/*England 1901–1902*
Light two-cylinder Pinart-engined 8 hp and 12 hp gear-driven cars from Foleshill, Coventry.

BROOKS/*Canada 1923–1926*
Over 300 of these two-cylinder steamers were built, all with four-door fabric sedan bodies.

BROTHERHOOD-CROCKER
England 1904–1906
Distinguished by a sideways pivoting accelerator, combined clutch/brake pedal and horn bulb in the centre of the steering wheel, the 20/25 hp Brotherhood-Crocker was built on Mercedes lines to the design of Percy Richardson, an ex-Daimler designer, by steam engineers

1904 Brooke 12/14hp phaeton

Peter Brotherhood. It was succeeded by Sheffield-Simplex.

BROUGH/*England 1912–1913*
The 8 hp Brough cyclecar had a flat-twin engine and pressed-steel chassis: it sold for £100. Its builder, W. E. Brough of Basford, Nottingham, was the father of George Brough of Brough Superior fame.

BROUGH SUPERIOR/*England 1935–1939*
George Brough, who had built motorcycles since 1921, was responsible for the Hudson-engined Brough Superior. Six- and eight-cylinder versions of this American engine were available and supercharging was a later option. In the last instance a version with the V-12 Lincoln-Zephyr engine was envisaged, but only one was built.

BROUHOT/*France 1901–1910*
'Marvellous qualities of endurance, comfort and speed' were attributed to the Brouhot from Vierzon (Cher), which started life with a rear-mounted twin-cylinder engine, but developed into a conventional touring car of 10 to 60 hp. Shaft drive and a shouldered radiator appeared in 1905, in which year Brouhots won two classes in the Coupe des Pyrenees.

BROWN/*England 1899–1911*
Brown Brothers, better known as suppliers of parts and accessories to the motor trade, also sold complete cars, starting in 1899 with quadricycles and tricycles. The 1902 8 hp Brown Voiturette was also available in component form; for 1904 this 'wonderful little car' was joined by a 12/16 hp four-cylinder. New for 1905 was an 18/20 hp four, apparently built for Brown by Star of Wolverhampton and in 1906 came a 40 hp six (6126cc) and a 25/30 hp four with similar cylinder dimensions (4084cc). Brown also sold the American Whitney steamer

The 'car that whistled like a swan', based on a 1913 Brooke

The Brouhot team for the 1905 Coupe des Pyrenees

1905 Brown 18/20hp

as the Brown-Whitney from 1899, and in 1910–11 offered the four-cylinder Albruna, available in 10/12 hp and 12/14 hp models.

BROWNIEKAR/*USA 1908–1910*
S. H. Mora, of the Mora Company, also headed the Omar Motor Company, which built this single-cylinder belt-drive 'juvenile motor car' intended for 'any intelligent boy or girl of eight years or more'.

BRULE-PONSARD/*France 1898–1901*
This '*avant-train*' power-pack for converting horse carriages used the weird Rozer-Mazurier three-cylinder 'compound' engine, in which the centre cylinder was powered by the exhaust gases of the outer pair.

BRUSH/*England 1901–1904*
Despite its name, the Brush Electrical Engineering Company built only petrol cars. Their 1902 'light Petrol Car' had a 10 hp twin-cylinder engine and sold — 'with lamps, horn, waterproof rugs, tools and spare parts' — for £420 ('less 5 per cent discount for cash'). There was also a 16 hp at £675. In 1904 Brush offered the coil-sprung Brushmobile, which was virtually identical to the contemporary Vauxhall.

BRUSH/*USA 1907–1913*
Alanson P. Brush designed this odd light car with a wooden chassis and axles, friction drive and coil springs all round.

BRUTSCH/*Germany 1951–1957*
Designed by former motorcycle- and car-racing driver Egon Brütsch, these cars were unorthodox and never reached quantity production. They included racing cars with Bugatti and Maserati engines, cars with the Ford 12M engine and also the 49cc Opelit-Mopetta.

1921 Bryan Steam Car

BRYAN STEAM CAR/*USA 1918–1923*
Bryan Steam Motors of Peru, Indiana, was a manufacturer of steam tractors and trucks. Between 1918 and 1923 a total of six steam

touring cars were built, most — if not all — made for company officials. A handsome sports sedan was announced for 1921 but failed to materialize.

BSA/*England 1907–1926, 1933–1936*
The early BSAs were, in effect, scaled-down Daimlers, this applying in particular to the sleeve-valve cars from 1911 onwards, a reminder of the company's take-over of Daimler in that year. However, an earlier 1908 model had been a copy of the Italian 40 hp Itala, so originality was never their watchword! A change came after the First World War with the vee-twin-powered Ten, though this lasted only until 1924, while sleeve-valve-engined cars continued until 1926. BSA re-emerged in 1933 with a car similar to the Lanchester Ten, the group having taken over the old-established concern in 1931.

BSA/*England 1929–1940*
BSA Cycles Ltd (the motorcycle division of BSA) produced a front-wheel-drive three-wheeler powered by a 1000cc vee-twin air-cooled engine in 1929. A fourth wheel was added in 1932 and the following year an 1100cc four-cylinder was fitted. This remained in production until 1940 (with a break in production in 1934), being re-named the Scout for the 1935 season.

BUC, BUCCIALI/*France 1922–1933*
The Bucciali brothers started making a small cyclecar under the name of Buc at Courbevoie. It was powered by a twin-cylinder two-stroke engine of 1340cc. It was followed in 1925 by a 1600cc SCAP-engined car available in two versions: 'Tourisme' and 'Quatre Speciale' supercharged. They also built a 1500cc six-cylinder car. In 1928 the Buccialis made cars which caused a great sensation: the TAN six-cylinder and an eight-cylinder front-wheel-drive with Sensaud de Lavaud automatic gearbox. This attempt was followed in the 1930s by the Double Huit, also fwd, powered by two straight-eight Continental engines mounted side by side. The last of these prototypes was made with a Voisin 12-cylinder engine. Very few of these fwd Bucciali cars ever reached the road.

BUCHET/*France 1910–1930*
The Buchet marque established its fame before the war making proprietary engines for automobile, aircraft and motor cycle manufacturers. Their first car, the 12/20hp, was presented in 1910 with a four-cylinder 1996cc engine. After the war they made 1131cc and 1551cc cars which remained in production, largely unchanged, until Buchet closed down. At the very end, a six-cylinder of 1737cc was introduced.

BUCKBOARD/*USA 1956*
The McDonough Power Equipment Co. of Georgia offered a lightweight, 3 hp air-cooled machine with a top speed of 15 mph.

BUCKBOARD/*USA 1960*
A 43 hp Ariel motorcycle engine powered an oak-framed, mahogany-panel-bodied, two-passenger car built by the Automotive Assoc. Co., White Plains, NY. Four-wheel independent suspension and steering gear came from Renault and the headlights turned with the front wheels.

BUCKINGHAM/*England 1914–1923*
A bullnosed, belt-drive cyclecar built in Coventry and designed by Captain Buckingham, inventor of the tracer bullet: inevitably, the coupé version was called the 'Palace'.

BUCKLE/*Australia 1955–1959*
Locally designed with a glass-fibre four-seater coupé body, the Buckle GT tourer employed a Ford Zephyr six-cylinder engine. The advanced design included fold-down rear seats, an adjustable steering column and electrically-operated door locks. The car was raced with distinction. Twenty were built, several still survive.

Buckle coupé, 1955

BUCKLER/*England 1947–1962*
One of the more prominent firms concerned with the manufacture of light, strong-bodied sports cars to which Ford mechanicals could be fitted. Their most successful car, the Buckler 90, had an all-enveloping body, weighed less than 9 cwt (1010 lb) and was fitted with a De Dion rear axle for ultimate road-holding.

BUCKMOBILE/*USA 1903–1905*
A 15 hp twin-cylinder roadster from Utica, New York.

BUFFALO/*USA 1901–1902*
Light, tiller-steered runabouts powered by petrol or electricity.

BUFFALO/*USA 1912–1915*
Formed by a merger of leading electric carriages (Babcock, Van Waggoner and others), the Buffalo Electric Vehicle Company offered elegant vehicles styled on petrol car lines under the slogan 'The Best of America'.

BUFFUM/*USA 1901–1906*
Built in Abington, Maryland, the Buffum is chiefly remembered for a spectacular flat-eight which appeared in 1904. Herbert Buffum also designed a lighting dynamo in 1905, but his ingenuity was not matched by his business acumen, and the company folded in 1906.

BUGETTA/*USA 1969 to date*
Powered by a 4949cc Ford V-8, this mid-engined car from Costa Mesa, California, has a one-piece moulded glass-fibre body with the choice of hard or soft top and two or four doors.

BUGATTI

BUGATTI/*Germany*/*France 1909–1956*
After nearly ten years of working for firms
such as De Dietrich, Mathis and Deutz,
Ettore Bugatti established himself in his own
premises at Molsheim, near Strasbourg. He
started with the ohc four-cylinder Type 13 of
1327cc. One of his early successes was the
'Bébé', made by Peugeot to Bugatti's design.
Pre-war, he also built fours of 1368cc and
5027cc, first with 8, later with 16, valves. In
1913 there was a 2906cc straight-eight. In
1922 came the first production eight-cylinder
1990cc Type 30. It was in 1924 that Ettore
presented the archetypal Bugatti, the eight-
cylinder Type 35 of 1990cc, subsequently
developed into versions such as the 35A
(1990cc) and the 35B (2261cc) or the 39A
(1492cc): all were supercharged. To meet
popular demand, Bugatti also evolved sports
models with a 1496cc four-cylinder engine.
The four-cylinder Type 40 and eight-cylinder
Type 43 were also good sports cars. On the
touring car front, Bugatti made the excellent
Type 44 (3 litres) and the Type 46 (5·3 litres).
He also made the fabulous Royales, whose
engines (eight-cylinder 12,762cc) were later
used in railcars. In 1931, Bugatti's first dohc
engine appeared on the Type 51 racing car
with eight-cylinders displacing 2261cc. The
last of the great line of racing cars from
Molsheim was the Type 59, made in 2·8-litre,
2·9-litre and 3·3-litre forms. The Type 55
was a fantastic 2·3-litre dohc sports car.
From 1934 up to the war, Bugatti made the
Type 57 of 3257cc, also available in
supercharged form as the 57S and 57SC. It
was the last of the production cars made by
'le Patron', who died in 1947. Some Type
101 models were built post-war, but
Hispano-Suiza took over the Molsheim
factory to make aircraft components.

*c.*1925 Bugatti Type 35A 'Tecla' in touring trim

1927 Bugatti Type 41, 'La Royale'

1928 Bugatti Type 43 straight-eight

Type 46 Bugatti, bodied by Neuss of Berlin for Prince Gustav Adolf

BUICK/*USA 1904 to date*

Scots plumber David Dunbar Buick built his first prototype in 1903 using his own ohv flat-twin engine, and started production (backed by the Briscoe brothers) in 1904. He soon ran out of finance, and Billy Durant took over. Buick was elbowed out in 1908, by which time the twin had been joined by three fours, of 2·7, 4·2 and 5·5 litres, all with ohv (Buick has never built a side-valve-engined car). The firm, by now one of the 'Big Four', was the cornerstone of Durant's 1908 formation of General Motors, and was managed by Charles Nash from 1910–12 and Walter Chrysler from 1912–20. Walter Marr designed the first Buick Six in 1914, and from 1919–26 Buick sales were the largest, in dollar terms, in the US car industry. Four-wheel brakes came in 1924, along with a Packard-like radiator; from 1925–30, a wide range of sixes from 3·1 to 5·4 litres was offered. A sales slide was spurred by the 1929 'pregnant Buick', and not halted by the introduction in 1931 of 3·6-, 4·5- and 5·7-litre straight-eights. The 1934 range had ifs and new styling, but revival of Buick's fortunes had to wait until 1936, when the new general manager, Harlow H. Curtice, and stylist Harley Earl, collaborated to produce a new line — Special, Century, Roadmaster and Limited — with more powerful engines, aluminium pistons and hydraulic brakes. Another line, the Super, was added in 1940. The 1942 Buicks had radical styling with full-width front fenders flowing into the rear fenders; this line was continued after the war, along with the toothy grille. In 1948 Buick became the first American manufacturer to offer a torque-converter drive — the famous 'Dynaflow' — on the Roadmaster. In 1949 came the first hardtop coupé, the Riviera. Buick remained faithful to straight-eights until 1953, when a short-stroke 5277cc was announced. This powered the limited edition Skylark which celebrated Buick's golden jubilee, in which year the company built its 7 millionth car. The Century appeared in 1954, capable of 110 mph with the V-8 unit; that season over 200 single and dual-tone colour schemes were available. Buick took third place in sales from the Plymouth in 1955–57, but drastic restyling in 1958, with lashings of chrome (including a 160-piece grille) failed to stop sales from falling below the 250,000 mark. The 1959 models featured compound-curve windscreens and canted fins fore and aft, with names including LeSabre, Invicta, Electra and Electra 225, all except the LeSabre having a new 6571cc engine. Styling was subdued for 1960, but Buick nevertheless fell to ninth place in sales. The Special compact with an all-alloy 3359cc V-8 appeared in 1961, followed in 1962 by a cast-iron V-6 of 3245cc (which supplanted the V-8 — sold to British Leyland — in 1964). The Riviera Sport Coupé of 1964 had V-8 power (6571cc or 6965cc), joined in 1966 by the 6965cc Skylark Gran Sport (succeeded in 1967 by the 6555cc GS400). The Riviera was restyled for the third time in 1971, with raked-forward front and boat-tail rear. Convertibles were a dying breed — two were built in 1972, one in 1973 and 1974 — and were then replaced by electric sunroofs. New bodies and an old name — Century (replacing Skylark) — appeared on the 1973 intermediates, with 5735cc or 7456cc V-8s. The Riviera was restyled in 1974, and the Apollo compact, with a 4097cc straight-six, launched. The V-6, dropped in 1967, was re-announced in 1975 in the subcompact Skyhawk, together with a new Skylark, Century and Apollo. A new Century, the Regal, became a series in its own right in 1977, with a turbocharged V-6, while the 1979 Riviera, with V-6 or V-8 power, shared the fwd all-independent suspension layout of the Olds Tornado and Cadillac Eldorado. May 1979 saw the launch of Buick's version of the GM X-car range.

1947 Buick Special sedan

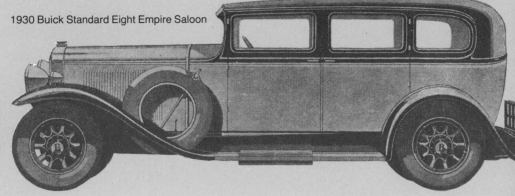

1930 Buick Standard Eight Empire Saloon

A Bedford-Buick in the 1913 Coupe de l'Auto

LA BUIRE / *France 1902–1930*

La Société de l'Horme et de La Buire was founded at Lyon in 1847, specializing in railway and tramway rolling stock, and was an early builder of steam carriages and traction engines. Their early success as car builders was achieved with the Type Fraignac, a Mercedes-like 20 hp with pair-cast cylinders, introduced at the 1904 Paris Salon at the behest of their most energetic agent, the engineer Fraignac. There was a 30 hp version with direct drive in third and fourth gears. The new 20/30 hp was one of the sensations of the 1905 Paris Salon. By 1907 there was a 15 hp six in the range also, with a 9500cc engine, and selling at £1200 in Britain as a chassis. Smaller sixes of 16 hp (3619cc), 24 hp (4786cc) and 30 hp (6374cc) joined it in a complex range for 1909, which also included five four-cylinder models from 12 hp to 28/35 hp. The big La Buires were actively campaigned in British sprint and hillclimb events by wealthy Stockport businessman J. A. Higginson, but otherwise the marque was not involved in racing. The immediately pre-World War One range went from an 8/10 hp four of 1726cc to a 24 hp six of 4767cc, all with notably long-stroke engines (the 4071cc 20 hp four had bore and stroke of 90mm × 160mm), but when the marque reappeared post-war its vital force was spent. Undistinguished fours of up to 2650cc constituted the remainder of La Buire's story, the only advanced feature being the addition of four-wheel brakes from 1922.

BUKH & GRY / *Denmark 1904*

Both Bukh and Gry had been working in car factories in the USA. Their one and only car, built at Horve, was exhibited at Tivoli in Copenhagen in 1905. It had a water-cooled 10/12 hp two-cylinder engine and friction drive. No more cars were built.

BULLOCK / *England 1972*

A rather ugly, open-top fun car designed by Andrew Ainsworth, the Bullock featured a glass-fibre body mounted on a pre-drilled box-section chassis. Power came from a Ford Anglia unit.

BURLAT / *France 1904–1909*

Burlat Frères of Lyon built cars with rotary X-formation four-cylinder engines, though their swansong was a rotary eight, incorporating two of these unorthodox power units in which, instead of ignition leads, there were curved contact strips against which the tops of the sparking plugs rubbed as they came round. Despite this, one Burlat was said to have covered 40,000 km.

BURNEY
England 1930–1933

Sir C. Dennistoun Burney, designer of the airship R 100, created this all-independently sprung, rear-engined streamline car, of which only a dozen (plus a prototype based on a back-to-front fwd Alvis chassis) were built, using Beverley-Barnes, Lycoming or Armstrong-Siddeley engines. The Prince of Wales bought one, and the design was taken up by Crossley. Unfortunately it overheated, and was not a commercial success.

1914 La Buire 15hp in the Melbourne-Sydney trial

BURNS / *USA 1908–1910*

The $800 Burns Hi-Wheel Buggy came from Havre de Grâce, Maryland. In 1908, Burns offered a 'transformable coupé' on their 18/20 hp high-wheeler chassis.

BURROW, STRUTT / *England/Germany 1900*

A three-wheeled, three-seater motor carriage whose makers claimed factories in London and Berlin. It had 'seat adjustable either to back or front at pleasure'.

BURROWES / *USA 1905–1908*

This Portland, Maine, manufacturer built a few cars, latterly a 30 hp four.

BURY / *USA 1927*

Billed as the first 'Bug' car, the Bury was an early attempt to market a miniature car of the Austin type on the American market. Designed by Charles W. Bury of New York City, the car sported a 73-inch wheelbase and in its two-passenger form was the smallest car in the USA at the time. Power was by a 1368cc Continental four-cylinder Model 'H-2' engine.

BUSH / *USA 1916–1924*

Like the Birch (also built in Chicago), the Bush was a car sold by mail order only. Built by various manufacturers, including Piedmont, a complete line of open and closed models wore the Bush emblem. Standard components were used throughout, four-cylinder cars using Lycoming engines and the sixes, Continentals.

BUSHBURY ELECTRIC / *England 1897*

Electric three- and four-wheeled cars built in the Star Cycle Factory at Wolverhampton. Some were controlled by reins.

BUSSON / *France 1907–1908*

The smallest six-cylinder car at the 1907 Paris Salon, the Busson-Bazelaire (built by de Bazelaire) had a 15/20 hp engine of 3318cc. The firm also sold six-cylinder Nagants as 'Busson-Dedeyns', and built a few voiturettes under their own name.

BUTTEROSI / *France 1919–1924*

The Butterosi, made in Boulogne-sur-Seine, had a sv four-cylinder engine of 1327cc.

BZ / *Germany 1922–1925*

One of the many small cars built after the Great War, the BZ had a 493cc flat-twin BMW motorcycle engine. It was a light — 300 kg — car with a two-seater body of Duralumin.

1964 Buick Wildcat

1979 Buick Road Hawk

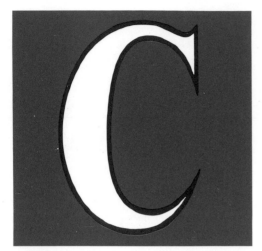

LE CABRI/*France 1924–1925*
A small cyclecar from Asnières with a sv 980cc Ruby engine. Few were made.

CADIX/*France 1920–1923*
Made at Cadix-Martinville, this car was Ballot-engined. Two engines were available, a 10 hp of 1593cc and a 12 hp of 2297cc. M. Jannel, the builder, was previously involved in manufacturing the Métropolitaine car in Paris.

CADOGAN/*England 1902–1907*
The first Cadogan cars had a 12 hp vertical-twin water-cooled engine and 'perfect construction of steering'. In 1907 Cadogan offered a twin-cylinder 14/16hp and fours of 16/20 hp and 28/32 hp under the name 'Leander'.

CAFFORT/*France 1920–1922*
The Caffort brothers of Marseilles started as marine-engine builders. They moved to Paris in 1921 to build a cyclecar using their own 1206cc four-stroke vee-twin engine. These were sold mainly as delivery vans.

1907 16/20hp Cadogan Landaulet

CADILLAC/*USA 1902 to date*
Originally the Henry Ford Company, this firm adopted the name of Antoine de la Mothe Cadillac, founder of Detroit in 1701, after Ford was replaced as chief engineer by Henry Leland, 'master of precision'. Leland practised rigorous interchangeability of parts, and his single-cylinder Cadillac (16,126 were sold between 1903 and 1908) won the 1908 Dewar Trophy in a spectacular demonstration of this, when three new Cadillacs were disassembled, their parts scrambled, and three cars built up from the pile of parts without any hand fitting. Durant took Cadillac into the new General Motors concern in 1909, by which time the firm was only building four-cylinder cars. In 1912, the 'self-lighting, self-starting, self-igniting' Cadillac with Delco electrics appeared, and won a second Dewar Trophy for this first practical, complete automotive electrical system. In 1914 Cadillac standardized on the 5150cc V-8 engine; during the War, Henry Leland and his son Wilfred left to found the Lincoln Motor Company, initially to build Liberty aeroengines, later to make fine cars. Cadillacs of the 1920s were, like so many of their contemporaries, well engineered but dull in appearance; a dynamically-balanced crank came in 1924, a year after four-wheel brakes. In 1928 a new 5·6-litre engine (based on the 1927 LaSalle unit) appeared, as did chromium plating and synchromesh gearchange. Chief engineer Ernest Seaholm's masterpiece, the world's first production V-16, was unveiled in January 1930; Fleetwood coachwork was standard, and 3863 of this ohv 7·4-litre were built, until it was replaced with a sv V-16 in 1938 (just 511 of these were built up to 1940). A V-12, using the V-8 chassis, was also listed until 1937; these were

W. J. Bryan's 1908 Cadillac 20/30hp four

1915 Cadillac V-8 tourer

1954 Cadillac Fleetwood 75

CALCOTT/*England 1914–1926*
The Calcott, with a shouldered radiator like the contemporary Standard, was the product of a famous Coventry cycle company. Pre-war cars had engines of 1460cc: post-war models had 1645cc power units. In 1926, Singer took over.

CALDWELL VALE/*Australia 1907–1913*
Few technical details have survived, except that this touring car had four-wheel drive and a 30 hp six-cylinder engine. One prototype had four-wheel steering, too. It appears that less than a dozen cars were built, but the company also made a fair number of trucks and tractors.

CALIFORNIA/*USA 1901–1903*
A 'stylish little runabout' on De Dion lines was the principal offering of this San Franciscan company, though they also claimed to build electric and steam vehicles.

1913 30hp 4wd, four-wheel steer Caldwell Vale

CALIFORNIA/*USA 1913*
A twin-cylinder 1130cc cyclecar with underslung chassis and friction drive, built in Los Angeles.

CALIFORNIAN/*USA 1920*
A handsome and sporty car, the Californian Six never really got off the ground: only one unit, a touring car, and part of another one encompassed the history of the company. A six-cylinder Beaver engine, wire wheels and a 134-inch wheelbase combined to give the Californian beauty and power. Listed price was $4500.

CALORIC/*USA 1902*
Built by the Chicago Moto-Cycle Company, this three-speed runabout had a curious 'hot air gas' two-stroke engine without carburettor or ignition system, which it was claimed 'will run without any gas internally, and so much gas cannot be used that it will not run'.

1915 Calthorpe Minor Sports

CALTHORPE/*England 1904–1932*
Like many other cars, the Calthorpe sprang from the bicycle industry. G. W. Hands' first car was a 10 hp four-cylinder, while later came the 16/20, a 2·8-litre car which Hands drove in the 1908 Irish Trials: a Calthorpe also came fourth in that year's TT. The company also entered for the 1909 Coupe des Voiturettes, achieving 8th and 9th places. These were powered by 1775cc fours by Alpha, though Calthorpe also fitted White and Poppe engines for their more conventional products. In 1913 came the 1094cc Calthorpe Minor, a well-made light car that continued to be produced well into the 1920s. The 10 was also produced in two- and four-seater variants, often fitted with handsome polished aluminium bodies by Mulliner of Birmingham, who very conveniently had works next door to the Calthorpe factory. Hands left the concern to produce the Hands light car of 1922 and a new model, the 12, appeared in 1923 and two years later came a shadowy 15·7 hp six. Though by this time Hands had returned to the Calthorpe fold, very few cars were made after 1927, though motorcycle production, which had begun in 1911, continued until 1939.

CALVERT/*USA 1927*
Prototypes only comprised 'production' of the Calvert, a small car using a six-cylinder engine supposedly of Calvert's own make. A chassis was theoretically available at $550 and open models were priced at $795.

CAMBER/*England 1966–c1968*
Six Camber GTs were built. Their distinctive glass-fibre bodies clothed Mini mechanicals nestling in a square tube chassis. Though reborn as the Maya GT, production of this Mini special was terminated following the death of its founder in a road accident.

1947 Cadillac Sedan

Cadillac's only deviation from the V-8 path. Stylist Harley Earl introduced a bold 'egg-crate' grille in 1941, and in 1948 came his legendary tailfins, inspired by the P-38 Lightning fighter plane's twinboom empennage. A new short-stroke V-8 of 5·4 litres appeared in 1949, and in 1950 Hydramatic four-speed automatic transmission, hitherto optional, was standardized on the 1950 Series 60 Special and 62, and on all cars except the 75 from 1952. In 1953, air conditioning was offered, and a limited edition convertible, the Eldorado, made its debut. Its successor, the 1957 Eldorado Brougham, was a $13,074 hand-built model with quad headlamps and self-levelling air suspension; just 904 were made (1957–60). Tailfins reached their apotheosis on the supremely vulgar 1959 Cadillacs, then gradually atrophied, until by 1965 they had almost disappeared. Comfort Control single-unit heating/air-conditioning appeared on 1964 models, all powered by the 1963-introduced 7030cc V-8. In 1967 came the razor-edged, front wheel drive Eldorado—President Nixon was to give Soviet leader Brezhnev a 1972 version as a gift—which by 1970 had the world's then-biggest production car engine of 8·2 litres. This unit was standard on all but one of the 1975 series. Following the energy crisis,

Cadillac introduced the Chevy Nova-based Seville, with 5·7-litre Olds power, to combat European luxury cars. Full-size Cadillacs had their engine displacement trimmed to 7 litres in 1978 (when Sevilles were specified with an on-board computer showing distance elapsed, fuel-to-empty and other information). The Eldorado emerged as a totally new car in 1979, shorter, and with improved handling, using a common power unit with the Seville (but still fwd).

1957 Cadillac Eldorado Classic Brougham

1979 Cadillac Eldorado

CAMBIER/*France 1898–1905*
Builders of one of the first petrol fire engines, Cambier of Lille built a 4 hp Benz-engined light car, as well as larger vehicles of 6, 8 and 12 hp with 'noiseless speed changing'.

CAMEN/*Italy 1927–1928*
Made in Sicily and financed by the Prince di Sirignano, the Camen was a short-lived ohv 1095cc four-cylinder car with a French Chapuis-Dornier engine. Some racing versions were built, but production was on a small scale.

CAMERON/*USA 1902–1921*
Frequently re-organized, and using a succession of factories, the builders of the Cameron believed in unconventionality. Their two-, four- and six-cylinder engines were air-cooled, with horizontal valves operated by long 'walking beams', while the curious back-axle/gearbox contrived to give direct drive on all three speeds. A water-cooled engine appeared in 1913, but 1919 saw a return to air-cooling, with valves operated by oscillating vertical shafts actuated by grooved cams.

CAMPBELL/*USA 1918–1919*
This was the successor to the Emerson built in Kingston, New York. Relatively few were sold, the entire line being limited to four-cylinder touring cars.

CAMPEADOR/*Spain 1967*
Available with 1300cc or 1500cc engines, the Barcelona-built Campeador resembled a scaled-down Ford GT 40.

CAMPION/*England 1913–1914*
An 8 hp cyclecar from a Nottingham motorbike maker.

CANADA GENERAL ELECTRIC
Canada 1899
Woods Electrics built in Peterboro, Ontario.

CANADIAN/*USA/Canada 1922*
Like the Brock, this was was to have been produced in Canada but the Windsor, Ontario, centre of operations failed to materialize and the prototype cars were actually built by Colonial Motors at Detroit, Michigan. This car had a pointed radiator and suspension similar to the Parenti, and was powered by a Continental six.

CANADIAN MOTOR/*Canada 1900–1902*
'Ideal for any first-class automobilist to drive', these elegant electrics could cover up to 45 miles on one charge of their batteries. They were built by an English-owned company in Toronto, and derived from Canada's first electrics designed and built by W. J. Still from 1893. In 1898 Still also built a 5 hp 'gasoline car' controlled by a steering column moving backwards and forwards to give forward or reverse motion.

CANADIAN STANDARD/*Canada 1913*
An American manufacturer, A. R. Walton, transferred production of four-cylinder, five-seater tourers from St Louis, Missouri, to Moose Jaw, Saskatchewan, but faded away after only pilot-build vehicles had been completed.

CANDA/*USA 1899–1903*
Built by the Canda Manufacturing Company of Cartaret, New Jersey, this 'Auto-Quadricycle' was built on the lines of the contemporary De Dion machines.

C & H/*England 1914*
Twin-cylinder cyclecars of 5/6 hp (£100) and 8 hp (£110).

CANNON/*USA 1902–1906*
Two- and four-cylinder models, up to 6·5-litres displacement, from Kalamazoo, Michigan.

CANTERBURY/*England 1903–1906*
This company sold a 6 hp De Dion-engined voiturette and a 12 hp Aster-engined Roi-des-Belges model styled on the Mercedes.

CANTONO (FRAM)/*Italy/USA 1900–1911*
Electric conversion units for horse-vehicles, built in Rome up to 1906, renamed Fram and built in Genoa until 1911. Coincidentally, it was licence-built in Canton, Ohio (1904–07).

CAP/*Belgium 1914*
An English-designed 8 hp JAP-engined cyclecar.

CAPEL/*England 1899–1901*
The designer of this tiller-steered 4 bhp twin-cylinder car, H. C. Capel, died of typhoid before it was completed. It incorporated many of his patented design features, including the use of long and extremely flexible springs and a curious four-speed transmission by leather-covered chains.

CAPITOL/*USA 1902–1903*
From Washington, DC, this corpulent 6 hp steam car seated three abreast, with the fourth passenger perched on the dashboard.

1901 Carde tonneau

CARDE/*France 1900–1901*
Built by a railway rolling-stock builder from Bordeaux, and equipped with two- or four-cylinder engines ('Jouasset-Gintrac's patent'), the Carde never passed the prototype stage.

CAR DE LUXE/*USA 1906–1910*
Sister marque to the Queen, the 40/50 hp, 6755cc Car de Luxe had overhead valves operated by one rocker per cylinder, actuated by a 'push-pull' rod and an unusual back axle, with the load taken by an I-beam dead axle carrying a separate differential unit.

1913 5hp vee-twin Carden

CARDEN/*England 1912–1925*
The pre-war Carden was a lethal monocar with centre-pivot steering and rear-mounted single or vee-twin engine. In 1919 it reappeared as a two-seater with a 707cc two-stroke flat-twin in unit with the back axle. The 1923 New Carden was available with two- or four-seat bodywork, at a basic price of £90: a £130 three-seat variant was sold as the Sheret.

CARDINET/*France 1900–1907*
Electric landaulets built in Paris. In 1907 the company offered a 20 hp petrol car, the 'Cardina'.

1923 Cardway tourer

CARDWAY/*USA 1923–1924*
The Cardway was named after Colonel Frederick Cardway, its designer and builder, and was produced with right-hand steering for export to Australia and New Zealand. A Continental six-cylinder engine was employed and wheelbase was 118 inches. Only six were completed.

CARHARTT/*USA 1910–1912*
The 'beautiful Carhartt' 35 hp was built by a Detroit company headed by cotton king Hamilton Carhartt: it had a double-drop frame and a pair-cast four-cylinder 4185cc engine.

CARLTON/*England 1900–1903*
A two-speed, single-cylinder air-cooled belt-driven 3½ hp voiturette was offered in 1900 — by 1902 a 10 hp shaft-driven vertical-twin was available, which had a 'combined carburettor and inlet valve for petrol or paraffin'.

CARMEN/*France 1907*
A 16hp model built in Paris. Only engines, apparently, were being offered by 1908.

CARPEVIAM/*England 1903*
This odd little two-seater 2¼hp three-wheeler was said to 'raise very little dust when running'. The car's curious name came from a quotation from Virgil: 'Carpe viam et susceptum perfice munus; adceleremus' (roughly: 'Life is short — enjoy it while you can').

CARROLL/*USA 1910–1913*
Despite much publicity in the automotive press concerning various models built by the Carroll Motor Car Co. of Strasburg, Pa., only one car was in fact ever built. This was a large touring car with a Continental six engine. The car was named after Carroll M. Aument who, with his brother, H. Chester Aument, operated an automobile agency in Strasburg.

CARROLL/*USA 1920–1922*
Although initial press releases announced that the Carroll would employ a Rochester six-cylinder engine, this was never used, and all Carroll cars were powered by a Beaver power plant instead. The disc-wheeled Carrolls were distinctive, with the radiator located to the rear of the front axle. Only roadsters and touring cars were produced, at prices up to $4000.

CARROW/*England 1919–1923*
Built at Whitley Bay, Northumberland, until 1921, then in Hanwell, Middlesex, this was a typical light car, with an 11·9hp Dorman engine (a Peters engine of similar rating was used on the Hanwell-built Carrows).

CARTER/*England 1913–1914*
A Birmingham-built cyclecar with air-cooled ohc engine.

CARTERCAR/*USA 1906–1916*
One of the more successful friction-drive cars, the Cartercar began with a flat-twin engine, which was still used alongside vertical fours in the 1909 range. In 1908, the company merged with the makers of the Pontiac high-wheeler: in 1909, they became part of General Motors. In 1912, there were two models, both pair-cast fours — the 4160cc Model R and the 5473cc Model S — with single chain drive. Byron Car-

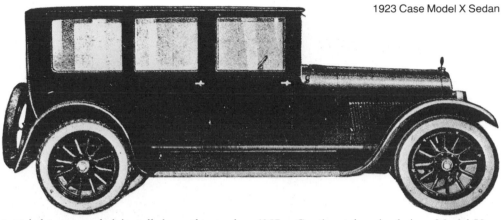

1923 Case Model X Sedan

ter tried to start a lady's stalled car, the crank kicked back, broke his jaw and caused gangrene from which he died. Hence his friend Henry Leland fitted Cadillacs with electric starters.

CARTERET/*France 1921–1925*
A small friction-drive 903cc Ruby-engined cyclecar made at Courbevoie by M. Vienne, who also made the Octo cars.

CARTER STEAM CAR/*USA 1921*
At least three of these cars — all touring models — were produced by the Carter Automobile Co., of Gulfport, Mississippi. They were powered by two small steam engines, one on each rear wheel. Wire wheels were standard and the wheelbase was 124 inches. Price was quoted at $2350.

CARTER TWIN-ENGINE/*USA 1907–1908*
Predecessor of the Washington, the Carter Twin-Engine had two separate 35hp power units, a somewhat extreme method of guarding against breakdown.

CASE/*Canada 1906–1909*
An air-cooled friction-drive car from Lethbridge, Alberta.

CASE/*USA 1910–1927*
Agricultural machinery manufacturer J. I. Case took over Pierce-Racine, and produced a three-car range — '25' (3439cc), '35' (5114cc) and '40' (5473cc) — of which the two smaller models had left-hand-drive. By 1918, there was a

4957cc Continental-engined six — Model U — available with 'Touring Family', 'All-Seasons Sedan' or 'Sport' coachwork. Model X, of 1922, had a smaller (3958cc) power unit: Model Y was a large-bore development of 5328cc. The last Case, the 'Jay-Eye-See', had the 3958cc engine and hydraulic four-wheel brakes, but after 1927 Case gave up car manufacture in favour of tractors and other agricultural machinery.

CASTLE THREE/*England 1919–1922*
This sturdy three-wheeler initially used a 1094cc four-cylinder Dorman engine coupled to a two-speed epicyclic gearbox. Later a more powerful 1207cc version was offered, while a four-wheeler was toyed with in the last year of production.

CASTOLDI/*France c1900*
A cycle maker from Lyon who also built motorcycles and voiturettes.

CASTRO/*Spain 1902–1903*
J. Castro's 'Fabrica Hispano-Suiza de Automobiles' succeeded la Cuadra, with Marc Birkigt again as chief engineer. Few cars were sold, mostly in the Barcelona area, before the firm closed down in December 1903. Three models were available, an over-square (190 × 120mm) twin of 6805cc, another twin of 2281cc and a 14hp four of 2217cc.

CAUSAN/*France 1923–1924*
This small cyclecar, designed by engineer Causan of Bignan fame, had a single-cylinder 349cc two-stroke engine. It was later made under the name of D'Aux.

CAVAC/*USA 1910*
A two-passenger roadster from Detroit, the four-cylinder Cavac had an underslung chassis.

CAVALIER/*USA 1926*
With its factory in Mount Vernon, New York, and headquarters in Baltimore, Maryland, the Cavalier advertised itself as the first of the 'Pony Cars'. A small car, the Cavalier sported a four-cylinder engine and a 98-inch wheelbase. The novelty surrounding this make was that the dealer would assemble the actual body style desired by adding or subtracting parts from the basic product. In any of four styles the price would be the same — $595 'agd' (at your garage door). Despite the novelty and imagination, the Cavalier never survived the first pilot models.

1926 Cavalier Roadster

1949 Caproni (Cemsa) roadster

CAVENDISH/*England 1906*
Assembled cars from Sheffield with 8/10 hp
Aster or 9 hp De Dion engines.

CCC/*England 1906–1907*
The Chassis Construction Company, of Taunton, Somerset, built live-axle 16/20 hp chain-drive models, sold through Gauthier & Co. of London.

CECO/*USA 1914*
An American monocar of neat design.

CEIRANO/*Italy 1920–1928*
All three Ceiranos—Giovanni, Matteo and Battista—were connected with cars. Giovanni created the SCAT before World War One and founded his own works at Turin after the war. The Ceirano was a middle-sized car, not unlike the Ansaldo. Most models had four-cylinder 1460cc sv—and later ohv—engines. In England, the Ceirano was known as the Newton-Ceirano, after being modified by the importers, Newton & Bennett. When the factory ran into financial difficulties, Fiat took it over.

CELERIPEDE/*England 1900–1901*
A motor tricycle built by John Thomas of High Barnet.

CELERITAS/*Austria 1901–1903*
Founded by wealthy Willy Stift (later of Gräf & Stift), the Vienna-based Celeritas works built Buchet-engined two-cylinder cars in limited numbers.

CELTIC/*France 1912*
A 2212cc 12 hp with double-shaft drive, built by Marcel Caplet in Le Havre.

CELTIC/*France 1927–1929*
M. Bignan was closely connected with the Celtic, a light car made in Paris. It had a four-cylinder engine of 700cc (later enlarged to 1085cc) and was made by the Compagnie Générale des Voitures, who also manufactured the Classic.

CEMSA/*Italy 1946–1950*
An 1100cc fwd saloon from the Caproni aircraft company, which failed to reach production.

CENTAUR/*England 1900–1901*
A four-seat front-engined 4½ hp *dos-à-dos* from Coventry, using belt transmission.

CENTAUR/*England 1973 to date*
A development of Dennis Adams's Probe 15, the Centaur was an extremely futuristic Impp-powered glass-fibre monocoque. A Mk II version lives on in the name of Pulsar 2.

CENTAUR/*USA 1978 to date*
Based on the discontinued Honda 600 minicar, the George Barris-styled Centaur was developed by Hybricon, Inc., of North Hollywood, Ca., as an answer to the fuel and environmental problems. It has two alternative power sources: Honda's conventional petrol engine driving the front wheels, two General Electric motors powering the rear. The owner starts the car moving electrically, and switches to petrol at around 30 mph. The combined petrol/electric range is a claimed 160 miles.

CENTURY/*USA 1899–1903*
Steam, electric and petrol vehicles were offered by this company from Syracuse, New York. The 1903 7 hp Century Tourist was a tiller-steered gas buggy on the lines of the Oldsmobile.

CENTURY/*England 1899–1906*
Although the first Century—like its cousin, the Eagle—was a tricar powered by a 2¼ hp single-cylinder engine, later models were conventional four-wheelers. From 1903, 8 and 12 hp two-cylinder and 22 hp four-cylinder Aster engines were fitted. Century fitted the gear quadrant of their 1902 9 hp Aster-engined model with an indicator lamp so that the driver could easily change gear after dark.

CERTAIN/*France 1907*
A belt-driven two-seater 'tri-voiturette' with a single-cylinder Lurquin-Coudert engine.

CERTUS/*Germany 1928–1929*
The Certus was made in very small numbers, mainly from French components, at Offenburg. SCAP supplied the sv 1170cc and 1476cc engines.

CEYC/*Spain 1923–1931*
The 4/10 cv CEYC was built by the Electronic and Communications Centre of the Spanish Army, using a 396cc two-cylinder duplex two-stroke engine devised by Captain of Engineers J. Hernandez Nunez. Two- and three-seat tourers and coupés were built — all for Army use.

CFB/*England 1920–1921*
Final drive by rubber belts was a novel feature of the CFB, which was powered by an 8 hp vee-twin engine.

CG/*France 1967–1973*
The CG was made at Brie Comte Robert by Chappe, Gesslin and Durand, using mostly Simca parts. The body was made of glass-fibre. They were only sold as sports-racing cars. The marque was succeeded by the Jidé.

CGV, CHARRON/*France 1901–1930*
In 1901 three ex-racing cyclists, Charron, Girardot and Voigt, began production of a four-cylinder 3300cc chain-driven car in Puteaux, followed by various models, including one of the very first straight-eights in the world, built in 1903. At that time, they sold their USA rights to Smith and Mabley. Most CGVs were chain driven and it was only in 1906 that the first shaft-drive model appeared. Girardot then left the factory, and the name was turned into Charron Ltd., after a British concern had taken over. For many years the Charron remained an old-fashioned car, with the radiator behind the engine. Notable among the various models manufactured between 1907 and the war were the 12 hp (2412cc) and 29 hp (5701cc) four-cylinders, the only six-cylinder (3619cc) and the tiny 7/10 hp (1592cc) introduced in 1912. At the outbreak of war Charron presented a new car, a 6 hp of 1056cc named 'la Charronette'. After the war, Charron resumed production with civilian models, having been one of the few French manufacturers continuing to make cars for the Army during hostilities. From a total of seven models in 1919, of which 'la Charonnette' was the most significant, production fell steadily over the years to three models. Then in 1925, a new 12/14 hp six (2770cc) appeared. The Charronette remained in production until the end, latterly bodied as a small van which could be quickly converted into a family tourer.

1907 Certain Tri-Voiturette

1904 CGV 15hp of French Premier Rouvier

CHABOCHE/*France 1900–1906*
M. Chaboche's twin-cylinder flash-boilered
steam cars came in two guises—a light
two/four-seater with paraffin- or petrol-fired
boiler and shaft-drive, or a heavy chain-driven
six/eight-seater with coke- or coal-fired boiler.

CHADWICK/*USA 1905–1916*
One of the great sporting marques, the Chadwick originated from Chester, Pennsylvania,
though production shifted to Philadelphia in
1906 and Pittsburgh in 1907. Lee Sherman
Chadwick's first production model was a pair-
cast four, but in 1907 came the first Great Six,
with a copper-jacketed engine of 'general simplicity of construction' and 11,581cc swept
volume. The 1909 60hp 'Semi-racer runabout'
had exhaust cutouts in the bonnet sides for
'speeding'. In 1911, the engine design was
altered from T-head to F-head, with the
overhead inlet valve in the centre of the combustion chamber. Some 1908 racing Chadwicks
had forced induction by centrifugal supercharger, but this did not appear in production.

CHADWICK/*USA 1960*
Weighing 680lb and powered by a BMW 13hp
single-cylinder air-cooled motor, the 87-inch
long Chadwick was designed as a shopping car.
Chassis was tubular, with independent front
suspension, and quarter-elliptic leaf springs at
the rear.

CHAIGNEAU-BRASIER/*France 1926–1930*
This luxury car was an attempt by the manager
of the Brasier works to make a car under his

own name. The engine was a straight-eight of
3079cc, and front-wheel drive was featured.

CHAINLESS/*France 1900–1903*
Shaft-driven voiturettes with Abeille motors of
10, 16 and 20cv, built, apparently, by a M.
Chain.

1915 Chalmers Six tourer

**CHALMERS-DETROIT,
CHALMERS**/*USA 1908–1924*
Hugh Chalmers, former vice-president of
National Cash Register, took over Thomas-
Detroit in June 1908, changing the name and
introducing a new F-head 30hp designed on
European lines. A 20hp appeared in 1909, but
was taken over by the newly formed Hudson
Motor Car Company. In 1911 the cars—and
the company—became known as plain 'Chalmers', and a 36hp four was added to the existing
models the following year. Chalmers's first six, a
pair-cast 56hp with compressed-air starting,
made its debut in 1911, and became known as
the Master Six. It was joined by the 30hp Light

Six in 1914. A new chief designer, C. C. Hinkley,
brought out a new ohc 6/40hp Model 32 six in
1915; it replaced the 4/36. A similar 6/30 model
appeared in 1916, Chalmers's best year, with
21,000 cars produced. Output fell to 12,000 in
1917, and Maxwell—now headed by Walter
Chrysler—took over, completely absorbing
Chalmers by 1921. Hydraulic band brakes on all
four wheels were added for 1924, but in January
that year the Chalmers was supplanted by the
new Chrysler four.

CHAMBERS/*Ireland 1904–1925*
One of the few cars to be built in Ulster, the
Chambers was made in limited numbers in the
Cuba Street Works, Belfast, starting with a
10hp twin, also marketed as 'Downshire'. In
1913 the firm was offering 11/15hp and 12/16hp
four-cylinder models with three-speed epicyclic
gearing. Only a 3181cc six was being built when
production ended.

CHAMEROY/*France 1907–1909*
A manufacturer of cars, light cars and voitur-
ettes with infinitely variable belt-drive, from Le
Vésinet (Seine-et-Oise).

CHAMPION/*England 1899*
A four-seater dog-cart powered by a 1¾hp De
Dion engine started by a pedal.

CHAMPION/*USA 1908–1909*
A 10/12hp tiller-steered high-wheeler 'roadster'
from East Chicago, Indiana.

CHAMPION/*USA 1917–1923*
The first Champions were built in Pottstown,
Pennsylvania, and drove through gearing
mounted in the rear wheel rims. Subsequently,
operations moved to Philadelphia where four-
cylinder cars, using both Herschell-Spillman
and Lycoming four-cylinder engines, were built.

CHAMPION/*USA 1920*
Not to be confused with the Philadelphia-built
car of the same name, the Champion of Cleveland, Ohio, was exhibited at an industrial
meeting in its home city in April, 1920, but failed
to survive the prototype stage.

CHAMPION/*Germany 1948–1956*
This Holbein-designed two-seater was built by
various producers in Germany and even Norway. It had 246cc double-piston TWN two-
stroke or 398cc Ilo and Heinkel twin-cylinder
two-stroke engines mounted in the rear. Maico,
still famous for motorcycles, took over production in 1956 and fitted 452cc Heinkel two-
stroke engines.

1951 Champion two-seater

119

Chandler's 1923 Cleveland Six 19.8hp

CHANDLER/*USA 1913–1929*
'The Marvelous Motor' was built in Cleveland; for most of its production span a 29 hp, 4736cc bi-block six of Chandler's own make was used, though in 1927 the monobloc Standard Six of 2954cc was offered, joined by two straight-eights the following year. From 1923 a constant-mesh 'Traffic Transmission' was used on the 29 hp six. Between 1919 and 1926 Chandler also built the ohv 3529cc Cleveland Six.

CHANNON/*England 1905*
Edward Channon & Sons of Dorchester built approximately six 10 hp cars using modified Brit stationary engines from nearby Bridport. The price was 225 guineas.

CHAPMAN/*USA 1899–1902*
A light 'sulky electromobile' with two ½ hp motors, built by the BelKnap Motor Company of Portland, Maine.

CHARLES TOWN-ABOUT/*USA 1958–1959*
Based on the Karmann-Ghia coupé body, the Charles Town-About was powered by two electric motors driving the rear wheels. Using a 48 volt electrical system, each motor developed 3·2 hp giving the car a 77 mile range. Top speed was a claimed 58 mph. Manufactured by the Stinson Aircraft Tool Corp., San Diego, Ca., the car was conceived by the company vice-president Dr. Charles H. Graves, whose name it bore. Torsion-bar suspension was used.

CHARLON/*France 1905–1906*
A belt-driven voiturette, 'built under Mahout licence'.

CHARRON-LAYCOCK/*England 1920–1926*
The 1460cc four-cylinder Charron-Laycock was so called because Charron Ltd. acquired a controlling interest in the railway equipment manufacturer W. S. Laycock of Sheffield. This 10/25 model was pricey: in 1925 the four-seater tourer cost £525, the saloon another £100.

CHARTER/*USA 1903*
James A. Charter's 'Mixed-Vapor' car operated on a mixture of petrol and water, the theory being that the ignition of the petrol in the cylinder would flash the water vapour into superheated steam.

CHASE/*England 1904–1905*
A 7 hp twin-cylinder 'four-wheel tandem car', the 'exquisitely designed' Chase from Anerley, SE London, pre-dated the cyclecar craze by several years.

CHATEL-JEANNIN/*Germany 1902–1903*
Despite the French name, these cars were made in Germany, as Mulhouse (Alsace) was then part of the German Empire. It was a very unorthodox design with 6·5 hp single-cylinder and 12 hp twin-cylinder engines.

CHATER-LEA
England 1907–1908, 1913–1922
Makers of cycles and components, Chater-Lea showed a four-wheeled 'Carette' at the 1908 Stanley Show. It had a 6 hp vee-twin engine mounted on the right of its coachbuilt body, with clutch and two-speed gear on a transverse shaft, which drove the left rear wheel by chain. An 8 hp light four was built from 1913.

CHATHAM/*Canada 1906–1909*
Starting with flat-twin Reeves-engined tourers, by 1907 Chatham was concentrating on a 25 hp four. In 1908 the company was acquired by a dentist named Cornell: production ended soon after.

CHECKER/*USA 1923 to date*
Up to 1948, when a 'pleasure car' was catalogued, Checker had catered solely for the taxi trade. Post-war models were much the same as pre-war designs, powered by a sv 3704cc Continental six, which was to remain Checker's main engine until 1965. The 1956 A8 was totally new, and its slab-sided modern appearance was uncompromisingly practical; ifs replaced the old beam axle. In 1958, an ohv six was offered on the new 12-passenger A9 'Airport Limousine' on a 189-inch wheelbase (there was also a smaller 9-seat version). In 1960, Checker surprisingly produced their first model for general public sale, the Superba, available as sedan or station wagon, but sharing body and mechanicals with the A8. The 1963 Town Custom Limousine was Checker's most prestigious model to date, with optional air-conditioning and centre division. From 1965, the base power plant was Chevrolet's 3769cc six, though various V-8s have been offered as options. A 1970 Ghia-designed prototype had not reached production in 1979, and the current Checkers still used the 1956 body, though the standard engine was now the 4097cc Chevrolet six, with a 5736cc V-8 available in the Marathon line.

1965 Checker limousine

CHELMSFORD (CLARKSON)
England 1899–1903
Successor to the elaborate Clarkson steamers of 1899–1901, the Chelmsford steam cars were built by the Clarkson & Capel Steam Car Syndicate of Moulsham Works, Chelmsford, Essex, who also supplied double-deck steam buses to the National omnibus fleet in London. Chelmsford steam cars were large, heavily built machines, usually featuring a distinctive curved

glass windscreen. They were described as 'Safe, strong, speedy, simple', and the passenger compartment could be heated by steam in cold weather. They also had the great advantage that 'a nice cup of tea can be quickly made by Steam at any time'.

CHELSEA/*USA 1914*
A four-cylinder 1557cc light car from Newark, New Jersey.

CHELSEA/*England 1922*
This electric car had the outward appearance of a petrol-engined vehicle, the under-bonnet area consisting mostly of batteries! A BTH electric motor was used.

1924 Le Mans Chenard-Walcker

CHENARD & WALCKER/*France 1901–1946*
The Chenard & Walcker factory, based in Asnières, started with tricycles and two- and four-cylinder light cars until it was forced to close its doors in 1907. Promptly resurrected under the name of Société Anonyme des Anciens Etablissements Chenard et Walcker in new premises in Gennevilliers, the firm presented two new models in 1908, a 14/16 hp (3020cc) and a 30/40 hp (5881cc). In 1912 they offered five different cars, from 7/9 hp (1592cc) to 20 hp (5881cc). More cars were presented the following year based on these engines, and a new six-cylinder 20 hp (4523cc) appeared. After the war, the factory resumed production with the 14 hp (3015cc) which remained in production for several years. It was followed in 1920 by a 12 hp (2650cc) and in 1921 by a 10 hp. In 1922 came the famous '3 litre' with a 2978cc engine. The ohc 2-litre, also of 1922, was the winner of the very first Le Mans 24 Hours Race in 1923, and 1924 saw the 22 hp straight-eight of 3945cc. In 1925 Chenard and Walcker launched a small 1095cc four-cylinder sports car with the much-admired streamlined 'tank' body, capable of 150 kph (94 mph) unsupercharged and 170 kph (106 mph) supercharged. Chenard & Walcker followed this with some medium cars of 1286cc and 1495cc. At the end of the 1930s Chenard & Walcker were struggling desperately to survive with the front-wheel-drive 'Aigle' with Citroën four-cylinder or Ford V-8 engines. They also made some rear-wheel-driven cars with Citroën engines. Though taken over in 1946 by Peugeot, Chenard remained independent for the next few years, producing light vans.

CHESWOLD/*England 1911–1915*
Former Adams designer E. C. Inman-Hunter was the progenitor of this Doncaster-built 15·9 hp four with dashboard radiator and worm drive.

CHEVROLET

CHEVROLET / USA 1911 to date

Billy Durant, recently ousted from General Motors, backed racing driver Louis Chevrolet (assisted by engineer Etienne Planche) to produce four- and six-cylinder prototypes in a Detroit garage. The six went into production for 1912, and 2999 units were sold that year. In 1913, manufacture was shifted to Flint, where a sister marque, the Little Four, was built; Louis Chevrolet resigned that year. The Little was phased out in 1915, but a similar design was followed in the new Model H Chevrolet with an ohv 2·4-litre four built by Mason. Chevrolet was by now so successful that Durant was able to exchange its shares for those of GM, thus regaining control of the group. Late in 1915, Chevrolet moved into direct confrontation with Ford by introducing the 490: by 1920, sales had soared to 150,226, but a financial crisis forced Durant out of GM for a second — and final — time. The 1923 Superior, succeeding the 490, offered better equipment than Ford at a slightly higher price, and sold 480,737 units in its first year. However, the 1923 'copper-cooled' Chevrolet was a disaster, and most of the 100 units released were recalled and destroyed. In 1927 Chevrolet became America's best-selling marque, producing over a million cars for the first time, and consolidated its lead with the new International Six, a 3·2-litre ohv unit launched in 1928. Ford regained the lead in 1929–30, but Chevrolet were back on top in 1931 and have maintained the lead virtually uninterrupted ever since. Master and Standard ranges appeared in 1933, with 'knee-action' ifs from 1934. The range was extensively redesigned in 1937, and endowed with the 3·55-litre 'Blue Flame' six. Pre-war designs lasted until 1949, when the Special and the De Luxe appeared, still with the old 'stove bolt six', and in 1950 Chevrolet were the first low-priced marque with a fully-automatic transmission, the two-speed Powerglide. The Corvette sports car of 1953 was totally new, with two-seat glass-fibre body and a new 'Blue Flame' six of 3·8 litres, plus Powerglide. Also brand new from the ground up, the 1955 Chevies had the marque's first V-8 since 1919. With fuel injection, this engine (in 4637cc form) became the first American production engine to develop 1 hp/cu in, in 1957. Chevrolet suffered a minor sales setback that year in face of the restyled Plymouth and Ford ranges, but recaptured the number one slot with all-new cars in 1958. Five different series were available on an x-member frame. The 4637cc engine was standard, but a 5702cc version with three two-barrel carburettors was a popular option. In line with other GM divisions, Chevrolet offered

Chevrolet 490, c.1918

1954 Chevrolet Bel Air sedan

1965 425hp Chevrolet Corvette Sting Ray

1971 Chevrolet Camaro SS Coupé

all-new bodies and frames for 1959, and now featured a 'gullwing' rear deck with huge peardrop tail-lights. At the end of that year, the dramatic styling was toned down, and the compact Corvair, Chevrolet's first unit-construction model, launched. Power was by a rear-mounted 2294cc flat-six and suspension was independent all round. Over 250,000 were sold in the first year. A totally new line, the Chevy II, appeared in 1962, with an ohv four of 2507cc or an ohv 3179cc six. A new 6702cc V-8 was available, and there was a performance version of the Corvair, the Monza Spyder, with a turbocharged engine. In 1963 the Corvette was completely redesigned, emerging as the Corvette Stingray, and in 1963 came the intermediate Chevelle with a 3179cc six or 4638cc V-8. Chevrolet's five separate lines were augmented by the division's belated answer to the Mustang, the Camaro, with 3769cc six or 5359cc V-8, a 5735cc V-8 being optional. The Corvair, condemned as 'unsafe at any speed' by consumers' champion Ralph Nader, was dropped in 1969. New for 1970 was the Monte Carlo, conservatively styled, with the 5735cc V-8. The 1971 Vega, with all-aluminium ohc four, pioneered Chevrolet's sub-compact revolution, and led to the 1975 Monza 2+2 hatchback, with optional 4293cc V-8. The 1971 Chevette rapidly became a best-seller; overseas GM subsidiaries built their own versions of this ohc 1393cc small car (though body panels and mechanical features were, oddly, not interchangeable). The Vega, which had even featured a Cosworth dohc four, was killed off in 1977. Economics forced greater interchangeability between GM lines, and the GM B-body was used on the 1977 Caprice/Impala range. However, the Corvette and Camaro continued with 1968 styling into 1979, except for a new Camaro Berlinetta, with a six or two V-8s available. In April 1979 the '1980' Caprice X-car was revealed as a replacement for the Nova, with a transverse four-cylinder engine driving the front wheels.

1980 Chevrolet Citation

CHIC/*Australia 1923–1929*
Though advertised as a 'Car for Australian Conditions', the Chic was a locally assembled tourer, using British mechanical parts and an Australian body. An unusual idea was the choice of two Meadows overhead valve engines. The four-cylinder 2·1-litre unit developed 40 bhp, the six-cylinder 2·7-litre developed 48 bhp. At least 50 Chics were sold and two are known to have survived. The chassis layout was conventional.

CHICAGOAN/*USA 1952–1954*
Using a two passenger glass-fibre sports body and a six-cylinder Willys engine, the Chicagoan was produced by Triplex Industries, located in Chicago. Only 15 examples were built over a two-year period, although, as the Triplex, it apparently continued into 1955.

CHILTERN/*England 1919–1920*
The short-lived Chiltern, powered by a Dorman engine, was built in Dunstable, Bedfordshire, and had Vulcan connections.

CHINNOCK/*England 1899–1900*
The Chinnock-Davis Manufacturing Co., of Penge, were cycle makers who built 3½ hp air-cooled single-cylinder voiturettes with two-seater dog-cart bodywork, and 2¾ hp tricycles.

CHIRIBIRI/*Italy 1913–1929*
Most Chiribiri cars—named after Antonio Chiribiri, the designer/manufacturer—were around 1·5-litres: 1593cc with a sv four-cylinder engine, 1453cc with an ohv motor and there was also a 'hot' 1485cc ohc racing car, designed by Englishman Jack Scales. Built in 1925, it developed 72 bhp at 5100 rpm. Sufficient funds to develop this excellent engine were not forthcoming. Gigi Platé drove one in 1926 at the Berlin Avus, but crashed in practice.

CHOTA/*England 1912–1913*
This 6 hp cyclecar preceded the Buckingham.

CHRISTCHURCH-CAMPBELL
England 1922
This assembled car had a 10·8 hp Coventry-Simplex engine and gearbox: only one was made.

CHRISTIE/*USA 1904–1910*
J. Walter Christie is predominantly known as being the first serious proponent of front-wheel-drive automobiles and built half-a-dozen racing cars between 1904 and 1908. The initial Christie racer of January 1904 had a transverse four-cylinder engine, the crankshaft taking the place of the front axle. Subsequent cars were all different from one another. Christie built two—possibly three—touring cars in 1905 and in 1909 built a taxicab. In 1911 be began producing front-wheel-drive tractor conversions for fire apparatus, and later made tanks.

CHRITON/*England 1905*
Built at Saltburn-by-the-Sea, Yorkshire, this was a horizontal-engined 1715cc 10 hp four.

CID/*France 1912–1914*
Constructions Industriels Dijonais (successors to Cottereau) were best known for the 8 hp Baby

Chrysler

CHRYSLER/*USA 1924 to date*
Walter Chrysler's gifted triumvirate of engineers—Breer, Skelton and Zeder—created a remarkable car to succeed the old Maxwell marque: its six-cylinder engine had a high-compression Ricardo-type head and four-wheel hydraulic band brakes were an innovation on a popular-priced car. $50 million-worth were sold in the first year. A four appeared in 1925 and a luxury Imperial Six was added to the range. Chrysler expanded rapidly: the De Soto and Plymouth marques were created in 1928, in which year Dodge was taken over. The company's reputation for innovation was sustained by the widely copied 'ribbon' radiators of the 1929 range. In 1929 a Cord L29-like radiator was adopted and two straight-eights of 3·9 litres and the 6·3-litre Imperial were announced. The 1932 models had automatic clutches and freewheels, synchromesh came in

1933, followed in 1934 by automatic overdrive. That was the year of the Airflow, a technical *tour de force* and commercial failure, which only lasted until 1937, though some of its advanced features were used on the more conventional Chryslers, which had moved the company into second place in the sales league. The 1942 models had a radical facelift, with full-width wraparound grilles, and the limited-production Town and Country was distinguished by external wood framing. Different grilles and trim were the only noticeable differences in the three post-war 1946 series; the C38 sv six, and the straight-eight C39 and C40 Imperial. The Town and Country was reintroduced, and standard transmission was the 1938-introduced clutchless 'Fluid-Drive'. New models celebrated Chrysler's 1949 Silver Jubilee, and in 1951 came the marque's first V-8, the famous ohv 'Hemi' of 5424cc, which

was the base engine in the New Yorker, Saratoga and Imperial series—and was also raced by Briggs Cunningham. The firm's first fully automatic transmission—PowerFlite—and AirTemp, the first recirculating air-conditioning system, appeared in 1953 models, restyled with a curved one-piece windscreen. 'Flight Sweep' styling by Virgil Exner on 1955 models revived flagging sales, with a long bonnet sloping down between well-defined wings and a windscreen wrapped-around at top and bottom. Two series—Windsor and New Yorker, both powered by the Hemi—were offered, Imperial becoming a separate division. There was also the limited edition 300 series based on the New Yorker, America's fastest and most powerful stock production car: in 1956 a 300B set up a world passenger car speed record of 139·9 mph. Tailfins reached their zenith on 1957 models, which had

1947 Chrysler Town & Country

1956 Chrysler 300B

1960 Chrysler 300F

1914 CID Baby

with single-cylinder Buchet engine and transverse front suspension, though big sleeve-valve fours were also offered.

CIEM/*Switzerland 1904–1906*
Convinced that the petrol engine was not reliable enough on its own, the Compagnie de l'Industrie Electrique et Mécanique of Geneva equipped their cars with electric motors as well as vee-formation engines with two or four cylinders. Vertical-twins and fours appeared at the end of 1905, and the following year the cars became known as 'Stella'.

CINCINNATI/*USA 1903*
A steam runabout with side-tiller steering and 'reachless running gear'.

CINO/*USA 1909–1913*
An ohv four built in Cincinnati.

CISITALIA/*Italy 1946–1965*
Famous for their fast single-seater racing cars, built after World War Two, with highly tuned

1928 Chrysler 72 Cabriolet

TorqueFlite pushbutton automatic transmission. New wedge head engines of 6276cc and 6768cc replaced the Hemi in 1959, and 1960 saw new unitary bodies; a 300C set a new speed record of 176·6 mph. The 1963 cars were little changed mechanically, but had all-new styling devoid of chrome. In 1964 a limited series of 50 gas turbine cars was built for evaluation purposes by Ghia; all but 10 were destroyed when the experiment ended in 1966. The 1965 models had sculptured side panels, slab-sided wings and minimal chrome, a style retained until 1969, when 'fuselage

styling' with a bulbous shape and narrow curved windows appeared. The last Chrysler convertible was built in 1970, and the Imperial line returned to the fold the next year, but poor sales caused the demise of this luxury car in 1975. Smallest post-war Chrysler, the Cordoba of 1975, was aimed for the 'personal luxury' market; in 1978 it gained a new 'Lean Burn' engine of 5211cc and a power sunroof. That year, too, the LeBaron model name, dating back before the war, was revived for a luxury compact with either a 3687cc six or V-8s of 5211cc or 5899cc. For 1979, the New Yorker/Newport series lost 360 kg in weight by extensive use of aluminium and engineering improvements including electronic spark control instead of 'Lean Burn', as well as an electronic feedback carburettor with catalytic convertor to reduce emissions.

CHRYSLER/*England/Scotland 1976–1979*
The old Rootes Group marque names were

suppressed after the Chrysler takeover in 1970, though the Sunbeam name has been revived on a hatchback, based on the Avenger floorpan. A 2·2-litre Lotus-engined performance version was launched in 1979.

CHRYSLER VALIANT
Australia 1962 to date
After initially importing US-made Valiants, Chrysler Australia embarked on local manufacture. Over the years, the design grew steadily away from the US counterpart. The early Valiants were highly successful, having more power (140 bhp) than rival Falcon and Holden models, but the Valiant's popularity diminished during the 1970s. The 1979 model came in three basic styles — sedan, waggon and van, with a choice of 4·3-litre six-cylinder engine or an imported 5·2-litre V-8. The design is conventional throughout, apart from the use of torsion bar front suspension. Up-market versions with the same mechanical specifications are called Regal and Le Baron.

1978 Chrysler Sunbeam GL

An Australian-built
1978 Chrysler Le Baron

123

four-cylinder 1098cc Fiat engines which developed around 60 bhp. Ex-racing driver Piero Dusio was the creator-manufacturer of these light cars with tubular frames, which were mainly sold to private customers. Dusio also built a range of sports cars with hotted-up 1089cc and 1346cc Fiat power units. In 1949, Ferdinand Porsche designed a 1492cc Grand Prix car for Dusio, with a 12-cylinder engine—with two superchargers—mounted in the rear of the tubular frame. At that time, Dusio ran out of money and transferred operations to Argentina, but never regained the position which he had held in Turin. Among his designers was an Austrian who soon became famous in his own right: Carlo Abarth. Another owner tried to resume Cisitalia production in Italy, but was not successful. His last cars had 847cc Fiat-based engines, while earlier attempts to revive the Cisitalia included the production of 1095cc, 1248cc and even 2760cc coupés. By 1965 nothing was left. Piero Dusio was equally unsuccessful in Argentina, where he built Jeep-like cars.

CITO/*Germany 1905–1909*
A bicycle and motorcycle factory which produced small Fafnir-engined two- and four-cylinder cars of 704cc, 1648cc, 1808cc, 2012cc and 2608cc. Some of the later cars had French Aster motors; Cito used many components of French manufacture.

CITUS/*Denmark 1900–1903*
Citus tri- and quadricycles were probably little more than modified De Dion Bouton products, even if the makers, Fyens Cycle Vaerk, Odense, tried to deny it. The name 'Citus Motor' was, however, cast on the crankcase of the single-cylinder air-cooled 2·5 hp engines.

1903 City & Suburban Grand Victoria

CITY AND SUBURBAN/*England 1901–1904*
The City and Suburban Electric Carriage Company supplied its vehicles—or Columbia electrics bearing its nameplate—to high society. Among its long list of illustrious clients were Queen Alexandra, the Dowager Empress of Russia, Dame Nellie Melba and the Countess of Wilton. Hire vehicles were based at Niagara, a former skating rink in Westminster. A wide range of formal coachwork was offered.

CLA-HOLME/*USA 1922*
The Cla-Holme was an eight-speed four-wheel-drive car. Only one prototype was produced.

CITROEN/*France 1919 to date*
Engineer André Citroën had spent many years in the automotive industry making gears; during the war he manufactured munitions. His first car, the Type A launched in 1919, had a sv 1327cc engine. In 1922 came the Type B of 1453cc. The same year saw the first of the famous Citroën expeditions with the Citroën-Kégresse half-track across the Sahara. It was also the year of the popular 'Cloverleaf' Type C of 855cc. This remarkable car was very popular, due to its low price and high reliability. Between May 1922 and May 1926, 80,232 Cloverleaves were built, but Citroën's record during the vintage period was for the C4 with 134,000 cars built in a little more than four years. Citroën introduced mass production on the American pattern into France. With the B10 in 1925, he introduced France's first all-steel body. The C-Series followed, of which the most interesting was the C6 six-cylinder available in two versions (2442cc and 2650cc). In 1934, Citroën presented the revolutionary 7 cv 'Traction Avant', but its development costs bankrupted him, and the firm was taken over by Michelin. Between 1934 and 1940 the factory made the Traction Avant in no fewer than 21 different versions, the three basic models being the 7 cv and 11 cv fours and the 15 cv six. It also presented a prototype of a sensational V-8-engined front-wheel-drive which never saw production. After the war, Citroën resumed production with the 11 cv and the 15 cv, sold only in black. At the Paris Motor Show of 1949, Citroën launched the amazing 2 cv, a strange and spartan car, front-wheel driven with a 375cc air-cooled flat-twin engine. For many years the Traction Avant and the Deux Chevaux were the only models; in 1954 the 15 cv was equipped with hydropneumatic suspension. The year after, Citroën presented the car of the new era, the immortal DS 19. The old 'Traction' nevertheless remained in production until 1957. A simpler version of the DS, the ID 19, was presented in 1956, and 1961 was the year of the Ami 6, a sort of 'super 2 cv'. The

1948 Citroën 2cv

CLAN/*England 1971–1976*
The clever all-glass-fibre monocoque Clan was conceived by a team of ex-Lotus men. With its unique looks, sturdy construction and eager performance, the Imp-powered car found success on road and track.

CLARENDON/*England 1902–1904*
This Coventry company built a 7 hp two-seater car as well as motorcycles.

CLARK/*USA 1899–1909*
A 6 hp twin-cylinder steam *dos-à-dos*—its controls were laid out so that the car could be driven from either the left or the right, depending on

1972 Clan Crusader

DS 21 followed the DS 19 in 1967, and the year after the Dyane appeared, still with the air-cooled flat-twin. In 1968 a strange vehicle left the works, the plastics-bodied Méhari, which resembled a Jeep. The most significant car of that year was the GS, with a flat-four engine, and 1969 saw the luxurious SM with the dohc Maserati V-6 of 2675cc. In 1975, the DS gave way to the CX 2000, later enlarged to 2200cc, 2400cc and 2500cc. Having come under the control of Puegeot, Citroën presented the LN, a marriage of a Peugeot body with a Citroën engine.

1928 Citroën B14 Cabriolet

1975 Citroën D Super

1978 Citroën LN

the driver's whim — from a marine engine and boiler-maker of Boston, Mass. In 1899, Clark also built the first four-wheel-drive, four-wheel-steer motor car, a light steamer designed by an inventor named Shaw, of Hyde Park, Mass.

CLARK/*USA 1910–1912*
Tourers of 30 hp and 40 hp were listed by this Shelbyville, Indiana, firm at $1400 to $1750

CLARKMOBILE/*USA 1903–1906*
A 7 hp wheel-steered 'gasoline buggy' — 'Easiest Rider built' — the Clarkmobile hailed from Lansing, Michigan, and was said to have been tested for two years before being marketed.

CLASSIC/*USA 1916–1917, 1920–1921*
A 3·2-litre Lycoming four powered this Chicago marque. Featuring a slanting windscreen, the Classic was only available in open form. Failing in 1917, the Classic reappeared three years later after re-incorporation with a factory at Lake Geneva, Wisconsin. Lycoming engines were again used, but these cars were more expensive than their Chicago forebears.

CLASSIC/*France 1925–1929*
Made by the Compagnie Générale des Voitures in Paris, the Classic was available with various engines: the 2120cc sv Sergant and a sleeve-valve unit of 1593cc. Classics were mainly used as taxis.

CLAUDE DELAGE/*France 1923–1927*
Having no relationship with the other Delage, these cars were made at Clichy with four-cylinder engines of 8 hp (1131cc), 10 hp (1847cc) and 12 hp (2297cc).

CLAUDIUS/*France 1903*
A voiturette 'remarkable for its low, yet elegant form', with a 4½ hp Aster engine on the rear axle, 'doing away with chains, belt or cardans'.

CLAVEAU/*France 1923–1950*
Made in Paris, all Claveau cars were highly unorthodox in design. The first was rear-engined, with a streamline body and independent suspension all round. The engines were a 9 hp flat-four and a 7 hp flat-twin of 739cc. The following model had front-wheel drive. A post-war V-8 prototype was never produced.

CLC/*France 1911–1913*
A single-cylinder 'valveless' voiturette with a circular radiator, built by MM. Cockborne, Lehucher and da Costa in Paris.

CLEM/*France 1911–1914*
The CLEM was assembled in Lyon using Belgian Fondu engines of 1131cc and 1327cc and Rolling (Dupressoir) chassis. It took its name from Mme. Clémence Servoz, wife of the first customer, a journalist.

CLEMENT, CLEMENT-BAYARD
France 1898–1922
Gustave-Adolphe Clément, having made his fortune in the cycle industry, floated the Clément-Gladiator-Humber ('Clediaber') company for Fr 22 million in 1896: the Humber connection was soon broken, but in 1898 the firm began building Clément and Gladiator cars. A new factory was built at Levallois-Perret (Seine) where the infamous Clément-Panhard, a beastly machine with centre-pivot steering and rear-mounted tube-ignition engine, was built alongside a tiny 2½ hp voiturette, also rear-engined. In 1901, 7 hp single- and 12 hp twin-cylinder cars designed by Marius Barbarou (who soon left to join Benz) were introduced; by 1903 a range of 9, 12 and 16 hp cars was available. The 12 and 16 hp were four-cylinders with automatic inlet valves, almost identical to the contemporary Gladiators, except with shaft instead of chain drive. In October 1903, Clément left the company, which was taken over by Harvey DuCros (of Dunlop tyres), and also lost

the right to make cars under his own name. He therefore changed his name to Clément-Bayard after *le chevalier sans peur et sans réproche*, whose statue stood in front of his factory at Mezières. Initially, Clément-Bayard cars were similar to the Clément-Gladiator, but in 1907 a 1·6-litre 10/12 hp model with unit gearbox and dashboard radiator was introduced. It was this type of high-quality light car which characterized the subsequent history of Clément-Bayard. Post-war, only 8 hp and 17·6 hp models were available; in 1922 the sole remaining Clément factory was taken over by Citroen for the manufacture of spare parts.

1899 Clément-Panhard

CLEMENT/*England 1908–1914*
After the foundation of Clement-Talbot, Clément-Gladiators were sold under the Clement name in Britain. All-British Clements were built in Coventry from 1908, based on contemporary Swift designs of 10/12 hp (twin), 14/18 hp and 18/28 hp (fours). A 12/14 hp four replaced the twin in 1913.

CLEMENT ET ROCHELLE
France 1927–1930
Another interesting attempt to make a car with independent suspension on all four wheels (this time by leaf-springs), the Clément et Rochelle was made in Clamart with an 1100cc Ruby.

CLENET/*USA 1976 to date*
Designed by French-born Alain Clenet after the style of Jaguar and Mercedes sports cars of the 1930s, each Clenet takes 1600 man hours to build and costs $50,000. A modified Continental MkV chassis carries an all-steel body, Ford suspension, brakes and engine, with MG doors and windscreen. Hand-rubbed walnut from 1200-year-old trees is used for the dash.

CLESSE/*France 1907–1908*
Friction-drive voiturettes and light cars were built by this firm from Levallois-Perret (Seine).

CLETRAC/*USA 1923*
Cletrac is an acronym for Cleveland Tractor, whose Cletrac tractors are famous throughout the world. Cletrac was affiliated with White, and the first Rollin cars (named after Rollin White) were built by Cletrac and consequently carried that name, although subsequent cars were marketed under the Rollin emblem.

CLEVELAND/*USA 1900–1901*
'Pretty, agreeable and practical' electric cars from the Cleveland Machine Screw Company.

CLEVELAND/*USA 1902–1909*
'The car without one weak spot' was a shaft-drive 6435cc four-cylinder 30/35 hp which completed the 1906 Glidden Tour with only two penalty points. Chassis were initially built by Garford: from 1908 they were of own make.

CLIFT/*England 1899–1902*
An electric victoria with an 'extra-special' top speed of 18 mph 'for quick manoeuvring in traffic'. Sinclair petrol cars of 5 hp (rear-engined) and 10 hp (front-engined twin) were also marketed by the same firm.

CLIMAX/*England 1904–1907*
'Pioneers of high-class cars at moderate prices', Climax of Coventry began production with a four-car range — 10/12 hp two-cylinder, 15 hp three-cylinder and fours of 16 hp and 20 hp, but in 1906 only 14 hp and 22 hp fours were listed. A 20 hp six appeared for 1907.

CLIMBER/*USA 1919–1923*
Featuring both four- and six-cylinder models of open and closed cars, as well as a handful of trucks, the Climber was the major effort made by the automobile industry in Arkansas. Using Herschell-Spillman engines exclusively, the cars were distributed by some ten agencies across Arkansas, Mississippi and Tennessee.

CLINTON/*Canada 1911–1912*
When its thresher factory burned down, Clinton rebuilt it as a car factory, but assembled less than ten four-cylinder cars with US engines.

CLIPPER/*USA 1956*
In 1956 the Clipper became a separate marque for a season (instead of a lower priced Packard) before it again became a Packard Clipper. Available in three series (Custom, Super and Deluxe) the Custom had Packard's superior Torsion-Level ride combining torsion-bar suspension with the electronic load-levelling system. This was offered as an option on the Super and Deluxe, which had coils at the front and leaf springs at the rear. The Custom Clipper used a 245 hp V-8 Packard engine, while the Super and Deluxe had a smaller 225 hp version. Electric windows and Twin Ultramatic transmission were optional.

CLOVER/*USA 1899–1900*
Lieutenant H. K. Clover, USN, designed the twin-cylinder two-stroke engine of this Omaha, Nebraska, car. Its silencer incorporated a 'Deodorizing preparation' of magnesia, lime and charcoal, to be renewed every 30 days.

CLUA/*Spain 1959–1960*
A 398cc twin-cylinder two-stroke powered this sporty utility model from Barcelona.

CLUB/*USA 1910–1911*
Several New York bankers, determined to eliminate the middleman, decided to combine and build a limited number of cars for themselves and others entering their club. Members could buy up to five $100 shares, allowing them to buy one 'Club Car' annually per share. The 40/50 hp Club was built by Merchant & Evans, of Philadelphia, and had an American & British engine. A dual-ratio back axle gave direct drive on the top two ratios.

CLUB/*Germany 1921–1925*
Club (of Berlin-Charlottenburg) fitted 1305cc 18 hp Atos engines into sporting two-seater cars. Top speed of the sturdy 760 kg car was around 70 km/h (43 mph).

CLULEY/*England 1922–1928*
Proprietary sv four-cylinder engines were used in the Coventry-built Cluley, the company initially having made bicycles. These 10 and 11·9 hp models were joined by the six-cylinder 16/40 in 1924. The final model was an ohv 14/50 though it never went into production.

CLYNO/*England 1922–1929*
Already famous as motorcycle manufacturers (their name came from the variable-ratio 'Clyno' belt-pulley, designed by the company's founders, Frank and Allwyn Smith), Clyno of Wolverhampton built three prototype 10 hp ohv sports cars in 1920 before the post-war slump killed the project. Re-formed in 1922, they launched a low-priced 10·8 hp Coventry-Climax-engined light car intended to compete with Morris; it proved an instant success. Early in 1924 a wide-track Colonial model (reflecting Clyno's interest in export markets) and an ephemeral Sports, with four-wheel brakes and external exhaust, were added to the range; at Olympia that year a refined Clyno range included 'Royal' tourer, two-seater and saloon. Right-hand gear change and balloon tyres were standard and four-wheel brakes were available. For 1926 an 11·9 hp four was added, initially with Coventry-Climax and then, from December 1925, with Clyno's own-make engine. Production peaked at over 12,000 in 1926, when Clyno was third-biggest British manufacturer, and a vast new factory was built in the Wolverhampton suburb of Bushbury. In September 1927 a new 8·3 hp Clyno 'Nine' appeared, designed by A. G. 'General' Booth, who subsequently designed the AJS Nine and the Hillman Minx. Like the other cars in the 1928 range, it had a new, square-

-- 1925 Clyno 10.8hp Sports

cut radiator. By February 1928, Bushbury was turning out 70 Nines a week, and in May 1928 came a luxury 12/35 hp, the wire-wheeled 'Olympic'. In an attempt to forestall the expected Morris Eight, Clyno launched the £112 'Century' Nine during 1928 (it had been planned as a £100 car). This basic machine's unpopularity with agents and public, coupled with the cost of Bushbury, helped to bring Clyno down in 1929, when a prototype monobloc straight-eight (derived from two Nine engines) had just completed its trials. R. H. Collier of Birmingham, who bought up the spares and goodwill, built another six 12/35s. A plan for the engine manufacturer Meadows to revive Clyno cars in the mid-1930s was scotched by their involvement in re-armament.

10.8hp Clyno Royal Tourer, 1927

CLYDE/*England 1899–1930*
G. H. Wait of Leicester built cars, motorcycles and 'tricarettes', mainly for local customers, for over 30 years. His 12/13 hp three-cylinder and 7/8 hp twin-cylinder cars of 1905 had transverse power units.

CM/*France 1924–1930*
Made by Charles Mochet, this was a tiny cyclecar with a single-cylinder 346cc engine mounted at the rear. The marque resumed after the war with the pedal-powered Vélocar Mochet.

CMN/*Italy 1919–1925*
Enzo Ferrari and Ugo Sivocci were with CMN at Milano-Pontedera, before they joined the much bigger Alfa-Romeo factory. CMN built a range of cars with 2180cc and 2960cc four-cylinder sv engines, but never gained any international fame.

COADOU ET FLEURY/*France 1921*
A small cyclecar made in Paris with a steel monocoque body and a 903cc sv Ruby engine.

COATES-GOSHEN/*USA 1908–1910*
Built four-cylinder cars of 25 hp and 32 hp.

COATS STEAM CAR/*USA 1922–1923*
Few of these $1085 three-cylinder steam tourers designed by George A. Coats were built. Never passing the prototype stage, the Coats boasted a two-speed and reverse gear with floor shift.

COCHOTTE/*France 1899*
A voiturette of untidy appearance, with an exposed water-cooled engine at the front.

COEY/*USA 1913–1917*
Coey of Chicago built the Coey Bear cyclecar and the six-cylinder Cocy Flyer sporting car.

COGNET DE SEYNES/*France 1912–1926*
An 1124cc four built in Lyon.

COHENDET/*France 1897–1914*
This company was founded by an American in Paris, C. R. Goodwin, after whom its 'Americaine' 792cc voiturette of 1910 was named. A 3½ hp single-cylinder air-cooled engine powered Cohendet's 'nice-looking carriage' of 1897, which was driven by a leather belt strengthened by steel links to prevent stretching. By 1905, one-, two- and four-cylinder models were available; Cohendet, who built a wide range of components, also offered to build cars from his clients' own designs.

COIGNET/*France 1912–1913*
MM. Coignet and Ducruzel, of Billancourt, built a varied range of belt-driven cyclecars with single-cylinder and twin-cylinder power units.

COLBURN/*USA 1906–1909*
The Colburn, from Denver, Colorado, was similar in appearance to the Renault, with the radiator behind a coal-scuttle bonnet. A 72 mph roadster was offered in 1909.

COLBY/*USA 1911–1914*
Underslung 40 hp four from Mason City, Iowa.

COLDA/*France 1921–1922*
Cars made in Paris with an 1847cc four-cylinder Sergant engine.

COLE/*USA 1909–1925*
J. J. Cole's carriage-building firm from Indianapolis started with a 14 hp flat-twin highwheeler, but soon turned to big, conventional four- and six-cylinder models. From 1913 these had electric starting and lighting. In 1915 Cole announced their first V-8, with a Northway power unit. The 1916 range was just Roadster, Sportster and Touring — one colour option was 'dustproof grey' — but by the early 1920s 'Sportsedan', 'Sportcoupé', 'Sportosine', 'Tourosine' and 'Toursedan' were also listed. Cole's penchant for appalling model names burst into full flower in their ultimate range with the 'Aero-Volante' and a saloon called, for some reason, the 'Brouette' — the French for 'Wheelbarrow'.

COLIBRI/*Germany 1907–1910*
Built by the Norddeutsche Automobilwerke (NAW) at Hameln/Weser, the small Colibri was a popular car, which was also exported in large numbers. The first model had an ioe 860cc twin-cylinder engine, the larger version a sv 1320cc four-cylinder. Later models were known as 'Sperber'.

COLLINET/*USA 1921–1922*
This was the successor to the earlier Collins built in Huntington, NY, but had a four-cylinder Wisconsin engine. Price in 1921 for the 132-inch wheelbase, wire-wheeled Collinet chassis was $5500. For 1922, this was reduced to $5000 although a six was quoted at $6500. A 1921 Collinet was exhibited late in 1920 in New York City. It may have been the only car actually built!

COLLINS/*USA 1920*
Built in Huntington, New York, by Albert H. Collins, the car featured a four-cylinder Herschell-Spillman engine and 120-inch wheelbase. Wire wheels were standard and the five-passenger touring car was listed at $2500. The car may have existed only as a prototype and became the Collinet for 1921.

COLLINS/*USA 1921–1922*
The Collins was built by the Collins Motor Car Co. of Detroit, Mich. (and later Cleveland, Ohio), by Richard H. Collins, former president of Cadillac. The car was absorbed into the Peerless line when Mr Collins affiliated with that company. Cars carrying a Collins nameplate were prototypes only.

COLOMBE/*France c1920–1925*
Though this firm from Colombes started with an assembled car using a Model T Ford engine and transmission, by 1923 they had introduced an odd fwd cyclecar with a 345cc single-cylinder engine, which, in single-seat form, set up world records in its class at Arpajon.

Colombe cyclecar, 1924

COLONIAL/*USA 1920*
Only one of these Colonials was built, but it is important in automotive history as the first car built in the United States with four-wheel hydraulic brakes. With an own-make straight-eight engine, the Colonial featured disc wheels and two side-mounted spare wheels, as well as a hard-top body (known in the United States as a 'California top') which could pass either as a touring car or a sedan at the whim of the driver, given a few seconds to arrange the windows.

COLONIAL/*USA 1920–1921*
The Chicago-based Colonial was nothing more than the Shaw automobile with another emblem. For some reason best known to Shaw, the Colonial name was substituted — briefly — before the car returned to its original 'Shaw' designation. Soon after it was bought by Yellow Cab and renamed 'Ambassador'.

COLONIAL/*USA 1921–1922*
Built in Boston, Mass., probably less than a dozen Colonials ever got on the road, despite the prediction of the company that they would produce 'in excess of 100 units' in their first year. These were handsome cars with a 130-inch wheelbase and six-cylinder engine by Beaver. Although a complete line of open and closed

1922 Colonial two-seater

body styles was advertised, probably only a few open models were actually ever built. A 12-cylinder model utilizing the Weidely engine was also proposed to augment the 1921 line but it is doubtful whether it materialized.

COLT/*USA 1907–1908*
The sporty six-cylinder Colt 40 hp was built at Yonkers, NY, and cost only $1500. Top speed was a claimed 60 mph, enabling it 'to run away on the hills from any runabout of the season, bar none'.

COLT/*USA 1958*
The Colt Manufacturing Co., of Milwaukee, Wisconsin, offered this two-passenger glass-fibre-bodied car powered by a one-cylinder four-stroke air-cooled engine with a top speed of 50 mph. It had automatic transmission as standard equipment.

COLTMAN/*England 1909–1920*
Though this 20 hp four-cylinder from the Mid-land Ironworks, Loughborough, is supposed to have remained in production until 1920, it appears only to have been built between 1909–13.

1899 Columbia Electric *dos-à-dos*

COLUMBIA/*USA 1898–1913*
One of America's leading manufacturers of electric vehicles, the Columbia and Electric Vehicle Company of Hartford, Connecticut, was part of Colonel Albert Pope's motor- and cycle-building empire. The 1899 models ranged from an electric phaeton (the original type of Columbia electric) through a *dos-à-dos*, a runabout, a victoria, a 'Daumon Victoria' and a brougham, to a 15-seat omnibus. Queen Alexandra of England used a Columbia Victoria around the grounds of Sandringham. The company began manufacture of 'gasoline carriages' in 1899. By 1904, a 12/14 hp twin and 30/35 hp fours designed by H. P. Maxim were available: the smaller models acquiring left-hand drive for 1905, while the larger cars retained right-hand control. In 1906, a big four of 40/45 hp was listed. The 1909 model, a 29 hp four, had the curious designation of 'Mark 48, Lot 3': perhaps prophetically, for Columbia became part of the United States Motor Company combine the following year; their last models were the Knight and Cavalier of 1911–13. Along with Courier, Stoddard-Dayton, Brush and Maxwell, Columbia went down with the collapse of the US Motor Company in 1913: only Maxwell was to resurface.

1919 Columbia Six tourer

COLUMBIA/*USA 1917–1924*
'Gem of the Highway', the Columbia Six was an assembled car of some quality which used a 24 hp Continental engine. It was noteworthy for its thermostat-controlled radiator shutters, 'a constant source of delight to the Columbia owner'. In 1923, Columbia took over Liberty.

COLUMBUS/*USA 1903–1904*
The Columbus Automobile & Manufacturing Company of Columbus, Ohio, were motor agents who also advertised 'machines reconstructed and special designs carried out'. Flat-twin cars were produced, sometimes known as 'Imperial'.

COMET/*Canada 1907–1908*
This Montreal-assembled 24 hp four used a Clément-Bayard engine and chassis: there were — briefly — a six and a 40 hp four. Its promoter eventually went on to open an orange-juice cannery.

COMET/*USA 1914–1915*
A tandem-seated cyclecar from Indianapolis.

COMET/*USA 1917–1923*
Comet produced several hundred cars during its brief existence. The first cars used Lewis engines but the company switched over to Continentals thereafter. All Comet cars were six-cylinder automobiles, excepting a smaller four of which only a handful was completed. Comet also built a Lycoming-powered truck. The company failed in 1922 and cars marketed as 1923 models were in reality left-over 1922 units.

COMET/*England 1921*
'Designed by an engineer with considerable racing experience in France', this was a 1593cc sports car.

COMET/*USA 1947–1948*
The General Developing Co., Ridgewood, NY, built 'the World's handiest run-around-in car'. The three-wheeled Comet had a 4½ hp air-cooled rear-mounted engine and a glass-fibre body on a tubular frame.

COMIOT/*France 1899–1904*
Reversing the usual trend, Comiot of Paris imported frames and transmissions for his tricycles and quadricycles from Eadie of Redditch.

COMMANDER/*USA 1922*
The Commander was actually a re-emblemed Ogren automobile, the proposed Commander company being a scheme to build the basic Ogren under a different name and management. One $5000 touring car was exhibited before the enterprise failed.

Hugo Ogren driving the 1923 Commander

COMMERCE/*USA 1922*
This was a truck company which built a ten-passenger touring car during one year. Billed as a 'charabanc', the Commerce open car used a Continental six-cylinder engine, sold for $2350, and if it looked very much like an open bus, it was not considered as such by its manufacturer.

COMMODORE/*USA 1921*
Built only in prototype form, the Commodore was a six-cylinder assembled car with a Herschell-Spillman engine and a 124-inch wheelbase. The price for the touring car, complete with wire wheels, was quoted at $2485.

COMMONWEALTH/*USA 1917–1922*
Formerly the Partin-Palmer, this was an assembled car built in Chicago, offering a complete line of open models and for 1921 a sedan and a taxicab. With the exception of a 'Victory Six' model in 1919, Commonwealth cars used four-

cylinder Lycoming or Herschell-Spillman engines. The make failed in 1922. An attempt to continue the passenger-car line as a luxury make under the 'Goodspeed' emblem came to nothing. The taxicab became the Checker cab.

COMPACT / England/France 1907
Sold by the Newmobile Car Company, the Compact car had British-built engines in French-made chassis.

COMPAGNIE FRANÇAISE / 1901–c1905
M. Onfray's Cie Française des Cycles et Automobiles, of Paris, built a range of cars including 6cv and 8cv single-cylinders, and twins of 9cv and 10cv, at prices from Fr 4000–Fr 9500.

COMPONENTS / England 1899
Built at 'Componentsville', Birmingham, these motor tricycles and quadricycles were known as 'Ariels' after 1900.

COMPOUND / USA 1903–1907
The power unit of the Compound was unusual — for a petrol engine — in having two high-pressure cylinders which exhausted, as on a steam engine, into a central low-pressure cylinder. Made by the Eisenhuth Horseless Vehicle Company, of Middletown, Connecticut, it survived only four years.

CONCORDIA / France 1903
This Parisian company offered a range of Buchet-engined cars from 10cv to 20cv, capable of running on petrol or alcohol.

CONCORDIA / Canada 1977
A wedge-shaped 'dream car' conceived by Ken Hill of Trebron Design as a 'teaching platform' in conjunction with Concordia University. It went into production in a limited run priced at $(Canada) 35,000–40,000.

CONDOR / Switzerland 1922
Only five Mag-engined cars (similar to the 5cv Citroën) were built by this Courfaivre (Jura) cycle manufacturer.

LA CONFORTABLE / France c1920
A tiny cyclecar with a single-cylinder two-stroke Train engine of 344cc.

CONNAUGHT / England 1949–1957
Best known for its racing cars, this Send, Surrey, firm began production with a Lea-Francis-based 1767cc sports car with full-width bodywork.

CONRAD / USA 1900–1904
Starting as makers of steam cars, Conrad (of Buffalo, NY) introduced a petrol-engined range in 1903. Alfred Sloan, later head of General Motors, owned one: 'it had a two-cycle engine with four cylinders . . . it was a lemon'.

CONSTANTINESCO
England/France 1926–1928
Romanian-born engineer Georges Constantinesco made a car with a 494cc two-stroke engine of his own design (as was the torque converter which replaced the gearbox and clutch). It never worked properly.

CONTINENTAL / England 1903
The Continental range — 6hp, 9hp singles, 12/14hp twin and 24hp four — was sold by a London Fiat agent. The 12/14hp, at least, was actually a French-built Henriod.

CONTINENTAL / Austria 1907–1910
The Continental Music Works of Hoffmann & Czerny, of Vienna, built a twin-cylinder 1162cc air-cooled voiturette which appeared at the 1907 Vienna Motor Show.

1907 Continental voiturette

CONTINENTAL / USA 1909–1914
A four-cylinder 5539cc engine powered this tourer from Franklin, Indiana.

CONTINENTAL / USA 1933–1934
The Continental was an unsuccessful attempt by the Continental Motors Corp. to sell the De-Vaux automobile under a new name and revamped design. Built in three basic models, one four and two sixes, the 'Beacon', 'Flyer' and 'Ace' constituted the line, with prices starting at $335. Despite the low price, attractive to the new car purchaser in the Depression, the cars did not sell and a total of only 3310 had been sold by 1 January 1934, when both the Flyer and Ace were dropped from the line and the four-cylinder Beacon was given a slight face-lift to designate it a 1934 model. Only 983 units were sold and the company ceased manufacture. Continentals were also sold in Canada under the Frontenac emblem.

CONTINENTAL / USA 1958
An obscure do-it-yourself glass-fibre sports car kit. Two models were available, the Sabre and the slightly larger Speedster, designed to fit small American or European chassis with the minimum of modification.

CONTINENTAL / USA 1956 to date
In 1956 a separate division of Ford built the Continental Mk II. The restrained chrome-free design (partly constructed by hand) was different from all others in the Ford range except for the Lincoln's 300hp V-8 engine. Designed as a 'status symbol', it cost almost $10,000. The Mk III of 1958 was a Lincoln Premiere with a different grille. For 1961 the Continental name was applied to a new range of Lincolns and remained as such until 1968, when a separate line of Continentals reappeared. The new Mk III was mass-produced and evolved into the Mk IV in mid-1971, followed by the Mk V in 1977. The styling and RR-type grille remained almost unaltered from 1968, but the 7538cc V-8 engine was replaced by a 6555cc unit in 1979. Elaborate trim by Pucci, Cartier or Givenchy is offered on limited versions.

1933 Continental Beacon Roadster

1933 Continental Ace De Luxe Sedan

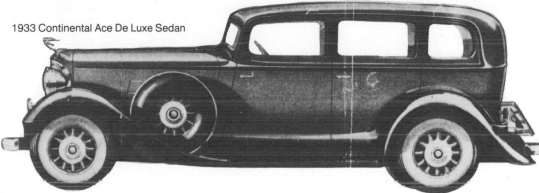

COOPER/*England 1909–1910*
The Cooper Steam Digger Company of King's Lynn, Norfolk, built this curious four-cylinder two-stroke, whose engine had rigid piston rods, cross-heads and connecting rods like a steam engine, and a three-speed gearbox driving through a dual-ratio back axle. Only six were built, of which one survives.

COOPER/*England 1922–1923*
A 1919 three-cylinder prototype preceded limited production of 1368cc Coventry-Climax-engined light cars in Coventry.

COPE-BOHEMIAN/*England 1905- 1906*
'The finest thing ever produced in tricars', the Cope-Bohemian was built in Manchester with 3½hp (air-cooled) or 4½hp (water-cooled) single-cylinder engines or a 6hp water-cooled twin.

CORBIN/*USA 1904–1912*
Built in New Britain, Connecticut, the first Corbins featured an air-cooled engine. The 1906 Model G 'High Powered Runabout' had a four-cylinder 24 hp engine and sold for $1800. Corbin cars were available with water-cooling as an option for 1908, apparently because of sales resistance to air-cooling. The 1908 30 hp six cost $2650 if air-cooled, $2500 water-cooled.

CORBITT/*USA 1912–1913*
A four-cylinder tourer built in Henderson, North Carolina.

CORD/*USA 1964–1973*
Glenn Pray of Tulsa, Oklahoma, made a plastic-bodied replica of the 1936 Cord. It used a Corvair flat-six air-cooled engine to drive the front wheels. In 1968 the third owners of the marque (it had gone to Philadelphia for a year) changed to rear-wheel drive, a Ford engine, a glass-fibre body and fixed headlights. Production was spasmodic.

CORINTHIAN/*USA 1922–1923*
The Corinthian car was built in two sizes, a 130-inch wheelbase Wisconsin-engined series with a touring car priced at $5000 and a similar body style with a 110-inch wheelbase at $985, powered by Herschell-Spillman. Very few of either model were produced.

CORNELIAN/*USA 1914–1915*
This cyclecar, built by components manufacturers Blood Brothers of Alleghan, Michigan, had all-round independent suspension by double transverse springs.

CORNILLEAU/*France 1910–1914*
Cornilleau first showed at the 1910 Paris Salon: the company's offerings were two four-cylinder models, one of 4942cc, the other of 2001cc.

CORNILLEAU-STE BEUVE
France 1905–1909
Cornilleau's 16/24cv four had engine and gearbox mounted as a unit in an aluminium casing which had side shields to keep the engine compartment clean. Well engineered and designed for ease of maintenance, the CSB was also built in England by Straker-Squire.

1931 Cord L29 Sedan

CORD/*USA 1929–1932, 1936–1937*
The first front-wheel-drive car to get into serious production in America, the Cord was introduced in November 1929 by the Auburn Automobile Co. of Auburn, Indiana, the third of the triumvirate of cars built by Erret Lobban Cord and designed to occupy a sales position between the Auburn and Duesenberg cars. The rakish, altogether beautiful and ahead-of-its-time Model L-29 Cord featured a 4894cc Lycoming straight-eight engine developing 125 bhp. The car's lines, strongly suggestive of the larger Duesenberg, adapted well to the car's height of only 61 inches and 137-inch wheelbase. Four standard models comprised the Cord L-29 line, including sedan, brougham, cabriolet and phaeton, at prices ranging from $3095 to $3295. In addition, two town-cars were built to special order, as well as some boat-tailed speedsters. Sleek, aesthetically pleasing and powerful as the Cord L-29 was, it could not have been introduced at a more inauspicious time, the introduction coinciding with the Stock Market Crash and sales, though consistent, were small. In early 1931, prices were reduced to $2395 to $2595—but to little avail—and the L-29 was phased out of production early in 1932 after some 4429 cars had been built. Late in 1935, the name was revived with the modernistic Model 810 which had been designed by Gordon Buehrig. Originally intended to be a smaller Duesenberg, a last-minute decision gave it the Cord nameplate and, like its predecessor, it was front-wheel driven. Of a unique modernistic design, its flat hood was adorned with wrap-around chromed louvres. Headlights were retractable and located in the wings. Powered by a 3547cc Lycoming V-8 engine, it developed 125 bhp at 3500 rpm. With a 125-inch wheelbase, overall height of the ultra-modern 810 was 58 to 60 inches. The car could be ordered in two sedan styles, as well as the two-seater 'Sportsman' and four-seater convertible sedan-phaeton. In 1937, the 810 gave way to the 812 which featured a supercharger, thereby upping the horsepower to 195! Added to the 812 line was a custom berline with glass division and lengthened

CORNU/*France 1905–1908*
Paul Cornu, designer of one of the first helicopters, built this curious voiturette with a complex tubular chassis and a separate single-cylinder engine, driving each rear wheel direct by belt, without any form of gear-change. The brake was actuated by the exhaust gas.

CORONA/*Germany 1905–1909*
Corona cars, built by a well-known bicycle and motorcycle factory at Brandenburg, were made under Maurer licence and had friction drive. Maurer also supplied the 1470cc single-cylinder 8 hp and 1526cc twin-cylinder 11 hp engines.

CORONA/*France 1920*
This was the first straight-12, with a pushrod ohv engine of 7238cc. A five-year guarantee was offered, but it is probable that no Coronas were sold.

CORONA/*England 1920–1923*
The two-seater Corona used a 9 hp flat-twin engine by Bovier, though in 1923 a 9·8 hp four-cylinder Coventry-Climax power unit was offered.

CORONET/*England 1904–1906*
Designed by MMC engineer George Iden's son Walter, these cars (8 hp single, 12 hp twin, 16 hp four) were assembled from British and French components in Coventry.

1905 16hp Coronet tonneau

CORRE/*France 1908–1914*
In 1908, J. Corré left the Corré-La Licorne company and built voiturettes of 8 hp, 10 hp and 12 hp under the 'Corré' or 'JC' marque at Rueil (Seine-et-Oise).

CORREJA/*USA 1908–1915*
A shaft-driven 40 hp four (5808cc) built by Vandewater & Co., of Iselin, NJ.

CORRE-LA LICORNE/*France 1899–1950*
The Société Française des Automobiles Corre was founded in 1901 in Levallois, and started production with motor tricycles and quadricycles. Various cars with proprietary engines were made until 1906. Up until then the cars were sold under the name of Corre. When M. Corre left the factory, the name was changed to Corre-La Licorne. The range was then a twin-cylinder (1727cc) and a 15/20 hp four (2544cc); however, the old single-cylinder De Dion-engined 8 hp model of 942cc was in production until 1912. After that date all Corres had four-cylinder engines. No fewer than nine models were available in 1914, from 7 hp to 25 hp. After the war, Corre-La Licorne moved to Neuilly; the first new model presented in 1919 had a sv Ballot engine of 1244cc. During the 1920s the main models were the Ballot-engined 9/12 cv (1692cc) and the 12/15 cv (2997cc) and the SCAP-engined 8/10 cv (1393cc). A 1492cc six was offered in 1927, and raced with success. La Licorne, bolstered in decline by the 5 cv (905cc) and the 8 cv (1450cc), moved to Courbevoie and made some conventional front-engined, rear-wheel-drive cars using the front-wheel-drive Citroën body. At the outbreak of the war, two new cars—a 6 cv and 8 cv—were made, but it was too late. After a prototype had been shown at the Paris Show in 1949, the works closed for ever.

COSMOS/*England 1906–1907*
A 'do-it-yourself' chassis to which the purchaser could fit an 8 hp or 10 hp engine of his choice.

COSMOS (CAR)/*England 1919–1920*
Roy Fedden, later of the Bristol Aeroplane Company, was responsible for the design of the three-cylinder radial rear-engined Cosmos. (It was a theme he later returned to with the experimental Fedden of the Second World War years.) The square (75 × 75mm) engine was also available in the CAR, though with a 5mm greater bore and stroke.

wheelbase. Prices of the 1936–37 Cord ranged from the $1995 of the 1936 sedan to $3575 for the supercharged 812 berline. Only 2320 810 and 812 Cord automobiles were made. The design, which was cited for its beauty by the Museum of Modern Art in New York City, subsequently was sold first to Hupp and finally to Graham and the last models of these two cars closely resembled the Cord in appearance. Since then at least three different concerns have built Cord replicas.

1937 Cord Convertible

A sporting 1924 Corre-La Licorne

M. Cottereau's family with his 1901 range

COSTIN / *England 1968–1972*
The name of engineer/designer Frank Costin has been linked with many projects. The Costin Amigo featured a plywood monocoque body/chassis unit, as first seen on the Marcos, with mainly glass-fibre panels. A total of seven cars was made, all but one being Vauxhall-powered.

COTAY / *USA 1920–1921*
The Cotay (the name was an acronym of its builder, the Coffyn-Taylor Motor Co. of New York City) was a sporting car built as a two-seater roadster only. It featured a four-cylinder air-cooled engine by Cameron, disc wheels and a wheelbase of 105 inches. Few were built.

COTE / *France 1908–1913*
Côte built a 3 hp voiturette in 1900: their 1908–13 range consisted of two-stroke two- and four-cylinder-engined cars of up to 16/28 hp.

COTTEREAU / *France 1898–1910*
The original Cottereaus were known as 'voiturines', their hillclimbing powers were 'a revelation'. In 1902, Cottereau of Dijon listed a 5 cv single-cylinder voiturette and tubular-chassis 7 cv and 10 cv vee-twins: the 'irréprochable' *tonneau riche* cost Fr 8000. There was also a 16 cv straight-four of 3191cc. The company was reorganized in 1906 — their 15 hp four was described as 'la plus chic voiture'. There were also two singles, a twin, two threes and another four. By 1910 the firm was experimenting with rotary-valve fours and sixes. From 1911, the marque was known as 'CID'.

COTTIN-DESGOUTTES / *France 1905–1933*
Cottin et Desgouttes of Lyon made many interesting cars from 1905: the best were the 9500cc six-cylinder of 1904, the four-cylinder series made from 1906 to 1914 using four different engines, and the 1908 six of 3619cc. After the war, Cottin-Desgouttes recommenced production with one model, the 14/16 cv (3216cc), promptly followed by a 18/20 cv (4071cc) and a 23/25 cv (5026cc). In 1924 a new range of cars appeared, with ohv engines of 2613cc, as well as the famous 2986cc three valves per cylinder model, the latter sometimes presented in a racing 'Grand Prix' version. In 1926 came the 2613cc 'Sans Secousses' model with independent suspension all round. The last Cottin-Desgouttes was a 3813cc sv six. Having always made luxury cars, Cottin-Desgouttes were victims of the Depression.

COUDERE / *France 1907*
A single-cylinder voiturette which won its class in the 1907 Evreux Trials.

COURIER / *France 1906–1908*
The 18/24 hp Courier had a Gnôme engine. A

M. Cottin in a 1907 Cottin-Desgouttes

major selling point of this model was its makers' claim that a Courier 'had been driven 8000 miles by a lady without any mechanical trouble'. There was also a 10/12 hp twin-cylinder Courier.

COURIER/*USA 1909–1913*
Related to the Stoddard-Dayton, this was a cheaper model with a 3245cc four-cylinder engine: from 1912 a 3638cc four was used, and the cars were known as Courier-Clermont.

COURIER/*USA 1922–1924*
Lineal descendant of the Maibohm, the Courier was built in Sandusky, Ohio, and featured full-pressure lubrication. Using a Falls six-cylinder engine, the 116-inch wheelbase Courier was noted for its trim sporty lines, closed models carrying cowl lights resembling small carriage lamps. Probably 1000 units were produced before the firm failed in 1924.

COUTERET/*France 1907*
A front-wheel-drive voiturette from Paris.

COUVERCHEL/*France 1905–1907*
Known as CVR following a move to Boulogne-sur-Seine from Neuilly in 1906, this firm offered cars from 12/16 hp to a 40/50 hp six.

COVENTRY MOTETTE
England 1896–1897
An Anglicized version of the Bollée voiturette built in Coventry.

1921 Coventry-Premier three-wheeler

COVENTRY-PREMIER/*England 1919–1923*
The original Coventry-Premier was a three-wheeler, powered by a water-cooled twin-cylinder engine. However, following a take-over by Singer in 1920 it acquired a fourth wheel and the following year a Singer Ten engine.

COVENTRY-VICTOR/*England 1926–1938*
The three-wheeler chain-driven Coventry-Victor naturally used its own proprietary engine, a side-valve flat-twin of 688cc. The make lingered on until 1938 by which time 850cc, 900cc and 1100cc engines were available.

1903 8hp Covert

COVERT/*USA 1901–1907*
Byron V. Covert of Lockport, NY, started in

1901 building steam cars, then progressed to light De Dion-engined runabouts which were exported to England as Covert-Jacksons.

COWEY/*England 1913–1915*
With a 10 hp Chapius-Dornier engine and friction drive, the Cowey from Kew was distinguished by pneumatic suspension with automatic levelling.

The chassis of the 1913 air-sprung Cowey

COX/*England 1967 to date*
The Cox GTM (Grand Touring Mini) went on sale in kit form in 1967 for the princely sum of £330, requiring only Mini mechanical parts to complete it. A stumpy car with glass-fibre body and strong backbone chassis the GTM had rear-mounted Mini power. About 250 have been built so far, initially under the Cox and latterly just the GTM banner.

COYOTE/*USA 1909–1910*
A sporty 50 hp eight-cylinder model from Redondo Beach, California.

CRAIG-DORWALD (AILSA CRAIG)
England c1902–c1906
About twelve cars of differing designs were built by this Putney engineering firm, starting with a single-speed 8 hp. Most used a two-cylinder Craig-Dörwald marine engine of 3539cc or four-cylinder derivative (an uprated '50 hp' four was used in a 1904 barouche for the Earl of Norbury). Marine engines were the company's *forte*: in 1904 they built a 12,127cc ohc six and a 150 bhp V-12 of 21,234cc.

1920 16-valve Craig Hunt

CRAIG-HUNT/*USA 1920*
Despite the fact the 'Sixteen Valves' Craig-Hunt was widely advertised in the automotive press, probably only one pilot model was made. The 'Character Car' resembled the Model T Ford in outward appearance, but had a conventional transmission.

CRAIG-TOLEDO/*USA 1906–c1907*
A $4000 three-passenger runabout.

CRANE/*USA 1912–1915*
Forerunner of the Crane-Simplex, this was a 9226cc four priced at $8000 in chassis form.

CRANE & BREED/*USA 1912–1917*
A 48 hp six was the 1912 offering from this Cincinnati company, which thereafter built mostly ambulances and hearses.

CRANE-SIMPLEX
USA 1915–1917, 1922–1924
One of the most prestigious and expensive cars built in America, Crane-Simplex (correctly, Simplex-Crane Model 5) produced about 500 chassis between its organization in 1915 and World War One when its factory was converted to war production. An enormous car, this successor to the earlier Simplex sported a six-cylinder engine with a displacement of 9238cc, and a wheelbase of 143½ inches. The $10,000 chassis carried coachwork from such custom body builders as Brewster, Holbrook, Quimby and Kimball and the car boasted 100 bhp at 1800 rpm. Following World War One, Crane-Simplex, along with Locomobile and Mercer, was absorbed by Hare's Motors; plans were announced in 1922 that a new Crane-Simplex would be made at the Locomobile plant in Bridgeport, Connecticut. Although the company technically existed, no cars were forthcoming.

1917 Crane-Simplex six-cylinder

CRAWFORD/*USA 1905–1923*
The Crawford was a highly regarded small-production car built in Hagerstown, Maryland, chain-driven until 1907 with transaxles being featured on the 1911–14 models. Later cars featured brass trim, disc-covered wooden artillery wheels and Continental six-cylinder engines. The Crawford interests were eventually purchased by the M. P. Moller Pipe Organ Co. of Hagerstown, which brought out a sporting version of the Crawford in 1922 called the Dagmar. The last Crawfords were sold in 1923, but Dagmar continued until 1927.

A surviving 1922 Crawford

CRAWSHAY-WILLIAMS
England 1904–1906
Four-cylinder Simms engines of 14/16 hp and 20/24 hp powered these handsome chain-drive cars.

CREANCHE/*France 1899–c1905*
In 1898 a Créanche tricycle won the Coupe des Motocycles: the following year a voiturette won the Louga–St Petersburg race. A Créanche electric car took first place in the 1899 Criterium des Voitures Eléctriques. The 1902 Créanche petrol cars (6 cv, 9 cv, 12 cv) were De Dion-engined: the two larger cars were based on the Chenard-Walcker, while the smaller was a carbon-copy of the De Dion Populaire.

CREMORNE/*England 1903–1904*
A steam car with a 25 hp horizontal four-cylinder engine, 'designed and constructed for solid rubber tyres'.

CRESCENT/*USA 1900*
This tiller-steered 'tri-moto' from the Western Wheel Works of Chicago had a single-cylinder engine driving the single front wheel.

CRESCENT/*England 1913–1915*
Birmingham-built cyclecars of 8·96 hp and 9 hp.

CRESCENT/*USA 1914–1915*
A conventional four-cylinder tourer from Cincinnati: the 1915 Crescents had either a 40 hp Northway four, or 60 hp six. Bodies were patterned on the Lancia.

CRESPELLE/*France 1906–1924*
M. Crespelle made his first cars with De Dion and Aster single-cylinder engines of 1694cc and 2199cc. These were followed by cars with 2982cc Janvier four-cylinder engines. After World War One, Crespelle used various four-cylinder Sergant engines: 1593cc, 2121cc and 2413cc. Before they closed in 1924 they also listed a 1327cc four. After production ceased, Crespelle remained in business making special ohv 'conversion kits' for production side-valve engines.

CREST/CRESTMOBILE/*USA 1899–1905*
Crest, of Cambridge, Mass., were engine manufacturers who built single-cylinder 2¼ hp and flat-twin 4 hp air-cooled engines on De Dion lines.

CREWFORD/*England 1920–1921*
Largely made of Model T parts, the Crewford used an underslung T chassis and Ford engine. Two- and four-seaters were offered.

CRICKET/*USA 1914–1915*
The engine of this Detroit-built cyclecar was on the running board, driving the right rear wheel.

CRIPPS/*England 1913*
A cyclecar with a water-cooled JAP vee-twin.

CRITCHLEY-NORRIS/*England 1906–1908*
Limited production of 40 hp Crossley-engined chain-drive cars was undertaken by this Lancashire bus builder.

CROMPTON/*England 1914–1915*
An aggressively pointed JAP-engined cyclecar, available as a monocar or two-seater.

CROSLEY/*USA 1939–1952*
Radio pioneer Powel Crosley's first small cars had a 580cc twin-cylinder engine, but in 1946 he returned to production in Marion, Indiana, using the Cobra (COpper BRAzed) sheet-steel

1904 22/28hp Crossley

1912 15hp Crossley chassis on test

CROSSLEY/*England 1904–1937*
Crossley of Manchester made four-stroke gas engines in the latter quarter of the 19th century, so it was only natural that they should turn to motor car manufacture. Their first model was a 22 hp four-cylinder car, while an even bigger 40 hp appeared in 1906. A later variation was a 20 hp model, this developing into the long-lived 20/25; after 1910 new 12 and 15 hp cars appeared. The latter model and the 25 hp car saw sterling service in the First World War, the Manchester firm being one of the few manufacturers to continue production throughout the hostilities. The faithful and uprated 25/30 continued in production until 1926, though the first new model of the decade was the 3·8-litre 19·9 hp which was available until 1925. That year saw the arrival of the company's first six, the 18/50, which replaced the 25/30; two years later its capacity was increased from 2·2 to 3·2 litres. Further six-cylinder models followed, the 2-litre in 1928 and the 20·9 hp Super Six of 1931. A sign of the times, however, was the Ten of 1932, having a Coventry-Climax overhead inlet/side exhaust engine of 1100cc; three years later came the Regis range of smaller cars, a Ten and 1½-litre six-cylinder with engines also by Coventry-Climax. They failed to pull the company round, and private car production stopped in 1937, though commercial vehicles were produced up until 1956.

15hp Crossley, c.1913

Crossley 18/50hp six, c.1928

engine, a 721cc four, originally developed for Navy generators. In 1949 it was succeeded by the more reliable CIBA cast-iron unit. The 1949 Crosleys were America's first disc-braked production cars (though the discs, prone to road salt damage, were replaced by drums in 1950). Four models were available: two-door sedan, station wagon, convertible and the nippy Hotshot roadster, which won the Performance Index at Sebring in 1950, and nearly won its class in the 1951 Le Mans 24-hour race. A Super Sports Roadster appeared in 1951, but sales had fallen to 4839 from the 1948 peak of 24,871, and Powel Crosley, having sunk $3 million into the venture, ended it in 1952 after only 1522 Crosleys had been sold that year.

1950 Crosley Hotshot

CROSSLAND STEAM CAR/*USA 1923*
This twin-cylinder steamer presumably existed only in prototype form. Specifications cite a 125-inch wheelbase and disc wheels, with the touring car priced at $1985.

1903 Crouan

CROUAN/*France 1897–1904*
A 6 bhp horizontal twin, the 1903 Crouan car was endowed with five speeds forward and everse—and the column-mounted gear lever also controlled the throttle!

CROUCH/*USA 1899–1900*
W. Lee Crouch, of New Brighton, Pa., built a handlebar-steered steam carriage, as well as the petrol engine for the car built by Doctor Booth of Youngstown, Ohio. Production was centred on Baltimore. From the spring of 1900, these cars were known as 'Columbia'.

CROUCH/*England 1912–1928*
The chain-driven three-wheeler 8 hp Crouch Carette was the first offering from this Coventry firm, though in 1913 a fourth wheel was added. The year 1922 saw the appearance of a front-mounted vee-twin (the first engine had been

centrally mounted) with shaft final drive. The following year a four-cylinder Anzani engine was offered.

CROWDEN/*England 1898–1901*
Formerly the manager of the Great Horseless Carriage Company, Charles T. Crowden invented the chain-geared front-driving cycle and had early experience with steam tramcars and fire-engines. The dog-cart, which he built in his works at Leamington Spa, had a 5 hp single-cylinder engine and three-speed belt transmission. In 1899 Crowden also built a steam shooting brake.

CROWDUS/*USA 1901–1903*
An obscure make of electric runabout built in Chicago, with speed control and braking operated by the steering tiller.

CROWDY/*England 1910–1911*
Crowdy took over Weigel in 1910, and continued the 20/30 hp and 30/40 hp Weigels under their own name. To these they added a 19/24 hp four and 29/34 hp six, aimed at 'the seeker after rational practical progress' with Cooper-Hewitt piston-valve engines and dashboard radiators. A curious body, the 'Canadian Canoe', with a driver's seat adjustable for height and rake, was a feature of these cars (and of another Hewitt-engined car, the Davy).

CROW-ELKHART/*USA 1909–1924*
The first Crow-Elkharts were 30 hp fours, the company's first six appearing in 1915 for $2250. Pricing policy changed totally in 1916, when the 19·6 hp Crow-Elkhart cost only $750 in its cheapest form. Six-cylinder engines re-appeared in 1919, this 4078cc model surviving until 1921, when production reverted to four-cylinder cars only. Some Crow-Elkharts were sold by Black under the name 'Black Crow': about 100 were built in Ontario in 1916–18 known as the 'Canadian Crow'.

CROWN/*England 1903*
A 5 hp light three-wheeled car sold by a Holborn firm.

CROXTED/*England 1904–1905*
Built in Herne Hill, South London, the Croxted car was available with either a 10 hp engine or a 14 hp four-cylinder power unit.

CROXTON-KEETON/*USA 1909–1910*
A brief-lived partnership between H. A. Croxton, of Jewel, and F. M. Keeton produced the 40 hp Jewel-based 'German-type' and the dashboard-radiatored 'French-type' Croxton-Keetons; the latter continued as 'Croxton' until 1914, with four- and six-cylinder engines.

1910 Croxton-Keeton 40hp tourer

CRYPTO-DUPRESSOIR
England 1906–1906
There were in 1905 two models of this assembled car: a De Dion-engined 8 hp single and a 10/12 hp with a two-cylinder Tony Huber engine. The 1906 twin-cylinder 8/10 hp Crypto-Dupressoir used a Bentall engine.

CSONKA/*Hungary 1909–1912*
This Budapest commercial vehicle works also built a few single-cylinder private cars with two-seater bodies and circular radiators.

LA CUADRA/*Spain 1898–1903*
Artillery captain Emilio de la Cuadra began by

8hp Crouch vee-twin, c.1922

building electric cars in his Barcelona factory, then, on a visit to Paris, he met the Swiss engineer Marc Birkigt, who designed first a petrol omnibus for La Cuadra, then a twin-cylinder car of 1101cc with shaft final drive. Few were built before lack of finance closed the factory.

CUBITT/*England 1920–1925*
The Cubitt was intended for mass-production along American lines. The engine was an or-thodox 2·8-litre four with four-speed gearbox and worm drive. The cheaply made body did little to enhance the vehicle's rather hefty appearance and the company later concentrated on making AC engines under licence.

CUDELL/*Germany 1899–1908*
The first Cudells had De Dion engines; from 1904 onwards own-make engines were used. Cudell was one of the pioneers in Germany and used single-cylinder engines of 402cc, 860cc and 942cc before the introduction of the Karl Slevogt-designed 'Phönix' models, big 6100cc four-cylinders developing 45 hp at 1400 rpm. Few of them were actually built, while a 2554cc four-cylinder of advanced design and excellent finish sold in large numbers. Experiments with new designs brought Max Cudell into financial difficulties. After 1905 the remains of the company were transferred from Aachen to Berlin, where Cudell's son Paul continued on a very small scale.

12hp twin-cylinder Cudell, 1903

CUMBRIA/*England 1913–1914*
The Cockermouth-built Cumbria light car was available in two models: a 964cc 8 hp twin-cylinder and a 1107cc 10 hp four.

CUNNINGHAM/*USA 1907–1937*
One of the most prestigious automobiles ever made in the United States, the Cunningham car initially appeared on the motoring scene as an electric in 1907. Manufacturer was the re-nowned carriage-building firm of James Cunningham Son & Co. Inc. of Rochester, New York, which had been in business since 1842. The first electrics were quickly succeeded by gasoline motor cars, assembled cars in the truest sense, with four- and six-cylinder types using engines by Continental as well as Cunningham's own four. After 1910, Cunningham began building cars from its own components and for five years they were put together alongside horse-drawn carriages, the latter being discontinued in 1915. By 1916, the Cunningham had become considerably larger and more powerful, with a new V-8 engine — and much more expensive. Pleasure cars were built, along with funeral

1921 Cubitt 15.9hp tourer

vehicles and ambulances, which had a reputation second to none. In its halcyon years — 1917 to 1927 — the Cunningham car occupied an enviable (if small) position in the American luxury car market, competing with such names as the American Rolls-Royce, largest McFarlan, Stevens-Duryea, Pierce-Arrow, Locomobile 48 and Packard Twin-Six, prices on closed Cunninghams frequently exceeding the $10,000 price tag. The make used its own coachwork almost exclusively, and quality was maintained up to the end of manufacture, although by 1931 the Cunningham was regarded by many as an anachronism. The last Cunninghams were built in 1931, although several of these were sold in 1932 and designated 1932 models. Cunningham then concentrated on its hearse and ambulance business, though continued to build an ever-increasing number of bodies for other chassis. The company also produced a number of town-car bodies for use on Ford V-8 chassis, the last of these being made in 1937. The company survives to this day as a manufacturer of crossbar switches.

CUNNINGHAM/*USA 1951–1955*
Wealthy sportsman Briggs Cunningham built his prototype C-1 sports car in 1951; it had a tubular chassis and was powered by Chrysler's new hemi-head V-8. It was closely followed by the C-2R in open and closed body styles, with the engine output boosted from 180 to 300 bhp. Three C-2Rs competed at Le Mans in 1951, but engine trouble put paid to their chances. The vastly improved C-4R, driven by Cunningham himself, came fourth in the 1952 Le Mans, and the torsion-bar-suspended C-5R came third overall the next year, with C-4Rs seventh and tenth. A 16-valve Offenhauser four powered the unsuccessful 1955 Le Mans contender, the C-6R. Cunningham, spending $50,000 annually

on his Le Mans attempts, called it a day. There was a production Cunningham car, too, the Michelotti-designed C-3 coupé, with automatic transmission and a 220 bhp hemi; there was also a 200 bhp road-going C-4.

CURRAN STEAM CAR/*USA 1923*
Curran was a builder of commercial vehicles and only two steam touring cars were made, using a three-cylinder motor and carrying a wheelbase of 128 inches.

CURTIS/*USA 1921*
A little-known Arkansas car, the Curtis used a Herschell-Spillman four-cylinder engine. Few were made.

CURTISS/*USA 1920–1921*
The Curtiss was a sporting car made in very limited numbers — perhaps as few as two — using a converted Curtiss OX-5 aircraft V-8 engine and a Phianna chassis. The car was made at Hammondsport, New York.

CUSSET/*France 1896*
Built at Levallois-Perret, this car had a single-cylinder horizontal engine with forced induction provided by a 'compressing cylinder' — the first supercharger?

CUTTING/*USA 1909–1912*
Successor to the C VI, the Cutting 40 was a shaft-drive four selling for $1650. A stripped chassis covered 200 miles at 65·75 mph in a race at Indianapolis in May 1910.

C VI/*USA 1907–1908*
Designed by Charles D. Cutting, the first 6178cc C VI 'Cutting Six' was completed in February 1907. The factory, at Jackson, Michigan, only built about 50 roadsters and tourers annually.

CWS/*Poland 1922–1929*
A 3-litre four built in Warsaw, equipped with four-wheel brakes.

CYCAR/*England 1920*
A. E. Parnacott of Penge, motor agent and prolific correspondent to the light car press, offered this 11·9 hp two/three-seater, 'proof against road shocks and guaranteed to run 50 miles per gallon'.

The curious 1921 Cyclauto

CYCLAUTO/*France 1919–1923*
A small three-wheeled cyclecar made at Sur-esnes by the Compagnie Française du Cyclauto. The engine was at the front of the tubular cycle-style frame, and the car was driven by the back axle. The first engine was a two-stroke twin-cylinder SICAM of 497cc, and they then used four-cylinder sv Ruby engines of 903cc and 950cc.

CYCLOMOBILE/*USA 1920*
A small car with a vee-twin Spacke air-cooled engine and a 90-inch wheelbase, the Cyclo-mobile was marketed as a two passenger wire-wheeled roadster at $425. The dummy radiator was the car's gasoline tank. The 1921 Manexall was a development of this vehicle.

CYKLON/*Germany 1902–1929*
Cyklon of Berlin was a pioneer motorcycle producer and, with their Cyklonette (1902–22), also a leading manufacturer of three-wheelers. Their final product was an 1825cc car nearly identical to a similar Dixi model, which also had components in common with some other factories — including NSU — which were then controlled by the Schapiro concern. For this concern, Cyklon also built from 1923 to 1927 a very popular 1300cc four-cylinder 20 hp car with a sv engine. The bodywork was made by Schebera, another factory belonging to Schapiro, who was also closely connected with Benz. The French Zedel works supplied some engines to Cyklon.

CYRANO/*France 1899*
A voiturette built under Elie Lacoste patents at Bergerac by Richard Popp, similar in appearance to that built by Lorenz Popp in Basle, Switzerland. It had a twin-cylinder engine with belt drive, and two- or four-seater *vis-à-vis* coachwork.

1899 Cyrano car from Bergerac

1919/20 Cunningham phaeton Model V-3

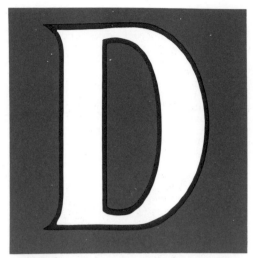

D.A.C./*USA 1922–1923*

Prototypes only were made of the V-6 Detroit air-cooled car. Featuring an own-make 2553cc engine, the car was mounted on a 115-inch wheelbase chassis. List price of the touring car was $1250.

DAF/*Holland 1958–1975*

Truck and trailer makers at Eindhoven, DAF introduced a twin-cylinder 600cc car — the 'Daffodil' — with 'Variomatic' belt drive at the 1958 Amsterdam Show. A 750cc development, the '33', appeared in 1962, followed in 1967 by the Michelotti-styled 850cc '44'. A four-cylinder 1100cc Renault engine was used on the '55' of 1968; a sports version appeared in 1969. Volvo of Sweden took a share in — and eventually control of — DAF after a 1974 reorganization. DAF's largest model, the 1300cc Marathon, formed the basis of a new model built as a Volvo.

DAF 44

DAGMAR/*USA 1922–1927*

One of the sportiest-looking automobiles of its time, the first Dagmar cars, a spin-off of the Crawford of Hagerstown, Maryland, featured disc-covered artillery wheels, brass trim and straight 'military' wings. Generally painted in pastel colours, the cars were produced in two sizes, featuring Continental or Lycoming six-cylinder engines. Several hundred Dagmars were manufactured. The make also acted as a base model for both the Standish automobile and the Luxor taxicab.

DAGSA/*Spain 1957–1959*

Defensa Antigas SA of Segovia built this 500cc saloon car, also available as a pickup.

DAIHATSU/*Japan 1954 to date*

Starting with the 540cc Bee three-wheeler, Daihatsu introduced their first four-wheeler, the 797cc Compagno, in 1963, adding a fuel-injected 958cc model in 1967. A 360cc minicar was also offered. In 1969 came the Consorte range — still in production ten years later — with 958cc and 1166cc engines. The 'Fellow Max', a 550cc flat-four, appeared in 1970, and in 1974 came the Charmont, with 1166cc and 1407cc power units.

DAIMLER/*Germany 1889–1902*

In 1885 Gottlieb Daimler, one of the great motoring pioneers, built his first — and last! — motorcycle, fitted an engine to a carriage in 1886, and in 1889 completed the 'Steelwheeler', with a 566cc vee-twin engine, designed by his assistant, Wilhelm Maybach. He exhibited this car at the 1889 Paris World-Exhibition and sold a production licence to Levassor; 1890 saw the foundation of the Daimler Motoren Gesellschaft at Cannstatt (now part of Stuttgart). Daimler then introduced his 1060cc two-cylinder belt-driven car, succeeded in 1897 by the 5507cc four-cylinder Phönix sports and racing car. This attracted the Consul-General of the Austro-Hungarian Empire at Nice, the wealthy Emil Jellinek, who influenced Maybach to design a lower-built, lighter car, which Jellinek called after his elder daughter, Mercédès. This appeared in 1901 — shortly after Daimler's death. Mercedes cars soon showed their supremacy, even over a new car designed by Daimler's son Paul, which was built at the Austrian Daimler factory at Wiener Neustadt.

1893 Cannstatt-Daimler phaeton (Chicago World Fair exhibit)

1897 Cannstatt-Daimler 'Phönix'

DAIMLER / *England 1897 to date*

Floated in 1896 by H. J. Lawson, Daimler of Coventry began production a year later with a 4 hp two-cylinder car based on the Panhard: one of these was the first car to travel from John O'Groats to Land's End. Over the next five years, a complex range of two- and four-cylinder cars was turned out under the aegis of J. S. Critchley; these were succeeded in 1902 by a three-car line-up designed by Edmund Lewis. One of the first buyers of the new 22 hp model was King Edward VII, whose purchase of a 6 hp in 1900 had marked the start of a long Royal patronage for Daimler. Up to 1908, fours and sixes of 3·3 to 10·4 litres were produced: then Daimler exchanged performance for refinement with the adoption of the Knight sleeve-valve engine. A merger with BSA in 1910 saw some rationalization of the two ranges. Post-war Daimlers, launched in

November 1919, were two 30 hp models and a 'special' 45 hp. Four-wheel brakes were standardized in 1924, as were thinner sleeve-valves for greater power outputs. Four '57 hp' Daimlers were built for King George V that year. In 1926 Daimler's chief engineer, Laurence Pomeroy, designed the complex 'Double-Six', a sleeve-valve V-12: Pomeroy also introduced, in 1930, the Fluid Flywheel which, combined with the Wilson preselector gearbox, gave a simplicity of control unrivalled until the advent of automatics. Sleeve-valves were phased out in the mid-1930s: Pomeroy introduced a 4·6-litre poppet-valve straight-eight in 1936, soon joined by three straight-sixes (though a few prestige poppet-valve V-12s were also built). Coil-spring independent front suspension appeared in the late 1930s on Daimler and their sister marque, Lanchester, acquired in 1931. The post-war range—

DB18 2·5-litre and DE27 4·1-litre sixes and 5·5-litre eight — was based on pre-war designs. A 3-litre six appeared in 1950; a four-cylinder variant, used in a new Lanchester 14, was the basis of the 1953 Daimler Conquest. A performance version, the 100 bhp Conquest Century, was current from 1954 to 1958. Also launched in 1953 was the 3-litre Regency, developed through a 3·5-litre version into the 3·8-litre Majestic of 1958, and Majestic Major 4·5-litre of 1960. In 1960, Jaguar bought Daimler, and the marque thereafter — apart from specialist models like the glass-fibre-bodied SP 250 sports designed by Edward Turner — was largely based on contemporary Jaguar bodies and running gear, though the pre-merger engines were used for a number of years. A V-12 Jaguar engine powered Daimler's 1973 Double-Six, while the limousine had a 4·2-litre XK power unit.

The Hon. John Scott-Montagu's 1899 12hp Daimler: passenger is Edward VII, then Prince of Wales

c.1909 Daimler 22hp phaeton

1977 Daimler Sovereign 3.4

1946 Daimler DD-18 2½-litre

DAIMLER-MERCEDES (BRITISH-MERCEDES)/England 1907–1908

The British & Colonial Daimler-Mercedes Syndicate of London commissioned these licence-built copies of the contemporary Mercedes from the Yorkshire Engine Company, locomotive engineers from Sheffield. Two models were available, a 35 hp four of 5322cc and a 50/60 hp six (7893cc). They differed from their prototype in mechanical detail, such as the use of a disc clutch instead of the famous Mercedes scroll clutch, and were considerably cheaper (chassis price of the 35 hp was £680, against £1010 for the comparable Mercedes). About 50 Daimler-Mercedes were built before the sales company's refusal to pay further royalties brought a lawsuit which ended the project.

DALIFOL/France 1896

A horizontal-engined petrol car from a firm better known for its steam motorcycles.

DALIFOL & THOMAS/France 1898–1899

Two separate De Dion engines powered this voiturette, built in the Dulac factory at Montreuil-sous-Bois. In 1899 came a motor tricycle with a 'Dust-proof' two-speed constant-mesh gearbox.

DALILA/France 1922–1923

A light car with all-round independent suspension on similar lines to the Citroën 2CV. Ruby engines of 903cc and 967cc were used.

DALLISON/England 1913

Weekly production of 50 of these five-speed, worm-drive cyclecars was envisaged.

DAMAIZIN & PUJOS/France 1910

Built chassis with a patented constant-mesh gear change. May also have been known as 'Dux'.

DANA/Denmark 1908–1914

The Copenhagen-built Dana cars had friction transmissions with belt final drive. Engines were first air-cooled single-cylinder Peugeots, then twin-cylinders from the same source. From 1913 a proper gearbox was used. The cars weighed only about 250 kg, and were popular as long as heavy cars were banned on Danish minor roads.

DANIELS/USA 1915–1924

One of the highest regarded motor cars of all time built in the United States, the Daniels of Reading, Pennsylvania, was built by G. C. Daniels, erstwhile president of Oakland. The car was powered by an own-make V-8 engine after 1919 and the stylish body styles for both open and closed models were in demand by the affluent. This was a large car with a high rounded radiator, identified only by the letter 'D' on the hubcaps. In 1923, the car was sold to a Philadelphia motor combine which attempted to assemble and sell a handful of Daniels sedans at $10,000, a considerably higher price than the earlier models. These later cars were not made with the care which had become associated with the Daniels name and the 1924 cars were the last of the line. Many of the closed models sported bodies by Fleetwood.

DANSK (DANSK FABRIKAT, CHRISTIANSEN)/Denmark 1901–1908

Cudell-engined three-wheelers and a prototype four-wheeler were built in 1899 by H. C. Christiansen, who was an enthusiastic cyclist and the owner of a Copenhagen cycle repair shop. In 1901 he founded the company, and at the 1902 automobile exhibition in Copenhagen nine cars were shown, ranging from 2 hp to 6 hp. Five cars were sold, having single-cylinder engines with two forward speeds. In 1902 Copenhagen's first taxi was delivered, but it was found to be too noisy and the rest of the fleet was fitted with Oldsmobile engines. Their first four-cylinder engine came in 1906 in a more civilized car with three-speed gearbox and shaft drive. Probably around 75 chassis were built, many of these commercials.

The 5cv Remi-Danvignes Sport 750

DANVIGNES/France 1937–1939

A small sports car made by a motorcycle agent in Paris. Two-seater and roadster bodies were available: power units were a 750cc twin or a 1100cc Ruby.

D'AOUST/Belgium 1912–1927

Light sporting cars were the *forte* of this Brussels-based firm. Their 1912 10/14 cv formed the basis of post-war production, along with a bored-out 2-litre sports model, which had fwb from 1924. There were also two light cars, a 6 cv and an 8 cv.

DARBY/USA 1909–1910

Billed as 'the simplest automobile on earth' the $800 Darby, from St Louis, was claimed to 'spin over the road like a monster touring car or dodge around city corners like a bicycle'.

A Darl'Mat Peugeot in the 1937 Le Mans race

DARL'MAT/France 1936–1950

Parisian Peugeot agent Emile Darl'mat made sports cars based on the Peugeot 302 chassis with the 402 engine which were successful at Le Mans. Made in very limited numbers, they were offered in three versions: roadster, coupé and drop-head coupé. After the war Darl'mat made several more cars based on the Peugeot 203.

Darmont-Morgan racer c.1923

DARMONT/France 1920–1939

Ex-Morgan racing driver and French agent for the Malvern three-wheelers, M. Darmont built replicas of the British trikes under his own name. These were powered by air- or water-cooled 1084cc vee-twins by Blackburne or JAP. Darmont also built some vee-twin-engined four-wheeled cars in the late 1930s under the name of 'Etoile de France'.

1920/22 Daniels 8 phaeton with victoria top

DARRACQ / *France 1896–1920*

Born in Bordeaux of Basque parents, Alexander Darracq sprang to notice when, in partnership with one Aucoc, he founded the Gladiator cycle company, selling out to a British combine five years later. His first motor cars were electric cabs, but the design was dismissed as 'worthless', and he turned to the manufacture of tricycles and quadricycles, then spent £10,000 on the acquisition of Léon Bollée's patents, and turned out a horrid belt-drive machine called the Darracq-Bollée. A neat voiturette appeared in 1900, this 6½ hp single being quickly followed by two- and four-cylinder models, which in 1904 acquired Darracq's distinctive chassis, pressed, together with its undershield, from a single sheet of steel. British capital reformed the company in 1905, and thereafter a complex range was available, from a 1039cc 8 hp single to an 8143cc 50/60 hp six. Disastrous fours with Henriod rotary valves appeared in 1912, a 2613cc 15 hp (uprated to 2951cc the next year) and a 3969cc 20 hp: these proved so unreliable that profits dwindled to almost nothing. M. Darracq quickly decided to retire (he had never really liked cars anyway, could not drive and did not like to be driven) and took a share in the Casino at Deauville. Darracq was taken over by Owen Clegg, who introduced a 1913 range based on his excellent Rover Twelve, with monobloc L-head engines of 2121cc and 2971cc: a 4084cc model was added in 1914. This was used by the French Army during the war, and was joined in 1919 by an advanced sv V-8 of 4595cc. A merger with Sunbeam-Talbot came in 1920, and Darracqs became 'Talbots' in France (but were still sold as 'Darracqs' or 'Talbot-Darracqs' in England until 1939).

1900 Darracq tonneau

1924 Talbot-Darracq 14hp

1905 Darracq 8hp 'Genevieve', star of the film

1907 Darracq 40hp six-cylinder

DARRIN / *USA 1946*

Howard 'Dutch' Darrin of Los Angeles designed and built this $1950 five-passenger car powered by a 90 hp Continental six-cylinder engine. The convertible body was constructed from four glass-fibre panels. Torsion-bar suspension at the front and semi-elliptic springs at the rear were used.

DARRIN / *USA 1955–1958*

Using the Kaiser-Darrin sports car frame (originally designed for the now defunct Kaiser company) car stylist Howard Darrin fitted a Cadillac engine to increase performance. Despite mechanical and styling alterations, only five of these $4350 cars were built.

DART / *USA 1914*

A vee-twin cyclecar built in Jamestown, NY, by the world's largest makers of voting machines.

DASSE / *Belgium 1894–1924*

Pair-cast 14/16 hp (2799cc) and 24/30 hp (4942cc) fours were offered by this Verviers firm — which had started with a belt-drive single-cylinder three-wheeler — in 1912. Few cars were built post-war, the firm turning to commercial and military vehicles, though two ohv fours, a 12/14 hp and a 30 hp were shown at the Brussels Salon.

DATSUN (NISSAN) / *Japan 1931 to date*

Originally Datson (from its three backers, Den, Aoyami and Takeuchi), Datsun was founded in Yokohama, though after the war production centred on the Tokyo area. Its main product during the 1930s (during which the Nissan company name was adopted) was an Austin Seven-based 750cc model (though a proposal to build the 10 hp Ford under licence came to nothing). Big cars based on the Graham-Paige appeared in 1937. Post-war, production resumed in 1947 with models again derived from Austin designs, then, in 1955, the 110 saloon appeared: its 1959 derivative, the 310, was the first of the Bluebird line. Also in 1959 the first Datsun 2000 appeared. A prestige model for the home market, the President, appeared in 1964, followed two years later by the Datsun 1000. In

1935 Datsun Type 14 Sedan

1966, too, Datsun merged with Prince Motors. Important new models followed: the 510 Bluebird, of 1967, with 1300cc and 1600cc ohc engines, the 1800 Laurel of 1968 and the 240Z sports six-cylinder, which was to win the East African Safari Rally twice. Then the 1000 was replaced by the 1200, and a new fwd model, the

100A Cherry, launched, finding its greatest favour in export markets. By the mid 1970s a comprehensive range included the Cherry, 120Y Sunny, 140J/160J Violet, Bluebirds of 1·6 to 2 litres, ohc 2-litre Laurel, 260Z Sports and the 3-litre straight-six and 4-litre V8 President.

1979 Datsun 280ZX

1979 Datsun Cherry coupé

LE DAUPHIN/*France 1941–1942*
This tandem-seated cyclecar was made during the first year of the German Occupation in Paris to provide a cheap and economic means of transport. It was available with 100cc and 175cc two-stroke Zurcher motorcycle engines or electrically powered.

DAVID/*Spain 1914–1922, 1951–1957*
José Maria Armangué, frustrated from representing Barcelona in a bobsleigh contest for lack of snow, fitted the sleigh with cycle wheels, starting a craze for engineless 'down cars' which became a dangerous pastime for young Barcelonese. A club was formed, and Armangué and his three brothers fitted a JAP engine and belt drive to a 'down car', creating a cyclecar which they christened the 'David'. A company — Fabrica Nacional de Cyclecars David — was formed on 14 July 1914, and was soon in full production, but now using vee-twin MAG engines. Later Davids also had four-cylinder Ballot power units. A noteworthy feature of the David was its independent front suspension. David cyclecars enjoyed many sporting suc-

1916 David

cesses. In 1917, José Maria Armangué was killed in a flying accident, and the company passed into the ownership of his collaborators José Maria and Ramon Moré. Oddly, the last production David cyclecars were taxis for Barcelona. The David company thereafter operated taxis and hire cars — mostly Citroëns — though in the Civil War some electric cars were built. Between 1951 and 1957 three-wheelers powered by a single-cylinder 345cc two-stroke engine were built in small numbers.

DAVID & BOURGEOIS/*France 1898*
This tiller-steered saloon had a 'square-four' engine developed by Paul Gautier.

DAVIS/*USA 1908–1930*
Starting with four-cylinder Continental-engined models, by 1914 this Richmond, Indiana, company was offering a 50hp Continental-engined six, and after 1915, built six-cylinder cars only. A small six, of 3670cc, was launched in 1915, and became the company's principal offering. The 1924 range had eccentric model names: 'Legionaire', 'Man O'War', 'Broudan'. An eight appeared in 1927 and like its sister marque, 'New York Six', had the Parkmobile easy parking device. The Davis also formed the basis of the Canadian Winnipeg (1923) and its successor, the Derby (1924–27).

DAVIS/*USA 1947–1949*
Built by Glenn Gordon Davis, this well-known three-wheeler could seat four people abreast. It had a four-cylinder 60hp Hercules engine, disc brakes all round, and aerodynamic styling with a detachable metal roof and push button operated doors. It was claimed that this untippable car could turn a smaller circle than standard cars at 55mph and that its top speed was 116mph, making it the fastest American car of its day. Seventeen prototypes were built but never reached production, due to Davis' conviction on a fraud charge.

DAVIS STEAM CAR/*USA 1921*
The Davis Steam Car only existed in prototype form — if that! The twin-cylinder Davis was announced as having a 120-inch wheelbase. The touring car was priced at $2300.

DAVIS TOTEM/*USA 1921–1922*
As many as ten Davis Totem cars were manufactured. The car boasted friction drive like the contemporary Kelsey and Metz and used a four-cylinder Herschell-Spillman engine. The five-passenger touring car was listed at $1695.

DAVRIAN/*England/Wales 1966 to date*
Now based in Wales, Davrian Developments first produced their dumpy, rear-engined sports car in West London. Its glass-fibre monocoque was designed to accept Hillman Imp subframes and engine, as well as Ford, Mini and VW units.

DAVY/*England 1909–1911*
An unorthodox Manchester-built car, the 12/18hp Davy had a 2·2-litre Hewitt piston-valve engine, 'two-speed clutch, and two-speed back axle' and two-seater 'Canadian Canoe' bodywork 'specially suited for Colonial use'. There was also a long-stroke 18/24hp 3·2-litre.

DAWSON/*England 1899–1901*
Like the vintage Dunelt motorcycle, the Dawson had a double-diameter 'top-hat' piston, though Mr. Dawson missed the supercharging potential of this layout. Instead, he used the lower piston to pump air into a reservoir, this compressed air being used to start the engine. A complex valve system also allowed the pumping piston to scavenge the cylinder at the bottom of each exhaust stroke and inject pure air at the start of each induction stroke.

1898 David & Bourgeois four-cylinder cab

DAWSON/*USA 1900–1902*
A twin-cylinder steam 'Auto-Mobile' from Basic, Virginia, capable of 25–30mph.

DAWSON/*England 1919–1921*
Ex-Hillman works manager A. J. Dawson conceived this handsome quality light car with an ohc 1795cc four and Bentley-like radiator: some 65 were built. Triumph took over the factory.

DAY-LEEDS/*England 1913–1925*
The first car built by Job Day of Leeds (makers of tea-packing machinery) was a twin-cylinder cyclecar of 804cc, succeeded in 1914 by a 10hp four-cylinder 1287cc light car, which formed the basis of post-war production.

DAYTON/*USA 1914*
This factory built three to four Spacke-engined cyciecars daily at its peak.

DAYTON ELECTRIC/*USA 1911–1915*
A complex range of electric cars from Dayton.

DB/*France 1938–1961*
Charles Deutsch and René Bonnet started with a Citroën-engined racing car before the war.

An early prototype DB sports

After the war they made a few more racing cars with Citroën engines but quickly turned to Panhard-engined 'Racer 500s', following those successful cars with a larger version, the 'Monomille' 750cc, built in sufficient numbers to justify their own junior formula in France. They also made some Panhard-engined sports-touring cars with glass-fibre bodies and engines from 850cc to 1300cc. After the end of their association in 1961 the two men made cars under two different names, CD and René Bonnet.

DEAL / *USA 1905–1911*
A four-seater high-wheeler with wheel steering.

DEASY, SIDDELEY-DEASY
England 1906–1919
Designed by E. W. Lewis, formerly with Rover, the original Deasy (made in Coventry) was a 4½-litre with ample braking and adjustable steering column. By 1909, however, two huge fours, of 8621cc and 11,947cc, headed the range. J. D. Siddeley joined Captain Deasy's company that year, and introduced the JDS 4084cc four with coffin-nosed bonnet and dashboard radiator, plus Lanchester worm-drive and cantilever rear springs. It was soon joined by a 2654cc 14/20 hp. On 7 November 1912, the company changed its name to Siddeley-Deasy and brought out two Knight sleeve-valve-engined models, a 3308cc 18/24 hp four and a 24/30 six of 4694cc, plus poppet-valve models of 1944cc and 3308cc. A poppet-valve 4962cc six was announced for 1914: war halted production, and the company merged with Armstrong-Whitworth in 1919 to form Armstrong Siddeley.

DE BAZELAIRE / *France 1908–1928*
Famed for their voiturettes, by 1909 De Bazelaire were offering a twin-cylinder 12/14 hp available in two chassis lengths with gearbox in unit with the differential. In 1910 a sports model

1905 Decauville landaulette

with a 1645cc engine and a Fischer slide-valve-engined six of 2540cc appeared. Other models used Ballot or Janvier engines — the 1914 Sport had a long-stroke (80 × 180mm) engine of 3619cc. After the war, De Bazelaire built a wide range of four-cylinder cars from 6 to 15 hp with SCAP, Ballot and Janvier power units.

DECAUVILLE / *France 1898–1911*
Narrow-gauge locomotive engineers of Petit-Bourg (Seine et Oise), Decauville acquired the rights to the Guédon car and christened it *La Voiturelle*; its two-cylinder De Dion-based engine drove the rear axle through naked and unlubricated two-speed gears. Sliding pillar ifs (and *no* rear suspension save the air in the tyres) characterized the Voiturelle, which was licence-built in Italy by Orio et Marchand, in Germany as the Wartburg. In 1900 a front-engined 5 hp model appeared, joined by a snub-nosed 8 hp twin with horseshoe-shaped dashboard radiator. A 3-litre four arrived in 1901; the neat 10 hp twin of 1902 with unit engine/gearbox construction inspired Henry Royce to build his first car. By 1906, the five-car range consisted of fours (12, 16, 24, 30 and 45 hp) but was cut to only the 12 and 16 hp in 1907.

DE CEZAC / *France 1922–1926*
A manufacturer from Périgueux who, after the Great War, built a handful of cars with 1203cc CIM and 1692cc Ballot engines.

DECHAMPS / *Belgium 1889–1906*
Déchamps of Brussels made Panhard-type cars of 7 hp (single), 9 hp (twin) and 20 hp (four). The 1902 Déchamps range was said to be the first to be fitted as standard with electric starters. From 1904 to 1906 they built the single ohc 15 hp and 25 hp Baudouin.

1902 Dechamps tonneau

De Dion Bouton

DE DION BOUTON/*France 1883–1932*
Comte Albert de Dion backed the mechanics Bouton and Trépardoux in the production of steam carriages during the 1880s and early 1890s. Trépardoux devised the 'De Dion axle' for power transmission on their heavy steam brakes, but resigned in 1894 because De Dion and Bouton were dabbling with petrol engines, which he regarded as heresy. Bouton's single-cylinder petrol engine of 1895 ran at speeds of up to 3500 rpm on test, and powered sporting tricycles, built until 1901. A quadricycle appeared in 1899, and was quickly supplanted by the rear-engined 3½ hp model D voiturette of 402cc. De Dion also produced engines in vast numbers for other

manufacturers — by 1904, over 40,000 power units had been completed at their Puteaux factory. By 1902, the rear-engined model had a 6 hp engine; it was then supplanted by the 8 hp Model K, with a front-mounted engine under a crocodile bonnet. This retained the neat two-speed expanding clutch transmission of its predecessor. Up to the war, all De Dions had *decelerator* pedals. The firm's first twin-cylinder car, the 12 hp S, came in 1903, and fours of 15 and 24 hp appeared two years later. By the end of 1906, all models had conventional gearboxes, and the last 8 hp single was made in 1908. In 1910, De Dion introduced the first production V-8 of any real merit, a 6·1-litre model, subsequently available with

swept volumes of 7 litres, 7·8 litres and 14·7 litres, the latter aimed at the US market. The De Dion axle was dropped in 1911, and the last single-cylinder engined model, the DE 1, was built in 1913. The V-8 was built up to 1923, alongside dated fours; then in 1923 came the ohv 12/28, with aluminium pistons and fwb available as an extra. In decline, the factory struggled on until 1927, and was temporarily closed down. It reopened with a new 2·5-litre straight-eight, offered alongside a 2-litre four, but few of either were sold, despite an uprating of the eight to 3 litres in 1930. The last car, an 11 hp, was delivered in 1932, but the company built trucks until the late 1940s, then became a service garage. The name was last seen on motorcycles in the 1950s.

1899 De Dion Quadricycle

1907 8hp single-cylinder De Dion Bouton

1907 De Dion Bouton 30/40hp

1923 De Dion Bouton 12/28hp

DECKERT/*France 1901–1904*
This Parisian firm offered a 6 hp single, 12 hp and 16 hp twins and a 20 hp four.

DE COSMO/*Belgium 1903–1908*
The designer of the first FNs, J. de Cosmo, was responsible for these pair-cast fours of 24/30 hp (sold in Britain as the Wilkinson) and 30/35 hp. A 45/55 hp six appeared in 1906.

DE CROSS/*USA 1913–1914*
A tandem-seat 1100cc vee-twin cyclecar.

1914 Deemster 10hp

DEEMSTER/*England 1914–1924*
The Ogston Motor Company of Acton, largely staffed by former Napier employees, was responsible for the Deemster, a light car of 1100cc capacity, with an engine of their own manufacture. Adventurous plans to manufacture the Deemster in America in 1923 at a price of $1100 came to nothing. In 1923 the Deemster succumbed to a proprietary engine, a 12 hp Anzani being available. Although it was never in the sports car league, no less a personage than Kaye Don raced a Deemster.

DEEP SANDERSON/*England 1961–1969*
Morgan devotee Chris Lawrence has been associated with a number of projects over the years, not least the Deep Sandersons. Fourteen of these rear-engined, Mini-powered 301 coupés were built, while various prototypes were raced at Le Mans.

DEERE/*USA 1906–1907*
Built by the famous plough manufacturer John Deere, of Moline, Illinois, this 'car of quality and style' sold for $2000.

DEERING MAGNETIC/*USA 1918–1919*
The Deering Magnetic was designed by Karl H. Martin, designer of both Roamer and Kenworthy and builder of Wasp motor cars. Featuring a Dorris six-cylinder engine and the Entz electric transmission—made famous by the Owen Magnetic—it sold for a substantially lower price. The car was probably over-priced for its time, some models selling in excess of $7000, and it failed before many units had reached their market.

DEETYPE/*England 1974 to date*
Conceived by automotive engineer Bryan Wingfield, with bodies built by Grand Prix Metalcraft Ltd., the Deetype is a beautifully fashioned and remarkably faithful replica of either the 1956 or 1957 (the choice is yours) Jaguar D-Type Le Mans cars. With laudable devotion, Wingfield constructs each car in his home workshop.

DE FRANCE/*France 1923*
A Ballot-engined light car from Vierzon (Cher). Two ran in the 1923 Bol d'Or.

1923 De France cyclecar

DEGUINGAND/*France 1928–1930*
After the closure of the Vinot-Deguingand works at Puteaux, the marque resumed production for a few years with a 735cc two-stroke four-cylinder 5 hp cyclecar designed by M. Violet, which were made alongside the Galba and Huascar.

DEHN/*Germany 1924*
Built soon after Germany's runaway inflation, this was a short-lived, simple cyclecar with an air-cooled 346cc motorcycle engine.

DELAGE/*France 1905–1959*
Louis Delâge started in Courbevoie with a single-cylinder De Dion-engined car. This was later followed by a 1460cc four-cylinder 9 cv, numerous 12 cv models and a six-cylinder of 2588cc, but it was not until the post-war period that Delage production became really significant. The first of the much-admired Delage cars was the CO of 1918, with a six-cylinder 20 cv engine of 4532cc. That car became the CO2 in 1921. The 1920s saw many racing successes for Delage: the most successful touring cars of the period were the DI of 2120cc and the GL with an ohc 30 cv engine of 5945cc. There then came a long line of six-cylinders like the ohv DM of 3174cc and the sv DR of 2516cc. In 1929 Delage presented their first straight-eight, the 4060cc D8, from which the D8S sports evolved. In 1932 came the D6 11 of 2100cc, and two years later the new eight-cylinder D8 15 of 2700cc. When Delage was forced to sell to Delahaye, some cars were continued, such as the 4300cc D8 100, the D8 120 and the 2700cc D6 70. After the war a six-cylinder model was advertised as a Delage by Delahaye, but the name eventually disappeared.

1907 Coupe des Voiturettes Delage

Delage six-cylinder – 1929 Paris Salon Exhibit

1920 Type CO 4½-litre six-cylinder Delage sports torpedo

1949 Delage D6 3-litre

DELAHAYE

DELAHAYE/*France 1894–1954*

Founded in Tours by Emile Delahaye, a pioneer of motoring, this company started by making belt-driven single- and twin-cylinder cars. The founder left the factory in 1901, one year after a second factory was opened in Paris. From 1908 Delahaye made more interesting cars with four cylinders like the 9 hp of 1460cc and the 12 hp of 2120cc, which were continued until the war together with a V-6 of 2565cc. Delahayes were exported, but also made under licence in Germany and America. After the war Delahaye was mainly involved in making lorries, motor ploughs and fire engines. Now little interested in cars, they nevertheless made some reliable models like the four-cylinder 1847cc and 2950cc and six-cylinder 4426cc. In 1934, Delahaye presented two new cars, the four-cylinder 12 cv (2150cc) and the six-cylinder 18 cv (3200cc). In 1935 came the most famous Delahayes, the six-cylinder ohv 3·2 Coupe des Alpes and the 3557cc '135'. In the same year Delahaye bought Delage, perpetuating that marque on cars built with Delahaye components. Delahaye was successful in racing, and the touring cars sold very well. Famous coachbuilders such as Figoni, Chapron and Letourneur et Marchand made lovely bodies for these cars. Delahaye was also involved in making lorries and armoured vehicles. After the war the 135 was resumed and the 175 of 4·5 litres was presented in 1948. In 1951 came the last new Delahayes: the Jeep-Delahaye, a very advanced vehicle, and the 235 of 3·5 litres. Hotchkiss took over Delahaye in 1954 and only built lorries. These were given the name of Hotchkiss-Delahaye for a few months, and were then known as Hotchkiss.

1896 Delahaye phaeton

1915 Delahaye 12/15hp Type 64

1930 Delahaye 16cv six-cylinder Type 122

1948 Delahaye 135MS

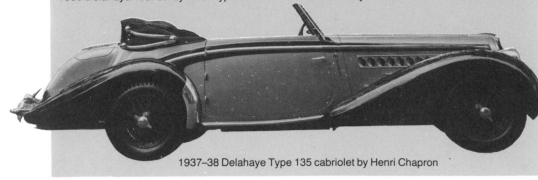

1937–38 Delahaye Type 135 cabriolet by Henri Chapron

DELAUGERE ET CLAYETTE
France 1900–1926

Delaugère et Clayette, of Orléans, started with a Romain-engined 2 hp tricycle. The 1902 Delaugères had 12 cv and 20 cv four-cylinder engines, and could run on petrol or alcohol. Chain drive was available until 1908. In 1911, Delaugère et Clayette presented a six-cylinder model of 4252cc, and in 1913 came a four-cylinder of 2723cc with a Fischer sleeve-valve engine. After the war, they continued with four-cylinder models of 1692cc, 2155cc and 3329cc, and a six of 4993cc. The works eventually collapsed, despite making small lorries.

1913 Delaunay-Belleville 40hp limousine

DELAUNAY-BELLEVILLE
France 1904–1950

This famous engineering firm from Saint Denis started with Marius Barbarou as engineer, building 16, 24 and 40 hp four-cylinder cars. But the six-cylinder engine was to become a feature of Delaunay-Belleville design, and the four-cylinder an exception. The marque was considered in France as the ultimate in cars and their round radiator — recalling the famous Belleville marine boilers — was well known. The smallest six-cylinder they made before World War One was the 12 hp of 2913cc and the biggest was the 45 hp of 7998cc. After the Armistice, Delaunay-Belleville resumed production with pre-war models, including the 1914 14/16 hp of 2129cc. In 1922 the 2613cc 12 hp four-cylinder acquired an ohc. By the late 1920s the Delaunay-Belleville had lost its 'prestige'; some unimportant models were made with American engines like the Continental straight-eight. The last true Delaunay-Bellevilles were the 3180cc and 3619cc ohv sixes. At the very end, after World War Two, Delaunay-Belleville built the tiny De Rovin cars in their works.

DE LA VERGNE/*USA 1895–1896*

A single-cylinder engine of 2234cc powered this Benz-derived car built by the New York Refrigerating Company. Its designer, La Vergne, built cyclecars in 1914.

DELCAR/*USA 1947–1949*

Built by American Motors of Troy, New York, the Delcar produced extremely compact delivery cars and station wagons. With a wheelbase of only 5 feet and a four-cylinder engine under the floor, the Delcar was able to utilize maximum carrying space in the smallest area.

DELECROIX/*Belgium 1899*

A twin-cylinder De Dion-engined voiturette which could be 'reversed at discretion'.

1924 Delfosse sports

1913 Delta voiturette

1903 Denis de Boisse 12cv chassis

DELFOSSE/*France 1922–1926*
Very few Delfosse cars were made at Marly-les-Valenciennes, but the range included a Chapuis-Dornier-engined 6/8 hp of 961cc, an 8/10 hp also powered by Chapuis-Dornier, an Altos-engined 1200cc and some six-cylinder CIME-engined cars of 3446cc.

DELIN/*Belgium 1899–1901*
Starting with an fwd voiturette with 2¼ hp De Dion engine, Délin progressed to a 3½ hp model with chain-driven rear axle, and also built larger chain-drive models.

DELLING/*USA 1923–1927*
Erik H. Delling, ex-Mercer designer, was behind this limited-production twin-cylinder steamer, available in open and closed models.

DELLOW/*England 1947–c1958*
Sturdy road-going competition cars designed primarily for use in Trials, Dellows had Ford mechanicals in a purpose-built chassis.

DEL MAR/*USA 1949*
The Del Mar prototype, from San Diego, Ca., resembled the contemporary Hillman. It used a four-cylinder Continental engine and a three-speed Warner transmission. Ford transverse leaf spring front suspension was used and either semi-elliptic or transverse springs at the rear.

DE LOREAN/*Northern Ireland 1979 to date*
Production of the exotic De Lorean DMC-12 sports car was due to begin at a purpose-built complex in West Belfast sometime in 1979. Of American origin but linked with Lotus and backed by £40 million of the British taxpayer's money, the De Lorean looks set for a bright future, with sales aimed at the USA.

1979 De Lorean

DELTA/*France 1905–1914*
M. de Colange, of Puteaux, Seine, built a range of Delta cars in 1905, but the marque was most active circa 1913 with a neat 10/12 hp light car with a 1470cc monobloc four-cylinder engine.

DELTA/*Denmark 1918*
Delta cars were assembled from parts bought in the USA. About 20 chassis were bought before the war, but they could not be delivered until after the Armistice. The engine had four cylinders and the radiator was rather similar to that of the Rolls-Royce.

DELTA/*USA 1925*
The Delta is one of the big American car mysteries. No one knows where or exactly when it was built. It is believed that this car, a touring model with six-cylinder Continental engine and 133-inch wheelbase, was a prototype constructed over a period of years up to 1925.

DE LUXE/*USA 1910*
A 'car on two wheels' from Cleveland.

DE MARCAY/*France 1920–1922*
A GN-like cyclecar with 1000cc Anzani vee-twin engine and shaft drive, built by a former aircraft manufacturer.

DEMEESTER/*France 1906–1914*
Leon Demeester of Paris built voiturettes with single-cylinder (358cc) and four-cylinder 10 hp (1303cc) power units in 1907. By 1912, fours of 10, 12 and 16 hp were listed, and the company also built the ultimate Sinpars.

DE MOT/*USA 1910*
This two-seater roadster from Detroit ('DEtroit MOTor') had a two-cylinder engine.

DENIS DE BOISSE/*France 1900–1904*
A 12 cv twin-cylinder light car with a patented double back axle was this marque's final product.

1902 Dennis 8hp phaeton

DENNIS/*England 1898–1914*
Cycle builders John and Raymond Dennis, of Guildford, Surrey, marketed motor tricycles in 1898, followed a year later by the rear-engined 3½ hp Speed King Light Doctor's Car, priced at £135. Car production, however, really began in earnest in 1901 with an 8 hp single and a 12 hp twin, both with tubular chassis and shaft drive. An Aster-engined 16/20 hp four appeared in 1903, as did a one-off 40 hp Simms-engined 'Gordon Bennett' racer. The 1904 season saw the introduction of a Dennis hallmark—a worm-drive back axle and in 1906 the marque standardized on White & Poppe engines (and eventually bought that company). Up to the outbreak of war, Dennis listed big fours of 18 to 40 hp (and a 60 hp six only built between 1909–11): their success in the commercial vehicle field caused private car production to be permanently suspended after 1914.

1952 Denzel-Sport with VW engine

DENZEL/*Austria 1948–1960*
Developed by ex-motorcycle racer Wolfgang Denzel at Vienna, these cars used basically VW and Porsche components. Denzel tuned the 1192cc VW engines for his hand-built sports cars and Porsche supplied 1290cc and 1582cc units.

147

DE P/*England 1914–1915*
Designer De Peyrecave had built the De P Duo cyclecar since 1910: the De P was a 1496cc Dorman-engined light car of sporting pretensions built in Deptford, London SE. A £136 cyclecar was also listed.

DERBY/*France 1921–1936*
Derby started by making a small 1000cc vee-twin Harley-Davidson-engined cyclecar. The second model, announced in 1921, had an 808cc Chapuis-Dornier engine. They later enlarged their production to Chapuis-Dornier-engined cars of 916cc and an ohv 950cc, also making sports cars with Ruby and 1100cc SCAP engines, some being supercharged. They also built larger cars with CIME engines of 1680cc, 1786cc and a 2·3-litre six. At the very end of production, Derby launched two front-wheel-drive cars, with four-cylinder and V-8 engines.

DERBY/*USA/Canada 1924–1927*
The Canadian Derby automobile was actually the American Davis with a different insignia for the Canadian market. Centre of Derby operations was Saskatoon, Saskatchewan, Canada. Total 'production' over four years of operation totalled 31 cars!

DER DESSAUER/*Germany 1911–1913*
Successor to MWD, the 'Der Dessauer' was produced in a big new factory at Dessau, which proved more expensive than the owners could afford. They produced a 2100cc 24 hp four-cylinder car in quite large numbers, but could not prevent financial disaster. Earlier models had 18 hp and 22 hp engines.

1913 Der Dessauer 2100cc four

DEREK/*England 1925–1926*
Four-cylinder side-valve and overhead-valve Chapuis-Dornier engines, rated at 9/20 or 10/25 hp respectively, were options available in the Derek light car, made in London's West Norwood.

DE RIANCEY/*France 1898–c1901*
A front-wheel-drive voiturette with an air-cooled flat-twin engine.

DE SANZY/*France 1924*
A cyclecar made in Paris with a single-cylinder two-stroke 350cc engine, wooden chassis and plywood body.

DESBERON/*USA 1901–1904*
Initially built steam trucks and 4 hp petrol 'pleasure carriages' on 'French lines'. Later cars were of 6·2 litres and of 12 hp.

DE SCHAUM/*USA 1908–1909*
From Buffalo, NY, this marque offered a 7 hp high-wheeler called 'Seven Little Buffaloes'.

DE SOTO/*USA 1913–1916*
From Auburn, Indiana, and unconnected with Chrysler's De Soto marque, this was a 55 hp six-cylinder selling at $2185.

DE SOTO/*USA 1928–1960*
Launched as a lower-priced running mate for the Chrysler, De Soto's first product was a 3·2-litre sv six. A 3·5-litre straight-eight appeared in 1930, with four-wheel hydraulic brakes. From about 1931, the marque was sold in Britain as a Chrysler. Its 1933 models featured all the Chrysler innovations such as 'floating power' engine mounting, while the 1934 models followed the Chrysler Airflow line with a 4-litre six featuring optional overdrive. Vee-bonnets were adopted in 1936, and a dummy radiator grille and rear-hinged bonnet featured on 1937 models. By 1939, ifs, a choice of two six-cylinder engines and steering-column gearchange were offered, with Vacumatic semi-automatic transmission available in 1941. Though the post-war models had bodies in common with Chrysler, the 1949 Carryall car-cum-station wagon was unique to De Soto. The L-head six was joined in 1952 by a 4525cc Firedome V-8, which sold 45,800 units in its first year, and soon outsold the sixes two to one. Attractive new styling heralded the 1955 FireFlyte series, with a 200 hp V-8 of 4769cc. From then on, V-8 engines powered all De Sotos, except for the export-only Diploma (a thinly disguised Plymouth). In 1956 came the limited-production Adventurer, with a gold-on-white paint scheme, gold trim and a 5595cc hemi-head V-8. New FlightSweep styling — and the low-priced FireSweep series, powered by a new 5326cc V-8 — boosted De Soto sales to a record 117,747 in 1957. However, poor quality control cut the next year's sales to 35,556. The new wedge-head V-8s (5916cc or 6276cc) boosted 1959 sales slightly, but not enough. The 1961 models, with canted fins, 'two-tier' grille and 5916cc engine, had only been out for four months before De Soto ceased production on December 18, 1960.

1929 De Soto K-series roadster

DE TAMBLE/*USA 1908–1913*
This 10/12 hp two-cylinder car was built by the Speed Changing Pulley Company, of Indianapolis, makers of the Carrico air-cooled four-cylinder engine, who also sold complete shaft-drive chassis to other manufacturers. For 1910, the four-cylinder 4-34 model was announced.

De Tomaso Pantera

DE TOMASO/*Italy 1959 to date*
Ex-racing driver Alessandro de Tomaso, born in Argentina, and his wife, American ex-racing driver Isabell Haskell, moved to Italy in the late 1950s. There De Tomaso built various prototypes — including racing cars. Today he owns Moto Guzzi and Benelli, two leading motorcycle factories and his Modena-based De Tomaso car works ... besides many other industrial interests. During an association with Ford came his first production car, the Mangusta, with a 4728cc V-8 Ford engine and a Ghia coupé body. Later, in 1970, the 5796cc V-8 Pantera appeared. It was a sports coupé with a top speed of 162 mph. The same year, the Mangusta acquired a bigger, 4949cc V-8 engine and there was now also the 5796cc Deauville, which had luxurious limousine bodywork. New in 1972 was the 'Longchamp', a luxurious coupé. Built in small numbers, these expensive cars are under steady development. By 1979 the range included the 300 bhp mid-engined Pantera L, the 330 bhp Pantera GTS, and the 300 bhp Longchamp and Deauville.

1933 De Soto SD-series

1958 De Soto Fireflite

DETROIT/*USA 1899–1900*

This was Henry Ford's first venture into commercial manufacture of horseless carriages, though he had already built two experimental cars. But the Detroit Automobile Company was short-lived, and no more than a dozen cars and vans were built. One of their more distinctive features was a 'single lever which by a forward and backward movement through the space of about 12 inches, starts the engine and controls the forward speeds and backup, doing away with the confusion arising from a multiplication of levers'.

DETROIT/*USA 1904–1907*

The Detroit 22/24 hp was a $1500 flat-twin with shaft drive whose main claim to fame was that its exclusive selling agent was John North Willys, subsequently of Willys-Overland.

DETROIT ELECTRIC/*USA 1907–1938*

Probably the best-known and best-selling electric car built in the United States, the Detroit Electric sold upwards of 1000 cars annually, prior to World War I, peak production being reached from 1912 to 1915. In 1920 a false bonnet was provided as an option for any buyer who disliked the boxy, 'museum showcase' appearance of the original design. Although to all intents and purposes the electric car was outmoded by 1920, a loyal but small clientele continued to purchase them. The final models featured Willys-Overland coachwork as a concession to modern design, but the older pattern featuring the fore and aft battery covers was still available, safety glass and balloon tyres being the only noticeable changes. A handful of the last Detroits used Dodge bonnets and grilles.

1914 Detroit Electric

DETROITER/*USA 1912–1915*

Also known as the Briggs-Detroiter, this was a 16/20 hp four-cylinder, which sold in Britain for £200. A 3·3-litre V-8 appeared in 1915.

DETROIT STEAM CAR/*USA 1922–1923*

Initially, this was advertised and marketed under the name 'Trask-Detroit', the name being changed for the 1923 model year. Very few of these twin-cylinder automobiles were built, all touring cars. The makes carried a 'Windsor' nameplate for cars to be sold in Canada.

DEUTZ/*Germany 1907–1911*

Ettore Bugatti designed this range of big cars with ohc engines of 4960cc, 6400cc, 9900cc and even 10,500cc at Cologne for Gustav Langen, who then headed the Deutz factory. After producing yet more big cars, Bugatti also created a small 1327cc four-cylinder in which he

1911 9900cc Deutz 38/65hp Type 8a

competed in some events, but which was never built at Deutz. It was with this design that he founded his own works at Molsheim (Alsace), although still continuing design and development work for Deutz. The last Deutz car had a 2600cc four-cylinder 30 hp engine; it was built in small numbers only, as these high-class Deutz cars were quite expensive.

DEVAUX/*USA 1931–1932*

The DeVaux was an economy car introduced at an economically inauspicious time and the hoped-for sales of this six-cylinder line of automobiles did not materialize. With only a few thousand units built, the DeVaux failed in 1932 after some 14 months of production. The assets of the company were taken over by the Continental Motors Co. of Detroit and Muskegon, Michigan, which marketed the cars for the remainder of that year as the Model 80 or DeVaux-Continental. The cars were facelifted and sold as Continentals in 1933 and 1934. In Canada, as a part of Canadian Durant, they were marketed as 'Frontenacs'.

DE VECCHI/*Italy 1904–1907*

Fast and comparatively sporting cars which proved successful in many sporting events. Engines—mainly ioe four-cylinder—were made by De Vecchi: 1908 models were a 16/20 hp (shaft-drive) and a chain-drive 18/24 hp. Ugo Sivocci, who was killed at Monza in 1923 driving an Alfa Romeo, was a De Vecchi driver in his early years.

DEVIN/*USA 1958–1960*

Devin Enterprises of El Monte, California, normally manufactured glass-fibre kits (starting price $295) suitable for small foreign car chassis. In 1959 they produced a complete car—the Devin SS—priced at $5950. Powered by a 220 hp V-8 Chevrolet engine it attained 60 mph in 5·6 seconds.

DEW/*USA 1928*

The Dew was named after the initials of its builder, D. E. Willis, who gained a kind of prominence by designing the Willis nine-cylinder car the same year as the smaller three-cylinder Dew. Like the larger car, only one pilot model was built.

DEWALD/*France 1902–1926*

Dewald seem to have built only one-offs to order until 1912, when a complex line-up was offered, ranging from 10 hp to 60 hp: the following year only 14 hp and 24 hp fours were offered. A straight-eight of 4·8 litres was listed in 1924.

The De Wandre Ford, an 'elegant spider'

DE WANDRE/*Belgium c1923*

A wire-wheeled sports car based on the Model T Ford.

DEWCAR/*England 1913–1914*

The original 482cc single-cylinder Dewcar cyclecar was as basic as could be, as its main chassis/body structure consisted of two planks on edge, joined at the front. It sold for £60, a high price considering the crudity of its construction. There was also a 6 hp vee-twin: these models were replaced by 4½ hp single and 8 hp twin Dewcars in 1914.

DEXTER/*France 1906–1909*

Sporting cars from Lyon with four- and six-cylinder engines of 50 to 100 hp.

1922 interior-drive DFP 12cv

DFP/*France 1906–1926*

The Doriot, Flandrin et Parant works in Courbevoie made lively single-cylinder 1100cc cars up to 1910, but from 1909 they had also offered an 8/10 cv four of 1874cc. From 1911 they abandoned proprietary engines to build their own, the 12/16 cv of 3015cc and the 10/14 cv of 2001cc. The latter was still being made when DFP restarted production after the war. Forced to return to proprietary engines, DFP made cars with 2001cc ohc Altos, 1847cc Sergant and even 1098cc CIME power units. In 1926 the DFP factory was bought by Théophile Lafitte.

DFR/*France 1924*

In 1924, the well-known motorcycle factory run by MM. Desert and De Font-Reaulx built a number of 893cc SCAP-engined light cars.

DIABLE/*France 1921–1924*
A three-wheeled, two-speed cyclecar from Paris with a twin-cylinder 1096cc engine.

DIAL/*England 1971–1974*
Many improvements were made to the futuristic mid-engined Dial Buccaneer before its demise. Final examples featured alloy space frame chassis, and lightweight bodies allowing exciting performance from almost any chosen power unit.

DIAMANT/*France 1901–1906*
'Combining all the improvements to date of any importance in motor engineering', the 1904 Diamant range consisted of a 12 hp twin and a 24 hp four-cylinder. (Also sold as 'La Française'.)

DIAMOND T/*USA 1905–1911*
Powerful touring cars (up to 70 hp) from a Chicago company later famed for its trucks.

DIANA/*England 1900*
A 5 hp three-seater voiturette built by Lewis & Lewis, Fulham, with 'new patent-speed-changing arrangement'. It sold at 165 guineas.

DIANA/*USA 1925–1928*
The Diana, introduced in mid-1925 as 'Queen of the Eights', was a companion car to — and built by — Moon. Powered by an eight-cylinder Continental engine, the car had a radiator copied from that of the Minerva. The cars were popular; one sporting model, a roadster, featured bronze radiator, wire wheels and bright bodywork. Prices ranged from $1595 to $2895 — plus a hardly seen town car, available to special order only, which retailed at $5000!

DIATTO/*Italy 1907–1929*
Diatto originally built a range of Clément-based two- and four-cylinder models. During the 1920s they built superb cars, partly designed by the famous Alfieri Maserati, who established his own factory in 1926. Together with his brothers, he also created a supercharged eight-cylinder ohc racing car, which eventually formed the basis for the first Maserati. Production Diatto cars had ohc 1990cc four-cylinder engines of advanced design and even had four-wheel brakes and four-speed gearboxes as early as 1922. There was also a 2980cc four-cylinder Diatto, which was built in limited numbers.

DIAZ Y GRILLO/*Spain 1914–1922*
The Diaz y Grillo (or D y G) was a sporting light car built in Barcelona. Initially a twin-cylinder Blumfield engine was used: latterly four-cylinder Ballot and MAG engines were employed.

DIEDERICHS/*France 1912–1914*
Though the Diederichs family had built prototype vehicles in 1878 and 1899–1901, production did not begin at Charpennes (Rhône) until 1912, using 10/12 cv Luc-Court four-cylinder engines.

DILE/*USA 1914–1916*
'Distinctively individual', the $485 Dile light car came from Reading, Penn.

DIM/*Greece 1977 to date*
The 594cc Dim, from Athens, is a two-door saloon with Fiat 126 mechanicals.

DININ/*France 1904–1907*
Long-range electric cars from Puteaux (Seine).

DINO/*Italy 1966 to date*
A mid-engined car built by Ferrari at Modena. Named after Ferrari's only son, Dino, who died young, the original Dino was a superb car with Pininfarina bodywork and Ferrari-designed 2418cc V-6 mid-engine. Following this 246 GT came the 246 GTS in 1972, which now had — like the 246 GT — an engine built by Fiat, of which Ferrari had become a part. A new Dino appeared in 1974: it was the 308 GT4 with a 2926cc, 225 bhp V-8 engine and a 2 + 2 seater coupé body. Today's Dino range includes the improved 308 GT4, with Bertone-designed and Scaglietti-built coupé coachwork, and a dohc 225 bhp V-8 engine. A smaller model, the 1975-introduced 208 GT4, has a 1991cc 170 bhp engine. This too is a mid-mounted V-8.

DINOS/*Germany 1921–1926*
Successor to the LUC built by Loeb of Berlin (1909–14), the sporting Dinos was designed and also driven by Robert Dunlop, whose Dinos factory at Berlin was financed by the Stinnes Group, which also controlled AGA, Rabag-Bugatti and Stolle. After the death of Stinnes, Dinos became part of AGA. Dinos built a 2100cc four and a 4050cc six; both had own-make ohc engines with detachable cylinder heads. Production was concentrated on the four.

DIRECT/*Belgium 1904–1905*
This 40/50 hp four-cylinder car from Brussels had no gearbox, but its clutch was said to give 'speed reductions by variations in pressure'.

DISK/*Czechoslovakia 1925–1926*
This car was a 660cc twin-cylinder two-stroke car, the first attempt by the Brno-Zidenice Arms Factory ('Z') to produce a small, cheap car. Designer was B. Novotny. Only a few were built before the factory introduced the 'Z' car.

DIVA/*England 1961–1966*
During Diva's five-year reign a number of front-engined and six mid-engined competition cars were built and raced with success. Only three genuine road cars were made. Known as 10Fs,

they were based on the front-engined GT, but featured heavier gauge bodies.

DIXI/*Germany 1904–1928*
Dixi ('I have spoken') cars succeeded the Wartburg in 1904, in which year they introduced a 2815cc four-cylinder. That year also saw a new single-cylinder of 1240cc and a twin-cylinder of 2468cc. A 6800cc four-cylinder came into production in 1907. There were many more models built, including a 1320cc four-cylinder with side valves. Improved versions of 1568cc appeared after the war. Two six-cylinder models of 2330cc and 3557cc appeared in the mid-1920s. Before the war, the 'Wartburg' trade mark was changed to 'Dixi' and in 1927 it was this factory which acquired the licence for the manufacture of the Austin Seven. They built it at Eisenach but ran out of money, and BMW of Munich took over the design and the works.

1928 Dixi 3/15hp (licence-built Austin Seven)

DIXIE FLYER/*USA 1916–1923*
The Dixie Flyer was an assembled automobile using Lycoming and Herschell-Spillman four-cylinder engines throughout its relatively brief life. In 1922 Dixie Flyer and Jackson were both absorbed by National and the Dixie Flyer became the National Model 6-31 for 1923, after existing '1923' Dixie Flyers had been sold.

DKW/*Germany 1928–1966*
Founded by Jörge-Skafte Rasmussen, DKW built its first two-stroke motorcycles in 1919, and, after building SB and DEW electrics, used a similar wood-framed chassis-less construction on its first petrol-powered DKW two-stroke cars at their Berlin-Spandau works in 1928. The first cars had 584cc twin-cylinder engines, followed in 1930 by water-cooled V-4 models with two-stroke engines which had 780cc and —

1931 DKW 584cc Sportwagen

1962 DKW Junior 741cc

later—992cc engines. The first front-wheel-drive two-stroke 490cc and 584cc two-cylinder models left the works in 1931. Up to 1939 DKW produced two-stroke cars in 684cc and V-4 1047cc versions. They were good, but not always very economical. In 1928 Rasmussen bought engine production equipment from Rickenbacker in the USA and afterwards produced big six- and eight-cylinder engines for Audi and other firms. In 1932 DKW became part of the Auto Union Group, consisting of DKW, Audi, Horch and Wanderer. After 1945, all these works became nationalized, as they were geographically in an area which became the DDR. New Auto Union factories in West Germany at Ingolstadt and Düsseldorf came into being in 1949 and built fwd DKW cars with 684cc twin-cylinders and soon after three-cylinders of 896cc. They were again two-stroke cars with water-cooling and vertical cylinders in line. They developed 23 bhp and 34 bhp, while later three-cylinder versions developed 38 bhp and also 40 bhp. The Auto Union DKW '1000' of 1957 got a new three-cylinder 980cc engine which had 44 bhp, afterwards 50 bhp at 4500 rpm, while the 'Special' was supplied with 55 hp motors. They were two-stroke cars with fairly thirsty engines. The trend led to four-stroke engines and to the first 'New' Audi. Mercedes (Daimler-Benz) bought the works in 1958 and sold it to VW in 1965, by which time Mercedes had developed the first engine for the Audi. The last two-stroke DKW was produced in February 1966.

1922 Doble Phaeton

DL/*Scotland 1913–1915*
A 10 hp monobloc 1307cc four-cylinder from Motherwell: an 8 hp was also available.

DMC/*England 1914*
Taking its name from the local area of ducal seats, the Dukeries Motor Company of Worksop, Nottinghamshire, built two models of cyclecar, a 578cc 4½ hp single-cylinder and a 964cc twin.

DOBELLI/*Italy 1904*
A 'mechanical prodigy' from Rome, the Dobelli was a monstrous 180 hp two-seater with five forward speeds, which Friswells of London offered for sale. Its huge four-cylinder engine had a displacement of 31,625cc, valves 114mm in diameter, and was accommodated under a 5ft 6in long bonnet.

DOBI/*Spain 1919*
A Madrid-built cyclecar with a British Douglas flat-twin engine.

DOBLE/*USA 1914–1932*
Abner Doble's first production steam cars appeared in 1915–17, advertised as 'Doble-Detroits'; the war halted the project, and production did not restart until 1924, in Emeryville, California. But his zeal for perfection prevented production from ever attaining anything like the anticipated momentum, and no more than 45 Doble steamers were built. However, in its final form the Doble could reach a full head of steam in under 90 seconds from cold, could run 1500 miles on 24 gallons of water, thanks to an efficient condenser, and had a 75 bhp four-cylinder engine giving exceptional acceleration and hill-climbing powers.

The 180hp Dobelli, a 'mechanical prodigy'

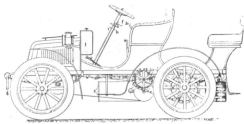

1901 Gaillardet (Doctoresse)

DOCTORESSE/*France 1899–1902*
Designed by Gaillardet, these 6 cv and 12 cv cars from Suresnes took their odd name from the fact that 'like a doctor, they were always ready to render service'.

DODGE/ *USA 1914 to date*

Built at Hamtramck, Detroit, the Dodge car was a 3·5-litre four with a dynastarter which operated automatically if the engine stalled. By 1916, the marque was America's fourth biggest; by 1920 the 'Dependable Dodge' was second only to Ford. All-steel coachwork was adopted as early as 1916, stop-lamps and anti-theft locks were offered from 1923. The new Senior Six, with hydraulic fwb, appeared in 1927; the four was replaced by a cheaper 'Victory' six in 1928, in which year Chrysler bought the company for $126 million. A Chrysler-based straight-eight appeared in 1930, as did a 2·6-litre six. The eight was dropped in 1933, but Senior and Victory Sixes were now lavishly equipped. Dodges never adopted Chrysler's 'Airflow' styling, but were otherwise closely patterned on the sister marque; 1936 saw automatically engaged overdrive standardized on the Senior Six. Though the post-war cars used the basic pre-war designs, styling was freshened-up, with fenders swept into the doors and a chequerboard grille; all models used the 3769cc six. All-new models — Wayfarer, Meadowbrook and the top-of-the-line Coronet — appeared for 1949, with

1916 Dodge touring car

1929 Dodge Standard Six

1967 Dodge Dart GT convertible

the 3769cc six coupled to Fluid-Drive transmission (as before) or with the new option of GyroMatic semi-automatic transmission. In 1953 came Dodge's version of the Chrysler hemi-head V-8, the 3949cc Red Ram, initially only available in the Coronet, but by 1955 standardized on Royal and Custom Lancers and optional across the rest of the range. The 1957 range had Virgil Exner's 'Forward Look' styling with high fins and compound-curved windscreens, and unitary construction arrived on the 1960 range. Standard models were renamed Matador and Polara, and the intermediate Dart range — Seneca, Pioneer and Phoenix — was launched. The faithful L-head six was replaced by an ohv slant six of 3687cc, standard in Seneca and Pioneer. Dodge styling had lost its fins by 1962, when the Lancer compact (based on the Plymouth

Valiant) made its bow, powered by a 2785cc six; it only lasted two seasons, the Dart taking over as Dodge's compact in 1963. The most expensive 1963 model, the new Custom 880, shared a Chrysler bodyshell. In 1966 came the performance Charger model, with a 5211cc V-8 as standard, and units up to a 425 bhp V-8 of 6891cc as options; these engines also powered the handsome 1968 Charger, capable of 0-60 mph in 4·75 sec. Only available for 1969, a limited edition performance model, the Charger-based Daytona, had a long aerodynamic nose and two huge stabilizer fins. The popular Dart series carried Dodge into the 1970s, while on the performance front the Charger was joined by the Challenger, with the slant six as standard and the V-8s up to the 425 bhp version optional. Top of the range was the luxury Monaco. In 1972, Dodge introduced the Mitsubishi Colt of 1598cc to the US market, where it sold quite well. In 1975, the Charger was totally redesigned, with a bodyshell in common with Chrysler's Cordoba; its performance image was traded for a 'personal luxury car' specification. New for 1976 was the Aspen compact with the 3687cc six (or optional V-8s of 5211cc or 5899cc), which supplanted the Dart, and offered a sporty 'Super Coupé' with front and rear spoilers. A new Challenger appeared for 1978, based on the Colt, with 2540cc 'Silent Shaft' engine, four-wheel disc brakes and five-speed manual transmission. Also new for 1978 were the Diplomat (based on Chrysler's LeBaron) and the luxury Magnum XE, derived from the Charger SE. But the big news of 1978 was the Omni fwd compact, with a 1753cc VW engine (rumours suggest Chrysler will soon produce their own small four); a 2+2 hatchback version appeared for 1979, in which year the Monaco luxury model was replaced as Dodge's flagship by the St Regis.

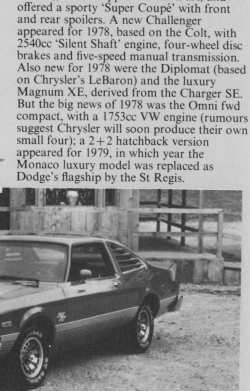

1979 Dodge Aspen R/T

DODGESON/*USA 1926*
John Duval Dodge, son of John F. Dodge (one of the original Dodge Brothers who built the Dodge Brothers car), was engineer and designer of the Dodgeson which featured a 3167cc straight-eight rotary-valve engine producing 72 bhp at 3000 rpm. Prototypes were built and experiments were made. Although the Dodgeson was pronounced a success, the car never went beyond the experimental stage.

1913 Dodson
12/16hp tourer

DODSON/*England 1910*
Built in two models, a three-speed 12/16 hp and a four-speed 20/30 hp, the Dodson was 'practically a replica of the Renault', built in Huddersfield by David Brown Limited. Up to late 1912, the obsolescent quadrant gear change was standard.

DOHERTY/*Canada 1895*
Stove-maker Tom Doherty of Sarnia, Ontario, actually built and operated a three-wheeled prototype car worked by a giant clock spring.

DOLLY/*England 1920*
A four-cylinder water-cooled engine was the motive power of the Dolly. A slanting engine/gearbox unit obviated the need for a universal joint in the propeller shaft.

DOLPHIN/*England 1906–1909*
The Dolphin used a two-stroke engine designed by Harry Ricardo: this had separate pumping and working cylinders in vee-formation. The prototype had a 12/15 hp 'twin' power unit, but the majority of the dozen or so cars produced had 28/30 hp engines with four working cylinders. Most of the orders received seem to have come from indulgent members of the Ricardo family.

DOLSON/*USA 1904–1907*
The 'mile-a-minute' Dolson, from Charlotte, Mich., had a 60 hp engine: 20 and 28 hp models were also listed.

DOME-O/*Japan 1978 to date*
A limited-production 'dream car' built by a group of enthusiasts.

DOMINION/*Canada 1910–c1915*
A 3942cc 35 hp four built in Walkerville, Ontario, to the design of E. W. Winans, formerly with Regal in Detroit. As New Dominion, the firm struggled on for three years after a 1911 liquidation.

DOMINION/*Canada 1914*
This American-backed company planned to assemble six-cylinder cars shipped from Britain at the port of St John, New Brunswick, ice-free all year round.

DONNET/*France 1924–1933*
The small Donnet was the successor to the Zedel. They tried to survive by producing a small 7 cv of 1098cc and an 11 cv of 2120cc. In 1926 Donnet presented a six-cylinder model of 1866cc. Marcel Violet built a small car like his Huascar for Donnet, with a 750cc twin-cylinder two-stroke, but shortly afterwards the works passed into the hands of Simca.

DONOSTI/*Spain 1923*
A 3-litre 16-valve sports car built by the Garage Internacional of San Sebastian.

DORA/*Italy 1899–1907*
This Genoa firm built a few electrics.

Doré fiacre, 1898

DORE & BOUISSOU (DORE)
France 1898–c1900
The steering-pivot of this twin-cylinder carriage also acted as a shaft for the pinion driving the front axle. A petrol car was later built under the 'Doré' name, and the Doré motor was used as the basis of an ingenious fraud by Walter K. Freeman, the 'auto-acetylene swindler' (late of Sing Sing) who claimed it as a new type of motive power to attract credulous investors.

DOREY/*France 1906–1907, 1912–1913*
A French-Canadian resident in Paris, Dorey built both chassis and complete cars: in 1906–07 single (De Dion) cylinder and four-cylinder voiturettes, and in 1912 a twin cyclecar.

DORIGNY/*France 1898*
The 'Inseparable' was a rear-engined tricycle seating two side-by-side on saddles, each with their own handlebars and brakes.

DORMANDY/*USA 1903–1905*
All told, only four Dormandy automobiles were built, combining the talents of a mechanic in a buggy works and an employee of a shirt factory! Four-cylinder air-cooled engines were used for all the cars, the last of them being a Frayer-Miller. The cars were built at the request of J. K. P. Pine, president of the United Shirt & Collar Co. of Troy, New York, and were used by Mr. Pine, his two sons, and Gary Dormandy, an employee and the builder of the cars.

DORRIS/*USA 1905–1926*
George P. Dorris was an early automobile manufacturer in St Louis, Missouri, who had produced several lines of cars from 1897 to 1905 named after the city of their origin (see St Louis). Thereafter all Dorris cars (and commercial vehicles) carried the name of their maker. After World War I, the Dorris became one of the country's better known luxury automobiles, limited production notwithstanding. Prices of the cars in the 1920s ran as high as $7000 for closed models and although 'production' as such ceased in 1923, Dorris cars could be obtained on special order until 1926.

DORT/*USA 1915–1924*
In 1886, J. Dallas Dort, a clerk in a hardware store, invested $1000 for a half-share in the new Durant-Dort carriage company, which soon became America's biggest, producing 150,000 vehicles in 15 plants, and went into the motor business in 1903, producing the Buick car. Dort began building cars under his own name in 1915. The first Dorts were 2720cc Lycoming-engined fours: the 1918 Model 11 had a 3146cc Lycoming, and one pedal-operated clutch and parking brake, the other the 'emergency' brake. The 1921 range was totally re-styled, with an angular radiator shell: this, however, was supplanted by a rounded, nickeled radiator a couple of years later. An ohv 3205 six joined the range in 1923 and became the sole Dort chassis in 1924.

DOUGLAS/*England 1913–1922*
A 10 hp flat-twin light car built by the famous Kingswood, Bristol, motorcycle company.

1920 Douglas 8hp cyclecar
at Brooklands

DOUGLAS/*USA 1918–1920*
The former Drummond car, the Douglas featured an eight-cylinder Herschell-Spillman engine. The few cars sold in 1920 were in all probability left-over 1919 models.

DPL/*England 1907–1910*
A 12/15 hp bonnet-less landaulet with flat-twin engine built by Dawfield, Philips, of West Ealing, Middlesex.

DRAGON/*USA 1907–1908*
A son of the tramcar builder J. G. Brill, of Philadelphia, built this four-cylinder car, using proprietary components. In January 1908, the company changed hands: only 35 hp two-seater roadsters were available to the public, as the main output became taxicabs.

DRAGON/*USA 1921*
Although the Dragon looked almost identical to the contemporary ReVere, there was no connection between the two. A 3620cc Midwest four-cylinder engine was used. Wire wheels were standard and open models only were available, although plans were made for a taxicab. Probably no more than a dozen units were completed.

DRAKE SIX/*USA 1922*
Built by the Drake Motor & Tyre Mfg. Co., of Knoxville, Tenn., only a single prototype of the car (and one of a truck) was produced. The car featured a six-cylinder Herschell-Spillman engine, was equipped with disc wheels and was otherwise conventional throughout. Wheelbase was 127 inches and the touring car was listed at $2195. A smaller model was planned but never built.

DREYHAUPT/*Germany 1905*
A simple car with a two-cylinder 10 hp De Dion engine built in very limited numbers. Most parts were supplied by other companies.

DRIGGS/*USA 1921–1923*
The idea of the Driggs car was to emphasize economic value in size with meticulous detail in construction or, as its slogan stated, 'Built with the Precision of Ordnance'. Using a four-cylinder own-make engine of 1596cc, the 104-inch wheelbase Driggs was available in two open body styles as well as a coupé and a sedan. Relatively few were manufactured. In 1915–16, the company built the Driggs-Seabury cyclecar, as well as Ritz, Sharon and Twombly light cars.

DRI-SLEEVE SPECIAL/*England 1971–1972*
Whether Ettore would have approved of it or not, the Dri-Sleeve replica of his type 37 Bugatti was built to exactingly high standards. A ladder chassis, housing a Cortina engine, supercharged or unsupercharged, was clothed in a mixture of aluminium and fibre-glass. Despite anomalies like the large alloy wheels the flavour was unmistakably Bugatti. Six were sold.

DRUMMOND/*Scotland 1908–1909*
The first Drummond was built as a personal car for D. M. Drummond of the North British Ironworks, Dumfries: 16/20 hp cars of similar design were marketed in 1908 and 1909.

DS/*England 1978*
Costing around £120, the DS Spyder kit does for the Triumph Spitfire what the Arkley does for the Sprite/Midget — gives a fresh, individual look to ageing or rusting examples.

DSPL/*France 1910–1914*
Failed aeroplane builder Comte Pierre D'Hespel, of Premesques, near Pérenchies (Nord), built sporting four-cylinder cars with shaft drive. A 2815cc 12/13 hp DSPL was shown at the 1912 Paris Salon. D'Hespel not only built his own engines and coachwork, but also patented wheels with detachable rims.

DSR/*France 1908–1909*
This Parisian model had its epicyclic gearbox incorporated in the back axle.

DUAL-GHIA/*USA 1955–1958*
Gene Casaroll, head of Dual Motors, a haulage firm in Detroit, used Chrysler components, the 5162cc Dodge D-500 with engine and bodywork designed by Ghia, to make this Italian assembled car priced at $7646. Available either as a four passenger hardtop or convertible, the cars had Powerflite transmission, radio, heater and English leather upholstery. Rising costs put an end to production in 1958 after approximately 117 cars had been built.

DU BOIS/*England 1903*
This London-based company offered an 11 hp petrol car and a 10 hp Steam Tonneau ('the most attractive steam car on the market').

DUCOMMUN/*Germany 1903–1905*
Another small car factory in Alsace, Ducommun of Mulhouse built three models, all with square (110 × 110mm) engines. There was a twin-cylinder of 2088cc and two distinct four-cylinder models of 4179cc. All had four speeds and shaft drive.

DUCROISET/*France 1897–1900*
Built on the 'Berret' system, the 8 hp twin-cylinder Ducroiset of 1898 had a three-speed

belt-drive transmission, and was sold in Britain as the 'Hercules'.

DUDLY BUG/*USA 1914–1915*
A bullnosed two-seater cyclecar from Menominee, Michigan.

DUER/*USA 1907–1908*
Rope final drive characterized this 12/15 hp high-wheeler from Chicago.

DUESENBERG/*USA 1966 to date*
One car was built by Ghia to the design of Virgil Exner in 1966 in an attempt to revive the Duesenberg car. In 1971 the Duesenberg Motor Corp., Gardena, California, launched a replica of the SSJ short-wheelbased Duesenberg of 1936. Though identical in appearance to the original, it was, however, built on a modified Dodge truck chassis, powered by a 6210cc Chrysler V-8 engine and bodied in aluminium. Costing $50,000, it is thought that 25 cars had been built by 1977.

DUFAUX/*Switzerland 1903–1909*
Charles and Frederic Dufaux were well-known motorcycle makers from Geneva who had a 12·8-litre straight-eight racing car built in the

DUESENBERG/*USA 1920–1937*
Fred Duesenberg's Model A of 1920 was America's first straight-eight, current until 1926, when the similar Model X appeared and E. L. Cord took over. Under his aegis, Duesenberg developed the luxurious Model J of 1928, with a 6883cc Lycoming eight with twin ohc operating four valves per cylinder. One of America's most luxurious cars, it cost $8500 in chassis form ready for coachwork by leading *carrossiers*. Top speed was a claimed 116 mph. In 1932 came the '320hp' SJ, with a centrifugal supercharger: two short-chassis 'SSJ' speedsters were also built. The collapse of Cord's empire dragged down Duesenberg: unsuccessful attempts to revive the marque in 1947 and 1966 only resulted in prototypes.

1935 Duesenberg SJ Roadster

Piccard-Pictet works with the aim of competing in the 1904 Gordon Bennett Cup. It was joined in 1905 by a 26·4-litre 150 hp four which set up a flying kilometre world speed record of 156·5 km/h at Salon. That year, too, the Dufaux built a successful petrol-powered helicopter. The first touring Dufaux cars appeared in 1905, built in a new factory at Balexert, a suburb of Geneva. These had four-cylinder 35 cv engines: in 1906 a 16 cv of 4084cc also appeared. At least one straight-eight 70/90 cv limousine was built. An association with the Italian marque Marchand was agreed in 1907, but the Marchand-Dufaux lasted less than two years.

DU FURAN/*France 1907*
'Quadrivoiturettes' from this maker of cycles and car components appeared at the 1907 Paris Salon.

DUHANOT/*France 1907–1908*
Best known as builders of taxicabs, Duhanot of Paris began production with a six-model line-up, hastily reduced to three soon after the launch. Duhanot's most endearing feature was a tubular radiator which revolved like the blades of a fan. The 1908 range consisted of 12/14 hp and 17/20 hp fours, with conventional coolers.

D-ULTRA/*England 1914–1916*
A 995cc Lister four-cylinder engine powered this Clapham company's principal offering, a two-seater light car: 8 hp Chater-Lea twin-cylinder models were also listed.

DUMAS/*France 1899–1902*
A Paris-built car with a twin-cylinder 2083cc power unit: a 4½ hp three-wheeler was also built.

DUMONT/*France 1912–1913*
A short-lived friction-drive 1335cc single-cylinder voiturette built at Asnières (Seine), and also sold by Gregoire.

DUNALISTAIR/*England 1925–1926*
A mere four examples of this Nottingham-built car were made. A 14 hp Meadows engine and gearbox were used.

DUNKLEY/*England 1896–1925*
Dunkleys of Birmingham were best known as pram manufacturers, but from 1896 built a series of gas-propelled cars of curious design. These went into full production in 1901, equipped with take-off pipes so that they could refill from any convenient street lamp. They were built for four or five years. In 1911 Dunkleys

The gas-powered 1902 Dunkley

built a cyclecar called the Alvechurch, after the street in which their factory was located. In 1923, they introduced a design which beat even the gas cars for eccentricity: this was the motor-pram, powered by the Pramotor power pack, which resembled a scooter, with the front wheel replaced by the pram. Top of the range was the 'Saloon Pramotor', which at 135 guineas cost more than a Model T Ford. A 750cc version appeared in 1924, the year before production ended.

1937 Duesenberg SJ Rolston convertible sedan

1929 Duesenberg J town car

1929 Duesenberg J Club Sedan

8hp Duo cyclecar, 1914

DUNN/*USA 1914–1918*
A $295 15 hp vee-four roadster from Ogdensburg, NY—'a wonder of speed and handling'.

DUO/*England 1912–1914*
The original Duo cyclecar was a 964cc vee-twin: in 1914 a three-car range — 747cc single, 1085cc twin and 1093cc four — replaced it.

DUPLEX/*USA 1908–1911*
Two cylinders, two flywheels, two friction drives, two propeller shafts and two crown wheels and pinions earned this Chicago-built 18/20 hp car its name.

DUPLEX/*England 1919–1921*
The first Manchester-built Duplex had a 10 hp sleeve-valve engine with two parallel rows of four cylinders: production models used a 1½-litre Coventry-Climax.

DUPONT/*USA 1915*
The DuPont car of 1915 was the former Sphinx under a different company and name (see Sphinx). This DuPont bore no relationship to the later Du Pont car built from 1920 to 1932.

DUPONT/*USA 1920–1932*
Wealthy industrialist E. Paul DuPont's company built just 537 luxury cars, starting with a 4·1-litre sv own-make four, followed by proprietary sixes, notably by Wisconsin and Herschell-Spillman. Best-known DuPont was the Model G Speedster, with a 5·3-litre Continental straight-eight, bullnosed radiator grille and Woodlite headlamps: its top speed was 114 mph. The ultimate DuPont cars were assembled in the Indian motorcycle factory.

DUPRESSOIR/*France 1900–1914*
Paul Dupressoir of Maubeuge (Nord) built chassis and components. He began production in 1899 with De Dion-engined tricycles and quadricycles, as well as a 'motor forecarriage'

for converting 'small carts' into motorcars. The company's original car was a single cylinder voiturette with de Dion or Aster power unit, but in 1905 the 'Rolling' models of 6 to 24 hp were introduced. Production was delayed by a fire which destroyed the factory in June 1905. Shown at the 1905 Paris Salon were two 'Rollings', a special taxicab chassis of 12/14 hp and a 16 hp touring car.

DURANT/*USA 1921–1932*
Sister marque to Eagle, Flint, Locomobile, Princeton, Rugby and Star in Billy Durant's 'Second Empire', the Durant had an ohv four-cylinder engine and a tubular 'backbone' reinforcing its chassis. Production peaked early, reaching 55,000 in 1922 and falling thereafter. An Anstead-engined six was listed in 1922–23. Production reached a hiatus in 1927, restarting in 1928 with a redesigned range of four- and six-

cylinder models. Two sizes were offered in 1930, and Continental engines were used in the 1931 Durants. Sales fell to 7270 that year, and the firm collapsed early in 1932. Canadian Durants were sold as 'Frontenacs'.

DURKOPP/*Germany 1898–1927*
A producer of bicycles, sewing-machines and later motorcycles and ball-bearings, Dürkopp of Bielefeld in Westphalia built their first cars on Panhard & Levassor lines. They were known in England under the 'Watsonia' trade mark, in other countries as 'Canello-Dürkopp' cars. Many different models came into being, with two-, four-, six- and even eight-cylinder engines; there was a 'six' already in 1904, an eight-cylinder prototype in 1905. There were four-cylinder cars from 14 hp to 100 hp and there were even three-cylinder models built under Belgian Dasse licence. There were Kaiserpreis racing cars with 7450cc engines, big fours of 13,077cc (150mm bore and 185mm stroke) and also small 1560cc four-cylinder versions. The famous 2540cc P10 four-cylinder (built from 1914 to 1922) and the 2080cc P8 developing 32 hp at 2500 rpm preceded the last Dürkopp passenger car, the 3006cc six-cylinder P12.

DUROCAR/*USA 1907–1909*
Los Angeles was the home of this car, which had a horizontal 26 hp twin engine beneath the seat.

DURYEA/*USA 1893–1916*
'A carriage, not a machine' was the proud slogan of America's first production car. The brothers Charles and Frank Duryea built their first 'Power Wagon' in 1893, and following a quarrel, Frank began production in Springfield, Illinois, in 1895. Thirteen Benz-like cars were built in 1896, and two of them ran in the 1896 London–Brighton Emancipation Day run, making Duryea America's first exporter, too. But the company folded in 1898, and Charles took over, building—from around 1900—baroque three- and four-wheelers with 'one-hand control' (the two gears were selected by moving the steering tiller—whose grip was also a hand throttle—back and forth) and trans-

1903 Duryea Power Surrey

verse three-cylinder engines with desaxé cranks. These ingenious machines were also licence-built in England from 1904–07 and in Belgium. From 1908 the American company (which had moved to Reading, Pa., in 1903) produced the crude Buggyaut high-wheeler, with two-speed friction drive selected by moving the whole engine in the frame. By 1916, the three-wheeled friction-drive Duryea Gem cyclecar was being built by Cresson-Morris of Philadelphia.

DUTTON/*England 1970 to date*
From its humble beginnings in a Sussex pig farm, Tim Woolley's low budget sports car company has gone from strength to strength. From the P1 to Malaga, the simple Lotus Seven style machines have followed the same format. Hundreds of kits have now been sold.

DUX/*Germany 1905–1926*
Dux originated from the Polyphon-Werke at Leipzig, which originally built the American Oldsmobile under licence as the 'Polymobile'. Dux produced a variety of sturdy cars designed by Gustav Schürmann, which included 1546cc, 2038cc and 2597cc sv four-cylinder models, including sports cars. Two models dominated production to the end, when Dux was bought by Presto. These models were a 4680cc four-cylinder developing 50 bhp at 1500 rpm and a 4440cc six-cylinder.

D-WAGEN/*Germany 1924–1925*
Made at the Haselhorst factory of the Berlin-Spandau-based Deutsche Werke, the 1290cc four-cylinder D-Wagen was a four-seater touring car. Their principal products were D-Rad motorcycles. After 1925, the factory assembled American Durant and Rugby cars, and was eventually bought by DKW for the manufacture of their two-stroke cars.

DYKE/*USA 1901–1904*
A. L. Dyke, the 'Gasoline Doctor' of St Louis, began by selling his 'Automorettes' in kit form for $350 or complete for $600. He made his own engines of 3 to 10 hp, and from 1906–07 collaborated in producing the 35 hp DLG.

DYMAXION/*USA 1933–1934*
A 'geodesic' three-wheeler with teardrop styling and rear-mounted Ford V-8 conceived by architect Buckminster Fuller. Only three were made.

DYNA-VERITAS
Germany 1950–1952
Handsome cabriolets using the 744cc flat-twin engine and most other components of the fwd Dyna-Panhard. Producer of Dyna-Veritas cars was Veritas, a factory best known for its bigger sports and racing cars.

D'YRSAN/*France 1923–1930*
Another French three-wheeler, made in Asnières by the Marquis Siran de Cavanac, using Ruby and SCAP engines of 750cc and 1100cc plus independent front suspension by leaf springs. At the end of production, the D'Yrsan works made a few four-wheeled cars with Ruby and SCAP engines, some supercharged for racing. They also made motorcycles.

1972 Dutton B-Type sports

1950 Dyna Veritas cabriolet

1926 D'Yrsan (Raymond de Siran de Cavanac at the front)

157

1978 Eagle coupé

EADIE / *England 1898–1900*
Eadie of Redditch built motor tricycles and quadricycles with 2¼ hp De Dion engines.

EAGLE / *England 1901–1913*
Ralph Jackson started building 'Ralpho' cycles at Altrincham, Cheshire, in 1885, then in 1899 founded the Century Engineering & Motor Company to build his design of three-wheeler, the 'Century Tandem'. He sold the company and the design in 1901 to a London businessman called Begbie, who imported Aster engines into Britain, but continued building the tricars in Altrincham under the name Eagle. The two makes even appeared on different stands at the 1904 Crystal Palace Show. Light cars with a similar epicyclic transmission to the Eagle Tandem appeared in 1903, a two-cylinder 9 hp competing in that year's ACGBI reliability trials. There was also a fearsome 'Racer' version of the Eagle Tandem, with a 16 hp engine, capable of 'over 80 mph'. The company was wound up in 1907, but Jackson continued to assemble cars (now called 'New Eagle') in a nearby electricity generating station. This continued until 1910, when Jackson founded a garage. In 1913 he produced a prototype cyclecar, the Eagle Runabout, with a vertical twin two-stroke engine and pedal-controlled epicyclic transmission.

EAGLE / *England 1913–1914*
The Eagle Motor Manufacturing Company, which built a £109 999cc twin and a £175 1131cc four, preceded the Beverley-Barnes.

EAGLE / *USA 1915*
Three- and five-passenger electric coupés from Detroit.

EAGLE / *USA 1923–1924*
A brief attempt by Durant to market a car in the $800 price range. Pilot models only were built before the project was dropped. A six-cylinder Continental engine was employed on the Eagle, which had been planned to fill the gap between the Star and the Durant Four.

EAGLE / *England 1979 to date*
A very pretty, front-engined two-seater sports car with more than a hint of Fiat X1/9, the Eagle features Leyland 1100/1300 subframes bolted to a purpose-built, steel-tube chassis. The body is moulded in glass-fibre, has burst-proof doors and a built-in roll-over bar. Alternative power units include Ford Fiesta and Simca.

EARL / *England 1903*
Possibly a French import, the 11 hp Earl was sold by the Great Central Garage of London whose telegraphic address was 'Squirting'!

EARL / *USA 1905–1909*
Earl began with a 15 hp flat-twin car with flitch-plated oak chassis and friction drive. Production started in Milwaukee in January 1906, and in mid-1907 the company moved to Kenosha, where a 20 hp twin and 22 hp four were announced. By January 1908, 81 Earls had been completed.

EARL / *USA 1922–1924*
The Earl was simply the continuation of the Briscoe. The Earls, of which some 2000 units were marketed, were four-cylinder cars with engines of their own design and make. Wheelbase was 112 inches: the touring car was listed at $1095.

EASTMAN / *USA 1899–1902*
H. F. Eastman, of Cleveland, Ohio, built America's first all-steel car, the three-wheeled 'Electro Cycle' in 1899. Its battery and electric motor accounted for three-quarters of its weight. A four-wheeled version was built in Detroit.

EASTMEAD-BIGGS / *England 1901–1904*
With an 8 hp Simms engine, the Eastmead-Biggs had a patent chassis 'whereby flexibility is obtained without the use of universal joints'. It was also sold as the 'Velomobile'.

L'ECLAIR / *France 1907–1908*
A Parisian car manufacturer who exhibited a 20 hp four at the 1907 Paris Salon.

ECLAIR / *France 1920–1925*
Made by Lebeau and Cordier in Courbevoie, this tiny cyclecar was powered by a 7/9 hp Anzani 500cc vee-twin and had a two-speed gearbox in the back axle.

ECLIPSE / *USA 1900–1903*
A three-cylinder shaft-drive steam runabout from Boston.

ECLIPSE / *USA 1905*
A single-cylinder 1688cc engine powered this epicyclic geared tourer from Milwaukee.

ECLIPSE / *England 1906*
A coachbuilt 5½ hp tricar with a vee-twin engine from the makers of the XL-All motorcycle.

ECONOMIC / *England 1921–1922*
The spindly Economic three-wheeler was propelled by a 200cc twin-cylinder engine, driving by chain to the offside rear wheel.

1903 Earl tonneau

ECONOMY / *USA 1906–1909*
'One of the busiest factories in Joliet, Illinois' built this high-wheeler.

ECONOMY / *USA 1917–1921*
An assembled six-cylinder automobile, the Economy used a Continental engine and other standard components. It was connected 'businesswise' with the Vogue, which was built in the same town of Tiffin, Ohio. The earliest Vogue models were frequently described as 'Economy-Vogue' cars.

ECONOOM / *Holland 1913–1915*
Only 85 of these light cars were built in the Amsterdam factory of Hautekeet & Van Asselt, using Ballot engines and MAB chassis imported from France.

EDISMITH / *England 1905*
Edwin Smith, of the Circus Garage, Blackburn, Lancashire, built cars under this name, with Tony Huber and De Dion power units.

EDIT / *Italy 1923–1925*
Designed by Mascheroni of Milan, the Edit was a cyclecar-like small car with a 10 hp twin-cylinder engine. It was available with a three-seater body and also as a two-seater sports car.

EDMOND / *England 1920–1921*
A two-cylinder 5/7 hp engine by Coventry-Victor powered the Edmond cyclecar, built by the Shand Motor Company of Lee Green.

EDMUND / *England 1920*
C. Edmund & Co. built motorcycles at Chester between 1907 and 1923; in 1920 a shaft-driven cyclecar put in a brief appearance.

EDSEL / USA 1958–1960
Launched in a blaze of publicity to plug the gap between the Lincoln and Mercury lines, the Edsel proved to be Ford's most costly mistake, losing between $250-350 million in its short lifespan. Four Series — low-priced Ranger and Pacer with a 5916cc V-8 and 'upper-medium-priced' Corsair and Citation with a 6719cc V-8 — were available in 18 models. Pushbuttons in the steering wheel hub controlled the automatic transmission, standard on the costlier models, and the front-end styling, with its vertical 'horsecollar' grille, was controversial. A sales recession coincided with the Edsel's launch, and only 60,000 were sold in the first year, falling to 44,000 in 1959. Completely restyled for 1960, and only offered in the Ranger Series, the Edsel was now basically a Ford with a Pontiac-like grille, and only 2846 were sold before the division ceased operation.

EDWARDS / USA 1912–1914
Forerunner of the Willys-Knight, this New York-built tourer had a 4523cc four-cylinder sleeve-valve engine and an overdrive fourth speed.

EDWARDS / England 1913
This cyclecar had huge airscoops in its bonnet for cooling its 8 hp Precision vee-twin eng·

EDWARDS / USA 1949–1955
E. H. Edwards, of San Francisco, built a sports car endeavouring to combine the best of European and American engineering. A tuned Ford V-8 engine powered the Edwards, which had an aluminium body on a tubular chassis with all-round independent suspension. For racing (where it proved successful) the leather hard top and windshield were removable. Later models used glass-fibre bodies and 205 hp Lincoln V-8 engines with GM Hydramatic transmission.

EGG / Switzerland 1898–1919
Rudolf Egg built his first car in 1893, and between 1896–98 was responsible for the Egg & Egli, a three-speed tricar with a single-cylinder De Dion engine and two-speed belt drive. From 1898, he built Benz-derived four-wheelers at Zurich, but production was halted by a fire in 1905 which destroyed both factory and completed vehicles. In 1914, Egg cars reappeared, based on the Moser voiturette, and in 1918–19 Moser also built a four-cylinder Zurcher-engined Egg, with gearbox in the back axle.

EGO / Germany 1921–1927
This marque sprang to fame in 1923, when young Rudolf Caracciola won a race at the Berlin Stadium on an EGO. The EGO range included four-cylinder models of 1016cc, 1290cc and 1320cc, the last with ohv.

1958 Edsel Citation

1960 Edsel Ranger

EHP / France 1921–1929
The Etablissements Henri Précloux made light cars and cyclecars of 903cc, 959cc and 1094cc. After 1924 they presented a 1203cc CIME-engined version. They occasionally entered racing events, and built an ohc 1500cc engine for that purpose. The last models had sv CIME six-cylinder engines of 1792cc. They sold very well. EHP were regular entrants at Le Mans from 1925 to 1928.

EHRHARDT / Germany 1905–1924
Gustav Ehrhardt, son of Heinrich Ehrhardt of Wartburg (Dixi) fame, built cars at Zella-St Blasii and at Düsseldorf. These were two- and four-cylinder models of high quality — and also high prices. The biggest was a 7956cc four-cylinder model, which by 1913 had four-wheel brakes. After 1918, the factory built a 40 hp four-cylinder and 55 hp six-cylinder with ohc engines, luxury cars of the highest calibre.

1922 Ego 4/14hp

The EHP of Lenoist/Doré in the 1925 Le Mans

EHRHARDT-SZAWE/*Germany 1924–1925*
The Szawe was one of the most luxurious cars ever built in Germany; when the Szawe works at Berlin-Reinickendorf closed down, Ehrhardt took over the limited manufacture of the 2570cc 10/50 hp ohc Szawe car: a six-cylinder which was designed without regard to cost. Even the radiator was made from German silver.

EISENACH/*Germany 1898–1903*
Predecessor of the Wartburg, Eisenach mainly built electric cars. Soon after production of petrol cars commenced, the factory adopted the 'Wartburg' name.

EJYR/*England 1907–1914*
In 1907 E. J. Y. R. Rutherford, of Newbury, Berkshire, built a prototype flash-boilered steam car, and went into production later that year with a three-cylinder 30/40 hp steamer on petrol car lines, which cost £575 with side-entrance bodywork. After 1908 the cars were known as 'Rutherfords', and the price cut to £535. By 1911, the price was down to £400. An improved model with the spiral tube condenser forming the bonnet sides appeared in 1912, but the Highclere Motor Car Syndicate, who built the cars, went into liquidation soon after.

EKSTROMER/*England 1905*
Ekstromer were battery manufacturers who also offered a range of electric vehicles, including a light two-seater, said to have a range of 100 miles.

1905 Ekstromer Electric

ELAN/*France 1898–1900*
The original 'Elan' had an air-cooled vertical-twin engine and two-seater coachwork by Kellner.

ELCAR/*USA 1915–1931*
The Elkhart Carriage Company, of Elkhart, Indiana, had been in business over 30 years before they produced their first car, the 30/35 hp Elkhart of 1905–09. It was followed by the 4·2-litre Sterling (1909–11) and the 1911 Komet. The Elcar appeared in 1915: two models were offered in the early days, a Lycoming-engined four and a Continental-engined six. A straight-eight, again Continental-engined, appeared in 1925. In 1930, the company became involved with the Reverend Alvah Powell's complex Lever engine, though only four Elcar-Levers were actually built. A lucrative contract supplying El-Fay taxis to a New York operator came to a sudden end when he was gunned down, and a project to market the 1930 Elcar as a revived Mercer for 1931 ended after only two prototypes had been built.

ELCO/*USA 1915–1916*
A 30 hp touring car from Sidney, Ohio, with a 1852cc Davis power unit.

ELDREDGE/*USA 1903–1906*
A light two-seater runabout with left-hand drive, built by the National Sewing Machine Co., of Belvedere, Illinois.

ELECTRA KING/*USA 1961 to date*
Built by Billard & Zarpe of the B & Z Electric Car Co., Long Beach, California, the Electra King had a 45 mile range on a single charge. Powered by a 1 hp DC electric motor and five 6 volt batteries the car could cruise at 18 mph. In 1972 Robert E. McCoy, an electronics engineer, bought the project. Three- and four-wheel versions are currently offered with a choice of four electric motors. Cruising speeds vary from 16 to 29 mph and the range from 18 to 36 miles.

ELECTRICAR/*France 1920–1921*
An urban car with a ½ hp electric engine made by M. Couaillet of Paris. It was a single-seater, three-wheeler car with a single front wheel.

ELECTRIC CARRIAGE AND GARAGE CO/*England 1902*
Formal electric vehicles—Landaulette, Victoria, Coupé—designed for town use.

ELECTRICIA/*France 1901*
A tiller-steered electric phaeton designed by Contal.

ELECTRIC MOTIVE POWER
England 1897
A heavy electric phaeton capable of running 20 miles on one charge.

ELECTRIC VEHICLE/*USA 1899*
These electric cabs were widely used in New York. They pioneered the use of pressed-steel

1898 Cail (SAAC), immediate fore-runner of the Elan

1919 Elcar Six

wheels, and had front-wheel drive and brakes and rear-wheel steering.

ELECTROGENIA/*France 1903–1905*
'No breakdowns' was the optimistic promise of this '4 kilowatt' petrol-electric (known as Champrobert in 1902) from Levallois-Perret.

ELECTROMOBILE/*England 1901–1920*
This London maker of electric town carriages offered a contract hire scheme as early as 1904. From 1903, the motor was mounted on the rear axle. Design changed little before World War One: in 1919 a new model, the 8/12 hp Elmo electric, with a short bonnet, appeared.

ELECTROMOTION/*France 1900–1909*
Electric cars with hub motors, built at Neuilly-sur-Seine.

ELECTRON/*France 1907–1908*
An electric car shown at the 1907 Paris Salon.

L'ELEGANTE/*France 1903–c1907*
De Dion-like cars of 4 hp to 12 hp. Paris.

1920 Elfe cyclecar

ELFE/*France 1920–1925*
Made in Levallois by M. Eugène (founder of the Bol d'Or race), the Elfe started as a cyclecar with passenger accommodation in tandem—the driver being in front—and the 987cc vee-twin Anzani 984cc was mounted centrally in the chassis. M. Mauve also made some touring cyclecars with 704cc two-stroke vee-twin Vapor engines.

ELGE/*France 1924–1925*
A marque created at Bordeaux by Roger Louis Maleyre, a pioneer of aerodynamics. Very low and light, and remarkably streamlined, Elgé cars used CIM engines. Maleyre also built a prototype propeller-driven car which proved to be a one-off design. Total production was about 30 cars.

1925 Elgé coupé

ELGIN/*USA 1916–1925*
Starting as a four-cylinder, the Chicago-built Elgin adopted a 2954cc ohv six in 1918, subsequently uprated to 3205cc. The 1922 Elgin six offered a Cutler-Hammer magnetic gearshift.

ELIESON/*England 1898*
An electric dog-cart with a narrow-tracked front axle.

ELITE/*USA 1901*
Built by D. B. Smith, of Utica, NY, this steam car — and its sister marque, the 'Saratoga Tourist' — were said to be 'the handsomest vehicles every built': the press just called them 'singular'.

ELITE/*Germany 1920–1928*
The first Elite was a 3130cc four-cylinder with a sv 45 hp engine. In 1922, Elite introduced a luxurious touring car, the 4600cc six-cylinder developing 70 hp at 2000 rpm. A sporting version was raced successfully by Walter Öster-reicher; it had a 90 hp engine. Smaller models had sv six-cylinder engines of 2360cc, others 3128cc power units. In 1927, Elite merged with the Diamant motorcycle works and in 1928 came under the Opel banner. Opel built motor-cycles in the Elite plant too.

ELIZALDE/*Spain 1914–1928*
Arturo Elizalde opened a garage in Barcelona in 1909, manufacturing automobile components. Backed by the Biada brothers, he began building cars in 1914, and by 1915 Alfonso XIII had a 20 cv Biada-Elizalde cabriolet in his stable. A 25 cv sports version of this car was marketed as the 'Reina Victoria': it was the first Spanish car with four-wheel brakes. In 1920 the 19/30 cv Model 29 was announced, with an ohv 3817cc four-cylinder engine: similar models were built

1920 Elizalde 18/20hp Reine Victoria

until 1927. But the sensation of 1920 was the magnificent 50/60 cv straight-eight Tipo 48, one of the first cars of this configuration to go into production. Its 8143cc power unit with four valves per cylinder incorporated a tyre pump which could also be used for vacuum-cleaning the interior of the car. There was a 5181cc straight-eight Gran Sport version capable of 160 km/h, too. Elizalde built lorries and aero-engines as well as cars.

ELKA/*Italy 1912–1914*
Driving an Elka, Lucca was sixth in the 1914 Targa Florio. The Elka was really a Laurin & Klement, assembled by a small Italian company which imported components of these Austro-Hungarian cars, forerunners of the Skoda.

1921 Elite 10/38PS

ELLEMOBIL/*Denmark 1909–1910*
In a 1909 catalogue from J. C. Ellehammer, Copenhagen, two different types were offered for sale. Both had air-cooled twin-cylinder engines and friction drive in combination with belt or chain drive. Ellehammer was a famous aviator and in 1905 he had built a flat 11 hp three-cylinder engine for a helicopter, but it was never used for that purpose. In 1913 the engine was modified and put into an experimental car, together with another invention, a hydraulic clutch. There was no production of this car, and few of the earlier models were built.

ELLIOT/*USA 1897–1900*
Built in Oakland, California, this was a rotund 4 hp motor victoria.

ELMORE/*USA 1900–1912*
Elmore, of Clyde, Ohio, never built anything except two-stroke-engined cars, starting with a 5 hp 1667cc twin-cylinder runabout with tiller steering and chain drive. A new range of shaft-driven cars with front-mounted two- and four-cylinder engines appeared in 1906, joined the following year by a 24 hp three-cylinder. The company, absorbed by General Motors in 1909, ceased operations three years later, when four-cylinder cars of 30 hp and 50 hp were made.

ELSWICK/*England 1903–1907*
The round-radiatored Elswicks were assembled cars using four-cylinder engines of 13/20 hp and 26/30 hp and a 26/30 hp six.

ELVA/*England 1955–1968*
Elva was formed by Frank Nichols to build competition cars, but unexpected success led to early thoughts of road versions. Over 2000 Elvas were eventually made, the most famous of which were the various Mks of Courier and the stillborn, Fiore-styled Elva BMW GT160.

L'ELYSEE/*France 1903*
A 'high-class French car' imported into London by Henry Whitlock Ltd.

ELYSEE/*France 1921–1925*
Made by M. Bonnet in Paris, these were light cars and cyclecars of 779cc, 950cc and 1995cc.

EMERALD/*England 1903–1904*
A 4 hp light car from West Norwood, London.

EMERAUDE/*France 1913–1914*
A friction-drive Buchet-engined cyclecar.

EMERSON/*USA 1916–1917*
The Emerson was a four-cylinder light car produced in limited numbers only as touring models. In 1918 it became the Campbell and was marketed under the latter name through 1919, when it went out of business.

EMERY/*England 1963*
Though Paul Emery's name appeared on many successful racing cars, his pretty GT road car was short-lived. Sadly, only four of these Imp-powered, mid-engined two-seaters were built. Their glass-fibre bodies were bonded to the neat space-frame chassis for ultimate strength.

1906 Elswick 24hp

EMF/*USA 1908–1912*
The 'million-dollar' Everitt-Metzger-Flanders Company was launched in June 1908: the EMF 30 car, designed by William E. Kelley, had a unit engine/gearbox and was planned for an initial production of 12,000 a year at a price of $1250 for tourer, demi-tonneau, and roadster.

EMILE PILAIN/*France 1930–1935*
Made in Levallois by Emile Pilain, these were 5 hp light cars with a sv 950cc engine.

EMMS/*England 1922–1923*
A 10·8 hp 1368cc Coventry-Climax-engined light car from Coventry, the Emms cost £285.

EMPIRE/*USA 1901–1902*
Built in Sterling, Illinois, the Empire steamer had a vee-twin engine geared to the right-hand rear wheel.

EMPIRE/*USA 1910–1919*
'The little aristocrat', the four-cylinder Empire 20 was a shaft-drive race-about from Indianapolis. More conventional bodies were later available: the marque announced its 1916 35 hp in April 1915. Final products were a four of 3865cc and a six of 3670cc.

EMPIRE STEAM CAR/*USA c1925–1927*
The three-cylinder compound engined Empire Steamer was designed by Carl Ubelmesser and built by the Gruban Machine & Steel Corporation of New York City. Only one was built — and it was not entirely completed.

1924 Endurance steam car

1908 Empress 16/20hp Roi-des-Belges

EMPRESS/*England 1907–1911*
Built in Manchester, the Empress had a circular radiator and bonnet like the Delaunay-Belleville. It had a four-cylinder rotary-valve engine of 18/24 hp: there were also six-cylinder Empress cars of 24/30 hp and 30/36 hp.

EMSCOTE/*England 1920–1921*
A 961cc vee-twin engine, in unit with a three-speed gearbox, powered these Warwick-built cyclecars with centre-pivot front axles.

EMW/*Germany 1945–1956*
The East German EMW was a slightly modified BMW built at the pre-war Eisenach BMW works, which were nationalized after the war. The engines were similar to the pre-war BMW 326 and 327 — and even the BMW emblem was used on this BMW-like car. It was not until 1952 that the name EMW was first used and the body shape changed slightly. The factory also built the AWE sports-racing cars, which were successfully driven by Barth and Rosenhammer.

ENDERS/*France 1911–1923*
A tiny cyclecar designed by M. Violet with a two-stroke 500cc engine.

ENDURANCE/*England 1898–1901*
The 'New Endurance' car, of similar general design to the Benz, had a rear-mounted horizontal single-cylinder engine and was chiefly notable for its 10-inch water orifice, designed to be filled straight from a stable-yard bucket, the water tank forming a dummy bonnet.

ENDURANCE STEAM CAR
USA 1922–1924
The Endurance had its origins with the Coats Steamer. It started in the east, but shifted operations to Los Angeles, California, where a single touring car was made. Thereafter Endurance moved to Dayton, Ohio, where one sedan was completed before the firm failed.

ENERGIE/*France 1899–1902*
The Société l'Energie, of Paris, originally built the Renaux motor tricycle. By 1902 they were making 8½ hp light cars powered by vertical-twin Buchet engines.

ENFIELD/*England 1906–1915*
The car-making side of Royal Enfield became a separate entity, the Enfield Autocar Company, in 1906. The first cars to leave their Redditch factory were a short-lived 16/20 hp and a 24/30 hp, both four-cylinders. Enfield was soon acquired by Alldays & Onions, and an Alldays-engined 18/22 hp with a round radiator appeared in November 1907: it had a Hele-Shaw multi-plate clutch, and remained in production

1913 Enfield 18.4hp Phaeton

until 1910, in which year a new 16 hp was announced. In 1909 came an Enfield version of the 10/12 hp twin-cylinder Alldays, built in the new Enfield factory at Sparkbrook, Birmingham. Biggest of the Enfields was the 1909–10 30/35 hp, with a 6107cc power unit. In 1913 there were two Enfield 'Autolettes', an 8 hp twin and a 9 hp four, both with Alldays counterparts. The 14·3 hp, 18·4 hp and 24·9 hp Enfields of 1913–14 had neat flush-sided torpedo coachwork and detachable wheels.

ENFIELD/*England 1973–1976*
Over 100 Enfield electric cars were sold, 61 going to the Electricity Council for evaluation. A very good attempt at a mass-production electric vehicle, the Enfield was 8 inches shorter than a Mini. Under its dumpy glass-fibre body were Hillman Imp suspension at the front and a live-axle at the rear. Power came from a 48V, 6 Kw DC motor fed by eight 12-volt batteries. The maximum speed was 40 mph and the range 40 miles.

ENFIELD-ALLDAY/*England 1919–1925*
The result of a union between the Enfield and Alldays & Onions car companies, the Enfield-Allday was an unconventional device powered by a five-cylinder sv 1½-litre radial engine designed by A. W. Reeves and A. C. Bertelli. It also had a tubular backbone chassis. Orthodoxy triumphed in 1923, however, with the 10/20 having a 1½-litre water-cooled four-cylinder.

ENGELHARDT/*Germany 1900–1902*
This small, long-forgotten Berlin-based factory built a single-cylinder 6½ hp vehicle.

ENGER/*USA 1909–1917*
Starting with a high-wheeled twin-cylinder car, by 1911, Enger, of Cincinnati, were making a $2000 four-cylinder 40 hp. In 1915 they announced one of America's first V-12s; the ohv 1916 version of this car could be run as a six by cutting out one bank of cylinders.

ENKA/*Czechoslovakia 1928–1929*
Made by Kolanda & Spol at Prague, this Novotny-designed 499cc single-cylinder two-stroke two-seater had bodies made by the Aero factory, which was much better equipped for car production than Kolanda. In 1929 Aero took this design for manufacture in its own works: this was the first car to bear the Aero trade mark.

ENSIGN, BRITISH ENSIGN
England 1913–1923
Building four-cylinder cars in 1913–14, the British Ensign company from Willesden introduced an advanced 38·4 hp ohc six of 6795cc in 1919. A couple of cars with Crown Magnetic transmission were built, but only completed after the firm had gone broke.

ENTROP/*Holland 1909*
Before 1909, Entrop of 's Gravenmoer built over 1500 bicycles, but their car production amounted to only four units.

ENTYRE/*USA 1910–1911*
A 7·7-litre four from Oregon, Illinois.

1973 Enfield Electric

ENV/*France 1908*
This English aeroengine company had a French factory at Courbevoie (Seine) where an 8168cc 40 hp V-8 car with electrolytically deposited copper water-jackets was also built in 1908. It had a two-speed gearbox and a dual-ratio back axle. The factory later housed the Alda car.

ENZMANN/*Switzerland 1957–late 1960s*
Enzmann bought new VWs, cut off the bodies and fitted them with elegant glass-fibre coachwork produced by a boatyard at Grandson.

EOS/*Germany 1922–1923*
Made by Rossineck & Co. in Berlin, the small Eos had an 18 hp three-cylinder two-stroke engine. It was raced by the designer Rossineck without great success; reliability was not its strong point. The car was also known as 'Erco'; production was very limited.

EPALLE/*France 1910–1914*
Light cars of 8/10 hp (twin) and 10/12, 12/16 and 14/20 hp (fours) from St Etienne.

ERDMANN/*Germany 1903–1908*
Known as the FEG — which stood for Friedrich Erdmann, Gera — this car had an Erdmann-patented friction drive. The range of models included two- and four-cylinder cars of up to 22 hp. The proprietary engines came from Fafnir, Korting and Horch.

ERIC/*England 1911–1914*
The Northampton built Eric was one of the more substantial cyclecars, with a flat-twin 1088cc engine/gearbox unit mid-mounted in a tubular chassis driving the rear wheel by shaft.

ERIC-CAMPBELL/*England 1919–1926*
Built originally by aircraft manufacturer Handley Page, the Eric-Campbell was created by Hugh Eric Orr-Ewing and Noel Campbell Macklin, later of Silver Hawk and Invicta fame. A tuned Coventry-Climax engine of 1½ litres was fitted.

ERIC-LONGDEN/*England 1922–1927*
Vee-twin JAP engines of 8 or 10 hp powered the Eric-Longden, a rather GN-ish device with shaft drive. Later, in 1922, four-cylinder engines by Alpha and Coventry-Simplex were offered. Before World War One, Eric Longden ran a music-hall.

ERIE/*USA 1898–1901*
Builders of gasoline and steam motor carriages from Anderson, Indiana.

ERIE/*USA 1920*
This four-cylinder assembled car hailed from Painsville, Ohio. Reportedly, only one pilot model was completed.

ERNST/*Switzerland 1905–c1908*
Four-cylinder Aster-engined cars of 2438cc and 3547cc with Malicet & Blin chassis, assembled in Geneva by ex-Daimler engineer Gustav Ernst.

ERSKINE/*USA 1926–1930*
Named after Studebaker's president, Albert R. Erskine, the Erskine was advertised as a 'European motor car' and such it was, its overseas sales being markedly more successful than those in America. It featured a 2320cc six-cylinder engine, increased in 1928 to 2629cc displacement. By 1930, the Erskine had increased in size and more closely resembled the Studebaker. With a price approaching $1000, the Erskine was re-christened 'Studebaker Six' in May of that Year. Mr. Erskine committed suicide in 1933.

ESCULAPE/*France 1899*
'Worked by an improved De Dion-Bouton motor, strengthened by a water current', the two-seater Esculape was said by its makers, the Automobile Union of Paris, to be 'fast, silent and vibrationless'. It was probably none of these.

ESCULAPEUS/*England 1902*
This 'chainless' voiturette had a 5 hp Ader vee-twin engine and was designed for the use of medical practitioners, with a locker for their bag, plus full weather protection.

ESHELMAN/*USA 1953–1960*
Chester L. Eshelman Co., Baltimore, Maryland, manufactured a 54-inch long, 24-inch wide one-passenger runabout powered by a 70 mpg 3 hp Briggs & Stratton engine. Several gardening attachments were available, including a lawn sweeper, reel mower and trailer.

1924 Eric Campbell 8/20hp Sports

1919 Essex Speedster

ESPAÑA/*Spain 1917–1928*
Barcelona textile engineer Felipe Batlló's first car was perversely called the España 2: it had a four-cylinder Altos engine of 1847cc. It was followed by the España 3 of 3690cc with a four-cylinder ohv engine and four speeds forward: only two prototypes were built, one for Batlló's father, the other for Alfonso XIII. España 4 was a 4·5-litre prototype with a 16-valve engine, and a six-cylinder was also built. In 1928 España merged with Ricart.

ESPERIA/*Italy 1905–1910*
Built by the Societa Automobili Lombarda 'Esperia' at Bergamo, the Esperia cars were shaft-driven vehicles of 20 hp and 40 hp with ioe engines.

ESSEX/*USA 1918–1932*
Hudson's low-priced ($1595) and angular Essex line used a 2·9-litre four-cylinder ioe engine: a two-door sedan at $1295 was added in 1922, making the marque a best-seller. A 2·1-litre six succeeded the four in 1924, and was later uprated to 2·5 litres—the 'Super Six'. Four-wheel brakes were optional in 1927, standard the next year. The Challenger 18·2 hp Six of 1930 reinforced the marque's popularity. The 1932 Essex six had a 3·2-litre engine, V-radiator and Startix automatic starter, but was replaced the next year by a new marque, Terraplane.

EUCLID/*USA 1907–1908*
An air-cooled 20 hp three-cylinder two-stroke engine powered this car from Cleveland, Ohio.

EUCORT/*Spain 1946–1953*
A bold attempt at producing a 'popular car', the Eucort, from Barcelona, had a 764cc twin-cylinder engine. The last new Eucort was the Victoria of 1950, with a 1034cc three-cylinder engine.

EUDELIN/*France c1905–1908*
A Parisian manufacturer who built 14/16 hp and 25/30 hp four-cylinder cars. Eudelin also made an opposed-piston engine with a complex variable-stroke linkage. Eudelin's original power unit was a 'double piston engine with a single double throw crank directly below the combustion chamber'.

EUREKA/*USA 1900*
Ough & Waltenbaugh of San Francisco built this car with a 4408cc rear-inclined three-cylinder engine under the back seat.

EUREKA/*France 1906–1909*
A single-cylinder voiturette with friction transmission and belt final drive built at La Garenne-Colombes (Seine): it used 6 hp De Dion or 12 hp Anzani engines.

EUREKA/*USA 1907–1914*
A wheel-steered high-wheeler from St Louis, Mo., with a two-cylinder air-cooled engine.

EUROPEEN/*France 1899–1903*
Starting with light steamers, this Parisian marque soon turned to internal combustion: a 30 hp Européen ran in the 1903 Paris-Madrid.

EVERITT/*USA 1909–1912*
After Studebaker took over EMF, Everitt and Metzger built this 30 hp four, which featured a 'thiefproof' gear lever lock, also built in Canada as the Tudhope.

EVERY DAY/*Canada 1911–1913*
American-designed two-cylinder high-wheelers from Woodstock, Ontario.

EWING/*USA 1908–1910*
Designed by Louis Mooers, formerly with Peerless & Moon, the 20 hp Ewing, from Geneva, Ohio, was unusual in being sold with taxicab bodywork. About 100 were built.

EXAU/*France 1922–1924*
A cyclecar made in Paris by M. Kolbac and designed by Jacques Muller (later with BNC) with a sv 870cc SCAP engine.

EXCALIBUR SS/*USA 1964 to date*
Brooks Steven Excalibur SS, manufactured in Milwaukee, Wisconsin, is loosely based on the 1930 Mercedes SSK. Its 1500 parts are supplied by 250 manufacturers: it uses Chevrolet Corvette engines. Two models are available, a two-seater roadster and a four-passenger phaeton. Approximately 150 are produced per year, costing $20,000 each.

1973 Excalibur SS 7.4-litre

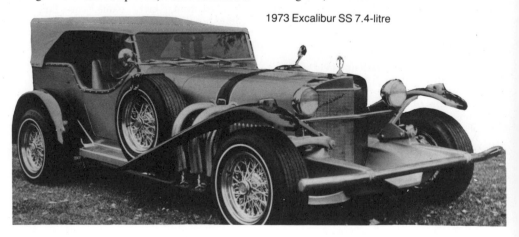

EXCELSIOR/*Belgium 1901–1932*
For its first few years Excelsior of Brussels built unremarkable light cars with proprietary engines—in 1905 one-, two- and four-cylinder Aster units were fitted. In 1907, however, engineer Arthur de Coninck took over, and the company was producing his 'Adex' six; soon after, Belgica was taken over. The classic Edwardian Excelsior, the bi-block 29/30 hp Adex six of 4426cc, appeared in 1911, accompanied by a monobloc 2951cc four. Normally built with sidevalves, these cars had ohv in their sporting incarnations. The six was produced until 1920, when de Coninck launched a new ohc model with his own design of diagonally compensated four-wheel brakes; this was developed into the magnificent ohc Albert Ier in 1922. This 5350cc six had triple Zenith carburettors and its cantilever rear springs incorporated anti-roll bars. An improved single-carburettor 30/100 hp version Albert Ier, with vacuum servo brakes, appeared in 1926, but in 1928 Impéria took over Excelsior and production ceased soon after, though a few Albert Iers were assembled from existing parts thereafter to special order.

1911 Excelsior tourer

EXCELSIOR/*England 1904–1905*
A 4½ hp tri-car from Bayliss & Thomas of Coventry, who built light cars from 1922.

EXCELSIOR
Switzerland 1905–1907
Designed by Rudolf Egg, the Excelsior was a 6 cv voiturette based closely on the curved-dash Oldsmobile, but with wheel steering. A round-radiatored four-cylinder, with a German-made engine, appeared in 1906.

EXCELSIOR/*France 1907*
A cycle and motorcycle maker from Bourgoin (Isère) who also built tricars.

EXCELSIOR-MASCOT/*Germany 1911–1922*
Only a few of these small cars were made by this Cologne-Nippes factory. They had two- and four-cylinder proprietary engines of 8 hp to 18 hp.

EXOR/*Germany 1923*
One of the many small post war German car makers, Exor used a four-cylinder 16 hp proprietary engine.

EXPRESS/*Germany 1901–1909*
Germany's oldest bicycle manufacturer also built—with some interruptions—cars and, after World War Two, motorcycles. The cars had 16 hp and 25 hp Fafnir engines. Express became part of the Sachs empire and the manufacture of motorcycles ceased some years ago.

EYSINK/*Holland 1903–1919*
The Eysink brothers built Holland's first indigenous car in 1897, only a year after the first two cars, a Benz and a Daimler, had arrived in the country. Production did not start in earnest until 1903, with a range of shaft-driven cars, of 10/12 hp, 16/20 hp and 20/30 hp. A 30/40 hp six was also built. A 6/8 hp light car, announced in 1912, survived until 1919. Peak production of Eysinks was around 50 a year. The firm continued building motorcycles until 1957.

FAB/*Belgium 1912–1914*

Successor to Vivinus, the FAB ('Fabrique Automobile Belge') offered two four-cylinder models, of 2121cc and 3563cc.

FACEL-VEGA/*France 1954–1964*

Last of the French builders of luxury cars, the Forges et Ateliers de Construction de l'Eure et Loire in Pont-à-Mousson was formerly a body builder for Simca, Ford and Panhard. They started to build complete cars in 1954 using Chrysler V-8 engines of 4·5 litres, and then of 5·8 and 6·3 litres. In 1957 Facel presented a *voiture de prestige*, the 'Excellence'. They also made a smaller model—the Facellia—originally fitted with a Facel-built dohc four-cylinder 1600cc engine. This unreliable engine caused great consternation among Facel's customers, and was mainly responsible for the failure of Facel-Vega, In 1962 the 1600cc engine was replaced by the Volvo 1800, but too late to restore confidence.

1961 Facel-Vega Facellia

FADAG/*Germany 1921–1925*

A Düsseldorf bicycle and motorcycle producer, whose cars were designed by Dr. Ing. George Bergman, Fadag offered four-cylinder models of 16, 18, 25, 30 and 32 hp. An ohc 50 hp with 2650cc Siemens & Halske engine was the only six-cylinder built by Fadag.

FAFAG/*Germany 1921–1924*

A sporting ohc 976cc four-cylinder built in limited numbers. Fafag's own-make 16-valve engine developed 40 bhp on alcohol fuel in racing-form; the top speed was around 82 mph. A Fafag racing driver was Count Hachenburg.

FAFNIR/*Germany 1908–1926*

A leading manufacturer of proprietary motorcycle and car engines, Fafnir of Aachen built four-cylinder cars with own-make ioe engines of 1520–2496cc. Of advanced design, Fafnirs also gained successes in races with such drivers as Caracciola, Uren, Müller, Hirth and Utermöhle. The ultimate model, built 1923–1926, had a 1050cc ohv engine developing 50 bhp at 2500 rpm. Supercharged racing cars with this engine developed 80 bhp.

A racing Fafnir with special radiator cowl, 1922

FAGEOL/*USA 1916–1917, 1921*

The Fageol was an enormous automobile produced by a successful firm of commercial vehicle and bus manufacturers in an attempt to seize the super-luxury car market. The cars, sporting a 142-inch wheelbase, were powered by a six-cylinder ohv Hall-Scott engine with a displacement of 13,514cc. Very few were made: an attempt to market the car as late as 1921 was abortive, the company mounting several bodies on a single chassis in an unsuccessful attempt to win the approval of the affluent.

FAIRFAX/*England 1906*

The 7/9 hp twin-cylinder Fairfax, built in Chiswick, had 'the engines placed well forward under the driver's footboard' and a constant-mesh gearbox simple enough, it was claimed, to be operated by a child.

Mk II Fairthorpe TX GT, 1968

FAIRTHORPE/*England 1952 to date*

Following the three-wheeler Atom there has been a succession of unusual glass-fibre-bodied sports cars from this unique company.

FAIRY/*England 1907*

Built by the forerunners of the Douglas Motorcycle Company, the Fairy Tricar had a 6/8 hp flat-twin engine.

F.A.L./*France 1907*

Light cars built by Coll'habert et Sénéchal, of Saint-Cloud (Seine-et-Oise).

FAL-CAR/*USA 1909-1913*

Successor to Reliable Dayton, this was a 35/40 hp four—'trim, classy, speedy and efficient'—with the choice of three body styles.

FALCON/*USA 1914*

A cyclecar built in Ohio.

FALCON/*USA 1922*

The Falcon was built in limited numbers in the Halladay factory and was, in a sense, a smaller Halladay with a different design and original name. Using four-cylinder engines of its own make as well as by Rutenber, the Falcon featured a 115-inch wheelbase and a price range from $1295 to $1595.

FALCON/*Germany 1922–1926*

The first Falcon was a 1459cc four-cylinder with a unit-design 18 hp long-stroke engine, which two years later was uprated to 1520cc. The last car made by Falcon was a 1496cc four-cylinder developing 36 hp at 3600 rpm: racing versions had tuned 45 bhp engines and competed in the Avus race in 1922. The works at Ober-Ramstadt were bought in 1927 by Röhr, who built there in 1934–35 the 1·5-litre Zoller two-stroke racing cars.

1962 Falcon Competition sports-racer

FALCON/*England c1950–1964*

Well-known re-clothers of 1950s Fords, Falcon eventually progressed to making complete cars. However, for various reasons neither the 515 or 1000 was a success and shortly before Falcon's closure the original and very pretty Caribbean Ford 8/10 replacement body was still their most saleable product—over 2000 were sold.

FALCON-KNIGHT/*USA 1927–1928*

The Falcon-Knight was a link in the chain of John North Willys' automotive empire and, although technically an independent, it was little more than a companion car to the Willys-Knight 70 and the Whippet Six. Using a six-cylinder Knight sleeve-valve engine and a wheelbase of 109½ inches, a complete line of closed and open coachwork was available. Prices ranged from $995 to $1250. Artillery wooden wheels were standard on all models, except the Gray Ghost roadster, luxury car of the line, which sported wire ones. A unique accessory available on the roadster was a special top to keep the rain off rumble-seat passengers. The last cars were marketed as 1929 models.

FALKE/*Germany 1899–1908*
Early Falke models were based on French Decauville designs with De Dion engines, later ones had two- and four-cylinder Fafnir engines from 704cc to 1501cc. Production of these cars was on a limited scale.

FANNING/*USA 1902–1903*
This Chicago company built a 'fetching' electric runabout as well as petrol cars.

FARCOT ET OLIVIER/*France 1907*
Builders of power units for cars and aeroplanes, this Parisian firm also offered a chassis with 'progressive speed change'. Taxis were built in some numbers.

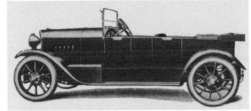
1923 Falcon (Germany) Type CA6 6/22PS

FARMACK/*USA 1915*
An ohc 20hp four built in Chicago: the two-seater cabriolet cost $1155. It was succeeded by the similar Drexel (1916–17), which also added a dohc 16-valve 3-litre.

FARMAN/*France 1902*
Henry Farman, later a pioneer aviator, built a light car in 1902, but then joined his brother Dick building 'BF' engines of 10, 12, 16, 24 and 45hp with single-cast cylinders which they supplied to builders of motor cars and launches.

FARMAN/*France 1920–1931*
The Farman brothers decided to build a luxury car in their aeroplane works after the war. The engine was an ohc straight-six of 6597cc. To this model A6B was later added the NF, with a larger engine of 7069cc. Very few of either model were made.

FARNELL/*England 1897*
Albert Farnell, a Bradford cycle agent, built this 1¼hp car with tubular chassis, four-speed transmission and independent front suspension. In 1906, Farnell sold the TH 28/36 and 30/40 hp cars.

FARNER/*USA 1922–1923*
Although the name and specifications were published widely, it is unlikely that the Farner progressed beyond the planning stage. Trade journals of the time listed the car as being powered by a Continental six-engine, and quoted a 115-inch wheelbase and three available body styles—touring car, coupé, and sedan—with prices ranging from $1095 to $1295 fob Streator, Illinois.

FAST/*Italy 1919–1923*
Designed by Ing. Orazi, the Fast had an ohc 2960cc four-cylinder engine. It was an exclusive car built in limited numbers, which disappeared after a short production period.

FASTO/*France 1924–1931*
One of the few cars made in the Puy de Dôme, Fasto started with a 10hp four-cylinder of 1598cc, followed with another 10hp of 1693cc and a 14hp of 2397cc. In 1930, Fasto only offered a 9hp four-cylinder of 1616cc.

FAUBER/*USA 1914*
A low-built cyclecar with steel-faced wood body/chassis unit and an 8/10hp twin-cylinder engine.

FAUGERE/*France 1898–c1901*
The Faugère was a spidery two-seater powered by a horizontal twin-cylinder engine, which could be started from the driver's seat by a lever. Top speed was 25kph (15mph).

FAUN/*Germany 1924–1929*
Famous for big lorries and municipal vehicles, Faun of Norimberk succeeded Ansbach, building light cars with ohc four-cylinder engines of 1410cc and 1550cc. The last models had Perrot four-wheel brakes.

FAURE/*France 1941–1947*
M. Faure made a batch of little urban electric cars during the German Occupation.

LE FAVORI/*France 1921–1923*
A tiny three-wheeled cyclecar made in Paris, with a 987cc twin-cylinder engine.

FAY/*USA 1921*
The Fay was built (or plans were under way for it to be built) as an export venture, but details of its construction are not known.

FD/*Belgium 1923–1929*
Light cars using 1·1-litre Ruby, 1½-litre CIM or 2-litre Altos engines.

FEDERAL/*USA 1901–1905*
A steam carriage built in Brooklyn, with all-steel bodywork.

FEDERAL/*USA 1907–1909*
A wheel-steered high-wheeled motor buggy, originally from Chicago, later from Rockford, Illinois.

FEJES/*Hungary 1923–1928*
The entire Fejes car was built up from pressed and welded iron sheet—even the 1244cc ohv engine. Plans to produce this Budapest utility vehicle in England as the Ascot were stillborn.

FELBER/*Switzerland 1975 to date*
This company is based at Morges and builds a Michelotti-styled Lancia-engined roadster, and the FF Ferrari V-12 sports model; latest model is the Pontiac Firebird-based Excellence Cabriolet/Coupé.

FELDMANN/*Germany 1905–1912*
Fafnir supplied the twin-cylinder 804cc engines for Feldmann's 'Nixe' voiturette. Other models built from 1908 onwards had ohv 2120cc four-cylinder engines developing 25bhp and, in a sporting version, 40bhp.

FEND/*Germany 1958–1961*
Produced the FMR Tiger, a sporting four-wheeled version of the Messerschmitt cabin-scooter. It had a 493cc twin-cylinder Sachs two-stroke engine, developing 19·5bhp at 5000rpm, mounted ahead of the rear axle, plus a four-speed gearbox. Only 240 were built.

EL FENIX/*Spain 1901–1904*
Domingo Tamaro Y Roig, who had worked with La Cuadra, built a few twin-cylinder petrol-engined cars under this name at Barcelona before joining Turcat-Méry in 1904.

FERGUS/*Ireland/USA 1920–1923*
The Fergus was the culmination of an earlier (1915) car of the same name built in Ireland by Joseph Ferguson, Senior. At least one car, and probably as many as nine or ten, were practically hand-fashioned at the company's headquarters in Newark, NJ. The car featured a high-revving six-cylinder engine with overhead valves and overhead camshaft, springs housed inside deep frame members and cantilever springs all round. It also boasted complete pressure lubrication. A sedan was priced at $8500.

1931 Farman saloon

1947/48 Ferrari 166

FERRARI / *Italy 1946 to date*

The great Enzo Ferrari, closely connected for many years (until the end of 1938) with Alfa Romeo, built a few sports cars bearing his own name and his prancing horse badge, 'inherited' from World War One air ace Francesco Baracca, in 1940, but real car production did not start until after the end of World War Two. In 1969, Ferrari became part of the Fiat empire, but Enzo Ferrari stayed on as head of his works at Maranello, near Modena. Some Fiat parts were used on his very early sports cars, but when Colombo designed new cars after the war, they were a 'pure' Ferrari product with dohc 1·5-litre, 2-litre and 2·5-litre V-12 engines in various stages of tune. After 1950, Lampredi designed 4·5-litre and also 2-litre (4 cylinder) sports and racing cars for Maranello, where V-12s of 4·1 litres, 4·5 litres and even 4·9 litres were built. Many superb and powerful sports cars have left the Maranello works over the years, some developing over 400 bhp. Ferraris won Le Mans, as well as many championships all over the world, and built numerous fast cars with V-engines from 6 to 12 cylinders with double ohc valve gear. Recently, Ferrari has

1965 Ferrari 275 Spyder

FIAT / *Italy 1899 to date*

Giovanni Agnelli, Count Biscaretti di Ruffia and Count di Bricherasio headed the Fabbrica Italiana Automobili Torino, which started business by absorbing Ceirano, on whose payroll was the talented designed Faccioli who created the first Fiat car, with a horizontal twin-cylinder 3½ hp engine. When the directors insisted that Faccioli should design a new model with the engine at the front instead of at the back, Faccioli resigned, and was replaced by Enrico, who in 1902 brought out a 1·2-litre four-cylinder model which owed much to the recently introduced Mercedes. The years up to 1914 saw a succession of four-cylinder models of between 1846cc and 10,082cc, as well as sixes of 7408cc and 11,034cc. However, Fiat (known as F.I.A.T. up to the end of 1906) did not essay a popular mass-produced

1899 Fiat 3½hp Victoria

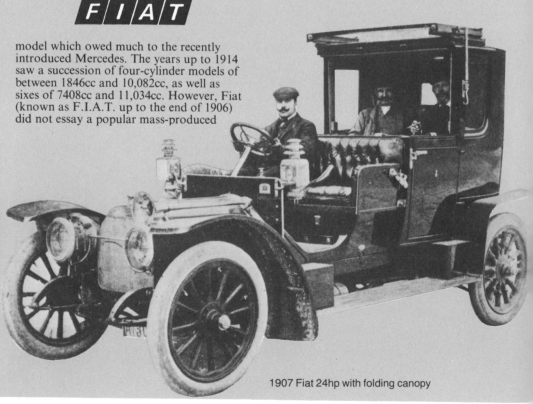

1907 Fiat 24hp with folding canopy

adopted flat-12 engines in his Formula 1 racing cars. In 1955 Ferrari took over the 2·5-litre F-1 Lancias; from 1961 onwards, Ferrari competition cars have been rear-engined. There have, however, been many superb front-engined production models, like the 275 GTB with a 300 bhp 3·3-litre V-12 and the 300 bhp 4-litre V-12 330 GT and GTC. Then there have been the 2-litre mid-

engined 180 bhp V-6 Dino GT, and 365 GTB 4 with a 4·4-litre 352 bhp V-12 and, recently, the mid-engined dohc 2·9-litre 352 bhp V-12 plus, more recently, the mid-engined dohc 2·9-litre 308 GTB/GTS and the 4·8-litre V-12 400 and 400 GT, successors to the 365 GT; these are coupés with Pininfarina bodywork. Another modern Ferrari, the BB 512, houses an ohc 4·9-litre flat-12 engine.

FERRIS / *USA 1920–1922*
The Ferris is a good example of an expensive, beautifully built assembled automobile. Continental six-cylinder engines were used for all models, the Series C20, C21, 60 and 70 displacements ranging from 4078cc to 5328cc. Disc wheels were used exclusively for the first two years — wire wheels were optional in 1922 and a 130-inch wheelbase was standard. Four open and two closed models comprised the catalogue offerings. An estimated 935 cars were produced in three years of manufacturing.

FERVES / *Italy 1965–1970*
A Fiat-based multi-purpose car with a rear-mounted 499cc two-cylinder in-line engine.

1969 Ferves Ranger 500cc

FIAL / *Italy 1906–1908*
This Milanese manufacturer offered a 6/8hp twin and a 10/12 hp four.

1976 Ferrari GT4

model until 1912, when the 1846cc 'Tipo Zero' was launched. Post-war came the Cavalli-designed 501, with a four-cylinder 1·5-litre engine, of which more than 45,000 had been built by 1926. Alongside this, Fiat produced a very few examples of one of their few flops, the hyper-luxury V-12 6·8-litre SuperFiat, of 1921–23; the 4·8-litre six-cylinder Tipo 519 was listed until 1929. In 1925 came a more modern light car, the 509, with an ohc 990cc engine, of which over 90,000 were sold up to 1929. The other principal models of the late 1920s were the 1440cc Tipo 514, the 2516cc Tipo 521 and

the 3740cc Tipo 525, the latter two being six-cylinder models. A major step forward came in 1932, with the introduction of the Tipo 508 Ballila (named after a Fascist youth organization), a 995cc ohv four developing 25 bhp in touring form, 36 bhp in its rare and desirable sporting form. It was licence-built in Germany by NSU, in Czechoslovakia by Walter and in France by Simca (who also offered a very fast version tuned by Gordini). The backbone-framed 1500 of 1936, with its aerodynamic bodywork and Dubonnet-type ifs, led later that year to the immortal 'Topolino'

(Mickey Mouse) Tipo 500, with its four-cylinder 570cc engine mounted ahead of the radiator; this tiny two-seater continued almost unchanged until 1948. At the outbreak of war, Fiat's best-selling models were the 500 (priced at £120 in England) and the 1100, or Millecento, while the biggest model then available was the 2852cc six, which cost £795 in Britain. Little of novelty appeared in the immediate post-war years, until the advent of the over-square 1400 four-cylinder in 1950. The last of the Topolini, the ohv 500C, was replaced by the new 633cc rear-engined '600' in 1955; this →

1922 Fiat 519 sedanca de ville

1932 Fiat 'Balilla'

continued from previous page

unit-construction saloon sold a million by 1960. A twin-cylinder 'Nuova 500' appeared in 1957, with a 499cc ohv power unit. Over 3 million examples of this model were built before it gave way to the derivative 126 in 1972. In the same vein as the 500 and 600 was the 850, with a rear-mounted four-cylinder in-line engine. In 1966 came one of Fiat's most popular models, the 124, with engines of 1197cc and 1438cc, which formed the basis of big licence-production deals, especially in Eastern Bloc countries. A dohc 1608cc four, the 125, appeared in 1967, alongside the 1481cc 1500L, the six-cylinder 1795cc 1800B and 2279cc 2300; the Dino Spyder and Coupé with the 1987cc Ferrari-built dohc Dino V-6 had been launched in 1966. In 1969 Fiat took over Lancia and Ferrari; Abarth was acquired in 1971. That year, Fiat launched the fwd 127, with a 903cc ohv transverse four (a 1049cc version

is also available); the 128 is another fwd model, with 1116cc and 1290cc power units. The successor to the 124, the 131 Mirafiore, is available with 1297cc or 1585cc engines in various stages of tune. There is also a dohc 1995cc Abarth version, with irs and a five-speed gearbox, developing 140 bhp and capable of reaching almost 145 mph in racing guise. A conventional 'middle-class' car, the 132 has dohc four-cylinder power units of 1585cc and 1995cc. Fiat also introduced in 1973 a series-production mid-engined sports car, the X1/9, with a 1290cc power unit and wedge-styling. Fiat today is far more than a car manufacturer, with interests as diverse as aircraft, shipbuilding, tourism, roadbuilding and machinery. At the end of 1977, Fiat numbered 270 manufacturing facilities, including 35 car plants, in 22 countries, plus affiliated operations in others.

1952 Fiat 8V aerodynamic coupé

1955 Fiat 600

1938 Fiat 2800 Cabriolet

1979 Fiat Strada 65CL

FIAT / *USA 1910–1918*
This American-financed company built big four-cylinder Fiats under licence at Pough-keepsie, New York, in a factory which even had its own foundry. Initially, the 5899cc Type 54 was built: from 1912 a Poughkeepsie-designed 'Type 56' was available, with a monobloc 8553cc engine. But the most famous American Fiat was the Type 55, a monstrous 9026cc four whose top speed was only 62 mph. In 1918, Rochester-Duesenberg took over the plant for aeroengine manufacture.

FIF / *Belgium 1909–1914*
Built by Felix Heck, of Etterbeck, near Brussels, the FIF was a voiturette of sporting pretensions.

FILIPINETTI / *Switzerland 1967–late 1960s*
Motor museum owner and Minister Georges Filipinetti, of the Chateau Grandson, was responsible for these 1600cc VW-powered sports coupés styled by Sbarro.

FILTZ / *France 1899–c1908*
Filtz began production with a voiturette powered by a curious power unit with two horizontal pistons each driving separate vertical crank-shafts geared together. This power unit was also used by Turgan-Foy, and supplying engines to other manufacturers seems to have been Filtz's main activity, though the firm (from Neuilly-sur-Seine) was still exhibiting its own-make chassis at the 1907 Paris Salon, offering powers of 10 hp to 130 hp, though the cars on display were of 12/16 hp, 20/25 hp and 35/40 hp.

FIMER / *Italy 1948–1949*
One of the many mini-cars built after World War Two, the Fimer had a 246cc two-stroke motorcycle engine in the rear: few were made.

FINA-SPORT / *USA 1953–1954*
Perry Fina created the Fina-Sport using a 210 hp Cadillac V-8 engine and Hydramatic transmission on a Ford chassis. Convertible and hardtop styling was by Vignale.

FINLANDIA / *Finland 1923*
Just two Finlandia cars, large vee-radiatored tourers, were built by coachbuilder P. J. Heik-kila: a fire engine was mounted on the same chassis for use in Helsinki.

FINLAYSON / *Australia 1900–1907*
The Finlayson brothers of Tasmania built a successful steam buggy in 1900, then produced nine larger petrol vehicles, including a bus.

The Finlayson, built in Tasmania c.1900

1903 Firefly 8hp tonneau

FIREFLY/*England 1903*
This Croydon firm built 6 hp ('Genuine De Dion engine') and 10 hp cars.

FIRESTONE-COLUMBUS/*USA 1907–1915*
Starting with high-wheelers, by 1909 this company had progressed to a 26 hp 'Mechanical Greyhound' roadster.

FISCHER/*Switzerland 1909–1919*
Martin Fischer broke away from Turicum at the end of 1908 and began development of a four-cylinder voiturette, still with friction drive. Production began late in 1909 in the former Weidmann factory; after 70 cars had been built, Fischer used an ingenious four-speed gearbox in which a pinion on a cardan shaft engaged with internally toothed gears to give direct drive in every ratio. In 1911, Fischer launched a 33 cv sleeve-valve four of 2724cc with half-moon-shaped sleeves 'rounding off' oval bores; a six-cylinder (4086cc) appeared in 1914. Only two of these were built after the war and Fischer closed down, though the six was built under licence in the USA. A 1919 cyclecar with a vee-twin MAG engine and, again, friction drive, proved a short-lived project.

FISSON/*France 1895–c1898*
A two-seater car with a Benz engine.

FISSORE/*Italy 1977 to date*
Basically a Fiat 127, the Fissore Scout 127 is delivered with a variety of—mainly open—coachwork. The works are at Savigliano.

FL/*France 1908–1914*
Originally built by H. De la Fresnaye of Paris and Levallois-Perret, the FL light car was produced after 1910 in the Otto works.

FLAC/*Denmark 1914–1915*
Mammen & Drescher, of Jyderup, built 25 cars with American 10 hp four-cylinder engines of unknown origin. One or two cars used French engines.

FLAG/*Italy 1904–1907*
Made on the lines of the English Thornycroft cars, the FLAG had four-cylinder 18 hp and 30 hp and six-cylinder 45 hp 7772cc engines. FLAG also imported Thornycrofts into Italy; hence the close co-operation.

FLAGLER/*USA 1914–1915*
A $450 cyclecar from Cheboygan, Michigan, the sporty four-cylinder Flagler had shaft drive, not the customary belt.

FLAID/*Belgium 1920–1921*
This 10/12 hp light car was designed for export to Britain.

FLANDERS/*USA 1909–1912*
Sister marque to EMF, and sold through Studebaker, this was a 2450cc four, initially offered with two speeds, later with three.

LA FLECHE/*France 1912–1913*
An 8 hp friction-driven cyclecar from Guders Jack, Paris.

FLETCHER/*England 1966–1967*
Norman Fletcher Ltd. were boat builders by trade, but filled in a quiet period of production in 1966 with their version of the recently terminated Ogle SX1000. John Handley enjoyed success with a racing version, but only four cars eventually saw the light of day.

FLINT/*USA 1923–1927*
Billy Durant's Flint Six (designed by Zeder, Skelton and Breer, under Walter Chrysler's leadership) was named after America's 'Carriage Capital', though it was also built in Long Island City, NY, and Bridgeport, Connecticut. Four-wheel hydraulic brakes were fitted from 1925, except on the low-priced junior model.

FLORENTIA/*Italy 1903–1912*
Once a well-known make, who also exported cars to England. They had 4396cc, 5425cc and 9847cc four-cylinder and 6594cc six-cylinder engines. There were also 16 hp and 24 hp four-cylinder models, some built under French Rochet-Schneider licence. In later years, the Florence-based factory built marine engines. Among their designers were such famous men as Cattaneo, who afterwards headed the Isotta-Fraschini design department, and Antonio Chiribiri, who later built fast sporting cars.

FLORIO/*Italy 1913*
The forerunner of Beccaria cars, this marque was inspired by Cav. Vincenzo Florio, the famous Sicilian pioneer and founder of the Targa Florio. The model made was an 18 hp four-cylinder of 2951cc. Its price in England was £385. There were also a few racing cars made privately by Florio in Sicily.

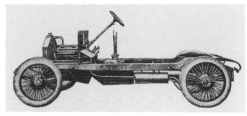

1913 Florio 18hp chassis

FN/*Belgium 1899–1939*
This famous armament factory from Liège began production with a twin-cylinder, two-speed voiturette, but by 1906 was building the Rochet-Schneider under licence. In 1908, an FN-designed 2-litre appeared, followed by a range of well-engineered light cars of 1245 to 1500cc. Though cars of up to 3800cc were built during the 1920s, the best-known vintage FN was the ohv 1300cc, which was available with front-wheel brakes; this model, and its 1400cc and 1625cc derivatives, enjoyed a number of sporting successes, and remained in production until 1933. A 3·2-litre straight-eight was current from 1930 to 1935, and the 2-litre 'Baudouin' model replaced the old 1625cc. There was also an aerodynamic saloon, the 'Prince Albert', with either 2·2-litre or 3·8-litre engines. Production effectively ceased in 1935.

FONCK/*France 1921–1925*
World War One flying ace René Fonck made these luxury cars in the Fraysse Unieux factory. The engines of the Fonck were designed by engineer Gadoux and built by CIME. They were ohc units, available in four-cylinder (2614cc) and eight-cylinder (5228cc) form. Later, Fonck produced a smaller ohc eight of 3303cc. Their customers were offered an unlimited guarantee.

FONDU/*Belgium 1906–c1912*
The first Fondu, a pair-cast 24/30 hp four of 4·8 litres, was the pattern for the Russo-Baltique. Fondu, of Vilvorde, Brussels, later offered monobloc fours of 1·7 and 2·1 litres, a 1·1-litre light car appearing in 1912.

FONLUPT/*France 1920–1922*
At their Levallois works, Fonlupt made a small number of the 1539cc four-cylinder 10 hp Sport and the 10 hp 2155cc Ville, also a four-cylinder. There was also an eight-cylinder of 4310cc. All these engines had ohc.

FORD/*USA 1903 to date*
Henry Ford's ambition of 'building a car for the great multitude' was reflected in his early twin-cylinder A, C and F models, though his backers forced him to build higher-priced, less-successful models (the four-cylinder B and the six-cylinder K). His first major success came with the modestly priced 15 hp Model N (1906) which paved the way for the immortal Model T of 1908–27, the 'car that put the world on wheels' — some 16·5 million were built in its 19-year life-span. Its successor, Model A, retained Ford's transverse suspension, but was much more conventional than the eccentric T, which up to its demise retained a two-speed epicyclic transmission and rear-wheel brakes only. Model A, the first production car with a safety glass windscreen, had four-wheel brakes and a three-speed sliding gearbox; a million were sold in its first 16 months, an all-time record still unbroken. It was followed by the 1932 AB and its more glamorous derivative, the 18F V-8, 'Ford's last mechanical triumph'. The flathead V-8 was Ford's mainstay in the 1930s, with progressive styling and mechanical updates, and the 1942 range was the basis of post-war production, though 1946 cars shared Mercury's 3916cc V-8 instead of using the pre-war 3621cc unit. A milestone was the 1949 line, the first Ford to feature ifs (rear suspension was semi-elliptic, another break with tradition). Three-speed Fordamatic transmission appeared in 1951, which year also saw the special edition V-8 Crestliner, succeeded by the Victoria hardtop. In 1952 a short-stroke six of 3654cc, to remain Ford's basic unit until 1964, appeared, and the 'Y-block' ohv V-8 of 3917cc followed in 1954. All-new styling, wraparound windscreens and bright two-tone paint dispelled Ford's traditionally conservative image on 1955 models, which included the immortal two-passenger Thunderbird 'personal car', an instant success. Also included in the 1955 line-up were the Fairlane Sunliner Convertible and the Crown Victoria, whose Skyliner hardtop featured a transparent plexiglass roof over the front seat. This hothouse roof gave way to the complex Skyliner retractable hardtop, offered from 1957–59, with total sales of 48,000. The restyled 1957 models — Custom and Custom 300, Fairlane and Fairlane 500 — offered a bewildering array of engines from 4457cc to 5113cc in a 21-model line-up. Introduced for 1959 was the top of the range Galaxies. The most successful of the compacts, the 2360cc six-cylinder Falcon, appeared in 1960, and a new intermediate Fairlane range, with a 2786cc six or 3622cc V-8, was launched in 1962. One of the most successful of all Ford models, the Mustang, appeared in 1964; this 2+2 personal sports car was powered by the 2786cc six as standard, with three V-8s up to 4736cc optional. The millionth Mustang was sold in 1966, in which year the fwd Bronco was added to the range, as was the Torino, with engines from 3277cc to 6391cc. In 1967 came the top of the range LTD, based on the Galaxie; by 1969, the Galaxie/LTD range totalled 21 models. The 1969 six-cylinder Maverick was Ford's smallest model until the advent of the Pinto two years later. Disc brakes were standardized throughout the range in 1974, when Ford offered cars with engines varying from 2294cc to a 7538cc V-8 standard in the T-Bird, and optional in the Torino, LTD and the new Mercedes-inspired Elite. The 1976 line-up was the Pinto, Maverick, Torino, Granada, Bronco, Mustang II, Thunderbird, Elite and the mighty LTD, which was 18 ft 7 in long, with most power options as standard. In 1978, the Fairmont replaced the Maverick; promoted as a 'European-style automobile', it was powered by engines from 2294cc to 4949cc. The Fiesta 1600 was imported from Europe, and a T-Bird-based LTD II appeared alongside the old LTD, which was down-sized to 17 ft 5 in for 1979. This left the 18 ft 3 in LTD II as the biggest Ford, with four-wheel disc brakes standard and 4949cc V-8 power, the 6555cc and 7538cc engines being dropped in the interests of fuel economy.

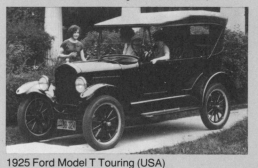
1925 Ford Model T Touring (USA)

1950 Ford Fordor Sedan (USA)

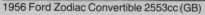
1980 Ford LTD four-door sedan (USA)

1956 Ford Zodiac Convertible 2553cc (GB)

1980 Ford Cortina GLS (GB)

1979 Fiesta Millionaire
(limited edition to celebrate
1,000,000 Fiestas) (FDR)

FORD/ *England 1911 to date*
The first Ford factory outside America opened in a former tramcar works at Trafford Park, Manchester, in October 1911, assembling Model Ts from imported components. Apart from local coachwork in 1912–14 and the use (at extra cost!) of a 14 9 hp engine built at Ford's Cork plant, instead of the 24 hp engine, in the Model A from 1928, cars followed the American pattern until February 1932, when the first 'European' small Ford, the Dearborn-designed 8 hp Model Y of 933cc, was exhibited at Ford's Albert Hall Show after a gestation period of only five months. Improved, it entered production at Ford's new Dagenham factory the following August, and formed the basis of Ford light car design until the 1950s. It was also built at Asnières (Paris), Barcelona and Cologne. In 1934 came the 1172cc Model C Ten, ancestor of the Prefect (1939–53). The Model Y became the first and only £100 saloon car in September 1935; its 1940 development, the Anglia, was produced until 1953, when its 10 hp export variant became the Popular, built in the former Doncaster Briggs Bodies plant until 1959. Dagenham built its first 30 hp V-8 in 1935, soon also offering a 22 hp version similar to the Matford Alsace. This provided the coachwork for the 1947–52 30 hp Pilot V-8. The first unit-constructed ohv Fords with ifs, the Consul four and Zephyr six, appeared in 1950, with convertible models and a deluxe six, the Zephyr Zodiac, available from 1953. That year unit-constructed 1172cc side-valve 100 E models of the Anglia and Prefect appeared. In 1959 came the lively 105E Anglia, with an ohv 997cc engine and reverse-rake rear window. Transitional models, the 1961 Consul Classic and Capri, heralded the MkI Cortina of 1962, which sold over a million before it was replaced in 1967 by a MkII version. There was even a Lotus version of the MkI and MkII Cortinas. The Corsair line adopted V-4 engines in 1965, followed by a V-4 and V-6 Zephyr and Zodiac MkIVs from spring 1966. In 1966–70, Ford's Advanced Vehicle Operations at Slough built 101 examples of the spectacular road-racing GT40. The Halewood, Merseyside, plant introduced the Escort in 1968 to replace the Anglia: 1100 and 1300cc engines were standard, with a 1558cc twin-cam engine fitted to the sporting version. The sporting Escort, in both MkI and MkII versions, became the most successful individual model in the history of motor sport, its victory in the 1970 World Cup Rally giving birth to the 1600cc pushrod-engined Mexico. The 1979 line-up consisted of the Fiesta (announced in 1976), the Escort, the Capri (MkIII versions of a 'personalized' model announced in 1969, but now imported from Cologne, as is the big-car Granada range) and a MkIV Cortina.

FORD/ *Germany 1925 to date*
From 1925 Ford assembled cars at Berlin-Plötzensee and in 1931 opened a new factory at Cologne, where the first cars were made to American designs. They included the 933cc Köln (model 19-Y) and the 3285cc four-cylinder Rheinland, which was really a re-bodied Model B. V-8 Fords were imported until 1934, then built at Cologne, using the 3618cc engine, and from 1939 Cologne also offered the smaller 2228cc V-8. The 1172cc Eifel (based on the English Model C-20 10 hp) of 1935–39 was a bestseller. The post-war 1172cc Taunus, nicknamed 'Buckel' (hunchback), was a developed version of the 1939 Taunus, which appeared in 1948, to be superseded in 1952 by an improved and modernized Taunus 12M, developing 38 bhp at 4250 rpm. The 15M, with a 1498cc ohv engine, appeared in 1955. New in 1957 was the 1698cc 17M, followed by 1758cc versions. A new Taunus with 1183cc and 1498cc engines appeared after 1962; this range had V-4 power-units and front-wheel drive. A 1280cc version, and also larger models with V-engines, were added in 1966 and 1967, while V-motors (including ohv V-6 1998cc and 2293cc engines) were also included in the range of rear-wheel-driven German Fords. Sixes of 2550cc were added in 1969, while 1968 saw the introduction of the 1098cc in-line four-cylinder Escort. A new 1285cc four-cylinder in-line Taunus appeared in 1970, followed in 1974 by a 1576cc version: the 1981cc Taunus still had the V-6 motor. The first Capris of 1969 had in-line and V-engines of 1288 to 2637cc, heralding a move towards total European rationalization (apart from some engine variations) of the Ford range: it was superseded by the improved Capri II in 1974, followed in turn by the four-headlamp Capri III in 1977. A new Consul/Granada range appeared in 1972: the 1978 Granada, built only in Germany, was the flagship of Ford's European range. In 1979 Ford's German factories also built the Fiesta, Escort, Taunus (identical with the British Cortina) and the Capri.

Ford France Védette, 1952

FORD/ *France 1947–1954*
Ford-France resumed production post-war in a purpose-built plant at Poissy (Seine), but the car they introduced, the 2158cc V-8 Védette, an American-styled full-width fastback with ifs, was sadly out of tune with post-war demands for economy. Elegant Facel-bodied Comète versions were available from 1952, but two years later Ford sold Poissy to Simca, who continued to build the V-8 as the Simca Védette.

FORD FALCON/ *Australia 1960 to date*
Ford Australia was originally established in 1925 to assemble Model T Fords, with local bodies. The company's manufacturing capacity steadily grew and in 1960 a locally manufactured version of the Ford Falcon was launched with a six-cylinder engine. Subsequent models have progressively grown away from US influence and, since 1965, the Falcon range has been unique to Australia. The 1978 models were offered in five body styles (sedan, coupé, waggon, utility and van), with six-cylinder and V-8 engines.

1978 Ford Falcon 500 (AUS)

FORDINETTE JD/*France 1922–1923*
M. Depreux made a small cyclecar (no connection with Ford) in Levallois powered by an 807cc four-cylinder Chapuis-Dornier engine.

FOREST/*England 1910–1914*
A friction-driven 8 hp vee-twin light car from Liverpool which sold for £165 complete.

FORMAN/*England 1905*
Forman of Coventry were engine manufacturers who also built a few chassis with their 14 hp four-cylinder power unit.

FORSTER/*Canada 1920*
A large right-hand-drive quasi-luxury automobile; the Forster plans called for a six-cylinder Herschell-Spillman engine and standardized components throughout, including disc wheels, Rolls-Royce-type radiator and a maple leaf emblem. Why the right-hand steering is anyone's guess although, at the time, four of Canada's provinces and Newfoundland (then a dominion) were still adhering to the left of the road. It did not matter in the long run, as the plans for the car failed to materialize.

FORTIER/*France 1898*
Two separate single-cylinder air-cooled engines powered this belt-drive voiturette.

FOSSUM/*Norway 1906–1907*
In 1906 M. H. Fossum of Oslo built his first car which had a twin-cylinder engine and looked like an American 'gas-buggy'. Soon after, he built a car which was more or less a copy of the contemporary Oldsmobile.

FOSTER/*USA 1899–c1904*
Piano makers Foster & Company, of Rochester, NY, put their first 5 hp steam car on the market late in 1899. At first, they built light tiller-steered steamers on Locomobile lines: in 1902 a heavier 15 hp model with wheel steering and a front-mounted engine was introduced.

FOUCHER & DELACHANEL/*France 1897*
An 'elegant voiturette' with a horizontal-twin engine and handlebar steering.

FOUILLARON/*France 1900–1914*
Fouillaron of Levallois-Perret used an ingenious infinitely variable belt drive throughout their existence, even racing a 5054cc Aster-engined 24 hp in the Paris-Madrid. Buchet and De Dion engines with one, two, three and four cylinders were also employed. Largest production model was the 16/20 hp of 3·7 litres.

FOURNIER/*France 1913–1924*
The small garage run by racing driver Fournier in Levallois started building light Ballot-engined cars before the war. Post-war, Fournier resumed production with a light cyclecar using a sv 995cc Train vee-twin engine and friction drive. Later, a sv 904cc Ruby-engined cyclecar and a larger version with a 1131cc Ballot engine appeared.

FOURNIER-MARCADIER
France 1963 to date
A small workshop in Lyon which makes small sports and racing cars using engines and parts from Renault and Simca. The body is made of polyester, and these vehicles are supplied either in kit form or as complete cars.

FOX/*France 1912–1923*
A Neuilly (Seine) firm which built monobloc fours of 9, 10/12, 12/15, 14/16 and 18 hp. Post-1919, a Chapuis-Dornier of 11·9 hp was fitted.

FOX/*USA 1921–1923*
Designed by Ansley W. Fox (designer of the famous Fox shotgun favoured by President Theodore Roosevelt on his big game expeditions), the Fox car threatened the Franklin for a time in its bid for supremacy among American air-cooled motor cars of the period. A larger and considerably faster car than the Franklin, the Fox was also considerably more expensive. Using a 4398cc six-cylinder engine of its own design, the Fox was popular with bootleggers during America's 'Great Experiment' of Prohibition. Unlike the Franklin, the Fox was not prone to overheating. Production was small, however, and relatively few Fox sedans, coupés and phaetons were seen on the highway. Prices ranged from $3900 to $4900.

FOY-STEELE/*England 1913–1916*
A handsome bullnosed radiator adorned this Coventry-Simplex-engined 12 hp sold by ex-racer Charles Jarrott, a co-founder of the Automobile Association. 'Foy' steel alloy was used in its chassis, hence the name.

FRAMO/*Germany 1932–1937*
Closely connected with DKW at Zschopau, Framo was owned by J. S. Rasmussen (founder of DKW), but did not join the Auto Union. Framo was a large accessory factory which built the 198cc and 298cc Piccolo cars with modified DKW two-stroke engines. There were also three-wheeled Framo models, with two-stroke engines up to 596cc.

FRANCO/*Italy 1905–1912*
Attilio Franco was a small producer at Sesto San Giovanni who became known when Cariolato's Franco won the 1910 Targa Florio (184·8 miles) in Sicily, in front of the Sigma driven by De Prosperis. The engine of the Franco cars was a 6·8-litre 28/40 hp four-cylinder.

FRANCON/*France 1922–1925*
This firm, which specialized in making stationary and marine engines, built light cars with a two-stroke engine, first of 458cc, then of 622cc and 664cc, with friction drive.

FRANGAR/*France 1907*
M. Rutishauser of Paris was the manufacturer of this 12/15 hp model.

FRANKLIN/*USA 1902–1934*
Every Franklin ever built had air-cooling, most had full-elliptic suspension and, until 1927, all had wooden chassis. The first cars to leave the company's Syracuse, New York, factory had transverse four-cylinder engines with overhead valves; a model with a conventionally disposed engine of four or six cylinders under a circular bonnet appeared in 1905, and from 1907 featured automatic ignition advance and retard. A new bonnet design and full pressure lubrication were 1912 improvements. In 1915 a Franklin was driven 860 miles across America in bottom gear without overheating; that year's Franklins were probably the first American production cars with aluminium pistons. In 1922, the Renault-style bonnet was replaced by a sloping dummy radiator; 1925 saw the handsome De Causse-styled Series LL, which included an electric primer for its carburettor. However, four-wheel brakes did not appear until 1927 when the 26 hp Airman model was announced; Atlantic flyer Charles Lindbergh had four of this model. Custom bodies designed by Ray Dietrich proliferated on Franklin cars in the late 1920s, but failed to arrest falling sales. By 1932, the wooden chassis had been phased out: that year a 95 mph Dietrich-styled V-12 appeared, but failed to sell, and the last Franklin, the Olympic, was a Reo in all but power unit.

1908 Franklin 18hp

FRAYER-MILLER/*USA 1904–1910*
Famous air-cooled cars from Ohio: a 24 hp four and 6522cc six were the principal offerings.

FRAZER/*USA 1946–1951*
Billed as Kaiser-Frazer's luxury offering, the Frazer was powered by a 3703cc 'Supersonic' sv six, designed by Continental but built by K-F. Two models were offered — a four-door sedan and top of the range Manhattan, with interior trim rivalling Cadillac and Lincoln. A convertible was available from 1949, and 1951 models included the dual-purpose Vagabond with rear hatch and fold-down back seat. A total of 151,983 Frazers was built before production of Frazer (and Kaiser) cars ended.

FRAZER NASH/*England 1924–1960*
Archie Frazer-Nash's highly individual chain-driven sports car was a logical extension of the earlier GN with which it shared a similar transmission layout. This had a dog-clutch gear change, separate chains for each of the three forward speeds and a solid rear axle. Quarter-elliptic springs were another inheritance. A variety of proprietary engines was fitted. Initially a Powerplus was listed, though this was succeeded by the 1½-litre side-valve Anzani unit. This in its turn was replaced by the ohv Meadows. From 1934 an ohc 1½-litre four-cylinder

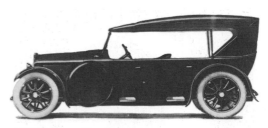

1922 Fremont Six phaeton

1925 Frazer Nash Super Sports in the Six-Hour
Trial at Brooklands

power unit was also fitted, latterly known as the
Gough (after its designer, Albert Gough). This
particular engine was fitted to the Shelsley and
TT Replica models, though in the former instance yet another engine variant was available,
the dohc 1667cc six-cylinder Blackburne. In
1929 H. J. Aldington took over the company,
and in 1934 began importing the German BMW
car; clearly the days of the archaic chain-drive
cars were numbered, though a trickle continued
to be made up until 1939. By contrast, the post-
war Frazer Nash was a far more sophisticated
product, using as its power unit the 2-litre pre-
war BMW 328 engine, jointly developed by the
Bristol Aeroplane Company and the Aldington
brothers. This was mounted in a tubular chassis
with transverse leaf independent front suspension and torsion bar rear suspension. In 1948 the
High Speed Model appeared and from that
derived the Le Mans Replica (following a 3rd
placing in the 1949 24-hour classic). A win in the
1951 Targo Florio made the Frazer Nash the
only British car to have won victory laurels on
the twisting Sicilian circuit. Latter-day 'Nashes
were fitted with BMW V-6 2·6-litre engines
though the capacity was later increased to 3·2
litres. The marque's last appearance was at the
1959 Motor Show, production ceasing the following year.

FREDONIA/*USA 1902–1904*
The 9 hp Fredonia, from Youngstown, Ohio,
had a curious single-cylinder valveless engine
with a pre-compression chamber to force the
fuel-air mixture into the combustion chamber.

FREIA/*Germany 1922–1927*
Designed and raced by Ernst Schuh, the Freia
was an underslung limited-production sports
car, with 1320cc or 1472cc sv four-cylinder
engines. The factory was at Greiz.

FREJUS/*Italy 1909–1924*
Made by Diatto at Turin, the Fréjus was a small
car initially built under licence from Clément-
Bayard of France. An own-design small car
with a 1350cc four-cylinder engine followed.

FREMONT/*USA 1921 1922*
The Fremont was intended for export, but
whether any cars were actually built and sent
abroad is speculative. Specifications called for a
six-cylinder Falls engine and standard com-

ponents throughout. According to promotional
literature, the cars carried cycle-type fenders,
door steps and horizontal louvres on the hood,
an unusual mode of design as early as 1921–22.
Fremont also built a truck under the Fremont
emblem, and All-American trucks were assembled at the Fremont factory in Fremont, Ohio.

FRENAY/*Belgium 1914*
A vee-radiatored 10/12 hp four of 1460cc, from
Liège.

FRICK/*England 1904 1906*
Alfred Dougill of Leeds built a number of rear-
engined cars from 1896–99: he also made the
Lawson Motor Wheel for converting horse-
carriages and the 1900–04 Loidis. The Frick
had friction transmission, the principal model
being an 8/10hp twin of 2190cc. A 7 hp single
(1095cc) and 12/18 hp three-cylinder (3285cc)
were also listed. A hand-wheel on the steering
column operated dual friction wheels 'through a
system of compound levers'.

FRIEDMAN/*USA 1900–1903*
'The equal of any $1200 gasoline automobile',
the Chicago-built $750 Friedman Road Wagon
was a typical gas buggy, with a 6 hp flat-twin
four-stroke engine and tiller steering.

FRIEND/*USA 1920–1922*
A small-production light automobile, the
Friend was successor to the Olympian and was
produced in small quantities. Using its own-
make four-cylinder engine and with a wheelbase
of 112 inches, Friend offered a roadster touring
car, coupé and sedan, with prices from $1285.

FRITCHLE/*USA 1904–1917*
In 1905, this electric car maker listed a $2500
'Torpedo Roadster' with Renault-type bonnet.

FRONTENAC/*USA 1906–1912*
During 1906 the Abendroth & Root Company
of Newburgh, NY, built an initial batch of 40 to
50 touring cars using a 40 hp pair-cast four of
5877cc, carried in a pressed-steel subframe.

FRONTENAC/*USA 1922–1924*
There is much natural confusion over the 'Frontenac' name as it has been used frequently, both
in the USA and Canada. Frontenac Motors
Co./Frontenac Motors Corp. produced two
distinct automobiles in 1922 and 1924 respectively. In 1922 they announced a 3225cc four-
cylinder car with wire wheels. The car never
survived the prototype phase. In 1924, a highly
attractive eight-cylinder sleeve-valve sport
phaeton was shown. This car, with a 5864cc
displacement, featured wire wheels and four-
wheel hydraulic brakes. Like its 1922 predecessor, this car was designed by Louis Chevrolet
and only appeared in prototype form.

FRONTMOBILE/*USA 1917–1918*
An early attempt to build a front-wheel-drive
'Safety Motor', the Frontmobile came from
New Jersey. A sharply dropped chassis behind
the engine gave a very low build, there was a
complex push-pull gear mechanism, and
suspension — cantilever at the front, transverse
full-elliptic at the rear — was just weird.

FROUSSART/*France 1907*
An obscure marque from Charleville in the
Ardennes, shown at the 1907 Paris Salon.

FRP/*USA 1914–1918*
Designed by Finley Robertson Porter, the FRP
is historically important as being the second car
designed by Porter, the first having been the T-
head Mercer. The FRP, of which an estimated
nine units were made, boasted a 170 bhp engine
and a $5000-and-up chassis with coachwork
available either from Holbrook or M. Armstrong. A Mercedes-type vee-radiator was distinctive and the car was by far the most powerful
automobile in America in the stock car category
of the time. The FRP was the lineal predecessor
of the Porter car of 1919–22.

FUCHS/*Austria 1921–1922*
This was an ephemeral sports car, made by the
Inzersdorfer Industrie Werke. It had a sv 1180cc
four-cylinder engine and was designed by Hans
Fuchs, who also raced his products along with
his works drivers Littman and Teutscher.

FULDAMOBIL/*Germany 1950–1960*
Single-cylinder Ilo and Sachs engines powered
this light three-wheeler, fitted first with a composite wood/alloy body, with all-steel construction from 1953 and bodied in glass fibre
from 1957.

FULLER/*USA 1908–1910*
High-wheelers with two- or four-cylinder
engines, from Angus, Nebraska.

FULLER/*USA 1909–1911*
This Jackson, Mich., factory built both high-
wheelers and conventional cars. Their 1910
Model 30 roadster had a two-speed epicyclic
gear and sold for $1065.

FULMINA/*Germany 1913–1926*
The Hofmann-designed Fulmina-cars were
made in limited numbers at Friedrichsfeld, near
Mannheim. They had sv four-cylinder engines
of 2595cc and 4212cc.

FUSI FERRO/*Italy 1948–1949*
This Fusi-designed car, a 1086cc eight-cylinder,
was built in very limited numbers.

FUTURA/*England 1971*
The Futura was dreamt up by Jem Cars, makers
of the Mini-Jem. Based on a VW floor-pan, the
car carried a highly eye-catching body, the
nose of which hinged sideways to allow entry
from the front. However, development of the
Futura drained the company's resources to the
point of liquidation.

GABRIEL/*France 1912–1914*
Four-cylinder cars of 9/12 hp, 13/18 hp and 20/30 hp built in Paris.

GADABOUT/*USA 1913–1915*
Looking like a mobile wastepaper basket, this four-cylinder cyclecar from Newark, NJ, had a body woven from 'waterproof reeds'.

GAETH/*USA 1902–1911*
'The best $3500 car on the market', the 6423cc 35/40 hp 1909 Gaeth was a powerful four-cylinder from Cleveland, Ohio. It succeeded a 25/30 hp horizontal three-cylinder.

1907 Targa Florio Gaggenau

GAGGENAU/*Germany 1905–1911*
Known also as SAF (for Süddeutsche Automobil Fabrik), Theodor Bergmann's works had, in Josef Vollmer, one of Germany's leading designers of the era. They built the 567cc single-cylinder Lilliput, followed by four-cylinder cars of 4991cc and 8830cc. Gaggenau also built high-efficiency racing cars and, eventually, aero-engines. Gaggenaus were superb, low-built cars which won many sporting events. Otto Hieronymus was one of their designer-driver aces. Georg Wyss eventually bought the works and concentrated production on commercials, though he also continued manufacture of cars, which he, too, drove in sporting events. There was a close co-operation with Benz at Mannheim, and in 1910 Benz bought the Gaggenau factory.

GAINSBOROUGH/*England 1902–1904*
The 16 hp Gainsborough car had a horizontally opposed engine with only one double-ended piston to each pair of cylinders, acting on connecting rods outside the cylinders.

GALBA/*France 1929–1931*
Another Violet-designed small car built in Courbevoie, with a two-stroke 564cc engine.

GALE/*USA 1904–1910*
Starting with a typical single-cylinder gas buggy, with wheel steering and a dummy bonnet, the Western Tool Works, of Galesburg, Illinois, had progressed by 1907 to a 24/26 hp model which, they boasted, 'climbs hills like a squirrel and eats up the road like an express train'. Gale cars were distinguished by their tilting bodies, for easy access to the mechanism.

GALLIA/*France 1903–1908*
Elegant electric carriages from Paris, capable of 26 km/h. The company also made Dixi petrol cars under the name 'Régina'.

GALLIOT/*France 1908*
A tandem two-seater sporting voiturette designed by Norbert Galliot, with either a single- or three-cylinder mid-mounted engine — a kind of proto-cyclecar!

GALLOWAY/*Scotland 1921–1928*
Arrol-Johnston's light car, the Galloway had a 1460cc four-cylinder engine and three-speed gearbox. This 10·5 hp model was designed by T. C. Pullinger and lasted until 1925, being replaced by a 12 hp model with a pushrod overhead valve engine. Originally based at Tongland in Kirkcudbright, production was transferred to Heathall, Dumfries, in 1923.

GALT/*Canada 1911–1913*
Based on the US Alpena, the Canada Tourist and Roadster used the same 30 hp and 25 hp Hazard engines: in 1912, the Galt became Canada's first car with electric starting.

GALT/*Canada 1913–1927*
Starting by assembling ten cars from components left by the defunct Galt company, this new firm used the profits to develop two petrol-electrics, but gave up trying to find backers in 1927. One of these cars often provided emergency electric power for the local cinema.

GAMAGE/*England 1900–1915*
Gamages was a well-known London department store who sold a wide range of cars and motor tricycles under their own name, though most of these vehicles were certainly Continental imports. The 1903 Gamage (with either 7 hp Aster or 6 hp De Dion power unit) was, for instance, very similar in appearance to the Regal. In 1915 a Chapuis-Dornier-engined light car was offered.

GAMMA/*France 1921–1922*
This minor manufacturer from Courbevoie listed three different models, of 1131cc, 1593cc and 2297cc, with Ballot and Altos engines. The first Gamma (or Gamma-Hebe) was apparently built in 1914.

GAR/*France 1922–1931*
M. Gardahaut started by making a vee-twin cyclecar in Clichy, but quickly turned to sports cars with various proprietary engines: 1100cc Ruby, SCAP and Chapuis-Dornier, and 1500cc SCAP. More interesting were his own-make ohc 733cc four and an ohc eight of 1374cc, often supercharged for racing.

GARANZINI/*Italy 1924–1926*
Racing motorcyclist and motorcycle manufacturer Oreste Garanzini also built a few cars with ohv 1194cc four-cylinder proprietary engines.

GARBATY/*Germany 1924–1927*
Garbaty's factory at Mainz built a few ohv four-cylinder cars, whose 1205cc engine developed 25 bhp at 2500 rpm.

GARDNER/*USA 1919–1931*
Formerly the St Louis Chevrolet assembly plant, the Gardner carriage works introduced a Lycoming-engined 3153cc 'Light Four' in 1919. Six- and eight-cylinder models appeared in 1924, and the marque's sole offering from 1926–29 was a 4273cc eight with expanding hydraulic four-wheel brakes and centralized door locking. A new six appeared in 1929: a front-wheel-drive prototype was exhibited in 1930.

GAREAU/*Canada 1910*
Only three of these 35 hp worm-drive fours were built as the Montreal firm could not raise enough working capital.

GARFORD/*USA 1908–1912, 1916*
Garford, of Elyria, Ohio, who built trucks from 1902, and from 1905 supplied the chassis for Studebaker, Rainier and Cleveland cars, decided late in 1907 to build a car under their own name. This was a 6098cc 40 hp four with shaft drive and geared-up fourth speed. They built Willys-Knights from 1913–15, but made a brief reappearance in 1916.

GARRARD/*England 1904*
A 'Suspended Tri-car' from the makers of the Clément-Garrard motorcycle.

1904 Garrard Tricar

GARRARD & BLUMFIELD
England 1894–1896
A 'neat and well-fitted' electric carriage built in Coventry.

GAS-AU-LEC/*USA 1905–1906*
The 40/45 hp Gas-au-Lec petrol-electric, from Peabody, Mass., had a copper-jacketed four-

cylinder engine with electromagnetically-operated inlet valves.

GASLIGHT / *USA 1960–c1961*
An odd replica of the 1902 Rambler powered by a single-cylinder 4 hp air-cooled engine and selling at around $1495.

GASMOBILE / *USA 1900–1903*
Starting with 'strictly high grade motor carriages', by 1902 the Automobile Company of America was building a 35 hp 'luxurious and Frenchified' phaeton, selling at $6000. In November 1901 Gasmobile exhibited — and sold — a six-cylinder tonneau at the New York Show.

The 1948 Gatford 4-litre Sports Roadster

GATFORD / *Netherlands 1948–1950*
Also known as the 'Gatso', this Mercury V-8-engined aero-styled coupé was sponsored by rally driver Maurice Gatsonides: triple headlights and clear plastic 'cockpit' were features.

GATTER / *Czechoslovakia 1929–1932*
There were eight Gatter brothers: two worked for Austro-Daimler, and subsequently created the small Gatter two-seater with a wooden frame and an air-cooled 344cc Villiers two-stroke engine. Few were built.

LA GAULOISE / *France 1907*
This firm from Issy-les-Moulineaux (Seine) built single- and four-cylinder voiturettes.

GAUTIER / *France 1902–c1907*
Ch. Gautier — formerly of Gautier-Wehrlé — of Courbevoie, Seine, built chassis, with or without power units, which could be finished by motor agents who would claim the result as 'entirely their own manufacture'. Gautier also offered a 'Popular' three-seater car — 'defies competition'. Gautier were the sole agents for Malicet & Blin chassis and components. In 1904 they announced a four-cylinder Mutel-engined light car, 'silent and cheap'. A landaulette demi-luxe and double phaeton were shown at the 1907 Paris Salon.

GAUTIER WEHRLE / *France 1894–1904*
Known from 1898 as the 'Société Continentale d'Automobiles', this company began by making bodies for Serpollet. Their twin-cylinder petrol

1898 Gautier Wehrlé, driven by M. Wehrlé

cars of 1896 had handlebar steering, shaft drive and independent rear suspension, the rear wheels being driven through universally jointed cardan shafts — the first time this method of transmission had been seen on a car.

GAYLORD / *USA 1910–1912*
The Gaylord 'Utility Car' had a 3295cc four-cylinder Oswald engine and could be converted into a pick-up by removing the rear seats: a demi-tonneau was also listed.

GAYLORD / *USA / Germany 1955–1956*
Manufactured in Germany by Spohn, and styled by Brooks Stevens, the Gaylord featured a retractable hardtop. Only five were built, three powered by Cadillac and two by Chrysler engines. Priced from $10,000 to $17,500, standard equipment included vacuum and electric power brakes, PAS, automatic transmission, leather seating, and radio.

GAZ / *Russia 1930 to date*
Licence-production of Ford Model A cars and trucks began in Moscow in 1929 but was soon transferred to the new Molotov car works near Nijhni Novgorod (later Gorky), built with Ford technological aid in an attempt to 'fill the Russians full of capitalism'. This Gorky Automobil Zavod began building 'Russki-Fords' in 1930, and was still using the Model A engine in Jeep-like vehicles long after the war. The GAZ-A was supplanted by the GAZ M-1 in 1936 — this had a Russian-designed grille and transmission, but a 1933 Ford body. A 3·5-litre six-cylinder version, GAZ M-11, appeared in 1938, forming the basis for wartime command cars. A new 2·1-litre model, the 'Pobieda' (Victory), designed by Andrei Litzgart, was built from 1946; it had unit construction and independent

front suspension, and a four-wheel-drive version, M-72, appeared in 1955. In 1958, the Pobieda was supplanted by the M-21 Volga, with a 2·5-litre engine. From 1950–57, the Gorky Works also built the straight-eight ZIM luxury model for middle-ranking Communist officials; this was replaced by the Chaika ('Seagull') based on the vulgar Packard Patrician. The 1978 Chaika was favoured by President Brezhnev. A MkII Volga appeared in 1968.

GB / *England 1922–1924*
So called because it was built by George Baets, this three-wheeler used a 5/7 hp Coventry-Victor twin-cylinder driving the rear wheels.

GC / *France 1908*
A 9 hp built by Guyot & Cie, of Paris.

GEARLESS / *USA 1907–1909*
Big friction-drive cars of up to 75 hp (known as 'Olympic' from 1909), built in Rochester, NY.

GEARLESS STEAM CAR / *USA 1921–1923*
Gearless was one of several companies who attempted to market a successful steam automobile in the early 1920s and succeeded better than many other contenders for the same market. Featuring two separate two-cylinder double-acting side-valve steam engines, the Gearless sported wire or wood wheels. Four Gearless officers were charged with mail fraud and the company failed. At least eight cars — all open models — and possibly as many as 15 or 20, were manufactured and sold before operations ceased in 1923.

GEERING / *England 1899–1904*
A crude paraffin-fuelled car with a 3 hp twin-cylinder engine, built in Rolvenden, Kent.

GEHA / *Germany 1910–1923*
Electric fwd three-wheelers from Harhorn of Berlin, part of the Elite group from 1917.

Geha electric phaeton, c.1913

GEIJER / *Norway 1926–1930*
A/S C. Geijer & Co, of Oslo, was essentially a coachbuilding company, but assembled about 20 cars out of parts imported from the USA. Both four- and eight-cylinder cars with hydraulic brakes were built. The frames were manufactured in Norway, and in a more sound economic climate, it is quite possible that the company could have enjoyed success, as the product was robust and reasonably cheap.

GELRIA / *Holland 1899–1906*
Gelria, from Arnhem, began with a front-engined single-cylinder 4 hp car with chain drive. A 6 hp twin appeared in 1901, but only a few cars were built after 1902.

GEM / *France 1907–1909*
Racing driver Léonce Girardot ('the eternal second'), formerly of CGV, headed this Parisian company and designed the 20/24 hp petrol-electric car which it produced. The later models used Knight sleeve-valve engines.

GENERAL / *England 1902–1905*
This South London firm built mainly 6½ hp and 12 hp cars with Aster or Buchet engines, though 30 hp (Simms) and 40 hp (Buchet) models were offered towards the end of their activities. A 40 hp racer with an aggressively pointed snout was built in 1902.

GENERAL ELECTRIC / *USA 1898–1899*
Built in Philadelphia, these electric vehicles followed horse-carriage practice in design and construction, 'the company believing that any radical changes should come by degrees to avoid public aversion to riding in objectionably conspicuous vehicles'.

GENESTIN / *France 1926–1929*
Even though relying largely on local custom, the Genestin (made in Fourmies in the north of France) was very successful. Genestin cars had various proprietary engines — mainly SCAP and CIME units of 1100cc and 1500cc, and also an 1808cc straight-eight, sometimes supercharged for racing.

GENEVA / *USA 1901–1903*
Built in Geneva, Ohio, this was a typical Locomobile-type steamer whose makers announced an initial production of 100 vehicles.

GENTRY / *England 1974 to date*
For those who cannot afford a real MG TF, the RMB Gentry offers some consolation. Based very obviously on the Abingdon car, the Gentry body is designed to clothe a Herald/Vitesse chassis — though a purpose-built model is available. Over 200 Gentrys have been made.

GEORGES IRAT / *France 1921–1946*
Georges Irat made very nice cars in the vintage period, starting by making their own engine, an ohv 1990cc four-cylinder, which gave way to a 2985cc six-cylinder in 1926. They turned to Lycoming engines with six and eight cylinders in 1929, when they moved from Chatou to Neuilly. Having been partly taken over by Ruby in 1934, they then moved to the Ruby works in Levallois, where they made a very successful fwd Ruby-engined roadster, followed by a fwd Citroën-engined roadster. Though a prototype was presented after the war, it was never put into production.

Front-wheel-drive Georges Irat sports, 1935

GEORGES-RICHARD; RICHARD-BRASIER / *France 1897–1905*
The first Georges-Richards were crude copies of the Benz, with alarming chain-and-sprocket steering and belt drive, but by 1900 the Ivry-Port factory was offering the Belgian Vivinus built under licence, and in 1901 a shaft-drive voiturette appeared. The designer Brasier joined the company in 1902 and produced larger Richard-Brasier cars on conventional lines, mostly with chain drive, culminating in the excellent racing cars which won the Gordon Bennett Trophy for France in 1904 and 1905. Georges Richard left in 1905 to build the Unic, and the marque became plain 'Brasier'.

A Georges Richard 8hp in the 1900 1000 Miles Trial

A Georges Roy Berline Grand Luxe, 1914

GEORGES ROY / *France 1906–1929*
Built at Bordeaux, Georges Roy cars always had medium to large power units. Starting with an 1140cc single, a 2941cc twin and a 4561 four, Georges Roy added a massive six of 10,179cc in 1907, one of no less than 16 models launched in seven years. In the 1911 catalogue, three basic models were listed, two four-cylinders (12 and 16 hp) and a 20 hp six. In 1925 the company offered only one chassis, a 10 hp, and three *de luxe* coachwork options — tourer, 'Caddy' two-seater, and interior drive. Light trucks were also offered.

GEORGE WHITE / *USA 1909*
These 14 hp twin-cylinder shaft-driven high-wheelers came from Rock Island, Illinois.

GEP / *France 1913–1914*
An 8 hp Anzani-engined light car from Gennevilliers.

GERALD / *England 1920*
The Gerald cyclecar used chain- and belt-drive, power coming from an 8 hp JAP engine mounted lengthwise in the chassis.

GERALD / *France 1920–1923*
SCAP-engined 1481cc cars made in Clichy.

GERMAIN / *Belgium 1897–1914*
Germain of Monceau-sur-Sambre began by building the 'Daimler-Belge' under licence from Cannstatt; from 1901 cars of 'improved Panhard' pattern were offered. The first Germain 'Standard' appeared in 1903; it was a 2917cc chain-drive 18 hp L-head with separate cylinders, and was soon joined by similar models of 3810cc, 5734cc and 9811cc. In 1905 came the

28 hp shaft-driven 'Chainless' with T-headed cylinders and a distinctive oval radiator. The 3834cc six of 1907 had a ball-bearing crank: there was also a 60 hp six of 8822cc and a monstrous chain-drive '80 hp' four of 12,454cc. The 1912 range had full pressure lubrication and included an ohc 15 hp and a 20 hp Knight sleeve-valve model.

GERONIMO/*USA 1917–1920*
The Geronimo was named after the famous Indian chief of the same name, and was one of the few makes to hail from Oklahoma. With a factory at Enid, the Geronimo began life as a four-cylinder automobile, but a year after its entry into the automobile spectrum adopted a Lycoming six and used it until the end of production. Geronimo never built any closed models; several hundred — perhaps even 1000 — cars were built before the company went to the happy hunting grounds.

GHIA/*Italy 1966–1968*
The famous coachbuilders, then owned by Alessandro de Tomaso, built the 450/SS, a very sporting cabriolet with 235bhp V-8 4500cc Plymouth Barracuda engine. Few were built.

GIAUR/*Italy 1949–1954*
Sports and racing cars with partly modified Fiat 746cc engines and Fiat chassis components were Giaur's main offering. There were also models from 498cc up to 1098cc. One of the directors of Giaur was racing driver Taraschi.

GIBBONS/*England 1921–1926*
The belt-driven Gibbons was built in Chadwell Heath, Essex, and offered with three engine variants: 349cc Precision and 488cc Blackburne (both single-cylinder) and 688cc Coventry-Victor twin.

GIBSON/*USA 1899*
A tiller-steered Stanhope powered by a 12 hp carbonic acid gas engine said to weigh 32 lb.

GIDEON/*Denmark 1913–1919*
The first Gideon cars, from Horsens, were presented at the end of 1913 and were available in three sizes, all with four-cylinder engines. Passenger car engines developed 9·7 hp and were entirely Danish-made. The only imported parts were carburettors and magnetos: 129 vehicles were produced, but only 17 were passenger cars.

GILBERN/*Wales 1958–1977*
There have been some chequered careers in the motor industry, but that of Gilbern probably caps them all. The production of some fine cars was interspersed with changes in management and an almost constant threat of liquidation. The last car, the glass-fibre-bodied, Ford-powered Mk III Invader was a sturdy, well-equipped GT car that, marketed by the right hands, could well have saved Wales' only long-standing car manufacturer from the history books.

GILBERT/*England 1899–1901*
Gilbert & Son, of Birmingham, devised a two-stroke engine with two cylinders of different diameters on a common axis, capable of running on 'light or heavy petroleum'.

GILBURT/*England 1904–1906*
A light 6 hp twin-cylinder car with a tubular chassis and chain drive.

1905 Gilburt 6hp light car

GILCHRIST/*Scotland 1920–1923*
An ohv version of the 11·9 hp Hotchkiss engine used in the Morris powered this light car from Govan, Glasgow: total Gilchrist output was around 20..

GILLET/*England 1926–1927*
A £100 car that used an 8 hp four-cylinder ohv engine and had just enough room for two adults and two offspring.

GILLET-FOREST/*France 1901–c1908*
This firm, whose factory was at St Cloud, near Paris, built 8 hp and 10 hp cars, including a Traveller's Brougham with cupboards for samples and a 10 hp Duc-Tonneau, perhaps the first car to have a heater as standard equipment. The company last exhibited at the 1907 Paris Salon.

GILYARD/*England 1912–1916*
A 10 hp Chater-Lea-engined 1267cc cyclecar which sold for £105.

GINETTA/*England 1967 to date*
The highly enthusiastic Walklett Brothers have produced a variety of competition and road cars over the years, the most successful of which is without doubt the rear-engined, Imp-powered G15, over 500 of which were made. But in 1979, back in their original factory, they were pri-

1972 Gilbern Invader Mk III

marily concerned with refurbishing G15s and developing their new open-topped glass-fibre sports car, the G23, which was powered by the Ford 2·8-litre fuel injection engine.

1973 Ginetta G21

GIRLING/*England 1911–1914*
Apart from a JAP-engined prototype, the three-wheeled Girling cyclecars were powered by a single-cylinder 95 × 95mm engine of the company's own make. Friction drive was employed; 110 Girlings were shipped to Australia in 1911–1913. Albert Girling later devised the famous Girling braking system.

GITANE/*England 1962*
The first six Gitanes had rear-mounted Mini-Cooper engines tuned to 83 bhp, and a claimed top speed of 130 mph. Plans to develop a light alloy Gitane engine were stillborn.

The 1962 Gitane prototype

GJG/*USA 1909–1911*
Assembled from imported components, including a 'Renault-type' 40 hp four-cylinder engine, the GJG was available with either 'cruiser torpedo' or 'pirate runabout' coachwork.

GKN FFF100/*England 1972*
Commissioned by GKN, the FFF100 was built to test the performance and durability of some of their components, including the Maxaret anti-lock braking system and the Ferguson four-wheel drive system. It was a formidable beast, with William Towns-styled glass-fibre body hiding a modified Jensen four-wheel-drive chassis, powered by a much modified 7-litre Chrysler engine of some 600bhp. The car recorded 0–100mph in 6·5 sec and 0–100 mph and back to rest in a mere 11·5 sec.

The GKN FFF100 coupé, 1972

GLADIATOR/*France 1896–1920*
Aucoc and Darracq's Gladiator cycle company was acquired by British capital in 1896, and began building spidery, handlebar-steered 4 hp voiturettes in their Pré-St-Gervais factory. Wheel steering and Aster engines of 2½ hp and

3½ hp were used from 1899. By 1901, a 6½ hp Aster-engined Gladiator was available, joined later that year by a 12 hp twin, still Aster engined, with an armoured wood chassis. The 1902 range went from a 3½ hp quadricycle to four-cylinder cars. By 1903, fours of 2·1 litres and 2·7 litres of Gladiator's own make were available; the range was very similar to the sister marque, Clément. The 1906 line-up was complex, to the extent that models sold in France had armoured wood chassis, while models for the British market had pressed-steel frames! That year, Gladiator's first six, a 5·5-litre, appeared. From 1908–09, Gladiators were supposedly also built in Birmingham by Austin. In 1909, Vinot & Deguingand took over, and from then on only the radiators distinguished the two marques (though Gladiator built no more sixes). At the end of 1911, Gladiator offered a 10/12 hp, a 15·9 hp, and a 25/30 hp of 1693cc, 2212cc and 4166cc respectively: a 15/20 hp of 2614cc was added in 1913, but no new models appeared before production ended in 1920.

1902 12hp Gladiator rear-entrance tonneau

GLAS/*Germany 1955–1966*

Old-established manufacturers of agricultural machinery, from 1951 to 1954 Glas built the Goggo scooter, and from 1955 to 1969 the small Goggomobil with 247cc, 296cc and 395cc two-cylinder two-stroke engines. In 1958 appeared the first 'real' Glas cars with 584cc and 688cc ohv flat-twin engines. Bigger models with ohc four-cylinder in-line engines of 992cc, 1189cc, 1290cc and 1682cc followed. The last Glas-built cars had ohc 2580cc and 2982cc V-8 engines, beautiful sporting four-seater coupé bodywork by Frua, and De Dion rear axles. Unfortunately these superb cars led the company into financial difficulties. Glas could not afford to spend millions of Deutschmarks on the more up-to-date equipment needed for economical production of these high-class luxury cars. In 1966 BMW took over the Glas works at Dingolfing.

1966 Glas 1700 four-door saloon

GLASSIC/*USA 1966 to date*

Jack Faircloth and his son built a glass-fibre replica Model A Ford using International Harvester components and a four-cylinder Scout engine. Production moved to West Palm Beach, Florida, in 1972 when Fred Pro bought the project. Available as a roadster or phaeton with Ford automatic transmission and powered by a 210 hp Ford V-8 engine, the Glassic (now renamed Replicar) cost $14,950 in 1979.

GLEASON/*USA 1909–1914*

A high-wheeler succeeding the 'Kansas City'.

GLEN/*Canada 1921–1922*

A three-cylinder cyclecar from Toronto with a Rolls-Royce-like radiator.

GLIDE/*USA 1903–1920*

The 1903 Glidemobile, designed by O. Y. Bartholomew, was a single-cylinder 1930cc tiller-steered runabout, joined by a 12 hp twin in 1904. This had a spring-mounted motor subframe and steel-spoked artillery wheels. A 30 hp four-cylinder Glide appeared in 1906, and a 45 hp Rutenber-engined six in 1907. In 1911, a 5806cc single-cast four was listed, and in 1912 came a monobloc 36 hp four at $1550. The year 1916 saw the last new Glide, the 6-40, which continued unchanged, except for an increase in engine bore, until production ended in 1920.

GLOBE/*England 1913–1916*

Built by sanitary engineers Tuke and Bell, the 'torpedo two-seater' Globe cyclecar was propelled by a single-cylinder 1039cc Aster engine. The clutch pedal moved the back axle forward, first slackening the driving belt, then forcing the driving pulley against a brake block.

GLOBE FOUR/*USA 1921–1922*

A conventional assembled car of the time, the Globe Four used a four-cylinder Supreme engine. Production was limited to roadsters and touring models.

GLORIA (GLORIETTE)/*Austria 1933–1936*

Offered for 3600 Austrian schillings in 1936, the two-seater Gloriette—designed by former Delta-Gnom motorcycle designer Hans Pitzek—was a modern little car. It had a backbone-chassis and an ohv 795cc four-cylinder engine. Lack of money prevented production on a large scale. Pitzek lacked sufficient facilities, although he was backed by leading Vienna car-dealer and racing driver, Bernhard Kandl.

GLOVER/*USA 1908*

The Glover, from Chicago, was driven by a fifth wheel in the centre of the car, which could be forced down on to the road for extra traction.

GLOVER/*USA 1920–1921*

Like a number of other automobiles made in the United States at the time, the Glover was built

exclusively for export, to the order of Glover's Motors Ltd., Leeds, Yorkshire. In all probability, the Glover was little more than a Seneca car, built in Fostoria, Ohio, equipped with a Rolls-Royce-shaped radiator. The four-cylinder Glover used a Leroi engine. Wheelbase was 114 inches and wire wheels were standard.

GM/*France 1924–1928*

Gendron et Michelot made some very good CIME-engined cars, a 1099cc four-cylinder and a 1500cc six, in their Paris works.

A GM in Le Mans trim, 1925

GMCC/*England/France 1903*

The General Motor Car Company of London and Paris offered an unlikely range consisting of a 6 hp Light Runabout (120 guineas) and a 40 hp, four-speed touring car which weighed 19½ cwt and cost 1500 guineas.

1920 GN on the Brooklands Test Hill

GN/*England 1910–1925*

H. R. Godfrey and Archie Frazer-Nash's cyclecar originally used 1100cc JAP and Antoine vee-twins, but by 1911 they were able to offer an engine of their own manufacture. Transmission was by belts and chains, though chain and dog clutch layout was later standardized. After World War One a new steel chassis replaced the original ash one while sporting variants were offered—the tuned Légère and Vitesse with a 1087cc overhead camshaft engine, the latter being a revived 1913 GP model. Godfrey and Frazer-Nash left in 1922, the GN rather losing its cutting edge as four-cylinder water-cooled engines were offered. Power units by DFP and Anzani were among those used, though only a handful were made.

GN/France 1919–1922
After World War One the Salmson company in Boulogne-sur-Seine entered the automobile industry by making a cyclecar of British GN design. The vee-twin engine was of 1086cc. They sold very well, and paved the way for proper Salmson cars two years later.

French-built GN-Salmson, 1921

GN-GIOVANELLI/France 1922–1923
When Salmson stopped building GNs, a Parisian agent, M. Giovanelli, decided to build more cars using the remaining parts. Instead of the vee-twin, he fitted the ohc four-cylinder Nova engine of 950cc.

GNOM/Czechoslovakia 1921–1924
Wealthy hat-manufacturer and racing driver Fritz Hückel built various sporting Gnom cars, and helped to found the Nordmährische Automobil Gesellschaft, where a few small two-seater 5 hp cars on Opel Laubfrosch lines were built, using Opel engines.

GNOME/France 1907
These were 12 hp and 18/24 hp cars, built by a famous engine manufacturer from Paris.

GNOME (NOMAD)/England 1925–1926
Devoid of suspension, and with integral steel/plywood body/chassis, this 343cc friction-driven Villiers-engined cyclecar from London was understandably short-lived.

GNOME ET RHONE/France 1919–1920
This well-known aeroengine company presented a 40 hp ohc six-cylinder car of 6000cc just after the war, but were more successful in making motorcycles.

GODET/France 1919
The Godet Triauto was an 8/10 hp two-seater three-wheeler: though M. Godet showed at the 1919 Salon, he only built one car.

GOBRON BRILLIÉ

GOBRON-BRILLIE/France 1898–1930
Gobron and Brillié started at Boulogne-sur-Seine building rear-engined cars. Brillié left the association in 1903 but his name remained until the war. From the early days, Gobron-Brillié cars were equipped with a very strange engine with two pistons working in the same cylinder, the explosion taking place between them. M. Guichard, the designer, claimed that this engine was able to work with any fuel—including brandy or whisky! In 1904, a racing Gobron was the first car to exceed 100 mph. Until 1906, most production cars had tubular frames and twin-cylinder engines of 2290cc or four-cylinder units of 4580cc. They also made more classic engines with side valves. In 1911, Gobron-Brillié introduced two big cars with inlet over exhaust engines of 8165cc and 9123cc. After the war, Gobron-Brillié restarted with the fantastic 35 cv six-cylinder of 7490cc, still with the two pistons per cylinder and—to add some more complications—sleeve valves! More reliable were the few 1495cc Chapuis Dornier-engined cars presented in 1922. At the end, Gobron-Brillié tried to sell 1327cc and 1500cc cars in small numbers, the latter under the name of 'Turbo-Sport' with a Cozette supercharger.

Dureste on a Gobron-Brillié in the 1907 Coupe de la Presse

GODIVA †England 1900–1901
Payne & Bates of Coventry, who built the Stonebow, also offered a similar vehicle under the name Godiva, with a twin-cylinder 9 hp engine. Two- and four-cylinder models of 7 hp–25 hp were listed in 1901. They later built some Internationals.

GOGGOMOBIL/Australia 1958–1961
Essentially a local version of the German product, the Australian Goggomobil had a glass-fibre body and imported components. Produced as a sedan, coupé and two-seater sports car, the diminutive design was powered by a twin-cylinder two-stroke engine developing 17 bhp. With an overall weight of only 8 cwt, the car accelerated strongly and could reach 55 mph. More than 5000 were produced, but the arrival of the Morris Mini made the car uncompetitive.

An Australian-built Goggomobil, 1958

GOLIATH/Germany 1950–1963
Borgward had produced three-wheeled Goliath vans since 1931. In 1950, Goliath cars with 688cc two-cylinder two-stroke engines were offered.

886cc versions with fuel injection developed up to 50 bhp, a 1093cc version with an ohv flat-four engine gave 55 bhp at 5000 rpm. All Goliath cars had front-wheel drive and the engines ahead of the front axle.

GOODCHILD / *England 1913–1915*
A 10 hp, 1327cc light car sold by T. B. Goodchild of London.

GOODSPEED / *USA 1922*
The Goodspeed was a spin-off of the Commonwealth — an attempt to keep the make afloat under a new name, geared strictly for the luxury market. Two sporting open phaetons were built, and displayed at the auto shows in New York and Chicago. A 5178cc six-cylinder own-make engine was used. Wire wheels were fitted and wheelbase was 124 inches. The venture failed. Commonwealth's taxicab line became the Checker, which exists to the present day.

GOODYEAR / *England c1922*
Model T Ford engine, gearbox and axles formed the basis of the Goodyear, the remainder being British. Even the engine was mildly tuned!

The 1922 Goodyear sports was Model T Ford-based

GORDANO / *England 1947–1949*
The Gordano, which took its name from Clapton-in-Gordano in Somerset, never progressed beyond the prototype stage. Construction consisted of a box-section chassis capped with light-alloy bodywork. Suspension was fully independent, with damping variable from the driving seat. Power came from a Wolseley engine. Sadly, Joe Fry, one of the designers, lost his life in a racing accident and no more was heard of the project.

1947 Gordano

GORDINI / *France 1936–1957*
'Le Sorcier' Gordini started his career by making 'specials' evolved from Simca and Fiat, both sports-racing two-seaters and monoposti. It was only in 1951 that he made the first proper Gordini, using his own engines. He made 1500cc 2-litre and 3-litre racing cars, but his 2.3-litre sports car presented at the 1952 Paris Show never reached the public. Confined to motor racing, he closed his works in 1957 and joined Renault as a consultant engineer, creating the Dauphine 'Gordini' and Renault 8 'Gordini'.

The Gordon cyclecar, 1912

GORDON / *England 1912–1917*
Later to achieve fame as makers of shock absorbers, Gordon Armstrong of Beverley, East Riding, Yorkshire, built a range of vee-twin JAP-engined cyclecars with cantilever suspension and the odd feature of supplementary coil ignition on one cylinder only (normal ignition was by magneto) to assist starting. The tubular chassis and body frame were integral.

GORDON / *England 1954–1958*
A sub-utility three-wheeler built by a subsidiary of Vernons Football Pools, the Gordon had a 197cc Villiers two-stroke engine driving the right-hand rear wheel only.

GORDON-KEEBLE / *England 1964–1969*
The Gordon-Keeble was arguably ahead of its time, and only 100 or so of these fine cars were built. With its origins in the even shorter-lived Gordon GT of the late 1950s, the Gordon-Keeble featured a multi-tubular chassis topped with a handsome Bertone-designed body. Power came from a 5·3-litre Chevrolet Corvette engine of some 300 bhp.

1966 Gordon-Keeble coupé

GORDON MINIATURE / *England 1903–1904*
Sold at 125 guineas complete, the spidery Gordon Miniature was built by a firm of motor and cycle agents in the Seven Sisters Road, London.

GORET / *France 1898*
The radial three-cylinder engine of this voiturette operated on a 'six-stroke' cycle — ('intake and mixing', 'compression', 'explosion', 'exhaust', 'intake of scavenging air', 'exhaust of scavenging air').

GORM / *Denmark 1917*
Karl J. Schmidt of Copenhagen produced only 16 cars. Of these, 14 had four-cylinder — probably JAP — engines and two had Perkins engines. Drive was through friction transmission and chain. These cars were also known as AFG (Automobil Fabrik Gorm).

GOTTSCHALK / *Germany 1900–1901*
Gottschalk, the predecessor of the Berlin Motorwagen-Fabrik, built a limited number of 4 hp cars with De Dion engines.

GOUJON / *France 1896–1901*
A four-seater voiturette with an air-cooled 3½ hp single-cylinder engine.

1898 Goujon 3½cv *vis-à-vis*

GOVE / *USA 1920–1922*
Built by the Gove Motor Truck Co. of Detroit, the Gove automobile did not proceed beyond the prototype phase. Gove cars had six-cylinder engines and wire wheels. Price of the touring car (which never went into production) was $2150.

1967 GP Centron

GP / *England 1967 to date*
A strong survivor of the UK 'Buggy' era, GP have been responsible for a variety of fascinating products, including the Centron GT car, the fixed-head, four-seat Ranchero and an ever-improving range of buggies, now sold mainly to Arabs. All these cars have featured well-finished, stylish glass-fibre bodies for fitting to VW mechanicals.

GRACIELA/*Argentina 1960–1961*
Developed from a Peronist 'people's car', the 1954–55 Justicialista (only built in prototype form), this three-cylinder Wartburg-engined saloon was built in a government aircraft factory at Cordoba.

GRACILE/*France 1906–1907*
There were four models of the Gracile: a 10/12 hp two-cylinder, a 12/14 hp four-cylinder, an 18/24 hp four and a 30 hp four with dual ignition.

GRADE/*Germany 1921–1928*
Aviation pioneer and two-stroke engine designer and manufacturer, Hans Grade produced engines, motorcycles, cars and aeroplanes. His cars had bodywork on aircraft principles. The two-stroke engines were of deflector-type three-port design; they were vertical twins of 808cc and 980cc.

GRAF & STIFT/*Austria 1907–1938*
This was the 'Rolls-Royce of Austria'. Stift was earlier connected with the manufacture of Celeritas cars. After he founded the Gräf & Stift factory in 1902, he built cars for five years on behalf of Arnold Spitz. In 1907, the first Gräf & Stift car appeared. It was the ambition of Willy Stift to build big cars of the highest quality regardless of cost, while the Gräf brothers— Karl, Franz and Heinrich — were the technical experts behind this ambitious venture. In 1897 the Gräfs built a voiturette with the engine in the rear, but it was never manufactured commercially. After 1908, production concentrated on big 4240cc, 5880cc, 7320cc and even 7684cc four-cylinder models. A new, smaller model of 1940cc appeared in 1922: there was also a new ohc 7745cc six-cylinder capable of 90 mph. The

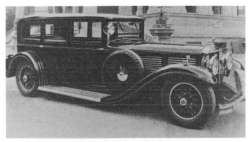

1930 Gräf and Stift SP 6-litre limousine

last Gräf & Stift cars were a 3895cc six and the fantastic SP8 with an ohc 5988cc eight-cylinder engine, which developed 125 bhp at 3000 rpm. Armbruster, Kellner, Jech and other coachbuilders created superb bodies on these cars. The factory also produced lorries during World War One and in the 1920s some interesting sports-racing cars with ohc 7070cc and 7745cc six-cylinder engines. In addition to their own designs, the Vienna factory also built Ford, Citroën and Minor cars under licence. The Gräfford was a Gräf & Stift-built Ford V-8 of the mid-1930s.

GRAHAM/*USA 1903*
The Chicago-built Graham Roadster was available with a choice of electric or petrol engines at a price of $850.

1923 Grade cyclecar

GRAHAM-PAIGE
USA 1928–1940
The three Graham brothers took over Paige in 1928, and continued the old Lycoming-engined 8-85 Straightaway Eight alongside three Continental sixes of 3128cc, 3666cc and 4740cc: these were, briefly, also built by a Graham branch factory in Berlin. Graham-Paige was the 12th largest US car company in 1928, but from then on its market share fell. The 1932 Blue Streak range, with vee-grille, pontoon wings and rear axle slotted through the chassis to keep the height down, was a trend-setter, but did not help sales: nor did the adoption of a centrifugal supercharger on the 1934 4350cc Custom Eight. This formed the basis for an English sports saloon version, the Bertelli-bodied Graham British Special of 1935–36. From 1936, Graham-Paige concentrated on six-cylinders of 2780cc and 3679cc, known as Crusader and Cavalier, and the superseded Special Six body dies were sold to Nissan (builders of the Datsun), who also used Graham engines. A new supercharged Graham-Paige appeared in 1937, followed in 1938 by the controversial 'shark-nosed' 3·5-litre six, a range of surpassing ugliness, with the option of 'Vacumatic' gear-shift and overdrive. The firm's last model, the Graham Hollywood, used Cord 810/812 body dies and a Hupmobile chassis; in 1945 the moribund Graham-Paige company was absorbed by Kaiser-Frazer.

1930 Graham-Paige

GRAHAM-WHITE/*England 1920–1924*
A 3½ hp 348cc single-cylinder engine with kick-start propelled the Buckboard cyclecar, though later a water-cooled 1100cc Dorman was used.

GRAMM/*Canada 1913*
Twin-cylinder, belt-drive cyclecars built in Walkerville, Ontario.

GRAND/*England 1903*
Sold by the Motor Vehicle Engineering Company, who also marketed Ader cars under the name 'Pegasus', the 10 hp and 16 hp Grand cars were probably French imports.

GRAND NATIONAL/*England 1900*
After 25 years as cycle manufacturers, H. F. Copland & Co. of SE London went 'earnestly in for the Motor Industry' with a 2¾ hp De Dion-engined 'Motor Quad'.

GRANT/*USA 1913–1922*
The first Grant automobiles were four-cylinder cars, but by 1915 the make changed to sixes and this policy was retained until the end of the line, a Walker engine being used. Wheelbase was 116 inches and several thousand Grant Sixes were manufactured before the company ceased production. The 1525cc Grant four was sold in England as the Whiting-Grant.

GRANTA/*England 1906*
From the same makers as the Westminster, the 28/34 hp car had four separately cast cylinders, 'seven point suspension' and shaft drive.

GRAY/*USA 1922–1926*
The Gray was an inexpensive car which attempted to seize the part of the market dominated by the Model T Ford, presumably aimed at the owner who liked economy but preferred conventional transmission. Featuring a four-cylinder engine of its own design, a 100- to 104-inch wheelbase and a complete line of open and closed body styles, the company did relatively well for a time, 1923 production reaching 30,000 units. Four-wheel brakes were added for 1926, the last year of production. Prices ranged from $490 up.

GRAY-DORT/*Canada 1915–1925*
This was the US Dort built under licence by a carriage and sledge-building company from Chatham, Ontario, using the four-cylinder Lycoming engine till the end of production. The 1922 Gray-Dort Special had, it was claimed, the first factory-fitted automatic reversing lamp.

GRAY LIGHT CAR/*USA 1920*
Only one Gray was built. This Colorado product featured a twin-cylinder Harley-Davidson motorcycle engine. It was a two-passenger roadster.

GREAT EAGLE/*USA 1910–1918*
Big 5·8-litre four-cylinder cars from Columbus, Ohio.

GREAT SOUTHERN/*USA 1910–1914*
This Birmingham, Alabama, firm made 30 hp and 50 hp fours, in two- and five-seat open models.

1910 Great Western 40 roadster

GREAT WESTERN/*USA 1908–1916*
'The Car that awoke Motordom' came from Peru, Indiana. Initially a twin and a 50 hp four were offered, but by 1910 a 40 hp four was the standard model, priced at only $1600 but 'able to go and come back where many cars fear to tread'.

GREEN/*England 1906*
Gustavus Green was a famous manufacturer of engines for everything from motorcycles to airships. Some of his power units incorporated radiators in their water-jackets. In 1906 he showed a 26/30 hp chassis with 'many novel features' at the Agricultural Hall Exhibition.

GREGOIRE/*France 1903–1923*
Starting—briefly—with an 8 hp single, 12 hp twin and 20 hp four, Grégoire of Poissy, near Paris, soon switched to building refined voiturettes, the most famous being the 1905 8 hp twin, built until 1912. There was also a 15 hp four. An 18/24 hp six appeared in 1909. In 1912 Grégoire marketed the Dumont (q.v.) under the name Grégoire-Dumont. In 1911–12, Grégoire experimented with overhead camshafts and hemi-spherical combustion chambers; they also produced some aerodynamic two-seaters and saloons, mostly on the 3217cc 16/20 hp chassis. This was also encumbered with extraordinary double and triple berline bodies with switchback roof and four-pane side windows. The sporting 14/20 hp of 1913 formed the basis of post-war production, acquiring ohv in 1921; production ended in 1923. The 1919 Grégoire-Campbell was, in fact, a Bignan-Sport built in the Grégoire factory, and the last 'Grégoire' was actually built by Hinstin at Maubeuge, with an 1100cc CIME engine. Britons knew it as the 'Little Greg'.

GREGOIRE/*France 1945–c1962*
J. A. Grégoire, pioneer of the front-wheel drive with the Tracta, presented some cars under his own name after the war. In 1945, a 600cc flat-twin prototype evolved into the 'Dyna' Panhard. The 2-litre flat-four of 1947 was made by Hotchkiss under the name of Hotchkiss-Grégoire; from this were developed some Chapron-bodied roadsters sold under Grégoire's own name. More recently, Grégoire has presented an electric car prototype.

1907 Grégoire 7hp in the Coupe des Voiturettes

GREYHOUND/*England 1904–1905*
A three-speed tricar with 3½ hp Antoine or 3 hp Fafnir engine, built in Ashford, Middlesex.

GRICE/*England 1927*
The Grice was powered by a rear-mounted 680cc air-cooled JAP engine and was a three-wheeler. Made by GWK of Maidenhead, it never went into production.

GRIDI/*Germany 1923–1924*
A basic car with an 865cc single-cylinder engine and a two-seater body, the Gridi was built in very small numbers.

GRIFFIN/*England 1976 to date*
A 'poor man's Reliant Scimitar GTE', the Griffin has the unlikely base of the Morris Minor van. The professionally laminated body is well conceived, however, and features a removable estate hardtop.

GRIFFITH/*USA 1964–1967*
The Griffith used glass-fibre bodies (shipped from England) on a tubular frame. Amazing acceleration was provided by 200 hp Ford V-8 engines. Selling at $4,800, a total of 285 Griffiths were built.

1920 Griffon 987cc cyclecar

GRIFFON/*France 1906–1924*
A well-established bicycle and motorcycle manufacturer in Courbevoie, Griffon first made cars in 1906 with single-cylinder Aster and Buchet engines. In 1920, after many years of interruption, they made a cyclecar. This had a vee-twin Anzani engine of 987cc, and was of true motorcycle inspiration.

GRISWOLD/*USA 1907*
The Griswold from Detroit was a friction-drive twin-cylinder model.

GRIVEL/*France 1897*
A tubular-framed quadricycle with a rear-mounted vertical-twin air-cooled engine.

GROFRI/*Austria 1924–1927*
Like the German Pluto, the Austrian Grofri was built under Amilcar licence. These sporting cars used sv 903cc and 1074cc four-cylinder engines; some racing versions had Roots-type superchargers. Bernhard Kandl, Karl Sarg and opera-singer Käthe Rantzau were prominent competition drivers of Grofris.

GROSE/*England 1899–1900*
These were Northampton-built versions of the Benz.

GROSVENOR/*England 1908*
A 40 hp four-cylinder of 7433cc, the Grosvenor

had a brazen laurel wreath attached to its radiator honeycomb.

GROUESY/*France 1923–1924*
A tiny belt-driven sports/racing cyclecar made in Sartrouville with a 985cc vee-twin.

GROUP SIX/*England 1972–1975*
John Mitchell's substitute for a dreamed-of road-going McLaren, the Group Six kit car featured a sporting, self-coloured glass-fibre body for adding to the traditional VW mechanicals.

1902 Grout (Weston) steamer filling its boiler

GROUT/*USA 1898–1913*
Better known as builders of steam carriages (sold in England as 'Westons'), Grout Brothers of Orange, Mass., also built twin-cylinder petrol-engined 'automobile carriages', which were among the first cars to be equipped with an electric lighting outfit powered by a dynamo. The 1903 Grout came complete with cowcatcher. W. L. Grout was originally the maker of the 'New Home' sewing machine, produced at the rate of one a minute. He and his two sons owned the entire $250,000 capital of the company, which employed 123 workers in 1905. Petrol cars followed the steamers in 1905 until the end of production in 1913. The 1909 Grout was a 35 hp four-cylinder, with shaft- or chain-drive optional.

GRP/*France 1924–1930*
Made in Paris by Georges and René Pol, the GRP was normally seen as taxis and commercial vehicles with 1693cc and 1892cc engines.

GS/*England 1976 to date*
Built by GS cars of Bristol, the GS Europa is basically a reclothed Lotus Europa with attractive glass-fibre body featuring flying buttresses for improved vision at the rear. A dozen or so had been built by the end of 1978.

1926 Grofri (Amilcar) 20 PS

GSM/*England 1960–1961*
There were big plans for the GSM Delta. Well sorted suspension hung on a stiff ladder chassis ensured good roadholding, while a light body and the facility of Ford engines in various states of tune ensured good performance. However, the car was more successful on the race tracks than the road and only 35 or so open cars and a couple of the intended fastback were completed.

Guédon, 1895, ancestor of the Decauville voiturette

GUEDON/*France 1897*
This voiturette, built at Bordeaux by naval architect Guédon and Cornilleau, is believed to have been the first car with direct drive. The driver could start it without leaving his seat by turning a hand-wheel mounted on his right. Decauville put this design into production as the 'Voiturelle'.

GUERRAZ/*France 1901*
A range of voiturettes with C-spring rear suspension and 1357cc Bolide engines.

GUERRY ET BOURGUIGNON/*France 1907*
A 'tri-voiturette' built by a Parisian cycle company.

LE GUI/*France 1906–1914*
A voiturette with a double-dropped chassis, a four-cylinder 1593cc engine and a four-speed gearbox, was the first Le Gui ('little fellow'): by 1908, fours of 1·8–3·1 litres and a 5·5-litre six were available. From 1911 10 hp (1726cc) and 15 hp (2650cc) fours were available, the 15 hp being cut to 2121cc for 1912.

GUILDFORD/*England 1920*
The chain-driven Guildford, built in the Surrey town of the same name, used a Blackburne 8 hp vee-twin engine and chain drive. A speculative venture, it was never marketed.

GUILICK/*France 1914–1930*
Makers of proprietary chassis in Maubeuge who normally supplied other car 'manufacturers', Guilick also occasionally issued motor cars under their own name with various proprietary engines: CIME, Ruby, Ballot, SCAP and Altos units from 1100cc to 2000cc.

GURGEL/*Brazil 1966 to date*
A plastics-bodied utility vehicle with a VW engine.

GURIK (GEA)/*Sweden 1905–1909*
Gustaf L. M. Ericsson worked as an apprentice at the Franklin Company in the USA. When he returned to Sweden in 1904 he started building

stationary engines and boat engines in Stockholm. Plans were laid for a large six-cylinder car and one prototype was built. The engine was built up from three German Fafnir twin-cylinder engines. The car was nicknamed *Ormen Långe* (The Long Snake, after a common name for Viking ships), but there was no production. At the automobile exhibition in Stockholm in 1907 the company exhibited both imported cars and cars built at the factory. These were called Gurik and came in two sizes, 12/14 hp and 16/20 hp, both with four-cylinder engines. It is not known if the engines were bought from outside suppliers, or if they were built in Sweden. Probably very few cars were produced, though one is preserved.

GUTBROD/*Germany 1933–1954*
Founded 1926 as the Standard motorcycle factory, Gutbrod built, from 1933 to 1935, the Ganz-designed 'Standard-Superior', a rear-engined car with 398cc and 498cc engines. The more advanced 'Gutbrod-Superior' entered the market in 1950, and 7726 of these cars were made. Most had 593cc two-stroke twin-cylinder engines: a similar 663cc version was offered latterly, the final models having fuel injection.

GUY/*France 1904–1907*
The Guy (built by J. Lamy of Paris) was a two-speed voiturette with a 7 hp four-cylinder engine.

GUY/*Canada 1911*
A 30 hp of high quality built by a carriage and hearse maker from Oshawa, Ontario.

GUY/*England 1919–1925*
Guy Motors of Wolverhampton, commercial vehicle makers since 1914, went into the luxury car market in 1919 with their 4-litre V-8 with detachable heads and side valves. This 20 hp car was joined in 1922 by a model with a conventional 2- or 2½-litre in-line four-cylinder engine. These failed to attract a market and after 1929 the company reverted exclusively to commercial vehicle production, though in 1929 they acquired Star, another Wolverhampton motor manufacturer.

GUYOT SPECIALE/*France 1924–1931*
Racing driver Albert Guyot made a few racing cars with Burt-McCollum sleeve-valve engines. He also made some touring cars with 3500cc six-cylinder and 5200cc eight-cylinder American Continental engines.

GUYSON/*England 1975*
Named after the Guyson shot-blasting concern who sponsored its manufacture, the Guyson E12 was in fact a re-bodied Jaguar E Type. Moving far away from the E Type's own curvaceous lines, the William Towns-designed replacement panels were remarkable for their flatness. Only two cars were made, one for Jim Thompson, director of Guyson, and one for Towns himself.

GWALIA/*Wales 1922*
This 9 hp Alpha-engined car from Cardiff had an odd suspension by bellcranks and coil springs.

GWK/*England 1911–1931*
The GWK, made by Grice, Wood and Keiller, was a friction-drive cyclecar, utilizing a two-cylinder rear-mounted Coventry-Simplex engine. Production was centred at Datchet, Buckinghamshire, but transferred to Maidenhead in 1914. The original engine was briefly retained after World War One, though soon replaced by a Coventry-Climax four-cylinder of 1368cc. Engine power was again increased in 1924, when a 1½-litre power unit was fitted. Grice had left the concern in 1920 to make the similar Unit, and although GWK had gone out of production in 1926 he tried to resurrect the concern in 1930.

1913 GWK 8hp two-seater . . .

. . . and its friction-drive chassis

GWYNNE/*England 1922–1929*
Manufacturers of centrifugal pumps, Gwynne Engineering first produced the Albert car (for which they had made engines) and from 1923 the cars were known as Gwynne-Alberts. The Gwynne Eight of the same year was a different confection, having an ohv 950cc four-cylinder engine designed by Spaniard Arturo Elizalde. Later a larger engine, a 1247cc Ten, became available, and a 1021cc sports Eight.

1975 Guyson

HAASE / *USA 1904–1905*
Tiller-steered twin-cylinder cars of 6 hp and 8 hp from Milwaukee.

HACKETT / *USA 1916–1919*
'A prideful car, distinctively different', the $888 Hackett 'Ultra Four' was built in Jackson, Mich., as successor to the Argo. In 1920, it was reborn as the Lorraine.

HAG (HAG-GASTELL) / *Germany 1922–1927*
Cars of advanced design with ohc 1305cc four-cylinder engines. When the Darmstadt HAG factory closed down in 1925, production was resumed at the Gebr. Gastell railway-carriage works at Mainz-Mombach, where sports-racing cars with 1496cc engines were also built in small numbers. Harry Stumpf-Lekisch was the leading Hag-Gastell racing driver.

1924 HAG 1305cc touring car

HAGEA / *Germany 1922–1924*
A little-known 1017cc four-cylinder Steudel-engined car with friction drive.

HAL / *USA 1916–1918*
H. A. Lozier, brother of E. R. Lozier, left the Lozier company in 1913 to build the HAL Twelve, which had a 6383cc V-12 engine with cylinders cast in threes. Prices ranged from $3600 for the tourer to $5000 for the Limousine and Town Car.

HALL / *England 1918–1919*
An unusual device, the Hall was built by H. E. Hall and Company of Tonbridge, Kent, with a 20·6 hp horizontal eight-cylinder engine. A Talbot radiator and Studebaker rear axle were incorporated. Only two Halls were made.

HALLADAY / *USA 1905–1922*
The first dozen years of manufacture of these cars designed by L. P. Halladay was centred on Streator, Illinois. The cars were subsequently made in Lexington, Attica and Newark, Ohio. For a small-production assembled car, the Halladay was singularly long-lived, nearly all of them using a Rutenber engine. Four-cylinder models were phased out permanently in 1914 in favour of sixes. Control of the Halladay was gained by Albert Barley who, in 1916, three years following his acquisition of Halladay, introduced the Roamer. Barley sold Halladay in 1917 to concentrate his attention on the Roamer, and the Halladay survived as a manufacturing entity through 1921. Although 1922 models were built, these were probably pilot models only. In addition, a handful of smaller Falcon cars was made by Halladay until production was terminated early in 1922.

HALLAMSHIRE / *England 1900–1907*
The early cars built by Durham, Churchill & Company, of Sheffield, used a 'friction clutch change speed and reverse gear', apparently an epicyclic transmission adapted from a marine unit. In 1902 the range consisted of a 7 hp and 14 hp, while in 1905 there were a 5/8 hp and a 10/16 hp. The last year of car production was 1907, when an Aster-engined 14/18 hp was offered, still with the same two-speed transmission. Thereafter, the company concentrated on its 'Churchill' commercial vehicles.

HALL & MARTIN / *England 1905*
A 10/12 hp car with twin-cylinder Aster engine and armoured wood chassis, built in Croydon, Surrey.

HAMLIN-HOLMES, HAMLIN
USA 1919–1929
This company attempted to perfect and market a front-wheel-drive car between 1919 and 1929. Approximately one experimental model per year was completed in this span of years, none looking exactly like another; a production model, announced in 1923, failed to get beyond the experimental stage. One racing version of the car did manage to get into the Indianapolis 500 race in 1926. The name was simplified to 'Hamlin' for 1930. The 1930 Hamlin was very similar in design and appearance to the front-wheel-drive Gardner of the same year. While the Gardner prototype was actually built, there is some doubt concerning the Hamlin.

HAMMER / *USA 1905–1906*
Like its counterpart, the Sommer, this was a 12 hp twin-cylinder light car, though Hammer did bring out a 24 hp four-cylinder in 1906. The two marques had cloned off the 1902–04 Hammer Sommer.

HAMMOND / *England 1919–1920*
The Hammond, made at Finchley, London, had a long-stroke 2243cc engine and was designed to sell at about £400. Very few were built.

HAMMOND MOUTER / *France 1912–1913*
A cycle builder from Paris who offered two voiturette models, both four-cylinders, one of 1888cc, the other of 2474cc.

HAMPTON / *England 1911–1933*
Starting life in Hampton-in-Arden, Warwickshire, the Hampton then moved to King's Norton, Birmingham, and finally to Stroud in Gloucestershire. The 1912 Hammond was the 12/16 model, with a 1726cc four-cylinder engine, while two years later a short-lived twin-cylinder two-stroke was announced and cyclecars powered by Precision or Chapuis-Dornier engines were offered. A Dorman 1496cc engine was fitted to the 10/16 of 1919; this was later increased to 1795cc. From 1923, Meadows engines were used, and in 1928 a six-cylinder model, the 15/45, appeared at the same time as a new 9 hp car. An excursion into unreality came in 1930 with an order, at the height of the Depression, for 100 straight-eight engines and chassis from the German Röhr concern. The subsequent model was offered with the 2262cc straight-eight, mounted in its own or in a Hampton chassis.

1913 11.9hp   Hampton two-seater

HANDLEY-KNIGHT, HANDLEY
USA 1921–1923
The Handley-Knight was one of a handful of American automobiles which used the Knight sleeve-valve engine, a four-cylinder type being used on this make. Early in 1923, the Knight engine was discontinued, the name was abbreviated to Handley and prices were sharply reduced. Successor to the Handley-Knight, the 1923 Model 6-40 Handley used a six-cylinder Falls engine and a pointed radiator, whereas the 6-60 retained the conventional flat radiator and featured a six-cylinder Midwest motor. Like the earlier Handley-Knights, the cars were distinguished by small handles or loops on the headlights, and, despite the fact that Reo also boasted this feature, the Handley slogan was 'If it carries handles, it's a Handley'. Checker Cab bought out the make in May 1923.

HANDS / *England 1922–1924*
After G. W. Hands had produced the Calthorpe light car, he produced a vehicle under his own name with a 1100cc Dorman four-cylinder engine. It was joined in 1924 by a 15 hp overhead camshaft six, later to emerge as a Calthorpe after Hands returned to his own company.

HANOMAG / *Germany 1924–1939*
The little 499cc Hanomag, with its rear-mounted 10 hp single-cylinder, water-cooled engine, was the first true German 'people's car', popularly known as the 'Kommisbrot' ('army loaf'): it had an all-enveloping body — a lever between the two seats acted as starter. It was a cheap, but well-made car which performed well in rough and hilly country. It was even raced

with success and competed in many long-distance events. A more conventional 745cc Hanomag four-cylinder superseded the Kommisbrot. Further Hanomag cars had ohv four-cylinder 896cc, 1089cc, 1299cc and 1494cc engines. From 1934 to 1939, an ohv 2241cc six-cylinder was offered and a diesel-engined 1910cc four-cylinder was available from 1937 to 1939. Hanomag also built cars for the German Wehrmacht during the war, but did not re-enter car manufacture after 1945.

1938 Hanomag 1½-litre

HANOVER/*USA 1921–1924, 1927?*
Hanover was an export-line cyclecar built in Hanover, Pennsylvania. Approximately 800 to 900 of the air-cooled, twin-cylinder Hanover roadsters were marketed. Some six water-cooled cars were reportedly produced during the 1927 calendar year.

HANSA/*Germany 1905–1939*
Founded by August Sparkhorst and Dr. Robert Allmers at Varel, Hansa bought the Westphalia car works at Bielefeld in 1913 and the next year merged with Hansa-Lloyd of Bremen. Early Hansa cars were much influenced by French products, mainly the Alcyon voiturette. There were De Dion-engined 720cc single-cylinder models, called 'HAG', also available in 1050cc versions, as well as a 1360cc twin-cylinder. Fafnir supplied 1410cc four-cylinder engines to Hansa, who also produced sports cars, including an ohv 2494cc model. From 1910 onwards, Hansa built RAF cars under licence. The pre-Great War range also included 1550cc, 1796cc, 2080cc and other models up to a 3815cc four-cylinder 55 bhp model. In 1920 Hansa, Hansa-Lloyd, NAG and Brennabor formed the GDA, the 'Gemeinschaft Deutscher Automobilfabriken'. Between the two wars, Hansa offered sv 2063cc four-cylinder 36 hp models and

Continental-engined six- and eight-cylinder versions of 3262cc and 3996cc respectively — there was even a 4324cc model with one of these USA-made eight-cylinder engines. All these cars were made at the Varel works, while the Bremen-built Hansa cars, available from 1930 onwards, had sv 2098cc and 3253cc four-cylinder engines, a 2577cc six-cylinder as well as ohv models with 1088cc and 1640cc own-make engines. New 3485cc and 1962cc ohv six-cylinder models appeared in 1936 and 1937; the last car, already called 'Borgward', was the 2247cc six-cylinder, built in 1939. The rear-engined 498cc twin-cylinder two-stroke built in 1934–35 also belongs to the complicated Hansa story. An earlier version with a similar 348cc engine was produced in small numbers only.

HANSA-LLOYD/*Germany 1914–1929*
Three 4082cc four-cylinder Hansa-Lloyd cars gained renown in the 1914 Alpine-Trial. Improved versions of this model with 50 hp at 1700 rpm appeared on the market in 1921. Another model with 4500cc, called 'Treff-Ass', boasted 65 bhp at 2400 rpm and was followed in 1926 by a big ohc eight-cylinder of 5220cc which developed 100 bhp at 3000 rpm. This excellent big car was the last Hansa-Lloyd. After 1930 only lorries were built, in conjunction with NAG.

HANSON/*USA 1917–1923*
One of the few cars built in the southern United States, the Hanson was an assembled car, featuring a Continental engine and other standardized components. Several hundred units were produced and like other southern-built assembled automobiles, notably Anderson, the car enjoyed sales outside its own region. Both open and closed models were sold.

HANZER/*France 1900–1902*
Hanzer of Petit-Ivry built a range of 5cv and 6½ cv single and 9cv twins, all with crocodile bonnets: one example survives. From 1902 the cars were sold as 'Durey-Sohy'.

HARDING/*Canada 1911–1912*
A 20 hp four on Hupmobile lines built in London, Ontario.

HARDING/*England/France 1912*
Aeronautical engineer H. J. Harding, who built monoplanes closely based on the Blériot XI, also made a 9 hp JAP-engined 'quadcar' in his Paris workshop.

The sole surviving Hanzer, a 1902 5hp

HARDING/*USA 1915*
The Harding, built in Cleveland, Ohio, was one of the first 12-cylinder cars on the American market. Unfortunately, only one touring car was made before operations ground to a halt.

HARDMAN/*England 1906*
'Specially built for British Roads', the Hardman cars emanated from Liverpool. The range consisted of 18/20hp, 25/30hp and 40/50hp models.

HARDY/*England 1905–1906*
A 6 hp Stevens-engined tricar 'fitted with an appliance preventing side roll whilst turning a corner', supplied as a chassis and kit of parts 'to complete to customer's own satisfaction'.

HARISCOTT/*England 1920–1921*
This obscure sports car from Bradford, Yorkshire, used a 1½-litre side-valve Coventry-Climax engine. It was so called because the makers were Harrison, Scott and Co.

HARPER RUNABOUT/*England 1922–1926*
Built in the Avro aeroplane factory at Manchester, this was a three-wheeled, single-seat, £100 runabout with a single-cylinder 269cc Villiers engine (giving 90–100 mpg) and integral body-chassis construction.

HARRIGAN/*USA 1922*
The Harrigan Six was an assembled car; the prototype was apparently built in Cleveland, Ohio. Plans called for a factory either in Jersey City or Hoboken, New Jersey. The car used a Continental engine; the touring model was priced at $1490. The Rolls-Royce-shaped radiator did not lie flush with the hood, but rose above it in the style of the McFarlan.

1913 Hansa 15.9hp sporting tourer 'Typ E'

1928 Hansa-Lloyd ohc 5220cc straight-eight four-door saloon

HARRINGTON/*England 1901–1902*
A four-seater 7 hp single-cylinder 'Panhard system' car offered by the London coachbuilders Offord.

HARRISON/*USA 1904–1907*
The 1906 Harrison, from Grand Rapids, Michigan, had a four-cylinder engine which could run in either direction, thanks to two sets of exhaust cams controlled by the driver. Inlet valves, perhaps mercifully, were automatic. The cylinders could also be made to fire in pairs 'for greater power on hills'. An acetylene-powered self-starting system and four-speed constant-mesh transmission were also featured.

HARRIS SIX/*USA 1923*
An ambitious local project: no cars were actually produced at the Menasha, Wisconsin, plant of the Harris Six until a bankruptcy court ordered as many cars as possible be manufactured and sold from existing parts. Probably less than ten were made, disc-wheeled sport phaetons powered by Waukesha or Continental engines. Wheelbase was 120 inches and price was $1485.

A Beautiful Car Embodying Remarkable Qualities At a Very Moderate Price.

1923 Harris Six 4078cc sport phaeton

HARROUN/*USA 1917–1922*
The Harroun, built in Wayne, Michigan, honoured the name of Ray Harroun, who won the first Indianapolis '500' in 1911 at the wheel of a Marmon Wasp. This was a low-priced automobile with its own make of four-cylinder engine, selling in the $1200 price bracket.

HART/*England 1900–1903*
Ernest W. Hart, of Luton and London, was a motor agent who also marketed electric carriages. Their 1900 *La Toujours Contente*, with a 2½ hp Löhner-Porsche electric motor in each hub, was the first four-wheel-drive motor car. In 1903 Hart offered a 40 hp petrol-electric.

HARTNETT/*Australia 1949–1955*
Designed by French engineer Jean Grégoire (and similar to the British Kendall), the Hartnett was a front-wheel-drive design which made extensive use of aluminium. It had four-wheel independent suspension, rack-and-pinion steering and an air-cooled horizontally-opposed engine. Plans were made to sell 10,000 a year, but serious difficulties arose when an outside contractor failed to deliver body panels. Some 120 rolling chassis had been completed when Hartnett took the contractor to court. These chassis were fitted with hand-built timber station wagon bodies. Hartnett won a protracted law suit, but the project died.

1915 Harvard two-seater

HARVARD/*USA 1915–1920*
This was a two-passenger roadster, marketed for export only and manufactured first in Troy, New York, then in Hudson Falls, New York, and eventually in Hyattsville, Maryland. Harvards were all built with right-hand drive: most, if not all, were produced for the New Zealand market. A hidden compartment for the spare wheel in the rear deck was an innovation. A four-cylinder Model motor was used throughout the car's six-year production.

HASBROUCK/*USA 1899–1901*
Stephen Augustus Hasbrouck designed a very complex 'convertible compound explosive engine' in 1899. His Hasbrouck Motor Company of New York were builders of launches and yachts with 'gasoline motive power', who also fitted their power units to carriages which could be 'operated by any intelligent person . . . its speed is gauged from one mile per hour to as fast as one may care to go'.

HATAZ/*Germany 1921–1925*
One of the better small German cars, the 972cc Hataz had a Steudel-made four-cylinder sv engine. Sports versions were available with a similar ohv unit and two-seater bodywork.

HATFIELD/*USA 1917–1924*
An assembled car, the Hatfield's only probable claim to fame was its 1917 suburban car, forerunner of today's station wagon. The earlier models used a four-cylinder G. B. & S. engine, later models using both four- and six-cylinder engines by Herschell-Spillman.

HAUTIER/*France 1899–1905*
'Young engineer' Hautier designed this marque's 'Espérance' engines which followed an 1899 electric car. The 1902 models had not only electric lighting, but also an underslung circular radiator beneath a conventional bonnet. Catalogues that year included a cut-out model of the 1903 four-cylinder: first prize for the best finished model was a new Fr 9000 twin-

1921 Haynes roadster

cylinder Hautier! Hautier's ultimate range consisted of 20 hp and 30 hp models with frames pressed from a single sheet of steel and constant-mesh gearboxes.

c.1901 Hautier 'La Silencieuse' 8hp twin

HAVERS/*USA 1908–1914*
Powerful six-cylinders from Port Huron, Michigan: 1914 models had a 55 hp engine of 6178cc.

HAWK/*USA 1920*
Only one pilot model was built by the Hawk Motor Co. of Detroit. This featured disc wheels and a five-passenger touring body.

HAY/*USA 1899–1900*
Walter Hay, of New Haven, Connecticut, claimed this 6 hp four-cylinder 4212cc Stanhope phaeton would run 'without oil or water'. It operated on an 'eight-stroke' cycle, with two out of four revolutions occupied in 'cooling and purifying' the cylinders.

HAY-BERG/*USA 1906–1908*
Assembled cars from Milwaukee, using an ohv air-cooled 20 hp Carrico four-cylinder engine of 3925cc.

HAYES/*England 1904*
A 'newly invented Balanced Engine and new Ratio Velocity Gear' were this car's main features.

HAYNES, HAYNES-APPERSON
USA 1898–1925
Elwood Haynes, of Kokomo, Indiana, the inventor of stainless steel, made his first car in 1894, and for many years claimed it as America's first motor vehicle. However, production did not begin until 1898, when Haynes teamed up with the Apperson brothers, building boxy cars with tiller steering and a rear-mounted flat-twin engine. The Appersons broke away in 1902 to set up on their own, though the cars were still called 'Haynes-Appersons' two years later. Wheel steering appeared in 1903: these were among the first left-hand-drive American cars. Haynes cars adopted a front-engine position in 1904, though still using a 12 hp flat twin: a five-seater aluminium-bodied Roi-des-Belges cost $2550. A vertical-four engine of 35/40 hp appeared in 1905, last year of the flat-twins; only big pair-cast fours were available between 1906–14, in which year the company's first six appeared. This was the Model 27, with electric gear-shift and a pair-cast engine of 7763cc. A 60 degree V-12 appeared two years later, with two monobloc cylinders giving a swept volume of 5909cc. The 'Light

189

Twelve' remained in production until 1921. The last Haynes was the Model 60, a 5219cc six, available with roadster, tourer or sedan bodywork.

HB/*USA 1908–1909*
A 10hp high-wheeler built by H. Brothers of Chicago.

HCE/*England 1912–1913*
An underslung cyclecar with 6hp Buckingham engine.

HCS/*USA 1920–1925*
Harry C. Stutz left his Stutz Motor Car Co. in Indianapolis in 1919 to head a new concern in the same city, the first HCS automobiles being introduced for 1920. A relatively expensive machine, the HCS resembled the Hispano-Suiza and was highly regarded by sporting car aficionados. The cars were powered by a four-cylinder Weidely engine; in 1924, this was augmented by a Midwest six. The Weidely four was dropped for 1925 which was the last year of HCS passenger-car production. The company remained in business as a taxicab manufacturer into 1927.

HE/*England 1920–1931*
Financed by Herbert Merton and designed by R. J. Sully, the HE was built in Reading, Berkshire, by the Herbert Engineering Company. The first model was a sv 1795cc four, though it was soon succeeded by the 14/20 of 1920; two years later a sporting model, the 14/40, appeared. A six-cylinder model, a 15·7hp of 2·3 litres, was added in the 1927 season. The four was dropped in 1928 and a 1½-litre six appeared in 1930, a few being sold in supercharged form, though it featured quarter-elliptic springs all round, a sign of the times!

1927 HE Six at Brooklands

HEADLAND/*England 1898–c1900*
Front-wheel-drive electric broughams and phaetons 'of not unpleasing appearance'.

HEALEY/*England 1946–1953*
A highly accomplished driver and experienced engineer, Donald Healey formed plans for the production of a car bearing his name whilst in

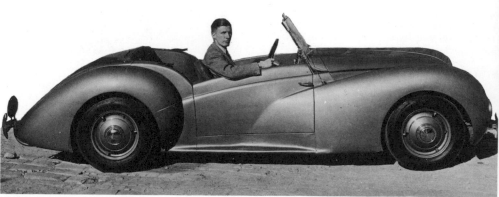
1948 Healey Westland two-seater

the employ of Humber; he had already left his stamp at Triumph, being responsible for the birth of both the Gloria and Dolomite. Production of both the Elliot (closed) and Westland (open) grand touring Healeys began in October 1946. Later, yet more sporting models were produced, the Nash-Healeys finishing with distinction at Le Mans and the Healey Silverstones finding great favour with the club racers at home. The Nash was the most widely produced of the Warwick-built Healeys, 253 being made altogether, as against 105 Silverstones.

HEBE/*Spain 1920*
A 6/8 cv cyclecar built in Barcelona: unusually for this type of vehicle, saloon bodies were offered.

HEDEA/*France 1912–1924*
Made in Paris by M. Accary (and sometimes sold under his own name) these were medium-sized cars with 1795cc Chapuis-Dornier engines.

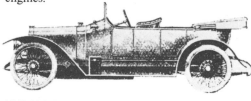
1919 10/12hp Hédéa tourer

HEIFNER/*USA 1920–1922*
Located first in Chester, Penn., and later in Geneva, Ohio, the Heifner was developed into a few pilot models at best and just drawing-board plans at least. Announced were six-cylinder models featuring a Continental engine in 1920 and 1921 and a Wisconsin four for 1922. The six-cylinder models, in touring car form, were listed at $3595.

HEILMANN/*France 1897–1900*
Monstrously complex, the Heilman (from Le Havre) had a twin-cylinder opposed-piston engine driving a dynamo which powered hub motors. In 1899, this maker of electric locomotives offered a four-wheeled electric *avant-train* to convert horse carriages.

HEIM/*Germany 1921–1926*
Made by former Benz engineer and racing-driver Franz Heim, these 20hp, 30hp and 40hp

touring cars had own-make four-cylinder engines of 1569cc, 2009cc and 2100cc with side valves; 1924 saw the introduction of an ohc 2385cc six-cylinder. Production of Heim cars was limited, especially of an ohc 1960cc sports six-cylinder, which was built in 1925–26.

HEINE-VELOX/*USA 1906–1909, 1921–1922*
The initial phase of the car carrying this name was a conventional four-cylinder type built by the Heine-Velox Motor Co, of San Francisco, California. The second line of automobiles—enormous and highly expensive machines—was produced by the Heine-Velox Engineering Co, of the same city. These later cars rode on a wheelbase of 148 inches and used a modified Weidley V-12 engine with 6383cc displacement. Hydraulic four-wheel brakes were included and both open and closed models were built. Price of the five-passenger touring model was $17,000, making it America's most expensive motor car at the time.

HEINIS/*France 1925–1930*
Made in Neuilly by M. Heinis, these cars were offered with various engines, from an ohc 799cc four designed by Heinis, through various proprietary 1100cc, 1170cc, 1690cc and 1947cc units to a 5000cc Lycoming eight.

HEINKEL/*Germany 1955–1958*
Formerly famous for their military aircraft, Heinkel built three-wheeled 174cc 'bubble cars'; from 1957 a four-wheeled minicar with ohv 198cc and 204cc single-cylinder engines was also available. In 1958 Heinkel sold the design and production equipment to Ireland and England respectively.

HELBE/*France 1905–1907*
The Helbé ('LB', for Levêcque and Bodenreider, its constructors) was an assembled light car using De Dion engines of 4½hp, 6hp and 8hp and Delage components.

HELIOS (NORDEN)/*Sweden 1901–1906*
Södertälje Verstäder built railway rolling stock, but started importing Kuhlstein, NAG, Protos and Ducommun cars from Germany. Any of these cars could probably have been sold under the Helios name in 1901–02. From 1902 the American Northern car was assembled and marketed as Norden. The venture was not profitable and production ceased in 1906.

HELIOS/*Switzerland 1906–c1907*
A short-lived marque from Zurich whose 18/24 cv shaft-drive cars were built in the Weidmann factory.

HELIOS/*Germany 1924–1926*
A small car with a water-cooled 972cc flat-twin MI (afterwards Mehne) engine.

HELVETIA/*France 1898–c1900*
Built at Combs-la-Ville (Seine et Marne) by the Swiss engineer Jacques Fischer-Hinnen, this was a light electric car — a Helvétia was the first car seen in Prague.

HENDERSON/*USA 1912–1915*
'More car for less money' was the slogan of this Indianapolis-built 4·6-litre four with electric lighting and starting. The sons of the company's founder made the famous Henderson four-cylinder motorcycle.

HENNEY/*USA 1920–1930*
The majority of passenger automobiles built by this funeral car manufacturer were formal sedans built either as emergency ambulances, invalid cars or automobiles to accommodate mourners at funerals, and used the conventional ambulance/hearse chassis. A handful of disc-wheeled sport phaetons were destined for West Coast sales in 1920 and in 1930 the company built four convertible sedans, featuring a long chassis and wire wheels. All four units were sold to funeral directors and were priced at $5000.

1920 Henney Sport Phaeton

HENOU/*France 1923*
For one year, M. Henou of Paris sold some 1843cc cars made by Guilick in Maubeuge.

HENRIOD/*Switzerland 1896–c1899*
Fritz Henriod of Bienne built a steam tricycle in 1888; in 1893 he built a single-cylinder car on Peugeot lines. Production began with a rear-engined 4 cv car, shown at the Exposition Nationale in Geneva in 1896, in which year Fritz was joined by his young brother Charles-Edouard. In 1896, too, came a car with rear-mounted flat-twin engine and a transmission consisting of a crown-wheel with three concentric sets of teeth engaged by a sliding pinion. In 1898 Charles-Edouard broke away to set up in France, and Swiss production ended.

HENRIOD/*France 1898–c1911*
Charles-Edouard Henriod began production at Neuilly-sur-Seine with cars similar to the last

Swiss-built Henriods, with flat-twin air-cooled engines mounted at the front of the chassis. Seven models were offered. Among Charles-Edouard's later inventions was a 'valveless' engine which Darracq built under licence (and which almost ruined them). 'All the elements of mystery' were contained in the 1909 Henriod 30/40 hp chassis, which had an air-cooled engine. There was no visible gearbox, the propeller shaft running direct from clutch to rear axle. In fact, the clutch contained a three-speed epicyclic transmission operated by pedal. 'No fewer than seven pedals figure on the footboard', commented a press report. 'They are not in line, however, three of them being double, with a rocking motion, so that the heel and toe may work one or other of a pair. It must be conceded that the simplicity of the transmission is somewhat discounted by the intricacy of control'. The marque survived until at least 1911, building a four-cylinder 'valveless' 2614cc car with friction drive to the design of one G. Aubrespy.

HENRY/*USA 1910–1912*
'Built to sell on its merits', the Henry 35 came from Muskegon, Wisconsin.

HENRY BAUCHET/*France 1903*
A 5/8 cv twin-cylinder light car from Rethel (Ardennes) sold direct to the public, possibly succeeding l'Ardennais.

HENRY-DUBRAY/*France 1901*
A 5 cv three-seater voiturette from Paris, noted for its 'softness in rolling'.

HENRY J/*USA 1951–1954*
The Kaiser-Frazer Company introduced the Henry J in 1951 in an attempt to bolster its sagging fortunes. An ugly compact car designed by American Metal Products, with additional styling by Howard Darrin, the Henry J was powered by Willys-built L-head four- and six-cylinder engines. Although available only as a two-door, four-passenger fastback coupé, 82,000 cars were sold. Sales had slumped by the end of 1952 when a new model — the Vagabond — was introduced. Willys merged with Kaiser in 1953 and the Henry J was dropped in 1954, having sold 120,000 cars.

1951 Henry J – 'functional beauty without frills'

HENSCHEL/*Germany 1900–1906*
There was no connection between this Berlin machine factory and the famous Henschel locomotive works. They produced electrically driven cars and a small 6 hp petrol car in limited numbers.

HERALD/*France 1901–1906*
Hérald secured one of the biggest fleet orders of their day, to supply 100 chassis for 'motor hansoms' for London. 14 hp, 18 hp and 24 hp models were available: Queen Wilhelmina of the Netherlands had a 24 hp Hérald limousine in 1905.

HERALD/*Germany 1903–1906*
An 'unlucky' car, because the Herald — built by Otto Weiss & Co., of Berlin — had so much in common with the 1140cc single-cylinder Maurer-Union that Weiss lost a court action and had to cease car manufacture.

HERBERT/*England 1916–1917*
An 11·9 hp SUP engine powered this Hampton-like light car assembled in London by Herbert Smith.

1916 11.9hp Herbert coupé

HERCULES/*Switzerland 1900–c1902*
Hercules cars, built in Menziken (Argovie), were heavy wagonettes with single-cylinder 6 cv and four-cylinder 12 cv engines. From 1902 on, trucks only were built.

HERDTLE & BRUNEAU/*France 1905*
Certainly the smallest four-wheeled passenger vehicles ever were the motorized roller skates produced by this motorcycle maker. Each skate had a 1 hp motor; the controls were fixed to the skater's belt, and linked to the skates by flexible cables. Top speed was claimed to be a brakeless 66 kph. Hardly surprising, motor skating failed to catch on as a pastime.

HERES/*France 1910*
A four-cylinder 2413cc car with cone clutch and live axle, built in Paris.

HERFF-BROOKS/*USA 1914–1916*
A 40 hp four and 50 hp six, selling at $1100 and $1375, were manufactured in this company's 'one great plant in Indianapolis'. A 25 hp, selling at $765, was added for 1915.

HERING/*Germany c1900–1903*
Hering, makers of construction equipment and steam pile-drivers at Ronnebourg, offered a range of two- and four-cylinder cars with crocodile bonnets and armoured-wood chassis.

HERMES/*England 1903*
Built by the Autocar Construction Company, the 25 hp Hermes was developed from the Accles-Turrell and had a 'sliding body', giving easy access to the four-cylinder horizontal slow-speed engine and transmission.

HERMES/*Germany 1904–1907*
The Hermès (or Hermès-Simplex), was designed by Ettore Bugatti and built by E. E. C. Mathis at Graffenstaden in Alsace. There were 45 hp (7433cc) and 60 hp (8261cc) four-cylinder models, as well as a limited number of 25 hp and some 90 hp (12,064cc) racing versions. They competed in many events: drivers included Bugatti, Gustav Langen, Emile Mathis, De Vizcaya and Robert Dunlop.

1905 Hermes 50hp tourer

HERMES (HISA)/*Italy/Belgium 1905–1909*
This was a Belgo-Italian factory with works at Liège and Naples. Racing driver and financier Baron de Crawhez was behind these 4192cc four-cylinder cars, which were of up-to-date design and excellent quality. Production was on a limited scale only. There was no connection between this factory and the Bugatti-designed Hermès-Simplex.

HERMON/*England 1936*
The Hermon featured André Girling coil-spring independent front suspension and was closely modelled on the 1½-litre British Salmson.

HERON/*England 1924–1926*
The Heron was unusual in having an 11·9 hp Dorman engine mounted transversely amidships with chain drive to the rear axle and a Consuta copper-sewn plywood body built by flying-boat manufacturers S. E. Saunders. Later cars had a conventionally mounted engine of 10·8 hp.

HERON/*England 1960–1964*
Heron Plastics had been involved in re-clothing Austin Sevens at one time and the body for the Heron Europa was in fact a widened, generally modified version of one of those early designs. Underneath lay a Ford nestling in a backbone chassis. In 1962 the kit was a mere £580. Following early promise and a flirtation with Monteverdi, Heron scrapped the project after 12 years.

HERRESHOFF/*USA 1909–1914*
This Detroit company built a conventional four-cylinder model, which sold at $950 in roadster form with a mother-in-law seat. The 30 hp Herreshoff chassis 'gave an impression of originality which is dissipated, almost wholly, by detail consideration'. It had a 30 hp 2199cc engine.

HERRESHOFF/*USA 1914*
The work of yacht designer Charles Frederick Herreshoff, this 16 hp light car was built in Troy, NY: it was seemingly unconnected with the Detroit Herreshoff.

HERSOT HELICE/*France 1920–1924*
Better known as a brake manufacturer in Limours, Hersot made some unusual cars with propellers like aeroplanes.

HERTEL/*USA 1895–1900*
'One of the lightest hydro-carbon motor vehicles on the market', the 1899 Hertel, built by the Oakman Motor Vehicle Company, of Greenfield, Massachusetts, scaled 500 lb in running order. The independently sprung front wheels were carried in cycle forks, and a single lever not only controlled the friction drive (by vee-pulleys on to a 'driving rim' inside each rear wheel), brake and throttle, but was also used to start the twin-cylinder 2¼ hp engine.

1899 Hertel 2½hp

HERTZ/*USA 1925–1927*
The Hertz was the first car made purely for rental and was the ancestor of today's Hertz rental car system. Under Yellow Cab aegis, it first appeared in 1925 as a successor to the Ambassador D-1 and survived in both open and closed models until late 1927. It featured Continental six-cylinder engines, disc-wheels, Buick-shaped radiator and 114-inch wheelbase.

HEWETT/*England 1905*
A 24 hp four-cylinder tonneau 'suitable for private use or traveller's business'.

HEWINSON-BELL/*England c1900*
Six of these crude Benz copies with wheel-steering were apparently built in the Southampton area.

HEWITT/*USA 1906–1907*
Hewitt used the same design of 'pedals-to-push' gearing as its related marque, the English Adams, and used identical 10 hp horizontal single and 7423cc V-8 engines, though there was also a pair-cast four with an optional sliding gear-change.

HEWITT-LINDSTROM/*USA 1900–1901*
Chicago builders of electric vehicles ranging from light Stanhopes to stage-coaches.

HEXE/*Germany 1905–1907*
Built in Hamburg, the Hexe ('Witch') was patterned on the Nagant — fours of 18/20 hp, 24/30 hp and 40/45 hp, and a 35/40 hp six were available.

HEYMANN/*USA 1898–1902*
A tiller-steered two-seater from Melrose, Mass.

HFG/*England 1920–1921*
Using a 9 hp flat-twin engine, mounted transversely on the near side of the car, the HFG was a short-lived essay by C. Portass and Son of Sheffield.

HH/*Germany 1906–1907*
A long-forgotten producer of cars known as 'Ferna', with engines from 10 hp to 28 hp; most had Fafnir four-cylinder engines.

HIDLEY STEAM CAR/*USA 1901*
Definitely one, and perhaps as many as four, Hidley automobiles were made. The centre of operations was Troy, New York.

HIGHGATE, HMC/*England 1903–1904*
The 1903 HMC Popular had a choice of 6½ hp Aster or De Dion engines, and sold at 170 guineas, while the 1904 Highgate light car ('only 125 guineas') had a 6 hp De Dion.

HIGHLANDER/*USA 1920–1921*
Sometimes listed as 'Hylander', this assembled car used a Continental six-cylinder engine. It was built in 1920 and 1921 by Midwest Motors, with the former Stafford Car factory of Kansas City, Missouri as headquarters. With a 120/125-inch wheelbase, the touring car was listed at $1975.

HILDEBRAND/*Germany 1922–1924*
Assembled a few three-seater cars with 15 hp Steudel four-cylinder engines.

HILL & STANIER/*England 1914*
A 6 hp cyclecar built in Newcastle upon Tyne.

HILLE/*Germany 1898*
A copy of the De Dion tricycle with a 1¼ hp air-cooled engine.

HILLEN/*Holland c1913*
An ephemeral marque from Jutphaas.

c.1901 Hewinson-Bell dogcart

HILLMAN/*England 1907–1976*
William Hillman, a cycle manufacturer of 10 years' standing, commissioned Louis Coatalen to design his first car for the 1907 Tourist Trophy. The 24 hp four-cylinder model was eliminated following a crash. Coatalen left to work wonders at Sunbeam, and Hillman settled down to producing modest and unspectacular models: these included a 9·7-litre six-cylinder

car and a 6·4-litre four, though at the other extreme a 9 hp 1357cc car was more successful, spanning the war years and finally being discontinued in 1925, by which time it had grown to 1·6 litres. A 14 hp model came out in 1926, and two years later the company was taken over by the Rootes brothers: a 2·6-litre straight-eight was an uncharacteristic offering for the marque. A landmark for Hillman came in 1932 with the appearance of the 1185cc Minx, while the sporting market was not neglected with the 1933 Aero Minx. There were some six-cylinder models, but by 1939 production was rationalized and only the four-cylinder Minx and 14 hp models were offered. The Minx soldiered on after the war and for 1949 received full-width bodywork and the following year a 1265cc engine. Overhead valves came late to the Minx, 1955 seeing their adoption with a 1390cc engine. The faithful Minx remained in production until 1970, by which time it was powered by a 1725cc engine. The company's entry into the small-car market came with the Imp of 1963, which had a rear-mounted 875cc all-aluminium overhead camshaft engine and all-independent suspension, though it never achieved the hoped-for sales. The American Chrysler Corporation attained a majority interest in Rootes in 1964 and one outcome of this take-over was the 1294cc Avenger of 1970. It was no surprise when the Hillman name ceased to appear in 1976, being replaced by the Chrysler trade mark. In 1978 Chrysler's British operations were acquired by the French Peugeot-Citroën group as part of their take-over of Chrysler-Europe.

1908 25hp Hillman-Coatalen Roi-des-Belges

The 1920 Speed Model Hillman 10hp

1955 1390cc Hillman Minx

HILTON/*USA 1921*
A curiosity in that it was only available in coupé form, the 114-inch wheelbase Hilton sold at $2375. Head office was at Philadelphia, with the factory at Riverton, New Jersey. All Hiltons featured a four-cylinder Herschell-Spillman engine and wire wheels.

HINDUSTAN/*India 1942 to date*
Morris-based cars built in Hooghly, West Bengal, starting with the Hindustan 10. The current Ambassador range was introduced in 1957, based on the contemporary Morris-Oxford.

HINES/*USA 1907–1910*
William R. Hines, of the National Screw and Tack Company, of Cleveland, Ohio, built his first car in 1902, and soon became an advocate of two-stroke engines. The first production Hines was completed in April 1907: it used an over-square four-cylinder two-stroke engine of 4170cc. A three-cylinder engine was also built.

HINO/*Japan 1953–1967*
Formerly building only commercials, Hino began assembling the Renault 4 cv under licence in 1953, introducing its own design, the rear-engined 893cc Contessa 900, in 1961. The line was revised by Michelotti in 1964, with cars up to 1300cc. Hino merged with Toyota in 1967.

HINSTIN/*France 1921–1926*
Made both by M. Hinstin in the SUP works in Mezières and by Guilick in Maubeuge, these were light cyclecars with 1099cc CIME and 1094cc Ruby engines. Some light cars with 1500cc SCAP engines were also offered.

HISPANO ALEMAN/*Spain 1979 to date*
Built two sports cars, one similar to the Mallorca but with Ford Fiesta 1300cc engine, the other a BMW-powered BMW 328 replica.

193

Hispano Suiza

HISPANO-SUIZA/*Spain 1904–1938*
Succeeding Castro, Fabrica La Hispano-Suiza de Automovils recorded its Swiss designer, Marc Birkigt, in its title: production was, again, in Barcelona. At first, the Castro four was continued under the Hispano-Suiza name, then, in late 1906, two pair-cast fours of 3·8 and 7·4 litres were introduced, followed by two big sixes in 1907. Already, the young King Alfonso XIII had a Hispano in his stable, the first of some 30 he would own. A racing Hispano built for the 1910 Coupe des Voiturettes sired the famous 3620cc Alfonso XIII sports model (Queen Ena of Spain gave her husband one for his birthday). By 1912, a Paris factory was in operation, and it was here that the famous 6·5-litre ohc H6 of 1919 was principally built, though Barcelona did turn out a limited number as the T41 (T56 8-litre from 1928: the T49 used the same chassis but a 3750cc six-cylinder engine. In the 1920s Barcelona also built the ohv T30 4·7-litre (1914–24) and T16 3089cc (1921–24): the 2500cc T48 was built for the Government public services. Between 1932 and 1943, Barcelona built a series of six-cylinder models, the last of which was the T60RL, introduced in 1934, a depressing machine with servo-assisted Lockheed hydraulic brakes and central gear-change.

HISPANO-SUIZA/*France 1911–1938*
To satisfy its fashionable French clientele, Hispano-Suiza opened a Parisian assembly plant at Levallois-Perret in 1911, moving to larger premises at Bois-Colombes in 1914. It was the French factory which produced the immortal 32 cv H6B in 1919, with its ohc light-alloy engine of 6597cc, joined in 1924 by the even more exciting Boulogne sports derivative, of 7983cc. The H6B was built under licence by Skoda of Czechoslovakia from 1924–27. In 1930, Hispano took over Ballot, who built the 4580cc Junior six-cylinder. In 1931 Hispano-Suiza, loftily ignoring the Depression, brought out the magnificent Type 68 V-12 of 9425cc; it was later developed into the 11,310cc Type 68 *bis*. A six-cylinder version, the K6, succeeded the Junior in 1934. Post-war, the French factory built a fwd prototype using a Ford V-8 engine, which never reached production.

A line-up of 20/24hp Hispano-Suizas in Barcelona, *c.*1905

*c.*1922 Hispano-Suiza H6B Torpédo Scaphandrier

15.9hp Hispano-Suiza, 1914, in racing trim

An H6B Hispano-Suiza tourer, *c.*1923

HISPANO-GUADALAJARA
Spain 1918–1923
Hispano-designed vehicles—mostly military trucks—were produced in the Guadalajara factory, which operated independently from Barcelona until 1923. Some 8/10 hp light cars were built, also known simply as 'La Hispano'

HISPARCO/*Spain 1924–1929*
Carlos Perez del Arco designed this Madrid-built 6/8 hp sporting light car. Four-wheel brakes, three-speed gearbox and a four-cylinder 961cc engine were features of the specification: about 100 Hisparcos were built, some being sold through a Parisian agency.

HITCHON-WELLER/*England 1904–1906*
Fitted with the Hitchon Patent Change-Speed Gear, this 9 hp light car was built in Accrington, Lancashire. Later models were known as 'Globe', and a 14 hp White & Poppe engine became available.

HL/*France 1911–1924*
Designed by H. L. A. Hainsselin, the HL ('Europe's reply to America') was a bullnosed four-cylinder with coil-spring independent front suspension, close-fitting cycle wings and a two-speed gearbox in unit with the back axle. Two engine sizes were available, 2121cc and 3092cc. Also sold as Hainsselin, this marque offered a 2413cc four of similar design post-war.

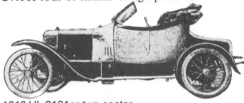
1913 HL 2121cc two-seater

HMC/*England 1913*
An 8 hp Chater-Lea-engined cyclecar from Hendon.

HOBBIE ACCESSIBLE/*USA 1908–1909*
The Hobbie was one of the many high-wheeled cars which were being sold at the same time. Featuring a twin-cylinder air-cooled engine, it had tiller steering and solid tyres. It was one of the relatively few Iowa-built cars, its factory being located in Hampton.

1910 Hobbie Accessible high-wheeler

HOFFMAN/*USA 1901–1904*
A 'general utility car' from a firm of bicycle builders in Cleveland, Ohio, the 8 hp Hoffman became the Royal Tourist in 1904.

HOFFMAN/*USA 1931*
A novel front-wheel-drive Lycoming-engined straight-eight shown in Detroit early in 1931. Only two prototypes were built.

HOLCAR/*England 1897–1905*
Michael Holroyd-Smith, an inventor 'determined to break away from the conventional', first made a high-built phaeton with tiller steering and massive unsprung chassis, the body being carried on full-elliptic springs. Holroyd-Smith's 1901 car had a 90 degree vee-twin, and transmission by 'employing cones with a specially-devised linked belt'. The United Kingdom Inventions Association (Telegrams 'Ghostology') of London offered the Holcar, designed by Holroyd-Smith, as well as a 'rotary steam motor' in 1903.

1978 Holden Kingswood sedan

HOLDEN/*Australia 1948 to date*
After 18 years of assembling Vauxhall and Chevrolet models, General Motors Holden launched Australia's first mass-produced car in 1948. The light six-cylinder four-door sedan was typically American in concept, powered by a 60 hp engine. It was an immediate success. More than 4 million Holdens have since been sold. The 1978 range consisted of sedans, waggons and panel vans, with a choice of six-cylinder and V-8 engines. In 1969 GMH also launched a smaller car called Torana. Originally based on the Vauxhall Viva, it grew in size and is now produced with a 1·9-litre four-cylinder or a larger six-cylinder unit. The larger Holden is produced in several levels of trim, and in an extended wheelbase version known as the Statesman.

HOLDSWORTH/*England 1903–1904*
There were three models of the Birmingham-built Holdsworth—a chain-driven 4½ hp, a 6½ hp Aster-engined shaft-drive model and a 6 hp twin with 'patent transmission by connecting rods; pedal starting gear; twenty different speeds either forward or reverse'.

HOLLAND/*USA 1901–c1905*
Built cars of 1¼ hp to 12 hp, with one and two cylinders.

HOLLEY/*USA 1899–1904*
George H. Holley, of Bradford, Pennsylvania, built tiller-steered three- and four-wheeler cars.

HOLLIER/*USA 1915–1921*
Built by the Lewis Spring & Axle Co., of Chelsea, Michigan, the Hollier was initially available with a V-8 engine of its own design. A smaller model with Falls six-cylinder engine was introduced for 1917, and later, Continental sixes were substituted. All Hollier automobiles were open models.

HOLMES/*USA 1918–1923*
The Holmes was a well-built, highly regarded, relatively expensive automobile which ranked second to Franklin in air-cooled car sales at the time. Using an ohv six-cylinder engine of its own design and make and with a wheelbase of 126 inches, the Holmes line constituted both open and closed models. A planned four-cylinder did not materialize. In six years of business, Holmes manufactured an estimated 2700 cars.

HOLSMAN/*USA 1902/1909*
The Holsman Automobile Company of Chicago claimed to be the 'oldest, largest and most practical manufacturers of carriage automobiles in the world'—all demonstrably untrue—and built spindly belt-drive high-wheelers with a minimum of mechanical refinement.

HOL-TAN/*USA 1908*
Moon of St Louis built this European-styled four for Lancia agents Hollander & Tangeman of New York.

HOLYOKE/*USA 1899–1903*
Gas-engine makers of Holyoke, Mass., who turned to making complete motor vehicles. Matheson took over the factory.

HOMER LAUGHLIN/*USA 1916–c1918*
This was a V-8 with the odd combination of friction transmission and front-wheel drive, the friction disc being linked to the front axle by twin chains.

HONDA/*Japan 1962 to date*
The world's biggest motorcycle manufacturers, Honda of Hamamatsu brought out the twin ohc S500 Sports at the 1962 Tokyo show: 360cc and 500cc engines were available, and before long there was an 800cc version too. In 1966 saloons of 360cc and 600cc were introduced, and in 1969 came the Honda 1300, with single ohc and front-wheel drive. A stratified-charge engine, the CVCC, was available in the 1973 Civic. A

1903 Holley Motorette

larger model, the Accord, came next, with a 1600cc engine: this was the subject of controversial negotiations in 1979 whereby BL (formerly British Leyland) planned to build it as a 'Triumph' model in Coventry as a stop-gap until their LC10 mid-range model became available in the early 1980s.

HONG-QI / *China 1959 to date*

The Hong-Qi ('Red Flag') prestige limousine is built by the Number One Automobile Plant in Changchun, Manchuria. The first model, Hong-Qi 72, appeared as a prototype in 1958, and was produced in small numbers until 1966, when the Ca 770 series was launched. Powered by a 5652cc V-8, it is said to be capable of 118 mph. In 1958, the same factory introduced the 1·5-litre Dong Feng ('East Wind'). Standard colour, appropriately, was red.

1968 Honda N360 saloon

Hong-Qi's small car, the 1958 Dong Feng

1979 Honda Prelude 1600cc coupé

HORBICK / *England 1902–1909*

Horsfall & Bickham, of Pendleton, Manchester, were manufacturers of textile machinery who diversified into car manufacture with twin cylinder shaft-drive cars of 8 hp and 10 hp 'built to the exact specifications of public demand'. A 6 hp Horbick Minor 'with patented combined change-speed and transmission gear' appeared in 1904. The 1905 Horbick Minor was a 10/12 hp three-cylinder; also new was a 15/20 hp L-head four capable of 35 mph. In 1907 came two six-cylinder models, of 2714cc and 8102cc. Horbick, however, were too successful: when demand began to outstrip their production capacity, they decided to give up car manufacture altogether rather than expand their works, and again concentrated on textile machinery manufacture.

HORCH / *Germany 1899–1939*

August Horch was one of Germany's pioneer car manufacturers who produced 5 hp and 10 hp twin-cylinder cars. In 1902, he moved to Reichenbach and designed in 1903 a 20 hp four-cylinder car with shaft drive. A 22 hp version appeared in 1904, after Horch had again moved production, to a new factory at Zwickau in Saxony. In 1905 a 40 hp 5800cc Horch went into production and 1907 saw the first six-cylinder model, a 7800 65 hp, on the market. Horch cars, very successful in sporting events, soon became very popular and production continued to rise. New models included ioe four-cylinder cars of 1588cc, 2080cc, 2608cc, 3175cc, 4700cc and 6395cc. And there was even an 8440cc four-cylinder ioe version, which was built in small numbers. There were also Horch cars with sleeve-valve engines, made under Knight licence. In 1909 August Horch left the works, and Georg Paulmann took over the design of

Horch 850 5-litre straight-eight cabriolet, 1934

Horch cars, which now also included a 2582cc model, a small car for that period and therefore called 'Pony'. After the war, Horch built cars including 8/24 hp, 10/30 hp, 15/45 hp, 18/55 hp, 25/60 hp and 33/80 hp models, all exhibited by the Zwickau-factory at the 1921 Berlin Show. Quantity production came in 1924 with a 10/50 hp ohc four-cylinder model of 2630cc, which succeeded a sv 2630cc four-cylinder; 1926 saw the first 3132cc dohc straight-eight in production, followed by a 3378cc version. A capacity increase to 3950cc brought 80 hp at 3200 rpm, but from 1931 onwards there were also new single-ohc straight-eight Horch cars, designed by Fritz Fiedler, with engines from 3 to 5 litres. Another new car in the early 1930s was the sv 6021cc V-12 Horch with a 120 hp engine and ZF-Aphon four-speed gearbox. Most Horch cars belonged to the luxury class and often had exclusive bodywork by Gläser, Neuss,

Armbruster and other leading coachbuilders: 1933 saw the introduction of new sv V-8 models of 3004cc, 3227cc, 3517cc and 3823cc. There was also the 850, with an ohc 4946cc straight-eight motor, which developed 100 bhp at 3400 rpm, while a 'hotter' version, the 951A, developed 120 bhp at the same number of revolutions. Less demanding customers got V-8s of 3517cc and 3823cc. In Zwickau, Horch built from 1933 to 1939 the rear-engined, Ferdinand Porsche designed, Auto Union Grand Prix racing cars. Horch built high-class, beautiful cars until the war, but in 1945 the original Auto-Union became defunct: the name 'Horch' is still waiting for a rebirth in Germany. To be correct, in 1946 there was the rebirth of a Horch in East Germany, at Zwickau, but as the name Horch belongs to the West German Auto Union, the East Germans had to drop it and call the new car 'Sachsenring' instead.

HORLEY/*England 1904–1907*
The 8 hp MMC-engined 'Hundred Guinea' Horley of 1904–06 was one of the first cars to approach a £100 price tag: it was also known as the 'No-Name'. Uprated to 9 hp in 1906, it was replaced next year by a 904cc twin at £121.

HORNET/*England 1905–1906*
The Hornet (sold by Horner & Sons of London) was a cheap (£131 complete) car with a massive 24 hp 3078cc twin-cylinder engine. There was also a 48·6 hp four of 6158cc at £263. Coyly, the company advertised these as '9 hp' and '18 hp'.

HORNMOBILE/*France 1912*
Offered a complex, if ephemeral range — 5 hp single and fours of 10, 11, 15 and 20 hp.

HORSE-SHOE/*France 1908*
Built by Glaenzer & Cie, of Paris, the Horse-Shoe was available in two models, a one-cylinder 8 hp and a 12 hp twin: both had radiator surrounds in the shape of a horseshoe — complete with nails.

HORSTMANN/*England 1914–1929*
The original Horstmann had a 1-litre four-cylinder engine with detachable cylinder head and horizontal overhead valves, though the gearbox was tucked away in the rear-axle. After the war, the company offered 1368cc or 1498cc Coventry-Climax engines and in 1921 the Horstman (the Germanic final 'n' was tactfully dropped) power unit was dispensed with. Sydney Horstmann also pursued a racing programme and tests were conducted at Brooklands with a supercharged side-valve Anzani power unit. Sports and Super Sports models were offered, being slightly modified racing types. The 1½-litre Anzani power unit was standardized in 1923, and in 1924 an 1100cc Coventry-Climax engine was offered. Technical advances included front-wheel brakes on racing cars in 1921, the aforementioned supercharging two years later and Lockheed hydraulic brakes in 1925. In the final year of production the 11 hp Anzani and 9/25 hp models were available.

1915 Horstmann coupé

HOTCHKISS/*France 1903–1954*
Connecticut Yankee Benjamin Hotchkiss had established his arms factory at St-Denis, 6 km north of Paris, in the 1870s. It filled in the slack period of peace by making motor components, and produced its first car in 1903, though a factory fire nearly halted the project permanently. This round-radiatored 17 cv four was followed in 1906 by a 7·4-litre six. A quality light car, the 2·2-litre 12/16 hp, appeared in 1912, and the next year a five-car range of three fours (12/16, 16/20 and 20/30 hp) and two sixes (20/30 and 40/50 hp) was catalogued. Post-war, Hotchkiss essayed a super-luxury car, the 6·6-litre Type AK, with ohv operated by a miniature crankshaft, but only one was built. From 1923–28, the refined 2·2-litre Type AM was the company's sole offering, gaining pushrod ohv by 1926. In 1928 came a new six, the AM 80, which was to be the basis for all subsequent Hotchkiss sixes, and which was offered until 1923 with torque-tube transmission instead of the traditional 'Hotchkiss drive' by open propeller shaft. In 1933 came the sporting AM80S 3·5-litre, based on the car which had won the 1932 Monte Carlo Rally (an event which Hotchkiss also won in 1933, 1934, 1939, 1949 and 1950). The sporting Paris-Nice of 1934 commemorated a sporting victory by Hotchkiss. A 1937 merger with Amilcar produced the Grégoire-designed Amilcar-Compound, which never saw serious production, and after the Armistice the pre-war 686 model was reintroduced, joined in 1949 by a new 13 cv four. From 1952, the 2-litre fwd flat-four Hotchkiss-Grégoire was built in small numbers alongside the 3·5-litre (which had acquired ifs in 1949). There was a temporary merger with Peugeot, a permanent one with Delahaye, and in 1954 the company ceased producing cars in favour of commercial vehicles and licence-built Jeeps.

1905 17cv Hotchkiss

1950 Hotchkiss Grégoire

1913 Hotchkiss 40/50hp six, with touring body by Gill of London

HOTCHKISS/*England 1920*
A British offshoot of the famous French company, the Coventry firm is usually remembered as building engines for William Morris's famous 'Bullnose' model. However, they did experiment with a car of their own, with a 1080cc vee-twin ohv engine, but it never went into production.

HOUK/*USA 1917*
A short-lived beetle-backed phaeton from a famous maker of wire wheels.

HOULBERG/*Denmark 1919–1920*
The maximum weight allowed on smaller Danish minor roads was 450 kg and that law bred a special type of car. One was the Houlberg, first produced in Odense in 1913. The car had a four-cylinder 5/12 hp Ballot engine, shaft drive and hand- and footbrake on the rear wheels. It is possible that an even smaller model with a Dutch Eysinck engine was built. Altogether 25–30 cars were made.

HOUPT/*USA 1909–1912*
Racing drivers Harry S. Houpt and Montague Roberts were behind this high-speed marque from Bristol, Connecticut. A 40 hp four of 9344cc and a 60 hp six (14,016cc) were available, and the cars were entered for many sporting events.

HOWARD/*USA 1903–1905*
The Howard started operations in Troy, New York, but operations were moved to Yonkers, New York, shortly thereafter. An expensive automobile, the 25/30 hp touring-car was listed at $5000 and closed models (listed as 'available') at a considerably higher figure.

HOWETT/*England 1912–1913*
A vee-twin cyclecar with 'eccentric steering'.

HP/*England 1926–1929*
This 500cc motorcycle-engined three-wheeled cyclecar, built by Hilton-Peacey Motors of Woking, Surrey, sold for only £65.

HPS/*England 1903–1904*
A 6 hp De Dion-engined light car on Panhard lines, said to be capable of 35 mph, was the Hyde Park Motor Stores' first offering. Two- and four-cylinder models were listed in 1904.

1949 HRG 1500

HRG/*England 1936–1956*
So called because of the involvement of E. A. Halford, G. H. Robins and H. R. Godfrey (of GN fame), the HRG was a spiritual successor to the Frazer Nash, though with a shaft-driven rear axle instead of chains. Initially, the 4ED 1496cc Meadows ohv engine was used and in 1939 an 1100cc single overhead camshaft Singer engine was fitted, to be followed shortly by a 1½-litre power unit from the same manufacturers when supplies of the Meadows engine dried up. After the war, the 1496cc Aerodynamic model made a brief appearance, though this was soon dropped in favour of the traditional chunky 1930s style bodywork. A final fling came in 1955 when an all-independent-suspension disc-braked model with twin overhead camshaft was announced but never proceeded with.

HUASCAR/*France 1930–1932*
Made in Courbevoie in close relationship with Deguingand and Galba, these cars were Violet-designed, with a water-cooled twin-cylinder two-stroke engine of 627cc.

HUBBARD/*England 1904–1905*
A 4½ hp coachbuilt tricar with front-wheel brakes, built in Coventry.

HUDLASS/*England 1897–1902*
In 1896 Felix Hudlass, aged 21, spent an inheritance (intended for his training as a doctor) on equipping a motor works, even though he had never seen a car. His first car, with a vertical-twin monobloc engine at the front and two-speed belt drive, appeared the following year, but after a few months was dismantled, and parts incorporated in a second car, which followed Benz lines, with a horizontal single-cylinder engine of 2813cc mounted at the rear. About 20 of this type were built between 1897 and 1899. By 1902 Hudlass was building 6 hp and 10 hp single-cylinder cars, and 12 hp and 20 hp twins with front engines, but a fire at his coachbuilders destroyed much of his stock. As he was not insured, he sold out, and joined Weller Brothers of Norwood, who went into liquidation in 1903. Hudlass was chief engineer of the Royal Automobile Club (formerly the ACGBI) from then on until he retired in 1947.

HUDSON/*USA 1901–1902*
A light tiller-steered steamer from Hudson, Michigan.

1956 Hudson Hornet V-8 hardtop

HUDSON/*USA 1909–1957*
Detroit store magnate J. L. Hudson gave his name to this marque, whose first offering, a 2534cc four of unremarkable design (by Howard Coffin), proved an instant success, pushing Hudson to seventeenth place in the US sales league by the end of 1910. The first Hudson six, the 6-litre Model 6–54, arrived in 1912; two years later Hudson were claiming to be the biggest manufacturer of sixes in the world. The four, by now of 4324cc, was dropped in 1916, and a one-model policy adopted with the 4730cc Super-Six, available in a wide range of body styles, and classy enough for President Hoover to order a landaulette. From 1927–30, the Super-Six engine had inlet over exhaust valves, but after that nothing except side valves were used on any Hudson. Hudson-Essex group sales were third biggest in the USA in 1929, but tailed off after that, despite the introduction of a new straight-eight in 1930. The six was phased out the next year, but the eight was to remain in production until 1954. In 1932, six eight-wheeled tourers were built for the Japanese Government. From 1934–38, after the demise of Essex, Hudson and Terraplane had much in common, and in 1935 the 'Electric Hand' electric gear shift became optional; 1936 saw the 'safety engineered chassis' with hydraulic

1916 Hudson Six-40 Town Car, 'in fashionable Grosse Pointe, Michigan'

brakes backed up by an emergency mechanical system. Hudson emerged from the war with a continuation of its 1942 models, but broke new ground with the unit-construction Step-Down design of 1948, offered in five series, from the low-priced Pacemaker to the high-priced Commodore Eight. Engines were a 4293cc six and a 4162cc V-8. The Hornet series used the old L-head six of 5047cc, and from 1951–54, this model was virtually invincible in stock car racing. Sales had peaked in 1950, however, and Hudson lacked the finance to re-tool. The 1953 compact Jet was abandoned when Hudson merged with Nash to form American Motors in 1954. After that, Hudson shared Nash's body-

shell; top of the line was the Hornet Custom Hollywood, with Packard V-8 power (replaced in 1956 by the new 180 bhp AMC V-8). The smaller Wasp used Hudson's old 3310cc six.

HUDSON / *England 1975*
A one-off electric town car built by John Hudson of Doncaster, the Hudson was capable of 40 mph and had a range of 28 miles. Its power came from 3 cwt (336 lb) of lead-acid batteries.

HUFFIT / *France 1914*
An 'absolute cyclecar', powered by a 1206cc Clement-Bayard twin, with 'sporting Alfonso XIII' body.

HUFFMAN / *USA 1920–1925*
The Huffman was an assembled car built in Elkhart, Indiana, offered as line of models all featuring a Continental six-cylinder engine throughout its solid, but rather dull history. A 120-inch wheelbase was featured. The 'K' series, introduced in 1923, was built until 1925, the last Huffmans being equipped with disc wheels and four-wheel brakes.

HUGOT / *France 1897–1905*
A voiturette driven by rear-mounted 2¼ hp De Dion or Aster single-cylinder engines. A few 697cc single-cylinder voiturettes appeared in 1905.

HUMBER

HUMBER / *England 1898–1976*
Thomas Humber's bicycle business was established in Coventry in 1868. It was therefore no surprise that the company's first vehicles to be powered by an internal-combustion engine were tricycles and quadricycles. These led to the Humberette of 1903, with a tubular frame and a single-cylinder 5 hp engine. By 1905 the range of Humbers included two- and four-cylinder cars ranging from the 5 hp to a 10/12 hp four. A three-cylinder 9 hp put in a brief appearance in 1903–04. But from 1905 the→

1913 8hp vee-twin Humberette cyclecar

1904 Humber 5hp Olympia Tricar

A 1915 11hp Humber two-seater

c.1921 15.9hp Humber Tourer

continued from previous page

two-cylinder cars were dropped, the range consisting of 10/12 and 16/20 models, with a 15 hp appearing in 1907. It was back to twins in 1908, and 1913 saw the Humberette name revived for an air-cooled vee-twin 8 hp (later examples were water-cooled). Mention should be made of the team of cars F. T. Burgess designed for the 1914 Tourist Trophy race. These used four-cylinder 3·3-litre twin overhead camshaft engines, but suffered teething troubles in the race and failed to show their mettle. The post-war years saw the company establish a reputation for themselves by producing solid, well-mannered cars. Side-valve engines were favoured up until 1922, but after this date overhead inlet/side exhaust engines appeared, the 8/18 of 1923 being a typical

example. Other excellent fours, a 9/20 and 14/40 hp, consolidated the company's position by 1927, that year also seeing the appearance of a fashionable six: the 20/55 hp model. However, 1930 saw the take-over of the company by the Rootes brothers and the appearance of two more sixes, the 2·1-litre 16/50 and 3·5-litre Snipe. The final departure of the overhead inlet/side exhaust engine came in 1932, Humber settling down to their traditional role of providing cars for the upper middle classes. The following year came the 1·7-litre four-cylinder 12 hp, though by the end of the decade the company was only producing six-cylinder models, the 4·1-litre Super Snipe and its variants being made during the Second World War. After the war, production of

these side-valve sixes continued, the Snipe and 4·1-litre Pullman range being augmented by a 2-litre four-cylinder engine of Hillman origins in the Hawk. Overhead valves did not appear on the Super Snipe and Pullman until the 1953 season, while the Hawk did not acquire them for another year; 1959 saw the re-emergence of the Super Snipe (it having been dropped for a short time) with a 2·7-litre engine, though this was later upped to 3 litres. The ailing Rootes Group was taken over by the Chrysler Corporation in 1964, the Sceptre of that year being a more luxurious version of the Hillman Minx, this having a four-cylinder engine of 1·7-litre capacity. This was the only upholder of the Humber name, the re-styled Sceptre being phased out in 1976.

1936 Humber Snipe

1953 six-cylinder Humber Super Snipe

HUMPHRIS/*England 1908–1909*
The Humphris Patent Gear was a final drive using a disc with four concentric rings of holes; pegs on the drive shaft gave the different ratios, with direct drive in every gear: 'guaranteed saving of 20 per cent in power'. Four-cylinder engines of 10/12 hp and 12/16 hp were used.

HUNGERFORD/*USA 1929*
The Hungerford, or Hungerford Rocket, was America's first successful rocket automobile and the first to be licensed for operation on public highways. Built by two eccentric clair-voyant brothers in Elmira, New York, the Hungerford was based on a 1921 Chevrolet chassis with a special rocket hookup and pumps built by the Gould Pump Co. of Seneca Falls, New York. The car never materialized beyond the prototype stage, but the one pilot model is extant to this day. The Hungerford had to be brought to a halt before being converted to rocket propulsion or *vice versa*. Teardrop styl-ing was used not unlike the Dymaxion.

HUNTER/*USA 1920–1921*
Little is known of the Hunter car of Harrisburg, Pa. At least one car is known to have been completed, a six-cylinder touring car with 121-inch wheelbase and an announced price of $2250.

1915 Hupmobile 15/18hp four

HUPMOBILE/*USA 1908–1940*
Bobby Hupp and E. A. Nelson designed the original Hupmobile, a 2·8-litre Detroit-built runabout with two-speed transmission. Selling at $750, it was an instant success, and by 1913 production was up to 12,000: a development of

1925 Hupmobile 16.9hp four-cylinder touring

this model was still in production in 1925, when it was joined by America's first low-priced straight-eight, with contracting Lockheed hydraulic brakes. A 3·2-litre six replaced the four in 1926. In 1929, Hupmobile took over Chandler, and built its lower-priced range in their Cleveland factory. The handsome Hupmobiles of 1932–33 were followed by an aerodynamic range, with a three-panel D-shaped windscreen (a proposed front-wheel-drive model was stillborn). By 1936, the range had been trimmed to a 4-litre six and a 5-litre eight; cast aluminium wheels were standard. In the summer of that year production was suspended for several months: the revived eights had automatic overdrive. Hupmobile's last venture was a rear-wheel-drive adaptation of the Cord 810/812. That having failed, they abandoned car production and moved into car spares, kitchen equipment and electronics.

1933 Hupmobile Six Three-Window Coupé

HUPP-YEATS / *USA 1911–1916*
The Hupp-Yeats electric coach was a costly luxury vehicle selling at up to $5000. 'Richest imported tapestries and leathers', and gold-plated fittings were this marque's distinctive features.

HURLINCAR / *England 1913–1916*
Hurlin & Co were motor agents ('two doors from the Hackney Empire') who built an 8 hp JAP-engined cyclecar in 1913, followed the next year by a vee-radiatored 10 hp four-cylinder light car.

HURST / *England 1896–1907*
George Hurst, 'Autocar Builder', claimed his 1903 12 hp two-cylinder and 24 hp four-cylinder were 'manufactured throughout' in his Holloway workshop. In 1906, Hurst was offering a 15/18 hp four-cylinder and a massive 30 hp six-cylinder of 5638cc. By 1907, this had been enlarged to 40 hp and 5883cc and was known as the Hurmid, as Hurst was now in partnership with a man called Middleton.

HURTU / *France 1896–1929*
The Conpagnie des Cycles et Automobiles Hurtu started making pushbikes and motor-cycles, and entered the automobile field as sub-contractors for Bollée. In 1900 they built the first true Hurtu cars, with single-cylinder De Dion and Aster engines. In 1907, Hurtu had three basic models, the 14 cv (1244cc) and 24 cv

(4502cc) four-cylinders and the 8 cv single-cylinder of 942cc. After 1912, the single-cylinder was abandoned and all Hurtus had four cylinders. Until 1914, their principal lines were the 10 hp of 1693cc and the 12 hp of 1767cc. They resumed production after the war with the 12 hp, but the most significant Hurtu models in the vintage period were the 12/14 cv (2358cc) and the 10/16 Sport (2001cc) with ohv. The last new model, of 1328cc, appeared in 1925.

HUSTLER / *Antigua 1976 to date*
A multi-purpose low-cost 'fun car' with Hillman Imp power, built by Chrysler agents Arawak Motors at the rate of four per week.

HUSTLER / *England 1978 to date*
Arising out of an association between stylist William Towns and Jensen Special Products, the Hustler utility vehicle was by 1979 under construction in the old Jensen works at West Bromwich. The Hustler had an immensely strong, welded box-section steel frame with an integral roll-over cage to which replaceable glass-fibre body panels were bolted. The engine and running gear came from the Mini.

HUTTON / *England 1900–1905*
Jack Hutton began production in Northallerton, Yorkshire, with rear-engined belt-drive voiturettes, but a move south to Thames Ditton, Surrey, saw the introduction of conventional bi-block four-cylinder shaft-drive cars of 12 hp and 20 hp. In 1904 came a one-off curiosity, with an F-head bi-block engine whose pushrod ohv had variable lift controlled by a lever on the steering wheel. It was fitted with the Barber infinitely variable automatic transmission and hydraulic brakes, but was probably never completed: Hutton then concentrated on his Mercedes agency. The 'Hutton' cars built for the 1908 Tourist Trophy were actually four-cylinder cars built by Napier.

HYDROCAR / *USA 1901–c1902*
A twin-cylinder 4 hp model built by Colonel Pope's American Bicycle Company of New York. Early models had hub-centre steering.

HYDROMOTOR / *USA 1917*
Plans were announced for the Automobile Boat Co. of Seattle to manufacture William Mazzei's Continental-engined amphibious car. With a streamlined body, it was said to be capable of 60 mph on land, 25 mph on water.

A 1904 Hyler-White design, the English Mechanic

HYLER-WHITE / *England 1899*
T. Hyler-White designed a curious opposed-piston engine with two crankshafts geared together. He also designed the 'English Mechanic' steam and petrol cars which could be built from plans published in *The English Mechanic & World of Science* (and reprinted in *Horseless Age*). Two such cars survive.

HYUNDAI / *Korea 1975 to date*
The first all-Korean car, the Hyundai Pony 1200cc was exhibited in mock-up form at the 1974 Turin Show, and went into production the following year at a plant near the southern tip of the Korean peninsula, part of the largest heavy industry combine in South Korea, run by the Chung family. A four-door saloon of conventional design, the Pony was aimed at developing markets with a right-hand rule of the road. Of an annual production run of some 90,000 vehicles, around 13,000 were scheduled for export. An annual output of 300,000 was the target for the mid-1980s from a new factory.

1914 Hurlincar

I

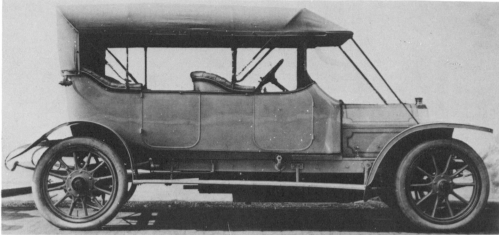

c. 1911 Impéria

IDEN/*England 1904–1907*
George Iden, formerly with Daimler, designed these four-cylinder 10/17 hp and 25/35 hp shaft-driven cars with 'Iden's frictionless radial gearbox'.

IENA/*Italy 1922–1925*
The 1096cc IENA was a sports car with a French four-cylinder Chapuis-Dornier engine.

IFA/*Germany 1948–1956*
Made at the pre-war Audi works, the East German IFA was virtually identical with the pre-war DKW Meisterklasse. It had a 684cc twin-cylinder two-stroke engine with front-wheel drive; another IFA had a 900cc three-cylinder two-stroke motor. The last IFA cars were made at the EMW (formerly BMW) plant at Eisenach. The IFA was succeeded by the Wartburg.

IKA-RENAULT/*Brazil 1955 to date*
Founded as Industrias Kaiser Argentina, this company, whose HQ is at Buenos Aires, introduced the Torino in 1966, using the 3770cc Kaiser Tornado engine in a Farina-styled body originally designed for Rambler. Various Renault models are also built.

ILFORD/*England 1902–1903*
A three-speed 5 hp light car from a firm of cycle makers in Ilford, Essex.

IMMERMOBIL/*Germany 1905–1907*
These 8 hp and 12 hp cars, incorporating many French components including De Dion and Reyrol engines, were built in small numbers in Hamburg.

IMP/*USA 1913–1914*
An air-cooled 10 hp vee-twin powered this belt-drive cyclecar built by McIntyre of Auburn, Indiana.

IMPERIA/*Belgium 1906–1948*
The first Impérias, built by Ateliers Piedboeuf of Liège, were designed by the German Paul Henze: these were fours of 3 litres, 4·9 litres and 9·9 litres. The next year, Impéria moved into the old Pieper factory at Nessonvaux. A monobloc

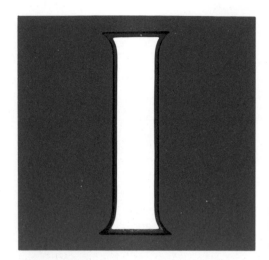

1905 Iden 25/30hp Landaulette

1927 Impéria 11/27hp

12 hp appeared in 1909, and in 1910 came a merger with Springuel. From about 1916, Impéria-Abadals were built at Nessonvaux. In 1921, three ohc 5·6-litre straight-eights were built, replaced by an ephemeral ohc 3-litre 32-valve four, capable of 90 mph. It was followed by the Couchard-designed 1100cc side-valve 11/22 hp four, one of the first cars to have a sliding sunshine roof. Its engine rotated counter-clockwise, and the transmission brake acted as a servo for the front-wheel brakes. Some Impérias were assembled in Britain at Maidenhead. A six of 1624cc appeared in 1937, available in three-carburettor Super Sports form from 1930. Impérias of 1934 on were merely four-wheel-drive Adlers with Belgian coachwork. In 1936, Impéria merged with Minerva. Post-1948, Impéria assembled Standard Vanguards under licence.

IMPERIAL/*England 1900–c1905*
Built at Hulme, Manchester, the 1901 Imperial was available in two-speed 3½ hp and three-speed 5 hp forms, with 'sloping wheel-steering'. In 1903, 8 hp and 12 hp models were offered.

IMPERIAL/*England 1904*
Formal electric carriages built by The Anti-Vibrator Company Limited of Croydon.

IMPERIAL/*USA 1906–1908*
Selling at $2500, the 5·5-litre Imperial Roadster from Williamsport, Penn., had a double-dropped chassis to give straight-line drive from flywheel to rear axle.

IMPERIAL/*USA 1907–1916*
From Jackson, Michigan, Imperial built a range of open tourers and roadsters. The 1914 range

1913 Imp cyclecar

consisted of five models with four engines—two monobloc fours (4882cc and 5212cc) and two bi-block sixes (5701cc and 6898cc).

IMPERIAL / *USA 1955–1971*
Though it still used Chrysler bodyshells, the Imperial was classed as a separate make from 1955: the range consisted of Custom, Crown and Newport and the lwb Crown Limousine. Power was by a Chrysler hemi-head V-8 of 5801cc. The 1957 Imperials had unique Virgil Exner styling, with skyscraper fins, and came with TorqueFlite transmission as standard; Imperial, Crown and LeBaron series were offered. The prestige Crown limousine was custom-built by Ghia of Italy; only 132 of these hand-crafted machines were made in the 1957–65 period. Sales peaked at 33,027 in 1957. The second best year (aided by all-new styling) was 1964, with 21,257 cars sold. There was a new chassis and new sheet metal in 1967, and in 1969 Imperial adopted Chrysler's 'tumblehome' styling. Though sharing the same sheet metal, Imperial continued to use a separate chassis up to 1971, when the marque returned to the Chrysler fold.

IMPETUS / *France 1900*
A C-sprung voiturette powered by a front-mounted De Dion engine, built at Pornichet-Plage (Loire-Inférieure) by Max Hertel (the same man who built the USA Hertel).

1928 Indian two-seater

INDIAN / *USA 1928–1929*
Only three or four experimental cars were built by the Indian Motorcycle Co. of Springfield, Mass. Two of these 85-inch wheelbase cars were equipped with twin-cylinder Indian engines, a four-cylinder Continental or a four-cylinder Chevrolet motor being used in the other car or cars. Wire wheels were standard. A roadster, coupé and one other body style were made.

INDUCO / *France 1922–1924*
Made in Puteaux, Seine, by M. Van der Heyden, this was a light car with a 1094cc Chapuis Dornier engine.

INNES / *USA 1922*
Successor to the earlier Simms car, less than 10 Innes cars were built by the American Export Co. of Jacksonville, Florida. The cars used both Supreme and Herschell-Spillman four-cylinder engines. The 'line' included a roadster, touring car and light truck.

INNES LEE / *England 1972–1973*
The Tom Killeen-designed Scorpion was a clever little monocoque two-seater sports car with a rear-mounted Hillman Imp engine. However, the company, based in Telford (Shropshire), never got the Scorpion into pro-

duction, despite an encouraging reception at the London Show in 1973.

INNOCENTI (LEYLAND) / *Italy 1961–1976*
Famous for many years for Lambretta scooters, Innocenti built the BMC (later British Leyland) Mini with 998cc and 1275cc engines under licence, following with other models, including the Regent (Allegro), with engines up to 1485cc.

INNOCENTI / *Italy 1976 to date*
Successor to Leyland Innocenti, the 'Nuova Innocenti', made at Milan by the De Tomaso Group, is still similar to the British Mini. It has Bertone-designed five-seater bodywork and is available with 998cc and 1275cc engines.

INTER / *France 1954*
A tandem-seat cyclecar with 175cc Ydral engine and rubber suspension.

INTERMECCANICA / *Italy 1971–1976*
This specialist producer first used 5766cc Ford Mustang V-8 engines followed by a 5354cc version. Another of these sporting luxury cars had a 2784cc six-cylinder Opel power unit. Production was mainly for export to the USA.

INTERNATIONAL / *England 1898–1904*
Until 1901, Oscar E. Seyd's company, based in Great Portland Street, London, modified Benz cars for the British market. From 1900, the Allard-built International Charette, a single-cylinder belt-drive model, was their mainstay, a twin-cylinder model built by Payne & Bates having proved unsuccessful. Imported models offered by International included the Armstrong (1902), Portland (1903) and Diamant (1904).

INTERNATIONAL / *USA 1914–1915*
A tandem-seated cyclecar selling at $380, built in Harvey, Illinois.

INTERNATIONAL BABY CARRIAGE
England 1904
A miniature motor car, belt driven and with a ⅛ hp electric motor, designed for children.

INTERNATIONAL HARVESTER
USA 1947 to date
In 1950 International, better known for trucks and farm vehicles, launched the Travelall wagon which was suitable for rough country and farming chores. The new model of 1957 gave more attention to styling. By 1961 the Travelall was available with two- or four-wheel-drive and

1973 International (IHC) 4wd Travelall

six-cylinder or V-8 engines. A new four-wheel-drive cross-country vehicle, the Scout, was offered with a wide range of open or closed bodywork. When off-road vehicles became a fashionable pastime in the 1970s, International built an extensive range of Scout models. The Traveler, a new model for 1977, featured six-cylinder in-line diesel engines built by Nissan of Japan.

INTERNATIONAL MOTOR WHEEL
USA 1899
This was a 'power pack' with a single driving wheel which replaced the front wheels of a horse-carriage to convert it into a motor vehicle. Various types of engine, from a single-cylinder two-stroke to a four-cylinder vee-twin with two crankshafts, were used.

INTER-STATE / *USA 1909–1918*
The Inter-State, from Muncie, Indiana, started life as a 4654cc four, but by 1913 the six-cylinder Model 45 of 6251cc was available. A cheaper model, the Touring-T, with a 3191cc Beaver four, was introduced in 1914, following a company reorganization, but in 1918 General Motors bought the Inter-State plant to produce the Sheridan.

1927 3-litre round-the-world Invicta

INVICTA / *England 1925–1938, 1946–1950*
Noel Macklin had already produced the Eric-Campbell and the Silver Hawk by the time the Invicta put in an appearance in 1925. The intention was to offer a sports car with American flexibility allied to traditional British quality. The Invicta's appeal was undeniable: low lines, handsome square radiator and bonnet with rivets clearly visible. Though the prototypes were fitted with 2·5-litre Coventry-Climax six-cylinder engines, production cars used the Meadows ohv 2·6-litre six which produced the right performance. The project was financed by Oliver Lyle (of Tate and Lyle fame) and Earl Fitzwilliam, previously of Sheffield-Simplex. Engine capacity was increased to 3 litres in 1926 and to 4½ litres in 1928, by which time the Meadows engine had been coaxed to deliver 100 bhp. Later, in 1930, the 4½-litre became available in two types: the high chassis and the graceful low chassis '100 mph' car with underslung chassis. Unfortunately, a win by Donald Healey in the 1931 Monte Carlo Rally and success in the Alpine Trial came at the height of the Depression and production tailed off, almost ceasing in 1935. This was not before efforts had been made to offer a more popular confection: the 1932 12/45 with an ohc Blackburne 1½-litre engine. A supercharged version, the 12/90, was announced the following year, though it achieved little success. Meanwhile

1948 Invicta Black Prince

Macklin had become involved with the Railton project and sold out to Earl Fitzwilliam: three new Invictas were announced for 1938, but these cars were nothing more than re-bodied Darracqs and the project was still-born. The Invicta name was revived after World War Two, the Black Prince model being designed by W. G. Watson, who had been responsible for the original Invicta of the 1920s. The new car was a vehicle of some complexity. The engine, based on a Meadows industrial unit, was a dohc camshaft 3-litre. Power was transmitted by a Brockhouse hydraulic torque converter (there being no gearbox). All-independent suspension by torsion bars was featured. The whole package was offered at £3000, though by the time production ceased in 1949 the price had spiralled to nearly £4000. The remaining spares were purchased by AFN Ltd. on the collapse of the enterprise.

IPE/*Germany 1919–1922*
A 12 hp small car with a sv 1017cc four-cylinder engine, made only in small quantities.

IPSI/*France 1920–1921*
Made in Asnières, Seine, these were 1100cc Ballot-engined cyclecars with friction drive.

IRIS/*England 1905–1915*
Named after the Greek goddess Iris, 'Speedy messenger of the gods', this Willesden marque later adopted the mnemonic 'It Runs in Silence'. From late 1905 a diamond-shaped radiator identified the Iris, built by Legros & Knowles: Ivon de Havilland, brother of the aviation pioneer, was associated with the marque until his premature death. Initially fours of 25/30 hp (4882cc) and 35/40 hp (6757cc) were offered, supplemented for 1907 by a 7310cc six. During the war they moved to Aylesbury, but produced no more cars.

1913 Iris 15hp Torpedo Phaeton

ISIS/*Czechoslovakia 1922–1924*
The Beutelschmidt-Ruzicka designed car had a German 769cc Baer two-stroke double-piston engine and was quite heavy. Other models had French Chapuis-Dornier 1100cc and 1500cc engines. Only 20 Isis cars were built.

ISO (ISETTA)/*Italy 1953–1976*
Iso's first motor vehicles were scooters and two-stroke motorcycles. Next, they built the Isetta 'bubble-car' with double-piston two-stroke engines of 236cc; it was also licence-built by BMW in Germany, VELAM in France and Isetta in Great Britain. Manufacture of big luxury cars commenced in 1961. Most had Ghia and Bertone-built bodywork and big Chevrolet V-8 engines. The range included the 5359cc Rivolta coupés and limousines. There was also the very sporting Grifo Lusso, a two-seater coupé. Others included the Lele, a Bertone-coupé with a 5768cc Ford V-8 engine, the Fidia and the Grifo. There was also the Grifo IR 9 Can-Am with a 7443cc Chevrolet V-8 and a top speed of 182 mph.

ISPANO-FRANCIA/*France 1920–1921*
Made in Biarritz by M. Pelladoux, the Ispano-Francia was a 16/20 hp car of very little interest.

ISUZU/*Japan 1953 to date*
Primarily truck manufacturers, Isuzu of Tokyo assembled Hillman Minxes during the 1950s. In 1969 General Motors, looking for a foothold in Japan, bought 34·2 per cent of Isuzu; the mid-1970s saw a three-car range — the 1·6/1·8-litre Gemini, the Florian (ohv 1·6/ohc 1·8-litre) and the Ghia-styled Coupé, available with a twin-cam, twin-carb 1800cc engine.

ISOTTA-FRASCHINI/*Italy 1901–1949*
Founded by Cesare Isotta and Oreste Fraschini, Isotta-Fraschini built a wide range of models in pre-Great War days, mainly four-cylinder cars up to 11,304cc. A six-cylinder, built in 1908, had 11,939cc. An Isotta-Fraschini, driven by Trucco, won the 1908 Targa Florio, and 1911 saw a small model with a 1·3-litre ohc engine, supposedly designed by Ettore Bugatti . . . a statement strongly denied by Isotta-Fraschini chief designer Cattaneo, who designed between the two World Wars the most famous model ever built by this car manufacturer: the straight-eight Isotta-Fraschini, the world's first series production straight-eights. Among them was the ohv 5623cc Tipo 8 of 1919, which was followed in 1924 by a bigger 7372cc version, Tipo 8A. Another eight-cylinder was the 1926 'Super Spinto' Tipo 8ASS, with a 135 bhp engine. Heavy steering spoiled these big Isottas. The last version, the Tipo 8B, was a big improvement, but only 30 were built from 1931 to 1939. After 1945, the factory tried to return to car manufacture, when Aurelio Lampredi designed in 1948–49 the rear-engined 3400cc Monterosa, which had a 120 bhp V-8 engine, an up-to-date design which never went into production.

1908 Targa Florio Isotta-Fraschini

iTALa

ITALA / *Italy 1903–1933*

Though Itala existed for 30 years, their heyday was unquestionably the period before the Great War. They had also two leading designers in Giulio Cesare Cappa and Matteo Ceirano. Their renowned early big four-cylinder racing cars had capacities of 16,666cc, 14,904cc and 12,045cc. Even production models had big engines of up to 12,924cc, though cars as small as 1942cc were listed. An 8336cc car, built in 1912, had a rotary-valve engine. New models came into being in 1920; a 2612cc (later 2811cc) four-cylinder and a 4423cc six-cylinder. In the mid-1920s, a sv 1953cc four-cylinder model became quite popular but was soon superseded by a 1991cc six-cylinder ohv version. There was also a short-chassis sv 2811cc sports version, which competed in many events. In 1926 Itala built a special racing car with a Hispano-Suiza engine and also a works racer with ohc 1094cc and 1450cc V-12 engines and Roots-type superchargers.

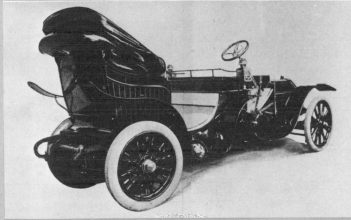

1907 40hp Itala 'state carriage'

1908 60/80hp Itala stripped for Brooklands racing

c. 1925 Tipo 8A Isotta-Fraschini

IVANHOE / *Canada 1903–1905*

Predecessor of the Russell, this was an electric runabout designed by H. P. Maxim.

IVEL / *England 1899–c1906*

'Smiling' Dan Albone was the inventor of the lady's safety cycle and built a pioneer petrol tractor: his Benz-engined light car had the body carried on C-springs, and the chassis was sprung on horn plates and coil springs like a railway locomotive. It was steered by a tiller on the driver's right, and application of the handbrake cut out the ignition.

IVERNIA / *England 1920*

A shadowy marque this, as it is not certain whether any were actually built! Specifications included a four-cylinder engine of 4579cc capacity.

IVOR / *England 1912–1916*

With a 12/16hp Ballot engine, the Ivor had a four-seat torpedo body of patented design.

IVRY / *France 1906–1907, 1912–1914*

Voiturettes, tri-voiturettes and tri-cars, all 5/6 hp two-speeders, were built in 1906–07 by this Parisian firm, which was actually the Ivry workshops of an electricity company. In 1912–14, four-cylinder cars of 12 hp and 16 hp were built.

IZARO / *Spain c1922*

Cyclecars of 600cc to 700cc built in Madrid.

205

JACKSON/*England 1899–1915*
R. Reynold Jackson's first offering was a belt-drive 'doctor's carriage' with a 3½ hp De Dion engine. After breaking with Mytholm in 1900, Jackson went to London and sold American Buckmobile, Century and Covert cars until 1903, when he brought out cars of his own assembly, with 6 hp or 9 hp De Dion engines in Lacoste & Battmann chassis. Singles were the main offering until 1909, though some of these had surprisingly long strokes—the 1909 Demon racer, with an aggressively pointed bonnet, had an engine of 104 × 213mm (1809cc). Four-cylinder models of 14hp and 17·5 hp appeared in 1909, a Chapuis-Dornier-engined light car and a JAP-engined three-wheeler in 1913.

JACK SPORT/*France 1925–1930*
Built in Paris by M. Corbeau (also a maker of motorcycles), the Jack Sport was a 410cc single-cylinder cyclecar.

JACQUEMONT/*France 1920–1925*
Made in Paris, this cyclecar was a close copy of the Bédélia. It had a single-cylinder 1100cc engine and was belt driven.

JACQUET FLYER/*USA 1921*
A high-priced sporting car, the Jacquet Flyer had a wheelbase of 124 inches, and wire wheels were standard. It was powered by a four-cylinder Wisconsin engine and a two-passenger roadster constituted its sole model. Few were made.

JAEGER/*Denmark 1907*
The Aarhus Pengeskabsfabrik had a prototype ready in 1907, and production was planned. The car had a water-cooled 7hp single-cylinder engine, and bodywork was a phaeton with four seats. The car was sold, but no more were built.

JAG/*England 1950–1956*
Sports cars with Ford V-8 and 1172cc Ten engines.

JAGUAR/*England 1945 to date*
The name Jaguar first appeared in 1935. It adorned a magnificent two-seater roadster introduced by the Swallow Sidecar Company at the London Motor Show. However, it was not until 1945 that (the now) Sir William Lyons founded Jaguar Cars Limited. Now part of the Leyland empire, Jaguar has made countless contributions to motoring history, not least by way of the XK roadsters which took the road and track by storm when introduced in 1948, its five Le Mans wins achieved by the subsequent C and D Type sports-racing cars, and the unparalleled value for money offered by the now legendary E Type. However, while it is the achievements of the Jaguar sports cars that are most easily recalled, the saloons were just as successful in their own way. The first Jaguars were difficult to distinguish from their SS counterparts; however, the first all-new saloon, the MkV, carried the legend a stage further. It is now hard to imagine, but the subsequent, even bigger Mks VII, VIII and IX were very successful competition as well as road cars. So too were the nimbler Mks I and II, perhaps the best sporting saloons of their time. By the advent of the Mk X in 1962, however, the emphasis was more on refinement, a quality that is the hallmark of today's XJ series. Arguably quieter than even a Rolls-Royce, today's Jaguars are still value for money.

JAMES/*USA 1909–1911*
A high-wheeled touring car with a 14/16 hp flat-twin engine.

JAMES & BROWNE/*England 1901–1910*
Though T. B. Browne was an early and enthusiastic owner of a Panhard, the first cars built

9hp James & Browne phaeton, 1902

by his company used horizontal power units. The 1902 model had a 9 hp twin-cylinder engine and four-speed transmission, while an 18 hp four appeared a year later. A feature of these cars was a six-seater aluminium tonneau body. There was a 'bonnetless' landaulette with under-floor power unit in 1903, too, aimed at superseding the electric carriage. In 1905 they announced an 8 hp bonnetless light car, while from 1906 luxury vertical-engined fours and sixes were sold under the name 'Vertex'.

JAMESON/*England 1973 to date*
Surrey engineer Paul Jameson has been responsible for two remarkable cars. The first, a glass-fibre-bodied, front-engined two-seater was powered by a 750 bhp Meteor tank engine, until the car was all but destroyed by fire. More exciting still, however, is an open two-seater

1946 Jaguar 3½-litre saloon

1951 Jaguar XK120 roadster

1979 Jaguar XJ12 5.3 Series III

with mid-mounted, blown Merlin engine giving some 1760 bhp. It is a six-wheeler with both rear axles driven.

JAMIESON/*USA 1902*
A tiller-steered two-seater with a twin-cylinder 7 hp engine and chain drive.

JAN/*Denmark 1915–1918*
The Copenhagen-built Jan type A had a four-cylinder engine of 1328cc and a three-speed gearbox. The cars were of entirely Danish construction and sported a handsome pointed radiator of hammered copper: 42 Type A Jans were built. The six-cylinder type E came after the war, but only two were built.

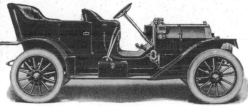
1910 Jackson (US) Model 40 tourer

JANEMIAN/*France 1920–1923*
Built in Bièvres, Essonne, by M. Janémian, these were rear-engined cars with chain drive. The 1096cc vee-twin was later enlarged to 1395cc.

JANOIR/*France 1921–1922*
A maker of motorcycles and sidecars in Saint-Ouen, Seine, M. Janoir also assembled some 965cc flat-twin-engined cyclecars.

JANVIER/*France 1903–1904*
This six-wheeler tonneau from Paris steered with its front two axles.

JANVIER/*France 1924–1926*
Well-known manufacturers of proprietary and stationary engines, Janvier et Sabin of Châtillon-sous-Bagneux made cars with 11 hp (1994cc) and 15 hp (2982cc) engines. They also built a 5-litre racing car in 1925.

JAP/*England 1904–1905*
This most famous of proprietary power unit makers built this 'novel and new pattern tricar' in their Tottenham works. It had side-by-side bucket seats and a front-mounted 4½ hp JAP.

JAPPIC/*England 1925*
This single-seater cyclecar by coachbuilders Jarvis of Wimbledon was chain driven and powered by 500cc or 350cc JAP engines. Hence the name!

JAR/*England 1913–1915*
A vee-twin Precision engine powered this light car sold by J. A. Ryley of Birmingham: its 'big car' styling was spoiled by a starting crank protruding beneath the nearside running board.

JAWA/*Czechoslovakia 1934–1939*
With 684cc twin-cylinder two-stroke engines and front-wheel drive, the Jawa was built under DKW (Auto Union) licence and was similar to the 'Meisterklasse'. A smaller 615cc model was

The Rolls-Royce Merlin-engined 1976 Jameson MkII

introduced in 1937: a 1990cc version never went into quantity production.

JAXON (JACKSON)/*USA 1903–1923*
'Our steam cars are strong, simple and ride like a Pullman', claimed the Jackson Automobile Company of Jackson, Mich., who built tiller-steered steamers similar in design to the Locomobile. They also offered a 6 hp petrol car under the Jaxon nameplate. Literacy later prevailed and, under the name 'Jackson', they remained in business until 1923, building large, conventional cars with a sporty image. An overhead camshaft engine was offered in 1910, in unit with the gear. Their 1914 range including the 'Sultanic' six, and 'Majestic' and 'Olympic' fours.

JBR/*Spain 1923*
A Barcelona dentist, José Bonniquet Riera, was behind this sporting cyclecar which won the 750cc class in the 1923 Armangué Trophy race. He later created the ephemeral 6/8 cv 969cc STORM, also built in Barcelona.

1979 Jeep

JBS/*England 1913–1915*
A twin-cylinder 8 hp JAP-engined shaft-drive cyclecar built by J. Bagshaw & Sons of Batley, Yorkshire. The 1915 models used a 10 hp four-cylinder engine.

JEAN-BART/*France 1907–1908*
Successor to the Prosper-Lambert, the Jean-Bart company built shaft-driven cars of 9 hp (single cylinder), and 16 hp and 40 hp fours.

JEAN GRAS/*France 1924–1927*
Jean Gras of Issy-les-Moulineaux, Seine, offered 1·2-litre fours and 1·5-litre sixes built in the Philos factory at Lyon.

JEANTAUD/*France 1893–1906*
Charles Jeantaud was a Parisian coachbuilder who built his first electric carriage in 1881. His output of electric vehicles included the first car

to set up a land speed record—39·24 mph (63·15 kph)—driven by the Comte de Chasseloup-Laubat, as well as coupés and hansom cabs, in which the driver sat high up at the rear. Some Jeantauds had an ingenious bevel-gear front-wheel-drive layout. In 1902–04, Jeantaud offered a range of petrol-engined cars which looked like Panhards of circa 1898!

JEECY-VEA/*Belgium 1925–1926*
A limited production light car from a famous Brussels motorcycle factory: power was by a 750cc Coventry-Climax flat-twin.

JEEP/*USA 1963 to date*
The Jeep found fame during World War Two and was the sole product of Willys-Overland after 1956. It was only recognized as a make in its own right after 1963, when it was taken over by Kaiser Corp. The range consisted of two- and four-wheel-drive station wagons and an updated version of the wartime vehicle. Four- or six-cylinder engines were available and in 1965 a

5·4-litre Rambler V-8 was offered. Having acquired Jeep in 1970, American Motors expanded the range for 1971 with the luxurious Jeepster series in station wagon, convertible and roadster forms. Engine options included a 145 hp six-cylinder and the 230 hp V-8, also offered in the Wagoneer. Almost all the mechanical components were redesigned in 1972 and by 1979 the range was a far cry from the wartime vehicle.

JEFFERY/*USA 1914–1917*
Succeeding Rambler, these were conventional fours and sixes; the firm was renamed 'Nash' after Charles W. Nash took over in 1917.

JEFFREY/*England 1968–1975*
Road-going developments of the successful Jeffrey racers, the J4 and J5 were neat front-engined Lotus Seven-style roadsters with glass-

fibre and aluminium bodies adorning tubular space-frames. Power came from a range of Ford engines. Performance was good, thanks to an all-up-weight of around 10 cwt.

JEM SPECIAL/*USA 1922*
Little is known of this make, but it is assumed to have been a one-of-a-type car built by or for John E. Meyer of New York City. Powered by a Continental six-cylinder engine, the Jem Special had a 128-inch wheelbase. Plans for further manufacture and sales came to nothing.

JENATZY/*France 1898–1903*
Belgian racing driver Camille Jenatzy was the first man to exceed 100 kph, on a streamlined electric racing car, *La Jamaise Contente*, of his own design. But the normal Jenatzy electrics, built by the Société Générale des Transports Automobiles of France, were square-rigged machines only capable of 12 kph.

*c.*1900 Jenatzy electric 'dog-phaeton'

JENKINS/*USA 1901–1906*
Builders of steam and petrol cars, Jenkins of Washington, DC achieved fame in 1901 with the 'Littlest Automobile Ever', a 3 ft-long electric victoria 'guaranteed to run for 2000 hours', made for Chiquita, the 26-inch high 'Cuban Midget' who appeared at that year's Pan-American Exposition.

JENKINS/*USA 1907–1912*
A 6546cc four from Rochester, NY.

JENNINGS/*England 1914–1915*
Built by the Jennings-Chalmers Light Car Company of Birmingham, this was a neat 1094cc Dorman-engined two-seater.

1914 Jennings (1098cc Dorman twin)

The Jensen brothers with their 1937 sports tourer

1948 Jensen Saloon

Jensen Interceptor Convertible, 1969

JENSEN / *England 1936–1976*

Body stylists Richard and Alan Jensen's first car was a 3·6-litre Ford V-8-powered model fitted with a two-speed Columbia rear axle. Other engine options were available, including the 2·2-litre Ford V-8 and straight-eight Nash units. Although a Meadows-engined 3·8-litre straight-eight was planned for post-war production, it failed to materialize and a 4-litre Austin six was substituted. This engine was used to power the Interceptor of 1950 and also for the glass-fibre 541 saloon of 1964. The company reverted to American engines for the 1963 CV8 — in this instance a 5·9-litre Chrysler V-8 — while 1967 saw the announcement of the FF. The engine was now 6·3 litres, but the really sensational aspect of the car was the Ferguson four-wheel-drive layout used in conjunction with the Dunlop Maxaret anti-lock braking system. In 1968 Jensen was taken over by merchant bankers William Brandt from the Norcros Group, who had acquired the company in 1959. An outcome of this move was that Kjell Qvale became president and Donald Healey chairman of the reconstructed company. Consequently, when Jensen announced their new sports car in 1972, it was under the name of Jensen-Healey. The engine was a Lotus-built 2-litre twin-cam 16-valve four-cylinder based on the Vauxhall single cam block. Regrettably, the model failed to live up to expectations and, although a GT was announced in 1975, the company ceased production the following year.

JEWEL / *USA 1906–1909*

A two-stroke runabout from Massillon, Ohio. In 1909 the products of the Forest City Motor Car Company were renamed Jewel-Keeton.

JEWEL / *England 1919–1938*

John E. Wood Limited of Bradford, Yorkshire, assembled cars to bespoke order for local customers. The 1922 Jewel was a 9 hp Coventry-Climax-engined 1088cc four-cylinder selling at £255. Meadows engines were used from 1924.

JEWETT / *USA 1922–1926*

Named after Paige's president, H. M. Jewett, the Jewett was to all intents and purposes a smaller and cheaper version of the Paige. The six-cylinder engines were of Jewett's own make or by Continental; in all an estimated 40,000 cars were manufactured. In 1926, the Jewett was continued under the Paige emblem.

JG SPORT / *France 1922–1923*

A small cyclecar made by M. Janvier, with 970cc Ruby engine and chain drive.

JIMINI / *England 1975 to date*

This strange-looking, four- or six-wheeled, Mini-based utility vehicle is one of several kits filling the gap left by the moribund Mini-Moke. About ten Jiminis are made per month.

JL / *England 1920*

A 1½-litre four-cylinder Decolonge engine powered the JL, a plywood-bodied light car from London's East Dulwich.

JMB / *England 1933–1935*

These three-wheelers could be had with two- or four-seater coachwork: a 497cc single-cylinder engine was fitted and final drive was, predictably, by chain.

JOEL-ROSENTHAL / *England 1899–c1902*

A London-built electric carriage with a separate 2 hp engine for each rear wheel.

JOHNARD / *England 1975 to date*

Johnard manufacture the Donington, a Bentley Special based on the old Mk 6 and available with either V-8 or six-cylinder Bentley engines. Made by restoration experts, the Doningtons feature exquisitely finished glass-fibre bodies with aluminium bonnet and wings.

JOHN O'GAUNT / *England 1901–1904*

Built by William Atkinson & Sons of Lancaster, the 4 hp John O'Gaunt was 'made to meet the requirements of people who do not require a high-priced car'.

JOHNSON / *USA 1905–1912*

Beginning with steamers, by 1907 this Milwaukee company was offering a range of three petrol cars, the biggest a 50 hp.

JONES / *USA 1915–1920*

A 3848cc Lycoming-engined six built in Wichita, which sold for $1150: factory capacity was 100 cars a month. From 1917, a Continental Six was fitted.

JONES-CORBIN / *USA 1902–1907*

The De Dion-engined Jones-Corbin from Philadelphia had double-chain drive and a honeycomb radiator. An 8 hp Runabout and a 9 hp Tonneau were offered, priced at $1000 and $1500 respectively.

JONSSON / *Sweden 1921*

Alfred Jonssons Motorfabrik, of Lidköping, specialized in marine engines, but experimented in 1902 with a twin-cylinder car. A more ambitious venture was the planned production of ten cars in 1921 — to be followed by series

production. Everything was made at the factory, except electrical system, fuel pump, instruments and tyres. The engine was a water-cooled side-valve of little more than 2-litres capacity. Only one car was built, with an aluminium touring body.

JORDAN / *USA 1916–1931*

Ex-journalist and advertising man Edward S. Jordan was given $300,000 to prove that the car market had not reached saturation point. The Jordan, a well-designed assembled car built in Cleveland, Ohio, always used Continental power units, initially a 4966cc six. By 1921 the 'Playboy' model was in the range, subject of one of the most famous advertisements in motoring history. Hydraulic four-wheel brakes were fitted from 1924, and in 1925 a 4408cc straight-eight was introduced. For 1927, 'the first truly fine American small car' offered a 'custom' range of 3259cc sixes with worm drive, which included 'Blue Boy' sports touring and 'Tom Boy' collapsible cabriolet, and the 'Air Line' 4380cc eight, still featuring a 'Playboy' coupé. Last new Jordan was the 5277cc Speedway Eight of 1930, with sporting coachwork and streamlined 'Woodlite' headlamps.

JOSWIN / *Germany 1920–1924*

Designer Josef Winsch modified war-surplus Mercedes six-cylinder, 12 spark plug aero-engines of 6462cc and 7269cc to power these big luxury cars built at his Berlin-Halensee works.

JOUFFRET / *France 1920–1926*

Made in Suresnes and then in Colombes, Seine, by M. Demeester, these cars were sometimes sold under his own name. They used 1172cc and 1616cc ohv engines from Ruby and SCAP. In 1923, Jouffret took over Sidea, and produced Sidea-Jouffret cars.

JOUSSET / *France 1924–1928*

Made in Bellac, Haute Vienne, by M. Jousset, these were CIME-engined sports and touring cars of 1099cc and 1496cc.

JOUVIE / *France 1913–1914*

A JAP-engined cyclecar from Paris.

1905 JP 16/20hp tulip-seat tonneau

JP / *France 1905*

The Prunello brothers of Puteaux, near Paris, offered a range of Gnôme-engined cars, shaft-driven 10/12 hp two-cylinder and 16/20 hp four-cylinder models and a 24/30 hp four-cylinder with chain drive.

JOWETT
England 1906–1954

Benjamin and William Jowett's light two-seater of 1910 was powered by an 816cc flat-twin engine, the basic layout remaining in production until 1954. It was the outcome of some years of experimentation, but having achieved their successful formula the Jowett brothers saw little reason to alter their specification. After World War One, the Jowett's engine was increased to 907cc while a four-seater, the Long Four, appeared in 1923, to be joined by a saloon version in 1926. Front-wheel-brakes finally appeared on most Jowetts in 1929, about five years after the rest of the industry! The faithful flat-twin was gradually refined, having received detachable heads in 1929. It was again increased in capacity to 946cc for

1937. Also, from 1925 it had powered the reliable Bradford van and continued to do so after World War Two right up until Jowetts ceased production in 1954, by which time it had been stretched to 1008cc. Not that the twin had everything its own way. In 1936 the Ten was announced, powered by an 1166cc flat-four engine. This engine configuration was used to power the Javelin of 1947, a modern design by Gerald Palmer, with bodywork inspired by the Lincoln Zephyr. Suspension was by torsion bar and road holding was excellent. Unfortunately, early cars were unreliable, which was particularly damaging on the export market. A sports car, the Jupiter, designed by Eberan von Eberhorst, appeared in 1950 with a space-frame chassis. It ran at Le Mans in 1950–52. Production of all models ceased in 1954.

c.1924 Jowett 7hp

A tiller-steered 1913 Jowett 6hp twin

1950 Jowett Jupiter Sports

J-P WIMILLE/*France 1948–1949*
A rear-mounted 22hp Ford V-8 powered the production versions of this aerodynamic saloon designed by racing driver Jean-Pierre Wimille. Production was no more than 20.

1948 JP Wimille coupé

JUHO/*Germany 1922*
This motorcycle producer tried his luck—unsuccessfully—with a small 400cc two-stroke.

JULES/*Canada 1911*
This 30hp four from Toronto had the strange feature of a horn button in the centre of the brake pedal. Only two were built.

JULIAN/*USA 1925*
Only one car was completed by Julian Brown of Syracuse, New York. It featured a five-passenger coupé body with the steering wheel mounted in the centre, and a 60hp radial engine mounted at the rear. The one car made had a custom body by Fleetwood: projected price of the 125-inch wheelbase Julian was $2500.

Junior R Phaeton

JULIEN/*France 1920–1926*
A tiny cyclecar from Blois, Loir-et-Cher, with a 174cc single and two-speed gearbox.

JULIEN/*France 1946–1950*
A small town car made in Paris by M. Julien, using a 325cc four-stroke and chain drive.

JUNIOR/*Italy 1905–1910*
Giovanni Ceirano built his Junior cars with 12/14hp twin- and four-cylinder engines of 3920cc and 6367cc Also known as 'FJTA'.

JUNIOR R/*USA 1924*
Only one car bearing this name was produced by General Motors for John J. Raskob Jr, son of the then president of the corporation. It consisted of components from Chevrolet, Oakland and Cadillac. The one-off touring car had disc wheels and a 111-inch wheelbase.

JUWEL/*Belgium 1923–1927*
Optimistic plans for mass-production of an 1100cc tourer having run aground, Juwel introduced an abortive fwd sports car in 1926.

JUZAN/*France 1897*
A light quadricycle on De Dion lines.

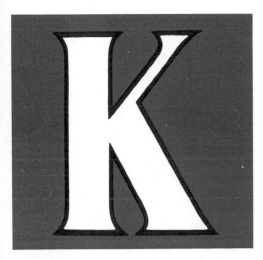

KAISER-DARRIN / *USA 1954*
Kaiser stylist Howard Darrin designed a glass-fibre-bodied sports car based on a Henry J chassis with sliding doors and landau top. Powered by a 90 hp six-cylinder Willys F-head engine, it had a top speed of 100 mph. Marketed by Henry Kaiser, only 435 examples were built. Darrin purchased the last hundred, fitted more powerful Cadillac engines, and sold the cars from his Los Angeles showroom.

KAMPER / *Germany 1905–1906*
Makers of proprietary engines, Kämper also built 8 hp four-cylinder cars of simple design.

KAN / *Czechoslovakia 1911–1914*
KAN built cars, designed by Alois Nejedly, with own-make water-cooled one-, two- and four-cylinder sv engines. Yearly production was 80 cars, of which the 1326cc four-cylinder two-seater was the best seller.

KANSAS CITY / *USA 1905–1909*
A 35 hp flat-twin with two forward speeds, the Kansas City car was said to be built on 'six years of practical experience', and to be 'artistic in detail'.

KAPI / *Spain 1950–1955*
A 2cv single-cylinder two-stroke engine powered this light three-wheeled runabout from Barcelona.

KARMINSKI / *England 1902*
The bonnet of the 7 hp Karminski came to a 'torpedo point'. In 1902 this Bradford-based firm said that they could not supply their similar 12 hp model 'owing to a contract by a Russian firm for a great quantity'.

1916 Kearns Model L 12hp tour

KEARNS / *USA 1908–1916*
Starting with the high-wheeled twin-cylinder Eureka buggy, this firm from Beavertown, Pennsylvania, progressed to trucks in 1910 and a 12 hp light car, Model L, in 1915 as well as the 1914 LuLu cyclecar.

KEETON / *USA 1908–1914*
Similar in appearance to the Renault, with a dashboard radiator and coal-scuttle bonnet, the Keeton (Croxton-Keeton in 1909–10) was advertised as 'an European type — at an American price'. The 1913 Keeton range, with a 48 hp six-cylinder engine, was available in three models — Riverside touring, Meadowbrook roadster and

KAC / *Denmark 1914–1917*
Probably at least four KAC cars were built by the Dansk Motor & Maskinfabrik, Copenhagen. They were of the typical Danish 'minor roads' type.

KAISER / *Germany 1910–1913*
Identical to the Braun, the Kaiser was built at the Justus Christian Braun fire-engine company's Premier works at Nürnburg. There was limited production of cars with 18 hp to 70 hp engines, some supplied by Fafnir of Aachen.

Kaiser

KAISER / *USA 1946–1955*
Millionaire shipbuilder Henry J. Kaiser and Joe Frazer of Graham-Paige commissioned Howard 'Dutch' Darrin to design two cars — the Kaiser and the Frazer. They hoped to break the Big Three's stranglehold on the US auto industry. A prototype of 1946 incorporated advanced engineering ideas but conventional mechanics were used in the first production models. The Kaiser had a box-section frame, coil-spring independent front suspension and live rear axle; it was powered by a Continental six-cylinder L-head engine. The cars proved to be very popular and by 1949 the range included a station-wagon-cum-sedan and a convertible with a power-operated hardtop. Attractively restyled in 1951 with lower lines and more glass, one of the Kaiser's safety features was the unique heart-shaped windshield which popped out of its socket if struck with more than 35 lb force. Kaiser sales reached twelfth place in the USA. No Frazers, but four Kaiser models—Manhattan, DeLuxe, Virginian and Special—were produced in 1952. Top of the range was the Kaiser Hardtop Dragon, introduced in 1953, featuring Hydramatic transmission, gold-plated exterior trim and a luxury interior. Sales then dropped and in 1953 Kaiser merged with Willys: a supercharger was offered as an option on the six-cylinder engine, but sales still continued to decrease. Production then moved to Argentina, where the marque was known as the was known as the Carabela.

1951 Kaiser with safety windshield

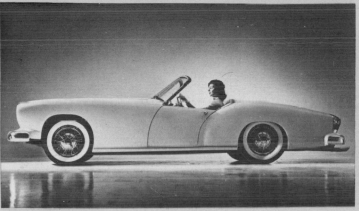

1954 Kaiser DKF-161 with glass-fibre body

Tuxedo coupé— at prices from $2750 to $3000 (including a 'lamp for changing tyres at night'). Keetons were built in Canada from 1913–15.

KELLER/*USA 1948–1949*
Successor to the Bobbi-Kar, George D. Keller Motors of Huntsville, Alabama, manufactured the Keller Chief and Super Chief. These cars used 49 hp Hercules or Continental four-cylinder engines, all-round independent suspension and Goodrich's Torsilastic rubber torsion bars. Kellers were available as a convertible with rear-mounted engine or as a station wagon with front engine. (A double bed was an option on the station wagon.) Only 18 examples were manufactured in 1949 but the station wagon was produced in Antwerp, Belgium, in 1954–55, as the PLM.

KELLNER/*France 1896*
A 3½ hp horizontal twin-cylinder engine propelled this belt-driven three-seater.

KELSEY/*USA 1921–1924*
C. W. Kelsey was a pioneer among American motor car builders, having built his first car, the Auto Tri, in 1898. He subsequently built the Spartan and the three-wheeled Motorette. Former sales manager of Maxwell, he formed his Kelsey Motor Car Co. in 1921 for the purpose of building friction-driven cars (Metz was then the only car of this type still being made in the USA). Both four- and six-cylinder models were featured between 1921 and 1923. In 1923 a four with a conventional transmission was added to the line and, in 1924, was the only Kelsey available. Kelsey also manufactured taxicabs.

Kerry also marketed tricars under their name; this is a 1905/6 Kerry Tricar Basket Forecarriage

KELVIN/*Scotland 1904–1906*
A 16 hp car built by the Bergius Car & Engine Company of Glasgow; only 14 were built.

KENDALL/*England 1912–1913*
An ephemeral worm-driven cyclecar from Sparkhill, Birmingham, the Kendall was available with either 945cc or 1042cc vee-twin power units.

KENDALL/*England 1945–1946*
An ill-fated attempt to build a 'people's car' based on the 954cc Grégoire flat-twin, sponsored by Denis Kendall MP, which failed after only a few cars had been built.

KENMORE/*USA 1909–1911*
Sold direct from its Chicago factory, the Kenmore was a pneumatic-tyred high-wheeler with detachable rear seat (ideal for 'farmers, salesmen, poultrymen, dairymen').

KENNEDY/*Canada 1909–1910*
Starting as a high-wheeler, by 1910 this 18 hp with a De Tamble flat-twin engine had normal wheels and tyres.

KENNEDY/*England 1914–1916*
A 1346cc own-make four powered this sporting belt-drive two-seater from Leicester.

KENSINGTON/*USA 1899–1904*
A light electric carriage— 'the successor of the horse'—powered by a 'patented storage battery', built in Buffalo, NY.

KENSINGTON/*England 1903*
A 10 hp twin and 20 hp four, probably French imports, were sold under this name, as was the Mildé electric.

KENTER/*Germany 1923–1925*
Kenter offered two models: a sv four with a 1060cc Steudel engine and an Atos-engined model of 1305cc.

KENT'S PACEMAKER/*USA 1900*
Colonial of Boston offered this steamer, which had one front steering-wheel and *three* rear wheels, the centre one of which drove, and an outer pair which could be raised to allow the machine to 'coast like a bicycle'.

KENWORTHY/*USA 1920–1922*
Kenworthy and Duesenberg share the honour of being the first production cars in the USA to feature four-wheel brakes and a straight-eight engine. In the case of Kenworthy, this was the company's widely touted 'Line-o-Eight', although the make could be obtained also with four- or six-cylinder engines (Rochester-Duesenberg and Continental respectively). The Kenworthy was a sporting car featuring either wire or disc wheels. Probably less than 200 cars were built in all.

KERRY/*England 1905–1907*
Motor factors East London Rubber Company sold 10/12 hp Tony Huber and Thames cars under this name (in the 1930s an open sports Model Y Ford was also called the 'Kerry').

KESSLER/*USA 1921–1922*
Using its own-make four-cylinder engine, the Kessler was otherwise an assembled tourer with wooden artillery wheels.

KESS-LINE 8/*USA 1922*
A spin-off of Kessler, probably only one phaeton was made on the Kess-Line chassis. This featured a 119-inch wheelbase, an own-make eight-cylinder engine and wire wheels.

KESTREL/*England 1914*
A typical 10 hp light car of its day, save for the friction drive. Few were built.

KEVAH/*France 1920–1924*
A small cyclecar built by Muller, Allen-Sommer and Robert at La Garenne Colombes, Seine, the Kevah had vee-twin 1100cc Train or MAG engines and was well made. In 1923, a four-cylinder 898cc sv Chapuis-Dornier-powered Kevah with three-speed gearbox appeared.

KEYSTONE/*USA 1899–1900*
Based at Lebanon, Pa., this company, predecessor of Searchmont, offered in 1899 a steam car with small three-cylinder radial engines built into each rear hub.

KEYSTONE/*USA 1915*
Using a Rutenber 55 hp six, the 1914 Keystone was designed by Chas C. Snodgrass and built in Pittsburgh.

KIA/*South Korea c1976 to date*
The Brisa, built in Seoul, is a four-door saloon with 985cc and 1272cc power units.

KIDDER/*USA 1901*
A twin-engined steam runabout from New Haven, Connecticut.

KIDDY/*France 1921–1922*
A small 398cc flat-twin cyclecar made in Paris by Jacques Bignan.

KIEFT/*England 1950–1961*
Best known for his 500cc racers, Cyril Kieft introduced a Gordon Bedson-designed sports-racer in 1953; MG, Bristol and Coventry-Climax engines were used.

KING/*USA 1910–1924*
Charles Brady King built Detroit's first car in 1895–96, and worked for Northern from 1902–08. His 1910 'Silent' 36 hp was a unit-constructed 5400cc model incorporating 14 patented features, including a pressed-steel front axle. In 1914 the first King V-8 appeared; two years later, eight-cylinder models were the firm's sole offering.

1960 8½hp single-cylinder King Midget

KING MIDGET/*USA 1946–1969*
A two-passenger steel and aluminium small car, the Midget first appeared in kit form. One-cylinder 8½ hp Wisconsin engines were used until 1966, when they were then replaced by the 9½ hp Kohler unit. Styling resembled the Jeep and was mounted on a perforated girder chassis with all-round independent suspension and a unique two-speed and reverse automatic transmission. Over 5000 King Midgets were manufactured before the Athens, Ohio, plant closed in 1969.

KINGSBURY JUNIOR/*England 1920–1927*
The Kingsbury Junior was powered by a flat-twin 1021cc Koh-i-noor engine. The power unit hailed from Scotland and was also used in the Rob Roy car.

1925 Kissel straight-eight Speedster

KISSEL
USA 1906–1931
'Every Inch a Car', the Kissel Kar, from Hartford, Wisconsin, began as a pair-cast 26 hp four-cylinder of 4952cc, increased to 5517cc for 1908. Apart from accessories, the entire car was made in the Kissel factory. A six of 8276cc appeared in 1909, and by 1912 the range consisted of fours of 30 hp, 40 hp and 50 hp, and the 60 hp six; prices ranged from $1300–$3000. By 1913 electric lighting and starting were standard; in 1917 a new range, the '100 Point Six', with a monobloc 4078cc available as tourer, sedan or staggered-door all-year Sedane, made its debut, as did a short-lived V-12. Conover T. Silver developed a 'Silver Special Speedster' six, and the 4660cc 'Custom-built Speedster' of 1919 was a direct development of this. Painted chrome yellow, it was named 'Gold Bug' as the result of a $5 contest in the *Milwaukee Journal*, whose editor owned one of the first of this model. There were 'Custom-built' tourings, 'urban-sedans', 'coach-sedans' and coupés, too. A Lycoming eight appeared in 1924. In 1929 came the 'White Eagle' speedster, with six- or eight-cylinder engine and internally expanding hydraulic brakes. Plans to revive Kissel to build a Lever-engined car in 1933 came to nothing.

KITTO / *USA 1903*
The Kitto Mobile Light Car was available with either an 1107cc 8 hp vertical twin or an 8 hp horizontal power unit.

KLAUS / *France 1894–1899*
A three-wheeled belt-drive tricycle, the Lyon-built Klaus incorporated a 'dead-man's handle' engine cut-out in the steering tiller.

KLEIBER / *USA 1924–1929*
The Kleiber was an assembled car produced by a well-known West Coast truck manufacturer. The cars were strictly assembled affairs, using proven components throughout, and were sold in small numbers on the Pacific Coast. Continental engines were used on the six-cylinder Kleibers until 1929, when a Continental eight was substituted. Two sedans marked the company's entire passenger-car output in this last year of production.

KLEINSCHNITTGER / *Germany 1950–1957*
A 123cc Ilo single-cylinder two-stroke engine powered this basic car built by ex-employees of East German factories who had emigrated to West Germany.

1950 Kleinschnittger 123cc two-seater

KLINE KAR / *USA 1910–1923*
The Kline Kar was initially built in York, Pennsylvania, with operations moving to Richmond, Virginia, in 1913. Although the company initially used engines of its own design and manufacture, the product gradually took on the aspect of an assembled car. Continental engines were used during the company's last years.

KLINGENBERG / *Germany 1898–1900*
Designed by Georg Klingenberg, a professor of the Berlin-Charlottenburg High School, this pioneer car did not go into serious production until NAG took over the design. The cars made by Klingenberg were (more or less) prototypes.

1929 Kleiber six-cylinder sedan

KLINK / *USA 1907–1909*
A 30 hp four of 4417cc built in Dansville, NY.

KNAP / *Belgium / France 1898–c1909*
A three-wheeled voiturette built in Liège with a 4 hp engine was Georgia Knap's first production car. He returned to Troyes (France) and built prototypes with up to six cylinders before settling on a single-cylinder four-wheeled voiturette in 1904.

KNICKERBOCKER / *USA 1901–1903*
This was the petrol car line built by the makers of the Ward-Leonard Electric.

KNIGHT JUNIOR / *England 1914*
A bullnosed 11 hp two-seater with a 1743cc engine built by Knight Brothers of Chelmsford, Essex, for motor agents Friswells of London. It sold for £185 complete.

KNIGHT OF THE ROAD
England 1902
A single-cylinder 5 hp voiturette intended for commercial travellers.

KNIGHT OF THE ROAD
England 1913–1914
From the same maker as the Knight Junior, this was a 15·9 hp 2654cc four-cylinder sold exclusively by Friswells at 350 guineas.

KNOLLER / *Germany 1924*
Produced a 980cc four-cylinder car in very small numbers.

KNOX / *USA 1900–1915*
The 'waterless' Knox was designed by H. A. Knox and built in the old Waltham Watch Tool Factory at Springfield, Mass. The first experimental Knox cars appeared in 1895–97. Production did not begin until 1899, initially by the Overman cycle company, the Knox company not being founded until 1901. These were three-wheelers with the famous air-cooled 'porcupine' engine, with pegs instead of fins on the cylinder. In 1903, a hydraulic damper was incorporated in the tiller steering. The 'waterless' Knox was built to special order until 1908, but by then big four-wheeled cars with four-cylinder engines

1910 Knox Tonneauett

cooled by water were the company's staple product.

KOCH/*France 1897–1901*
Paraffin-powered cars with a 6 hp opposed-piston engine.

KOCO/*Germany 1921–1926*
The GN-like Koco was a cyclecar with chain drive and an own-make twin-cylinder 1020cc engine with air-cooled or water-cooled horizontal cylinders. A second version had a sv 1303cc four-cylinder engine and often competed — with streamlined bodywork — in races.

KOECHLIN/*France 1910–1913*
An ex-Peugeot director backed this Courbevoie, Seine, marque, which appeared with an underslung 3-litre two-stroke racer in the 1911 Coupe des Voitures Legères; production models of 1912–13 were a 2·9-litre four and a 3-litre six, both with monobloc engines.

KOEHLER/*USA 1909–1915*
'The swellest-looking automobile it has been your good fortune to see', the Koehler 40 of 4649cc first appeared in 1909 at the low price of $1650, with 'Montclair Torpedo de Luxe' body.

KOMET/*USA 1911*
A four-cylinder car built by Sterling of Elkhart.

KOMET/*Germany 1922–1924*
The predecessor of the smaller Kenter, the Komet had a 1060cc Steudel engine.

KOMNICK/*Germany 1907–1927*
Strong cars for the bad roads in the northeastern part of Germany were the forte of this Elbing machine works. Early models had the radiator behind the engine like the contemporary Renaults. Komnick produced cars from 1520cc to 5536cc in the early days and an own-make ohc 2100cc four-cylinder from 1923 to 1927. Komnick also produced heavy lorries and agricultural machinery.

KONDOR/*Germany 1900–1902*
A bicycle works which produced 5 hp two-seater cars.

KORN ET LATIL/*France 1901–1902*
A fwd voiturette with Aster engine of 3½ hp (later 6 hp) designed by Latil, later well known for his fwd commercials.

KORTE/*England 1902–c1905*
Built in Leeds, the chain-driven 12 hp Korte had two cylinders, four speeds and an 'electric indicator showing stoppage in circulation'.

KORTING/*Germany 1922–1924*
Körting's limited production was of two models, sv four-cylinders of 1569cc and 2085cc with Basse & Selve engines.

KOUGAR/*England 1977 to date*
Traces of the Healey Silverstone and various Frazer Nashes can be seen in the beautifully finished, Jaguar-powered Kougar. Based on 'S' Type mechanicals, the lightweight Kougar has stunning performance as well as classic looks.

KRC/*England 1922–1924*
Made by White, Holmes and Company of Hammersmith, London, the KRC was a light car initially powered by a 10 hp vee-twin Blackburne engine. Later options included four-cylinder units by Coventry-Climax or Janvier.

KRIEGER/*France 1898–1909*
One of the best-known electric carriages, the Kriéger had hub motors on both front wheels, giving speeds up to 20 kph. The normal Kriéger body style was a formal coupé. This make used to undertake long runs on one charge to obtain publicity. Petrol-electrics appeared in 1904, and were produced, intermittently, using Richard-Brasier engines.

1915 3622cc KRIT tourer

KRIT/*USA 1909–1916*
Kenneth Krittenden was behind this four-cylinder popular car, the basic design of which remained much the same throughout its production life (save for an underslung model introduced in 1911). Like Ford, KRIT used vanadium steel for chassis components. Unkind critics claimed the name stood for 'Keeps Right In Town'.

KROBOTH (FAVORIT)
Czechoslovakia 1930–1933
This Sternberk-built 498cc single-cylinder car was designed by Gustav Kroboth, who made scooters after 1945 in Germany. Originally called Favorit, the marque was financed by Grohmann, a wool manufacturer, but few cars left the works before Grohmann lost interest in car manufacture.

KUHLSTEIN-VOLLMER
Germany 1898–1902
A power pack with a four-stroke engine which replaced the front wheels, axles and springs of horse-drawn vehicles to convert them into motor carriages — 'virtually a motor horse, to be harnessed to any vehicle at will'. In 1900 a rear-engined 5 hp twin-cylinder petrol model was announced. A twin-cylinder petrol car with three-speed 'belt, pinion and chain' transmission (clutch and speed change operated by a single lever) appeared in mid-1901.

KUHN/*Germany 1927–1929*
These were slightly modified Opel cars with Kühn-built bodywork. The best-known Kühn car was the 1916cc six-cylinder.

KUNISUE/*Japan 1910*
A few of these 8 hp twin-cylinder tourers were built in Tokyo. The radiator was a 'Japanese copy' of the Argyll pattern.

KURTIS/*USA 1949–1955*
Frank Kurtis, well known for his racing car designs, introduced his own, distinctive two-passenger Kurtis Sports in 1949. Bodies were of glass-fibre and steel on Ford running gear. About 36 Kurtis cars had been built when Muntz Motors took over the design, marketing it as the Muntz Jet. In 1954 Kurtis produced a road version of his Indianapolis racing car. This 500-S model could be ordered with various engines including Mercury's V-8. Also available was the 500-KK tubular chassis to which the buyer could add his own bodywork. Production ended after 18 model 500-Ms had been built. These had glass-fibre bodies, torsion-bar suspension and four-cylinder ohv supercharged engines.

KURTZ AUTOMATIC/*USA 1921–1923*
A Cleveland, Ohio, product, the Kurtz featured a preselector gear-change mechanism on the steering column; otherwise it was a typical assembled car, utilizing a six-cylinder Herschell-Spillman engine. The Kurtz car was made in limited numbers, but it was highly regarded and sold well.

KYMA/*England 1903–1905*
The New Kyma Car Company of Peckham built 6 hp twin-cylinder three-wheelers and four-cylinder light cars.

LABOR/*France 1907–1912*
Built for cycle manufacturers de Clèves et Chevalier, of Neuilly-sur-Seine, in the Weyher et Richemond works. The most popular Labor was the 20/30 hp four.

LACOSTE & BATTMANN
France 1897–1913
Builders of chassis and components, Lacoste & Battmann, of Levallois, Seine, rarely marketed cars under their own name, but supplied them to erstwhile 'manufacturers', e.g. Gamage, Napoléon, Speedwell and Jackson. De Dion and Aster engines were used. Their last offering was the Aster-engined 1·8-litre Simplicia.

LACOUR/*France 1912–1914*
Successor to Lurquin-Coudert, Lacour catalogued a Torpédo Sport vee-twin belt-drive cyclecar in 1912.

LAD/*England 1913–1926*
One of the longer-lived cyclecars, the LAD came from Farnham, Surrey, and was normally built as a single-seater with rear-mounted engine. Two models were available in 1923—a 350cc single (£78) and a 688cc twin (£110).

LADA (ZHIGULI)/*Russia 1970 to date*
Built in the Togliattigrad works (established with Fiat aid) the Zhiguli car is known outside Russia as the Lada. It is based on the obsolete Fiat 124, with engines of 1200cc to 1600cc. In 1978, a 4wd model, the Niva, appeared on Western markets.

LADAS/*England 1906–1908*
J. Bowen of Albert Street, Didsbury, Lancashire, showed this 7 hp two-seater, named after a Derby winner, at the 1906 Manchester Motor Show.

LAD'S CAR/*USA 1912–1914*
'More a real working toy than a go-anywhere motor car', this 3 hp single-seater was made by the Niagara Motor Co. of Niagara Falls, NY.

LAETITIA/*France 1922–1923*
Cyclecar made in Asnières, Seine, by M. Conelli with a 1000cc Anzani air-cooled engine.

LAFAYETTE/*USA 1920–1924*
The LaFayette was designed by D. McCall White, who was responsible for the Cadillac V-8 of 1915. The LaFayette, itself a V-8, combined luxury and breeding with endurance and excellent craftsmanship. An expensive car, with prices in the $4000–$7000 range, the powerful LaFayette (which was fast as well as luxurious), had an engine developing 100 bhp and thermostatically-controlled radiator shutters, a novelty in its time. LaFayette was absorbed by Nash Motors in 1923 and for a time was continued as Nash's luxury line.

LAFER/*Brazil 1972 to date*
The Lafer brothers of São Paulo built their first 'replicar' based on the MG-TD in October 1972, and by 1975 were building 350 cars annually. Apart from the VW-powered 'MP' replicar, they offer the modern-styled 'LL' 4097cc six-cylinder sports coupé.

LAFITTE/*France 1893–c1898*
A famous Bordeaux coachbuilder, Henri Lafitte built a few cars, starting in 1893. One, with a De Dion engine, competed in the 1898 Bordeaux-Biarritz race.

LAFITTE/*France 1923–1928*
Curious cyclecar from Genevilliers, Seine, with 736cc sv three-cylinder radial engine, later enlarged to 895cc. Instead of a gearbox there was a strange friction device: the engine pivoted to obtain the different ratios. Most Lafittes were sold as delivery vans.

A 2-litre Lagonda tourer, 1928

LAGONDA/*England 1906–1963, 1978 to date*
Wilbur Gunn was an American of Scots descent who began by building twin-cylinder tricars in the greenhouse of his home in Staines, Middle-

1962 Lagonda Rapide

sex. By 1907 the tricars had been superseded by four wheels, with four-cylinder 20 hp and six-cylinder 30 hp models being offered: much of the production went to Russia. In 1913 Gunn scrapped his previous models and decided to adopt just one line, an 1100cc 11·1 hp car with unit-construction gearbox and transverse front suspension, a marketing policy and design clearly inspired by the Ford Model T. Another progressive feature was the integral body/chassis construction. After World War One, the 11·1 became the 11·9, so that in 1920 Lagonda was clearly chasing the same market as Morris. As the 1920s progressed Lagonda gave up the unequal struggle, chancing their luck in the sports car field, 1927 seeing the appearance of the 2-litre dohc Speed Model; a pushrod 2-litre later appeared. From 1934 the Meadows six-cylinder 4½-litre engine was fitted, this engine powering the company's winning car at

1978 Aston Martin Lagonda

Le Mans in 1935. The twin-cam 1100cc Rapier also appeared in 1934, but the following year the company went broke and was purchased by solicitor Alan Good for £67,000. The Rapier was hived off and Good brought in W. O. Bentley as technical director. The range was refined and the Meadows engine quietened, but the V-12 of 1937 was Bentley's design (though the inspiration and much of the detail of this short-stroke 4½-litre engine came from ex-Rolls-Royce engineer Stewart Tresilian). Lagonda was sold to the David Brown group after World War Two, this 1947 deal allowing Brown to fit a Bentley-designed dohc 2·6-litre six-cylinder engine to the Aston Martin DB2 of 1950. The Lagonda marque name reappeared in 1961. The Rapide was DB-engined, but production ceased in 1963. An Aston Martin-based Lagonda with elaborate electronic controls began to reach private owners in 1978.

LAHAUSSOIS/*France 1907*
An obscure manufacturer from Paris, who offered both chassis and complete cars.

LAMBERT/*USA 1905–1916*
In 1891, John Lambert of Ohio City built — and attempted to market — America's first petrol car, a three-wheeler with a four-stroke single-cylinder engine. He built a number of proto-types powered by his Buckeye gas engines in 1898–1901, and began full-scale manufacture in 1902 with the Union car, a tiller-steered four-wheeler with friction drive. About 300 are thought to have been built before the Lambert Automobile Company was formed, taking over Union's Anderson, Indiana, factory. By 1910, production of the friction-drive Lambert cars was said to be running at 3000 a year: trucks and tractors were also built. Apart from engines of their own make, Lambert used Rutenber, Buda,

Atlas, Continental, Trebbert and Davis engines. The company manufactured armaments and military fire engines during World War One, and decided to diversify after the Armistice.

LAMBERT / *England 1912*
Built in Thetford, Norfolk, the Lambert was a three-wheeled cyclecar with a distinctive oval radiator.

M. Lambert with a 1953 Lambert 1100cc sports

LAMBERT / *France 1926–1954*
This small firm started in Macon, Saône-et-Loire, building 1100cc Ruby-engined cars with all-round independent suspension by leaf springs under the marque name 'Sans Chocs'. Lambert later moved to Reims, Marne, and built these sports/touring cars there until the war. After the war Lambert moved to Giromagny, Belfort, where he built fwd Ruby-engined cars.

LAMBERT & WEST / *England 1913*
An 8 hp cyclecar from Putney, London, designed by Warren-Lambert.

LAMBERT-HERBERT / *England 1913–1914*
This 1244cc light car was backed by motor agent and racing driver Percy Lambert, but his death at Brooklands in 1913, trying to beat his own 100 miles in an hour record, meant the end of the project.

LAMBORGHINI / *Italy 1963 to date*
Tractor manufacturer Ferruccio Lamborghini built his first cars as a hobby, using modified Fiat parts. When he saw a demand for big, exclusive sports cars, he founded his Bologna car factory. Among his creations was the 3929cc V-12 Miura of 1966 with a rear transverse engine. A smaller mid-engined model was the 2463cc eight-cylinder Urraco P 250, launched in 1970, like the dohc Jarama 400 GT, another V-12. While the Jarama was a 2 + 2 seater, the Espada 400 GT was a four-seater with Bertone bodywork. Development brought the 385 bhp Miura P 400 SV. The ultimate Urraco could be supplied with V-8 engines of 1994cc, 2463cc or 2996cc, with power up to 260 bhp. The latest Jarama 400 GTS model houses an improved 3929cc V-12 engine developing 365 bhp, while the mid-engined Lamborghini Countach LP 400/400S, a Bertone coupé, houses a similar 375 bhp motor and has a top speed of

187·5 mph. Lamborghini was sold in 1972 to a Swiss group, which continued production on a smaller scale.

1971 Lamborghini Miura P400

1979 Lamborghini Countach

![LANCHESTER]

LANCHESTER / *England 1895–1956*
The Lanchester brothers built the first truly all-British car in 1895: underpowered, it was rebuilt the next year with a balanced (two cylinders, two counter-rotating cranks, *six* connecting rods) power unit, air-cooled, and with Frederick Lanchester's famous wick carburettor. One valve per cylinder was both inlet and exhaust, thanks to a concentric 'crossover' disc valve. The experimental cars set the pattern for production vehicles, which began to leave the Lanchester Engine Company's Armourer Mills, Birmingham, factory in 1900: there was no bonnet, the driver sitting well forward behind a hinged leather dashboard, steering with a right-hand tiller. Cantilever springs had the same periodicity as a walking man; final drive was by Lanchester worm; compound epicyclic gearing gave three forward speeds. The first Lanchesters had 4035cc twin-cylinder air-cooled engines and incorporated a disc brake in the transmission; a water-cooled version appeared in 1902, a larger '18 hp' model in 1904. Rudyard Kipling was an early owner who reflected his enthusiasm for the car in his short stories. Also in 1904 came the first four-cylinder, the over-square '20 hp' of 2471cc. Though in engineering terms Lanchesters were a long way ahead of their contemporaries — they pioneered the rigorous interchangeability of parts — their

The 'wooden car', a 1925 Lanchester prototype

40hp Lanchester saloon, c.1924

very unorthodoxy created sales resistance. So in 1907 wheel steering became available. A '38 hp' six of 3295cc joined the 28 hp: it was to solve problems of six-cylinder vibration that Frederick Lanchester devised his famous crankshaft damper. Youngest brother George Lanchester took over as chief engineer and in 1914 produced a thoroughly conventional long-bonnetted 'Sporting Forty' 5560cc sv six, with half-elliptic front springs: a similar chassis was used on the 6178cc ohv Forty of 1919. Though it was so different from the pre-war Lanchesters, the new Forty was a worthy

1939 Lanchester 14 Roadrider De Luxe

LAMMAS-GRAHAM / *England 1936–1938*

A supercharged six-cylinder Graham engine powered this rather traditional-looking car built at Sunbury-on-Thames. The American power unit was of 3·7-litres capacity and produced 128 bhp. Only chassis were produced, body-builders including Abbott, Bertelli and Carlton.

1903 Lamplough-Albany steam car

LAMPLOUGH-ALBANY
England 1902–1905

A remarkably ugly steam car with petrol car styling and tiller steering. Mr Lamplough built his first steamer — with shaft-driven live axle! — in 1896. A petrol car was also marketed under the 'Albany' name.

LANCAMOBILE / *USA 1899–1901*

James H. Lancaster of New York designed this 'car of the explosive motor power class of the phaeton style, with a vis-à-vis foreseat'. It was said to be 'compact and speedy'.

rival for the Rolls-Royce 40/50 hp; it was joined in 1924 by an ohc 2982cc '21 hp' six. A 4440cc straight-eight was launched at the 1928 Southport Rally, again with ohc: it proved to be the last 'real' Lanchester, for in 1931 the company was acquired by Daimler, and Lanchesters became merely re-radiatored Daimlers. The 1932 'Ten' was still in production in the late 1940s, updated with independent front suspension; 1952 saw a '14', whose chassis was used on the six-cylinder Daimler-engined, Hooper-bodied Dauphin; 1956 saw the short-lived Sprite 1·6-litre with Hobbs automatic transmission.

LANCIA / *Italy 1906 to date*

Wealthy soup manufacturer's son Vincenzo Lancia worked for Fiat before founding his own factory at Turin (and continued to race for Fiat until 1908). His first production model, the 2543cc Alpha, appeared in 1907, joined in 1908 by the 3815cc DiAlfa, of which only 23 were made. Lancia ran through the Greek alphabet with the 3117cc Beta (1909), followed by the similar Gamma (1910) and the 4082cc Delta (1911). The 1912 Eta, also of 4082cc, was the first Lancia with electric lighting. The 4939cc Theta of 1914 was said to be the first European car with standardized electric lighting and starting. A development, the Kappa, with detachable cylinder head, was Lancia's first post-war model, a narrow-angle V-12 with monobloc ohc engine shown in 1919 failing to reach production. The Kappa was followed by the DiKappa and by the ohc V-8 TriKappa, but these were only a prelude to the classic Lambda, which made its public debut in 1922. This had a narrow-angle V-4 engine of 2124cc, sliding-pillar ifs and integral body/chassis construction. In 1926, the Seventh Series Lambda acquired a 2370cc power unit, enlarged to 2570cc on the Eighth Series of 1928–29. At the end of 1929, Lancia introduced the more conventional DiLambda, with a 3960cc V-8, and in 1931 replaced the Lambda with the 1925cc ohc V-4 Artena and the 2605cc V-8 Astura (later models were of 2972cc). Unit construction reappeared with the 1196cc

Augusta, which proved to have outstanding roadholding, and led to Vincenzo Lancia's last classic car, the pillarless Aprilia, introduced just before his death in 1937. A smaller development, the 1091cc Ardea, appeared a little while later. The Aprilia was built until 1950, when the Jano-designed Aurelia was announced, initially with a 1754cc V-6 engine, later enlarged to 1991cc, 2261cc and 2451cc. The Aurelia GT was also the basis for the sports-racing D23 and D24 models, with 2693cc and 2983cc dohc power units, some supercharged. In 1953 Gianni Lancia designed the 1091cc Appia V-4, but a couple of years later financial difficulties forced him to sell his company to Fiat. The Flaminia, powered by a development of the 2458cc Aurelia GT engine, succeeded the Aurelia in 1956, but a real sensation was caused in 1961 by the fwd Flavia, designed by Professor Fossia; it had a flat four engine of 1498cc, increased to 1798cc three years later. The Fulvia, another fwd model, succeeded the Appia as the smallest car in the Lancia range in 1964; by the end of the decade it was available with 1216cc and 1298cc engines. The Beta, first announced in 1972, was available in 1979 with ohc four-cylinder engines of 1297cc, 1585cc and 1995cc. It was sold alongside the 1999cc and 2484cc Gamma, which had flat-four dohc power units. The Stratos, a limited-production sporting model, had a mid-mounted dohc V-6 developing 190 bhp, and in 1979 won the Monte Carlo Rally for the fifth time.

20hp Lancia, 1907

1925 Lancia Lambda tourer

1976 Lancia Stratos

1978 Lancia Gamma coupé

LANDA/*Spain 1922–1935*
Built in Madrid, the Landa had a curious two-stroke engine. Two- and four-cylinders were the normal production: a conventional six-cylinder was sold to the Madrid funeral service.

L & E/*USA 1922–1931*
Although the car built by Lundelius & Eccleston of Los Angeles, California, was first announced in 1922, it probably was not publicly revealed for another two years. It was an 'axleless car', the touring car being powered by a six-cylinder air-cooled engine. Although plans called for a modern factory in Long Beach, Calif., this never materialized and subsequent production was on a strictly experimental basis. The 1932 model closely resembled a Franklin and was announced in October 1931. This car, probably the last, featured four transverse springs both at the front and rear to support the wheels, each rear wheel being driven by a short shaft with two universal joints, the shaft linked to a bevel gear and differential unit hung from cross members on a frame.

LANDINI/*Italy 1919*
Initially intended as a cheap way of training pilots, this vee-twin cyclecar was steered by foot, with gears and accelerator operated by the knees. Later models had more conventional controls.

L & P/*England 1909–1913*
Lloyd & Plaister, of Wood Green, London, supplied parts to Dolphin as well as building this 16 hp shaft-drive car and the Vox cyclecar. The company dated back to 1897, when Lloyd had been associated with Hurst and a few Hurst & Lloyd cars had been built up to 1900, when the partners went their own ways, and Lloyd joined with Plaister. Some of the remaining Hurst & Lloyds were sold as 'Lloyd & Plaister'.

LANDRY & BEYROUX/*France 1894–1902*
Sometimes known as the MLB, this marque started life with a rear-mounted 4 hp single-cylinder engine, though a vehicle of lighter construction appeared towards the end of production.

1898 Landry & Beyroux ('MLB') cab

LANDSEN/*USA 1906–1908*
An electric from Newark, NJ, with batteries housed under a dummy bonnet.

LANE/*USA 1899–1910*
Lane steamers, from Poughkeepsie, NY, were big, powerful twin-cylinder cars. The 1910 30 hp was a seven-seater 'which could easily challenge a train'.

1900 Lane Steam Wagon

LANE STEAM WAGON/*USA 1900*
The Lane Steam Wagon was built—possibly only as a prototype—by the Lane, Daley Co. of Barre, Vermont. This 3200 lb vehicle, equipped with three seats, could comfortably accommodate six passengers (or, without seats, a load of 2 tons) up the steepest gradients. Its safety features included a throttle which was self-closing in case the driver ever fell off the wagon. The company sold out in 1902 to the larger Daley Motor Wagon Co. of Everett, Mass., and no further self-propelled vehicles were manufactured.

LANZA/*Italy 1895–1902*
A candlemaker and motoring pioneer who built a few cars, mostly with twin-cylinder horizontal engines of his own design.

LASALLE/*USA 1927–1940*
Californian stylist Harley J. Earl 'created' this General Motors marque, a lower-priced running mate for Cadillac, with appearance features unashamedly cribbed from the Hispano-Suiza. It had a 5-litre V-8 engine, and acquired chrome plate and synchromesh in 1929: by 1930 its power units had grown to 5·8 litres. In 1934 it pioneered GM's controversial 'turret-top' styling and acquired a straight-eight engine, though a V-8 reappeared in 1937, when bodyshells were shared with Buick and Oldsmobile. By this time the LaSalle had nothing special to offer, and production ended in 1940.

LAUER/*Germany 1922*
One of the many small German cars built with limited facilities during the 1920s, the Lauer was a 15 hp four-cylinder vehicle.

LAUNCESTON/*England 1920*
The short-lived Launceston was built at Willesden Junction, London. A 12/20 hp model was offered for £300 in 1920.

LAUREL/*USA 1916–1920*
The Laurel was a minor American assembled car with a G. B. & S. four-cylinder engine, selling both in touring car and roadster forms, both priced at $895. This car had its name in script on either side of the bonnet.

LAURENCE-JACKSON/*England 1920*
An 8/10 hp JAP vee-twin powered this friction-drive 'streamline two-seater'.

LAURIN & KLEMENT
Czechoslovakia 1906–1928
Laurin & Klement built superb motorcycles from 1899 and cars from 1906 to 1928. The factory at Mladá Boleslav became part of Skoda in 1925, and from 1929 the Skoda trade mark was used. The first cars had vee-twin cylinder 7 hp and 9 hp engines. Later models used four-, six- and eight-cylinder engines. In 1907 a 4873cc straight-eight appeared. The factory also built buses and lorries, had agencies all over the world and gained many racing successes. In 1913 the RAF car works—and its Knight sleeve-valve engine licence—became part of L & K, who became increasingly preoccupied with aeroengines. A great variety of cars with engines up to 3·8 litres was made. Most had sv engines, but Knight sleeve-valve engines of up to 5 litres were also used.

1907 Laurin & Klement

1927 Laurin & Klement model 360

LAVIE/*France c1904*
A. Lavie of Paris built a few 6 cv twin-cylinder voiturettes, of which one still survives.

LAWIL/*Italy 1972 to date*
A mini car with either a 246cc twin-cylinder two-stroke engine or a 123cc single-cylinder model.

LAWRENCE/*England 1972 to date*
Syd Lawrence began building his Mk6 Bentley Specials because he was reportedly disgusted at the efforts of others. With well-finished glass-fibre bodies and alloy wheels, the SLs are a subtle blend of vintage and modern design.

LEACH/*USA 1899–1901*
There were three models of this steam car from Everett, Mass. — mail phaeton, Stanhope and delivery wagon.

LEACH/*USA 1920–1923*
A large assembled automobile, the Leach (initially termed 'Leach-Biltwell') was a popular car with Hollywood stars in the silent screen days. It was a large and expensive automobile: prices ranged from $5200 for the cheapest model. Open cars sold with the 'California top', the device combining a permanent top and sliding plate-glass windows. Sedans were also available; some of the sportier models included a golf bag and holder as standard equipment. A Continental six was the 'house engine' although an option could be had with a different six, which may have been designed by Harry Miller. Although Leach automobiles were shown in both New York City and Chicago, almost the entire output went to California buyers.

LEADER/*England 1904–1909*
Charles Binks, who achieved greater fame as a maker of carburettors, sold Leader and New Leader cars from 1904. The first models were 10 hp and 14 hp four-cylinders with pressed steel chassis, but by 1906 Mr Binks was offering a V-8 with a cubic capacity of 15·5 litres, almost certainly the biggest eight-cylinder car ever sold.

1907 Binks (Leader) Voiturette

LEA-FRANCIS/*England 1904–1906, 1920–1935, 1937–1953, 1960*
The first Lea-Francis had a three-cylinder 15 hp horizontal engine, though their manufacture was soon taken over by Singer. However, Lea and Francis, who had initially made bicycles, began making motorcycles in 1911, and in 1920 car production started up again, 11·9 hp and 13·9 hp models being offered. The year 1922 saw the appearance of a Coventry-Simplex-engined car of 8·9 hp, while the following year a Meadows ohv power unit was fitted. A sports car, the 12/40, was announced in 1925 and remained in production until 1935. In the early 1920s the company amalgamated with Vulcan of Southport and some of the heavier six-cylinder Vulcans were sold under the Lea-Francis name. Far more exciting was the Hyper Sports of 1928, having a Cozette-supercharged 1½-litre Meadows engine. The Ace of Spades model appeared in 1931, being powered by a 2-litre six-cylinder ohc engine. This remained in production until the company's demise in 1935, alongside the faithful 12/40. Lea-Francis was

1930 Lea-Francis 12/40hp fabric saloon

reconstituted in 1937 with two models of 1½- and 1·6-litre capacity and the engines by Hugh Rose (who had designed the Riley 12/4) bore a striking similarity to that unit. Production continued after the war, with the 14 hp 1·6-litre car predominating, smartly followed by a tuned sports model in 1948. In 1950 a new 18 hp 2½-litre car was introduced with torsion bar front suspension which had also featured on the earlier 14 hp model. But production dwindled and ceased completely in 1953. In 1960 the controversially styled Ford Zephyr-engined Leaf-Lynx was displayed at that year's Motor Show, but no orders resulted from this automotive kite-flying. In 1978, Barry Price of Studley, Warwickshire, announced that Lea-Francis was about to resume limited production with motive power supplied by Jaguar.

LEANDER/*England 1901*
Fitted with a De Dion engine, the Leander was built by Jas. Walmsley's Union Carriage Works of Preston, Lancashire. Its five-seater tonneau body, with 'V-shaped cut-wind, canopy of elegant design, luncheon basket and stick basket' won Dr. Hele-Shaw's special medal at the 1901 Royal Lancashire Show. 'Collins splendid unpuncturable tyres' were standard. There was also a 'Palatine' Siamese Phaeton with 'alternative light delivery van body suitable for wine merchant or the like'.

LEBRUN/*France 1896–1906*
A two-seater car with a rear-mounted Daimler engine was this firm's first offering.

LEC/*England 1913*
Built by a firm of telephone manufacturers, the Phonopore Company, of Southall, Middlesex, the LEC was a cyclecar with a water-cooled twin-cylinder 1003cc power unit.

LECOY/*England 1921–1922*
The friction-drive Lecoy was built in Harrow, Middlesex and powered by an 8 hp vee-twin JAP engine. The front coil springs were an unconventional feature.

LEGROS/*France 1900–1913*
René Legros, of Fécamp (Seine-Inférieure), initially built cars of 4 hp (single-cylinder) under

the 'La Plus Simple' label, followed by twins of 6 cv and 12 cv. From 1906, he offered two-stroke cars. Two models were available, a 10/12 hp twin and a 20/24 hp four. By 1912, the range had been expanded to two twin-cylinder and two four-cylinder models, still all two-strokes.

LEIDART/*England 1936–1938*
This Anglo-American model used the ubiquitous Ford V-8 as its power unit. Built in Pontefract, Yorkshire, the Leidart was also available with a Ford 10 supercharged engine.

1903 Lems No 1 Electric Runabout

LEMS/*England 1903–1904*
The London Electro-Mobile Syndicate offered a two-seater electric runabout ('40 miles on one charge') for 180 guineas.

LENAWEE/*USA 1903–1904*
A left-hand-drive tonneau with horizontal single-cylinder engine beneath the front seat.

LENHAM/*England 1969 to date*
Once known only for their meticulous restorations, the Lenham Motor Company expanded during the 1960s to produce glass-fibre panels and accessories for a variety of cars, as well as special bodies for Sprites and Midgets and their own Lenham GT, a futuristic mid-engined vehicle designed primarily for racing. Since 1978 they have made a spartan kit for rejuvenating tired and rusted Healey 100/6s and 3000s. The kit features an aluminium and glass-fibre body, special wheels, twin aero screens, an outside exhaust and handbrake lever and even vintage-style bonnet straps.

219

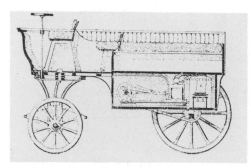

The 1863 Lenoir hydrocarbon carriage

LENOIR/*France 1862–1863*
Belgian inventor J. J. Etienne Lenoir built the first practical 'hydrocarbon carriage' in Paris in 1862, and made a number of short, slow journeys with it before selling it to Czar Alexander II

LENOX/*USA 1909–1918*
The 'uncommon' Lenox was, claimed its makers, 'the only car built in Boston'. Starting with electrics, the company eventually built elegant petrol cars in its Hyde Park factory.

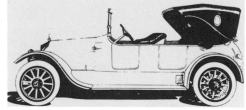

1917 Lenox Victoria

LEO/*France 1897–1898*
An early design by Léon Lefèvre, the Léo was a belt-drive car with a Pygmée paraffin engine.

LEO/*England 1912–1913*
A fwd 8 hp cyclecar sold by Derry & Toms of Kensington, London.

LEON BUAT/*France 1901–c1908*
Buat, of Senlis (Oise), who began by building 8 cv light cars designed especially for doctors, also offered a De Dion-like voiturette ('La Polaire') in 1902, as well as larger cars with 12 cv twin and 16 cv four-cylinder engines: all power units were supplied by Aster.

LEON LAISNE/*France 1920–1937*
The Léon-Laisne (Harris-Léon-Laisne from 1927) had tubular chassis side-members which housed hydraulically damped coil-springs giving all-round independent suspension. Power was by SCAP, CIME or Hotchkiss.

LEON PAULET/*France 1921–1927*
Made in Marseille, these were luxury cars powered by an ohc six-cylinder 3445cc engine, later enlarged to 3920cc. Very well made, they attracted a lot of local custom. The marque resumed during the war with some small electric cars.

LEON RUBAY/*USA 1922–1924*
Sometimes erroneously termed 'Rubay', this marque was named after Leon Rubay, a coach-work specialist who, like Brewster, had been a carriage builder. Leon Rubay cars were small (118-inch wheelbase) and used a four-cylinder engine of their own manufacture. In many ways the Leon Rubay was the same type of car as the contemporary Brewster, although it was cheaper, the sedan selling for $5200: it featured four-wheel brakes. Very few Leon Rubay automobiles were produced and the assets of the company passed to Rauch & Lang in 1924. The name Rubay is more commonly associated with bodies than with the specific make.

*c.*1900 Lepape with spider seat

LEPAPE/*France 1898–c1901*
'Elegant and comfortable', the belt-driven Lepape had its twin-cylinder engine at the front, behind glass windows, so that the driver could see it was working properly.

LEROY/*Canada 1902–1904*
Having built trial-and-error prototypes from 1899, the Good brothers of Berlin (Kitchener), Ontario, took the easy way out by copying the Oldsmobile for their production cars.

LEROY/*France 1927–1928*
A pioneer of the two-stroke in France, M. Leroy created some strange two-stroke engines for experimental purposes. With the assistance of the prolific M. Violet he made some sports cars in Courbevoie, Seine, with four-cylinder two-stroke engines.

LESTER SOLUS/*England 1913*
An 8 hp JAP-engined single-seat cyclecar.

LEUCHTERS/*England 1898*
A De Dion-type motor tricycle 'made entirely in Leeds'.

LEVERE-PORTAL/*France 1907*
M. Levère-Portal entered a 15 hp four-cylinder of his own construction in the touring class at the 1907 Evreux Trials.

LEWIS/*USA 1899–1902*
'Chicago inventor' George W. Lewis established a factory in Philadelphia in 1899 to build 'gasolene wagons' with horizontal single-cylinder 4178cc engines and friction drive by 'compressed papers'.

LEWIS/*Australia 1900–1906*
After building a single-cylinder buggy in 1900, Vivian Lewis produced a series of lightweight cars, as well as a range of motorcycles. Car production ceased in 1906 but the motorcycles were built for several more years.

LEWIS/*USA 1913–1916*
Designed by René Petard, who also designed the 1913 Mitchell, and backed by William Mitchell Lewis, of the Mitchell company, the Lewis—also known as 'LPC'—was powered by a long-stroke six of 5676cc.

LEWIS/*England 1923–1924*
A MAG 10 hp vee-twin engine powered the Lewis which was built in London's Abbey Wood. Although a four-cylinder model was announced simultaneously, neither vehicle went into production.

LEXINGTON/*USA 1909–1928*
Founded in Lexington, Kentucky, this manufacturer of quality assembled cars moved to Indiana within its first year. Only fours were built up to 1915, when the first six-cylinder models appeared, sixes remaining in production for the rest of Lexington's existence. Output peaked at 6000 in 1920; in 1921, Lexington adopted Ansted power units. The most popular Lexington models were the Lexington tourer and Concord sedan of the early 1920s: the Minute Man Six also traded on War of Independence legend surrounding the battle of Lexington-Concord, though the battle had no connection with the marque's Kentucky origins. Though Lexington went into receivership in 1923, small-scale output continued for five years.

LEY/*Germany 1906–1929*
Designed by Albert Ley, whose brother Rudolf had founded this company at Arnstadt (now East Germany), the first cars bearing the name Ley—also known as Loreley—had 1559cc four-cylinder engines. In 1907 a six-cylinder was in production. Other pre-war models included 1132cc, 1545cc and 2068cc four-cylinders and a 2599cc six-cylinder. There was a unique six-cylinder Ley (Loreley) with a small five-bearing sv 1559cc engine developing 18 hp at 1800 rpm. Ley returned to production in 1919 with a 3134cc 40 hp six-cylinder car, but afterwards concentrated on four-cylinder models with sv engines of 1530cc, 1990cc and 3070cc. Ley (Loreley) cars had a good reputation for quality and advanced design. Designer-Director Gockenbach tested, together with Rudolf Ley and Paul Jaray, Ley cars with Jaray streamlined bodywork; there was also the TO sports model of 1924, which housed an ohc 1498cc four-cylinder engine.

1920 prototype Leyland Eight

LEYLAND/*England 1920–1923*
Leyland Motors, who had been commercial vehicle builders since 1897, decided to enter the luxury car market with the Leyland Eight of 1920. Designed by J. G. Parry-Thomas, it was

the first British production straight-eight and was of 7·3-litres capacity. This magnificent car bristled with individuality. Servo-assisted brakes, leaf-valve springs and torsion-bar-assisted suspension were just some of its unusual features. Unfortunately, at a price of £3050 there were few takers and only 18 were built. Thomas, however, actively campaigned tuned examples at Brooklands.

LEYLAND/Australia 1973–1975
Leyland Australia was born out of the merger of the former Austin and Morris (BMC) subsidiary companies. In post-war years they had launched a series of locally designed cars, such as the Austin Lancer, Morris Major and Austin Freeway, all based on British designs. In 1970 the newly formed Leyland concern decided to compete against Holden and Falcon. Called the P76, the entirely new car proved to be a very large sedan with a 2825mm(9ft 3in) wheelbase, powered by a conventional six-cylinder engine. An optional Rover-based alloy V-8 was also offered. Body styling was by the Italian specialist Michelotti. Leyland Australia ran into sales difficulties and the manufacturing facilities were closed during 1975. By that time they had just started to build coupé versions of the P76 and six-cylinder versions of the Morris Marina.

LEYAT/France 1913–1925
This very strange car was remarkable for the use of a propeller at the front, and for steering by the rear wheels. Leyats used ABC motorcycle flat-twin engines at the beginning, later supplanted by a radial three-cylinder Anzani.

LIBELLE/Germany 1922–1924
Founded by ex-Daimler employees, this small factory at Sindelfingen built a few 990cc two-seater cars.

LIBERIA/France 1900–1902
The four-seater Libéria 'Light Voiture' had a 5 hp water-cooled Aster engine, a three-speed and reverse transmission and chain final drive. It sold in England for £250.

LIBERTY/USA 1916–1924
The Liberty Six had a 3394cc monobloc six, and sold for $1095. Included in the standard equipment were fitted tools and a clothes brush. The company was bought by Columbia late in 1923.

LIFU/England/USA 1899–1902
Henry Alonzo House, formerly with the Liquid Fuel Engineering Company, of Cowes, Isle of Wight, moved to Bridgeport, Conn., where he showed his paraffin-fired 'Lifu' steam carriage in 1899. The Cowes factory could build 30 heavy steam cars and 20 steam launches a year, and in 1899 a Birmingham branch factory was also established in the former Starley & Westwood Cycle Works at Adderley Park. House joined the Automatic Steam Motor Supply Syndicate of New York late in 1899, but the first American Lifu did not appear until 1901. Lifus were mostly heavy commercials, but a number of tiller-steered 10 hp cars were built.

LILIPUT/Germany 1904–1908
Designed by Willi Seck for Georg Wiss, owner of the SAF (Suddeutsche Automobil Fabrik), the 567cc single-cylinder 4 hp Liliput had friction drive. Plans to build it in large numbers, not only at the Gaggenau works but also at the Schilling arms factory at Suhl (which in the 1920s produced Rennsteig motorcycles), did not materialize.

LILLA/Japan 1923–1925
The Jitsuyo Automobile Company of Osaka built Gorham twin-cylinder light three- and four-wheelers from 1920, then produced the utilitarian Lilla and Lilla Peaton four-cylinder, which had 2-litre water-cooled engines.

LINCOLN/Australia 1919–1924
Built in Sydney, New South Wales, the Lincoln Pioneer Six featured a Continental six-cylinder engine and a radiator suggestive of the Packard. Wire wheels could be had at extra cost, although most Lincolns already had them. In 1923 the company was requested to drop its name by the Lincoln Motor Co. of Detroit, Mich., but the plea went unheeded and Australia's Lincoln went out of business a year later. Two examples survive.

c.1924 Lincoln phaeton

Clark Gable with his 1948 Lincoln convertible

LINCOLN/USA 1920 to date
Named after Henry Leland's boyhood hero, the Lincoln car appeared at the end of 1920, its fine engineering offset by dull coachwork styled by Leland's son-in-law, ex-milliner Angus Woodbridge. Power was by a 5·8-litre V-8, but many of the chassis components were bought-in assemblies. A bill for alleged tax arrears plunged Lincoln into financial crisis, and the company was bought by Ford, the Lelands resigning soon after. Under the control of Edsel Ford, the Lincoln soon acquired the elegance to match its engineering. Its rapid acceleration made it a favourite with police and gangsters alike, and a police model with four-wheel brakes (not generally available until 1927) was offered in 1924; that year, Calvin Coolidge became the first US President to own a Lincoln. Engine size was increased to 6·3 litres in 1928, and a further engineering innovation came in 1932 with the V-12 KB model, one of only seven V-12 cars on the US market. Sales, however, were disappointing, and in 1936 a new low-priced range, the ultra-streamlined Lincoln-Zephyr styled by John Tjaarda, made its debut. Of 18,994 Lincolns sold that year, 17,715 were Lincoln-Zephyrs. The Lincoln- →

A 'dream car' of the mid-1950s, the Lincoln Continental 'Nineteen Fifty-X

continued from previous page

Zephyr formed the basis of Edsel Ford's classic Lincoln Continental, a low-slung coupé first seen in March 1939. When America entered the war, the Lincoln-Zephyr ceased production for ever. But the Lincoln Continental and the Lincoln continued after the war, still with the flathead V-12 of 4998cc, until the Continental was finally dropped in 1948. (It reappeared as a separate marque in 1956.) The 1949 models featured new slab-sided styling and a sv V-8 of 5555cc. Completely new designs appeared in 1952, powered by an ohv 5203cc V-8; the Cosmopolitan was the only series listed, and was available in five series, including the Capri coupé and convertible. The all-new 1956 models had a long, low look and a 6030cc V-8; top of the range was now the Premiere. A 1957 facelift produced vertical dual headlamps and sharply pointed tailfins. The 'longer, lower, wider' 1958 models were over 19 feet long, weighed 4880 lb and were powered by a 7047cc V-8. But in 1961 came more

compact designs reminiscent of the 1956–57 Continental Mk II, offered only as four-door sedan or convertible, the latter unique in the industry. The same bodyshell was retained until 1969, Lincoln preferring detail improvement to drastic restyling (though the convertible was dropped in 1967, and 1968 saw the separate Mk III line introduced). In 1970 came a new Lincoln using many Ford/Mercury chassis components, with styling that was evolutionary rather than dramatic. Its coffin-shaped bonnet ended in a smaller grille flanked by retractable headlights. Power was by a 7538cc V-8, and the range consisted of a two-door coupé, four-door sedan and the more costly Town Car, soon joined by a Town Coupé. Changes to this range were minimal, though in 1979 a concession to 'down-sizing' was made by the adoption of a 6555cc engine. In mid-1977, the Mercury Monarch-based Versailles joined the Lincoln range; its 1979 version had a 4949cc V-8.

1979 Lincoln Town Car

LINDCAR/*Germany 1921–1925*
Though early examples of this well-made light car had air-cooled sv fours of 1299cc, most came with water-cooled proprietary fours, either a 1017cc Atos or a 1320cc Steudel.

LINDSAY/*England 1904–1908*
There were three models of the 1906–08 Lindsay, built in Woodbridge, Suffolk—a 12 hp, a 20 hp and a 28/30 hp. All had four-cylinder engines and were described as 'economical, reliable and powerful'. The marque took its name from Lindsay Scott, who had started with 3½ hp Minerva-engined tricars in 1904.

LINDSTROM/*USA 1899*
An electric buggy with separate motors driving each rear wheel through a ring gear.

LINGTON/*England 1920*
The short-lived Lington used a 10 hp vee-twin engine which could be pedal-started from the driver's seat. Shaft drive was employed.

LINON/*Belgium 1900–1914*
A two-seater lightweight voiturette, powered by a 3 hp De Dion engine with a water-cooled cylinder head, began this firm's activities. By

1912, an 8 hp single and fours of 10, 12, 14, 16, 20 and 22 hp were available.

LINSER/*Austria c1905–1907*
Built in Reichenberg, the 'pretty little' four-cylinder Linser had separate cylinders and 'all the organs of a large car'.

LION/*England 1905*
Built by Milbrowe Smith of Birmingham, this Aster-engined 16/20 hp car had sterling silver-plated brightwork.

LION/*USA 1910–1912*
Built at Adrian, Michigan, the Lion 40 had a 5312cc four-cylinder engine and came in runabout style as standard.

LION-PEUGEOT/*France 1906–1913*
Originally an independent venture by Robert Peugeot in the Peugeot cycle factory at Beaulieu-Valentigny (Doubs), the Lion-Peugeot is chiefly remembered for its eccentric long-stroke racing voiturettes, culminating in the 2815cc vee-twin V-5 (80 × 280mm) and 3451cc V-4 (65 × 260mm) of 1910. But there were also touring Lion-Peugeots—single-cylinder and vee-twins of up to 1·7 litres and,

following the absorption of Lion-Peugeot back into the mainstream company in 1910, a V-4 which appeared in 1911.

LIPSCOMB/*England 1903–1905*
The English Motor-Car Company of London made 6½ hp and 8 hp light cars with three-speed transmission and shaft drive, predecessors of the Bayley.

LIPSIA/*Germany 1922–1924*
Middle-sized cars with 1530cc and 1980cc four-cylinder engines produced in limited numbers.

LIQUID AIR/*USA/England 1899–1902*
Liquid Air's first factory opened at Boston, Mass., in 1899, claiming that cars could be built to run 100 miles on liquid air. *Horseless Age* called the system 'liquid moonshine'. The Boston company went into receivership in July 1901. Stock was $1·5 million, assets $7500, liabilities $4500. The Liquid Air car, apparently a modified Locomobile steamer, was demonstrated in London (where the company had a depot) by its designer Hans Knudsen in 1902: it was claimed to run 40 miles at 12 mph on 18 gallons of liquid air at a shilling a gallon.

LISTER/*England 1896–c1899*
A mysterious firm from Keighley, Yorkshire, which claimed to have exported 'two-passenger gigs' to the East Indies in 1896: in 1899 an oil-engined three-wheeler was completed.

LITTLE/*USA 1911–1913*
The Little Four, from Flint, Mich., was 'out of the ruck of American cars'. A neat two-seater runabout, which sold for 165 guineas in England, it had a bi-block 2128cc four-cylinder engine in unit with a two-speed gearbox. The company was acquired by Chevrolet.

LITTLE MIDLAND/*England c1905–1922*
A 7 hp two-seater which sold for 150 guineas complete in 1905 was the first of this Clitheroe, Lancashire, company's spasmodic offerings, the next being a 7 hp JAP-engined cyclecar produced in 1911; a modified version appeared post-war, built first in Blackburn, then in Preston.

LITTLE WONDER/*USA 1907*
There were four models of this wheel-steered single-cylinder two-stroke gas buggy—an 8 hp two-seater, a 'roomier two-seater', a 'Doctor's Phaeton' and a 10 hp Stanhope. The Doctor's Phaeton came complete with instrument case.

1907 Little Wonder Type 4

LIVER/*England 1900–1906*
Starting life as a Benz derivative, by 1906 the Liverpool-built Liver had become a conventional four-cylinder with pressed-steel chassis and Aster or PF engines.

1957 Lloyd Alexander saloon

LLOYD/*Germany 1906–1963*
Designed by Joseph Vollmer, the first Lloyd cars built by the Bremen-based NAMAG works had 3685cc and 2311cc four-cylinder engines. A 5520cc four-cylinder 50 hp car, plus a 60 hp version, came into production in 1910–11. As a result of the merger with Hansa-Lloyd and a co-operation with other factories after World War One, the name Lloyd disappeared until Borgward, now owner of the works, introduced the little 293cc Lloyd twin-cylinder two-stroke in 1950. It was followed by improved 248cc and 286cc versions. Like their successors with four-stroke engines, they had front-wheel drive. The four-stroke range with in-line twin-cylinder ohc engines included 596cc models. From 1959 ohv 897cc flat-four engines were available. The Lloyd disappeared with the collapse of the Borgward group.

LLOYD/*England 1936–1951*
The pre-war Lloyd used a rear-mounted 350cc single-cylinder engine. Post-1945 types had all-independent suspension and were powered by a 650cc two-stroke front-mounted engine, the device being driven by the front wheels.

LM/*France 1913*
Only two LM automobiles were built, designed by Charles L. Lawrance who, with Arthur Moulton and Sidney Breeze, had manufactured the BLM car in Brooklyn, NY, from 1906 to 1909. The engine was a four-cylinder affair which had ohv and peculiar auxiliary ported exhausts as in a two-cycle engine, controlled by a rotary valve.

LMB/*England 1960–1962*
Leslie Ballamy, famed for his ifs conversions of transverse-sprung Fords, built a series of 100 tubular chassis for Ford or BMC power; some, with Edwards Brothers glass-fibre GT bodies, were sold as EB Debonairs.

LMW/*Sweden 1923*
The Lidköping Mekaniska Verkstads AB planned to build an initial batch of three cars but only one was built. The engine was a French four-cylinder 18 hp CIME with a Cozette carburettor. The gearbox had three forward speeds and the total weight was 700 kg (1540lb).

LMX/*Italy 1970–1972*
A coachbuilder who fitted plastic coupé and cabriolet coachwork on cars equipped with 2293cc Ford V-6 engines. Supercharged 180 bhp versions were also available.

LOCKWOOD/*England 1921–1922*
Produced at Eastbourne, Sussex, the Lockwood was a miniature car intended for use by children.

"Locomobile"

LOCOMOBILE/*USA 1899–1929*
Founded to exploit the steam car design of the Stanley brothers, Locomobile (of Bridgeport, Connecticut) was soon, if briefly, America's biggest manufacturer, turning out 4000 cars by 1902. Their frail steam buggy was widely plagiarized, but in 1902 they built their first petrol car, a four-cylinder model designed by A. L. Riker. It was so successful that they gave up steam cars in 1903, and were soon established as makers of big, expensive petrol cars, including in 1904 the two-cylinder Type C 9/12 hp and the Type D 18/22 hp, a chain-drive four on Mercedes lines. These were followed by the Type E 15/20hp, the 40/45 hp Type F and the 30/35 hp Type H of 1905–06, as well as a replica of their Gordon Bennett racer, a 17·7-litre four. In 1911 came the 8-litre, six-cylinder Model 48 ('the Exclusive Car for Exclusive People'), which lasted until the end of production in 1929. In 1920, Locomobile was briefly linked with Mercer and Crane-Simplex, then, in 1923, became part of Billy Durant's final empire. New models, the 1925–27 Junior Eight and the luxury Model 90, appeared, and the Locomobile plant also built the low-priced Flint Six. The last Locomobile, Model 88, had a 4·9-litre Lycoming engine.

1901 Locomobile steam car

1904 16hp Locomobile touring car

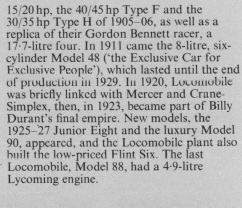

1928 Locomobile 8-70 straight-eight five-passenger sedan

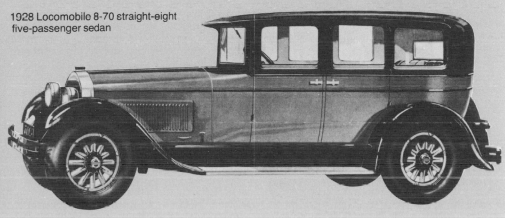

1911 Loeb sporting tourer

LOEB (LUC)/*Germany 1910–1914*

Loeb of Berlin was a leading car importer and dealer. Reissig designed their first LUC car, which had 2025cc four-cylinder Knight sleeve-valve engines, imported from Daimler at Coventry. Other models of this quality car, known either as Loeb or LUC, had four-cylinder engines of 2612cc, 3052cc and 4084cc. During World War One, Loeb built aeroengines, and after the war sold the factory to the Stinnes-owned Dinos company.

LOGAN/*USA 1903–1908*

A roadster from Chillicothe, Ohio, powered by a 24hp ohv air-cooled Carrico engine.

LOHNER/*Austria 1896–1906*

Viennese coachbuilder Jacob Löhner built a few Pygmée-engined petrol cars before turning to electrics in 1898, in which year Ferdinand Porsche joined the company, designing cars with electric motors incorporated in the front wheel hubs. Petrol-electrics on this principle were also constructed: in 1906 the patents were sold to Emil Jellinek of Mercedes.

LOIDIS/*England 1900–1904*

A shaft-driven light car with single-cylinder 9 hp Aster engine; it was named after the ancient Celtic settlement ('Caer Loidis') which was the foundation of its natal town, Leeds. Its makers, Dougill, also imported Lux cars under this name: they subsequently built the Frick.

LOMBARD/*France 1927–1929*

These sports cars made in Puteaux, Seine, had a wonderful dohc engine of 1093cc: some of them were supercharged, and did very well in races. In 1929 Lombard presented an ohc straight-eight of 2896cc, which never went into production. They were taken over by BNC and some of the racing Lombards had badge engineering inflicted on them.

Lombard dohc 1100cc

LOMBARDI/*Italy 1969–1971*

A two-seater coupé based on a Fiat 850 Special floorpan, with a 47bhp 843cc four-cylinder engine. Few of these cars were made. The company also rebodied the 903cc Fiat 127 and the 1991cc four-cylinder Lancia.

LONDONIA/*England? 1908*

Said to be of English origin, but probably imported from the USA, this marque was linked with the mysterious Owen. In 1908 an 8/10 hp twin, 20 hp four, 35 hp four and 30 hp six were listed—though the same photograph illustrated each in *The Autocar* Buyer's Guide . . .

The Canadian-built London Six, 1922

LONDON SIX/*Canada 1921–1925*

'Canada's Quality Car' used a 4078cc Herschell-Spillman engine and rode on laminated-wood disc wheels: bodies were initially supplied by an Ontario coffin maker. Plans to use this car as the basis of an automotive empire ended in insolvency for its promoter, William Stansell, after 98 cars had been built.

LONE STAR/*USA 1920–1922*

Sold by a truck and tractor firm in San Antonio, Texas, the Lone Star was available either as a four or a six, Lycoming engines being used in both models. The cars were actually built by Piedmont in Lynchburg, Virginia, along with such other assembled marques as Bush, Marshall, Norwalk Six and Stork Kar.

LONSDALE/*England 1901–1902*

Albert Lambourne, who later built the Old Mill car, designed this 463cc single-cylinder car with chain-driven ohc. Three were built, in Hove, Sussex.

LOOMIS/*USA 1900–1904*

A single-cylinder 2½ hp 'park carriage' selling at $450 was this Massachusetts firm's first offering (though Gilbert J. Loomis had built his first car, a steamer, in 1896): by 1901 only flat-twin engines were available, and in 1904 a three-cylinder was offered.

LORD/*England 1915*

An own-make flat-twin of 1068cc was fitted to this friction-drive light car from Surbiton, Surrey, which retailed at £100.

LA LORRAINE/*France 1899–1902*

A *vis-à-vis* built by Charles Schmid of Bar-le-Duc, Meuse, with infinitely variable belt-drive.

LORRAINE/*USA 1907–1908*

John O. Hobbs of Chicago built his first 'self-starting' car in 1903: the starter was powered by compressed air. The first Lorraine was completed in May 1907, and used Hobbs's 'elastic driving shaft' built up from 24 steel torsion rods; it had electric lighting. Four-cylinder engines of 30 hp and 50 hp were available.

LORRAINE/*USA 1920–1922*

This assembled car, successor to the Hackett, was built in Grand Rapids, Michigan. A four-cylinder Herschell-Spillman engine was used; a few hundred cars were assembled.

LORRAINE/*USA 1920–1923*

The Lorraine—produced by the Lorraine Car Co. of Richmond, Indiana—had no connection with its Grand Rapids counterpart, but rather was the ambulance and hearse division of the Pilot automobile. Continental motors were used and a small number of limousines was made in addition to hearses and ambulances.

LORRAINE DIETRICH

Germany/France 1896–1935

Old-established makers of railway locomotives in Alsace-Lorraine, De Diétrich et Cie started to build motor cars under licence from constructors such as Bollée, Vivinus or Turcat-Méry, at their Lunéville and Niederbronn plants. From 1902 Bugatti worked as their engineer at Niederbronn, where he designed a 5304cc four and a 50 hp racer with the seat behind the rear axle. In 1908 the marque name was changed to Lorraine-Dietrich. In 1909 they had a six-cylinder of 11,460cc, many four-cylinder models, from the small 12 cv of 2120cc to the big 60 cv of 12,053cc, as well as a twin-cylinder 10 cv of 1060cc. The following year, a 3619cc six-cylinder 15 hp was introduced. Most of these cars were made right up to the war, excepting the twin-cylinder. After the war, when Alsace became part of France again, Lorraine-Dietrich restarted production with the ohv 12 cv of 2297cc and ohv 15 cv six of 3445cc, as well as the 30 cv six (6107cc). The 15 cv Lorraine was the

c.1903 De Dietrich 30hp

1925 3-litre Lorraine Dietrich

backbone of production for many years, and eventually won the Le Mans 24-hour race. Before business ceased, Lorraine introduced the sv 20 cv six of 4086cc: it was a complete failure.

LORYC/*Spain 1920–1925*
Lacy, 'Ribas y Compana of Palma, Mallorca, gave their name to this sporting cyclecar designed by the Frenchman Albert Ouvrard, formerly with Hispano-Suiza. Ruby, SCAP and EHP engines imported from France were used.

LOS ANGELES/*USA 1914–1915*
A four-cylinder water-cooled cyclecar built in Compton, California.

1964 Lost Cause

LOST CAUSE/*USA 1963–1964*
Charles Peaslee Farnsley's 'Lost Cause' was basically a Chevrolet Corvair luxuriously modified by the Derham Custom Body works. Equipment included altimeter, mint julep cups and matching luggage.

LOTHIAN/*England 1920*
The Lothian apparently used a four-cylinder engine available in 10 hp and 11·9 hp variations.

LOTIS/*England 1908–1912*
Built in the old British Duryea factory at Coventry under the aegis of Henry Sturmey, founding editor of *The Autocar* (and inventor of the Sturmey-Archer hub gear for cycles), the original Lotis was a front-engined 22 hp four, soon joined by a single-cylinder 8 hp, 10/12 hp and 12/18 hp vee-twins with Riley engines and a 30/35 hp. Only the twins were built in 1909, and a totally new range (10/12 hp twin, 12/18 hp twin—with a different power unit—16/20 hp four, 20/25 hp four) was announced the next year. The range was reshuffled again in 1911 and in 1912, the last year of production.

LOUET/*France 1903–c1908*
This Parisian firm offered 'light cars for luxury or touring', with 25/30 hp and 30/35 hp four-cylinder engines. A six-cylinder had apparently been built in 1903.

LOUIS CHENARD/*France 1920–1932*
No relationship with the 'other' Chenard, this Colombes, Seine, works started with a sv 7/9 hp of 1244cc. In 1922 they launched an ohv 10 hp of 1693cc, followed in 1923 by a 7/9 hp Chapuis-Dornier-engined 1093cc and an ohv 10 hp of 1496cc, enlarged to 1525cc in 1925. These models remained until the end.

LOUTZKY/*Germany 1900*
A two-speed 3½ hp 'neat two-seated carriage' from Berlin: Herr Loutzky also built parcels carriers for the German post office.

LOYD-LORD/*England 1923–1924*
Although the Loyd-Lord began life with a 1795cc four-cylinder engine, 1924 examples were offered with supercharged two-stroke air-cooled two- and four-cylinder engines of mind-boggling complexity.

1913/14 Lozier seven-passenger tourer

LOZIER/*USA 1899–1917*
George A. Burrell, supervisor of the Lozier Cycle Company's Toledo plant, designed a three-wheeled carriage in 1899: when H. A. Lozier Sr. retired from the business in 1900, his

LOTUS/*England 1947 to date*
The Lotus legend started in 1947 when talented engineer Anthony Colin Bruce Chapman took to building 750 specials. Public demand for replicas led to the forming of Lotus Engineering in 1952 and, a few years later, the first production Lotus, the 6, since when Lotus has grown out of all recognition. Now many times World Champion Car Constructor as well as maker of up-market sports and GT cars, not to mention luxury yachts, Chapman has become a legend in his own time as well as a multi-millionaire. The first four Lotuses were all based on the Austin Seven. The Mk5 never happened but was to have been a 100-mph sports-racing car. The ubiquitous Mk7 lives on today, known simply as the Seven and built by Caterham Cars. The next road car was the pretty, glass-fibre Elite. This was effectively superseded by the Elan in late 1962, the Plus 2 version of which appeared in 1967. Shortly before, however, in December 1966, Lotus announced their first mid-engined road car, the Europa. Initially Renault-powered, it eventually sported the same Ford-based, twin-cam engine as its stablemates. Following special and expensive derivatives of the Elans and Europas, Lotus finally cut their ties with the enthusiast and launched an executive dream, the Elite, in 1974. With only the badge in common with the original car of the same name, it started a new era for this company which soon afterwards added the Eclat (a coupé version of the Elite) and the mid-engined Esprit to complete its range of fast, sleek rich man's toys.

1963 Lotus Elite

1973 JPS Lotus Europa

1973 Lotus Super Seven Mk IV

son, E. R. Lozier, and Burrell, set up the Lozier Motor Company in Toledo. However, production did not begin until 1905, when Lozier's Plattsburg, NY, factory introduced a pair-cast 40 hp four, selling at $5500–$6500 according to body. From 1907 Loziers were shaft driven, yet retained dummy chain-covers to add to their 'sporty' image. Best known of the early Loziers was the sporting 7450cc Briarcliff toy tonneau, named after the 1908 Briarcliff Trophy race (in which Lozier was not actually very successful). There was also a 9085cc pair-cast six version; like the four, it could be specified with Briarcliff, touring or limousine coachwork, at prices from $6000–$7000. Other exotic body styles graced Lozier cars—the three-seat 'Meadowbrook', seven passenger 'Riverside' touring and 'Knickerbocker Berlin'. Production shifted to Detroit in 1910: by 1914, prices were down. The Lozier '77' bi-block 6378cc six cost $3250 as a tourer, and the '84' monobloc 6044cc four was only $2100. But the price cuts failed to counter falling sales, and by 1918 'the quality car for quality people' had ceased production.

LOZIER / USA 1922
It is doubtful whether any cars were produced by the Lozier Motors Co. of New York City, although two models were quoted—a touring car at $8500 and a limousine at $10,000. Likewise it is doubtful whether the marque had any connection with the earlier Lozier.

LSD / England 1920–1924
A JAP vee-twin was the motive power of this rather ungainly three-wheeler which hailed from Yorkshire. Final drive was by chains.

LT / Sweden 1923
Anders Lindström of Torsby had very advanced mechanical ideas and his 20 hp fwd car had clean lines, a pointed radiator and was very well made. It is rumoured that Lindström was contacted by various sources who wanted to finance production, but he preferred to stay independent. The workshop, deep in the forests of Värmland in the western part of Sweden, burnt down after only three cars of a planned production of 50 were produced—one of them being exported to Norway.

LUCAR / England 1913–1914
A 1094cc light car from Brixton, London, with electric lamps.

1906 Luc Court landaulette

LUC COURT / France 1899–1936
The distinctive feature of the early Luc Courts from Lyon was the 'demountable chassis' devised by one Lacoin. The front part of the chassis could be detached from the bodywork

1896 Lutzman dogcart

and rear wheels and attached to a different body and wheels, 'the transformation taking place within a few minutes, without tools'. The year 1912 saw a three-car range, fours of 2155cc and 3631cc, and a 3233cc six. Post-war, Luc Court built mostly light commercials, plus a few 12 hp and 20 hp cars.

LUCERNA / Switzerland 1907–c1909
Garage-owner A. H. Grivel offered a range of assembled cars, using Aster engines and Malicet & Blin chassis—four-cylinders of 10/14 hp, 14/18 hp and 20/24 hp, and a 20/24 hp six.

LUCIA / Switzerland 1903–1908
Designed by Lucien Picker, the Lucia originally appeared as a 905cc four-cylinder with two speeds and shaft drive. From 1904, L. Picker, Moccand & Cie. built these cars in a new factory at Chêne-Bougeries, Geneva. Two models were available in 1905, a 12/16 cv twin and a 24/30 cv four. Picker devised a 'squish' cylinder head, akin to the Ricardo head of the 1920s, for these cars. About 100 Lucias were made.

LUDGATE / England 1904–1905
A two-seater 'light runabout' with 4 hp water-cooled engine and chain drive.

LUFBERY / France 1898–c1902
Charles-Edouard Lufbery's rear-engined vee-twin car combined epicyclic gearing with a three-speed belt transmission to give a primitive overdrive.

LULU / USA 1914
'More than a cyclecar', the $398 LuLu (made by Kearns) had a four-cylinder monobloc engine and three-speed gearing.

LURQUIN-COUDERT / France 1907–1914
'Voiturette-tricars' from a Parisian maker of industrial engines. A twin-cylinder ran in the touring class at the 1907 Château-Thierry hill-climb, and vee-twin cyclecars were built from around 1910.

LUTECE / France 1906–1907
A shaft-drive 14 hp four built by G. Cochot of Colombes (Seine) and shown at Olympia in 1906. Cochot had sold rear-engined 2½ hp voiturettes in 1900–01 under his own name.

LUTIER / France 1907
A four-cylinder car of unknown provenance.

LUTZMANN / Germany 1893–1898
One of the leading German car pioneers, Friedrich Lutzmann built his first car in 1893. From 1896 onwards came a production version with a 2540cc single-cylinder engine, which developed 5 bhp at 300 rpm. This car had a two-speed gearbox, chain drive to the rear wheels and a 23 mph top speed. Opel bought the Lutzmann design and the production equipment in 1898, transferring the operation from Dessau to the Opel bicycle works at Russelsheim.

LUVERNE / USA 1913–1919
In 1915, the 'Big Brown Luverne' 38 hp six sold for $2500 in seven-seater tourer form.

LUWO / Germany 1922–1923
Another car with a 1320cc four-cylinder Steudel engine, built in small quantities in Munich.

LUX / Germany 1897–1902
The early Lux cars (from Ludwigshafen-am-Rhein) had rear-mounted 604cc flat-twin engines. A later version had the power unit in front and a 'patent safety clutch'.

LUX / Italy 1906–1908
Small four-cylinder cars with own-make 10 hp or 16 hp engines were built in small numbers by this Torinese cycle works.

LUXIOR / France 1912–1914
The four-cylinder Luxior from Vincennes, near Paris, had a 1779cc engine and was one of the earliest light cars to be offered in saloon form. In 1912 Luxior also produced a 1767cc model with 'valveless pre-compression engine with super-imposed cylinders'.

LYMAN & BURNHAM / USA 1903–1904
Built for Lyman & Burnham of Boston by the Fore River Ship and Engine Company, of Quincy, Mass., this 12 hp twin-cylinder car had an odd throttle valve 'located in the cylinder casting and surrounding the inlet valve . . . said to be very sensitive'.

LYNX / England 1975 to date
Lynx Engineering's replica of the legendary D Type Jaguar. Like the Deetype, it is difficult to tell from the original. However, under the elegant panelwork is to be found pure E Type front suspension and a modified E Type arrangement at the rear. The choice is of long- or short-nosed body, 3·8- or 4·2-litre engine.

LYONS / USA / England 1920
Featuring a Rolls-Royce-type radiator and wire wheels, this car was manufactured in the United States for London & Midland Motors of London, for sale in the United Kingdom. It was powered by a Herschell-Spillman four.

LYONS ATLAS / USA 1913–1915
With Knight sleeve-valve engines and worm-drive rear axles, these Indianapolis-built cars were designed by Harry A. Knox.

LYS / France 1908–1909
Fernand Marx of Paris produced engines of 8/10 hp, 10/12 hp and 12/16 hp and components, as well as the complete Lys car.

MAB/*England 1906–1911*
A 16/20 hp car from cycle makers A. G. Fenn of Mortimer Market, London ('MAB' = Mortimer Auto Bikes).

MAB/*France 1925*
Makers of automobile components and chassis, Malicet et Blin in Aubervilliers, Seine, occasionally assembled ohc Anzani-engined cars.

MACDONALD STEAM CAR
USA 1923–1924
The MacDonald Steam Automotive Co., of Garfield, Ohio, flourished briefly as a builder (and rebuilder) of steam engines and other parts of existing steam cars. It also advertised a roadster termed the 'Steam Bobcat'. None was built, although one MacDonald sedan is known to have been made.

MACKENZIE/*England 1899*
Electric phaetons and dog-carts built in Lambeth and based closely on the Riker.

MAD/*France 1919*
A range of voiturettes from Levallois-Perret, Seine, shown at the 1919 Paris Salon.

MADELVIC/*Scotland 1898–1900*
Madelvic electrics were built at Granton, Edinburgh, but the vehicles proved impractical, and the company lasted less than two years.

MADISON/*USA 1915–1921*
Madisons were assembled cars made in Anderson, Indiana, in roadster and touring car form. One model was appropriately called the 'Dolly Madison' model, the mis-spelled first name (it should be 'Dollie') designed apparently to honour the wife of the fourth US President, James Madison. Rutenber four-cylinder engines were used throughout (excepting a Herschell-Spillman V-8 which was offered, only briefly, in 1916).

MADOU/*France 1922–1926*
This strange example of 'badge engineering' was a small batch of Marguerite cars sold under the name of Cora Madou, a famous actress of the day, as a special order by her rich boyfriend.

MADOZ/*France 1921*
Powered by a 175cc two-stroke engine and also known as the 'Propulcycle', this light cyclecar was built in Nanterre, Seine.

MAF/*Germany 1908–1922*
Air-cooled in-line four-cylinder cars designed by the works owner Hugo Ruppe (whose father and brothers owned the Piccolo-Apollo car factory). Hugo Ruppe left MAF in the early 1920s, designed the first DKW two-stroke engines and afterwards built Bekamo motorcycles in Berlin. The MAF was made at Markranstadt, near Leipzig. Pre-1914 models ranged from 1192cc to 1910cc. After the war, the range included an 1833cc version, some improved 1230cc pre-war models and also an ohc 3483cc four-cylinder car. Apollo took over MAF when production ceased.

MAG/*Hungary 1911–1934*
Built on German lines, the MAG cars were quite heavy and not always in line with the latest developments. Real production, on Hungary's first moving assembly line, started after World War One with 1790cc four-cylinder and 2407cc six-cylinder cars, which proved very popular as taxicabs. Udvarda drove one of the 'Mago-Six' models in the Monte Carlo Rally.

MAGENTA/*England 1972 to date*
A cheap, easy-to-build sports car, the Magenta features a rigid ladder frame, and a simple glass-fibre body designed to accept an MG 1100 subframe and running gear. Several Magentas have achieved success in rallying and over 200 kits have now been sold.

MAGNET/*England 1903*
A range of three cars — 12 hp twin-cylinder and 16 hp and 24 hp fours.

MAGNET/*Germany 1921–1924*
This Berlin-Weissensee firm produced motorcycles and three-wheelers pre-1914, and in the early 1920s offered a small 789cc four-cylinder car.

MAGNETIC/*England 1921–1926*
American Entz magnetic transmission was the distinctly novel feature of the Magnetic. Burt McCollum sleeve-valve engines of two capacities were offered, a four-cylinder of 2614cc and an eight of 5228cc. A 2888cc six-cylinder ohv power unit appeared in 1924.

MAIBOHM/*USA 1916–1922*
Built initially in Racine, Wisconsin, and later in Sandusky, Ohio, the Maibohm was a conventional assembled car, using a four-cylinder engine up to 1919 and a Falls six from 1918 to 1922, the four being dropped in 1919. Open and

1919 20hp Maibohm Six tourer

closed coachwork was available and bodies were built by Millspaugh & Irish. The Maibohm became the Courier in 1922.

MAICO/*Germany 1956–1958*
Still a well-known motorcycle factory, Maico produced an improved version of the little Champion car. The engines—452cc twin-cylinder two-strokes—were built by Heinkel, the bodywork by Baur of Stuttgart. The engine was behind the driven rear axle, the gearbox in front of it.

MAIFLOWER/*England 1919–1921*
This Model T Ford-based device was built by army captains M. Price and A. I. Flower. A newly fabricated rear end and alterations to the front transverse suspension were variations on the standard Ford chassis.

1921 22hp Maiflower two-seater

MAIL/*England 1903*
A four-seater 8 hp single-cylinder model and a six-seater 12 hp twin-cylinder coupé were sold by this short-lived company.

MAILLARD/*France 1900–c1903*
Two models of the Maillard were offered, a 6 hp and a 10 hp (uprated to 8 hp and 12 hp in 1901). These were also licence-built in Belgium as Aquilas.

MAISON PARISIENNE/*France 1897–c1898*
M. Laboure of La Maison Parisienne assembled Benz cars under licence for the French market. Some were sold under the name 'l'Eclair'. In 1898 the company's engineer, Serex, designed a flat-twin car, still on Benz lines, which ran in the Marseille-Nice Race.

1907 28hp Maja of Graf Hugo Boos

MAJA/*Austria 1906–1908*
Ferdinand Porsche designed this 4520cc four-cylinder car for the Jellinek-owned Osterreichische Automobil Gesellschaft. The name came from Jellinek's younger daughter; the older one was Mercédès. However, Maja cars— actually built by Austro-Daimler on behalf of Jellinek—failed to gain much popularity. Improved 'Maja' models were built by Austro-Daimler until World War One.

MAJESTIC/*France 1926–1930*
Big cars made in Paris by MM. Gadoux and Lelong with an ohv straight-eight engine of 2996cc. Few were built.

MAJOLA/*France 1911–1928*
From 1911–1914 the St. Denis, Seine, works only offered one 1327cc model. In 1914 they presented an ohc 984cc 6 hp car. In 1921 they announced a 1393cc model. The two latter models remained in production until the end, the ohc car being enlarged to 1086cc in 1922.

1919 6/12hp Majola.

MAJOR/*France 1920–1921*
Once again, M. Violet was responsible for the design of the Major cyclecar, built in Courbevoie, Seine. It was powered by a twin-cylinder two-stroke engine of 1060cc and featured a friction transmission. It was later sold under the name of Mourre.

1920 Major sporting cyclecar

MALCOLM/*England 1906*
The Yukon Motor & Engineering Company of Balham, South London, built 'Malcolm' engines with two, four or six separately cast cylinders. They also made the Malcolm car 'in all powers'. Their 6/8 hp twin had a pressed steel frame, chain drive and a honeycomb radiator.

MALCOLM/*USA 1915*
A New York-built 13 hp four of attractive appearance, retailing at $595.

MALCOLM JONES/*USA 1914–1915*
A four-cylinder water-cooled cyclecar from Detroit.

MALLALIEU/*England 1974 to date*
The Mallalieu Bentley Specials owe their name to Derry Mallalieu, a one-time Bugatti racer. Both the Barchetta and Mercia are based on the 1950s Mk6 chassis. Most are exported to America.

MALLIARY/*France 1901*
A 6 cv shaft-drive voiturette from Puteaux (Seine).

MALLORCA/*Spain 1975 to date*
A Lotus Seven-based sports car with 1438cc or 1756cc Seat engine.

MALVERNIA/*England 1897–1913*
T. C. Santler, who claimed to have helped Karl Benz design his first car and to have produced a car in 1887, built two Benz-like cars in his Malvern Link, Worcs., workshops in 1897. Front-engined light cars appeared in 1906 and 1913.

MANCH-ASTER/*England 1904–1905*
As its name suggested, this 20 hp Aster-engined car was built in Manchester. It was assembled by Bennett & Carlisle, predecessors of Newton & Bennett, who sold the NB car.

MANEXALL/*USA 1921*
The Manexall was merely the Cyclomobile fitted with a rear deck. To achieve this, the wheelbase was increased to 102 inches. Price was $475.

MANIC/*Canada 1969–1971*
Built in Montreal and Granby, Quebec, this was a glass-fibre sports car based on a Renault floorpan.

MANNESMANN/*Germany 1923–1929*
Made by the Mannesmann brothers at Remscheid, Mannesmann cars had 1289cc four-cylinder 20 hp engines. In 1927, a 2395cc ohv eight of advanced design was built, followed by a Rickenbacker-engined sv 5130cc eight (Rickenbacker engines were then made by the Rasmussen-owned Audi works). Before building cars, the Mannesmanns produced Mulag lorries.

MANON/*France 1903–c1905*
A light car with either a 6 hp or 9 hp engine built by H. Chaigneau of Paris, and sold in England as the Mohawk-Manon.

MAPLEBAY/*USA 1908*
An air-cooled 22 hp runabout from Crookston, Minn., with a Reeves four and friction drive.

MARATHON/*USA 1908–1915*
Built initially in Jackson, Tennessee, Marathon cars were produced in Nashville after 1910. The 1913 range included three big fours: a 2837cc 25 hp, a 4177cc 35 hp and a 6758cc 45 hp.

MARATHON/*USA 1920*
The Marathon of Elkhart, Indiana, was no relation to the Nashville Marathon. The Elkhart-built Marathon was strictly an export concern, though if any cars were actually made and/or exported, they were few indeed. The Marathon Company and the Crow-Elkhart Company, another Elkhart concern, were taken over by Century Motors and the Marathon became the Morriss-London.

MARATHON/*France 1954–1955*
This was a last attempt by Rosengart to re-enter the automobile field with a 750cc Panhard flat-twin-engined car.

MARAUDER/*England 1950–1953*
Built mainly from Rover parts, the Marauder was marketed by Wilks Mackie & Co. Ltd., of Dorridge, Birmingham. The 2103cc Rover engine was installed in a box-section chassis clothed with a handsome touring body. Several examples were built.

MARBLE-SWIFT/*USA 1903–1905*
A friction-drive two-seater with a 10 hp twin-cylinder engine, built in Chicago.

MARCA-TRE-SPADE/*Italy 1908–1911*
Four-cylinder ioe 24 hp cars with four-speed gearboxes, from a famous gunsmiths.

MARCHAND/*Italy 1898–1909*
This cycle and sewing-machine works at Piacenza first built a number of rear-engined Decauville-type cars, then progressed to front-engined cars, mostly four- and six-cylinder models of up to 60 hp.

1976 Mallalieu Bentley

1970 Marcos Mantis

MARCOS/*Wales/England 1959–1971*

Between them Jem MARsh and Frank COStin contrived to build one of the prettiest sports cars of all time, the Marcos Volvo (the same shell was subsequently fitted with a variety of Ford engines). Marsh alone must take responsibility for the ugly but nonetheless successful Mini-Marcos, also the Dennis Adams-styled Mantis with which Marcos were forced to close their books after 32 had been built. From the very first plywood Marcos to the perhaps ahead-of-its-time Mantis, Marcos were originators of the first order. The Mini-Marcos lives on, and is now built by D. & H. Fibreglass Techniques, while Marsh has bought back the moulds and some interesting examples of the other models and now spends his time restoring and making spares for his early creations.

MARCUS/*England 1919*

A cyclecar built by G. L. Marcus of Golders Green, North London.

MARENDAZ/*England 1926–1936*

Early Marendaz Specials used sv 1½-litre Anzani engines, sometimes in supercharged form; for 1932 D. M. K. Marendaz offered a small six of 1900cc. The following year a 2½-litre car, the 17/97, was announced. For 1935 a new 2-litre six by Coventry-Climax was marketed. Production of these handsome sports cars with flexible external exhaust pipes and Bentley-like radiators was transferred from south-west London to Maidenhead in 1932. Among pre-war drivers was Mrs. Alfred Moss, mother of future racing driver Stirling, who actively campaigned an attractive white two-seater.

MARGARIA/*France 1910–1912*

A 2297cc four-cylinder car shown at the 1910 Paris Salon, the shaft-drive Margaria sold for Fr 5000 in chassis form. In 1912, M. Margaria teamed up with M. Launay to build the SCAP.

MARGUERITE/*France 1920–1928*

Made by the Marguerite brothers in Courbevoie, Seine, these were light cars with Ruby and SCAP 1093cc engines. They were also sold under the name of Morano-Marguerite, Induco and Madou.

MARIE DE BAGNEUX/*France 1907*

A single-seat three-wheeler, M. Marie de Bagneux's belt-driven car weighed 100 kg (220 lb) and had a 1¼ hp De Dion engine.

MARIENFELDE/*Germany 1899–1902*

Owned by Daimler directors without Gottlieb Daimler's official consent, Marienfelde offered, among other models, a copy of the 5900cc four-cylinder Daimler. Daimler of Canstatt eventually took over the Marienfelde works and used them for the manufacture of heavy trucks

MARION/*USA 1904–1914*

Starting life as a transverse air-cooled 16 hp, by 1906 the Indianapolis Marion had acquired more conventionally positioned power units of 16 hp and 24 hp. The shaft-drive 1907 20 hp four-cylinder Marion had a two-speed Hassler gear incorporated in the differential unit. An experimental 9455cc V-12 was built in 1908. By 1913, Marions were being built in a former Willys Overland factory and operating a night shift to cope with their flow of orders. 'Much better finished and with better style than the average American car around this price,' the $1475 Marion had right-hand steering and central gear and brake levers.

MARION-HANDLEY/*USA 1916–1920*

An assembled six-cylinder car, the Marion-Handley was a continuation of the earlier Marion automobile. Continental engines were used, except for a few cars at the end of the company's existence which used a Rutenber. The company was reorganized and became the Handley-Knight, which in turn became the Handley and was finally absorbed by Checker.

MARITIME/*Canada 1912–1915*

The Maritime Six was — apart from two prototypes — no more than an assembled Palmer-Singer, from St. John, New Brunswick.

MARLBOROUGH

France/England 1906–1926

Though the chassis and engine of the Marlborough were French, the car was virtually unknown in that country, being assembled for sale in Britain by T. B. André (later famous as makers of Hartford shock absorbers) using Malicet et Blin chassis. First shown at Olympia in 1906 in single-cylinder 8 hp form, twin-cylinder 10/12 hp and four-cylinder 14 hp models by Gauthier & Co. (also agents for CCC), the early Marlboroughs had round radiators and bonnets. A change of direction came in 1912 with a near-cyclecar, the vee-radiatored 8/10 hp of 1094cc, which had grown into a more substantial light car by the outbreak of war. Postwar, a 1087cc CIME-engined version was offered, and there were a few sporting models with British Anzani and Coventry-Climax engines, the latter being a 2-litre six with four-wheel brakes announced in 1925, which never saw production. Some 2000 Marlboroughs were built in all.

1907 Marie de Bagneux tricar

MARLBOROUGH-THOMAS

England 1923–1924

Only a few of these exciting sports cars were built, T. B. Andre and J. G. Parry Thomas producing them from a shed at Brooklands Motor Course. The engine was a dohc 1½-litre unit; the use of leaf-valve springs was a distinctive Thomas feature.

1923–25 Marmon coupé, bodied by Hume

MARMON/*USA 1902–1933*

The Nordyke & Marmon Company of Indianapolis dated back to 1851. From 1902 to 1908, Marmon built pressure-lubricated air-cooled V-4s, designed by Howard Marmon, joined in 1908 by a 60 hp V-8. Big fours of 40/45 hp and 50/60 hp were introduced for 1909, and in 1911 the Marmon Wasp six-cylinder racer won the first Indianapolis '500' race. In 1914 two models—the four-cylinder '32' (5213cc) and the six-cylinder '48' (9383cc)—were listed. The advanced '34' ohv six (5565cc) was launched in 1916: a development was still in production eleven years later, alongside the 'Little Marmon' 3115cc straight-eight, which heralded an all-eight policy lasting until 1931, when the 8046cc alloy-engined V-16—one of the great American classics—appeared. It was the sole model offered in 1933, though a backbone-chassis V-12 was on the stocks. The Marmon name survived on trucks. From 1929–31, Marmon offered an eight at less than $1000, under the Roosevelt marque name.

c.1914 Marlborough 10hp two-seater

LA MARNE/*USA 1920*

The La Marne, successor to the Richard car, was an eight-cylinder automobile with a 128-inch wheelbase and a touring car price of $1485. Few of these cars were produced.

MAROT-GARDON/*France 1898–1904*

Starting with racing tricycles, by 1900 this firm from Corbie (Somme) had progressed to a 4½ cv 'miniature carriage'.

229

MARQUETTE/*USA 1912*
Succeeding Welch and Rainier, the Marquette was built in two models, with pair-cast engines of 6435cc and 6757cc, at prices of $3000 and $4000 respectively.

MARQUETTE/*USA 1929–1931*
A small side-valve six priced at $990–$1060, briefly produced by Buick as a separate marque.

MARQUEZ/*France 1930*
Streamlined fwd cars of which very few were made, using a straight-eight ohv SCAP engine of 2344cc.

MARR/*USA 1903–1904*
Marr of Detroit subcontracted an order for 100 Marr Autocars to the Fauber Manufacturing Company of Elgin, Illinois, but the marque died when the Fauber factory burned down in August 1904.

MARRIOTT/*England 1901–1902*
A 2¾ hp De Dion-engined quadricycle from St Albans, Herts.

MARS/*England 1904–1905*
A 4 hp White & Poppe engine powered this two-speed tri-car from Finchley, North London.

MARS/*Germany 1904–1908*
Famous for the Mars motorcycles of the 1920s (with 956cc Maybach flat-twin engines), Mars, of Norimberk-Doos, earlier produced cars with one- and two-cylinder Korting engines and Maurer friction drive.

MARSEEL (MARSEAL)
England 1919–1925
The Coventry-built Marseel was produced by D. M. K. Marendaz and one Seelhaft. A 1½-litre four-cylinder Coventry-Climax engine was used. In 1923 Seelhaft departed and the spelling was anglicized. The 1¼-litre 11/27 joined the 1½-litre, while an ohv six of 1750cc also put in a brief appearance.

MARSH/*England 1904–1905*
A 3½ hp Tri- Car from Kettering, the Marsh had the curious option of wheel or side-tiller steering, and could run on petrol or paraffin.

MARSH/*USA 1921–1924*
The Marsh was built in Cleveland and the first models built were powered by a four-cylinder Lycoming engine. Wheelbase was 114 inches. In 1923 this was extended by 3 inches and a six-cylinder Continental engine substituted. At best, Marsh was a hand-to-mouth proposition and only four fours and two sixes were built before the factory burned down in 1924, destroying two more cars.

MARSHALL/*USA 1920–1921*
The Marshall has always confused historians as it was actually a Norwalk, sold by a Chicago distributor named Marshall. The Norwalk, in turn, was manufactured by Piedmont and was similar to other Piedmont-built cars like the Lone Star, Stork Kar, Bush and Alsace. A four-cylinder Lycoming engine was used on all Marshall (and Norwalk Six) cars.

MARSHALL-ARTER/*England 1912–1915*
Formerly makers of the 'QED', Marshall-Arter of Hammersmith manufactured a handsome two-seater with 1244cc Chapuis-Dornier engine. engine.

MARTA/*Hungary 1912–1914*
To cope with the atrocious Hungarian roads, Marta cars were strong and heavy vehicles, based on Westinghouse designs. Built at Arad (which became part of Romania after World War One), Martas were offered with sv four-cylinder engines of 22 hp, 30 hp and 45 hp, the latter with chain drive.

MARTIN/*France 1907*
A manufacturer of voiturettes from Saint-Germain-en-Laye (Seine-et-Oise).

MARTIN/*Canada 1911*
Possibly the only car ever built in a church, this friction-drive high-wheeler sold only two.

MARTIN/*USA 1920–1922*
The Martin was a motorcycle which attempted to pass itself off in its sales pitch as an economical automobile in the same fashion as Ner-a-Car. It featured a twin-cylinder engine and sold for $250. Martin also built a clumsy-looking three-wheeler, the Scootmobile.

MARTIN/*USA 1927–1932*
Designed by Miles H. Carpenter, formerly of Phianna, and built by the M. P. Moller Company in Hagerstown, Maryland, this midget car underwent tremendous promotion between 1928 and 1932. Produced and promoted by Capt. J. V. Martin of aeronautic fame, the $200 Martin failed to excite anyone who could have aided the venture. With a four-cylinder Cleveland motorcycle engine, the disc-wheeled two-passenger Martin coupés — prototypes only — had 60-inch wheelbases. The crate in which the car was to be delivered would become its garage. The promoters also had plans for an export Martin which would be sold abroad under the name 'Dart' and the car's 1929 prospectus used the Dart name and insignia. Only two or three prototypes constituted the entire production of this ill-fated venture.

Max de Martini's 20hp Martini

MARTINI/*Switzerland 1897–1934*
This famous armaments factory also made stationary engines, and in 1897 built a rear-engined twin-cylinder car with tube ignition. Front-engined cars on Panhard lines appeared in 1899, and in 1903 Martini began building Rochet-Schneiders under licence in a new fac-tory at St-Blaise, which passed into English control in 1906 and was re-acquired by Swiss capital in 1908. Big pair-cast fours were their stock-in-trade, though ohv voiturettes of 1087cc appeared in 1908, and a team ran in that year's Coupe des Voiturettes at Dieppe. A sleeve-valve 25 hp was listed in 1913, and in 1914 came the 2614cc 12cv Sport, whose ohc engine boasted four valves per cylinder in hemispherical heads. The range was now from a 1357cc four to the 18 cv of 3563cc. In 1921, the first new post-war Martini, the 18/45cc type FN, appeared, and in 1924 the firm was acquired by the Swiss engineer Steiger, who brought out a 3·1-litre six in 1926. Two sixes of 15 cv and 20 cv were listed in 1929, but the following year licence production of the 2·5-litre Wanderer six began. Martini's last fling was a 4·4-litre monobloc six, type NF, which appeared early in 1931. Total Martini production was around 2000 cars.

MARVEL/*France 1905–1908*
Built in Paris, Marvel cars were conventional four-cylinder vehicles of 14 hp to 30 hp. Their last model was a 15 hp of 2799cc.

MARVEL/*USA 1907*
A short-lived 'Automobile Roadster' from Detroit.

MARYLAND/*USA 1900–1901*
A solid-tyred steam car from Luke, Maryland, with a 12 hp twin-cylinder engine.

MARYLAND/*USA 1904–1910*
Built by the Sinclair-Scott Company (manufacturers of canning machinery, farm equipment and car components), these ohc 3·3-litres were initially known as 'Ariels'. Total production was 100 cars.

MASCOT/*France 1906*
A range of two- and four-cylinder cars from 8 hp to 24 hp shown at Olympia in 1906.

MASCOTTE/*England 1919–1921*
A Peters engine of 1645cc initially powered the Mascotte, though later examples used a 1795cc version. Only a few examples of this London-built light car were constructed.

MASE/*France 1921–1924*
The Manufacture d'Automobiles, d'Outillage et de Cycles de Saint-Etienne made a small batch of sports cyclecars with an interesting 995cc ohc engine. They were also available with a 1097cc power unit.

1922 MASE 10hp Sports

MASERATI/*Italy 1926 to date*

The Maserati brothers—Alfieri, Bindo, Carlo, Ettore, Ernesto and Mario—were associated with motor cars from the very early days; Alfieri, Ernesto and Bindo built two 2-litre Grand Prix cars for Diatto in 1925, then took them over and linered them down to 1·5 litres when Diatto withdrew from racing a year later. The new car, driven by Alfieri, won the 1926 Targa Florio, its first race. Maserati made their name with racing cars with four, six and eight—even 16—cylinders of 1088cc to 4995cc, though road-going cars with detuned racing engines did appear during the 1930s. Even one of the fearsome *sedici cilindri* (two straight-eights mounted in parallel, with the crankshafts geared together) was converted into a road car. In 1937, Omer Orsi took over control, though the Maserati brothers stayed on until 1947, when they left to found OSCA. Racing cars were again the mainstay of the company after the war, most famous being the 250F, designed by Giaocchino Colombo in 1953, and raced until 1958 in various forms, by drivers including Moss, Hawthorn and Fangio. Then Maserati decided to withdraw from competition, and concentrated on a range of expensive sports cars, with the six-cylinder 3485cc 300S engine. However, the 1994cc and 2890cc 'Birdcage' Maseratis enjoyed some competition success in the early 1960s in private hands. In 1969, Citroën took over control of Maserati for approximately 1000 million lire; the Modena factory then built about two-and-a-half cars a day as well as some 30 engines for the Citroën Maserati SM grand touring model. In 1975, Maserati announced that it was going out of business, but was rescued at the eleventh hour by the De Tomaso group. It currently offers the mid-engined V-6 Merak, of 2965cc, and the smaller Merak 2000; a mid-engined 4719cc V-8 Bora; the 4930cc Khamsin V-8; and the dohc 4136cc V-8 Quattroporte, available with coupé or limousine coachwork.

c.1933 Maserati eight-cylinder sports

1979 Maserati Quattro Porte II

MASON/*USA 1906–1910*

'The swiftest and strongest two-cylinder car in America', the 1906 24hp Mason, from Des Moines, Iowa, sold for $1250, and was Fred Duesenberg's first design. In 1910, the cars became known as 'Maytags'.

MASS/*France 1903–1923*

Built in Courbevoie, Seine, for the English market, the Mass took its name from its importer, Mr Masser-Horniman (from 1912 it was sold in its homeland under the name of its constructor, Pierron). Initially, there were singles of 4½ hp and 6 hp, but in 1905 two- and four-cylinder cars appeared. The 1907 range was most complex, with a 573cc single, 1005cc twin and fours of 3403cc, 4787cc, 5420cc, 6872cc and the biggest Mass of all, the 30/40 hp of 8015cc. A monobloc 10/12 hp appeared in 1912, and in 1913 came a long-stroke six of 5429cc. The 1914 range were all Ballot-engined, culminating in a 5340cc four, but only a 2800cc 15·9 hp survived the war.

MASSEY-HARRIS/*Canada 1900–1902*

Canada's first series-production petrol vehicles, these were tricycles and quadricycles with De Dion engines.

MASTERBILT SIX/*USA 1926–1927*

Three Masterbilt cars—a seven-passenger sedan, a two-door sedan and a coupé—were built in all. An air-cooled car, the Masterbilt had a modified Franklin engine. Built by the Govro-Nelson Co. of Detroit, the car was designed by Victor Gorvreau, who had previously been associated with Pan.

1926–27 Masterbilt Six

MATAS, SRC/*Spain 1917–1925*

The first Matas cyclecars, with front suspension by a transverse spring, had 8/10 hp Dorman engines; soon Continental engines, imported from the USA, were being fitted. The design was subsequently sold to another Barcelona firm, Stevenson, Romagosa y Compana, who built the cars under the name 'SRC'.

MATCHLESS/*England 1906–1907, 1913–1929*

This famous motorcycle works at Plumstead, Kent, showed a 6hp twin-cylinder Fafnir-engined runabout at the 1906 Stanley Show. A three-wheeler cyclecar appeared in 1913, and, post-war, a very few integral-construction cyclecars with fwb and ifs appeared, powered by a flat-twin of 1250cc.

MATFORD/*France 1934–1939*

Henry Ford needed to expand his French production as his Asnières, Seine, plant was too small; Emile Mathis needed finance, and so these two individualists struck up an often stormy relationship which resulted in the production of the Ford V-8 at the Mathis plant in

1910 Mass 15hp two-seater

1939 Matford
13cv V8–F92A cabriolet

Strasbourg under the 'Matford' label. Initially the 30 hp V-8 was produced, then, in 1935, Dearborn created the 22 hp 'Alsace' engine for France (Dagenham also adopted it). Matfords were generally better styled than their British counterparts, and some handsome cabriolet models appeared. Mathis broke with Ford in 1939, but plans to transfer V-8 production to a Bordeaux factory were scotched by the outbreak of World War Two.

MATHESON / *USA 1903–1912*
The first Mathesons were built in the factory of the recently defunct Holyoke company, but in 1906 the firm moved to Wilkesbarre, Penn.

Initially a 24 hp ohv four was listed: by 1906 chain-drive fours of 40/45 hp and 60/65 hp were catalogued at prices ranging from $5000 to $7500. Chain drive was used on most models (except the 50 hp six of 1909) until 1910. By the end of production only the 5213cc 'Silent Six' was available.

MATHIEU / *Belgium 1902–1908*
Sold in England as the Beckett and Farlow, the Mathieu was claimed to be 'simple, reliable, noiseless . . . can be started without jerk'. One-, two- or four-cylinder engines were offered. At the 1907 Paris Salon, fours of 18/24 hp (3770cc) and 30/40 hp (6902cc) were exhibited.

MATHIS

MATHIS
Germany / France 1905–1950
Emile Mathis was a leading car dealer in Strasbourg, Alsace, handling Fiat, De Dietrich and Panhard-Levassor, among other makes. The first car marketed under his own name was the Hermès (or Hermès-Simplex) designed for him by the young Bugatti and built at Grafenstaden. Current for 1905–06, it was built in 28, 40, and 98 hp forms, all being Mercedes-like cars with chain drive. Then designer and racing-driver Esser created cars of 2025cc and 2253cc which were built under licence from Stoewer. The first true Mathis appeared in 1913, in the guise of the 951cc (soon enlarged to 1029cc) Babylette. A 1131cc version appeared in 1914, forming the basis of post-war production. Other pre-1914 Mathis included the Baby, with engine and gearbox

in unit, built in 1327cc and 1406cc models, plus two sv models of 1850cc and 3453cc and a 4·4-litre Mathis-Knight. The famous London store Harrods sold the Babylette under its own name. Post-war, with Alsace now in France, the small Mathis cars were built at a prodigious rate, and the marque soon became the fourth biggest in its new homeland. In 1921 came the vee-radiatored SB ohv 1·5-litre, developed from an ohc racer, while Mathis countered the 5 cv Citroën with a basic car of 760cc, which had electric lighting but no instruments or differential: like the other little Mathis, it featured a four-speed gearbox. Since 1920, Mathis had been experimenting with small sixes, the first production model — of only 1188cc — appearing in 1923. There was even a 1·7-litre ohc straight-eight in 1925, a depressing and gutless machine. After

producing a bewildering variety of small cars, Mathis pursued a single-model policy in 1927 with the 1·2-litre four-cylinder sv MY, joined the next year by the 1·8-litre Emysix. These stolid machines set the pattern for the early 1930s, though in 1930 there were bigger sixes of 2·4 and 4·1 litres, and 1931 saw two short-lived straight-eights. The larger of these, Type-FOH, was of 3 litres. The more modern Emyquatre, with ifs and synchromesh, appeared in 1933, but its Emyhuit sister had only just appeared when production of Mathis cars was ousted by the Matford. Mathis regained his factory just before the war, and resumed activity in 1946, after an attempt to interest the Americans in plastics-bodied cars. His post-war projects, an Andreau-styled three-wheeler and a 2·8-litre fwd flat-six, failed to reach production. His plant was bought by Citroën in 1954.

*c.*1913 Mathis Babylette 8hp

1935 Mathis 'Emyquatre' saloon

MATRA/*France 1965 to date*
Aerospace group Matra (Mécanique-Aviation-Traction) took over René Bonnet and continued to produce that firm's sports cars, becoming better known, however, for their Formula One racers. When their first own-design road-going car, the Matra 530, with V-4 Ford engine, failed to sell in sufficient numbers, Matra linked with Chrysler at the beginning of the 1970s to develop the Simca 1300-powered Bagheera sports coupé with three-abreast seating.

1905 Maudslay 15hp phaeton

MAUDSLAY/*England 1902–1914, 1923*
An offshoot of the famous engineering company founded by Henry Maudslay, this Coventry-based firm began production in 1903 with a 14 hp *en bloc* three-cylinder car with an overhead camshaft, thought to be the first application of this principle on a production car. A fully pressured lubricated crankshaft was another advanced feature. Standard bodywork included a 'convertible omnibus' rear section which lifted off to convert the car to an open tonneau, and the first-ever production shooting-brake, the 'All-Round' car, a solid-tyred car capable of carrying eleven passengers or '300 head of game, well hung'. Early Maudslays had 'coalscuttle' bonnets, but by 1905 a conventional radiator and bonnet were in use; later that year came the celebrated round radiator and bonnet which recalled the company's marine boilers. The three-cylinder Maudslay was built until 1906 (a 25 hp version was introduced in 1904, along with two big sixes, exactly double the capacity of the threes). A four-cylinder range had been announced in 1905, and after 1906 nothing else was made. The 1907 range consisted of a 20/30 hp and a 35/45 hp, both with four-speed gearboxes with overdrive top. Maudslay's most famous model was the 'Sweet Seventeen' introduced in October 1909, the last production Maudslay. After the war the firm concentrated on commercial vehicles, apart from an advanced 2-litre twin ohc 15/80 hp six with four-wheel brakes of which three examples would have been shown at Olympia in 1923, had not the show landaulette been destroyed at the coachbuilders. Chassis price was £825, but the decision was taken to shelve the project after prototypes only had been built.

MAURER/*Germany 1908–1909, 1923–1924*
A complicated story, because Ludwig Maurer, the founder of this factory, also founded Maurer-Union. His 1908 cars had 1520cc two-cylinder engines and friction drive. In 1923, a flat-twin two-stroke car followed a long succession of Maurer motorcycles.

MAURER-UNION/*Germany 1900–1908*
Ludwig-Maurer's original design was his famous friction-drive car, built first with 1140cc single-cylinder 6 hp, afterwards 8 hp, engines. There was also a vee-twin version. Four-cylinder cars were under development when the Nürnburg factory went broke. It was bought by C. J. Braun's Kaiser car works (associated with Premier). Soon afterwards, Maurer's wife Johanna 'founded' the new Maurer works on behalf of her husband. Many other car producers copied Maurer designs, especially the friction drive, though only a few, like Mars, actually bothered to pay for the Maurer licence.

MAUSER/*Germany 1923–1927*
A famous rifle and revolver manufacturer, Mauser first built a two-wheeler car, the 'Mauser-Einspurauto'. In 1923 came an ohv four-wheeler with a 1569cc four-cylinder engine.

MAVERICK/*USA 1953–1955*
Not to be confused with Ford's model of the same name, the Maverick was a large car with room for only three passengers. It used a Cadillac chassis and engine with a glass-fibre body. The floor was of marine plywood, the dashboard was spun copper and the seats were upholstered in plastic. About seven Mavericks were made before production ceased.

MAX/*France 1920–1926*
A small cyclecar made in Billancourt, Seine, with single-cylinder 350cc or vee-twin 483cc two-stroke engines. The smaller version had a friction transmission and the bigger, a conventional gearbox.

MAXIM/*England 1903–1915*
Sir Hiram Stevens Maxim of Maxim machine-gun fame built this car, sold in limited numbers only. In 1904 there were two models, a 2281cc 16 hp twin and a 24 hp four. The tonneau body was hinged at the rear, so that it could be lifted to inspect the mechanism for service or repair.

1904 Maxim 24hp and its lift-up body

MAXIMAG/*Switzerland 1922–1928*
Motosacoche, founded by the Dufaux brothers, was famed for motorcycles and Mag engines. They built ohc 5 cv four-cylinder voiturette engines of 1904cc from 1914, but did not make a complete car until 1922. The 5 cv Maximag was a sporting two-seater, still of 1094cc, but with side-valves. A four-seater 7 cv (1593cc) appeared shortly after. Some Maximags are believed to have been built in the Motosacoche branch factory in Lyon. Total output was around 200 cars. Some Maximags were built in the Motosacoche branch factory in Lyon using 1093cc Ruby engines from 1925–27.

MAXWELL-BRISCOE, MAXWELL
USA 1904–1925
Jonathan Dixon Maxwell and Ben Briscoe collaborated to create a 1647cc flat-twin runabout, followed by four-cylinder cars of up to 30/40 hp. In 1909, Maxwell-Briscoe was part of the United States Motor group, surviving its collapse in 1912, and producing Mascotte and Mercury models. Low-priced monobloc fours were the staple offerings thereafter. The 1921 'New Good Maxwell' was the prelude to Walter Chrysler's take-over in 1923 and the marque's replacement by the four-cylinder Chrysler two years later.

c.1915 Maxwell 25hp tourer

MAYBACH/*Germany 1921–1940*
After leaving Mercedes in 1907, Wilhelm Maybach collaborated with Graf Zeppelin to build aeroengines—particularly for airships—and his Friedrichshafen factory also made marine engines and motorcycle power units, before introducing a sv 5738cc six-cylinder car (the engine was also sold to Spyker in Holland). First shown in 1921, the Maybach originally had a two-speed pedal-controlled gearbox; Spohn, Glaser, Armbruster, Erdmann & Rossi and Voll-Ruhrbeck were among the coachbuilders who clothed this high-quality chassis with exclusive bodywork. An ohv 6995cc engine appeared in the W5 of 1926, available with a *schnellgang* auxiliary two-speed gearbox. A 6922cc V-12 made its debut in 1929, and was developed into the Zeppelin model of 1930. From 1931, a 7977cc V-12 was also available: some Zeppelins had the W5 six-cylinder; all had seven-speed gearboxes. The ohc SW series included the 3790cc SW38, current from 1934 to 1940; there were also 3·5-litre and 4·2-litre SW models. Always an expensive car, the Maybach could cost over DM 40,000 in V-12 Zeppelin form with custom coachwork.

1935 Maybach Type SW35 Sport Cabriolet

MAYFAIR/*England 1900*
The Sports Motor Car Company, South Kensington, offered a range of De Dion-engined voiturettes which were similar to the Belgian Pieper, and may indeed have been imports. Their 8 hp 'Sports Car' was the first car marketed under that title.

MAYFAIR/*England 1907*
In 1906–07 Craig-Dorwald sold a range of Mayfairs of 6 hp (single), 10 hp (twin) and fours of 15 hp and 28 hp.

MAYTAG/*USA 1910–1915*
Successor to the Mason, the Maytag—'the only whirlwind on wheels'—was built in Waterloo, Iowa, using 24/28 hp flat-twin and 35/38 hp four-cylinder engines. Six models were available, priced from $1250–$1750. Fred Duesenberg supervised the building of this marque.

MAZDA/*Japan 1960 to date*
The Toyo Kogyo Cork company, founded in 1920, built its first motor vehicle, the Mazda three-wheel truck, ten years later. Car production had to wait until 1960, when the 360 Coupé appeared. In 1962 came the 600, followed in 1964 by the 800 Sedan. The 1000 came in 1965, the 1500 in 1966: but most significant was the 1967 announcement of the Wankel-engined R-100. That year, too, came the 1800, while a new rotary-engined model, the RX-2, appeared for 1970. By 1977 a developed version of the Wankel theme, with Mazda's REAPS emission control system by thermal reactor and air injection, was available alongside conventionally engined cars of up to 1800cc. Most powerful 1978 Mazda was the 135 bhp Cosmo AP Limited Coupé, with a maximum speed of 118mph in overdrive fifth gear. In 1979 came a new rotary-engined sports, the RX-7.

MB/*England 1919–1921*
The three-wheeler MB hailed from Bolton, Lancashire, and used a 10 hp vee-twin Precision engine. Later a four-cylinder Coventry-Climax power unit was fitted to a four-wheeled MB.

McCUE/*USA 1909–1911*
Built in Hartford, Connecticut, the sporty McCue car claimed '67 pounds weight to the horse power'. McCues could also be bought in kit form.

McCULLOUGH/*USA 1899–1900*
From Back Bay, Boston, Mass., the $600 McCullough was a simple motor buggy said to cost only '¼ cent a mile to run'. It had two 2¼ hp 229cc air-cooled horizontal engines.

McCURD/*England 1923–1927*
McCurd had built commercial vehicles since 1912 and their light car had a sv four-cylinder 12/20 hp engine. Only a few were made.

McCURDY/*USA 1922*
Only one McCurdy was built by the Hercules Corporation of Evansville, Indiana. The car was named after the president of the corporation. It featured a 127-inch wheelbase, a Continental engine and wire wheels.

1925 McFarlan SV Coach-Brougham

McFARLAN/*USA 1910–1928*
The McFarlan automobile was the product of a carriage works which had turned to motor car manufacture and, from the first cars made, the product became larger, more expensive and more prestigious. Several makes of engine were used in those first cars up to 1916 and a large Teetor-Hartley type was adopted in that year. Although many standard components went into the manufacture of the McFarlan, it was never regarded as an assembled car in the usual sense. In the autumn of 1920, the 'TV' or Twin-Valve series was introduced, with enormous six-cylinder engines of McFarlan design and manufacture, requiring 18 spark plugs. A complete line of open and closed models commanded prices approaching as high as $10,000 per car. A few fire engines and ambulances were also built on the TV chassis. The engines of this model were similar to those used on the Maxim fire apparatus, built in Middleboro, Mass., and the Maxim Company served as New England distributors for the McFarlan. In 1924, the company introduced the 'SV' or Single-Valve six, a considerably less expensive car. It was not a success and was withdrawn in 1926. However, the Eight-in-Line series, which more closely resembled the big six, but used a Lycoming eight-cylinder engine, was introduced in 1926 and, like the larger car, was built to the end of production. The 1928 models were sleeker and lower than their forebears but few were made.

Some 235 cars were built in McFarlan's best year; total production was about 2090.

McGILL/*USA 1920–1922*
The McGill would have been a strictly conventional and uninteresting assembled car of its time had it not been for its four-wheel drive. It was promoted spasmodically around Fort Worth, Texas, where it was assembled, and the one pilot model probably constituted the entire production. The touring car featured a six-cylinder Continental engine and was to have sold for $2385.

McINTYRE/*USA 1908–1914*
Successor to the Kiblinger (1907–08), this was a typical high-wheeler with two-cylinder engines of 12/14 hp and 16/18 hp and a four-cylinder 28/32 hp with shaft drive. This company also built the Imp cyclecar.

McKAY/*Canada 1910–1914*
Based on the US Penn (because the company's engineer had no engineering experience), McKays used 30 hp and 40 hp engines. Some 25 cars were built at Kentville, Nova Scotia, and a further 200-odd in a new factory at Amherst.

McKENZIE/*England 1914–1927*
An expensive four-cylinder light car built in Birmingham, the McKenzie was unusual for its day in having a four-speed gearbox.

McLACHLAN/*England 1899*
An omnivorous 2⅓ hp motor capable of running on 'petrol, paraffin or benzoline' powered this car, available with three or four wheels. 'If its performances are as satisfactory as its simplicity is marked', commented *The Autocar*, 'it should meet with great success'.

McLACHLAN/*Canada 1899–1901*
Canada's first production petrol car, a friction-drive model on Benz lines, built in Toronto.

1973 McLaren M12 GT

1922 McCurdy Six

McLAREN/*England 1969–1970*
It was always a dream of the late Bruce McLaren to build his own road car. That dream came true with the M6GT, only three of which were eventually built. The cars sported mid-mounted 5-litre Chevrolet engines and five-speed ZF gearboxes. Plans by Trojan for limited production were dropped following McLaren's tragic death.

McLAUGHLIN/*Canada 1908–1942*
One of Canada's most highly regarded carriage builders, McLaughlin of Oshawa, Ottawa, wanted to build an all-Canadian car to avoid the high tariff on imported cars, but the illness of their designer nullified this plan. Instead, they began production of cars based on the four-cylinder Buick, but better-finished. McLaughlin became a wholly-owned subsidiary of General Motors in 1918: their cars were by then based on Oakland and Chevrolet as well as Buick chassis. In 1923 the company was renamed McLaughlin-Buick: its products were marketed as plain 'Buick' in England, where they attracted less import duty than the US version.

MEADOWS/*England 1958–1959*
Henry Meadows Ltd. had long been established as engine manufacturers when they appeared, somewhat surprisingly, with the Frisky Sport at the 1958 Motor Show. Designed by Gordon Bedson in association with Raymond Flower and the Italian coachbuilders, Michelotti, the Frisky had a ladder chassis featuring rubber torsion unit front suspension and a solid axle with motorcycle suspension units at the rear. Power came from a twin-cylinder two-stroke engine driving the closely coupled rear wheels

by chain. Maximum speed was said to be 65 mph.

MEDIA/*England 1913–1915*
Forerunner of the Rhode, the Media (from its makers, Meade and Deakin) first appeared as an 8 hp JAP-engined cyclecar, but in 1914 two light fours, a 1093cc 8/10 hp and a 1645cc 10/12 hp, both selling at £150, appeared.

MEDICI/*England 1904–1906*
A 10 hp twin-cylinder Tony Huber engine powered this 180 guinea voiturette built by J. J. Leonard of 20 Long Acre, London.

MEDINGER/*England 1913*
A 1-litre two-stroke twin powered this sporting cyclecar, designed by Emile Médinger.

MEGY/*France 1901–1903*
With a primitive 'automatic transmission' and clutch and brake operated by moving the steering wheel up and down, the Mégy bore promise of exceptional mechanical derangements.

LE MEHARI/*France 1927*
M. Reynaud of Nouzonville, Ardennes, made this strange cyclecar with two 350cc two-stroke engines, each one driving a belt to one rear

MELEN/*England 1913–1914*
A twin-cylinder Alpha engine of 1104cc powered this Birmingham-built light car.

MENARD/*Canada 1908–1910*
A 16 hp high-wheeler designed by Byron Covert for 'Moses' Menard of Windsor, Ontario, Canada's largest wagon dealer.

MENDIP/*England 1913–1920*
Founded at the time of the Napoleonic Wars, the Cutler's Green Iron Works of Chewton Mendip, Somerset, made steam and petrol commercial vehicles, before building 1269cc four-cylinder light cars, mainly for local consumption. One example survives.

MENEGAULT-BASSET/*France 1907*
Shown at the 1907 Paris Salon, this was a 'simplified automobile with new organs transmitting directly and integrally the motive power to the driving wheels and suppressing the clutch, gearbox, differential and other organs'.

MENON/*Italy 1898–1902*
Treviso-built, the Menon was an early motor vehicle with a 3½ hp single-cylinder engine. Production was on a small scale.

Mercédès

MERCEDES/*Germany 1901–1926*
Emile Jellinek, Austro-Hungarian Consul at Nice and agent for Daimler cars, which he sold to his wealthy acquaintances, persuaded Wilhelm Maybach to design him lower, lighter and more powerful cars, which Jellinek named after his elder daughter, Mercédès. The first Mercedes, the 35 hp, had a 5913cc four-cylinder engine and combined the most modern design features — pressed steel chassis, honeycomb radiator and gate gear-change — in a whole which finally broke with horse-carriage traditions and set the pattern for quality car design in Europe and America. The name Mercedes, chosen to improve the marque's sales prospects in France, was soon adopted by Daimler for their private cars. Developments of the 35 hp followed, under the name Mercedes Simplex; most famous were the 18/22 hp, the 6780cc

40/45 hp and the mighty 9240cc 60 hp, with overhead inlet valves and 80 mph performance; one of these won the 1903 Gordon Bennett Cup Race in Ireland when the official team of 90 hp cars had been destroyed in a fire which gutted the Cannstatt factory. Maybach left Mercedes in 1907, his last designs for the company being sixes of 9480cc and 10,178cc; he was succeeded by Paul Daimler. The marque dominated the international racing scene before World War One; touring models of the period included a wide variety of cars from 1570cc to a 9575cc four, as well as

Knight-engined models, the 4055cc Mercedes surviving until 1923. Apart from this, the post-war range included the 7250cc ohc six, which Paul Daimler used for his supercharging experiments in 1921–22, and two small ohc fours of 1568cc and 2600cc. Ferdinand Porsche became chief designer in 1923, and shortly before the 1926 amalgamation between Mercedes and Benz, he introduced a blown ohc six-cylinder of 6240cc, known as the 24/100/140, from its rated/unblown/blown power outputs. Porsche also created the Type K, developing 110 bhp unblown, 160 bhp blown.

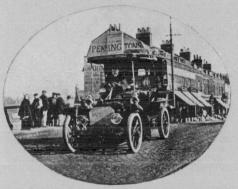

King Edward VII's 24/28hp Mercedes, c.1904

1907 120hp Mercedes of Baron Pierre de Caters

MERCEDES-BENZ/*Germany 1926 to date*
The newly amalgamated Mercedes-Benz group could draw on a wealth of technical experience, with Ferdinand Porsche heading a team which included Fritz Nibel and Nallinger (and later Rudolf Uhlenhaut and Max Sailer). First fruit of the merger was a 1988cc six-cylinder, followed by a 2968cc six, known as the Stuttgart and Mannheim respectively. World famous, though built in limited numbers, were Porsche's supercharged ohc six-cylinder sports cars, the 6250cc K, the 6789cc S and the 7020 SS, SSK and SSKL. Famous Mercedes of the 1930s were the 3444cc Mannheim six, the 4592cc Nürberg (enlarged to 4918cc in 1932), the 2560cc Stuttgart and the ostentatious straight-eight 'Grosser Mercedes, with a supercharged 7655cc ohv engine, built in its initial form from 1930 to 1937, and, with a more modern chassis and swing axles, from 1938. An 'economy class' Mercedes, the popular Type 170, with a 1692cc six-cylinder engine and independent front suspension, appeared in 1931, followed in 1933 by the 1962cc Type 200: but the rear-engined 'Heckmotor' 130H (a 1308cc four) of 1934–35 enjoyed no lasting success. Sporting Mercedes of the 1930s came with supercharged engines of 3796cc, 5018cc and 5401cc—all straight-eights. The last pre-war 540K developed 115 bhp unsupercharged, 180 bhp with the blower engaged. Backed by the German state propaganda machine, Mercedes racing cars (and Auto Union) won most of the major races of the 1934–39 era. Rebuilding after the war took some time, and the first post-war model, the 1697cc 170V sv four-cylinder, did not appear until 1947. Continuing a line begun before the war, Mercedes brought out a diesel-engined version of this car, the 170D. A breakaway from pre-war design came with the unitary-construction 180 series of 1954, but the classic Mercedes of that decade were without doubt the ohc six-cylinder 300S and 300 SL sports models of 2996cc of 1952 onwards, most famous in its original gull-wing coupé form. A sports-racing straight-eight derivative, the 300SLR, won many competition victories. The luxury Type 600, with an ohc V-8 of 6330cc, appeared in 1964. Since 1971, the six- and eight-cylinder S-class cars, with fuel-injection, have been flagships of the Mercedes fleet, though the diesel-engined models also sell well. The most powerful production Mercedes is the 6834cc ohc V-8 450 SEL model, with a 140 mph top speed. A milestone was passed at the beginning of 1979, when the cheapest Mercedes model passed the DM 20,000 price tag.

1930 Mercedes-Benz 36/220S supercharged

1956 Mercedes 300 SL coupé

1979 Mercedes 280SE

MERCER/*USA 1910–1925*
Succeeding the Roebling-Planche, the Mercer took its name from Mercer County, New Jersey, in which its factory at Trenton was situated. The first Mercers had T-head Beaver engines: a Speedster was the fastest 1910 model. Then chief engineer Finlay Robertson Porter produced a roadgoing adaptation of the Type 30-M racer—the immortal Type 35-R Raceabout, a stark two-seater designed to be 'safely and consistently' driven at over 70 mph. It was produced alongside more sedate Mercers, which initially had four speeds against the Raceabout's three. When Porter left in 1914 to build the FRP, he was succeeded by Erik H. Delling, who produced the F-head 22/70, which actually boasted a body with sides and a windscreen, as well as other effete items such as left-hand drive and central gearshift, and an optional hood. In 1918, Mercer became part of the Hare's Motors Group, with Locomobile and Crane-Simplex. Delling was replaced by A. C. Schultz, whose Series 4 and 5 Sportsters even had electric starters. A 5·5-litre ohv Rochester-engined development of these was the 'Car of Calibre's' sole offering in the last two years.

The L-head Mercer Raceabout, 1922

MERCER / USA 1931
The 1931 Mercer was an attempt to revive the earlier Mercer car and three of them were built and exhibited. A Continental straight-eight was used and the chassis was built by Elcar. The car was handsomely designed with a slight vee-radiator but the Mercer — and Elcar — failed shortly after the introduction of the new car.

MERCURY / USA 1897
An opposed-twin 4 hp *dos-à-dos* built on Benz lines, but with chain and pinion transmission.

MERCURY / England 1905
Also known as Ivanhoes, these 24 hp fours were built by a London Weigel agency.

c. 1922 Mercury 10hp on the Brooklands Test Hill

MERCURY / England 1914–1922
The original 12/14 Mercury from Twickenham had a 1944cc monobloc four-cylinder engine. A 10 hp of 1287cc with cantilever rear springing was shown at Olympia in 1919.

MERCURY / USA 1918–1920
A relatively light car, the Mercury carried a wheelbase of 114 inches and used a Weidely four-cylinder engine. This car had a door situated in the floor to give the driver ready access to the service brake mechanism, but otherwise differed little from the rank and file of assembled cars. Production was small. It was built in Hollis, New York.

MERCURY / USA 1920
Although full-page advertisements for this car were published in the automotive press, it is unlikely that any were built. Specifications called for a four-cylinder Rochester-Duesenberg engine. The four-passenger touring car of this Cleveland-based marque was priced at $6750.

MERCURY / USA 1922
Like its Cleveland counterpart of two years earlier, this car, reportedly made in Belfast, New York, was listed as being available, although it was probably never built. Theoretically available either as a four or a six, both engines were supposedly of Mercury's own manufacture. Price for the three-passenger coupé on the four-cylinder 128-inch wheelbase model was given at $4875, and $5625 for the similar body style on the 132-inch wheelbase six-cylinder chassis.

MERCURY / USA 1938 to date
Originally known as Ford-Mercury, this 3·9-litre V-8 model was intended to plug the gap between Ford and Lincoln. The 'Ford' was dropped for 1940 when a four-door convertible was introduced; it was not particularly popular. The 1942 models were restyled with a low, wide grille. Post-war, the marque image began a move upmarket with the 1949 models, which had a new 4179cc engine; automatic transmission became available in 1951, power-assisted steering in 1953. A year later came the first ohv V-8, a 4785cc unit later adopted by the Ford Thunderbird. From 1952 the Monterey name (initially seen on a vinyl-roofed hardtop of 1950) was applied to a new *de luxe* line. In 1954 came Lincoln-style ball-joint ifs and the Sun Valley, a transparent-roofed hardtop. Mercurys of the 1956–59 era were perhaps the most ornate cars of their day, notably the 1957 Turnpike Cruiser. Mercury's first car with other than a V-8 engine was the 1960 Comet compact, an enlarged Ford Falcon with the Ford 2360cc six. The new Ford short-stroke six was also available in the bigger Monterey, and three six-cylinder Mercurys were catalogued for 1962. A year later came the first V-8 Comet. Mercury gained a performance image in 1965 with the 320 bhp Comet Cyclone, and in 1967 came the Mustang-derived Cougar coupé, with a curious 'waterfall' grille. The 1969 Marquis Brougham shared the Lincoln Continental's bodyshell, though its engine displaced 7030cc to the Lincoln's 7538cc. By 1972, economy and rationalization were the keynotes; the latest Comet was little more than an upmarket Ford Maverick, while a small-car line was achieved by importing German Ford Capris. The 1972 range slotted carefully between Ford and Lincoln, the huge 7538cc Grand Marquis retaining Lincoln styling, while at the other end of the scale, the four-cylinder Bobcat paralleled Ford's 1540cc Pinto, and the Monarch was now a *de luxe* version of the Ford Granada. By 1977, the Marquis offered four-wheel disc brakes, but the Cougar name was now reserved for a humble Montego replacement. A 'brand new European-size compact' for 1978, the Zephyr, was just a rebadged Ford Fairmont. The 1979 line-up embraced the Capri, Zephyr, Monarch, Cougar and Marquis; the Grand Marquis offered tinted glass and 'coach lamps'.

MERCURY SIMPLEX / England 1904
A light car from the Anglo-French Motor Syndicate of Folkestone, Kent.

MEREDITH / England 1902
John Child Meredith, of Birmingham, who also built the Abingdon cars, offered a 10 hp two-cylinder, with 'a new system of gearing' as well as a 'Motor-car, smaller size'.

MERZ / USA 1914
A cyclops-headlamp cyclecar from Indianapolis, designed by racing driver C. C. Merz.

Film star Raymond Massey with his 1948 Mercury Sedan

1979 Mercury Marquis Brougham

MESSERSCHMITT/*Germany 1958–1961*
Aircraft-designer Willy Messerschmitt created the three-wheeled Messerschmitt bubble-car (and also the Fend-built FMR four-wheeled Tiger). A 493cc Sachs twin-cylinder two-stroke engine powered the three-wheeler.

MESSIER/*France 1926–1930*
Established in Montrouge, Seine, the Messier works made some cars chiefly remarkable for their pneumatic '*sans ressorts*' suspension. The engines were 1511cc and 1601cc four-cylinder CIME units. They also made a few cars with an American Lycoming straight-eight. The suspension quickly proved unreliable.

LE METAIS/*France 1904–1910*
Friction-driven light cars, with 8 hp single-cylinder engines, 10 hp two-cylinders or 12 hp four-cylinders, built at Levallois-Perret (Seine).

*c.*1913 car based on a 1908 Metallurgique

METALLURGIQUE/*Belgium 1898–1927*
Long established as locomotive and rolling-stock manufacturers, Métallurgique built their first prototypes in 1898 and opened a car factory at Marchienne-au-Pont in 1900. Chain drive gave way to shaft in 1902, and in 1903 ex-Mercedes designer Ernst Lehmann became chief designer. He produced a range of advanced design in 1905: these were Mercedes-like cars with pressed-steel chassis, high-tension ignition and the option of an electric lighting dynamo. A 10-litre 60/80 hp sports model was added in 1906, and in 1907 a handsome vee-radiator became a distinctive feature of the marque. The last two-cylinder Métallurgique appeared in 1908, and was replaced by a 12/14 hp four built in Germany by Bergmann. Big four-cylinder luxury cars like the 26/60 and the sporting 38/90 were Métallurgique's forte in Edwardian days: the 5-litre 26/60 continued after the war, with the addition of Adex four-wheel-brakes, along with the 15/20 hp and 20/40 hp, thanks to Métallurgique's skill in concealing their jigs and spares from the occupying German forces. The 15 hp was dropped in 1922, and succeeded by a new 1882cc 12 hp with pushrod ohv, designed by Paul Bastien. Impéria-Excelsior took over in 1929 and killed off Métallurgique: Bastien joined Stutz in America.

METEOR/*England 1903–1904*
A four-cylinder 12 hp tonneau built in Feltham, Middlesex, by the makers of the P & G. A Mutel engine was used on the 24 hp Meteor, while the 12 hp had a Blake twin-cylinder power unit.

METEOR/*USA 1908–1910*
'Three years preliminary testing' was said to have gone into this 50 hp four from Bettendorf, Iowa. 'All exposed woodwork is of Circassian walnut', boasted its makers.

METEOR/*USA 1914–1930*
Manufactured in Piqua, Ohio, Meteor roadsters and touring cars with both Model and Continental engines were built until 1916, in which year a V-12 Weidely engine was announced as an option (but probably never used). In 1916, however, the company started concentrating on the ambulance and funeral car market, its private car output being restricted to large sedans and limousines for funeral use as well as invalid cars. These were ostensibly routine sedans, but with the door pillars removed on one side to admit wheelchairs. Until 1930, passenger cars were built to special order. The company still exists.

METEOR/*USA 1919–1922*
The Meteor was an expensive car built in limited numbers at Philadelphia. Using a four-cylinder Rochester-Duesenberg engine, it had a 129-inch wheelbase, wire wheels and a vee-radiator copied closely from that of Austro-Daimler. An all-open line was augmented in 1922 with a sedan. Price of the four-passenger touring model was $5500.

1921 Philadelphia-built Meteor

METEOR/*Canada 1949 to date*
Built in Canada and retailed by Lincoln/Mercury dealers, the Meteor was Ford's attempt to gain a Canadian identity. Depending on corporate whim, this car was either a fullsize US Ford with distinctive grille and trim, or a Mercury with different trim and Ford interior. Two series were available in 1979, favouring the Mercury: the Rideau 500 and Montcalm, each with three models and powered by a 5752cc V-8 engine.

METEORITE/*England 1913–1924*
The Meteorite was one of the better pre-World War One light cars. It had a square-cut radiator and a 1244cc four-cylinder engine. The principal post-Armistice offering was a 1498cc four, though a 13·8 hp six appeared towards the end of production.

METROPOL/*USA 1913–1914*
A long-stroke 7329cc sporting car from Port Jefferson, LI.

METROPOLITAN/*USA 1922–1923*
A small-production car built in Kansas City, Missouri, Metropolitan's first cars featured a Continental six-cylinder engine, abandoned in favour of a smaller four of Metropolitan's own design. An eight was also announced, but probably failed to get into production.

METRO-TYLER/*England 1921–1923*
A 5/6 hp 698cc cyclecar from a London motorcycle manufacturer.

METZ/*USA 1908–1922*
Charles Metz devised the 'Metz Plan' to pay off the debts of the Waltham Company, which he had just acquired. Under this plan, the Metz car was sold for home assembly in 14 separate packages of $25–$27 each. The first packages were sold before the last were even designed, attracting complaints from some home assemblers who outstripped Metz's speed of manufacture. By the autumn of 1909, however, the first complete Metz cars were finished. They were simple runabouts with twin-cylinder 894cc air-cooled engines and friction drive. Only one model—a Roadster—was offered between 1909 and 1913. From 1910, the company offered complete cars. In 1911, a four-cylinder 22 hp engine based on the Model S Ford unit was introduced, enlarged to 25 hp in 1915. In 1919 an entirely new model, the 4786cc Master 6, with a conventional transmission, appeared, priced at $1495. In 1922, the marque was renamed Waltham.

MEYER/*France 1913*
A GN-like cyclecar built in Reims, Marne.

MEYER/*USA 1919–1920*
Built only to special order in touring car and truck form, the Meyer featured an airless tyre mounted on a cushion hub and a transmission in which the gears revolved only when engaged. The passenger car (only a few were made) used a six-cylinder engine—reportedly a Weidely—featured disc wheels and a 132-inch wheelbase. Price of the touring car was $6500.

1921 Meteorite 15hp tourer

MEYREL/*Germany 1908–1914*
The Meyrel brothers of Colmar were closely connected with La Buire. They built big, roomy cars; the 5340cc six-cylinder had a nine-seater body. The smaller 20 hp four-cylinder of 5192cc had 'only' seven seats. Another Meyrel was a 45 hp six-cylinder with an open torpedo body. Production of these cars was small.

MG/*England 1923 to date*

Few marque histories have been as blurred and misquoted as has the MG one. Nobody can state with certainty when the first MGs were produced, though the honour should probably fall to the six Raworth-bodied, two-seater sports cars the founder, Cecil Kimber, commissioned to be built on Morris-Cowley chassis in 1923. This was while Kimber was still Manager of Morris Garages – from where the MG name originated. The Hotchkiss-engined car so often and erroneously referred to as 'Number One' did not, in fact, appear for another two years, and was more accurately Kimber's first attempt at building a car solely for competition. The first model to be built in any numbers (about 400) was the 14/28 Super Sport, which came with either two or four seats and open or closed bodies. From then until 1952, when the Nuffield Group of which MG was a part amalgamated with the Austin Motor Company to form BMC, the prolific little firm at Abingdon, Berks., produced countless sports and saloon cars for both road and track, breaking record upon record on the way. Though they now bear the Leyland stamp, the 1979 MGBs and Midgets nevertheless owe much to their ancestry, of which the famous M, P and T Type Midgets and the larger K and N Type Magnettes are just a part. Today all MGs are sought after, not least the early racers with histories and the later classics such as the pretty TF and the fast, Twin-Cam MGA.

1955 MGA sports two-seater

1948 MG TC Midget two-seater

1933 MG Magnette saloon with novel sunshine roof

MGR/*France 1907*

Cars built by P. Morin et Cie of Suresnes (Seine). One competed in the 1907 Criterium de France.

MIARI E GIUSTI/*Italy 1896*

Builders of the Bernardi three-wheeler, a 624cc single-cylinder which was probably Italy's first petrol car.

MICHEL IRAT/*France 1929–1930*

These were Chaigneau-Brasier cars with a sv four-cylinder 1086cc engine sold under his own name by the son of Georges Irat.

MICHEL-UN/*France 1926*

These were 2120cc Donnet-Zedel-engined cars made in Neuilly, Seine, with gears controlled by a preselector on the steering wheel.

MICHIGAN/*USA 1908–1914*

W. H. Cameron, who claimed to have built over 100,000 cars of various marques by 1913, was the moving spirit behind the Michigan, with coachwork designed by John A. Campbell, 'whose body designs have been chosen by Kings'. Over 5000 Michigans had been built by the end of 1912, when the $1585 Michigan 40 was introduced; it had adjustable controls, electric lighting and starting and '14-inch deep Turkish cushions'.

MICRON/*France 1925–1930*

M. Jany of Toulouse made a lot of these small fwd 350cc and 500cc cyclecars, with water-cooled two-stroke engines. They were sometimes sold under the name 'Motocar'.

MICRON/*England 1968*

Following Marcos principles, the one-off Micron GT featured a plywood chassis bonded to a glass-fibre body, to which Mini subframes were attached. It featured gull-wing doors.

1975 'Golden Anniversary' MGB GT

MIDDLEBY/*USA 1908–1913*
An air-cooled four-cylinder 3295cc engine powered this $850 runabout built in the former Duryea factory at Reading, Pa.

MIDLAND/*USA 1908–1913*
'Unusual cars at common prices', Midlands were big 40 hp and 50 hp cars built in Moline, Ill.

1914 Miele 2292cc Landaulet

MIELE/*Germany 1912–1914*
Still a famous producer of washing-machines, Miele built excellent cars with sv 1565cc and 2292cc four-cylinder engines, designed by Professor Klemm, who became a famous aircraft designer and manufacturer after World War One.

MIER/*USA 1908–1909*
A 12 hp buggy from Ligonier, Illinois.

MIESSE/*Belgium 1898–1926*
Jules Miesse of Brussels built his first experimental steam car on Serpollet lines in 1896 and began production two years later. By 1902, the three-cylinder Miesse steamer was also being built under licence in Belgium, as the Turner-Miesse in 6 hp and 10 hp forms: a 20 hp followed next year. All had flash boilers, transverse engines and armoured wood chassis. Miesse began experiments with petrol cars in 1900, and abandoned steam entirely in 1907 when four-cylinder 24 hp and 35 hp monobloc six petrol cars were listed. However, Turner-Miesse steamers continued to be built until 1913. A valveless 20 hp, combining piston and slide-valves, appeared in 1912–13, as well as a worm-drive 15/18 hp. Post-war, an ohc 1858cc four was the standard offering, though there was also an ohc 3717cc straight-eight. In 1923–24, Miesse assembled the prototype Dunamis (Greek for 'power') sv straight-eight.

1902 Miesse steam car

MIEUSSET/*France 1903–1914*
Founded as fire pump manufacturers in 1867, Mieusset of Lyon built cars, trucks and motorboats, starting with a one-cylinder 8 hp: by 1905, 10 hp twin and fours of 16, 25, 40 and 60 hp were available, all of remarkably clean and robust construction. These continued until 1914.

MIGNONETTE/*France 1900*
Built by Wehrlé & Godard-Demarest of Neuilly (Seine), this 3 hp voiturette had aluminium coachwork and could be started from the driver's seat.

MIGNONETTE LUAP/*France 1898–1900*
A Bordeaux-built voiturette constructed by Paul Legendre, with a rear-mounted De Dion engine. The steering lever could be fixed in the centre with only the driver aboard, or moved to the side when a passenger was carried.

1898 Mignonette Luap

MIKROMOBIL/*Germany 1921–1924*
The Schorch-designed Mikromobil was a small car with a 7/9 hp air-cooled vee-twin engine. The last version had an 18 hp four.

MILANO/*Italy 1906–1907*
An unorthodox car with a 28 hp four.

MILBURN ELECTRIC/*USA 1914–1922*
One of the more prominent electric automobiles built in the USA, the Milburn was especially noted for its smooth lines and custom-type craftsmanship. Smaller and more delicate in appearance than such contemporary electrics as Detroit or Rauch & Lang, Milburns were popular and sold well. In 1919, a formal design, similar in appearance to conventional gasoline cars, was introduced. Between 7000 and 8000 cars were built: Milburn went out of business after a disastrous fire destroyed its Toledo, Ohio, factory.

MILDE ET MONDOS, MILDE
France 1898–1909
MM. Mildé and Mondos built a range of electric vehicles from light tricycles and a clumsy 'Mylord' victoria to omnibuses. From 1904, a range of Mildé petrol-electrics was built under the supervision of Fréderic Gaillardet, formerly of Doctoresse and Diamant, and latterly these were known as Mildé-Gaillardets. The 1908 range was a 12 hp twin and a 22 hp four.

MILLER/*USA 1915–1932*
Best known for his racing cars (many with front-wheel drive) and ohc racing engines, which he built from 1915, Harry Miller of Los Angeles also produced a couple of road cars in 1930–32, including a 400 bhp speedster with a dohc 5096cc V-16 power unit and four-wheel drive, at a reputed cost of $35,000.

MILLER-QUINCY/*USA 1922–1924*
The Miller-Quincy was a funeral car, a few units of which were built in sedan and limousine form. A Continental six served as motive power, wheels were disc and wheelbase was 130 inches. Price of the seven-passenger sedan was $2780.

MILLOT/*France 1901–1902*
Better known as makers of mobile saw-benches (some now restored as 'veteran cars'), Millot of Gray (Haute-Saône) also built 6/8 hp twin-cylinder cars and four-cylinders of 8 hp and 12 hp.

MILLOT/*Switzerland 1906–1907*
Four models were offered by this Zurich company. Two had shaft drive, a 25/30 cv four and a 35/50 cv six—and two were chain driven—a 40/50 cv four and a 70/80 cv six. Prices ranged from Sw Fr 15,000–Sw Fr 30,000.

MILNES/*England/Germany 1900–1902*
Sometimes known as 'CPC' ('Cannstatt-Paris-Coventry'), these 8 hp, 12 hp, 16 hp and 20 hp cars were actually built by the Marienfelde Daimler factory and bodied by tram manufacturers G. F. Milnes of Wellington, Shropshire. Milnes subsequently sold Cannstatt-Daimlers.

MILTON/*Scotland 1920–1921*
The friction-drive Milton was built in Edinburgh and engines were by Alpha or Decolange, of 9 hp and 10 hp respectively.

MILWAUKEE/*USA 1899–1902*
The 1899 Milwaukee was a typical American steam buggy, which had a twin-cylinder 6/7 hp 'marine type engine'. The company also supplied components for building steam cars. Their final offering was a 26 hp 'Racing and Touring Car' with a semi-flash boiler.

MINERVA/*Belgium 1904–1939*
Cycle maker Sylvain de Jong of Antwerp built an experimental car before the turn of the century: a Panhard-like prototype appeared in 1902, full-scale production starting two years later, with a range of two-, three- and four-cylinder cars of 1·6, 2·4 and 3·2 litres. There was also a basic single-cylinder model, the 636cc Minervette. Up to 1910, Minerva concentrated on big four-cylinders, including models of 3·8 and 5·9 litres: then they became the first marque in mainland Europe to adopt the Knight sleeve-valve engine, announcing a 38 hp dual-ignition 6·3-litre four (King Albert was an early patron),

1898 Mildé et Mondos 4cv Mylord electric

1924 30hp Minerva All-Weather Coupé

followed shortly by models of 2·3 and 4·25 litres. By the outbreak of World War One, the 38 hp had grown to 7·4 litres; there was also a 2·3-litre Fourteen. The first post-war model was the 1919 NN 20 hp four, joined in 1921 by a 5·3-litre 30 hp six, which acquired four-wheel brakes in 1923. The TT of 1923 had a sleeve-valve engine of under 2 litres and central gear-change. The 30 hp was succeeded by the Type AK 32/34 hp, with a proven sporting image, joined in 1930 by the Type AL straight-eight of 6616cc; but the 1930s saw a gradual decline into oblivion for 'the Goddess of Automobiles', which merged with Impéria in 1936.

LA MINERVE / *France 1899–1906*
'The transmission made by two chains enables any flexion of the frame without producing the unpleasant creaking of the different parts', ran a contemporary description of this 3 cv voiturette from Billancourt (Seine).

MINI-JEM / *England 1966–1975*
Like Mini-Marcos, the Mini-Jem was a direct development of test pilot Dizzy Addicott's Dart—a much modified racing Mini-van. Eventually known by the nickname of its original manufacturer, Jeremy Delmar-Morgan, the Jem was a very basic kit designed to accept Mini mechanicals—even the doors and glass had to be fitted by the customer. A change of management produced a far better MkII version, but after two further close calls, the design finally met its end after only 200 or so had been built.

MINIMUS / *Germany 1921–1924*
The Minimus was a small car available first with a vee-twin and later with a four-cylinder motor.

MINISPRINT / *England 1965–1966*
The Minisprint project, the brainchild of Dorset chemist Geoff Thomas, was masterminded by Neville Trickett and consisted of removing the bodies of unsuspecting Minis, cutting off 1½ inches from above and below the waistline, increasing the rake of both front and rear screens and modifying the nose to bring the whole car back into proportion. Over 100 Minisprints were built, most of which were exported.

MINISSIMA / *England 1973*
One of several design studies produced by the talented William Towns over recent years, the Minissima city car was first seen on the BLMC stand at the 1973 London Motor Show and featured a space-frame clothed in scanty glass-fibre bodywork.

MINOR / *Czechoslovakia 1945–1952*
Designed in 1937 at the Jawa works by Rudolf Vykoukal, the 615cc Minor (with a twin-cylinder two-stroke engine) was built after 1945 at the former Walter car works at Jinonice, near Prague. A sports version of this fwd car, with the engine enlarged to 745cc, was second in the 'Index of Performance' in the 1949 Le Mans. The car was also known as Aero-Minor.

MINOR-MEL / *England? 1910*
A 12/16 hp car (probably imported) sold by the Motor Exchange Limited, London.

MITCHELL / *USA 1903–1923*
Old-established carriage builders from Racine, Wisconsin, Mitchell began with a 7 hp runabout whose front-mounted 1419cc engine was air-cooled by a rotary blower. A four-cylinder model of similar design appear in 1904, and the option of air- or water-cooling was offered a year later. By 1912, Mitchell ordered four models of conventional design—fours of 3982cc and 4649cc, and sixes of 5973cc and 6974cc—which were superseded the following year by a new range designed by the Frenchman René Petard. These had very long strokes and consisted of 'Little Sixes' with the option of 152mm or 180mm stroke engines (5579cc or 6509cc) and a 9764cc 'Big Six'. A brief-lived V-8 was built in 1915–16, and from then on Mitchell sold monobloc sixes of conventional design. The 1920 model had a mildly raked radiator, which earned it the nickname 'the Drunken Mitchell'. Customer reaction, despite a reversion to vertical coolers, was such that Mitchell folded in 1923, and Nash bought the factory.

MITCHELL / *England 1906–1907*
Apparently unconnected with the American marque, this 'ideal car for town work' was a 14/20 hp bonnetless landaulette.

1906 'London Made' Mitchell 14/20hp Bonnetless Landaulette

MITSUBISHI / *Japan 1917, 1959 to date*
In 1917 Mitsubishi built a series of some 20 Fiat-based cars: but this major engineering corporation did not return to private car manufacture until 1959, when the twin cylinder ohv Mitsubishi 500 appeared. The first Mitsubishi Colt appeared in 1962: by 1966 the Colt range consisted of a three-cylinder two-stroke and pushrod fours of 1000cc and 1500cc. Also in 1962, the top-of-the-range Debonair six appeared. In 1966, a 356cc model, the Minica, was launched. In 1970, the ohc Colt Galant hard-top

and GTO appeared, joined a year later by the Galant Coupé and the 360cc ohc Minica Skipper. Developments of these models were the company's mainstay during the 1970s, along with the Lancer and Celeste ranges and the three- and five-door 1400 GLX with an eight-speed gearbox. In 1971, Mitsubishi entered into an agreement with Chrysler, whereby the US corporation took 35 per cent of a new joint company: Mitsubishi cars were sold in the USA and Britain as 'Colts'.

MJ / *France 1919–1920*
This short-lived marque from Neuilly, Seine, offered in 1920 two cars, a 12 hp twin-cylinder of 747cc and a four-cylinder 14 hp of 1368cc.

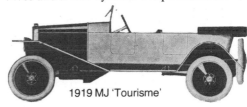

1919 MJ 'Tourisme'

MMC / *England 1897–1908*
The Motor Manufacturing Company was the 'flagship' company of H. J. Lawson's empire, with the most important concentration of production in his Coventry 'Motor Mills'. Daimler, in an adjoining building, made engines and chassis on the 'English Panhard' system, MMC making the bodies at first. George Iden became chief engineer in 1898, and rear-engined cars designed by him such as the horizontal-twin 10 hp Hampton Char-a-Banc and 4½ hp Princess appeared the following year. MMC also made tricycles and quadricycles with British De Dion engines of 1¾ hp and 2¼ hp. Production of front-engined cars, mostly on Panhard lines, survived the collapse of Lawson's operation: ousted from the Motor Mills by Daimler in 1905, MMC moved to Parkside, Coventry. A final move to Clapham, London, in 1907 produced only prototypes of a 35/45 hp six.

1902 MMC 12hp Rally Coupé

MOBILE / *USA 1899–1903*
John Brisben Walker broke away from Loco-mobile and built steam cars of identical design in a factory at Philipse-Manor-on-the-Hudson, New York.

MOBILE / *England 1903–1908*
The 1903 Birmingham-built Mobile was a 6 hp two-seater with De Dion single-cylinder power unit. Two years later a three car range was offered: a 20/22 hp four with Aster engine, a twin-cylinder Aster-engined 12/14 hp and an 8/10 hp, 'one of which has been driven from Birmingham to London on top speed'.

MODEL/*USA 1903–1907*
The Model, from Peru, Indiana, had a tilting body for easy access to its underfloor 24 hp engine. By removing the tonneau, it could be converted into a 'runabout with style' with a flat luggage deck. For 1908, the Model was known as the Star. In 1911, this company built three four-cylinder cars called 'Izzers' (not 'was-ers')!

MODEL A/*USA 1979 to date*
Announced in mid-1979, this was an ambitious plan to build 10,000 Pinto-engined replica 1928 Model A Fords in 1978–80, followed by replica 1955 Ford Thunderbirds.

MOHLER & DEGREES
Mexico/USA 1898–c1901
A box-like 2 hp car mounted on bicycle wheels, this was Mexico's first motor car (built by the country's first cycle manufacturers). By June 1899, Mohler was selling engines in Mechanicsburg, Pa., and in 1901 the partners were building engines and carriages at Astoria, LI.

MOHS/*USA 1967 to date*
Bruce Baldwin Mohs designed the Mohs Ostentatienne Opera Sedan manufactured by his company, Mohs Seaplane Corp., Madison, Wisconsin. It was an extraordinary vehicle with many safety features in addition to the Federal safety requirements: cantilever roof beams combined with roll bars, no side doors (entrance to the four-passenger car was from the rear) allowed full-length arm rests which concealed elbow-height chassis rails for side collision protection. Bucket seats swung laterally on turns (which kept passenger weight in the seats) and the seats also pivoted horizontally in the event of a head-on crash. An extensive range of standard equipment included a refrigerator, 24-carat gold inlay walnut grain dash, velvet upholstery and Holley carburettor conversion unit for butane operation. The automatic transmission was water-cooled and the custom-made tyres, filled with nitrogen, had a claimed life of 100,000 miles. Standard power came from a 4982cc V-8 engine, but a 8997cc International Harvester V-8 with five-speed manual box was optional. The Ostentatienne had an overall length of 246 inches and cost $19,600 or $25,000 according to engine size. Mohs introduced another unique vehicle with many advanced ideas in 1971. This eight-passenger dual cowl metal-topped convertible, named the Safari-Kar, had rear seats which converted into a bed! Five inches shorter than the Ostentatienne, it cost $12,000.

MOLINE/*USA 1904–1919*
From East Moline, Illinois, the Moline Automobile Company's early products included a 12 hp flat-twin selling at $1000 and a $1600 four-cylinder. By 1912 they were offering a 25 hp pair-cast four equipped with a self-starter, the Dreadnought '35', still moderately priced at $1700. Their ultimate offering was the four-cylinder 22·5 hp Moline-Knight sleeve-valve model.

MOLKAMP/*Germany 1923–1926*
A coachbuilder who took up manufacture of ohc 2650cc six-cylinder cars in the former Primus factory, Mölkamp also built an ohc 1420cc four-cylinder under Ceirano licence.

MOLL/*Germany 1921–1925*
Moll of Chemnitz produced 1595cc and 1960cc four-cylinder cars with Siemens & Halske engines, as well as a simple cyclecar, the 1924 Mollmobil with DKW two-stroke engines. Designed by Görke, the high, narrow Mollmobil had first a 164cc engine, later a 173cc power unit.

MONARCH/*USA 1905–1909*
A high-wheeled motor buggy with a 3·2-litre four-cylinder engine and epicyclic transmission.

MONARCH/*England 1912–1914*
An 8 hp cyclecar built by R. Walker & Sons of Tyseley, Birmingham, with air- or water-cooled Precision engines.

MONARCH/*USA 1914–1917*
Bobby Hupp was behind this assembled car, which used monobloc four- and six-cylinder Continental engines of 3153cc and 4730cc. Electric lighting and starting were standard. A Herschell-Spillman V-8 was added for 1915.

MONARCH/*England 1925–1928*
A 13·9 hp Meadows four powered this rare assembled saloon from Birmingham.

MONARCH/*Canada 1948–1961*
A Canadian Ford product based on the Mercury. It was discontinued for 1958 when the Edsel was introduced, returning in 1959 after the Edsel flopped. As standard Fords became more luxurious, Monarch production ceased.

MONDEX-MAGIC/*USA 1914*
This New York marque was powered by licence-built Fischer slide-valve sixes of 4·2 and 7 litres. Production was doubtless even more limited than its Swiss prototype.

MONET-GOYON/*France 1921–1926*
This well-known motorcycle manufacturer from Mâcon, Saône-et-Loire, made some awful cyclecars: the Automouche was a three-wheeler powered by a fourth wheel on which an engine was mounted; this power unit was also adapt-

1924 Mollmobil cyclecar

able to pushbikes. The 'Voiturette' Monet was a three-wheeler with an engine mounted on the front wheel. The true Monet-Goyon cyclecar was a four-wheeler with a 350cc Villiers engine: the company also made other three-wheelers with Mag engines of 750cc and 350cc Villiers units.

MONICA/*England/France 1969–1976*
A highly desirable and fully developed car that never quite went into full-scale production. A prestige four/five-seater with elegant steel body fixed to a strong independent chassis, the Monica was eventually powered by a 5·6-litre Chrysler V-8. Top speed was over 140 mph and the 0–60 mph time was 7·7 secs. Some 30–35 examples were made, 25 of them prototypes. When the limited French production run closed, there was talk of Panther being involved— much of the development had occurrred in England. Sadly, nothing materialized.

MONITOR/*USA 1915–1922*
The Cummins-Monitro Co. of Columbus, Ohio, marketed this low-priced ($795–$895) range, with 4–30 and 6–40 power units and '350 parts less than in the average car'.

MONITOR/*France 1921*
A cyclecar made in Suresnes, Seine, with a vee-twin side-valve 748cc engine and offered in single-seater as well as two-seater form.

MONNARD/*France 1899*
A light four-seater electric dog-cart.

MONOCAR/*France 1936–1939*
This small single-seater three-wheeler, powered by a 175cc two-stroke engine, was made in Paris.

1973 Monica saloon

MONOTRACE/*France 1925–1927*
This strange vehicle — half way between motorcycle and car — was built by the Société Française du Morgan Monotrace. It had a single-cylinder 510cc water-cooled engine. Small wheels held up the 'car' when it was at rest.

MONROE/*USA 1914–1924*
A four-cylinder 1969cc engine, in unit with the gearbox, initially powered this roadster, built until 1916 in Flint, thereafter in Pontiac. In 1917 a sedan was introduced: at $1850, it cost virtually twice as much as the roadster. The marque was acquired by Stratton in 1923, and both were then taken over by Premier.

MONTEVERDI/*Switzerland 1967 to date*
Basle garage owner Peter Monteverdi began production of his Chrysler V-8 engined 375S luxury model (and the sporting 400SS version) in 1967, joined in 1968 by the long wheelbase 375L. In 1971 the mid-engined Hai ('Shark') 450SS was unveiled: limited production of 375 and Hai-based models continues.

MONTIER & GILLET/*France 1897*
A lumpish tiller-steered steam waggonette with a boiler of curious design.

MONTIER SPECIALE/*France 1919–1935*
The Montier family, father and sons, made some good specials in Levallois using Ford spares and engines. They often raced their cars.

1924 publicity for the Montier Special

MOON/*USA 1905–1931*
Louis P. Mooers, late of Peerless, designed the first cars offered by Scots-born Joseph W. Moon, who ran a buggy factory in St Louis. The Model A Moon had a 30/35 hp Rutenber four-cylinder engine: by 1912 two four-cylinder models, of 5·2 and 5·6 litres, were made, joined the next year by a six. Continental sixes of 3·6 and 5 litres were offered in 1916, and the marque soon acquired an imitation Rolls-Royce radiator. The 1922 Moons had side-valves instead of ohv, and quarter-elliptic front springs, three-quarter elliptics at the rear. Four-wheel Lockheed hydraulic band brakes were specified in 1924, as were detachable disc wheels with detachable rims. In 1928, Moon offered a 4·4-litre straight-eight inherited from its defunct alter ego, Diana: this became the Windsor in 1929, in which year Moon became embroiled with the New Era Motors group. Moon built a few Ruxtons before finally waning in 1931.

MOORE/*USA 1906–1908*
The 'ball-bearing car' was a 40 hp four from New York with three spark plugs per cylinder — 'safe, speedy, reliable'.

MOORE/*USA 1916–1921*
Approximately 600 Moores were manufactured during the company's six-year existence. Moore automobiles were four-cylinder cars with a G. B. & S. engine and a price tag ranging from $550 in its earlier days to nearly $1200 in its final year of production.

1919 Moore

MOOSE JAW STANDARD/*Canada 1917*
Five local residents bought enough parts from the USA to build 25 Continental-engined luxury cars, but gave up after they each had a car, as they could not find buyers for the rest.

1930 Montier saloon based on the Model A Ford

MORA/*USA 1906–1910*
'The ideal gentleman's car', the Mora was built first in Rochester, NY, then in Newark, NY. A 24 hp roadster was listed initially, joined for 1908 by a 42/50 hp six, available as a tourer or as a 'racytype' built in a 'limited edition' of 100. In 1907 a 25 hp Mora took the 'World's Sealed Bonnet Record', covering over 10,000 miles.

MORELAND/*USA 1920–1924*
A Moreland passenger car was announced in November, 1919, by the Moreland Motor Truck Co., of Los Angeles, California, who said

1920 Moon 23.6hp tourer

operations would begin shortly at Burbank. Whether prototypes were ever made is not known. A 'DeLuxe' sedan was announced in 1924, but plans failed to materialize. The company ceased production of trucks in 1941.

MOREL & GERARD/*France 1897*
A quadricycle of basic design — virtually two bicycles linked by parallel cross-members carrying a single-cylinder engine.

MORENY/*France 1907–1908*
A manufacturer of cars and chassis from Montmartre, in Paris: the 14/18 hp Moreny had a four-cylinder engine of 2413cc.

MORETTE/*England 1903–1905*
B. E. Dickinson of Birmingham built this bathchair-like three-wheeler with 2½ hp or 4 hp engine driving the front wheel by friction roller.

MORETTI/*Italy 1945 to date*
Moretti first produced motorcycles, but soon concentrated on exclusive small cars with 350cc, 596cc and 746cc two- and four-cylinder engines with single- or twin-overhead camshafts and special bodywork. There were also Moretti cars with Fiat and Fiat-Abarth parts and some very 'hot' racing versions. A reorganization in 1962 led to a concentration of special bodywork and prototypes. Moretti's current models are Fiat-based and include the 126 'Minimaxi' and the 127 'Midimaxi' with 903cc and 1049cc engines and multipurpose bodywork.

MORGAN/*England 1904–1905*
Better known as coachbuilders, Morgan offered an 8 hp Electric Motor Phaeton in 1904. In 1905 Morgan announced the 24hp 'all-British' chassis, powered by a Mutel engine. At a chassis price of £750 (with formal coachwork adding another £250) it proved too costly, and only a handful was built before Morgan became agents for the German Adler and abandoned car production altogether.

MORGAN/*England 1910 to date*
The prototype Morgan three-wheeler was built in 1908–09 in the school workshops at Malvern College. H. F. S. Morgan, with the help of Mr. Stephenson-Peach, the engineering master, produced a design that in layout remained in production until 1950, while the independent front suspension is, in essence, still in use on current models. Production started in 1910, the car having a tubular chassis frame and sliding-pillar front suspension. Power was provided by an 1100cc air-cooled vee-twin JAP engine, which lived out in the open at the front of the car. Transmission was via dog clutches and chain drive. The successful formula was maintained after World War One with vee-twin power units — mainly by JAP or Blackburne — which were either air- or water-cooled. A refinement of the theme came in 1933 with the option of a four-cylinder Ford 8 engine. The 4/4, the first four-wheeled Morgan, appeared in 1936 with an 1122cc overhead inlet/side exhaust Coventry-Climax four. The 1·3-litre ohv Standard engine had been introduced just prior to the war and this remained until 1950, when the 2088cc wet-liner Standard Vanguard engine was

fitted, though the Plus Four of 1955 used the livelier TR engine. A year later the Series 2 4/4 appeared, using the well-proven sv 1172cc Ford engine which had powered the three-wheelers until their demise. This was followed by Dagenham's ohv 105E engine; the later Series V 4/4 used the 1498cc Ford power unit and the current model is still Ford-powered. By contrast, the Plus Four, after a succession of TR engines, ceased production in 1969. It was that year which saw the appearance of the Plus Eight, fitted with the 3½-litre V-8 developed by Rover, this being the other current model.

MORISSE / *France 1898–1914*

The first Morisse, from Etampes (Seine-et-Oise), was a light 2½ hp 'petite voiture' with belt front-wheel drive and rear-wheel steering; by 1904 a 9 hp similar to the contemporary Renault was available. Proprietary engines by De Dion, Tony Huber and Fossier were used. By 1914, monobloc fours of 9, 10, 14 and 16 hp were listed, sometimes known as SEM.

*c.*1913 Morisse two-seater

EL MOROCCO / *USA 1956–1957*

Reuben Allender offered a distinctive car at a reasonable price by converting 1956–57 Chevrolet Bel-Air hardtops and convertibles (powered by 4638cc V-8 engines) into a facsimile of Cadillac's limited edition Eldorado Brougham. Between 30 and 40 examples were built.

H. F. S. Morgan in a *c.*1920 Morgan Runabout

1960s Morgan Four Plus Four

MORRIS / *England 1913 to date*

Oxford cycle and motor agent William Morris sold his first car, the two-seater Morris-Oxford, in 1913. Costing £180, it was powered by a 1017cc engine by White and Poppe, with the gearbox in unit. Rear axle was by E. G. Wrigley, wheels by Sankey and bodywork by Raworth of Oxford. It was, in effect, an assembled job, but a good one. The Oxford was joined in 1915 by the 1496cc engined Cowley with engine/gearbox by the Continental Motors Company of Detroit, USA. Production began again in earnest after World War One with copies of the US engine being manufactured by Hotchkiss of Coventry. One major difference between the two engines was that the Coventry-built model had a cork clutch that ran in oil, one of the few contributions Morris made to detailed engine design! The 'Bullnose' Oxfords and the more austere Cowleys were destined to become the best-selling British cars of the decade. In 1921 Morris made a sensational series of price cuts and never

looked back. In 1923 an 1802cc engine was offered as an option in the Oxford, this being standardized from 1924. Both models remained in production until 1926, though the peak production year was 1925 when 54,151 cars were built, representing 41 per cent of new car production in Britain. The 1927 season saw the appearance of the less inspiring 'Flatnose' models, though the 2½-litre Empire model failed to woo the export market for which it had been designed.

1917 Morris-Cowley two-seater

Although a few sixes had been made earlier, it was not until 1928 that Morris adopted this engine configuration in a big way with an ohc 2½-litre car, a reminder that Wolseley, who were firm adherents to this engine layout, had been purchased the previous year. Morris's entry into the small-car market came in 1929 with the ohc 847cc Minor (also of Wolseley parentage). The ohc engine was dropped from the Minor in 1931 (though it had been successfully used in the MG Midget), being replaced by a simple side-valve unit, the two-seater version selling for £100. Lockheed hydraulic brakes first appeared on the six-cylinder Morrises of 1930 and during the following four years the whole range was converted. The early 1930s were poor years for Morris, and 1933 witnessed the appearance of the 1·3-litre 10/4: Morris hit the production jackpot again with his 918cc Series 1 Eight of 1935, a season in which, incidentally, he offered no less than 32 different models! The Eight continued in production until 1938, by which

time 250,000 had been built, making it the best-selling car of the decade. It was replaced for the 1939 season by the Series E Eight with completely new bodywork and faired-in headlamps. Although the Eight was Cowley's best-seller, the Morris range at this time boasted four other models, ranging from the 10/4 to the 3½-litre 25. All, with the exception of the Eight, were fitted with ohv engines; 1939 was also a significant year for Morris in that the Series M 1140cc Ten marked the company's first foray into integral construction. The immediate post-war years saw the reappearance of the pre-war Eight and Ten, though a major landmark came in 1948, with the announcement of the Issigonis-designed Minor, initially powered by the 916cc Series E engine, and featuring torsion bar ifs, rack-and-pinion steering and 14-inch road wheels. It remained in production until 1971 and was the first British car to sell over a million examples. The ohv Austin 803cc engine from the A30 was fitted from 1953 and the capacity progressively increased to 1098cc. The sv 1476cc Oxford and series MS Six, powered by an ohc 2·2-litre engine, also appeared at the same time as the Minor, and shared similarly styled bodywork. The creation of the British Motor Corporation in 1952 by the merging of the Austin and Morris companies inevitably resulted in rationalization, with the Cowley and more powerful Oxford receiving ohv Longbridge engines in 1954, the former 1200cc model appearing the same year. By 1959, the appearance of the Farina-bodied 1½-litre saloon meant that the differences between the Cowley and Longbridge products were less marked. The sensational Issigonis-designed front-wheel-drive 848cc Mini of the same year was sold under the Mini Minor name tag, while a logical progression was the best-selling 1100 of 1963, both those models later being available under the Austin banner. The year 1968 saw the engulfment of BMC by Leyland Motors to form British Leyland. A result of this new corporation was the Marina model of 1971, with a conventional engine and gearbox layout and rear-wheel drive, 1·3- and 1·8-litre engine options being available. The following year came the front-wheel-drive 2200 model. For 1979 the range consisted of 14 variations on the Marina theme.

William Cooper's one-off 1919 wooden-bodied sports Morris-Cowley

1926 Morris-Oxford touring car

1930 Morris Isis six-cylinder

1948 Morris Minor

1979 Morris Mini 1000

MORRIS & SALOM/*USA 1895–1897*
Morris & Salom's 'Electrobats' were front-wheel-drive electric cars and broughams, built in New York.

MORRISON/*England 1904–c1905*
A fwd 6 hp three-wheeler shown at the Crystal Palace in 1904. It was possibly of German origin.

MORRISS/*England c1908–c1914*
Prototype Morriss steam cars used American Mason engines, but the production models—four in total, recalled Frank Morriss, who, with his brother, specialized in repairing steam cars—used twin-cylinder slide-valve engines of Morriss's own manufacture.

MORRISS-LONDON
USA/England 1919–1921
The Morriss-London was an export car, built under the aegis of Century Motors (which had taken over both the Marathon Export Car and Crow-Elkhart). The Morriss-London was a continuation of the Marathon idea. Less than 100 cars, most of them just chassis, were exported, to be distributed by F. E. Morriss of London.

MORS/*France 1895–1956*
A pioneer of the French automobile and electrical industry, Emile Mors started by making air-cooled flat-twin engined cars, but soon progressed to V-4s with flexible engine mountings. By 1902, most Mors were water-cooled and chain driven, with the capacities ranging from 2·3 to 8 litres. In 1908, Mors presented the big four-cylinder 100cv of 12,831cc, and André Citroën became a director. From 1912, Mors adopted the Knight sleeve-valve engine for the 10/12 cv (2120cc), 14/20 cv (3308cc), 20/30 cv (4398cc) and 28/35 cv (7245cc). There were also some sv cars like the 20/30 cv six (5107cc), and four-cylinder 10/12 cv (2120cc) and 14/20 cv (3404cc). All the 1912 models remained in production until World War One. Post-war Mors resumed production with the sleeve-valve models only: a 14/20 cv Sport of 3562cc and a 12/16 cv of 1824cc, the latter engine being supplied by Minerva. After 1925, Mors only made components. During World War Two, they made some cheap electric cars, and in the 1950s they built scooters under the name of 'Mors-Speed'.

MORSE/*USA 1904–1911*
Designed by A. B. Morse, of South Easton, Mass., this marque started life as a vertical-twin. The ohv Morse engine had cylinders 'designed on the principle of a 30-30 rifle cartridge', with 'combustion chamber bigger than the cylinder proper'. For 1911, a 24 hp four was listed.

MORSE
USA 1914–1917
A fwd tandem-seat cyclecar from Pittsburgh.

MORT/*USA 1923–1926*
The Mort was actually a lower-priced line of the Piqua-built Meteor, marketed under its own emblem. Output included ambulances, funeral cars and a few sedans and invalid automobiles.

1914 Morriss steam car

An 18/24hp four-cylinder Mors wagonette, 1906

MOSER/*Switzerland 1914–1924*
Starting with vee-twin cyclecars, this manufacturer of motorcycles and engines from St Aubin (Neuchâtel) experimented with vee-twin three-wheelers in 1919–20, then began producing four-cylinder 1327cc light cars. However, after 1924 no more were built.

MOSKVITCH/*Russia 1947 to date*
The first Moskvitch ('son of Moscow') was built from pre-war Opel Kadett dies, though it was restyled in 1956 to become the Moskvitch 402 (there was also a 4wd model, the 410). A new range, the 407, appeared in 1958; the 1966 408 range represented a major step forward, with a four-cylinder 1·4-litre ohv engine, and was followed two years later by the 412 series, with

an ohc 1479cc engine. In 1978, two basic models were offered, the 2136/2138, with the ohv 1357cc engine, and the 2137/2140, with the 1479cc ohc unit.

MOTOBLOC/*France 1902–1930*
A company founded at Bordeaux in 1902 to exploit the designs of Schaudel, who was the first in the world to mount engine, clutch and transmission in one rigid casing—he called it 'le bloc-moteur'. In 1907 seven types of chassis were listed, from a 9 hp single to a four-cylinder 50 hp, with the option of shaft or chain drive. After the development by the company's chief engineer, Emile Dombret, of the bloc-moteur with flywheel between the middle pair of cylinders for smooth running, Motobloc specialized

in the production of strongly-built, powerful touring cars, which were exported to many countries. A six-cylinder model was particularly successful. Production was interrupted by World War One, during which Motobloc went into munitions manufacture, being taken up again after the end of hostilities with three models of chassis (one a light commercial) and two engines, of 12 hp and 15 hp.

1914 Motobloc chassis

Auguste Pons' 1907 Pekin-Paris Mototri-Contal, whose mudguards became an emergency bridge

1914 Motobloc 20hp six-cylinder sports

MOTOR BOB/USA 1914
A single-cylinder 2½ hp cyclecar from Buffalo, NY, sold for home assembly by 'boys from 12 to 15'.

MOTOR CARRIER/England 1904
A 6 hp 'pleasure car' which could be converted into an 8 cwt (900 lb) goods vehicle.

MOTORETTE/USA 1910–1911
The three-wheeled Motorette was designed and manufactured in Hartford, Connecticut, by C. W. Kelsey, automotive pioneer (see Auto Tri, Kelsey, Pilgrim and Spartan) and as many as 300 may have been made. The car sported two front wheels and a rear wheel and steering was by tiller. Initially air-cooled, the later cars were equipped with radiators. A tendency to roll on turns led Kelsey to develop the anti-sway bar. Price of the Motorette passenger-car model was $385, with a delivery van price being slightly higher. A special rickshaw body was developed for sales in Japan, where a number of Motorettes were exported. They also enjoyed sales throughout the United States, as well as Denmark, Mexico, Canada and Australia.

MOTORLAND MIDGET/England 1908
'Designed to supersede the tricar', the 7/8 hp single-cylinder Motorland Midget had a two-speed transmission and could attain 30–40 mpg.

MOTOTRI CONTAL/France 1907–1908
The high point of this company's existence was the entry of one of its three-wheelers in the 1907 Peking–Paris Race (though it failed to get very far). More elaborate than most tricars, the Paris-built Mototri Contal featured 'Roi-des-Belges' coachwork on its more costly models. Delivery tricycles were also made.

LA MOUCHE/France 1898–1902
A De Dion-engined voiturette built by Teste et Moret of Lyon-Vaise (Rhône).

MOURRE/France 1920–1923
Antoine Mourre started by building a six-cylinder 25 hp car named 'Pan American'. In 1921 he decided to make the Major cyclecar under licence, with Violet two-stroke engines (later with a 950cc Fivet four-cylinder four-stroke engine). These cars were sometimes sold under the 'Jack Enders' name.

MOUTETTE/France 1922–1925
Made in Paris by MM. Van der Eyken, Hurian and Vigy, these cars had 1327cc and 1328cc Altos engines, as well as 1495cc SCAP and 1093cc Ruby engines.

MOVEO/England 1931–1932
A 2973cc Meadows engine, available with supercharger if required, powered the Moveo, an ill-timed essay from Bolton, Lancashire. Other Meadows-engined options were listed, but none of these was built.

MOYER/USA 1911–1915
Initially offered with four- or six-cylinder engines, this car from Syracuse, New York, was later only available with a 5047cc four-cylinder engine.

MP/France 1908–1909
An imported French make, sold by J. E. H. Monypenny of London, the MP was a 30 hp four-cylinder of 5123cc, with a shouldered radiator reminiscent of the De Dietrich. A 16 hp four of 2011cc and a 45 hp six of 9784cc were also available.

1924 Mourre cyclecar

MPM/*USA 1914–1915*
A 44 hp eight-cylinder from Mount Pleasant, Michigan — hence the name!

MS/*France 1922–1925*
MM. Morain and Sylvestre started in Courbevoie, Seine, making a 961cc Chapuis-Dornier-engined light car. The company changed hands in 1924, and was taken over by MM. Martin and Blanco of Suresnes, Seine, who added a 1093cc model.

MSL/*England 1911–1912*
Assembled from imported French components by Motor Showrooms Ltd., these were a 10/14 hp of 1847cc and a 12/16 hp of 2121cc.

*c.*1898 Mueller-Benz Trap

MUELLER/*USA 1895–1900*
Mueller, of Decatur, Illinois, imported the Benz into the United States from an early date, and, indeed, competed with one in the 1895 Chicago Times-Herald race. The company later turned to manufacture of an 'improved' version of the Benz, with a tubular chassis which carried the cooling water from the single-cylinder engine at the rear to a tubular radiator on the front of the dashboard. Belt drive gave three speeds forward and reverse, and the standard bodywork was a four-seat *dos-à-dos*.

MULLNER/*Austria 1913*
A cyclecar with a 6 hp Zedel engine and chain drive.

MULTIPLEX/*USA 1912–1914*
Only 14 of this well-designed 50 hp four-cylinder were made by this Berwick, Pennsyl-vania, manufacturer, selling at $3600. A second Multiplex, a sports car with ifs and F-head Willys engine, appeared in 1954, but only three were built.

MUNTZ JET/*USA 1950–1954*
In 1950 Earl"Madman' Muntz, a zany character and astute businessman, purchased the tools and dies of the Kurtis Sports car and set up Muntz Motors to produce cars, first at Evansville, Ind., then in Chicago. The car was redesigned by Frank Kurtis and Sam Hanks, who lengthened the wheelbase to allow the installation of a rear seat. Numerous detail improvements went into the chassis and body, and production got under way in Illinois. Named the Muntz Jet, the first 28 cars used Cadillac 160 hp engines; later cars used 5195cc Lincoln V-8s with Hydramatic transmission. Top speed was a claimed 125 mph. Muntz was reputed to have lost around $400,000 on the 394 hand-built cars he produced.

MURRAY/*USA 1920–1921*
This car with a six-cylinder Continental engine was built by the Murray Motor Car Co. of Newark, New Jersey, and was a continuation of the earlier Murray Eight. John McCarthy subsequently took over the make and moved operations to the Boston area. As many as five or six of the Newark Murrays were sold.

MURRAY EIGHT/*USA 1916–1918*
Built in Pittsburgh, Pennsylvania, the Murray was a highly regarded and excellently built automobile at a reasonable price. Boasting such niceties as an electric clock as standard equipment and a slanting windshield, the car was distinguished by a Rolls-Royce-shaped radiator and precision coachwork, especially on its limousine and town-car models.

MURRAY SIX/*USA 1921–1928*
Also known as the 'Murray-Mac' (after its owner, John McCarthy), very few of these cars were produced — probably six or less — most, if not all, of these being assembled largely from existing parts. Beaver and (probably) Continental engines were used, and the five-passenger touring car was listed at $5000. Assembly was in Atlantic, Mass., near Boston. Around 1928, McCarthy built a handsome roadster in an effort to show and promote his venture, but he found no takers and the car remained his personal transportation for many years.

MUSTAD/*Norway/France 1917*
Clarin Mustad, of Oslo, was one of the automobile pioneers in Norway, and built sleeve-valve engines in 1909. In 1917 he built a prototype six-wheeled car with supplementary steering on the forward rear axle. The car had a four-cylinder engine, later replaced by a six-cylinder one, both built by the factory. The car was used up to World War Two, but was rebuilt in 1927. Mustad planned to sell the licence rights to Unic in France, but neither this, nor trials of the design as Paris buses, came to anything. However, a Duclair firm offered 7086cc Clarin Mustad six-wheelers until 1922.

MWD/*Germany 1911–1913*
Identical with 'Der Dessauer' cars, MWD stood for 'Motoren-Werke-Dessau'. Production concentrated around a sv 2100cc four-cylinder model.

MWF/*Austria 1905–1907*
When Wyner of Vienna closed down, MWF of Simmering continued the production of Wyner cars under their trade mark. They built cars from 9 hp to 40 hp, but concentrated on the smaller models. Manufacture was on a limited scale.

MYRON/*Czechoslovakia 1934*
A beautiful 796cc twin-cylinder two-stroke car, built at Zlin (now Gottwaldov), the Myron attracted many orders when exhibited at the Prague Motor Show, but was never produced. The reason was simple: the exhibited car, offered for less than 10,000 Kcs, had a specially built body by Fischer of Brno, which had cost 21,000 Kcs to produce!

MYTHOLM/*England 1900–1902*
Thomas Potter and J. W. Brown's Mytholm Cycle Works at Hipperholme, Halifax, built a three-wheeled car in 1897, followed by a four-wheeled prototype. They joined forces with R. Reynold Jackson in 1899, building some Jackson cars, but after Jackson's departure for London in 1900, a number of Mytholm cars were built. Chain driven, with steering-column gear-change, they had a 1357cc single-cylinder.

1918 Murray Eight Model 70T Town Car

1924 Murray-Mac six-cylinder

NACIONAL PESCARA/*Spain 1929–1932*
Raul, Marquis de Pescara, built a number of sporting 2948cc ohv straight-eights: a 3·9-litre straight-ten was also proposed in 1931.

NACIONAL RG/*Spain 1948*
Cuban engineer and aviator Ramon Girona built two-seater aeroplanes in his Barcelona factory, as well as streamlined twin-cylinder 740cc light cars with saloon or cabriolet coachwork.

NACIONAL SITGES/*Spain 1933–1937*
Built at Sitges, site of a Brooklands-inspired racetrack, the Nacional Sitges was a conventional four-cylinder saloon of 1235cc. From mid-1936, for political reasons, the marque was known as 'Popular Sitjes'.

1908 30/40hp Nagant tourer

NAGANT/*Belgium 1899–1927*
Starting with licence-built Gobron-Brilliés, Liègeois arms manufacturers Léon and Maurice Nagant then launched a 6872cc chain-driven 35/40 hp four of conventional design in 1906, followed in late 1907 by a 4589cc 20/30 hp. The 1908 season saw a 14 hp 'for the man of moderate means'. The 35/40 hp was discontinued in 1911, and in 1912 a new 10/12 hp appeared. Post-war production began in 1920 with a 16 hp four, shortly followed by an ohv sporting four of 1954cc with Adex four-wheel brakes. A supercharged Nagant was shown at the 1927 Brussels Show alongside the last production model, a sv six. Soon after, Impéria swallowed Nagant.

NAMELESS/*England 1908–1909*
'British-built all through', the Nameless was a low-priced (£290) 14 hp four from Hendon.

NAMI/*Russia 1927*
An air-cooled flat-twin powered this little four-seater, planned as the first mass-produced Soviet car. About 300 were built.

NANCEENE/*France 1900–c1903*
Built cars and lorries on Gobron-Brillié lines.

NAG

NAG/*Germany 1902–1934*
NAG, successor to AAG, initially continued the cars created by Prof. Klingenberg. His successor, Joseph Vollmer, designed two- and four-cylinder 10 hp and 20 hp cars, as well as commercial vehicles. A variety of models followed, including 5185cc and 7956cc four-cylinders and even an 1866cc twin-cylinder car. A 1570cc four-cylinder model (the 'Puck'), as well as 2071cc, 2579cc and 8384cc NAGs were later produced: the marque was favoured by the Kaiserin. The last NAG before World War One was a 2579cc four-cylinder. During the war, NAG built the 200 hp Benz aeroengine under licence; in 1919, it became a member of the GDA car production group together with Brennabor, Hansa and Hansa Lloyd. In 1920, Nag resumed car production with a sv 2536cc four-cylinder car, soon launching a sports version which won many races. An ohv 2640cc four-cylinder went into production in 1923, joined by six-cylinder

models of 3075cc and 3594cc from 1926 onwards. A joint venture with Protos, which NAG took over that year, these ohv sixes

1912 18hp NAG sports two-seater

were called NAG-Protos. In 1927 NAG took over Preston and Dux. Designer Paul Henze joined the Berlin NAG works in 1929, and created the 1930–32 ohv 3963cc six-cylinder and the ohv V-8 of 4499cc. Together with Bussein, Henze also designed a front-wheel-drive version of the big V-8 car in 1932. The last NAG was the fwd Type 220 built from 1933 onwards, with a 1468cc flat-four engine, developed by Bussein for Voran. Only a few had been built before NAG decided to concentrate on commercial vehicles, and merged with Büssing.

1921 NAG 10/40hp Sportwagen

NAPIER / *England 1900–1924*

Montague Napier's Lambeth works was famed for precision engineering long before its association with motor cars. The prototype Napier, a 2471cc vertical-twin, successfully competed in the 1900 1000 Miles' Trial; a 4942cc four appeared later that year, notable for a one-piece aluminium cylinder block with pressed-in iron liners and three atmospheric inlet valves per cylinder. From the start Napiers were sold and promoted by the forceful S. F. Edge. Napier pursued an active racing policy, which won the 1902 Gordon Bennett Trophy for Britain, and Napier Green became the official British racing livery. In 1903, Napier launched the first series-production six-cylinder car, the 4942cc 18 hp: initially, periodic vibration caused crankshaft whip and even breakage, which Edge euphemized as 'power rattle', but the overall smoothness and flexibility of the six proved strong selling points, and by 1906 there was a range of two

sixes of 40 hp (5001cc) and 60 hp (7753cc) and two fours — 18 hp (3160cc) and 45 hp (5309cc). The next year a 9653cc 60 hp driven by Edge averaged 65·9 mph for 24 hours on the new Brooklands race track, a record which stood for 18 years. Biggest production Napier was the 90 hp introduced in 1907 which had a swept volume of 14,565cc. A complex range of two-, four- and six-cylinder models was replaced by only

five models for 1912 — a 15 hp four and sixes of 30, 40, 45, 65 and 90 hp. World War One saw Napier building aeroengines, including the famous 'broad-arrow' Lion 12-cylinder designed by A. J. Rowledge, who was also responsible for the post-war Napier — a light-alloy ohc 6227cc 40/50 hp six. Only 187 were built out of a total of 4258 Napier private cars. A 1931 bid to acquire Bentley was thwarted by Rolls-Royce.

Interchangeable bodywork on the 1913 15hp 'Colonial' Napier

c.1913 30hp Napier touring car

The original Napier car, in the 1900 1000 Miles Trial

NAPOLEON / *France 1903*
A Lacoste et Battmann-based 5 hp car sold by Bernard Neave of Richmond, Surrey.

NAPOLEON / *USA 1916–1917*
An L-head 30 hp four from Napoleon, Ohio.

NAPTHOLETTE / *France 1899*
A light 2½ hp car on Decauville lines whose body could be 'removed in an instant and another one substituted'.

NARDI / *Italy 1947–1963*
Enrico Nardi created small racing, and sports

cars, using 498cc and 746cc BMW motorcycle engine components; he later employed modified Fiat and Lancia engines. An ex-Ferrari employee, he was an excellent engine tuner. Some of his racing cars had Giannini-designed 746cc dohc four-cylinder engines. His factory also produced tuning equipment for Fiat and other makes.

NARDINI / *France 1914*
An attractive light car designed to be sold on the English market by M. Nardini. Altos engines of 1244cc and 1779cc were used, and the chassis was reportedly very similar to the SUP.

1914 Nardini 1779cc chassis

Nash

NASH/*USA 1917–1957*

Charles W. Nash rose to become President of General Motors in 1912, but his ambition was to build a car under his own name. He therefore resigned and bought the Jeffery company in 1916, phasing out its name in favour of 'Nash' a year later. The first Nash car, an ohv 4-litre six, appeared in autumn 1917; it was joined by an ohv 2·5-litre four late in 1921, as Nash recovered from the 1920 recession. LaFayette and Mitchell were acquired, in 1922 and 1924 respectively, but the Mitchell's successor, Ajax, proved a flop. The Model 328 of 1928 was said to be 'America's cheapest seven-bearing six', helping to boost sales to 138,137, a record that would stand until 1949. The 1930 range covered 32 variants, including the all-new Twin-Ignition Eight of 3920cc, as well as the Single Six and Twin-Ignition Sixes, both of 3378cc; the Eight featured a starter operated by the clutch pedal. To counter sliding sales, Nash boosted their model range to 25 'First Series' body styles and 28 'Second Series' in 1932, and launched a 'Big Six', giving them two sixes and two eights, and, apart from GM, were the only US manufacturers to show a profit that year. The 1934 model had revised styling, with spatted wings, raked tails and rear-mounted spare wheels, and a low-priced LaFayette line was added. In 1934, the millionth Nash was built; drastic rationalization the next year brought the range down to two six-cylinder body styles and four eight-cylinder styles, with swept-tail 'Aeroform design'. The 1936 models had the option of conventional-styled models with a boot, and a rear seat which converted into a double bed. That same year's models also included the low-priced sv 400 six, of 3037cc or 3779cc, and the ohv Ambassador Six and Eight models. In 1937, Nash merged with Kelvinator refrigerators; a year later came 'Weather Eye' conditioned air heating and ventilation and vacuum-operated gearboxes. The 1940 models had a tall, narrow grille, curved inwards at the foot, and there was a limited edition of around 50 Nash Special convertibles styled by Count Alexis de Sakhnoffsky. The 1941 models featured an integral body/chassis, hailed as an American first; the new 2·8-litre '600' six was claimed to cover 600 miles on one 20-gallon tankful of petrol. After the war, Nash was quickly back in production, the 1945 cars being carry overs from 1942. An interesting 1946 model was the Ambassador Suburban Sedan, with wooden side panels. Airflyte styling distinguished the 1949 models, though enclosed wheels all-round made tyre changing almost impossible. All models employed unitary construction; seat belts were optional, and the front seatback dropped down to convert the interior into a double bed (mattress and curtains were options). Nash's best year was 1950, when they launched the first successful post-war compact, the Rambler, with the old sv six; Nash sales that season reached 175,722. The old 600 was replaced by the Statesman. A meeting on the *Queen Elizabeth* between Nash president George Mason and Donald Healey led to the English-built Nash-Healey, powered by a tuned Ambassador six, offered between 1951 and 1954. In 1954, Nash took over Hudson to form American Motors, with George Romney at the helm. He was not interested in full-size cars, and concentrated AMC's efforts on the Rambler. A 1955 restyling saw the option of Packard's 5244cc V-8 in the Ambassador, while 1956 saw the Ambassador with AMC's new 4097cc V-8. Sales fell to 9474 in 1957, despite flamboyant styling with dual vertical headlamps, and Nash was finally phased out.

1926 Nash Advanced Six Sedan with auxiliary Gruss air-springs

1932 Nash Six Convertible Victoria

1950 Nash Ambassador Super Sedan

1951 Nash Healey sports

EL NASR / *Egypt 1959 to date*

This company, with a factory at Helwan, offered licence-built versions of the Fiat 128 and 125 in 1979.

NATIONAL / *USA 1899–1900*

At least five Nationals, with 2½ hp, 5 hp or 8 hp twins, were built in St Louis in 1899.

NATIONAL / *USA 1900–1924*

'Electrically-propelled pleasure vehicles' occupied this Indianapolis firm until 1904, when they introduced a round-radiatored petrol car, with a 4649cc four-cylinder Rutenber engine, dropping 'Electrobiles' altogether in 1905. A year later came a six-cylinder model, but it was powerful big fours which really established National, who claimed their 7320cc 40 hp as 'the fastest stock car built': the 1912 Speedway Roadster commemorated the marque's victory in the Indianapolis '500' race that year. By 1913, electric starting and lighting were standard, as was an engine-driven tyre pump. The 1914 models had left-hand drive, and in 1915 a new model, with a 4966cc Continental Red Seal six, was launched, joined for 1916 by a 6064cc V-12 of National's own manufacture, listed until 1919. In 1920 came the 30 hp Sextet six which ran until the end of production. A 1922 merger with Jackson and Dixie Flyer led to some cars of these marques appearing as 'Nationals'.

NATIONAL / *England 1902–1906*

A tricar with a 4 hp MMC engine, the Manchester-built National had a coachbuilt body and wheel-steering.

NATIONAL / *England 1904–1912*

Rose Brothers, makers of tobacco wrapping machinery, built these cars of conventional design, with two, three and four cylinders— though a 15/17 hp five-cylinder was reportedly shown in 1904.

NAVARRE / *USA 1921*

A. C. Schulz, builder of the Navarre, had been associated with both Locomobile and Marmon, and plans had been made to build a quality luxury car. Only one car was made, a five-passenger sedan. This featured an own-make engine (a six) and a price tag of $6000.

NAW / *Germany 1908–1919*

Producers of NAW, Colibri and Sperber cars at Hameln/Weser, the works were bought by Selve.

NAZZARO / *Italy 1912–1922*

Felice Nazzaro, closely connected with Vincenzo Florio and Fiat as a very successful racing driver and technician, built these 20/30 hp cars with 4396cc four-cylinder engines. A smaller 12 hp car of 2092cc was made for British agents Newton & Bennett. The Nazzaro cars built for the 1919 French Grand Prix, with ohv four-cylinder 16-valve power units, retired with engine troubles. Nazzaro left the works in 1916 and eventually returned to Fiat. His successors produced a few 3480cc cars.

NB / *Scotland 1909–1912*

Successor to the Drummond, the North British was a 10 hp twin of 1652cc, which sold for £200.

NB / *Italy 1910–1915*

This was a 'semi-Italian' car, as the design and the finances came from the UK car dealers Newton & Bennett. There was reportedly a technical co-operation with Nazzaro, as both works were at Turin and Newton & Bennett imported Nazzaros. The four-cylinder NB cars had 2155cc engines.

NEANDER / *Germany 1937–1939*

Designer Ernst Neumann-Neander produced unorthodox motorcycles in the late 1920s, and afterwards created various small three- and four-wheeled cars, which never went into serious production. Between 1937 and 1939 he built a range of 1000cc sports-racing cars with JAP or Harley-Davidson vee-twin engines.

NEC / *England 1905–1920*

A famous 'bonnetless' car with all seats within the wheelbase, the NEC (built by the New Engine Company of Acton, London) had a horizontal power unit. There was originally a 30 hp four-cylinder, joined in 1906 by a 15 hp twin. The 30 hp, oddly enough, could be had with either two- or four-speed transmissions. For 1908, the 15 hp was bored out to create a 20 hp, and a 40 hp four of similar cylinder dimensions was offered alongside the 30 hp. Both the 30 hp and 40 hp were still theoretically available after the war, but these were almost certainly unsold 1914 models. The Mort brothers, J. G. and G. F., who owned NEC, also produced Roots-supercharged two-stroke aero-engines as early as 1910.

NECKAR / *Germany 1955–1968*

Made by NSU-Fiat at Heilbronn, the Neckar was really a Fiat 103 design with an ohv 1089cc four-cylinder engine. After 1966 the factory became independent from NSU, and concentrated on Fiat products.

LA NEF / *France 1899–1914*

A three-wheeled car built at Agen by Lacroix et de Laville, La Nef had a wooden chassis and tiller steering. According to the model, De Dion engines of 2¾ hp to 8 hp were used. Robust and easily driven, it was known as 'the country doctor's car'. Production was around 200.

NEGRE & RUFFIN
France 1896–1897

'Though the engine may be efficient enough to propel the vehicle', said a press description of the V-4 steam power unit used on this car, 'it is doubtful whether the system is all that is required by buyers'. In 1897, M. Nègre offered a steam car with cylinders in 'X' formation.

NELSON / *USA 1917–1922*

The Nelson was designed along European lines by Emil A. Nelson, who had previously been affiliated with Oldsmobile, Packard and Hupmobile. A relatively small car, the Nelson featured an ohc four-cylinder aircraft-type engine of its own make. Although production was limited, an estimated 350 to 400 cars had been produced by the end of 1920. Any 1921–22 Nelsons were presumably assembled from parts in hand. Most Nelsons were touring models, although some roadsters and sedans were built in earlier days, probably to special order.

NESSELSDORFER
Czechoslovakia 1897–1923

This pioneer factory completed its first 'President' motor car on 21 May 1898. From 1923 onwards, Nesselsdorf (now Kopřivnice) built cars which became known as 'Tatra'. Their most famous designer was Hans Ledwinka, who created some excellent cars, including the ohc 5328cc six-cylinder Type 'U', which was made from 1914 to 1923, when Ledwinka's famous twin-cylinder Tatra came into being.

1904 Nesselsdorfer 12hp phaeton

NEUSTADT-PERRY/*USA 1903–1907*
This 'combination car' from St Louis was furnished engineless so that the buyer could fit steam or petrol power to choice.

NEW BRITISH/*England 1921–1923*
The chain-driven New British used friction transmission and was powered by a 10 hp vee-twin Blackburne, either air- or water-cooled.

NEW CENTURY/*England 1903*
Made by old-established carriage-builders Henry Whitlock Ltd. in 7½ hp, 12 hp, 16 hp and 20 hp models.

NEW COURIER/*England 1898–1900*
The New Courier Cycle Company of Wolver-hampton built carrier tricycles and two-seater motor tricycles 'with patent starting gears'. Their 1900 three-wheeled 'Motorette' could be converted into a tradesman's box tricycle by removing the front seat.

NEW ENGLAND/*USA 1898–1900*
A tiller-steered two-cylinder steamer built at Waltham, Mass.

NEW ERA/*USA 1915–1917*
The 'Simplicity 16' was a $660 tourer built at Joliet, NY.

NEWEY ASTER, NEWEY
England 1907, 1913–1923
Newey of Birmingham and Leamington claimed to operate the biggest garage in the Midlands. They were agents for Siddeley, Star and De Dion, and in 1907 also built their own models with 10/12 hp, 20/22 hp and 24/30 hp Aster power units. With a 1324cc Aster engine, the 1913–23 Newey was a well-built light car with rotund two-seat coachwork.

NEW HUDSON/*England 1913–1924*
Built by a famous Birmingham motorcycle factory, the pre-war New Hudson was a 4¼ hp four-wheeled cyclecar: a vee-twin MAG engine powered their post-war three-wheeler.

1920 New Hudson
three-wheeled cyclecar

NEWMOBILE/*England 1906–1907*
'Specially designed to meet the requirements of the medical profession', the Newmobile was one of the first cars to feature unit construction of engine and gearbox. The constant mesh gears were engaged by a series of cone clutches.

NEW ORLEANS/*England 1900–1910*
The 'Orleans' recalls Bourbon connections with Twickenham, London, where this marque was made. The first New Orleans model was a 3½ hp licence-built version of the Belgian Vivinus—

there was also a 6 hp two-cylinder on similar lines—but by 1902 a four-cylinder 14 hp and 8 hp and 9 hp light cars were available. A 22 hp four appeared in 1906, a year after the company had become simply 'Orleans', the novelty presumably having worn off. By 1909, a 30/40 hp four and a 35/45 hp six were listed.

NEW YORK SIX/*USA 1928–1929*
Sold by the New York Motors Corporation, of Baltimore, Maryland, this car was actually built by the George W. Davis Motor Co. of Richmond, Indiana, and, with the Davis Eight, featured the unique Parkmobile, a jacking mechanism with small wheels allowing the car to be manoeuvred sideways in and out of parking spots. The car had a Continental engine and resembled Reo's Wolverine. Few were built.

NIAGARA/*USA 1915–1916*
Gustav H. Poppenberg, who owned the biggest piano warehouse in Buffalo, NY, backed this 36 hp four with 'motor yacht line' coachwork.

NICLAUSSE/*France 1906–1914*
Better known as makers of 'unexplodable boilers', J. & A. Niclausse of Paris introduced a 30 hp four-cylinder shaft-drive car in 1905, which remained current (though later uprated to 35 hp) throughout the marque's life. A 20 hp four appeared in 1908, followed by a 12/16 hp.

NIMROD/*England 1899–1900*
A De Dion-engined 'Roadster Motor Tricycle' built by a Bristol cycle manufacturer.

NIXE/*Germany 1905–1908*
Voiturettes made by Feldman of Soest (Westphalia), Nixe cars had ioe 804cc twin-cylinder Fafnir engines.

NOEL/*France 1920–1925*
Light cyclecars from Brienne-le-Château, Aube: one was a tandem two-seater with a 1089cc Anzani vee-twin engine. Noel also made a more conventional Ruby-engined 902cc cyclecar.

NOEL BENET/*France 1900*
This front-wheel-drive car from Offrainville, Seine-Maritime, was powered by a single-cylinder De Dion engine, and had front-wheel braking through the differential.

NOMA/*USA 1919–1923*
An assembled car with sporting lines, the Noma used a six-cylinder Continental engine (a Beaver power plant was also available). Low-slung and wire-wheeled, the Noma used step plates in place of running boards. An oval radiator was distinctive, reminiscent of the Brewster or Phianna. Although most of the several hundred Nomas produced were open models, a number of closed cars was also built.

NORDEC/*England 1949*
General engineers (they even offered model aircraft engines), the North Downs Engineering Company of Whyteleafe, Surrey, made the LMB ifs conversion for Fords and the Marshall-Nordec supercharger. These were both incorporated in this Ford Ten-powered sports car built in limited numbers.

NORDENFELDT/*France 1906–1910*
The Nordenfeldt first appeared in 1906 with a 24/30 hp Bariquand & Marre four-cylinder engine. Originally sold in England by racing driver Clifford Earp, the Nordenfeldt is somewhat of a mystery car, for its actual maker is unknown. Four-cylinder models of 12, 16, 20, 30/35 and 40/45 hp were listed during the Nordenfeldt's five-year production span.

NORFOLK/*England 1904–1905*
A. Blackburn & Co of Cleckheaton, Yorks., built about a dozen twin-cylinder cars of 1458cc and 1701cc.

NORIS/*Germany 1902–1905*
Made at Nürnburg, the Noris was a small car with one-, two- and four-cylinder proprietary engines up to 24 hp.

NORMA/*England 1914–1915*
A 10 hp four-cylinder light car with a 1460cc power unit, which sold for £178 complete.

NORSK/*Norway 1907–1911*
The first car from this Oslo firm was a single-cylinder 8 hp car with four-speed gearbox, which was presented in the spring of 1908. The second type of car had a twin-cylinder engine. Altogether around 10 cars were built.

1905 'Silent' Northern Limousine

NORTHERN/*USA 1902–1909*
Designed by Charles Brady King, the original Northern cars were typical gas buggies on Oldsmobile lines (King worked for Olds from 1900–02) with one- and two-cylinder engines. A folding steering column was a feature. In 1904 came the flat-twin 'Silent Northern', with a huge U-shaped silencer some 10ft in length and an epicyclic transmission controlled by a steering column lever. The 1906 ohv four-cylinder Northern had compressed-air-operated brakes, clutch and fuel feed. The company was absorbed by EMF in 1909.

NORTHERN/*England 1908–1910*
There were two models of the Northern, from Cleckheaton, Yorkshire—a 10 hp twin of 1759cc and a 20 hp four of 3518cc.

NORTH-LUCAS/*England 1923*
Ralph Lucas (of Valveless) and O. D. North collaborated to design this all-independent suspension car with unit-construction body/chassis and rear-mounted five-cylinder radial engine, built in the KLG spark plug factory.

253

NORTH STAR/*England 1920–1921*
This cyclecar built at London's Lee Green used a 4 hp single-cylinder Blackburne engine. It was belt driven and cost £159.

NORTHWAY/*USA 1921–1922*
Northway was a subsidiary of the Northway Engine Company, part of General Motors, which manufactured commercial vehicles as well as engines for other makes of car, including Oakland and Oldsmobile. Northway featured, naturally, a Northway engine for 1921, in which year a touring car sold for $4200. For some reason, the make opted for a Herschell-Spillman engine in 1922; few — if any — of these were sold.

NORWALK/*USA 1911–1922*
From Martinsburg, West Virginia, the 1911 Norwalk was a sporty car with an underslung chassis, riding on 40-inch wheels. It cost $3100. After 1916 a conventional chassis was used.

NOTA/*England 1972*
The Nota Fang was a basic little rear-engined alloy- and glass-fibre-bodied sports car with steel space frame; it had sold successfully in Australia before coming to the UK. Excellent performance from a choice of BMC A series engines was not enough to sell more than a handful of Notas in Britain.

NP/*England 1923–1925*
The NP (built at Newport Pagnell, Buckinghamshire) was made by a subsidiary of Salmons and Sons Ltd., the coachbuilders: 11·9 hp and 13·9 hp Meadows engines were used.

NSU-FIAT (NECKAR)/*Germany 1929–1973*
NSU had to sell its new Heilbronn factory to Fiat in 1929; Fiat cars assembled there were initially sold as NSU, later as NSU-Fiat cars. Best known were the 570cc (500) and 1089cc models. After World War Two, the works assembled the twin-cylinder 570cc, 479cc and

499cc Weinsberg and the 633cc and 767cc four-cylinder Jagst models. The cars were known as 'Neckars' after NSU resumed production in 1958. The factory is now the home of the German Fiat AG, which merely imports Fiats (as well as Russian and Polish Fiat-licence cars).

NUG/*Germany 1921–1925*
A small car produced in small numbers, the Niebaum-designed 960cc ioe four-cylinder NUG was one of the better cars of this period.

NYBERG/*USA 1912–1914*
Biggest of the Indiana-built Nybergs was a 5441cc six-cylinder seven-passenger tourer.

NYMPH/*England 1975–1978*
Designed by Bohanna Stables, the originators of the AC 3000, the Nymph was an open four-seat runabout of glass-fibre monocoque construction: 34 of these Imp-powered machines were built.

NSU/*Germany 1905–1929, 1958–1977*
Neckarsulmer motorcycles and bicycles were already well known when this company started building Belgian Pipe cars under licence. In 1906, they began production of a Pfaender-designed car with a 1420cc four-cylinder engine, followed by models of up to 2608cc. A vertical-twin voiturette of 1105cc appeared in 1909, a year which also saw the arrival of one of the most popular NSU cars of the period, the 1132cc four-cylinder, produced until 1913; there was also a 1550cc version. The biggest pre-war NSU was a

3300cc four. Introduced in 1913, the 1232cc 5/15 PS was still in production in 1926. Other models of the 1920s had four-cylinder engines of 2100cc and 3610cc, and sixes of 1567cc and 1781cc. Production was shifted to Heilbronn in 1927, but ceased when this had to be sold to Fiat. In 1934–35, however, the Neckarsulm factory produced some VW-like prototypes, with assistance from their English designer Walter Moore. But car production was not resumed until 1958, with the 583cc ohc vertical-twin Prinz, followed by an improved 598cc version.

Meanwhile, NSU had sold its entire motorcycle production set-up to Yugoslavia. In 1963, NSU created a sensation with the introduction of the first quantity-production Wankel-engined car, the Spider, developing 50 bhp from the equivalent of 500cc; it was built until 1967. The 1964 four-cylinder ohc 996cc Prinz was followed by models of 1085cc and 1177cc. Successor to the Spider was the elegant Ro80 saloon, produced for nearly a decade, despite some durability problems with early examples of its rotary power unit.

1913 8/24hp four-cylinder NSU

1908 NSU 10/20 PS phaeton

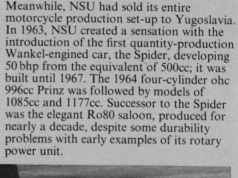

1976 NSU Ro80 with the Wankel rotary engine

O

OAKLAND / USA 1907–1932

The first car to leave Oakland's Pontiac, Mich., factory was a 20 hp twin, designed by Alanson Brush (and had his typical hallmark, an engine that cranked anti-clockwise). It had an epicyclic gear-change incorporated in the back axle. In 1909, Oakland became part of General Motors and introduced its first four. By 1912, fours of 3 and 4 litres were offered, followed in 1913 by a 5999cc 40 hp six, both with vee-radiators. A 5·5-litre V-8 appeared in 1916, as did an ohv 15/20 hp six of 2955cc, which soon became Oakland's sole model. It was succeeded in late

1929 Oakland All-American 6

1923 by a 3038cc side valve six with centralized chassis lubrication from the engine pump and four-wheel brakes. It was also the first Ducco-finished car: but the introduction of a sister marque, Pontia, in 1926, hit Oakland sales. A 1930 V-8, based on the Viking, was the last Oakland.

OBUS / France 1907–1908

A. Souriau of Montoire (Loire-et-Cher) built this voiturette.

OCENASEK / Czechoslovakia 1906–1907

A rotary air-cooled 16 hp eight-cylinder built in Prague, probably only in prototype form.

OCTO / France 1920–1928

M. Vienne, maker of the Carteret cyclecar, also made bigger cars in Courbevoie, Seine, under the 'Octo' name. The first model was a Ballot-engined 10 hp of 1592cc. In 1921 it was followed by a cyclecar with the 902cc Ruby engine. From 1923 to the end of production, Octo made only light touring and sports cars with 969cc Ruby engines.

ODENSE MOBIL / Denmark 1905

Two Odense Mobil cars were built, but probably were only Oldsmobiles with more comfortable bodies. It is not known if mechanical changes were also made.

ODETTI / Italy 1922–1924

Early Odetti cars had twin-cylinder two-stroke engines. Production was limited. One model had an interesting 'streamlined' two-seater racing body, another an open four-seater with a four-cylinder 12 hp engine.

OFELDT / USA 1899–1901

August W. Ofeldt, the Brooklyn steam and naphtha launch builder, offered tiller-steered carriages with vee-formation compound engines. In 1901 he offered an X-formation four-cylinder compound power unit.

OFFORD / England 1896

Well-known Kensington coachbuilders who also built an electric dog-cart.

1962 Ogle Mini

OGLE / England 1960 to date

David Ogle's first attractive replacement body was for the Riley 1.5. The subsequent Ogle Mini, later known as the Ogle SX1000, was a more commercial project, however, and 66 were completed before the manufacturing rights were sold to Norman Fletcher following Ogle's untimely death. Before he died, Ogle had designed the Daimler Dart-based SX250, which later became the prototype Reliant GT. Subsequently his company built the Triplex GTS, the prototype Scimitar GTE and Ogle Aston Martin. This was renamed the Sotheby Special after Aston Martin had decided against putting it into production.

1921-22 Ogren Sedan

OGREN / USA 1914–1923

A high-quality assembled car designed by Hugo W. Ogren, who had already created a number of successful racers and other cars under various marques. All Ogrens were six-cylinder cars with Beaver and Continental engines. No production statistics are available, but after output had been increased in 1920 the figure may have reached 400 units. Prices ranged from $3500 to about

$5700. An attempt to reorganize Ogren and move operations to Chicago under the name 'Commander' failed, with only one Commander touring car (actually an Ogren with a reworked emblem) displayed. The last Ogren cars were sold in 1923, but these were left-over 1921 and 1922 units.

OHB / USA 1904

O'Halloran Brothers of London, who imported the Crestmobile into Britain, disguised its cruder features under English-built bodywork and sold it as their own make.

OHIO / USA 1909–1913

A shaft-drive 40 hp four from Cincinnati.

OHIO / USA 1910–1918

Expensive electric broughams built in Toledo.

OHTA / Japan 1934–1957

This Tokyo firm built a prototype in 1922, but production began in 1934 with a sv 736cc four, reminiscent of the contemporary Model C Ford (then assembled in Yokohama). This model was built until 1939. Post-war, a range of small fours was offered until Kurogane swallowed Ohta in 1957 and halted car production.

OKEY / USA 1907–1908

A two-stroke three-cylinder 2·6-litre runabout built by Perry Okey of Columbus, Ohio.

1924 Oldfield sedan

OLDFIELD / USA 1924

Only a single Oldfield—a three-passenger coupé—was ever constructed. Built by the Kimball Truck Company for the Oldfield Motors Corporation of Los Angeles, the enterprise was headed by Berna Eli 'Barney' Oldfield, world-famous racing car driver, who had been heading the Oldfield Tyre Company. The car sported four-wheel brakes, balloon tyres, and was equipped with a six-cylinder Wisconsin engine, Barney Oldfield drove the car to Indianapolis in May 1924 to promote sales; on his return to the West Coast the Wisconsin motor was removed and an eight substituted. The project petered out at this point after the Kimball Truck plant, Oldfield, and an apathetic public collectively lost interest in the venture.

OLD MILL / England 1914–1915

Albert Lambourne's Old Mill Works, at Brighton, Sussex, built a number of 10 hp four-cylinder light cars, complete with windmill mascot with revolving sails.

OLDSMOBILE/*USA 1896 to date*

Olds built few cars until 1899, when copper and lumber magnate S. L. Smith bought the company to give his two sons a lucrative hobby. Original plans were for a $1250 luxury car with pneumatic clutch and electric starter, but it failed to sell and Ransom Olds then designed the immortal single-cylinder tiller-steered Curved-Dash Oldsmobile, which made its debut in 1901. By 1904, production of the 'Merry Oldsmobile' had reached 5000; that year Ransom Olds left the company, soon to found Reo. By 1905, flat-twin and wheel-steered variants of the Oldsmobile were available; the next year saw a vertical-twin two-stroke, the 20/24 hp 'Double-Action' Model L, and the company's first four, the 26/28 hp Model S. A 7400cc six was introduced in 1908, when the ailing company was acquired by General Motors. In 1910 came a colossal 11,469cc six, so tall that it needed two-tier running boards! By 1912, the biggest Olds was 'only' 6997cc; an efficient 4-litre V-8 with aluminium pistons arrived in 1916, surviving until 1923. From 1921–23 an ohv four with the same 2·8-litre engine as Chevrolet was available. A one-model policy prevailed until 1929, with a 2774cc six with Buick-like radiator; from 1927 it boasted fwb and chromium plating. The low-priced Viking V-8 was offered from 1929–31. A new 3933cc straight-eight appeared in 1932, and 1935 saw the controversial 'turret-top' styling. A reputation for technical innovation was maintained with the option of GM's first production automatic transmission in 1938, though it reportedly 'didn't become reliable' until 1940. The pre-war sixes and eights were continued for the first three post-war seasons—even in 1948, three-quarters of cars sold had the Hydramatic transmission. Along with Cadillac, the top of the range Olds 98 received GM's first new post-war body in 1948, with split curved windscreen and wraparound rear window, but a new power unit did not materialize until the next year. This was Gilbert Burrell's short-stroke ohv 4965cc Rocket V-8, initially developing 135 bhp and giving 240 bhp by 1965. 'Autronic Eye' automatic headlamp dipping came in 1953; 1958 saw quad headlamps, exaggerated tailfins and a short-lived air-springing option. The 1961 F85 compact had an aluminium V-8 of 3523cc; sporting derivatives included the 185 bhp Cutlass range and the 1963 Jetfire, available with turbocharger. Bigger Oldsmobiles used 6457cc V-8s from 280 to 345 bhp. In 1964, the F85's V-8 had been replaced by the more economical Buick V-6, and there was a range of full-size Jetstar eights of 5407cc, also aimed at economy. The Toronado sports coupé of 1966 was the first successful fwd automatic (with drum brakes, as originally specified, it proved too fast for its chassis). Its 6965cc V-8 (7456cc from 1968) drove the front wheels through silent-tooth chains. By 1971, Oldsmobile was still listing three lines of convertible (Cutlass Supreme, 442, Delta 88) and all but the cheapest models had front disc brakes. A compact model, the 1973 Omega, was the equivalent of the Pontiac Ventura, with which it had a 4097cc six and 5736cc V-8 in common. The 1975 Starfire had Chevrolet, Pontiac and Buick sister models; that year's Delta Royale was Oldsmobile's last convertible. Five-speed transmissions were available on 1976 Starfires and Omegas, and the Cutlass claimed to be America's best-selling model, with 515,000 registrations. An important technical breakthrough of 1978 was an optional 5·7-litre diesel engine. An all-new, scaled-down Toronado headed the 1979 range.

1904 Curved-Dash Oldsmobile

c.1923 Oldsmobile

1953 Oldsmobile Ninety-Eight sedan

1980 Oldsmobile Omega Brougham

OLYMPIAN/USA 1917–1921
A small-production assembled car, the Olympian sported a four-cylinder engine of its own make, touring cars and four-passenger roadsters being the only models available. The Olympian became the Friend car in 1920, and Olympians sold in 1921 were 1920 left-overs.

R. F. Oats in a 2-litre OM at Brooklands, c. 1926

OM/Italy 1918–1934
Successor to Züst, OM built some excellent sporting cars until this old-established machine factory, founded in 1899, became part of the Fiat empire. OM at first took over the existing 4170cc Züst-design: their own cars had 1496cc, 1991cc, 2216cc and—eventually—2325cc four- and six-cylinder engines. Some had ohv heads, a few boasted Roots-type superchargers. OM won the first Mille Miglia in 1927.

OMAHA/USA 1912–1913
An underslung chassis was used on the 3818cc four-cylinder Omaha.

OMEGA/France 1900
Tubular-framed voiturettes of 3 cv or 5½ cv, built by the Kreutzberger brothers of Paris, who supplied folding pushbikes to the French Army.

OMEGA/Germany 1921–1922
Predecessor of the Omikron, the sv 796cc four-cylinder Omega was a basic cyclecar, built in small numbers.

OMEGA/England 1925–1927
In 1926, this 980cc JAP-engined three-wheeler from a Coventry motorcycle maker took six world class speed records, covering over 297 miles in six hours.

1925 Le Mans Oméga-Six

OMEGA-SIX/France 1922–1930
Very few Oméga-Six cars left the Boulogne-sur-Seine works. They had engines designed by the engineer Gadoux. One was an ohc six-cylinder of 2915cc, the other a 1991cc six.

OMIKRON/Germany 1922–1925
Omikron took over where Omega at Berlin-Charlottenburg left off. They built a Pingel-designed 960cc four-cylinder with Steudel sv engine and also a sporting ohc 1042cc two-seater model.

OMNIA/Holland 1900–1911
This Voorburg firm built a range of two-, three- and four-cylinder models from 10 hp to 55 hp. After 1910, the 18 hp Spyker was built under licence. No more than 100 Omnias of all kinds were produced.

OMNIMOBIL/Germany 1904–1910
Fafnir of Aachen, who had built the 1902 Aachener, supplied a 353cc single-cylinder engine (and, later, two- and four-cylinder units) along with nearly all the necessary components for building complete cars. These Omnimobil sets led to a couple of new 'makes' from enterprising assemblers. Complete Fafnir cars were available from 1908.

1914 Omnium light car

OMNIUM/England 1913–1914
Initially a £135 twin-cylinder 'miniature car'. A 1094cc four was launched in January 1914.

1905 One of the Best Voiturette

ONE OF THE BEST/England 1905
A 9 hp light car built by a jack manufacturer named Adams from Tunbridge Wells, Kent.

ONLY/USA 1909–1913
An early production sports car, the Only took its name from its huge ohv 3380cc single-cylinder engine, with a bore of 130mm and a stroke of 254mm. Guaranteed top speed was 60 mph.

ONNASCH/Germany 1924–1925
Small cars with sv 746cc MI (later Mehne) flat-twin engines.

OPEL/Germany 1898 to date
The founder of the Opel cycle and sewing machine works, at Russelsheim, Adam Opel died in 1895. His sons bought Lutzmann and produced the first Opel car, 'System Lutzmann', in 1898. In 1900 they started importing Renaults and also Darracqs (for which they acquired the production licence). From 1902, Opel-designed cars (initially twin-cylinder 1884cc models) were offered alongside Opel-Darracqs of up to 8008cc. The Opel range was always very wide and by 1914 four-cylinder models from 1392cc to 10,200cc were offered, the latter having a 100 hp three-valve ioe engine and four-speed gearbox. In the 1920s young Fritz Opel won races on Opel motorcycles and Opel cars and in 1928 drove the first Opel racing car powered by rockets at the Avus race track. Models built in the early 1920s included 1984cc and 3430cc fours and a six-cylinder 5598cc model. After installing a moving assembly line in 1924, Opel built the Citroën 5 cv-like 951cc four-cylinder 'Laubfrosch' in large numbers. Priced at 4000 Gold Marks, it sold in large numbers. A 1016cc 14 hp model followed, while other models included excellent sixes of 1735cc, 1924cc, 3540cc and 4170cc. From 1929 Opel also offered the eight-cylinder 5972cc Regent, built on American lines: understandably so, because General Motors of Detroit had taken control of Opel in 1928. New small Opel fours appeared, including the 1074cc Kadett and 1488cc Olympia: the Kadett became a best-seller. Among six-cylinder Opels were the 2473cc Super-Six and Kapitän and the 3626cc Admiral, all with ohv engines. When World War Two broke out, Opel was the leading European car manufacturer, selling the small versions in large numbers; some 107,000 Kadetts were built from 1937 to 1941. The first Opel car→

1907 40hp Opel owned by Victor Leon

continued from previous page

after the war was the pre-war Olympia, now with an ohv 1488cc four-cylinder engine, which entered production in 1947. The first new 2473cc six-cylinder Kapitän arrived in 1948. Other models included the Rekord and the 1200. The year 1962 saw a new, modern Kadett with a 993cc four-cylinder engine. New 1963 Rekord models had 1488cc and 1680cc ohv four-cylinder motors. Later, four-cylinder engines up to 1897cc and six-cylinder power units of 2586cc were available in the Rekord. Six-cylinder Kapitäns and Admirals had engines up to 2784cc, while other big Opel cars, including the Diplomat, housed Chevrolet-built V-8 motors. The 1979 Opel range consisted of Kadett, Ascona, Manta, Rekord, Commodore and Senator/Monza models, with a variety of engines from 1196cc to 2969cc. There is also an Opel branch factory in Argentina.

1956 Opel Kapitan

1979 Opel Monza

OPES/*Italy 1948–1949*
A front-wheel-drive 'People's car' with a three-cylinder radial engine of 748cc, built in small numbers.

OPPERMANN/*England 1896–1907*
Carl Oppermann, whose works were in Clerkenwell, built both front- and rear-wheel-drive electrics. He claimed his 1902 electric broughams and landaulettes could run 50 miles on one charge.

OPUS/*England 1966–1968*
One of stylist Neville Trickett's more light-hearted designs, the Opus was a hot-rod, loosely inspired by the Model T Ford and utilizing Ford Anglia components.

OREL/*France 1905–1914*
From Argenteuil (Seine-et-Oise), Orel offered 8/10hp twin-cylinder and 12/14hp four-cylinder cars, with chain or shaft drive.

ORIAL/*France 1920–1923*
The Office de Représentation Industrielle et Automobile in Lyon was mainly a motorcycle manufacturer, but also made some Senechal-inspired cyclecars with sv 902cc Ruby engines.

ORIENT/*USA 1899–1909*
The Waltham Manufacturing Company, of Massachussets, were famed cycle builders before they introduced a De Dion Bouton-engined tricycle, which could be converted into a quadricycle by removing the front wheel and forks and replacing them with a frame carrying two wheels and a seat. Steam cars were also built from 1897–99. In 1900 came a light wheel-steered car, The Victoriette, and a tiller-steered Runabout. Aster engines were used. In 1902 the company introduced the Orient Buckboard, a lightweight two-seater relying on the spring in its wooden plank flooring for suspension.

1898 4hp Orient Express

ORIENT EXPRESS/*Germany 1896–1903*
Designed by Josef Vollmer, the single-cylinder 1922cc Orient Express, built at Theodor Bergmann's Gaggenau works, was similar to the early Benz, but had four-speed belt drive, ten handles and one pedal (which worked the warning bell). Improved versions had two- and four-cylinder power units up to 16hp.

ORION/*Switzerland 1900–1910*
Orion of Zürich began production with six front-engined single-cylinder *vis-à-vis* cars, then concentrated on making lorries.

ORIX/*Spain 1952*
Powered by a 610cc flat-twin engine, the Orix looked very like the VW Beetle.

ORPINGTON/*England 1920–1924*
The Orpington was a truly assembled car containing Model T Ford components, a 1½-litre Coventry-Simplex engine and Moss gearbox.

ORSON/*USA 1909*
'One hundred men interested in financial, railroad and industrial affairs' organized this company to build cars for themselves ('and later for

*c.*1905 OTAV voiturette rebuilt as a cyclecar in 1912

the general trade'): its showrooms were, appropriately, on Wall Street.

ORYX/*Germany 1907–1922*
Successor to BMF, the Berlin-based Oryx works produced 1555cc four-cylinder cars, was taken over in 1909 by Dürkopp and afterwards built an 1830cc four-cylinder car. Enlarged to 2080cc, the last Oryx was built at the Dürkopp works.

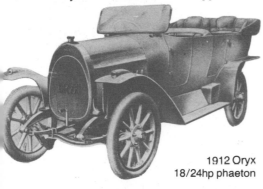

1912 Oryx
18/24hp phaeton

OSCA/*Italy 1947–1967*
The Maserati brothers sold their works to the Orsi family in 1937, but stayed on until 1947, when they left and founded a new factory, OSCA. The first design was a 4472cc V-12 racing engine for existing 1.5-litre Maseratis. OSCA built 1093cc and 1350cc four-cylinder, as well as 1987cc six-cylinder, sports and racing cars with ohc and dohc engines: there was also a 1490cc six-cylinder. In the late 1950s, a fast 749cc 'Four' was added, capable of 115mph. Some of the last 1492cc dohc machines could reach 145mph, the 1987cc version nearly 162mph. In 1966, the Maseratis retired and sold everything to MV-Agusta.

OSMOND/*England 1899–1900*
A Birmingham-built motor quadricycle.

OSTERFIELD/*England 1907–1909*
Despite its Germanic name, the Osterfield — 'for the man of moderate means' — was built by Douglas S. Cox, of South Norwood, London. There were three models, a 2596cc four, a 3893cc six and a straight-eight of 5191cc, at a chassis price of £850.

OTAV/*Italy 1901–1914*
Max Türkheimer was a pioneer of the Italian motor industry. He built motorcycles and cars, and imported British Ariel machines. He had been commercially connected with Ariel since 1897, so his early products used various Ariel-built parts. His cars had single-cylinder and, later, four-cylinder 2786cc engines. A versatile man, Türkheimer was also involved with the Torino-built Junior cars.

OTOMO/*Japan 1924–1927*
Having built two experimental Ales cars in 1921, Junya Toyokawa produced an air-cooled 944cc light car, joined in 1926 by a 24 hp model.

OTRO FORD/*Spain 1922–1924*
As its name cheekily implied — 'Another Ford' — this was a Model T Ford-based marque in the same mould as the English Mayflower.

OTTO/*France 1901–1914*
Starting with a 10 hp horizontal-engined twin and a vertical-engined 20 hp four, Otto of Paris offered, in 1902, two 10 hp models, a twin and a four-cylinder. In 1907 a 30cv model was shown at the Salon de l'Automobile, and in 1910 they took over the FL, built under Serex licence, with a 12 hp four-cylinder 2011cc engine. An 18 hp six appeared two years later.

OTTO/*USA 1910–1912*
'Highest grade at any price', the Philadelphia-built Otto sold for $2000. Fours of 4.2 to 5.1 litres were offered.

OTTO/*Germany 1923–1925*
Designed by Gustav Otto, son of the famous inventor of four-stroke gas engines Nikolaus Otto, the luxurious 4.9-litre Otto car was built in small numbers. The Munich factory produced Flottweg bicycle engines and motorcycles between the wars. It was later bought by BMW.

OURS/*France 1906–1909*
Round-radiatored cars built in Paris; their motto was 'Perfection — Solidity — Economy'. The 1908 range consisted of a 10/12 hp twin-cylinder, a 14/16 hp three-cylinder, a 20/24 hp four-cylinder and a 30/35 hp six-cylinder.

OUZOU/*France 1900–1901*
Soncin-engined 4 hp and 6 hp voiturettes from Paris.

OVERHOLT/*USA 1908–1909*
A four-seater motor buggy with friction drive, built in Galesburg, Illinois.

O-WE-GO/*USA 1914*
A tandem-seat $385 cyclecar from Owego, NY.

OWEN/*England 1895–c1936*
Owen (whose works were said to be in Birmingham), originally mechanical and marine engineers, claimed to have built a 5 hp single-cylinder car with five-speed chain-and-belt transmission as early as 1895: their showroom was at Carrick House, Comeragh Road, London, W.14. Production was, at best, spasmodic; indeed, there is some speculation whether they did in fact build any cars at all! They were (they claimed) principally makers of engines, gearboxes, axles, brakes and wheels for the motor trade. In 1920 they listed the 2994cc 20 hp (with only one forward speed!) and the 40 hp Owen-Dynamic, a 3216cc petrol-electric. Other marques associated with Owen were the Twentieth Century Voiturette (1901), Parisia, Londonia, Twentieth Century and Owen's Gearless (1905–06), as well as Orleans, Atalanta, Italiana and Owen's Petelecta. Owen's cars could well have been re-badged examples of other makes. A 1921 5302cc V-8 seems to have originated in America, and the last Owen was the 60 hp of 1925 (listed until 1936 in some sources) with a 7634cc straight-eight.

OWEN/*USA 1910–1914*
Noted for its high 42-inch pneumatic-tyred wheels, the 50 hp Owen had a 5912cc four-cylinder engine and left-hand drive.

OWEN MAGNETIC (CROWN MAGNETIC)/*USA 1914–c1921*
Ray M. Owen, of Baker Raulang, devised a magnetic transmission based on the Entz system used in oil-engined battleships: it was used in a 38 hp six-cylinder luxury car. Design rights to this 'Car of a Thousand Speeds' were sold to J. L. Crown, who began production at Wilkes-Barre, Pa., in 1920. He brought a Crown Magnetic to England soon after, and the Owen transmission was fitted to a few Minervas, two Ensigns and a few Magnetics. But the Crown Magnetic proved too complex and expensive; steep hills could cause 'magnetic drag' which brought the 2½-ton (5600-lb) car to a standstill, and production ceased.

OWEN-SCHOENECK/*USA 1915–1916*
A 5.2-litre Herschell-Spillman-powered four from Chicago.

OXFORD/*England 1899*
A 2¼ hp light belt-driven three-wheeler sold in Oxford Street, London.

OXFORD/*Canada 1914–1915*
The six Pontbriand brothers — plus two cousins — ran Oxford Car & Foundries Ltd., of Maisonneuve, Montreal, which built four pair-cast sixes to the design of H. M. Potter.

PACIFIC/*USA 1914*

A 13 hp two-cylinder cyclecar from Portland, Oregon.

PADUS/*Italy 1906–1908*
Voiturettes with 6 hp (single) and 10 hp (twin) engines, built in Turin.

PAGE/*USA 1905–1907*
A twin-cylinder air-cooled runabout from Providence, RI.

PAGE/*USA 1921–1924*
The Pagé (or Victor Pagé) 'Aero-Type Four' automobile, despite a total production of five units, commanded a good deal of attention in the American automotive press in the early 1920s. Photographs were published of a well-advanced-in-design car, available as a four-passenger roadster or a four-passenger coupé. These cars were built by Major Victor W. Pagé, a former textbook writer on automotive subjects, instructor in the American Expeditionary Force during World War One as a pilot trainer, and editor of *Scientific American* Magazine. The cars had an air-cooled four-cylinder engine and were displayed at the 1922 New York Automobile Show, but failed to go any further. Pagé built a smaller air-cooled car, the Utility.

French advertising for the 1919 Paige Six

P A C K A R D

PACKARD/*USA 1899–1958*

Convinced that he could build a better car than the new Winton he had just bought, electrical equipment manufacturer James Ward Packard began production of single-cylinder cars with automatic ignition advance at Warren, Ohio, in November 1899. His company was taken over in 1901 by Detroit businessman Henry B. Joy, under whose aegis the first Packard four, designed by the Frenchman Charles Schmidt, appeared in 1903, the year the factory moved to Detroit. Schmidt's 1904 Model L four-cylinder was the first to bear Packard's distinctive yoked radiator; the firm's first six appeared in 1912, confirming Packard's reputation as a maker of high-priced luxury cars. In 1916, inspired by the pioneering aeroengines designed by Sunbeam in Britain, engineer Jesse G. Vincent produced the V-12 Packard Twin-Six for the 1916 model year; this 6950cc model accounted for almost half that year's sales, and was current until 1923,

by which time 35,046 had been built. US President Warren Gamaliel Harding was the first to ride to his inauguration by car — in a Twin-Six. A 4395cc Single-Six appeared in 1921, followed in June 1923 by the Twin-Six replacement, the Single Eight of 5681cc, with four-wheel brakes and four-speed transmission. This model gave Packard supremacy in the luxury car market, and was produced in various Series designations. The six was dropped in 1928; that year limited production of a Speedster Eight based on the new Sixth Series began, lasting into the Seventh Series, but only 220 of this performance model were built in all. Eights remained the company's mainstay during the 1930s (though 5744 examples of a new Vincent-designed 7298cc V-12, again designated Twin-Six, were made up to 1939). A moderately priced Packard Eight, the 120, had the marque's first ifs, and sold for only $990 in its cheapest form; its appearance in 1935 was followed two years later by a six,

1928 Packard Eight 526 convertible coupé

which boosted production to an all-time record of 109,518 in 1937. The luxury eights, the Senior Series 160 and 180, ran through until the war, when, in a gesture of US-Soviet goodwill, their body dies were sold to Russia, resulting in the 1945 ZIS-110 series. This meant that Packard had no luxury car immediately post-war to compete with Lincoln and Cadillac, relying on a warmed-over version of its 1941-introduced Clipper

1903 Packard 12hp single-cylinder tonneau

1951 Packard Patrician 400, with Ultramatic transmission

PAIGE, PAIGE-DETROIT/*USA 1908–1927*
The 25 hp Paige-Detroit of 1908 had a 2172cc three-cylinder two-stroke engine in unit with a two-speed gearbox. 302 cars were built in 1908–09, after which four-cylinder four-stroke engines were adopted. The 2896cc '25', current until 1914, was succeeded by the 4118cc '36'. From 1915 only sixes — a Rutenber of 3771cc and a Continental of 4967cc — were used. In 1916, a moving assembly line was installed in the plant. From 1921, the 'Most Beautiful Car in America' had an elegant plated radiator like a shouldered Bentley cooler this looked especially well on the handsome Daytona roadster of 1922–26. The 1927 range consisted of three sixes and an eight: next year the marque became 'Graham-Paige'. From 1923–26, Paige built the Jewett.

PAKYAN/*Iran 1974 to date*
Chrysler UK Hunters exported in kit form for assembly by Iran National.

PALLADIUM/*France/England 1912–1925*
'A remarkably good car at a remarkably low

15/26hp Palladium Streamline Torpedo

series, ranging from the 4015cc Clipper 6 to the DeLuxe Clipper and Super and Custom range, with eights of 4621cc and 5834cc. Unfortunate slab-sided styling based on the old body earned 1948 Packards the nickname 'Pregnant Elephant'; three series — Eight, Super Eight, Custom Eight — with either 4720cc or 5359cc engines were offered, the six being relegated to taxis and export models. Sales reached a post-war peak of 104,593 in 1948, then began to fall. Packard's own automatic, the Ultra-matic Drive, appeared in spring 1949. The first all-new post-war Packards arrived in 1951; this 'Twenty-fourth Series' consisted of the 200, 200 DeLuxe, 250, 300 and 400. The 4720cc engine was standard on the Clipper 200, 250 and 300; the high-priced 400 Patrician had the 5359cc engine (optional on other models) as standard. A new president, James J. Nance, was determined to revive the ailing company and return to luxury cars, so the low-priced Clipper became a separate marque, and in 1953 some Derham-bodied Patricians and a series of 750 Caribbean convertibles were produced. In June 1954, Packard bought Studebaker, which was in dire financial straits; three months later came revolutionary new 1955 Packards, cleverly re-skinned on the old body, with a brand-new 5801cc V-8 and 'Torsion-Level' suspension linking all four wheels. 'Twin-Ultramatic' transmission was standard. Production rose to almost 70,000, but the millstone of Studebaker dragged Packard down. The Curtiss-Wright Corporation took the group over as a tax loss, and the last true Packards appeared in 1956, a new Executive model attempting to bridge the gap between Clipper and Packard lines. The 1957-58 Packards were no more than Studebakers using left-over Packard components; the bizarre Hawk (of which only 588 were built) had a wide-mouthed glass fibre snout.

price', the Palladium was originally built in France for sale in England. There were three models, with Chapuis-Dornier engines, a 1725cc 10/12 hp, a 2121cc 12/22 hp and a 2651cc 15/20 hp. Two new models were added in 1913, an 18/30 hp (3664cc) and an eight-cylinder 20/28 hp of 3451cc, twice the capacity of the 10/18 hp four. That year, Palladium production was switched to Twickenham. A complete *volte-face* came in 1919 with a chain-driven flat-twin-engined cyclecar of 1331cc. It was replaced in 1922 by a 1496cc four-cylinder 12 hp with a Dorman engine. A sports version was listed from 1923.

PALMER/*USA 1899–1900*
Marine engineers of Mianus, Connecticut, who sold engines and components and built at least one complete motor car.

PALMER-SINGER/*USA 1908–1914*
'Built in small quantities and sold to the select few', Palmer-Singers (built by the sole agents for Simplex) were initially available in 'Four-Thirty' (4185cc) and 'Six-Sixty' (9583cc) forms. A dashboard-radiatored 28/30 hp 'Skimabout' was listed in 1908. Fast and powerful, Palmer-Singers achieved some sporting success, but when failure loomed, tried desperately to re-kindle public interest by announcing their 1915 range in 1913.

PALMERSTON, PALM/*England 1921–1923*
A 688cc Coventry Victor-engined light car built by the Palmerston Motor Company of Boscombe, Hants: the later Palm was a 9 hp.

PAN/*USA 1917–1922*
The Pan takes an important place in American automotive history as a car built in what became one of the greatest automobile swindles in history from the viewpoint of stock sales. The builder of the car was Samuel Conner Pandolfo, who founded 'Pan-Town-on-the-Mississippi',

today St Cloud. An ambitious promoter, he built the town and everything in it, including what was probably the first motel. The Pan factory was a model of modern efficiency and the promotional catalogue of the car was probably the most elaborate ever printed in automotive history. The Pan featured a four-cylinder motor and body styles were restricted to open models. Seats were collapsible to form a double bed. Before the Federal Government stepped in to investigate the Pan stock manoeuvres, which ultimately sent Pandolfo to prison, some 737 cars had been manufactured.

PAN-AMERICAN/*USA 1918–1922*
'The American Beauty Car', built in Decatur, Illinois, was distinguished by a white-painted radiator shell; it was powered by a six-cylinder Continental engine and aimed to bring luxury car individuality to the popular car market.

PANDA/*USA 1955–1956*
The Panda was produced for two seasons only by Small Cars Inc., Kansas City, Mo. It was a small two-passenger runabout on a 70-inch wheelbase. A choice of two engines was offered: a 582cc four-cylinder Aerojet or a flat-twin 1098cc Kohler.

P & G/*England 1903*
An electric car built by Pritchetts & Gold, who also marketed the Meteor petrol car.

PANDORA/*England? 1903*
Sold either as a chassis or in kit form for home assembly, the 7 hp Pandora was marketed by Danny Citroën, London Minerva agent, who also sold the Vesta 'car set'.

PANEK/*Czechoslovakia 1921–1922*
The designer, a Laurin & Klement dealer at Rakovník, built a few 12 hp twin-cylinder cars of interesting design, but had no facilities for manufacture in large quantities.

Hippolyte Panhard's 1892 phaeton, which he drove from Paris to Nice

1913 Panhard-Levassor 15hp

PANHARD ET LEVASSOR
France 1889–1967

Having acquired French rights to the Daimler engine, the engineers Panhard et Levassor built their first car in 1891. It was rear-engined, but Levassor soon developed the basic layout of front engine beneath a bonnet driving the rear wheels which was followed by most subsequent constructors. The Daimler vee-twin was succeeded in 1895 by Panhard's 2·4-litre vertical-twin Phénix engine, their mainstay for many years. In 1898, Panhard introduced a four-cylinder power unit. Successful in racing, Panhard won the 1894 Paris-Rouen, 1896 Paris-Marseille-Paris, 1898 Paris-Amsterdam and the 1899 Tour de France. Panhard built a wide range of cars in the early 1900s, including a 1·8-litre three-cylinder 8/11 cv. In 1906 they presented a 50 cv four-cylinder of 10·5 litres and a six-cylinder of 11 litres. In 1909, Panhard had no fewer than four

different models: a 25 cv six of 4962cc, four-cylinder 15 cv (3380cc) and 10 cv (2412cc) models and a Phénix twin-cylinder of 1206cc. In 1910 the Phénix disappeared; new models included a six-cylinder 28 cv of 6597cc and a four-cylinder 25 cv (5231cc) as well as a 4398cc 20 cv with a Knight sleeve-valve engine. Another sleeve-valve model, of 2613cc, came in 1912. From that date, the sleeve-valve Knight engine was dominant at Panhard: a 35 cv of 7363cc was soon added to the line-up. In 1914, the first Panhard sleeve-valve six, a 6597cc 30 cv, was presented. After the war, Panhard resumed production with the 2280cc 10 cv poppet-valve model but soon returned to Knight-engined cars. In 1922 they introduced a small version of the 10 cv sleeve-valve of 1187cc. In 1925 all Panhards were sleeve-valve engined, from the four-cylinder 10, 16 and 20 cv to the eight-cylinder 35 cv (6355cc); that year, the 10 cv was enlarged to

1480cc. In 1927 another six-cylinder, the 2344cc 20/60 cv was made. Another eight-cylinder Panhard was built in the 1930s but this 5-litre car proved a failure. The range at that time was based on the 16/45 cv 1·8-litre and the 18/50 cv 2·3-litre. A futuristic touch came with the astonishing Dynamic of 1937: it had three seats at the front with the steering in the centre, backbone chassis and faired-in headlamps and wheels. It was offered in 2·5-litre, 2·7-litre and 3·8-litre forms. After the war, a complete change in policy resulted in the small fwd 610cc air-cooled flat-twin 'Dyna', enlarged to 750cc in 1950 and 800cc in 1952. A sports car, the 'Junior', was evolved from the Dyna in 1952. The last Panhard was the 24CT coupé launched in 1964. When Citroën took over Panhard in 1967, the factory was forced to stop making cars but the production of armoured cars under the Panhard name still continues.

1948 Panhard Dyna

1963 Panhard PL 17

PANTHER/*Germany 1902–1904*
A Magdeburg bicycle works which built cars with one-, two- and four-cylinder De Dion engines. Vormbaum, who owned the factory, sold the car manufacturing side to Dürkopp in 1904.

PANTHER/*England 1906*
F. M. Russell & Co., of London, showed the 14 hp Panther Roi-des-Belges, with a 'Kosmoid' engine, at the 1906 Olympia Show.

PANTHER/*USA 1909*
A tiny single-cylinder $300 car.

PANTHER/*England 1972 to date*
Arguably the motoring success story of the 1970s, Bob Jankel's Panther concern has produced an enormous collection of memorable machinery in a remarkably short space of time. Bearing more than a passing resemblance to the Jaguar SS100, the Panther J72 set the exacting standard for a company that would never look back. Interpretations of the Ferrari FF, the Bugatti Royale and Lancia D24 followed swiftly. The latter, powered by a modern Jaguar engine, was the hit of the 1974 London Motor Show. Other Panther creations include the one-off, three-seater, Jaguar-powered Lazer, the Rio (a specially bodied and extremely expensive Triumph Dolomite Sprint) and the astonishing 8·2-litre turbocharged Cadillac-engined six-wheeler. There is even a popular Panther now, the visually Morgan-like, Vauxhall-powered Lima.

1903 8hp Paragon

PANTHERE/*France 1920–1925*
M. Bogey (also the maker of the Violet-Bogey) built these cyclecars with sv 902cc Ruby engines in Paris.

PANTZ/*France 1900–1901*
Belt-driven 6 hp and 9 hp cars with twin-cylinder horizontal engines.

PAPILLON/*France 1904*
A long-wheelbase car with a 6 hp De Dion engine. This Parisian company also made motorcycles.

PAPILLON/*France 1921*
A cyclecar made in Paris by the French agent for Matchless and Velocette motorcycles. The engine was the sv 902cc Ruby.

1978 Panther six-wheeler

PARABUG/*Scotland 1972*
One of countless Volkswagen-based kit cars, the Parabug was a go-anywhere fun vehicle. The makers claimed it could be built in 50 hours.

PARAGON/*USA 1903–1907*
An 8 hp wheel-steered 'gas buggy' which sold in London for £230.

PARAGON/*England 1914*
A vee-twin 9 hp cyclecar from Manningtree, Essex.

PARAGON/*USA 1920–1921*
There is some mystery as to the origin of the Paragon, for although the company was initially located in Connelsville, Pennsylvania, and moved to Cumberland, Maryland, in 1921, the five prototype models were probably built in Ohio. The Paragon was powered by a four-cylinder ohv engine of its own design and had a Packard-like radiator. The touring car was listed at $3500, although the Paragon failed to get into production.

PARAMOUNT/*England 1951–1956*
Built in open and closed forms, the sporting Paramounts were based on a simple ladder chassis and powered by Ford engines from 1172cc to 1508cc.

PARENT/*France 1913*
From Maisons-Alfort (Seine), these light cars used 704cc (single) or 905cc (four) power units.

PARENTI/*USA 1920–1922*
The Parenti automobile was designed without axles, with transverse springing used instead: all cars featured a plywood unit body and frame construction. Initially with an air-cooled V-8 engine of its own design, Parenti substituted a Falls six later on. Production was limited and sales were poor. In 1922, the Buffalo-based car was sold to the Hanover Motor Car Co., of Hanover, Pennsylvania.

PARKER/*Canada 1922–1923*
Essentially the US Birmingham, but with conventional axles and suspension, the Montreal-built Parker also used the Haskelite Fabrikoid-covered plywood body. A handful of these 'Royal Sixes' was built before the company closed its doors in autumn 1923.

PARNACOTT/*England 1914*
A. E. Parnacott's cyclecar had a curious foot-operated chain-starting device.

PARR/*England 1901–1902*
Leicester-built 5 hp and 8 hp light cars with chain drive.

A Paramount roadster, c.1954

PARRY/*USA 1910–1912*
'In the spring a Parry is as irresistible as gravitation' carolled the Indianapolis makers of this 32/36 hp car. But even a change of name to 'New Parry' in 1912 failed to attract sufficient customers to make the marque viable.

PARTIN-PALMER/*USA 1913–1917*
This Chicago company offered a $975 six-cylinder 38 hp (originally plain 'Partin') and, in 1914, a $495 four-cylinder 20 hp. The marque was succeeded by the Commonwealth in 1917.

PARVILLE/*France 1927–1929*
Small fwd electric cars made in Paris.

PASCAL/*France 1902–1903*
Baron Henri de Rothschild, who worked as a doctor under the pseudonym 'Pascal' in the hospitals of Paris, backed this Mercedes-like 24 hp car: profits went to charity. The engine 'turned without trepidation or noise'.

Dr Rothschild's 1903 Pascal in the Algerian Desert

PASCO/*England 1908*
A 12 hp four-cylinder car with 'patent automatic gears, in which a reverse lever entirely takes the place of the ordinary change speed'.

PASING/*Germany 1902–1904*
Produced Klingenberg-designed cars under licence in small numbers. By 1903 the Pasing was outdated.

PASSAT/*England 1910*
M. B. Passat, of Wimbledon, built the first-ever 'flying car', a machine with two sets of bird-like wings which could be folded back and the machine driven along the road under its own power. Lack of finance killed the project.

PASSY-THELLIER/*France 1903–1907*
The Parisian Passy-Thelliers used De Dion, Buchet and Aster engines of 9, 12, 20 and 24 cv. The company claimed to have built the first voiturette to reach 100 kph. Later cars were known as Mendelssohns, from a director, M. Mendelssohn-Bartholdy, who was related to the famous composer.

PATERSON/*USA 1908–1924*
From the 'carriage capital' of Flint, Michigan, Paterson began production with a 30 hp four-cylinder. By 1919 they were building an undistinguished six-cylinder range with a 25 hp monobloc power unit, at prices ranging from $1265 to $1795.

PATHFINDER/*USA 1911–1918*
In 1914, the Indianapolis-built Pathfinder Six was available in two models, the 'Leather Stocking' and the 'Daniel Boone': a 'La Salle' was added in 1915.

PATIN/*France 1898–1900*
This electric dog-cart had a complex friction drive giving two speed ranges in addition to the normal controller mechanism.

PATRIA/*Germany 1900–1901*
This cycle manufacturer produced De Dion-engined cars for a short period.

PATRIA/*Spain c1919*
A Barcelona-built cyclecar with a motorcycle power unit.

PAUL MENARD/*France 1923*
A Humber agent in Clamart, Paris, Paul Menard assembled some cars from Humber parts and sold them under his own name.

PAUL SPIEDEL/*Switzerland 1915–1922*
Starting with a tandem-seated cyclecar with a four-cylinder Chapuis-Dornier engine, Paul Spiedel of Geneva subsequently built sporting 8 hp voiturettes with Müller-Vogel engines of two and four cylinders. Lack of finance restricted total output to 15 cars.

PAWI/*Germany 1921*
Paul Wilke's car had a 1598cc four-cylinder engine, but enjoyed no commercial success.

PAWTUCKET/*USA 1900–1902*
A twin-cylinder steam car built in three models by the Pawtucket Steamboat Company, RI.

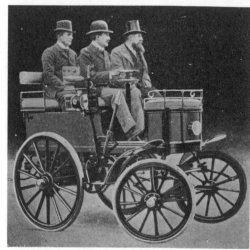

c. 1899 Patin dogcart

PAX/*France 1907–1909*
Another minor manufacturer from Suresnes, Paris, who built 10/14 hp and 18/24 hp four-cylinder light cars.

PAYDELL/*England 1924–1925*
A 13·9 hp Meadows four powered this little-seen car from Hendon.

PAYNE-MODERN/*USA 1907–1909*
Designed by Gilbert J. Loomis, the Payne-Modern — whose front springs were tilted up at the front by 15 degrees for easier riding — was backed by an oil millionaire; air-cooled vee-formation single ohc engines of four (3707cc), six (5500cc) and eight (7413cc) cylinders and a constant mesh gearbox controlled by a steering-column lever were used. Prototypes were built from 1904.

PAYZE/*England 1920–1921*
Built at Cookham, Berkshire, the Payze used a 10 hp Coventry-Simplex engine. The price in 1920 was £450.

PDA/*England 1913*
Built by Pickering, Darby and Allday, of Birmingham, this ephemeral 8 hp cyclecar had a choice of air- or water-cooled JAP engines.

PEARSON-COX/*England 1908–1916*
Pearson and Cox, of Shortlands, Bromley, Kent, were among the more successful British steam car (and motorcycle!) makers. Their cars were three-cylinder models with shaft drive, which sold for £380.

PECK/*Canada 1912–1913*
An expensive ($4000) electric brougham from Toronto.

PEEL/*Isle of Man 1962–c1968*
A 49cc DKW moped engine powered this tiny single-seater, which had a handle at the back so that it could be lifted into the narrowest parking places.

1913 Pearson-Cox steam car

c.1924 Peerless 5.4-litre V-8 tourer

1929 Peerless Six-81 3.7-litre Sedan

PEERLESS/*USA 1900–1931*

Peerless of Cleveland turned from cycles and clothes-wringers to motor cars with single-cylinder 'Motorettes'. Their 1902 range, designed by Louis P. Mooers, was more advanced, with twin-cylinder engines, shaft drive and side-entrance bodies. Two T-head fours (24 hp and 34 hp) appeared in 1903. Much useful publicity was provided by the 11,120cc 'Green Dragon'

racer of 1904, driven by Barney Oldfield. Now regarded as a prestige marque, Peerless launched their first six in 1907. Self-starters were standardized in 1913, and in 1915 a V-8 — 'The Equipoised Eight' — ousted the sixes; a six-cylinder Peerless was not built again until 1924. A Continental six — the first non-Peerless engine — appeared in 1925, and a Continental V-8 was adopted in 1929. Restyling by Count

Alexis de Sakhnoffsky failed to halt sliding sales, and the 1931 7·6-litre V-16 never saw production. After the repeal of Prohibition, Peerless re-emerged as the brewers of Carlings Ale.

PEERLESS (BRITISH PEERLESS)
England 1902–1904
The shaft-drive 8 hp single-cylinder Peerless Voiturette appeared at the 1902 Cordingley show in London's Agricultural Hall and offered 'three speeds forward and one reverse on one lever'. 10 hp and 12 hp twin-cylinder models were available in 1904.

PEERLESS/*England 1958–1962*
Designed by Bernie Rodger and produced by Peerless Motors of Slough, the four-seater Grand Touring Peerless was powered by a Triumph TR3 engine. The multi-tubular chassis was clothed in a shapely alloy body. A racing version finished in 16th place at Le Mans in 1958.

PEEWICK/*England 1963*
Very much a one-off, the Peewick was Chris Lawrence's idea of what the Peerless should have been. Its use of many Peerless as well as Warwick components led to the car's unusual name. Based on Lawrence's own tubular chassis, the Peewick, powered by a Triumph TR3 engine, was capable of well over 110 mph.

PEGASO/*Spain 1951–1957*
Enasa, the Spanish state truck company, took over the old Hispano-Suiza factory at Barcelona, to produce Pegaso commercials; in 1951 they also began limited production of a Ricart-designed V-8 luxury sports car of 2474cc, introduced at the 1951 Paris Salon, and claimed to be 'the fastest car in the world'. The Z-102 Pegaso could achieve 250 kph (156 mph), and at Jabbeke in Belgium, set up flying kilometre and mile records of 243·079 and 244·602 kph respectively, in September 1953.

Pegaso Z-102 coupé, 1951

PEKRUN/*Germany 1909–1911*
Made by a machine factory at Coswig in Saxony, only one model was in the Pekrun production programme. It was a 2594cc four-cylinder, 'without valves' according to the catalogue. The car had friction drive and a planetary three-speed gearbox.

PELHAM/*England 1904–1905*
Taking its name from the Pelham Street Garage, Kensington, this two-seater voiturette had a 6½ hp De Dion engine.

PENN/*USA 1910–1913*
Two models — fours of 30 hp and 45 hp — were available of this Pittsburgh marque.

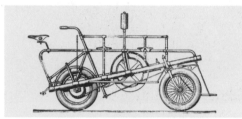
1896 Pennington three-wheeled Torpedo Autocar

PENNINGTON/*USA*/*England 1894–1900*
Edward Joel Pennington was a 'mechanical charlatan' from America who built a tubular framed 'Victoria' powered by a parallel-twin engine with minimal cooling: the design had two other Pennington trade marks — large section pneumatic tyres in lieu of suspension and 'long-mingling spark' ignition. Speed was controlled by metering the amount of petrol dribbled into the cylinders — there was no carburettor. Initially, these vehicles were built by Kane &

1894 Pennington Victoria

Company of Chicago: late in 1895 Pennington sailed to England and sold his British patents to Harry J. Lawson's Great Horseless Carriage Company. They produced a handful of motorcycles and three-wheeled 'Torpedo Autocars', long-stroke crudities devoid of cooling. The 1898 National Cycle Show saw an even weirder Pennington, the Raft Victoria, with front-wheel drive, rear-wheel steering and rope transmission: a one-off de luxe version was built by Stirling, but managed to consume 72 spark plugs between Manchester and Nuneaton on an abortive trip to London. In 1899, Pennington returned to America to promote a new company, building a few four-wheeled Torpedoes.

PENNSY/*USA 1916–1919*
A 30/35 hp four from Pittsburgh.

PENNSYLVANIA/*USA 1907–1911*
A 50 hp ohv four of 6098cc powered the 1907 $2800 Pennsylvania, from Bryn Mawr. A 25 hp four was added for 1909.

PERFEX/*USA 1912–1914*
The Perfex, from Los Angeles, had a 3247cc G.B. & S. four-cylinder engine.

PERFEX/*England 1920–1921*
An English version of the make from Los Angeles, the English Perfex used the same power unit as its American counterpart, a 22·5 hp G.B. & S.

PERL/*Austria 1921–1928*
Perl produced small cars with 898cc sv (afterwards ohv) four-cylinder engines. The factory also produced lorries and car bodies; it was eventually taken over by Gräf & Stift.

LA PERLE/*France 1913–1927*
Starting pre-war with a twin-cylinder cyclecar, Louis Lefèvre and his brother built light cars with Bignan and Altos engines in MAB chassis in the 1920s. A racing version, with supercharged six-cylinder Causan engine, could attain 160 kph (100 mph).

PERREAU/*France 1921*
Made in Epinay, Seine, this car had a four-cylinder 1495cc engine.

PERRY/*England 1913–1916*
Forerunner of the Bean, this marque was produced by a Birmingham cycle components firm, and appeared initially as a 6·4 hp vertical-twin of 875cc, followed in 1915 by an 11·9 hp four of 1795cc.

PESTOURIE ET PLANCHON
France 1921–1922
This light car made in Paris was virtually a three-wheeler, as the rear wheels had a very narrow track. The engine was a four-cylinder of 904cc.

PETERILL/*Belgium 1899*
A lightweight carriage built in Antwerp, powered by a twin-cylinder Aster engine.

PETER-MORITZ/*Germany 1921–1925*
The first P-M was an air-cooled 1218cc twin-cylinder, made at Eisenberg in Thuringia. Production was afterwards transferred to Naumburg/Saale, and a 1305cc water-cooled flat-twin engine was specified.

PETERS/*USA 1921–1922*
A small air-cooled twin-cylinder car, the Peters was built in Trenton, New Jersey. All cars were equipped with wire wheels and the three styles available — two-passenger speedster, roadster and station wagon — were priced at $345. Peters became a division of Romer Motors Corporation in 1922, and although listings vary — some put the car as late as 1926 — it is unlikely that any Peters cars were made after 1922.

PETIT/*France 1908–1909*
A voiturette powered by a 6cv Aster engine, weighing only 350 kg (770 lb).

PETREL/*USA 1908–1912*
A Wisconsin make with a 30 hp 4687cc engine, the earliest models having friction transmission with chain final drive. There was a sister marque, the F-S, with 22 hp, 30 hp and 40 hp engines.

1914 Perry 6.4hp twin-cylinder coupé

1895 Peugeot 3½hp *vis-à-vis*

The Peugeot 201 team in the 1933 Tour de France

PEUGEOT
France 1889 to date

Armand Peugeot built his first steam car in 1889, and from 1891 made Daimler-engined cars with rear engines in tubular chassis, they sold very well for the era. In 1896 Peugeot started to make his own engines. In 1902 the 758cc 'Bébé' was presented, and, two years later, Peugeot offered cars from 1·7 litres to 7·1 litres. Their first six-cylinder, a 10·4-litre, appeared in 1908, followed the next year by a smaller six of 3317cc. In 1912, Bugatti designed a new 855cc four-cylinder 'Bébé', and the same year Peugeot also made a V-4 of 1725cc. At that period, the dohc Peugeot racers designed by Ernest Henry were victorious in many events, including the French Grand Prix and the Indianapolis 500. At the outbreak of the war, Peugeot's staple products were the model 153 12 cv of 2613, and the 7 cv of 1452cc. After the war, Peugeot resumed production with these two models, to which were added the 10 cv of 1525cc and the 25 cv six of 5954cc. The popular 667cc 'Quadrilette' was introduced in 1920, giving way in 1923 to the 5 cv, this

model being enlarged in 1925 to 719cc. During the 1920s, there also was the sleeve-valve 18 cv of 3827cc, and—in 1927—a 3·8-litre six. The basic model was the 201 of 1100cc: it lasted for 10 years before giving way to the 1500cc 301. The last of the pre-war Peugeot six-cylinders, the 601, appeared in 1936; a year later came the streamlined Peugeot 402 which lasted until the war, alongside the 302 and 202. During the Occupation, Peugeot experimented with the electric-powered VLV. After the war, production restarted with the 202, and in 1947 Peugeot presented the 1·3-litre 203. The next step was the 403 of 1955, with a 1500cc engine. The 404 came in 1960, with a 1600cc engine. All these cars were also available in diesel form. A smaller car—the 1100cc 204—was launched in 1965, to be replaced in 1969 by the 304 with a 1300cc engine. The 504 was born in 1968. In the 1970s Peugeot took control first of Citroën, then of Chrysler Europe. The most recent models are the V-6-engined 604 and the 104, a small car also sold with a Citroën engine as the Citroën LN.

1948 Peugeot 203 Berline grand luxe

1979 Peugeot 104S

PEUGEOT-CROIZAT/*Italy 1906–1908*
Peugeots from the single-cylinder 5 hp to the 50 hp four assembled by a Torinese firm.

PG/*France 1921*
The origins of this 1495cc car are unknown.

PHANOMEN/*Germany 1913–1927*
Phänomen was originally a leading producer of motorcycles, three-wheelers and cars . . . the three-wheeled Phänomobil, with a 1536cc air-cooled four-cylinder engine mounted above the small front wheel, was commercially the most successful Phänomen product. An earlier version had a sv 880cc vee-twin motorcycle engine. The two car models built pre-war had 2580cc and 3968cc four-cylinder engines: a sv 2612cc was made from 1920 to 1924. In 1927 an ohc 3128cc four-cylinder was constructed at the Zittau Phänomen works. The factory was nationalized in 1945, and built Robur trucks.

1900 Phebus-Aster 3½hp, designed by Noé Boyer

PHEBUS/*France 1899–1903*
The original 'Automobilette' built by Noé Boyer's Phébus company (linked with Clément-Gladiator-Humber) had a 2¼ hp Aster engine. It was followed by the 3½ hp Phébus-Aster voiturette.

PHELPS
USA 1903–1905

Externally orthodox in appearance, the 1903 three-cylinder Phelps had a backbone chassis containing the two-speed gearbox and drive shaft and a body that could be lifted up to reveal chassis and engine.

PHENIX/*France 1912–1914*
Built by Prunel Frères, Dumas et Cie, formerly makers of the Prunel car, the Phénix light car was available in two models, both with four cylinders, and using a common chassis. One had a 1460cc engine, the other a 2121cc power unit.

PHIANNA/*USA 1916–1922*
The Phianna was successor to the SGV; the first Phianna cars incorporated some SGV components. Named after Phyllis and Anna, twin daughters of one of the group who had purchased the SGV interests, the car was from the

first a low-production, prestigious make, featuring an oval radiator and laminated walnut and ash fans located co-axially with the flywheel. An own-make four-cylinder engine was used. Phianna was sold to Miles Harold Carpenter in 1918; he continued the high quality of the make. The radiator was changed to a square Rolls-Royce type in 1919 and the make became a favourite for numerous heads of state, although production was very limited. By 1920, the Phianna five-passenger touring car was selling for $9500. The make failed in 1921 and remaining stock was used to assemble a few units which were sold as 1922 models. Carpenter ultimately designed experimental cars, using a Curtiss OX-5 aircraft engine, and, later, the Dart (Martin) midget car.

PHILIPIN/*Sweden 1946*
After the war the Swedish agent (Philipsons of Stockholm) for Auto-Union/DKW had problems with deliveries from Germany. However, during the war, planning had started for a small fwd four-seater saloon, with a licence-built twin-cylinder DKW engine of 700cc. A wooden prototype (it is still preserved) was built, but the economic situation and the news of the coming Saab car stopped the project.

PHILIPP/*England 1904*
Philipp & Co. were manufacturers of motor car components who also offered a twin-cylinder complete chassis.

PHILOS/*France 1912–1922*
The Société des Automobiles Philos of Lyon started in 1912 with a 1592cc Ballot-engined car, followed in 1914 by a smaller (1130cc) model. After the war Philos resumed with Altos-engined cars of 7/11hp (1328cc) and 14hp (1779cc) and another 1592cc Ballot-engined 14hp similar to the pre-war model.

PHOENIX/*USA 1899–1901*
Designed by R. M. Owen, this two-cylinder 3907cc petrol car was available with passenger or delivery wagon bodywork. It was built by a firm of contract carpet cleaners from Cleveland, Ohio.

PHOENIX, BARCAR/*England 1903–1908*
A mechanically minded medico, Dr W. H. Barrett, and Mr C. C. Cardell, took over the Hudlass business in 1902 and began production of Hudlass's design under the name of Phoenix (after the Phoenix Works founded by Hudlass in 1896). In 1904 they began using the name Barcar, and later that year announced a curious three-cylinder Barcar with 'an impulse every stroke', with the central cylinder working off the exhaust gases of the outer pair. In 1907 Barcar moved to Altrincham, took over the factory where Eagle cars had been built, and concentrated on building motorboat engines.

PHOENIX/*England 1903–1928*
J. Van Hooydonk started with the famous Phoenix Trimo three-wheeler on motorcycle lines: in 1905 came the Quad-Car runabout, with wheel-steering and 7/8hp twin-cylinder Fafnir engine. In 1908 came a true light car, with a 10hp two-cylinder engine and circular bonnet,

joined in 1910 by a 13hp, still with two cylinders; the 1913 Phoenix had a dashboard radiator and 11·9hp four-cylinder engine. After the war, it received a frontal radiator, and was joined in 1920 by an 18hp 3064cc four with overhead camshaft. In 1922 came the ohv 1795cc Meadows-engined 12/25, which sold for £425 against the larger car's £575. A six, again Meadows-engined, appeared in 1925. Van Hooydonk is said to have ended his days as a piano-tuner.

1923 12/25hp Phoenix Allweather

PHONIX/*Hungary 1905–c1912*
An ohv 40hp four-cylinder Phönix car from Bodvinecz & Heisler, of Budapest, was shown at the 1907 Vienna Exhibition. Based on the Cudell, the Phönix preceded the MAG.

PHRIXUS/*France 1924–1931*
Made in Paris by M. Oppenheim, the Phrixus was a cyclecar with friction transmission and available with sv 1094cc Altos or ohv 807cc Chapuis-Dornier units. Some of these cars were sold under the 'OP' name.

LE PIAF/*France 1951–1952*
A few of these cars, powered by a 175cc two-stroke engine, were made in the Livry-Gargan, Seine, works.

PICCOLO/*Germany 1904–1912*
Made by Ruppe & Sohn at Apolda, the Piccolo was the predecessor of the Apollo. Piccolo cars were air-cooled: the first model had a 704cc vee-twin engine. From 1908, the capacity was increased to 794cc. Other models of the Piccolo and Apollo-Piccolo were an 846cc vertical-twin, a 624cc single-cylinder, an in-line four of 1608cc and a 1575cc V-4. The last model, before the name Piccolo disappeared, was an ioe in-line 1770cc four with separate — still air-cooled — cylinders.

PICK/*England 1898–1925*
Jack Pick of Stamford, Lincolnshire, started production with his 'No 1 air-cooled Motor Voiturette' with a two-speed gear of his own design and belt final drive. It was soon joined by 'No 2 water-cooled Motor Dogcart', with a 4½hp engine. By 1903 a 6hp flat-twin and a gear-driven 12hp were available. The 'New Pick' appeared in 1910, with a 22·4hp four-cylinder engine of 3600cc (a 20hp 3232cc version was listed in 1913–14), and continued to the end of production, when a doorless 'Sporting Pick' model with drainpipe exhaust, geared to 40mph at 1000rpm, was listed. Mr Pick subsequently turned to greengrocery.

PICKARD/*USA 1908–1912*
The three Pickard brothers, from Brockton, Mass., built their first car, a 5hp single, in 1903.

The 1908 Pickard had an ohv four-cylinder air-cooled 25hp engine and a composite oak/steel chassis.

PIC-PIC/*Switzerland 1905–1924*
Hydraulic engineers Piccard-Pictet of Geneva began building cars designed by Marc Birkigt (and very similar to the recently introduced Hispano-Suiza) for the Société d'Automobiles de Genève. While the marque was known as SAG in Switzerland until 1910, in export markets it always seems to have been 'Pic-Pic'. The first cars were shaft-driven pair-cast 20/24hp and 35/40hp fours, a 5655cc six appearing in 1907. In 1910–12, Pic-Pics of 14/18hp and 18/22hp were introduced. Single-sleeve-valve engines appeared in 1912, and front-wheel brakes and hydraulic shock-absorbers were used on the firm's 1914 Grand Prix cars, which introduced the handsome shouldered vee-radiator used on the post-war Pic-Pics (one of the GP cars was rebodied as a coupé by the London Improved Coachbuilders of Lupus Street, London). The firm was reformed after a financial crash in 1919 and taken over in 1921 by the Ateliers de Charmilles, who sold off the car-building activities to a group of financiers. But the 3-litre sleeve-valve shown at the 1924 Geneva Salon proved to be the last of the Pic-Pics.

1908 Pic-Pic racing car converted to road use

PIEDMONT/*USA 1917–1922*
Although the Piedmont was a relatively successful small-production assembled car in its own right, it is far better known for its manufacture of cars for other firms (Alsace, Bush, Norwalk, Lone Star, Marshall, and Stork Kar). Piedmont cars were available in open and closed models, powered by four-cylinder Lycoming or six-cylinder Continental engines.

PIEPER/*Belgium 1899–1903*
Piéper were cycle makers from Liège, whose first two-seater voiturette appeared in 1899. 'Once seen, always admired', the Piéper had either a 3½hp single or 6hp twin-cylinder engine with belt drive, and was aimed at the lady motorist.

1905 7hp Pick

PIERCE-ARROW / *USA 1901–1938*

George N. Pierce began business in Buffalo, NY, in 1865 making birdcages and squirrel cages and progressed to shaft-drive cycles *via* cycle spokes. His company built an unsuccessful steam car in 1900, followed by a De Dion-engined quadricycle. Their first production model—the De Dion-engined Motorette—was designed by Yorkshireman David Fergusson, who came over with Pennington in 1899. Later in 1902 came a 15 hp twin, the Arrow, and in 1904 Fergusson introduced a Mercedes-inspired 24/28 hp, the 3770cc Great Arrow. Next year 30 hp and 40 hp Great Arrows were added, and Pierce-Arrow won the 1000-mile Glidden Tour reliability trial for the first of four times in succession. From 1905, cast

aluminium body panels were used, and the first Pierce (the marque adopted the name Pierce-Arrow in 1909) six-cylinder made its debut in the 1906 Glidden Tour: by 1910 only sixes were available, the biggest being the gargantuan '66' of 11,700cc (uprated to 13,514cc in 1912, making it America's biggest-ever production car—1638 were built in ten years). The marque's distinctive fender headlamps appeared with the 1913 'Second Series', which also ended annual model changes. The 1918 'Fifth Series' 47 hp had pair-cast cylinders and four valves per cylinder, but was soon replaced by a revised monobloc version. In 1920, Pierce-Arrow finally dropped right-hand steering. For 1925, a 'cheap' model, the Series 80, the first four-wheel-braked Pierce-Arrow, was

introduced. The Series 81, which replaced it in 1928, had unfortunate Art Deco styling by James R. Way, and sales suffered, precipitating an ill-starred merger with Studebaker. The new 5998cc straight-eight of 1929 was an excellent car, and 8000 were sold in its first year: but by 1932 sales had crumbled to 2692, despite an exciting new V-12 (a prototype set up a new 24-hour record, broken in 1933 by a production V-12 at 117mph). An ultra-streamlined 'Silver Arrow' was built for the Chicago World's Fair in 1933, shortly after a consortium of Buffalo businessmen had bought Pierce-Arrow back from Studebaker. The outstanding 1936 range—Model 1601 eight and Models 1602 and 1603 twelves—failed to halt the sales slide.

1923 Pierce-Arrow Twin-Valve Six

1929 Pierce-Arrow straight-eight

PIERCE-RACINE / *USA 1901–1911*

A. J. Pierce of Racine built his first gas engine in 1884: the Pierce company claimed to have built its first car in 1894 and the second in 1899. In 1901 20 8 hp 'detachable seat surreys' were sold at $800 each, and in 1903 some 150 twin-cylinder cars were sold. The first four-cylinder Pierce came in 1905: fours of 30 hp (3678cc) and 40 hp (5738cc) were produced. Case took over the company in 1911, and continued manufacturing the cars under their own name.

PIERRE ROY / *France 1902–1909*

No connection with its contemporary, the Georges Roy, this car from Montrouge (Seine) started life as a 10/12 hp twin-cylinder shaft-drive car on Renault lines, with lateral radiators and a crocodile bonnet. Pierre Roy drove one of his creations to a class victory in the 1903 Dourdan speed trial. Later, four-cylinder cars of 14/20 hp and 24/30 hp were offered. At the 1908 Paris Salon, 10/14 hp four-cylinder cars were exhibited.

PIGGINS / *USA 1909*

The 'Practical' Piggins was a big six of 36 hp or 50 hp from Racine, Wisconsin.

PIGGOTT / *England 1899–1901*

A motor quadricycle with the option of tube or electric ignition.

PILAIN / *France 1894–1898*

François Pilain worked for Serpollet, then moved to Lyon to build Serpollet steam three-wheelers under licence at La Buire. He set up on his own in 1893, building his first tiller-steered phaeton early in 1894. In 1898 he joined Vermorel as Director General, with his nephew, Emile Pilain, as assistant.

PILAIN (SLIM-PILAIN) / *France 1902–1920*

Made in Lyon by François Pilain, these cars had initially two- and four-cylinder engines. In 1903, the twin-cylinder was dropped. Pilain's four-cylinder models were the 20 cv of 5701cc and the 40 cv of 8621cc. The year 1909 saw the introduction of the 12/15cv of 2120cc, which continued until 1920. A 15/18 cv six 2389cc was announced in 1913 alongside a long-stroke (85 × 185mm) 18/24 cv four of 4199cc. After the war, Pilain's most significant models were the 11 cv of 1725cc, the 15 cv of 1888cc, and the 15 cv of 2484cc, made under the name of SLIM-Pilain, for the Ste. Lyonnaise d'Industrie Méca-

nique et Automobile, whose factory Pilain had taken over in 1920. The finest cars made by Pilain were the ohc 3817cc and the 4 268 12 hp, with four overhead valves per cylinder controlled by two camshafts in the crankcase. A distinctive feature of this marque for many years was a pneumatic starter.

PILGRIM / *England 1906–1914*

The twin-cylinder 11·9 hp Pilgrim, built by the Pilgrims' Way Motor Company of Farnham, Surrey, had a Renault-type bonnet and, unusually, featured front-wheel drive.

PILGRIM OF PROVIDENCE / *USA 1911*

A prototype which C. W. Kelsey had planned to construct in Providence, RI, but built at his factory in Hartford. It was a four-cylinder car of conventional design and was scrapped when the Motorette failed and the factory was closed.

PILOT / *England 1910–1914*

'A £150 car and course of instruction FREE' was the prize offered in a monthly competition run by Motor Schools Limited, owners of Pilot Motors. Alternatively, you *could* buy a Pilot, a 10·5 hp two-seater with five-speed friction drive.

PILOT/*USA 1911–1924*
Big Teetor six-cylinder engines of 55 hp and 75 hp powered the 1914 Pilots, 'champions of the road and hills'. In 1921–24, Herschell-Spillman sixes of 4078cc were also available.

PILOT/*Germany 1921–1925*
Of advanced design, the 1098cc Pilot had an ohc 16-valve unit-design engine and was made by a railway carriage factory. Production was limited, and the car became known mainly in south-west Germany.

PINEDE/*France 1898*
A light 3 cv twin-cylinder voiturette selling at Fr 4000–6000.

PINNACE/*England 1912–1913*
Forerunner of the Norma, this JAP-engined cyclecar was shaped like a ship's pinnace, with a sharp bow!

PIONEER/*USA 1907–1911*
High-wheeled shaft-drive runabouts (20 hp two-cylinder, 28/30 hp four) from El Reno, Oklahoma.

PIONEER/*USA 1915*
The Pioneer was a 14 hp four from Troy, NY.

PIPE/*Belgium 1898–1914*
One of Belgium's best-engineered cars, the Ghent-built Pipe began the century as a 6 hp twin on Panhard lines, joined in 1902 by a 15 hp four. A few petrol-electrics were built in 1904–05, but the 1904 Paris Salon saw the introduction of pushrod ohv in a hemispherical head, on four-cylinder cars of 3770cc and 8302cc. There was an apparent gap in production in 1908–10, though Pipe built some V-8 airship engines during that period. The 1910–11 model was a small side-valve, and long-stroke side-valve fours saw the marque through to the end of private car construction.

1907 50/60hp Pipe

PIPER/*England 1967–1976*
Well over 120 Ford-powered, glass-fibre-bodied Pipers were built during the life of the company, many of which survive today. Though not particularly successful, the mid-engined GTR race version looked fantastic. Later plans to market replicas on VW chassis did not get far.

PITT/*England 1902–1904*
The Pitt Yorkshire Machine Company, of Liversedge, built these 'Durable and perfect' 5 hp, 9 hp and 12 hp crocodile-bonneted cars.

PITTSBURGH/*USA 1899*
A 3 hp twin-cylinder 'gasolene runabout' with a top speed of 18 mph, predecessor to Autocar.

PITTSBURGH SIX/*USA 1908–1910*
'Simple, powerful and efficient', the 70 hp Pittsburgh Six car had a side-valve engine of 9147cc and shaft drive. A 'small' 40/45 hp (6570cc) six was added for 1910.

PIVOT/*France 1904–1908*
The 1905 Pivot, from Puteaux (Seine), had a 24/30 hp power unit with 'three double cylinders, three pistons, six compression chambers, cranks set at 120 degrees.' . . . The 1908 16/20 hp and 24/30 hp were conventional four-cylinder cars.

PLANET/*England 1904–1907*
Built a range of shaft-driven cars with engines of 6 hp to 24 hp.

PLASS/*USA 1897*
Reuben Plass, who claimed to have built his first car in the 1860s, offered this rear-engined phaeton with an 'L'-shaped tiller for steering with hand or foot.

PLASSON/*France 1910*
The 2413cc four-cylinder Plasson, built in Montmartre, ran on paraffin. Its makers claimed it was the 'sole paraffin motor sold at the same price as a petrol motor'.

LA PLATA/*France? 1906*
The 8/10 hp La Plata had a twin-cylinder Aster Engine, and though it was probably an import from France, had Sheffield-built coachwork.

PLAYBOY/*USA 1946–1951*
War prevented production until 1946, although an experimental Playboy had been running in 1940. It was a practical little car with an overall length of 155 inches. Height was a mere 54 inches and the car featured an all-metal folding top which stowed away behind the three-passenger seat. Powered by a 40 hp four-cylinder Hercules engine, it used a Warner Gear automatic transmission and self-adjusting brakes. The unitary body was undercoated and the Playboy sold for $985. Louis Horwitz, president of the Playboy Motor Car Corp., had expected annual production to be 100,000 but only 90–100 cars were built in Tonawanda, NY.

1968 Piper GTT

PLUTO/*Germany 1924–1927*
Made by the gigantic Ehrhardt group at the Zella-Mehlis/St Blasii works, the Pluto was a French Amilcar built under licence, with 970cc, 1054cc and 1111cc four-cylinder sv engines. Supercharged racing versions were also built which, driven by Gockenbach, Mederer, Friedrich and von Einem, won many sporting events.

PLYMOUTH/*USA 1910–1911*
A heavy friction-driven 50 hp from Plymouth, Ohio, mostly built with commercial bodywork, though at least one tourer appeared.

PLYMOUTH/*USA 1928 to date*
Chrysler 'went into the low-priced field with the throttle wide open' with the 1928 Plymouth Four, demand exceeding supply to such an extent that a second factory had to be built by 1929; the 1930 Plymouth U sedan cost the same as comparable Ford and Chevrolet models, and offered a radio as an option. The all-new 1931 Plymouth PA, with eight different body styles, was followed by the PB of 1932, and the marque's first six, the PD, costing only $495. The 1933 models featured an automatic clutch which operated every time the throttle was released. On 10 August 1934, production reached the first million. Unlike Chrysler and DeSoto, Plymouth never produced an Airflow model; their styling emphasized safety features, such as padded seatbacks and recessed controls, though one odd 1936 model, convertible from sedan to ambulance to hearse 'in a matter of seconds', seemed to be carrying things too far . . . Sealed-beam headlamps were standardized on 1940 models, and the 1942 Plymouth 14C had full-width styling. A development of this, the 15S, formed the basis of post-war production up to 1949, when all-new styling in three series was introduced—the P17 DeLuxe, P18 and P18 Special DeLuxe, all with the same 3569cc sv six. Some export markets knew the Special DeLuxe as the 'DeSoto Diplomat' or 'Dodge Kingsway'. Conservative styling lost Plymouth their third place in sales to Buick, so the 1955 cars were longer and lower, with a new 4621cc Hy-Fire V-8, unique to Plymouth. (The sv six was finally replaced in 1960.) Sales rose to a record 742,991 in 1955, but the third place in sales was not regained until 1957, when Virgil Exner's FlightSweep styling appeared, with more glass, less chrome and taller tailfins than the opposition. The Fury performance model

1931 Plymouth PA sedan

Plymouth Volare compact

1962 Plymouth Fury Hardtop

had a potent V-8 of 5211cc, optional on other models, and Plymouths adopted the Chrysler group's torsion-bar front suspension. A new 5736cc V-8 appeared in 1958, but production fell to half the 1957 level, due to poor quality control. The 1960 models had engines up to 6276cc, new styling and unitary construction; fins were bigger than ever, though they were to vanish a year later. A brand new compact, the Valiant, with the new Slant Six of 3687cc, was launched. But Plymouth again lost third place, this time to AMC's Rambler. New and unusual styling graced the 1962 big Plymouths; models included Belvedere, and Fury I, II and III. The Belvedere Satellite performance model offered a 6981cc V-8 of 425 bhp. The Barracuda fastback appeared in 1964, and was totally redesigned in 1967, with the Slant Six as standard. That year, 38 models and a staggering variety of engine options were offered. The Belvedere intermediate formed the basis for the performance GTX, as well as for the 1968 Road Runner (its horn sounded like the cartoon character from which it took its name!) claimed to be the world's fastest coupé with a top speed of up to 160 mph. A limited edition 'Super Bird' Road Runner (1200 were built) was even faster. The 1970 Duster, with 3244cc Slant Six or 5572cc V-8, was known as the 'pocket Road Runner'. Top of the 1971 range was the Sport Fury with Brougham luxury interior, as the 1966-launched VIP had been dropped, as indeed had the Belvedere, replaced by the Satellite Coupé, Custom and Sebring. The 'Plymouth Cricket' was an imported Chrysler-UK Avenger. By 1975 cars like the Road Runner, Satellite and Barracuda had disappeared, victims of the 1973 oil crisis, while the Fury came in three sizes — 'intermediate, large and full-size' — Valiant and Duster still being offered. A new line of

compacts, the Volare, appeared in 1976, completely supplanting the Fury line by 1978. For 1979, the Volare was the biggest Plymouth, with standard engines up to a 5211cc V-8 and models including a Road Runner; a Police Package offered a 5899cc V-8 and 120 mph top speed. New was the fwd 1716cc Horizon with all-round independent suspension, while the Sapporo and Arrow were Mitsubishi imports sold under the Plymouth banner.

PM/*Belgium 1922–1924*
A 1795cc Peters engine powered this light car from Liège, which had business ties with Carrow of England.

PMC/*USA 1908–1909*
A 12 hp high-wheeled buggy built by the C. S. Peets Mfg. Co., of New York.

PODEUS/*Germany 1911–1914*
The Podeus machine works at Wismar produced two models: 2248cc and 2536cc sv fours.

POLSKI-FIAT/*Poland 1948 to date*
Originally assembling the Russian Gaz Pobieda under licence as the Warszawa, this state-owned company began building the Fiat 125 P under licence in 1968. The modern Polonez uses Polski-Fiat 125 running gear, and there is also a Polski-Fiat 126 P.

POLYMOBIL/*Germany 1904–1909*
Based on the Curved-Dash Oldsmobile, the 1563cc three-seater Polymobile 'Gazelle' was made by the manufacturer of the Polyphon, a coin-in-the-slot clockwork musical box which was the remote ancestor of the juke box. A twin-cylinder version of 1356cc appeared in 1908: a four-cylinder 20 hp was built in small numbers.

POMEROY/*USA 1923–1924*
Designed by L. H. Pomeroy (who had designed noteworthy models for Daimler and Vauxhall), the Pomeroy was built at the Pierce-Arrow plant in Buffalo, New York, as the successor to the earlier Aluminum-Four. This had been built experimentally under Alcoa aegis to demonstrate the value of aluminium as a practical metal for motor car manufacture. Perhaps as many as ten Pomeroy cars were produced in all. These were not available to the public, the five-passenger sedans being used exclusively for testing purposes.

PONDER/*USA 1923*
Only one Ponder — a touring car — was ever built; this was presumably only a Bour-Davis with a different radiator emblem, as it succeeded the Bour-Davis, which had been built in Shreveport, Louisiana, since 1919.

1914 La Ponette 1592cc two-seater

LA PONETTE/*France 1909–1925*
This very small car builder started in 1909 with a single-cylinder 697cc car which looked like a small Renault. In 1911, it was followed by a four-cylinder 1592cc Ballot-engined car, which remained in production until 1920. Some minor models were also made, with various proprietary engines until the Société des Automobiles la Ponette, from Chevreuse, Yvelines, collapsed in 1925.

PONSARD-ANSALONI/*France 1898*
Also known as 'Brulé', this was a power-pack conversion for horse-carriages, with a twin-cylinder Roser-Mazurier engine.

PONTIAC/*USA 1907–1908*
Another of the legion American high-wheelers, this twin-cylinder had friction drive.

PONTIAC/*USA 1926 to date*

'The chief of the sixes' was designed by Ben H. Anibal as a low-priced running mate for Oakland; it was so successful that it ousted the older marque entirely. Indeed, it was — and is — the only marque created (rather than acquired) by General Motors to last more than a couple of seasons. The original sv 3064cc six lasted until 1930, when a Marquette-based 3277cc ohv six appeared. The last Oakland, an Olds Viking-based V-8 of 4104cc, became a Pontiac for 1932, but failed to last, and was quickly succeeded by America's first under-$600 straight-eight, a 3654cc unit which even briefly supplanted the six. 'Knee-action' ifs was introduced in 1934, as were 'turret-top' bodies. For 1935, 'Silver Streak' styling was launched as 'the most beautiful thing on wheels'; the British importer, Kaye Don, offered English-built coupé versions. A new look came with the 1941 Torpedo range, sold alongside the Streamliner and Streamliner Chieftain. The first post-war redesign came in 1949, with fastback (Streamline) and notchback (Chieftain) bodies. But that year's Canadian Pontiacs were basically Chevrolets with Pontiac grilles. The first Catalina hardtops appeared in 1950, dual-range Hydramatic transmission in 1952, wraparound rear windows and power steering in 1953. The sv eight was replaced by an ohv V-8 of 4703cc in 1955, and the sixes relegated to Canadian production. Only 3700 of the sporting Safari station wagon were built. There was a brief flirtation with fuel injection in 1958, while the wide-track Pontiacs of 1959 had extravagant tailfins as well as a 'tail grille' matching the front-end styling. A more compact model, the unit-construction Tempest, appeared in 1961, with an oversquare four of 3179cc and swing-axle irs and manual or automatic transaxle. It was replaced by a more conventional Tempest by 1964, though its 'Le Mans' version sired the legendary GTO, with 6555cc or 7456cc V-8 power, and offering 125 mph for $3000 in 1966, when over 95,000 GTOs were sold. Almost as fast, if less sporting, was the 1963 Grand Prix, and by 1968 there was a family

1935 Pontiac 28hp six-cylinder

1946 Pontiac Six Station Wagon

of small sporting coupés, the Firebirds, with a small ohc six (replaced in 1970 by a pushrod unit, also used on the 1971 Ventura compact). For 1973, low, wide lines rather than high performance characterized Pontiac's new intermediates, the Grand Ams two- and four-door hardtops. Fastest cars were now the Trans Ams coupés, and disc front brakes were standard on all but the Ventura and the cheapest Firebirds. The inevitable sub-compact — the Astre — appeared in 1975, evolving into the Sunbird (with optional five-speed manual gearbox) a year later. The Ventura range now included a hatchback, and big cars offered V-8s of 5 litres as standard, with 5·7- and 6·6-litre units optional. The immensely complex 1979 range included the Sunbird, with a choice of two four-cylinder Pontiac engines, Buick's V-6 or Chevrolet's 5162cc V-8; Firebird sport coupés up to 6604cc; the Phoenix intermediate; the Le Mans range; and full-size Pontiacs, only available with automatic transmission.

1967 Pontiac Le Mans hardtop coupé

1979 Pontiac Firebird Trans-Am

PONTS-MOTEURS/*France 1912–1913*

A twin-cylinder 1081cc power pack, built in Paris for transforming horse vehicles into motor vehicles 'in a few hours, without modification'.

POPE-HARTFORD/*USA 1903–1914*

Chain-drive 10hp single-cylinder two- and four-seaters were the first cars offered in this mid-priced range from the Pope group, though a 16hp shaft-driven twin with flitch-plated wooden chassis was available in 1905. The Model F of 1906 had a 28/30hp four, and sold for $2500: standard colour scheme was purple lake. By 1912, the range had become complex: seven models were available on the 36hp four-cylinder chassis and seven on the 44·6hp six, including 'pony tonneaux' and 'Front Door Roadsters'. Such uncoordinated marketing policies led to the fall of Colonel Pope's cycle and car empire in 1913.

POPE-TOLEDO/*USA 1903–1909*

The luxury range in Colonel Pope's line-up, 'the silent mile-a-minute car' succeeded the Toledo Steamer, though all its products had four-cylinder petrol engines. Prices initially ranged from $3500 for the 20hp to $7500 for the 60hp racer: a peaked radiator shell was a distinguishing feature of the Pope-Toledo. The last Pope-Toledos were big 50 hp fours of 6500cc, selling at $4250. The company was taken over in 1909 and production of Pope-Toledos ceased. John Willys bought the plant for Overland.

POPE-TRIBUNE / USA 1904–1907
This was Colonel Pope's economy line: the initial models were chain-drive 10 hp single-cylinder runabouts, followed in 1905 by a 12 hp front-engined twin with shaft drive.

POPP / Switzerland 1898
Lorenz Popp of Basle offered two models of twin-cylinder car, financed by the Benz agent for Switzerland. Hardly surprisingly, these were largely Benz-inspired. Inlet valves were automatic, but a chain-driven overhead camshaft actuated the exhaust valves.

POPULAIRE / France 1899
A light rear-engined voiturette with three-seater bodywork.

PORON / France 1898
A rear-engined opposed-piston 'motorcycle' with friction drive and tiller-steering.

PORTER / USA 1900–1901
'The only perfect automobile', the Porter steam Stanhope from Boston, Massachusetts, sold for $750, and was 'controlled by one lever only, as in times of danger several levers are confusing'.

1920 Porter Town Car

PORTER / USA 1919–1922
Successor to the FRP, the Porter was one of the most costly automobiles in the United States, some models costing upwards of $10,000. Using an ohv four-cylinder engine of its own design and make, the Porter, with a displacement of 6516cc, produced 140 bhp at 2600 rpm, making it the most powerful car in America at the time. With a 142-inch wheelbase and the option of wire or wood wheels, a total of 34 Porter motor cars was constructed; coachwork was provided by Brewster, Holbrook, Demarest and Blue Ribbon.

PORTHOS / France 1906–1914
This Billancourt firm began with a 24/30 hp four, joined for 1908 by fours of 14/18 hp and 40 hp and sixes of 40/50 hp (6842cc) and 60 hp (8143cc). A straight-eight Grand Prix racer of 10,857cc found no production parallels, and in 1909 production was suspended until 1912. Then 16 hp and 24 hp fours, and 20 hp and 30 hp sixes were offered, joined in 1914 by a 10 hp.

PORSCHE
Austria/Germany 1948 to date
After his post-war release from internment in France, Ferdinand Porsche settled in Gmünd, Austria, where he created the first Porsche cars, with 1086cc VW-based engines and sporting light alloy roadster bodywork. However, he found working conditions at Gmünd too difficult, with shortages in materials, components and skilled labour. Porsche cars were then relatively cheap, and demand high, so, after building 50 of this original model 356, Porsche moved to Stuttgart-Zuffenhausen in Germany. The rear-engined model 356 appeared in many guises, with engines from 1096cc to 1966cc; coupés, cabriolets, speedsters and convertibles were offered. It was succeeded by the 1965–69 Porsche 912, with a light-alloy 1582cc engine, still a flat-four; a year earlier, the famous ohc flat-six 1991cc Porsche 911 had made its debut, available from 1969 onwards with larger power units, of which the ultimate development was a 2993cc unit. From 1972–75, the Carrera was available, with a 2687cc flat-six developing 260 bhp; it was concurrent with the 1969–75 mid-engined Porsche 914, available with fours of 1795cc and 1971cc or the 1991cc six. The 1979 Porsche range consisted of the front-engined 924, with an in-line water-cooled four-cylinder engine of 1984cc, the rear-engined 911SC, with the 2993cc flat-six in 180 bhp form, the 911 Turbo, with a 3299cc six equipped with Bosch K-jetronic fuel-injection, and the front-engined 928, with a 4474cc V-8 power unit.

1960 Porsche 356B Coupé

1979 Porsche 911 Turbo 3.3-litre

1977 Porsche 928 4.5-litre V-8

PORTLAND/*France/England 1913*
Claiming dual nationality, the Portland was sold in two models, a £95 6/8 hp one-cylinder two-seater and a 10 hp four-cylinder (£145). The firm's telegraphic address was 'Skidlessly'.

POWELL SPORTSWAGON
USA 1955–1956
Made in Compton, Calif., by the Powell Corp., the Sportswagon was based on 1940/1950 Plymouth mechanical components. Bodies were made of metal and glass-fibre. Models included station wagons and pickups.

POWERDRIVE/*England 1956–1958*
One of the better-looking post-Suez economy cars, the Powerdrive had a three-abreast aluminium body and 322cc Anzani engine. It later reappeared as the Coronet.

PRADO/*USA 1920–1922*
Using an 8237cc Curtiss OX-5 aircraft engine, converted for passenger-car use and similar to the V-8 power plants used on Curtiss and Wharton cars, the Prado sported disc wheels. Available in chassis form or 'open types', an estimated nine were built. Chassis price: $9000.

PRAGA/*Austria/Czechoslovakia 1907–1947*
This leading Bohemian engineering works' first products were based on French Renault and Charron designs; after the war, when its Prague base had become part of Czechoslovakia, Praga became the new country's leading producer. A range of sv fours was produced during the 1920s, including the 850cc and 994cc Piccolo models, the Alfa (1243cc), the Mignon (2300cc) and the Grand (3800cc). By the end of the decade, the Alfa and Mignon had become sixes of 1790cc and 2636cc respectively, and the Grand a straight-eight of 3585cc. In the early 1930s, new models appeared: the 995cc Baby, the 1450cc Lady and the 1660cc Super-Piccolo, most of these designed by František Kec. The immediately pre-war range consisted of two light fours, the 1128cc Piccolo and 1660cc Lady, and two sixes, the 2492cc Alfa 23 and the 3485cc Golden, the latter having a six-speed gearbox. Praga cars competed successfully in international trials. A few light cars were built after the end of the war.

LE PRATIC/*France 1908–1908*
Monobloc-engined cars of 8/10 hp (twin-cylinder) and 16/20 hp (four-cylinders) built in Paris.

PRATT, PRATT-ELKHART
USA 1911–1917
The Elkhart Carriage and Harness Company entered the motor business with a four-cylinder 40 hp model. A 50 hp six appeared later.

PREMIER/*USA 1903–1925*
'First in rank among motor cars', the Premier from Indianapolis was conventional in design, but always well engineered. Air- or water-cooling were optional from 1903–07, and a transverse air-cooled four was listed in 1904. Big fours and sixes were built, notably the 4-40 and 6-60, with pair-cast cylinders: capacities were 5473cc and 8210cc. In 1913 a convoy of 12 Premiers drove across America: from that year only six-cylinder cars were offered. The Premiers of 1919–21 had the Cutler-Hammer magnetic gear-shift, controlled by a lever on the steering wheel: the monobloc alloy six-cylinder power unit of 4838cc had overhead valves and aluminium pistons.

PREMIER/*England 1906–1908, 1911–1913*
Though its sponsors claimed that 'ceaseless thought and tireless energy' had accompanied the creation of the 20/24 hp Premier of 1906, in fact it was really an imported Marchand from Italy. A 25/30 hp six was also available. This Birmingham company *did* build a car of their own, later in the same year, with a 10/12 hp two-cylinder Aster engine, which sold for £150 with two seats, £200 with four. By that time, too, they were acknowledging the Marchand's true parentage. A year later, the firm was concentrating on its agencies for Humber and Marchand, and on the manufacture of hoods and windscreens, and the 10/12 hp was dropped soon after. In 1911–13, the PMC, a tiller-steered three-wheeled cyclecar with a 6 hp JAP engine, was built by Premier.

PREMIER/*Germany 1913–1914*
A small two-seater car with a sv four-cylinder 1030cc engine, built at the J. C. Braun factory at Nürnberg (which also produced Kaiser cars).

1912 Pratt 40 tourer

PREMIER/*Austria 1913–1914*
Basically an English factory which had produced motorcycles since 1908. Since 1911 they had owned a German branch at Nürnburg, which in 1913 moved to Eger (now Cheb) which became part of Czechoslovakia. The car was a small 4/12 hp four-cylinder, whose design came from the Braun works. Few were built.

PREMIER/*India 1944 to date*
The Premier Padmini, built in Bombay, is based on the obsolete Fiat 1100; over 17,000 were produced in 1977.

Chassis of the 1906 Premier (England) 20/24hp four

PREMOCAR/*USA 1921–1923*
One of the relatively few American cars built in the Deep South, the Premocar hailed from Birmingham, Alabama. In its first year it offered both four- and six-cylinder models, the former with a Rochester-Duesenberg engine and the latter with a Falls. The four was dropped for 1922, but the six, designated the '6-40' or 'Magic Six', was continued through the last year of manufacture. Few Premocars were built.

PRESCOTT/*USA 1901–1905*
A. L. Prescott, maker of 'Enameline' stove polish, was behind the manufacture of this twin-cylinder tiller-steered steam car.

PRESTO/*Germany 1909–1927*
This cycle and motorcycle works' first cars had French four-cylinder Delahaye engines. Among the first own-design models was a 6238cc four-cylinder with a long-stroke (100mm × 200mm) engine and a smaller 4920cc model. Quantity production led to smaller 2340cc and 2078cc four-cylinder cars. Production of Presto cars increased after the war, when this Chemnitz factory joined the GDA group. Top model was now a 2350cc four-cylinder developing 30 bhp, followed by an improved 40 bhp version in 1925. The last Presto cars were ohv six-cylinders of 2613cc and 3141cc. In 1926 Presto bought the Dux works and became part of the NAG group in 1927. NAG sold the Chemnitz works to Auto-Union in 1934.

1933 Praga Lady Saloon

PRETOT/*France 1896–1899*
A two-cylinder 5 hp two-wheeled 'power pack'
for converting horse-carriages to horseless carriages, built under Kühlstein-Vollmer patents.

PRIAMUS/*Germany 1899–1921*
When Priamus at Cologne ran into financial
difficulties in 1921, they were taken over by
Molkamp. In their early years, Priamus had
produced single- and twin-cylinder cars, followed by fours of 1592cc to 3052cc. Production
was never on a large scale.

PRIMA, PRIMA-LUX/*France 1906–1909*
Léon Lefèbvre, designer of the Bolide, was
behind the Prima marque. A 10 hp single and
fours of 15 hp and 20 hp with unit-constructed
engine/gearbox were the staple offerings.

Engine of the 1907 Prima 10hp voiturette

PRIMUS/*Germany 1899–1904*
Kaiser, a famous manufacturer of sewing-
machines and bicycles, also built three-wheeled
vehicles with De Dion-type own-make engines.
Small cars with two- and four-cylinder engines
up to 12 hp were available from 1902 onwards.

PRIMUS/*England 1903*
The 'noiseless' Primus was built in Brixton, and
cost 175 guineas in 5 hp form, with 7 hp and 9 hp
models also available. It was said to be 'very
reliable, steady and fast'.

PRINCE/*Japan 1952–1966*
Post-war, the Tachikawa Aircraft Company
built Tama electrics, then brought out the 1·5-
litre Prince. The ifs-equipped Skyline appeared
in 1955, the first Japanese car to be sold in
Europe (from 1957). In 1961 came the 1·9-litre
Gloria, later available with engines up to 2·5
litres. The Prince Royal heralded the merger
with Nissan (Datsun) and the rationalization of
the two ranges.

PRINCEPS/*England 1902–1903*
A 4¼ hp 'Bijou voiturette' from a famous Nottingham motorcycle maker.

PRINCESS/*England 1906*
The 3261cc Princess, made by the Century
Motor Company of Willesden Junction, Lon-
don, had a magneto and coil ignition.

PRINCESS/*USA 1914–1919*
This was a coal-scuttle-bonneted 1599cc light
car built in Detroit. A four-cylinder L-head
1557cc engine was used. A Golden, Belknap &
Schwartz-engined 30 hp four, of conventional
appearance, was launched for 1915.

PRINCESS/*England 1923*
Shock absorber manufacturers Streatham
Engineering Co. Ltd. were responsible for the
Princess, a light car using an 8·9 hp vee-twin air-
cooled engine.

PRINCETON/*USA 1923–1924*
The Princeton automobile was William C.
Durant's bid to bridge the gap between his Flint
and Locomobile cars. Only two or three were
probably ever built, all designated 1924 models.
The Princeton was an impressive car for the
price, its 128/132-inch wheelbase sedan selling
for $2485. An Ansted six-cylinder engine was
employed. Similar in appearance to the Flint,
the make was discontinued before production
could be started.

PRINETTI & STUCCHI/*Italy 1899–1901*
The great Ettore Bugatti worked with this
company when they built motor tricycles,
motorcycles and some twin-cylinder cars. While
still very young, he subsequently moved to De
Dietrich in Alsace.

PROD' HOMME/*France 1907–1908*
Builders of cars with 18 hp opposed-piston
engines à la Gobron-Brillié, Prod'homme's factory was at Ivry-Port (Seine).

PROGRESS/*England c1898–1903*
Progress were cycle makers, who turned to
building a voiturette based on the De Dion.
Their final offerings were a 9 hp De Dion-
powered car and 6¼ hp and 12 hp models with
Aster engines, which reappeared in 1904 as the
West-Aster.

PROGRESS/*England 1934*
The three-wheeled Progress from Manchester
had a 980cc flat-twin engine. It was manufactured by Haynes Economy Motors Ltd.

1916 Princess (USA) light car

PROJECTA/*England 1914*
A vee-twin JAP engine powered this
monocoque-bodied cyclecar from Hendon,

PROSPER LAMBERT/*France 1901–1906*
From Nanterre, Seine, the Prosper Lambert was
said to be 'most beautiful, most elegant, least
expensive'. Starting with a single-cylinder De
Dion-engined 7 hp model, by 1905, 9 hp and
12 hp models were available, at prices from
Fr 4950 to Fr 7900. In 1907, the marque
changed its name to Jean-Bart.

PROTOS/*Germany 1899–1926*
Mrs Lilli Sternberg was a well-known pioneer
motorist, whose husband Alfred founded the
Protos factory at Berlin. His first design was a
749cc single-cylinder voiturette, which was followed by his three-cylinder 'Kompensengin'.
From 1904 Protos — already finding favour as
Berlin taxicabs — were available with four-
cylinder engines of up to 45 hp. A 100 hp six-
cylinder racer was built in 1905; though it did
not enter production, it paved the way for a
45 hp six. That year, too, Sternberg sold Protos
to Siemens-Schuckert and Crown Prinz Wilhelm bought a six-cylinder Protos. A wide
variety of Protos cars, from 1501cc to a five-
bearing 6838cc six, were built up to the outbreak
of war. The first models to appear after 1918
were an ohv 2612cc four and the sv 4137cc
'16/46'. Then came a sv 2596 four, which was the
basis of all Protos production up to 1926, when
NAG took control. After the take-over, some
NAG models were sold as 'NAG-Protos'.

1922 Protos 16/46hp sporting tourer

PRUNEL/*France 1900–1907*
Prunel, whose factory was at Puteaux, Seine, offered a four-car range in 1903, consisting of the 'Apollo' single-cylinder 6 hp, which, like the slightly larger 9 hp, had a De Dion engine, and two Aster-engined cars, a 12 hp twin and 16 hp four. By 1905 they were offering a 24/30 hp four of 4942cc, but by 1906 were concentrating principally on the manufacture of large commercial vehicles. The Prunels were also connected with Gnôme, Gracile and JP cars, and the 1912–14 Phénix. Prunel cars were sold in England by a gunpowder and ammunition manufacturing works in Hendon.

PTV/*Spain 1956–1962*
Automoviles Utilitarios SA of Manresa built 1250 of these minicars, powered by a 246cc single-cylinder two-stroke engine of their own make, before turning to the production of dumper trucks.

PUBLIX/*USA 1947–1948*
The Publix was a three-wheeled convertible with the single wheel at the front. Its aluminium body was attached to an aluminium tube frame. The engines (also of aluminium) ranged from 1·7 to 10·4 hp. The overall length was 72 inches and weight varied from 150 to 250 lbs.

PUCH/*Austria 1906–1923*
Puch was already a well-known manufacturer of bicycles and motorcycles when he engaged the well-known German designer Slevogt to produce a prototype; tests were also carried out with French cars before the first Puch car, a well-conceived 7 hp voiturette, made its bow. Puch's Graz factory followed this with a 25 hp four, both models achieving some sporting success. A 9 hp twin was added to the range then, in 1909, Slevogt designed an ohc 3992cc four. Other Puch models included a sv 1580cc four, another sv four of 4400cc and the sporting Alpenwagen, with a 40 bhp sv four of 3560cc. The final Puch had a 1588cc four-cylinder engine and a four-speed gearbox; it formed the basis of works racers produced in 1921–22 which gained many successes driven by Kirchner, Weiss and Zsolnay. Car manufacture ceased when Ing Marcinello produced the first of the famous double-piston Puch motorcycles.

PULLCAR/*England 1906–1908*
The fwd 14/16 hp Pullcar from Preston had a 'patent encyclic' gear operated by pedals.

PULLMAN/*USA 1903–1917*
Built by the Hardinge Company to A. P. Broomell's design, the 1903 Pullman was a complex six-wheeler, succeeded by the conventional 'York' range in 1905. The 1908 models were a 40 hp four and a 30 hp six. Pullman built cars up to a 60 hp 8603cc six with compressed-air starting (1912), and from 1915 offered the Cutler-Hammer push-button magnetic gear-change system.

1903 Pullman

PUMA/*Brazil 1964 to date*
Founded under the name Luminari, this São Paulo company started with the DKW-engined Malzoni, introducing the Puma GT in 1966. It gained VW power in 1968. From 1974 there was also a 4-litre GM-engined Puma GTB.

PUNGS FINCH/*USA 1904–1908*
These were powerful touring cars built by a Detroit gas engine factory. For 1908, the Model 35 Runabout of 5808cc and the Model 50 of 6435cc were catalogued: prices ranged from $2500 to $5000.

PURITAN/*USA 1902–1903*
Built in Salem, Massachusetts, the 6 hp Puritan Steamer had a folding steering column for easy access to the driver's seat.

PY/*France 1899–1900*
Andre Py was manager and designer for the Compagnie des Automobiles du Sud-Ouest, who built this Bollée-like motor tricycle. It had front-wheel drive and rear-wheel steering.

PYRAMID/*England 1914*
A JAP-engined 8 hp cyclecar built by Payne's Engineering of Chiswick.

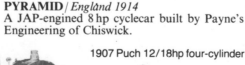
1907 Puch 12/18hp four-cylinder

QUADRANT/*England 1905–1906*
In 1905 Quadrant of Birmingham exhibited a chassis with a four-speed Lloyd 'crossed rollers' gearbox, giving direct drive on all speeds.

QUEEN/*Canada 1901–1903*
A gas buggy from Toronto with a single-cylinder 824cc engine.

QUEEN/*England 1904–1905*
'The car for the million or the millionaire' was sold by Horner & Sons of Mitre Square, London. 12 hp and 16 hp models were offered, at prices from 235 guineas to 275 guineas.

1906 Queen (USA) 26/28hp touring car

QUEEN/*USA 1904–1907*
Chain driven one-, two- and four-cylinder cars built by Blomstrom, who also made the Gyroscope car. The 1906 Queen was available in three models — 14 hp and 18 hp twins, 26/28 hp four.

QUICK/*USA 1899–1900*
This otherwise conventional tiller-steered gas buggy was the first American car to have an overhead camshaft power unit. The twin-cylinder engine had a chain-driven ohc and developed a heady 4 bhp at 700 rpm.

QUINBY/*USA 1899*
Electric carriages 'on the Leitner system' with two 2½ hp motors geared to the rear wheels.

QUO VADIS/*France 1921–1923*
A cyclecar made in Courbevoie, Seine, with a twin-cylinder Train engine.

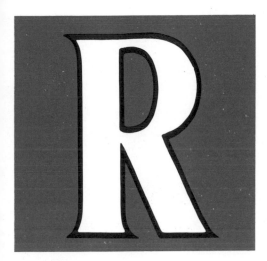

R

RABA/*Hungary 1912–1914*
Made by the Hungarian Machine Factory at Raab (Györ), the Raba was the 3·8-litre 45 hp Praga 'Grand' built under Praga licence, in limited numbers. Raba also imported many foreign makes, including Benz, Panhard and Austro-Daimler.

1924 Rabag (licence-built Bugatti) sports phaeton

RABAG/*Germany 1922–1925*
Rabag built French Bugatti Types 22 and 23 under licence. These were ohc 16-valve 1453cc and 1496cc ohc four-cylinder cars. Special racing cars were imported from Molsheim and equipped with Rabag radiators. Rabag did not produce many more than 100 cars in all.

1907 Radia voiturette

RADIA/*France 1907–1908*
It is not known whether this company from Levallois-Perret (Seine) was connected with the Radia (or l'Automotrice) built in Bergerac; at the 1907 Paris Salon three Radias were exhibited, a shaft-driven 14/18 hp four-cylinder voiturette, and cars of 20/30 hp and 30/40 hp.

LA RADIEUSE/*France 1907*
Voiturettes built at Bayeux (Calvados) by M. E. Marie, and shown at the 1907 Paris Salon.

RADIOR/*France 1920–1922*
M. Chapolard, Rochet-Schneider agent in Bourg-en-Bresse, assembled some 1592cc Ballot-engined cars, sold as Radiors.

Chassis of the 1907 RAF

RAF/*Austria 1907–1913*
The Reichenberger Automobil Fabrik was founded by the great pioneer Baron Theodor von Liebig and two wealthy wool-manufacturers, Alfred Ginskey and Oskar Klinger. They built superb, expensive cars to a very high standard. From 1912 onwards, Knight sleeve-valve engines were built under licence; in 1913 Laurin & Klement bought the RAF works. Most RAF cars were big ones, with engines ranging from 30 hp to 70 hp.

RAGLAN/*England 1899*
A virtual carbon copy of the Benz, built in Coventry.

1939 Railton 21.6 Fairmile

RAILTON/*England 1933–1949*
The Railton was a cheap and fast sporting car, though a Yankee at heart. The work of Reid Railton, it was originally based on the 4-litre Terraplane 8 chassis, though from mid-1934 a Hudson straight-eight of 4·2 litres was used. However, the British coachwork disguised the origins, while the riveted bonnet was reminiscent of the Invicta, Noel Macklin being concerned with both projects. The Hudson straight-eight engine, despite its crude internals (such as splash-lubricated big-ends) gave the Railton a top speed of about 90 mph. Increased costs resulted in a smaller model appearing in 1938, fitted with 2·7- and 3·5-litre sixes, also by Hudson. A baby Railton of the same year was fitted with a Standard engine of 10 hp, however. A handful of cars was made after World War Two.

RAINIER/*USA 1905–1911*
The first Rainiers were 22/28 hp and 30/35 hp fours built by Garford; after 1907 this Saginaw, Michigan, company built its own chassis. The last Rainiers were 45/59 hp fours.

RALEIGH/*USA 1920–1922*
Built first in Bridgeton, New Jersey, and later in Reading, Pennsylvania, the Raleigh was a typical assembled car of its time. Raleighs used Herschell-Spillman six-cylinder engines and had a wheelbase of 122 inches; the five-passenger touring car cost $2750. Probably less than 25 cars were made and, although a four-cylinder model was announced in 1921, it was not forthcoming.

RALEIGH/*England 1933–1936*
The famous Nottingham cycle company built a few four-cylinder cyclecars circa 1916, but true production did not begin until 1933, with the 742cc vee-twin 'Safety Seven' three-wheeler, which subsequently became the first Reliant.

An 1100cc Rally sports two-seater

RALLY/*France 1920–1933*
This Colombes, Seine, works started by converting Harley-Davidson sidecar outfits into cyclecars. In 1922 they built proper cyclecars, still with the 987cc Harley-Davidson vee-twin. The same year, Rally presented their first four-cylinder-engined car, followed by many with various French proprietary engines (SCAP, Chapuis-Dornier or Ruby) from 900cc to 1100cc. In 1931, Rally presented cars with modified Salmson chassis and dohc 1300cc Salmson engines.

RALPH LUCAS/*England 1901–c1908*
Lucas's first car was a curious paraffin-powered two-stroke car, with a piston and crankshaft at either end of its single cylinder. The speed of the engine was controlled by a button in the steering wheel, and the coachwork was of pressed steel. The Lucas 1908 two-stroke design was the origin of the Valveless.

1905 Rambler Surrey Type One

RAMBLER/*USA 1900–1914, 1950 to date*
Thomas B. Jeffery, born in Devon in 1845, emigrated to America aged 18; in 1879 he built

his first Rambler cycle. His son Charles built two tiller-steered runabouts in 1900, followed by a left-hand-drive wheel-steered car in 1901. Model C of 1902 was the first production model, a crude, spidery single-cylinder buggy with tiller-steering. The 1904–08 model had a secondary 'steering wheel' which operated the throttle. A twin-cylinder, patronized by Teddy Roosevelt, appeared in 1905, and a 40 hp four followed in 1907. Production was limited to 2500 cars in 1910 'to assure maximum quality'; a customer that year traded six cows for a new Rambler. Thomas Jeffery died while visiting Pompeii in 1910. The 1911 models had locking petrol taps and adjustable steering columns, and electric lighting was standardized in 1913: the cars were renamed Jeffery in 1914. The name was revived in 1950 by Nash Motors and continued after the creation of American Motors in 1954 (see American Motors).

R & V KNIGHT / USA 1920–1924

Built by the R & V Division of the Root & Vandervoort Engineering Co., of East Moline, Illinois, the R & V Knight was successor to the Moline-Knight. A highly regarded make, it was produced at the rate of 500 to 750 units per year, in both four- and six-cylinder models. A full line of open and closed models was available at prices ranging from around $1650 to $4000.

RANGER / England 1913–1915

An 8 hp Precision-engined cyclecar from Coventry.

RANGER / USA 1920–1923

Ranger was a limited-production assembled car company specializing in four-cylinder models until 1922, when a six was introduced in addition to the existing line. Some of the roadsters and touring cars on the larger model chassis carried such names as 'Pal o'Mine', 'Commodore', 'Blue Bonnet' and 'Newport' and were distinguished with full sport treatment, including aluminium door steps, cycle fenders and side wind-wings. Prices were as high as $3500. Few of the sixes were built, however, and the 1923 line would have used the four only, had the company not failed before it could be put into production.

RAOUVAL / France 1899–1902

Similar in design to Léon Lefèvbre's Pygmée, the power unit of this car from Anzin (Nord) was an 8 hp twin of 2851cc.

RAPID / Switzerland 1899

This was the Egg & Egli tri-voiturette under a different name. A trailer with two extra seats was available as an option.

RAPID / Italy 1904–1921

Giovanni Ceirano created these cars, which were built with a variety of four-cylinder engines from 2110cc to 9847cc. Most models were of advanced design with four-speed gearboxes and a very sophisticated rear suspension.

RAPID / Switzerland 1946

A backbone chassis was used on these streamlined three-wheelers from a mowing-machine works at Dietikon near Zürich, powered by a rear-mounted opposed-piston MAG engine. Only 36 were built.

LA RAPIDE / England 1919–1920

Built in south-west London, La Rapide was an unusual cyclecar in that its engine, an air-cooled 8 hp JAP, was mounted outside the body, drive being transmitted to the offside rear wheel.

RAPIER / England 1935–1940

The Rapier was originally a Lagonda design, and was sold by the Staines company until the firm was placed under receivership in 1935. The model had a dohc 1104cc engine, a progressive layout for a car with a chassis price of £270. In fact the original intention was to produce the engine in an aluminium alloy, but cast iron was eventually used on grounds of cost. The new management under Alan Good did not want the Rapier, so a new company, Rapier Cars Ltd., was formed by the designer Tim Ashcroft, W. H. Oats and N. Brocklebank, to buy the design and manufacture it under the name of Rapier. It was available in supercharged form from 1936, and in all about 300 examples were made.

RATIER / France 1926–1930

The Ratier factory from Montrouge, Seine, better known for aircraft components, nevertheless made some interesting ohc 746cc-engined cars. They later made motorcycles.

RATIONAL / England 1901–1906

Designed for solid tyres, the Rational had a 10/12 hp horizontal twin-cylinder engine and constant-mesh gearbox. Some of London's first taxis were Rationals.

RATIONAL / England 1911

Using Fafnir motorcycle cylinders mounted on a specially cast crankcase, K. J. McMullen assembled a 2030cc 14 hp car in his Berkshire stables, aided by his butler and an odd-job man named Scroggins. A V-6 of 2640cc was also listed. The worm final drive was confected from traction-engine steering-gear. A sales leaflet was issued, though whether any Rationals actually found buyers is doubtful.

RAUCH & LANG, RAULANG
USA 1905–1928

One of the best-known builders of electric carriages, Rauch & Lang of Cleveland concentrated on town-cars. In 1916 they joined Baker, and from 1919 the cars were known as Raulangs. By 1922 production had been shifted

1908 25/30hp Rapid landaulette

to the Stevens-Duryea factory at Chicopee Falls. A few R & L petrol-electric cabs were built here together with a handful of Raulangs, before the company reverted to its former trade of coachbuilding (it made the bodies for the first mass-produced station wagon, the 1929 Model A Ford).

1907 20hp Ravaillier amphibious car

RAVAILLIER / France 1907

Perhaps the first successful amphibious car, this 20 hp device had a steel hull, chain drive and solid-tyred disc wheels.

1868 Ravel steam carriage

RAVEL / France 1868

The Ravel steam waggon was an oil-fired steam automobile, built under French Patent 82263 J. R., issued September 2nd, 1868 to Joseph Ravel, a Swiss engineer noted for building railways in Spain. The steamer carried its single cylinder and drive boxed in below the seat. Even in this early development of the self-propelled carriage, at least one and perhaps more persons met their death when the Ravel went out of control and overturned. Its builder and his Basque wife were the parents of Maurice Ravel, the French composer.

RAVEL / France 1900–1902

This voiturette from Neuilly-sur-Seine had a twin-cylinder engine mounted on the back axle, which it drove through a two-speed gear.

1925 Ravel 2484cc sports tourer

RAVEL/*France 1923–1928*
The Société Anonyme des Automobiles Ravel of Besançon, Doubs, bore no relationship to the Ravel veteran. They made an ohv four-cylinder of 2297cc, later enlarged to 2484cc. In 1925 they presented a smaller version with a 1460cc engine.

RAW/*Germany 1913–1914*
The name stood for the small Reissiger Automobil Werke, near Plauen (Vogtland), which produced a 2418cc four-cylinder car, and was also known as Siegfried or Reissig.

RAYFIELD/*USA 1911–1915*
Dashboard-radiatored 18 hp fours and 22 hp sixes, built in Springfield, Illinois.

RAYMOND/*France 1924–1926*
This was a car assembled in Paris with a Model T Ford engine of 2863cc.

RAYMOND MAYS/*England 1938–1939*
Produced by racing driver Raymond Mays from his home at Bourne, Lincolnshire, the Raymond Mays used a 2·6-litre Standard V-8 engine. Independent front suspension was by double transverse leaf springs. Only five examples were built before the outbreak of war.

RCC/*England 1906*
A 6 hp light car 'for the man of moderate means', this £135 two-seater was built by the Road Carrying Company of Liverpool.

1913 RCH 15.9hp roadster

RCH/*USA 1912–1916*
R. C. 'Bobby' Hupp left Hupmobile in 1911 to build this 15·9 hp light car with an L-head 2553cc four-cylinder engine. The *de luxe* RCH sold in England for only £225 in 1912, complete with 12-inch electric headlights, an advanced touch.

REAC/*Morocco 1953–1955*
This was a local attempt to build sports cars with Dyna-Panhard engines and glass-fibre bodies.

READ/*USA 1913–1914*
An $850 five-seat tourer from Detroit, the Read had a four-cylinder 3261cc engine.

READING/*USA 1900–1903*
The Reading steam car was built in Reading, Pennsylvania. The 1902 model had a 5¾ hp four-cylinder single-acting engine with a rotary valve, which 'enabled the operator to start, stop and reverse with a single lever'. This make was also known as the Saracen, and was taken over by Meteor Engineering of Reading.

READING/*USA 1910–1913*
Succeeding the Middleby (which continued as a Reading model), this marque offered a 6065cc 40 hp water-cooled sporting model: it was said to have the biggest monobloc engine in America.

REBER/*USA 1902–1903*
A vertical-twin engine powered this tonneau from Reading, Pa., forerunner of Acme.

REBOUR/*France 1905–1908*
'Luxury touring cars' and cabs were built by this firm from Puteaux (Seine). Their model range consisted of 10/12 hp, 18/22 hp, 20/25 hp and 40/50 hp cars, all with pair-cast four-cylinder engines. The Rebour was sold as the 'Catalonia' in Spain.

1904 Redjacket touring car

RED JACKET/*USA 1904*
Built in Buffalo, NY, this twin-cylinder car took its name from a local Red Indian chief.

REDPATH/*Canada 1903–1907*
The Redpath Messenger was a light 1173cc single-cylinder car whose production was abruptly halted when the Toronto factory burned down.

REEVES/*USA 1905–1912*
Milton O. Reeves, 'President People's Savings and Trust Company, Vice-President Reeves Pulley Company, of Columbus, Indiana', invented an infinitely variable belt drive with expanding pulleys and a rawhide belt stiffened by riveted-on strips of iron and leather. He built five cars powered by Sintz two-stroke engines in 1896–1899. In 1905 came 12 hp and 18/20 hp air-cooled fours, followed by water-cooled

fours and an air-cooled six the following year. The company's products retrogressed into a high-wheeled 'Go-buggy' which ceased production in 1910. Then came Milton Reeves's immortal hobby-horses, the Octoauto and the Sextoauto. The Overland-based Octoauto had four axles and eight wheels, and was claimed to ride like 'a Pullman Palace-Car'. The similar Sextoauto had only one front axle. Overland and Stutz cars were used as the basis for this model. Modern multi-wheeled racing car designs imply that perhaps Milton Reeves was not so crazy after all.

REFORM/*Austria 1906–1907*
Thein & Goldberger of Vienna first built motor-cycles, then a few small cars containing a 996cc vee-twin motorcycle engine.

1903 Regal 8hp light car

REGAL/*France 1903–1904*
Built in Paris for O. C. Selbach of London, the 1903 Regal had a 6 hp De Dion engine. By 1904, 8 hp, 12 hp, 20 hp and 24 hp Regals were also available.

REGAL/*USA 1907–1918*
Though Regals with conventional chassis were available, the best-known model was the 3258cc Underslung, produced until 1914. The marque was imported into Britain as the 'Seabrook-RMC'. Around 300 Regal V-8s were built in 1918; the last production Regal was the 2982cc 'High Power Four' of 1917–18, though London agents Seabrook showed an RMC six at the 1919 Olympia Show.

1914 Regal Underslung

REGAL/*Canada 1915–1917*
Differing from its US prototype in using Lycoming engines and more rotund coachwork, the Regal from Berlin (Kitchener), Ontario, was backed by Henry Nyberg, whose Indiana factory had just closed: 20 hp and 30 hp fours and a 40 hp V-8 were available.

REGAS/*USA 1903–1905*
The 12 hp Regas, from Rochester, NY, had a vee-twin engine with air-cooling by slotted tubes 'on the Bunsen burner principle'. The Regas was one of the first side-entrance four-seaters on the American market.

REGENT/*England 1899–1900*
A Birmingham cycle company who built a tricycle with an Accles-Turrell engine.

REGENT/*Austria 1899–1910*
These cars were identical with the Bock & Hollender cars. When the works ceased car manufacture, a new company bought the remains and founded WAF.

REGINA/*France 1903–1908*
These were licence-built Dixi cars of 17, 26 and 40 hp from the Société l'Eléctrique, of Paris, who also made the Gallia and Galliette electric cars. They also built cycles, motorcycles and tricars.

REGINA/*France 1921–1925*
A small cyclecar made in Paris, this three-wheeler had a single front wheel, and was rear-engined with a four-cylinder 902cc Ruby unit.

REGINETTE/*France 1920–1921*
A Paris-built copy of the Briggs & Stratton Flyer. Only the Briggs & Stratton engine was imported.

1907 Regner voiturette chassis

REGNER/*France 1905–1908*
Originally a belt-driven voiturette built in Paris. By 1908, big cars of 12/16 hp and 24/30 hp were also marketed.

REKORD/*Germany 1904–1908*
Willi Schulz drove a 45 hp Rekord in the 1905 Herkomer Trial; these Berlin-built cars used French components, especially Aster engines and Gladiator chassis.

RELIABLE DAYTON/*USA 1906–1909*
A 'simple and powerful' two-stroke engine of 1104cc powered this $500 high-wheeler with 'piano box body'.

RELIANCE/*USA 1903–1907*
Selling at $1250, the Reliance was a 'large roomy five-passenger' 22 hp touring car.

RELIANT/*England 1935 to date*
Reliant started their career as three-wheeler manufacturers and even today, the Robin, the latest in a string of such designs, accounts for a large percentage of the company's business. The Les Bellamy-designed Sabre was their first four-wheeler, with four- and six-cylinder Ford engines. The Ogle-designed Scimitar and its hatchback successor, the GTE, have found far greater popularity. In 1975 a four-wheeled derivative of the Robin called the Kitten appeared.

RELYANTE/*England 1903*
Relyante petrol cars were 6 hp and 12 hp models based on the De Dion: the Relyante steamer was an imported Serpollet.

REMINGTON/*USA 1900–1901*
From the famous typewriter company, the four-

RENAULT/*France 1898 to date*
Louis Renault made his first car — a De Dion-engined vehicle of 273cc — in 1898, in the backyard of his parents' house. Having received orders from potential customers, he founded Renault Frères in Billancourt, Seine, with his two brothers Fernand and Marcel. From 1900, Renault fitted 500cc De Dion engines, and then made twin-cylinder models such as the 1060cc 8 cv and the 4398cc four-cylinder 20 cv. Many of the twin-cylinder Renaults were used as taxis in Paris and London, where they survived for many years. The first six-cylinder Renault, a 50 cv 9·5-litre, was presented in 1908. In 1912 Renault Frères offered no fewer than 15 different models, of which the best was the six-cylinder 40 cv of 7539cc. The following year a smaller six-cylinder — the 4523cc 22 cv — appeared. By the outbreak of war, Renault had become one of the most important manufacturers of cars in Europe. During the war the Renault taxis became the legendary 'Taxis de la Marne' and Renault pioneered the building of light tanks. After the Armistice, the twin-cylinder Renaults survived for only a few months in production, as Renault resumed manufacture of most of the pre-war models. In 1923 Renault launched a new model to compete with the 6 cv Citroën: this was the 951cc 6 cv 'KJ'. The same year came the six-cylinder JY of 4222cc, later enlarged to 4766cc. The 40 cv still continued, but since the war had been enlarged to 9123cc. In the

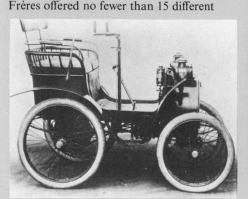

First production Renault, the 1898 1½hp

1911 Renault 20/30hp saloon

cylinder Remington ran on a mixture of hydrogen and acetylene.

REMINGTON / *USA 1914–1915*
A four-cylinder cyclecar with a preselector transmission designed by Philo E. Remington, whose grandfather had founded the Remington arms company. A V-8 was used in 1915 cars.

1976 Renaissance coupé

RENAISSANCE / *Canada 1976*
Le Vicomte Classic coachbuilders of St Sauveur des Monts, Quebec, planned a limited edition of 50 of this 1930s-styled four-seat luxury coupé, powered by a 6559cc Ford V-8. The massive chassis was formed from 6·5-inch steel channel.

RENE BONNET / *France 1962–1965*
After Deutsch left D B, René Bonnet continued to build sports cars with Renault 850 and 1100cc engines, front-engined like the Le Mans or rear-engined like the Djet. He also made some racing cars. When Bonnet was taken over by Matra in 1965, the Champigny, Val-de-Marne, works continued to produce cars for a while under the name of Matra-Bonnet, then as 'Matra'.

RENEGADE / *England 1971 to date*
One of the more streamlined VW-based buggies, the Renegade was first seen at the 1971 Racing Car Show. Over 100 have been sold.

RENFERT / *Germany 1924–1925*
A little-known 776cc twin-cylinder two-stroke two-seater, made in small numbers.

RENFREW / *Scotland 1904*
A 16/20 hp four from Glasgow.

REO / *USA 1904–1936*
Ransom E. Olds retired from Oldsmobile in 1904, but was persuaded to head a new company, producing a single-cylinder gas buggy: there was also a twin-cylinder model. An unsuccessful four appeared in 1906: Reo's next

four was, claimed Ransome Olds, 'pretty close to finality'. He called this 'Reo the Fifth' his 'farewell car', but went on to produce four- and six-cylinder models, concentrating on the six-cylinder Model T in 1920: this car was underslung at the rear. A new 25 hp Flying Cloud six replaced this car in 1927, also available as the Wolverine. The 1931 season saw a Flying Cloud Eight, as well as the Sakhnoffsky-styled Custom Royale Eight, and in 1933 Reo, who had already pioneered synchromesh, offered a two-speed automatic transmission.

1907 Reo 18hp

1924 Renault NN tourer

late 1920s there was also a sv six of 1500cc, and many commercial vehicles. A complete change came in 1929 with the firm's first straight-eight, the 7100cc 'Reinastella', soon followed by the 'Nerva'. Nevertheless, none

of the Renaults of the time—the 'Monaquatre', 'Monasix' or 'Vivaquatre'—was modern compared with the marque's arch-rival Citroën. Renault had only just moved the radiator to the front of the car, having persisted with dashboard radiators for a quarter-century. The immediate pre-World War Two range was from 951cc to a 5·4-litre straight-eight. After the war, Renault was taken under government control and became the Regie Nationale des Usines Renault. They resumed production with the 'Juvaquatre', and later with the rear-engined

Renault 4cv at the 1946 Paris Salon

'4cv' of 760cc, which lasted until 1961. The 'Frégate', introduced in 1951, was the last of the front-engined, rear-drive cars made by Renault. The Dauphine came in 1956 and a 'Dauphine Gordini' was presented the following year. In 1959 came the Floride, and three years later the 747cc R4 with front-wheel drive. After an attempt to build the American Rambler under licence, the 956cc R8 arrived, giving way later to the 'R8 S', the 'Major' and the 'Gordini'. The R16 was presented in 1965, followed four years later by the R12 and then the R6 in 1970. The R15 and R17 came in 1971 and then the unsuccessful R12 'Gordini'. Latest in the line in recent years are the Rodeo (a sort of plastic Jeep), the R5 and the sporty R5-Alpine ('Gordini' in the UK), the R14, R18, R20 and R30.

1978 Renault 18 TS

REPUBLIC/*USA 1911–1916*
A 'classy' 35/40 hp whose four-cylinder T-head engine had a desaxé crankshaft.

RESTELLI/*Italy 1924–1925*
Small producer of advanced four-cylinder cars of sporting appearance, with ohv engines of 1368cc.

REVELATION/*France 1922–1923*
A cyclecar made in Paris, using Train or Villiers engines. It had a wooden chassis.

1920 ReVere speedster

REVERE/*USA 1917–1926*
One of America's prestige sporting cars, ReVere cars were powered by four-cylinder Rochester-Duesenberg engines exclusively until 1924, when the Monson, also a four and based on the Rochester-Duesenberg power plant, was sub-stituted. In that same year, a six-cylinder Continental was also available. Several ReVeres were built to special order for heads of state, including King Alfonso XIII of Spain. The last cars of this make were equipped with balloon tyres and four-wheel brakes, as well as a rudi-mentary power-steering system, this being effec-ted by dual steering-wheels, one within the other, which had a lower ratio to expedite parking.

REVOL/*France 1922*
Made in Fontenay-aux-Roses, Seine, this cycle-car was available with 990cc Train or 1100cc Anzani engines.

REVOLETTE/*England 1905*
This was a three-wheeler built by the New Revolution Cycle Company of Birmingham.

REX/*England 1901–1914*
Starting with a 900cc single-cylinder voiturette, Rex were soon producing a complex range of cars and tricars (Rexette tricars were the main offering from 1903–1906), and in 1906 three- and four-wheeled Airettes were available. Rex-Simplex 12 hp twin-cylinder cars were current from 1904–05, followed in 1906 by the 18/22 hp four-cylinder Ast-Rex; in 1906 came the vee-twin AiRex. A model known as the Remo was current between 1905–07; the 1908–09 Remo range consisted of round-radiatored fours of 2556cc and 2799cc. Thereafter, the company concentrated on motorcycles, apart from a 1912 vee-twin cyclecar and a 1914 1100cc Dorman-engined light car.

REX (REX SIMPLEX)/*Germany 1901–1924*
Richard & Hering at Ronneburg (Saxony) was a manufacturer of bicycle parts who built cars with De Dion and Fafnir proprietary engines. They built models from single-cylinders of

698cc to four-cylinder cars of 7440cc. Post-war, only fours of 3176cc and 2467cc were built. After Richard & Hering began mass-production of car wheels in 1921, Elite took over pro-duction of the larger Rex-Simplex model.

REYONNAH/*France 1951–1954*
M. Hannoyer in Paris made this strange folding car with a 175cc two-stroke Ydral engine.

1907 Reyrol (Passe-Partout) 7hp voiturette

REYROL (PASSE-PARTOUT)
France 1901–1930
Based at Neuilly until 1906, and at Levallois-Perret, Seine, thereafter, Reyrol started with a 5 hp single-cylinder voiturette, progressing to more substantial vehicles with 4½ hp De Dion and 6 hp Buchet engines by 1905. Armoured-wood chassis had been replaced by pressed steel in 1907, in which year three 942cc cars ran in the Coupe des Voiturettes under the marque's *alter*

1904 Rex 8hp tonneau

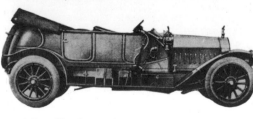

1912 Rex-Simplex touring car

ego, Passe-Partout. At the 1908 Paris Salon, Reyrol showed an 8/12 hp four-cylinder, and in 1910, a 2121cc four was listed. Post-war, cars of 1·5 and 2·3 litres were offered: the type 'Passe-Partout' of 1927 had a 1·1-litre Chapuis-Dornier engine and fwd.

RH/*France 1920*
Raymond Holbet, of Rueil, Seine, made some 10 hp Ballot-engined 1449cc cars.

RH/*France 1926–1927*
M. Hébert of Levallois, Seine, was mainly a builder of chassis, but also made some complete 1098cc CIME-engined cars.

RHEDA/*France 1897–1898*
A 2½ hp horizontal engine powered this tricycle carriage built at Saint Cloud.

RHEMAG/*Germany 1924–1926*
A sporting two-seater with an ohc four-cylinder 1065cc engine and Fulmina-Perrot four-wheel brakes. It had a 60 mph top speed, and was also available with three- and four-seater bodywork.

1925 Rhode 9hp tourer

RHODE/*England 1921–1931*
Built by F. W. Mead and T. W. Deakin, the Rhode light car used an engine specially manu-factured for it. This was a 1087cc four-cylinder with overhead camshaft, an unusual feature for

a light car. For 1924 a larger 1232cc engine was offered and in 1926 it was quietened by the introduction of pushrod ohv, and designated the 11/30 hp. A completely new car, the Hawk, initially powered by an ohc version of the 11/30 hp engine, appeared in 1928; it was subsequently powered by a 1½-litre Meadows.

RIBBLE/*England 1904–c1908*
Southport-built tricars with 5 hp Forman or 8 hp MMC power units: 10/12 hp and 12/16 hp four-cylinder four-wheelers followed.

RICART, RICART & PEREZ, RICART-ESPAÑA/*Spain 1922–1930*
Wilfredo Pelayo Ricart, pioneer aviator and engineer, began production of fast 1500cc four-cylinder ohc 16-valve racing cars in conjunction with Francisco Perez, but the venture only lasted a year. Thereafter Ricart built sporting cars—1500cc fours and a well-engineered 2401cc six—under his own name. In 1927 a 1601cc four and a 1486cc six were shown at the 1927 Paris Salon. In 1928 Ricart merged with España to form Ricart-España. Apart from a new 2400cc six, Ricart-Españas were similar to the Ricarts.

RICHARD/*USA 1914–1917*
The long-stroke 7362cc engine of the $1850 Richard, from Cleveland, was rated at only 25 hp, but developed a claimed 96 bhp, giving the car an 80 mph performance.

1905 Richardson 14hp tonneau

RICHARDSON/*England 1903–1907*
The cars produced by this manufacturer from Saxilby, near Lincoln, consisted of a 6½ hp Aster-engined single-cylinder two-seater, a 12/14 hp twin and an 18/29 hp four, all with speed controlled by variable-lift inlet valves.

RICHARDSON/*England 1919–1922*
JAP or Precision vee-twin engines powered this friction-drive cyclecar from Sheffield.

RICHELIEU/*USA 1923*
Designed by Newton VanZandt (formerly with ReVere), the Richelieu was similar to the ReVere, although heavier. Like ReVere, it used the Rochester-Duesenberg four-cylinder engine. High, rounded radiators, similar to Daniels, distinguished the Richelieu, and open and closed models were offered from $3950 to $6000. An estimated 25 to 50 cars were produced in two years of business. In 1923 the Richelieu interests were bought by Salvatore Barbarino, who later built the Barbarino car.

RICHMOND/*USA 1908–1914*
Air-cooled fours of 22 hp to 30 hp powered these cars from Richmond, Indiana, up to 1911; big water-cooled fours were used after that.

RICHMOND/*England 1913*
A 10/12 hp four-cylinder two-seater with under-slung rear axle.

RICKENBACKER/*USA 1922–1927*
'The car worthy of its name' carried the 'Hat-in-the-Ring' insignia of its promoter, Captain Eddie Rickenbacker, top-scoring American air ace of World War One. Three years of development by Harry Cummingham, Barney Everett and Walter Flanders were behind the six-cylinder Rickenbacker, with its double flywheels for smooth running and—from 1923—internal expanding four-wheel brakes. This was the first time this feature had been used on a medium-priced American car, and rival manufacturers started a 'whisper campaign' about the alleged dangers of too-powerful brakes, fearful that they, too, would have to face the cost of fitting front-wheel brakes. Despite handsome styling, sound engineering and the pioneering use of two-tone paint schemes, the Ricken-backer was unequal to such pressure. After Walter Flanders' accidental death, Captain Eddie called a halt to production.

RICKETTS/*USA 1908–1909*
Brownell engines with four cylinders (35 hp) and six cylinders (50 hp) powered these touring cars from South Bend, Indiana.

RICKSHAW/*England 1975*
The brainchild of Roy Haynes of Witham, Essex, the four-seater open-top electric Rick-shaw ran on 12 batteries and was capable of covering 50 miles between charges at up to 30 mph.

RIDDLE/*USA 1920–1926*
A highly respected firm of hearse and ambulance manufacturers, this erstwhile carriage firm started building motorized emergency vehicles of these types on its own chassis in 1916, previously having mounted coachwork on White chassis. In 1920, it began limited manufacture of sedans, either conventionally designed for the use of bearers at funerals, or pillarless on one side to allow passage for wheelchairs. All of these cars were built to special order only and, like the commercial vehicles, used Continental six-cylinder engines.

RIDER-LEWIS/*USA 1908–1909*
'The biggest little car ever built', the 1909 ohc 3707cc Rider-Lewis 30 hp four sold for $1000. The same firm built the single ohc 4942cc $2500 'Excellent Six' in their Muncie, Indiana, factory.

RIDLEY/*England 1902–1907*
These 3½ hp and 4½ hp voiturettes had a two-speed rear axle, incorporating a reverse gear. The company, based in Coventry, was wound up in 1904, and John Ridley worked for Horbick and Arrol-Johnston before starting production again in 1905 in Paisley, Scotland, with 4, 5, 6 and 7 hp cars. The first few chassis were built by Horbick. The new company folded in December 1907.

RIDLEY/*England 1914*
An 8 hp 'carette' from Woodbridge, Suffolk.

RIESS-ROYAL/*USA 1921–1922*
This was a continuation of the Bell '6-50' with minor differences. Only prototypes were built.

RIKAS/*Germany 1922–1923*
An unlucky attempt to produce a small 900cc four-cylinder car with inadequate resources.

1900 Riker Electric Victoria

RIKER/*USA 1896–1901*
Andrew Riker's company was one of the most famous manufacturers of electric vehicles, built in a wide range of styles and sizes, which all featured an unusual hub-centre steering layout. Riker's first petrol car, a 1667cc twin-cylinder, appeared in July 1901: he later designed petrol cars for Locomobile.

1921 Riddle Invalid Car

RILEY / *England 1898–1969*

Although the first Riley was a neat four-wheeled voiturette with a single-cylinder engine, production vehicles were initially motor tricycles; tricars were made until 1907. Four-wheelers followed, powered by 1034cc vee-twin engines. This capacity was increased to 2 litres from 1908. Although these were still in production by the outbreak of World War One, a 2·9-litre four was now also available. Post-war Rileys initially used a sv 1½-litre engine, the Redwing sports version of 1923 being a particularly handsome variant. However, the really sensational model of the 1920s was Percy Riley's Nine of 1927, particularly the fabric-bodied, high-waisted Monaco saloon, complete with boot (an unusual feature for the date). The engine was outstanding, an 1100cc four-cylinder with twin camshafts set high in the block, actuating inclined valves by pushrods in a hemispherical head. This proved a highly tunable layout, without the complexity of overhead camshafts, and remained a feature of Riley engine design up until 1957. In 1928 a touring version of the Nine appeared, and also the low and lively

Brooklands model, inspired by J. G. Parry Thomas. A six-cylinder variant of the Nine theme was inevitable: this, the 1·6-litre Fourteen, came in 1929. The 1930s saw many variants on the four- and six-cylinder engines, the distinctive fastback Kestrel and more conventional Falcon appearing in 1933. Not surprisingly, the Riley engine layout lent itself admirably to competition activities: one instance was successive wins in the BRDC 500 Mile race at Brooklands in 1934-35-36. Sporting models were the 9 hp Imp, the six-cylinder MPH and, later, the 1½-litre 12/4 four-cylinder engine appeared in 1934 and was produced alongside the faithful Nine. Two years later a 2½-litre long-stroke four was marketed. Financial storm clouds were gathering, however, and William Morris took over the company in 1938. The new broom saw that only the 1½- and 2½-litre cars remained in production, these engines also powering the post-war cars. The 2½-litre Pathfinder of 1954 retained the classic Riley engine, though this ceased in 1957. Remaining models were merely badge-engineered BMC variants, mainly on the Mini and 1100 theme.

1924 Riley Redwing 11.9hp four-seater

1934 Riley Imp

1962 Riley Elf

RIP / *France 1908–1912*

Ominously named voiturettes from Rive-de-Gier (Loire), with transverse coil springs all round, independent rear suspension, and the choice of 5/6hp single- or 10/12hp four-cylinder engines.

RITZ / *USA 1915*

This two-seater 12/15 hp light car was built by Driggs-Seabury, and had a two-speed transmission in the back axle.

RIVIERRE / *France 1912–1913*

Successor to the Mototri-Contal, this was a four-cylinder 1460cc two-seater torpedo with transmission by 'lateral shafts'.

ROADABLE / *USA 1946–1947*

Built in Garland, Texas, by the Southern Aircraft Division, Portable Products Corp., the Roadable could be converted into an airplane in five minutes by the addition of 30 ft wings, tail and propeller. A 130 hp six-cylinder air-cooled engine drove the three-wheeled vehicle while the rear-wheel drive was used in conjunction with the propeller for take-off. A top speed of 110 mph in the air, combined with a 600-mile range, was claimed.

ROADSTER / *USA 1902–1904*

'No experiment but a full-grown Automobile', the '8 full horsepower' Roadster from the Flint Automobile Company of Flint, Michigan, was claimed to be a great favourite with physicians. It sold for $950.

ROAMER / *USA 1916–1930*

Designed externally to resemble the Rolls-Royce, the first Roamers were powered by Continental sixes, Rochester-Duesenberg fours became available in 1921 and remained the power unit until 1925. Thereafter, with a few Continental sixes marketed in 1926, the make used Lycoming eights exclusively. The Roamer was built by Albert C. Barley (who had been producing the Halladay car) and was designed by Karl H. Martin (who would also design the Deering Magnetic and Kenworthy and build the Wasp). Production slackened after 1926, and the Roamers found fewer and fewer buyers. Cars sold as 1930 models were actually left-over models from 1929.

1923 Robe prototype

ROBE / *USA 1923*

The Robe was built in Nansemond, Va., by W. B. Robe, who had built a cyclecar in Portsmouth, Ohio, in 1914, and J. D. Strong. Using a four-cylinder engine of its 'own' manufacture, according to the announcements (but in fact probably a Continental), the 106-inch wheelbase Robe featured full leaf springs on either side of the body. At least one test chassis and one touring car are known to have been built — this may well have been the total production.

ROBERTSON / *England 1915–1916*
An alarming-looking three-wheeled cyclecar from Manchester, powered by 965cc JAP or Precision vee-twins.

ROBINSON / *USA 1900–1904*
'Modelled after the best French designs', the Robinson (or 'Pope-Robinson'), from Boston, was available with two- or four-cylinder engines, including a 5000cc 'fast touring carriage'.

ROBINSON / *England 1907*
Only three Robinsons were built out of a projected total of six. As the four-cylinder 12 hp engine was cooled by its own exhaust gases, which passed through a 'radiator' before being directed onto the cylinder heads by a copper cowl, this shortfall is perhaps understandable.

ROBINSON & HOLE / *England 1906–1907*
A four-cylinder 16/20 hp model with gate-change three-speed gearbox and shaft drive, built in Thames Ditton, Surrey.

ROB ROY / *Scotland 1922–1926*
This cyclecar originally used a 9 hp flat-twin engine, which also powered the Kingsbury Junior. It later graduated to four-cylinder engines by Dorman and Coventry-Climax.

ROCHDALE / *England 1952–1968*
Stylish glass-fibre-bodied fixed-head sports cars, the Rochdales sported a number of engines over the years. Some 400 Olympic Phase 1s and 2s were built. Many have survived and retain an enthusiastic following.

ROCHESTER / *USA 1901–1903*
A $600 tiller-steered light steam carriage.

ROCHET, ROCHET-PETIT
France 1899–1905
This Parisian company bought the design of their first car, a 6/8 hp 'of Daimler type', from Edouard Rossel of Lille, adding a 12 hp in 1900: the 4½ hp Aster-engined Rochet-Petit appeared in 1902.

1902 10hp Rochet

ROCHET *France 1907*
Tricars and 'tri-voiturettes' from Albert (Somme).

ROCHET FRERES / *France 1898–1901*
A Lyon-built voiturette with front-mounted De Dion engine.

1907 Rochet-Schneider 20hp

ROCHET-SCHNEIDER / *France 1894–1932*
This well-known Lyon factory started by making Benz-like cars, then built cars inspired first by Panhard, and subsequently by Mercedes. In 1909 they had nine different models, of which two were six-cylinders, of 30 cv (7135cc) and 45 cv (10,857cc), and which were chain driven. In 1914 Rochet-Schneider had six different models, the largest being the 50 cv four of 7238cc; there were also two six-cylinders, an 18 cv (3619cc) and a 28 cv (5228cc), all with sv. The company made lorries for the Army during the war, and resumed production in 1918 with pre-war models like the 14 cv, 18 cv and 30 cv. The first new car to be made was the 1920 sv six-cylinder of 6126cc. It eventually acquired ohv, and in 1926 was replaced by another six, of 3769cc, enlarged in 1930 to 4561cc. From 1932 Rochet-Schneider switched to building lorries and buses, as their old-fashioned four-cylinder models had become more and more difficult to sell.

ROCKAWAY / *USA 1902–1903*
A basic single-cylinder chain-drive runabout from Rockaway, New Jersey, selling for $650.

ROCK FALLS / *USA 1917–1926*
A manufacturer of funeral cars, Rock Falls produced a limited number of sedans and large limousines. Continental six-cylinder engines were standard throughout and the eight-passenger limousine was listed at $4500. Less than 50 — probably much fewer — were built per year.

1919 Rock Falls sedan

ROCKNE / *USA 1931–1933*
The smallest of the Studebaker line, the Rockne six made its bow on the automotive scene in 1931, ostensibly to fill the gap previously occupied by the Erskine which had been withdrawn a year before. It was named after Knute Rockne, football coach at Notre Dame University (located in South Bend, Indiana, like Studebaker). It was felt that a hero's name would sell cars, Knute Rockne having been employed by Studebaker in addition to his professional activities on the football field. Whether it was the fact that the car had been launched in a Depression year, whether it was that the great Rockne was killed in a plane crash before the car had actually been introduced, or whether the car was somewhat over-priced ($585 to $675) for its size, the Rockne never really caught on. Some 30,000 to 35,000 Rockne cars were sold before the make was quietly phased out in 1933.

ROCKWELL / *USA 1909*
An 18/20 hp four 'specially designed for taximeter work'.

ROEBLING-PLANCHE / *USA 1909–1910*
Designed by the French engineer Planche, the Roebling-Planche was built in the Walter factory and financed by the Roebling family, builders of the Brooklyn Bridge. The marque became the Mercer a year later.

ROGER / *France 1888–1896*
Emile Roger — perhaps the world's first motor agent — assembled Benz cars for the French market, but the venture ended with his death.

ROGER / *England 1920–1924*
The friction-drive Roger used a 10.8 hp Coventry-Simplex engine. Later, in 1923, the option of shaft drive was available.

ROHR / *Germany 1927–1935*
Founded by one of Germany's most capable designers, H. G. Röhr, the factory built very advanced ohv eight-cylinder cars of 2250cc and 3287cc, some of them supercharged. Röhr left in 1930 to join Adler; Porsche's design office at

1933 Rohr 3.3-litre straight-eight

Stuttgart created an improved 100 bhp eight-cylinder Röhr in 1934. An air-cooled ohv flat-four 1486cc Röhr car built under Tatra-licence had appeared in 1933. The Röhr works at Ober-Ramstadt also built the 1934 Zoller-designed 1496cc two-stroke racing cars.

LE ROITELET/*France 1921–1924*
A fwd cyclecar made in Paris with a twin-cylinder 749cc engine.

ROLAND/*France 1907*
Tricars from an Albert (Somme) cycle works.

ROLL/*France 1922–1923*
Cyclecar made in Paris with a 990cc four-cylinder Ruby engine.

1925 3-litre Rolland-Pilain at Le Mans

ROLLAND-PILAIN/*France 1906–1931*
Established in Tours, Rolland-Pilain started in 1906 with a 20 cv four-cylinder model of 2211cc. In 1910 they experimented with sleeve-valve engines, and introduced a 1500cc model. In 1913 they added a 20 cv of 3969cc and a big 60 cv of 6902cc. At the outbreak of the war, they were only building the 20 cv and the 10 cv (1924cc). They restarted production after the war with these old models, but in 1921 presented the ohv 12 cv of 2297cc, with brakes on all four wheels. In 1922 Rolland-Pilain raced a 2000cc straight-eight, and 1924 saw the 2008cc 11 cv ohv four, the best model ever made by the firm. The following year came the 1924cc 10/12 cv. At the very end, Rolland-Pilain experimented with American Continental engines.

ROLLIN/*USA 1923–1925*
Designed and built by Rollin White, chief engineer of the White Company, the four-cylinder Rollin was planned as an economical automobile to capture a share of the low-priced market. Its engine was similar to that of the Cletrac tractor — a White subsidiary — and the first Rollin cars were not only built in the Cleveland Tractor plant, but shared the Cletrac emblem. The 112-inch wheelbase, disc-wheeled Rollin was just a bit too high-priced for the market for which it had been intended. Output in 1924, its best year, was some 6500 units, but total production probably failed to reach 10,000 before the car was discontinued in 1925.

ROLLO/*England 1911–1913*
'The best thing in motor cycles, not the poorest in motor cars', the Birmingham-built Rollo was nevertheless a typical cyclecar, with an 8 hp JAP engine and chain-cum-belt drive. There were three models: a tandem seater 'for two or more'; a Sociable, 'for those who prefer to sit side by side'; and a Mono-car (70 guineas).

ROLLS-ROYCE/*England 1904 to date*
Manchester electrical engineer Henry Royce built a batch of three Decauville-inspired 10 hp twin-cylinder cars under his own name in 1904; Lord Llangattock's surprising son, the Hon. C. S. Rolls, was looking for a light car of quality to sell alongside the Continental imports in his West London motor agency; the two combined to create a motoring legend. After producing sound two-, three- and four-cylinder models of 10, 15 and 20 hp, not quite so good sixes of 30 hp and a dreadful V-8 (the 'Legalimit'), in 1906 Rolls-Royce launched the immortal 40/50 hp six, known from 1907 as the 'Silver Ghost'. Even though its design was sound rather than original, it was built with Royce's consummate devotion to the highest engineering ideals. The Ghost survived until 1925 (joined in 1922 by a 20 hp) and was supplanted by the ohv New Phantom, a

The first twin-cylinder Rolls-Royce, 1904

transitional design which gave way to the more comprehensively revised Phantom II in 1929. That year the 20 hp grew up into the 20/25, succeeded in 1936 by the 25/30 (which developed into the Wraith in 1938). The Phantom III of 1936–39 was a magnificent V-12 of 7341cc, often marred by clumsy coachwork, and whose engine, with hydraulic tappets, was prohibitively costly to overhaul. Post-war, Rolls-Royce moved from Derby (where they had been based since 1908) to Crewe, and restarted production in 1947 with the Silver Wraith, followed in 1949 by the Silver Dawn, first Rolls-Royce to have standardized steel coachwork. The six-cylinder engine line continued until 1959, followed by a 6231cc V-8, used both on the Silver Cloud and Phantom V models (the Phantom IV had been a 16-off 5675cc straight-eight). Integral construction and all-round independent suspension came with the 1965 Silver Shadow, direct ancestor of today's costly and magnificent Corniche and Camargue models. (In 1979, the cheapest Rolls-Royce cost over £30,000.)

ROLLS-ROYCE/*USA 1920–1931*
Rolls-Royce of America, Inc., was formed in Springfield, Mass., in 1920, to build and supply Rolls-Royce cars. Some 50 highly trained craftsmen were moved with their families and possessions to Springfield before operations began there. Between 1921 and 1929, some 2601 chassis left the Springfield works, both 'Silver Ghost' and 'New Phantom' models. Eventually the domestic Rolls-Royce became as much an American product as any other domestic car. The 12-

1912 'London-Edinburgh' Rolls-Royce 40/50hp

ROLUX/*France 1938–1952*
Builder of the New-Map motorcycles in Lyon, Martin made some light cars with 125cc and 175cc two-strokes, also sold as 'New Map'.

ROM CARMEL/*Israel 1958 to date*
Initially known as the Sabra, based on Reliant designs, from 1966 to 1971 this Haifa company was in partnership with Triumph of Coventry.

Late 1970s production is 1800 glass-fibre-bodied cars annually: the four-door Rom 1300 uses a Ford Escort engine.

ROMER/*USA 1921–1922*
Built in Danvers, Massachusetts, the Romer was an assembled car using a Continental six-cylinder engine. The five-passenger touring model was priced at $1975; other body styles including a speedster, roadster, coupé and two-door sedan, as well as a small truck, were available. Production was limited and passenger-car production was terminated in late 1921 (although truck production continued into the following year).

c. 1921 Springfield Rolls-Royce Silver Ghost Town Car

volt electrical system was changed to 6-volt and the four-speed transmission was dropped in favour of a three. In 1925, the steering wheel was moved to the left. The 'New Phantom' did not appear on the American scene until 1926, the same year Rolls-Royce bought Brewster & Company, coachbuilders. Most subsequent Springfield cars carried custom coachwork by this firm. When the 'Phantom II' was introduced by Derby, the Springfield operation ceased actual new car production due to lack of finance. However, in 1930–33 it managed to assemble some 350 additional—and now outmoded—cars from existing parts. In addition, it imported 121 Phantom II chassis and sold them in left-hand drive form and mounted with Brewster coachwork. In 1934, Rolls-Royce of America, Inc., was dissolved and its place taken by the newly organized Springfield Manufacturing Co., which assembled Brewster cars until 1936.

1914 Ronteix, sold in Britain as the Cummikar

RONTEIX/*France 1907–1914*
Ronteix of Paris built a 'suspended voiturette' in 1907, as well as tricars and fore-carriages. Their early cars used a curious multi-ratio crown-wheel and pinion like the Sizaire-Naudin, though from 1913 a normal gearbox was fitted. Four-cylinder engines and shaft drive placed the 905cc Ronteix on a higher technical plane than many of its contemporaries.

ROOSEVELT/*USA 1929–1931*
The Roosevelt, smallest of the Marmon line of cars, was announced on New Year's Day, 1929. Featuring a radiator emblem depicting the head of President Theodore Roosevelt, horizontal hood louvres, and a choice of wire or wood wheels, the Roosevelt was the only American straight-eight costing under $1000 at the time. In 1930, the Roosevelt-head insignia was dropped and the car was renamed the Marmon-Roosevelt.

ROOTS & VENABLES/*England 1895–1904*
J. D. Roots was one of the pioneers of British motoring. All his cars ran on 'heavy oil' (paraffin), which then cost 5½d a gallon, against 11d for 'motor spirit'. His earliest trials took place on the Continent to avoid the repressive British laws. 'The car would have been an instantaneous success', recalled a contemporary, 'but for the intensely objectionable smell it gave off when starting and occasionally running'.

ROPER-CORBET/*England 1911–1913*
A four-cylinder 14/16 hp model which sold for £350 complete.

1933 Rolls-Royce 20/25hp saloon

Rolls-Royce Camargue

Rolls-Royce Silver Shadow II

1948 Rosengart Supertrahuit ST8

ROSENGART/*France 1928–1955*
L. Rosengart started in Neuilly, Seine, just before the Depression with Austin Sevens built under licence. They were very similar to the British models, except that the bodywork was adapted to the French taste. In 1932, the chassis was lengthened, and a small 1100cc six offered. In the years preceding the war, Rosengart made some fwd 'Supertraction' cars based on the Adler Trumpf and, later, on the Citroën. After the war Rosengart resumed production with some pre-war models, and introduced the 'Supertrahuit' with Mercury engine (a complete flop). The 1954 Sagaie with a 750cc air-cooled flat-twin came too late to save the company.

ROSS/*USA 1905–1909*
This was a big, powerful five-seater steam car on petrol car lines, with a 25 hp twin-cylinder engine and shaft drive.

ROSS/*USA 1915–1918*
Ross, of Detroit, built V-8s of 29 hp and 34 hp.

ROSSEL/*France 1896–1899*
Petrol cars with Daimler-based engines; their designer later built steam tractors for canal barges.

1898 Rossel 3½hp

ROSSEL/*France 1903–1926*
Rossel was a Peugeot director who produced cars under his own name, the first production model being a 3958cc four (though a 4 hp racer was made in 1896). By 1907 a six was available too, and in 1908 a '100cv' Type Ventoux was listed. The 1910 line-up consisted of fours of 2799cc, 4181cc, 6333cc and 8016cc, and sixes of 3317cc, 6272cc and 7464cc, and the bigger cars retained chain drive until the war. Post-war models were undistinguished, and the Sochaux, Doubs, factory was sold to Peugeot in 1926.

ROTARY/*USA 1922–1923*
This car was powered by a six-cylinder rotary-valve engine of its own manufacture and the touring-car was priced at $6000. Designed by Eugene Bournonville, the car was widely promoted, though probably only one (possibly another two) pilot models were built. The car featured wire wheels and rode on a 130-inch wheelbase. The $6000 was reduced to $3800 in 1922, but this may have been a sacrifice to dispose of the existing model.

ROTHWELL/*England 1902–1916*
The Eclipse Machine Company of Oldham, Lancashire, produced a range of cars, including a single-cylinder 9hp and a 10/12hp twin-cylinder with steering-column gear-change.

LA ROULETTE/*France 1912–1914*
An 8/10 hp vee-twin cyclecar from Courbevoie.

ROUSSEL/*France 1908–1914*
Builders of light cars, voiturettes and taxicabs at Charleville-Mezières in the Ardennes. Four-cylinder 10 hp and 12 hp engines were available.

ROUSSEY/*France 1949–1951*
Made in Meudon, Seine, by the Roussey brothers (also makers of motorcycles), these were fwd small cars with 750cc flat-four engines.

ROUXEL/*France 1899–1900*
Rouxel built a De Dion-engined tricycle and a two-speed voiturette with a 2¼ hp Aster engine.

ROVER/*England 1904 to date*
Rover built the first true safety bicycle in 1888, but apart from an early electric tricycle and a De Dion-engined bathchair, did not venture into car production until 1904, when a neat 8 hp model designed by Edmund Lewis appeared, using a great deal of cast aluminium in its construction, particularly in its backbone chassis frame. A more conventional 6 hp appeared the next year, as did two four-cylinder models, the 10/12 and the 16/20, the latter a neat monobloc of 3199cc which won the 1907 Tourist Trophy Race. Sleeve-valve Rovers of 8 hp (single-cylinder 1042cc) and 12 hp (four-cylinder 3764cc) were announced for 1911, in the

1911 Rover 12hp tourer

In the 1920s De Rovin built this neat sporting cyclecar

both with tubular chassis, that of the 10 hp being braced so that it would not fold in two!

ROYAL ROEBUCK / *England 1900*
A motor quadricycle built by J. F. Janes in London, and exhibited at the 1900 National Cycle & Motor Show at the Crystal Palace.

ROYAL RUBY / *England 1913–1914*
A vee-twin 10 hp JAP engine powered this cyclecar built by a famous cycle company from Altrincham, near Manchester. In 1927, they offered a single-cylinder 5 hp three-wheeler.

ROYAL TOURIST / *USA 1904–1912*
Successor to the Hoffman, the Royal Tourist was a 'practical motor car with an intrinsic value', available in 16 hp twin-cylinder and 32 hp four-cylinder form, with aluminium coachwork. By 1906 a 40 hp was also offered.

ROYDALE / *England 1908*
The Roydale (the name was said to be an anagram for 'Learoyd') came from Huddersfield: 18 hp and 25 hp models were made.

ROVIN / *France 1946–1951*
Racing driver and maker of motorcycles, M. De Rovin built small cars with single-cylinder 260cc engines and flat-twins of 425cc, later enlarged to 462cc. They sold well, mainly in Paris.

ROYAL ENFIELD / *England 1899–1905*
'Built like a gun' was the motto of Royal Enfield, who built their first De Dion-engined tricycles and quadricycles in 1899. By 1904, cars of 6 hp (single) and 10 hp (twin) were available,

R.T.C. / *England 1922–1923*
The belt-driven R.T.C. was powered by an 8·3 hp air-cooled vee-twin Blackburne engine. It was manufactured by René Tondeur Co. Ltd., of Croydon, Surrey.

autumn of which year an excellent 2297cc 12 hp designed by Owen Clegg made its bow. It formed the basis of post-war production, joined by the Rover Eight, a 998cc flat-twin designed by J. Y. Sangster. These basic models were succeeded by the four-cylinder Nine and the P. A. Poppe-designed 14/45, a 3·4-litre six shown in 1923 having proved unsatisfactory. The ohc 14/45 (uprated to 16/50) did not sell well, and was replaced in 1928 by the 2-litre 'Light Six', which formed the basis of 1930s production in capacities up to 2·7 litres. A rear-engined 839cc V-4, the Scarab, with an £85 price tag, failed to reach production in 1931, and thereafter Rover

stuck to its solid middle-class image. In 1948 new ioe four- and six-cylinder models, the P3 60 and 75, with ifs for the first time, appeared, as did the 4wd Land-Rover. October 1949 saw the P4 75, with full-width styling and 'Cyclops' central headlight: it sired a range which lasted until May 1964. In 1963 came the radically different Rover 2000,

available from 1968 with the GM-designed light-alloy 3·5-litre V-8 also found on its luxury P4 stablemate. The 4wd Range Rover, aimed at a more sybaritic market than the Land-Rover, appeared in 1970, and 1976 saw a new Rover 3500, with Ferrari-like styling: it subsequently became available with Rover's in-line sixes as well.

1926 Rover 14/40hp Saloon

1963 Rover 110

1977 Rover 2600 six-cylinder

RUBURY-LINDSAY/*England 1920–1921*
Designed by J. M. Rubury, formerly chief designer of Sheffield Simplex, and built in Argyll's London service depot, this light car had a three-cylinder radial air-cooled engine of 1230cc.

RUBY/*France 1910–1922*
The 1910 Ruby range from this famous engine manufacturer of Levallois-Perret (Seine) consisted of a 6/8 hp single and a 10/14 hp four. These cars were sold in England from 1910–1912 as 'Elburns'. An 8/10 hp twin was added in 1914, when the cars were known in Britain as 'Tweenies'.

RUDGE/*England 1912–1913*
This famous Coventry cycle and motorcycle maker briefly marketed a long-stroke (85mm × 132mm) 750cc belt-drive cyclecar.

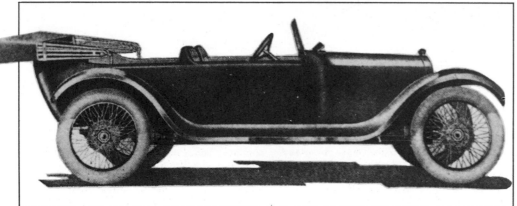

1917 Ruler Four

RULER/*USA 1917*
A 'frameless' car from Aurora, Illinois, with a four-cylinder 2720cc ohc engine and a three-point-suspended 'cradle' in place of a chassis.

RULEX/*England 1904*
A curiously styled voiturette, with either 3½ hp or 4½ hp Rulex engine and belt drive.

RUMPF/*Belgium 1899*
A three-seater car with a twin-cylinder 6½ hp engine built in Brussels.

RUMPLER/*Germany 1921–1926*
Dr. Edmund Rumpler was a genial and versatile designer, bursting with unorthodox ideas. He

1921 Rumpler streamline saloon

created superb aeroplanes and cars, including the advanced 'Teardrop', for which he designed an ohv 2579cc six-cylinder double-radial engine, built for him by Siemens of Berlin. Mounted in the rear, the power unit developed 36 bhp at 2000 rpm. Benz bought his design and also built the rear-engined 2-litre 'Teardrop' sports and racing cars. An improved Rumpler design, built in 1924, had an ohv 2595cc 50 hp engine; a front-wheel-drive car appeared in 1926.

RUSSELL/*Canada 1906–1915*
The Russell was Canada's finest pre-World War One car: its constructors, Canada Cycle & Motor Co. of Toronto, had earlier built cars under the name Ivanhoe (1903) and Queen (1901–03). Its fame really dated from the introduction of Knight sleeve-valve engined fours and sixes in 1909. The plant was eventually acquired by Willys-Overland.

RUSSELL/*USA 1946*
Former Ford employee Raymond Russell designed and built this unusual car which had 7 to 15 forward and reverse speeds. It was claimed to have more low gear power than any other vehicle of the time. The Russell used a hydraulic drive and the main motor fed oil through four single motors, one for each wheel.

RUSSO-BALTIQUE/*Russia 1909–1915*
A railway rolling-stock factory at Riga built T-head cars — initially of 4053cc, later of 4849cc and 5036cc — to the design of the Swiss engineer Potterat. In 1911, Ing. Valentin, of the German Rex-Simplex company, came to Riga to design a 7238cc 40/60 hp model; small L-head fours of 2212cc and 3686cc were built from 1911–15. In 1912, a 4502cc Russo-Baltique won the distance prize in the Monte Carlo Rally. Total production was 521 cars.

RUSTON HORNSBY/*England 1919–1924*
Ruston and Hornsby of Lincoln were a well-established firm of agricultural engineers who built Clerget and BR2 aeroengines during World War One. Their first car, the A1, was a sturdy affair with a straight-forward 2·6-litre four-cylinder engine of 15·9 hp and three-speed gearbox. The A3 of 1920 had a slightly larger engine of 3-litre capacity. A smaller 15 hp model appeared in 1923, but car production ceased the following year.

RUTTGER/*Germany 1920–1922*
Produced a limited number of 10/40 hp four-cylinder cars with ohv 2524cc Fafnir engines.

RUXTON/*USA 1929–1931*
The brainchild of financier Archie M. Andrews, a Hupmobile director, this was a low-slung front-wheel-drive model powered by a 5·5-litre Continental straight-eight. Production began in 1930 in the Moon and Kissel factories, with tourers from Raulang and sedan bodies built by Budd, using British Wolseley dies allied to garish interior trim by stage designer Joseph Urban. Between 300 and 500 cars were built before the collapse of Moon and Kissel brought Ruxton down as well.

RYJAN/*France 1920–1926*
M. Henry Janssen started making cars in Chatou, Seine, with a 2297cc four-cylinder. In 1923, he presented a new SCAP-engined 10 hp of 1693cc, later reduced to 1616cc. Taken over by M. Grillet in 1925, the marque ended with Altos-engined cars of 1995cc.

RYDE/*England 1904–1906*
Starting with a 14/16 hp three-cylinder, this West Ealing company added an ephemeral 10 hp flat-twin in 1904.

RYKNIELD/*England 1903–1906*
'An Engineer's Job', the original Ryknield from Burton upon Trent was a 10 hp twin with a pressed-steel chassis. A 20 hp four was introduced in 1904, and a 15 hp three-cylinder added to the range the following year. The project was backed by members of the Bass brewing company.

RYNER-WILSON/*England 1920–1921*
The stillborn Ryner-Wilson was to have been powered by a six-cylinder 2290cc engine. Dry sump lubrication was employed. The car, however, never advanced beyond the prototype stage.

Rytecraft Scootacar photo taken at Brooklands, 1937

RYTECRAFT/*England 1934–1940*
The tiny Scootacar started as a fairground attraction, and the first road-going models had 98cc Villiers engines and only one speed, though later models had three-speed gearing and 250cc Villiers engines. Used mostly for publicity purposes, some Scootacars were built as midget replicas of Vauxhall and Chrysler Airflow cars. In the 1960s, a Scootacar was driven round the world by motor book dealer Jim Parkinson.

SABA/*Italy 1926–1928*
A Fiat-like car with an ohv four-cylinder 983cc engine in unit with the gearbox, the SABA had a top speed of 45 mph. Very few of these 'Stelvio' models reached the market.

SABELLA/*England 1906–1914*
A. T. Warne of Leytonstone first showed the single-seat Sabella (designed by Fritz Sabel) at the 1906 Stanley Show. 'For doctors, travellers, golfers and professional men', it was a single-seat four-wheeler with a 5 hp twin-cylinder engine, whose speed was controlled by varying the valve-lift. It cost £85, and Warne also offered a hand-propelled Sabella for £2.10s. A 10 hp twin-cylinder car appeared in 1907, and a sporting cyclecar designed by Warne in 1912.

SABLATNIG-BEUCHELT
Germany 1925–1926
The Sablatnig-designed 1496cc four-cylinder car was one of many short-lived German creations of the early 1920s.

SACHSENRING/*Germany 1956–1959*
Made by the nationalized Horch works at Zwickau (East Germany), the Sachsenring had an ohv 2407cc six-cylinder engine. Originally known as Horch, the name had to be changed because the Horch title is still owned by the now West German Auto Union.

SAF/*Sweden 1921–1922*
Svenska Automobilfabriken's idea was to assemble American components into a 'Swedish' car at their Bolinäs factory. In 1919 negotiations started with American manufacturers and in 1921 the first assembled cars left the factory. The engine was a four-cylinder Continental with a three-speed gearbox. Rear springs were cantilevers, and the only body type was a five-seater tourer. Production was planned on a grand scale, but probably only 25 cars were produced. 'Rather bad' quality made them hard to sell.

SAFIR/*Switzerland 1907 c1909*
Commercial vehicles mostly were built by the Zürich firm, but they also offered big shaft-driven four-cylinder 30 hp and 50 hp touring cars built under Saurer licence.

SAAB/*Sweden 1949 to date*
In 1945 the Svenska Aeroplan AB, of Linköping, decided to go into car production; noted for their advanced aircraft design, they employed much of that technique on the car they built. It had unitary construction, an aerodynamic body, and the engine was a transversely mounted two-stroke twin of 764cc with a marked resemblance to the pre-war DKW unit. The car was front-wheel driven and had all-independent suspension. Initially, only a two-door saloon was offered. Cars were shown in 1947, but production started in late 1949. The model name was Saab 92, changed to 92B in 1952 when small body changes were made. The Saab 93 of 1955 had a three-cylinder 748cc engine and coil-spring suspension. Sports models, called Granturismo 750, were also built, mainly for export. The 1959 Saab 95 was a station waggon with an 841cc engine, also used in the 1960 Saab 96 with redesigned rear-end. There were also several sports versions. Saab had many rally successes, among them Monte Carlo Rally wins in 1962 and 1963 and the RAC Rally 1960–1962. In 1966 a small glass-fibre GT coupé, the Sonett II,

was launched. The 1967 Model 96 had the German Ford V-4, but the two-stroke engine was still available: the 96 was still being produced in Finland at the end of the 1970s. In 1969 the all-new Saab 99 started production. The engine was a Triumph-designed 1·7-litre ohc four, later enlarged to 2 litres; in 1972 full production of the engine started in Saab's Södertälje plant. Later versions were the 110 bhp fuel-injected EMS and the 140 bhp Turbo of 1977. The 900 has been available from 1978; it is a long-nosed version of the 99, with mechanical refinements.

1950 Saab 92 saloon

1979 Saab Turbo saloon

SAGE/*France 1900–1906*
Sage of Paris made a wide variety of two- and four-cylinder touring cars, from 10 hp to 50 hp.

SAGER/*Canada 1911*
Though illustrations of this 30 hp four were released, probably no cars, nor the 'extensive factory' at Welland, Ontario, were completed.

ST JOE/*USA 1908–1909*
St Joe took over the bankrupt Shoemaker Automobile Company, founded in Elkhart, Indiana, in 1906, and continued production of 'pleasure and commercial cars' under their own name. Leading line was a 40 hp selling at $2500.

ST LOUIS/*USA 1898–1907*
The products of 'America's pioneer motor car manufacturers', George P. Dorris, were also known as 'Rigs that Run'. The 1899 St Louis

1903 St Louis 9hp tonneau

'gasoline stanhope' was made in the first purpose-built car factory west of the Mississippi, and had a 6 hp horizontal-twin engine. Their ultimate offering, following a move from St Louis to Peoria, Illinois, was a $2500 four-cylinder 32/36 hp.

ST LOUIS/*USA 1922*
The name on this car was changed from Neskov-Mumperow for obvious reasons; however, there is little reason to believe that anything more than pilot models ever appeared. These were sporting cars with advanced lines and used Weidely four-cylinder engines. Price of the four-passenger touring model was $3500.

SALAMANCA/*Spain 1904*
A Paris-made single-cylinder 8 cv engine and transmission were used to build this wagonette.

SALISBURY /*USA 1896*
A clumsy four-seater car built by the Horseless Carriage Company of Chicago, Wilber S. Salisbury's car had a twin-cylinder 3 hp engine and three 48-inch wheels.

SALISBURY/*England 1903*
The 10 hp twin-cylinder Salisbury — there was also a 7 hp single — offered the advanced feature of a four-speed gearbox.

SALMON/*England 1912–1914*
From the same factory as the ACE and Baguley, the Salmon was an 11·9 hp four-cylinder model with bulbous coachbuilt body. An 8·1 hp model similar to the ACE was also offered.

Salmson cyclecars (derived from the GN), 1922

SALMSON/*France 1921–1957*
Well-known aeroengine manufacturer, the Société des Moteurs Salmson started by building the British GN under licence: they launched their first Salmson in 1921, and fitted it with a 1086cc engine with four 'push-pull-rods', which controlled both the inlet and exhaust valves. At the same time, engineer Petit evolved a racing version with dohc. In 1923, Salmson presented an 8/10 hp of 1194cc, then in 1930 they started the S4 series with a dohc 1500cc engine which was finally developed to 2·3 litres in the last new Salmson models made in 1953. Salmson cars won many sporting events.

SALVA/*Italy 1906–c1908*
The Societa Anonima Lombarda Vetture Automobili of Milan offered fours of 16/25 hp and 28/45 hp, plus a 60/75 hp six.

SALVADOR/*Spain c1918*
A cyclecar, with independent front suspension by parallel leaf springs, rack and pinion steering and a vee-twin MAG engine.

SAM/*Italy 1924–1929*
This Leghorn factory was first connected with the three-wheeled Vaghi cyclecar. SAM afterwards built sporting 1056cc two-, three- and four-seater voiturettes with four-cylinder sv and ohc engines of their own make. Fritz Jackl of Czechoslovakia drove SAM cars in hillclimbs.

SAMPSON
USA 1904, 1911
The Alden Sampson Company manufactured the chassis for the 1903 Moyea, a licence-built 18/22 hp Rochet-Schneider, and continued this car under their own name. The company later became the truck division of the United States Motor Company, but built a number of 35 hp touring cars in 1911, with pair-cast 5734cc four-cylinder engines.

SAMSON/*USA 1920*
The Samson Tractor Co., of Janesville, Wisconsin, a division of General Motors, built one passenger car, a nine-passenger touring model powered by a Chevrolet FB engine. It had auxiliary seats which could be removed, thereby converting the car into a truck!

SANCHIS/*France 1906–1912*
Enrique Sanchis, a Spanish engineer on a government mission to France, built a number of V-4 voiturettes with chassis and body skeleton pressed as one unit, ready for steel panelling to be riveted on.

SANDFORD/*France 1922–1939*
An Englishman in Paris, Malcolm Stuart Sandford, made some lovely Morgan-inspired sporting four-cylinder Ruby-engined three-wheelers from 900cc to 1100cc, some of them supercharged. He also made some flat-twin 950cc Ruby-engined three-wheelers and four-wheelers.

Sandford three-wheelers in action, c.1924

S & M/*USA 1913–1914*
Strobel & Martin, of Detroit, built this luxury six-cylinder touring car, which became the Benham in 1914.

S & M SIMPLEX, SIMPLEX
USA 1904–1914
Mercedes agents Smith & Mabley introduced 18 hp and 30 hp luxury cars in 1904 to beat the 40 per cent tax on imported models, but the S & M Simplex was a victim of the 1907 slump. The Simplex name was bought by Herman Broesel, who financed a Mercedes-inspired model designed by Edward Franquist and was built from the finest materials available. Best-known was the T-head 50 hp: in 1911 a 38 hp, 7·8-litre shaft-drive model appeared. The 1912–14 75 hp of 10-litres was probably America's last big chain-drive car. In 1914 the marque became Crane-Simplex.

1912 chain-driven Simplex

SANDRINGHAM/*England 1902–1905*
'Royal Motor Repairer' Frank Morriss showed a 10 hp car of his own make at the 1903 Cordingley Show in London.

1926 Salmson 1100cc Grand Prix sports two-seater

S & S / *USA 1924–1930*
Successor to the earlier Sayers, this car was a sideline of the Sayers & Scoville Company of Cincinnati, Ohio, builder of Sayers & Scoville hearses. It was available primarily as a pallbearers' car, large sedan or limousine. Continental six-cylinder engines were used until 1928, when eights of the same make were substituted. The model designations included 'Brighton', 'Elmwood', 'Gotham' and 'Lakewood'. All were available to the general public.

SANDUSKY / *USA 1901–1903*
'Mud, sand and hills shrink before it' was the optimistic slogan of the Sandusky Runabout from Sandusky, Ohio.

SANFORD / *Spain 1902–1903*
A four-seater car with an alcohol-powered engine shown at the Madrid 'Alcohol Exhibition' in December 1902.

SAN GIORGIO / *Italy 1906–1907*
Big six-cylinder cars from 25 hp to 60 hp produced under Napier licence, using many English components.

SAN GIUSTO / *Italy 1922–1924*
This very advanced cyclecar, with rear-mounted 738cc four-cylinder engine, central backbone chassis and independent suspension on all wheels, enjoyed no commercial success.

SANTAX / *France 1922–1927*
Small cyclecar made in Paris with Anzani single-cylinder engines of 125cc and 500cc.

SANTOS-DUMONT / *USA 1902–1904*
Named after the famous Brazilian aeronaut, the air-cooled flat-twin Santos-Dumont from Columbus, Ohio, was styled on De Dion Bouton lines and sold for $1500. A 20 hp flat-four appeared in 1904, selling for $2000.

SARA / *France 1923–1930*
The Société des Applications du Refroidissement par Air made some interesting air-cooled cars with four-cylinder 1098cc engines which sold well. However, in 1927 they presented the ill-fated SARA 6, an 1806cc six-cylinder model.

SAS / *France 1927–1928*
This Paris-based works presented a range of four CIME-engined cars in 1927: a 10 hp of 1496cc and a 12 hp of 1616cc, and two six-cylinders of 1211cc and 1492cc.

SAURER / *Switzerland 1897–c1918*
The first Saurer gas-engines were built in the company's Arbon workshops in 1888; a single-cylinder opposed-piston engine powered the first Saurer car of 1897–98. Sent to Paris, it formed the basis of the design of the Koch car. Serious production began in 1902, and from 1904 Saurer cars — 24/30 hp fours of 4398cc — had air-braking similar to that used on Rovers, utilizing movable cams which prevented the exhaust valves opening. Also offered in the 1904–14 period were 30/35 hp (5321cc) and 50/60 hp (9236cc) single-cast fours. Car production was gradually phased out in favour of the trucks for which Saurer are still famous, but in 1934 Saurer began assembly of Chrysler cars.

SAUTEL ET SECHARD / *France 1903*
A three-wheeled 'nouvelle voiturette' from Gentilly, which combined steering, clutch, braking and gear-changing on the pivoting steering column.

SAUTTER-HARLE / *France 1907–1912*
Pioneer motoring journalist W. F. Bradley was an enthusiastic owner of a Sautter-Harlé, built in Paris. The first of this marque were 16/20 hp fours, and a 10/12 hp two-cylinder; in 1910 12 hp and 18 hp fours were also listed.

SAVA / *Belgium 1910–1923*
The Société Anversoise pour Fabrication des Voitures Automobiles, of Antwerp, began production with an 18 hp, 2011cc monobloc four with a worm-drive back-axle. At the end of 1912 a 1966cc 18/26 hp appeared, with the odd layout of side inlet, overhead exhaust valves, and four or eight sparking plugs. The 1913 range consisted of a 14/18 hp (2474cc) the 18/26 hp (now 2957cc) and a 36/50 hp four, also with eoi head, which sold for £610. The company suffered badly in World War One, and there was little post-armistice activity until 1923, when the 1915 model (based on the 1914 Tourist Trophy cars)

1914 SAVA 36/50hp sports two-seater

made a belated appearance, just in time for the firm to be taken over by Minerva.

SAVER / *England 1912*
A 'gearboxless' tandem-seater from Manchester, with 14 hp Hewitt piston-valve engine.

SAVIANO SCAT / *USA 1960*
Weighing 1700 lb, the Saviano Scat used body steel twice as thick as that of most cars. It was a two-door four-passenger Jeep-type vehicle built on a welded rectangular tube frame. The two rear seats could be folded out of the way to provide extra cargo space. The doors were removable, as was the top, which was available in either steel or canvas. A 25 hp Kohler air-cooled engine provided power.

SAVOY / *England 1900*
With a water-cooled $3\frac{1}{2}$ hp De Dion engine, the Savoy voiturette, from the same firm as AMC and Carlton, sold at £198.

SAXON / *USA 1913–1923*
'The car that makes both ends meet', the Saxon was once one of Detroit's most popular products. The original Saxon was a four-cylinder light car selling for only $395. It was built by a company started by Hugh Chalmers and Harry (no relation to Henry) Ford. It sold well, and in 1915 a $785 Saxon Six was added to the range. By 1916, production was running at 27,800 annually, but the four-cylinder roadster was dropped the following year, and Saxon sales, which had reached tenth place in the US sales league, began to fall off. By 1921 the Saxon, now an ohv four known as the Saxon-Duplex, had become one of the most expensive cars of its type. The inevitable demise followed swiftly.

1923 SARA 1098cc air-cooled two-seater

1915 Saxon Six tourer

SAYERS/*USA 1917–1923*
A division of Sayers & Scoville, noted for hearses and ambulances, this assembled car was highly regarded from the standpoint of its body workmanship. Continental six-cylinder engines were used throughout its seven-year production. Although open models constituted the greater percentage of Sayers Six cars built, coupés, sedans and limousines were also available. In 1923, the Sayers was succeeded by the larger and more expensive S & S line, which was continued into 1930.

SB/*Germany 1920–1923*
The first little Slaby-Behringer cars were battery-electrics, but there were later cars with 169cc DKW two-stroke single-cylinder engines. Slaby also designed the first DKW cars.

SBARRO/*Switzerland 1973 to date*
Best-known for their replicas of the BMW 328 powered by modern four- and six-cylinder BMW engines, Sbarro are based at Les Tuileries de Grandson, near Lausanne.

SCACCHI/*Italy 1912–1914*
An advanced 3815cc four-cylinder with the engine in unit with a four-speed gearbox, known in the UK as Storero or Caesar.

SCAMP/*England 1976 to date*
A Mini-based kit car on the lines of the obsolete Mini Moke: the Mk 2 version is offered with gull-wing doors.

SCANIA/*Sweden 1901–1911*
Maskinfabriks AB Scania, Malmö, was formed in 1900 to produce bicycles, but in 1901 the first car was built. The initiative was taken by the manager, Hilding Hessler, and the car was constructed mainly by Anton Svensson and Reinhold Thorssin. The first series was produced in 1902, when six cars were built with German twin-cylinder Kämper engines. One was driven to the Stockholm Automobile Exhibition in 1903, quite a sensation in those days of bad roads. Mostly lorries were built, but passenger-cars with one-, two- or four-cylinders, from 5hp to 20hp, were also produced. From 1908 there were new types of engines, from 12 to 45hp. In 1911 the firm merged with Vabis.

SCANIA-VABIS/*Sweden 1911–1929*
After the merger between Scania and Vabis, the new company based in Södertälje mostly used the Vabis-designed four-cylinder engines. Three sizes of engines were mainly built, of 22, 30 and 50hp. Cars were exported to the other Scandinavian countries, and also to Russia and Australia. The main production was lorries of various sizes, and from 1924 Scania-Vabis concentrated on these, though three or four cars were assembled in 1929 from old model parts, even though the bodies looked fairly modern.

SCAP/*France 1912–1929*
The Société de Constructions Automobiles de Paris bore no relationship to the maker of proprietary SCAP engines, though some later models used these power units. In their Billancourt, Seine, works, they started by making Ballot-engined cars of 9hp (1460cc), 11hp (1725cc) and 14hp (2814cc). A 20hp (3810cc) was presented in 1914. After the war they resumed with a 12hp of 2538cc. In 1923 came a 1098cc SCAP-engined model. In 1925, the company presented a 10hp (1485cc) model, and a new SCAP-engined car of 1098cc came in 1926.

SCAR/*France 1906–1915*
The Société de Construction Automobile de Reims first built an 18/20hp four of 2·5 litres, joined in 1907 by a 4·1-litre four and a 6-litre six. The 1910 models had dashboard radiators, and ranged from a 1·3-litre twin to a 2·4-litre four and a 3·6-litre six. Long-stroke fours of 2·1, 2·8 and 3·2 litres were the marque's ultimate offerings.

SCARAB/*USA 1934–1939*
Developed from the prototype Sterkenberg, designed by John Tjaarda (later designer of the Lincoln Zephyr), this was a limited production streamline monocoque sedan with a rear-mounted Ford V-8 engine. Designer was aero-engineer William B. Stout.

SCARAB/*USA 1958–1963*
Barbara Hutton's son, Lance Reventlow, built several versions of the Scarab as competition cars. They employed modified components from various production cars, including the Corvette. One Scarab, using a 1958 Corvette 385 hp engine, had phenomenal acceleration and a top speed of almost 161 mph.

SCAT/*Italy 1906–1914*
Giovanni Ceirano's SCAT was a superb car, whose production was partly financed by Newton & Bennett of Manchester. The range included cars with 2722cc, 2949cc, 3052cc, 4710cc and 4483cc four-cylinder engines and four-speed gearboxes. The SCAT was also successful in races: Ceirano won the 1911 and 1914 Targa Florio, Snipe-Pardini the same event in 1912.

SCH/*Belgium 1927–1928*
A light cyclecar exhibited by a commercial vehicle maker at the 1927 Brussels Show.

SCHACHT/*USA 1901–1913*
The first Schachts were flat-twin friction-drive high-wheelers, but a 40hp four-cylinder model appeared in 1909. After 1913, the company concentrated on trucks.

SCHAUDEL/*France 1897–1902*
A car built in Bordeaux by a former arms manufacturer, who applied the methods of his profession, such as strict interchangeability of components in its construction. Schaudel was, moreover, inventor of the unit-construction engine/gearbox layout. Manufacture of his designs was taken over by Motobloc from 1902; about 150 Schaudels were built.

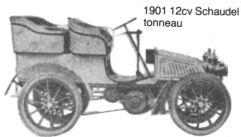

1901 12cv Schaudel tonneau

SCHAUM/*USA 1901–1905*
W. A. Schaum's first engines had twin cylinders with separate cranks geared up to a central driving shaft.

SCHEIBLER/*Germany 1901–1907*
In 1901, Scheibler of Aachen built a 6hp car with pivoted floor so that the owner, a paralytic ex-cavalry officer, could be hauled into the vehicle in his wheelchair. This engine and car factory produced a variety of two- and four-cylinder cars with engines up to 6786cc, as well as a range of commercial vehicles.

1914 SCAT 22hp limousine

SCEPTRE
USA 1979 to date
A 6·6-litre Ford V-8 powers this 'pseudo-classic' built in Santa Barbara, California. It has outside exhausts and solid silver emblems, and sold (as a limited edition of 250–300) at $50,000 in 1979.

SCHILLING/*Germany 1905–1906*
Suhl in Thuringia (now in East Germany) was the home of the Schilling arms factory, where 12hp cars with four-cylinder Fafnir engines were built. They were also known as VCS or Rennsteig cars.

SCHMIDT/*France 1910-1911*
A manufacturer from St Quentin (Aisne) who exhibited at the 1910 Paris Salon.

SCHULER/*USA 1924*
Price of the only Schuler model, a small two-passenger vee-twin roadster, was $245. Though it was advertised in the press of its city of manufacture, Milwaukee, Wisconsin, it is doubtful if many — or even any — were actually sold.

SCHULZ/*Germany 1904–1906*
Limited production cars with engines up to 28 hp. Schulz, the designer-manufacturer, competed in many sporting events.

SCHURICHT/*Germany 1921–1925*
A Bavarian manufacturer of small four-cylinder cars with Breuer proprietary sv engines from 12 hp to 20 hp.

SCHWANEMEYER/*Germany 1900–1901*
'With motor-gear and axle combined', the Schwanemeyer was the forerunner of Fafnir. Its immediate successor was the Aachener.

SCIMITAR/*USA 1956*
Brook Stevens Associates built three cars based on Chrysler components: a station wagon with a sliding roof, a convertible and a town car.

SCIROCCO/*England 1961–1963*
A stylish replacement body for the Ford Popular, the production Scirocco was a development of the gull-wing doored, Ford 100E-powered car, built by Peter Hammond for his own use. Only about ten were made.

SCOOTACAR/*England 1957–1964*
Longer-lived than many of the breed, this odd tandem-seat bubblecar had three wheels and a Villiers engine, initially of 197cc, later of 324cc.

SCOTSMAN/*Scotland 1922–1923*
The Glasgow-built Scotsman had an option of three four-cylinder engines, a 10 hp, an 11 hp, or a 45 hp ohc unit.

SCOTSMAN/*Scotland 1929–1930*
Built in Edinburgh, the second make to bear the name Scotsman used a French six-cylinder air-cooled SARA engine. The well-proven Meadows 4ED was fitted later.

SCOTT/*France 1912*
A Parisian marque — 15 hp and 24 hp fours of 2120cc and 3780cc were listed.

SCOTT SOCIABLE/*England 1921–1925*
The Scott Company had been making their famous water-cooled models from 1909 and their Sociable, an offset three-wheeler, was an inevitable development of this work. Power was naturally supplied by the company's water-cooled 578cc twin-cylinder two-stroke engine, drive being transmitted to the offside rear wheel by shaft.

SCOUT/*England 1904–1923*
Dean and Burden Brothers of Salisbury began production with a 6 hp twin and 12 hp four.

Scout cars enjoyed mostly local acclaim, though they did enter a 14/16 hp in the 1905 Tourist Trophy, and an 18/20 hp the following year. In 1907 production of the two-car range was said to be 100 a year, and in 1908, from a new factory, Scout offered a 12 hp twin, 15 hp four and 30 hp six of 4390cc, enlarged the next year to 5638cc. Post-1909 production seems to have been negligible, though a monobloc 1870cc 10/12 hp appeared in 1910, and a few 15·9 hp cars were assembled by the firm and its successors after the war.

SCRIPPS-BOOTH/*USA 1914–1922*
The son of an author, James Scripps-Booth was a talented artist who, in 1908 (aged 20), conceived a gigantic two-wheeled car (supported at low speeds by retractable auxiliary wheels) and completed its design while on his honeymoon in Paris in 1911. Financed by his uncle, a builder of marine engines, he built this 'Bi-Autogo' in Detroit in 1912, at a cost of $25,000. It had a 6306cc V-8 engine and weighed 3200 lb. Predictably, its steering was awesomely heavy, and only the prototype (which still survives) was completed. The following year, Scripps-Booth built a prototype tandem-seat cyclecar inspired by the Bedelia, which went into production as the 'JB Rocket' in January 1914. The Scripps-Booth Cyclecar Company was sold at the end of 1914 to the Puritan Machine Company of Detroit, who continued production under their own name for a short while. Scripps-Booth then introduced a luxury light car based on European practice and designed by Bill ('Simplicate and add lightness') Stout, who later became a famed aeronautical engineer, responsible for the immortal Ford Trimotor aeroplane. The Sterling-engined Scripps-Booth Model C was said to be the first American car to have a horn-button in the centre of the steering wheel. It also had electrically-operated door locks, though these were prone to jam on open models. Scripps-Booth owners included the king of Spain, the queen of Holland, Winston Churchill and Count John McCormack, the singer. In Au-tumn 1916, a new Scripps-Booth — Model D — appeared, powered by a Ferro V-8 engine designed by Alanson Brush. Roadsters and town cars were available. James Scripps-Booth resigned over company policy in October 1916; sales fell the following year as a result of production difficulties. By the end of 1917, Scripps-Booth had been absorbed by Chevrolet, to become part of General Motors in July 1918. Thereafter Scripps-Booth cars were no more than Oaklands with a 40 hp Northway six-cylinder engine, and were phased out in 1922 at Alfred P. Sloan's express order, the plant being turned over to production of Buick sedans. James Scripps-Booth tried to get back into the motor industry in 1923 with a low-slung luxury car called the Da Vinci, with an Argyll single-sleeve-valve engine, but failed to sell his designs (though he claimed that Stutz had pirated them). In 1930, he built a one-off belt-drive cyclecar, the Da Vinci Pup.

SEABROOK/*England 1917–1928*
Originally formed in 1896 to make cycle components, Seabrook of London imported the American Regal Underslung, before building a four-cylinder light car under their own name, with a monobloc 1796cc four-cylinder engine.

1922 Seabrook two-seater

1915 Scripps-Booth Model C

SEAL/*England 1912–1924*
A curious JAP-engined three-wheeler, resembling a motorcycle combination, but steered from the sidecar.

SEARCHMONT/*USA 1900–1903*
'America's leading automobile', built at Searchmont, Philadelphia. Seven different models were built, with prices up to $2500. Designer was Lee Sherman Chadwick, and racing driver Charles Fournier headed the company.

1903 Type VII Searchmont tonneau

SEARS/*USA 1908–1912*
Mail order king Richard Warren Sears spent some of his company's $50 million annual revenue in putting a flat-twin Motor Buggy on the market late in 1908. It sold for $395 complete, 'shipped and crated so as to secure the lowest possible freight rate', but it used an obsolescent formula, and purchasers wanted more than tiller steering and a 25 mph top speed. The introduction of a closed model, the 'Cozy Cab', did nothing to increase sales, and by 1912, having lost $80,000 on the automobile division, Sears stopped selling complete cars and turned instead to mail order accessories and components. In 1952–53, Sears marketed the Henry J compact as the 'Allstate'.

SEAT/*Spain 1949 to date*
Starting life as the Spanish subsidiary of Fiat in 1919 (from 1931 the cars were known as 'Fiat-Hispania'), Seat was owned by the Spanish state industry holding company INI from 1949 to 1979, when Fiat took over the majority shareholding. Seat cars were largely based on Fiat prototypes, like the 600, 850 and 1400, though in 1979 Lancia models were introduced with 2-litre Seat engines.

SEATON-PETTER/*England 1926–1927*
A short-lived £100 twin-cylinder two-stroke four-seat tourer, built by Petter of Yeovil.

SECQUEVILLE HOYAU/*France 1919–1924*
Secqueville-Hoyau of Gennevilliers, Seine, offered only one model, the 10 cv four of 1244cc.

1921 Secqueville-Hoyau 10hp two-seater

SECURUS/*Germany 1906*
A two-speed tricar built in Berlin by Max Ortmann.

SEIDEL-AROP/*Germany 1925–1926*
The Seidel-designed car was another doomed attempt to produce a good small car using inadequate facilities. It had a sv 1020cc four-cylinder engine.

SEKINE/*USA 1923*
The Sekine was probably only a prototype, the design of I. Sekine, an importer who had plans to build a small car for the Japanese market. Without a differential, the drive was, according to a brochure 'taken from a four-cylinder engine, angled at 17 degrees from the longitudinal axis of the car to the left rear wheel and thence through fabric universals to the right wheel by the way of a shaft'.

SELDEN/*USA 1906–1914*
George B. Selden, who claimed to have invented the motor car in 1877, did not go into production until 1906. His cars were conventional fours of 28/30 hp, which sold for $2000.

SELECT/*France 1920*
Made in Paris, these were V-8-engined cars of which little is known.

SELF/*Sweden 1916, 1919, 1922*
The two young Weiertz brothers, Per and Hugo, of Swedala, built three different cyclecars in 1916, 1919 and 1922. Some parts were re-used, but engines were changed from a one-cylinder to a four-cylinder and, finally, to a twin-cylinder. The four-cylinder engine was of German manufacture and seems to have been the best.

1921 Selve of Frau Hedi Hof

SELVE/*Germany 1919–1929*
Basse & Selve was a manufacturer of light-alloy car engines; when Sperber at Hameln was up for sale after World War One, Walther von Selve bought the works in 1919 and started manufacture of his own Selve cars with — of course — own-make engines. Chief designers were Lehmann, Slevogt and Henze, who created some excellent cars, including 1569cc and 2085cc four-cylinder and 2850cc and 3075cc six-cylinder models.

SENECA/*USA 1917–1924*
Seneca assembled open models only, with half of each year's production being exported. Four-cylinder LeRoi engines were used until 1922 — thereafter, Lycoming fours. Several hundred units a year were built; the Glover, built for export to the United Kingdon, was probably also made by this Fostoria, Ohio, concern.

Robert Senechal driving a 1922 Senechal sports car

SENECHAL/*France 1921–1929*
Aviator and racing driver Robert Sénéchal started making cyclecars using various French proprietary engines, in 'Sport' and 'Grand Sport' form, with capacities ranging from 900cc to 1100cc. Taken over by Chenard & Walcker, he made the 1500cc 'Torpille' Chenard-Sénéchal.

SENSAUD DE LAVAUD/*France 1926–1928*
A strange car with automatic transmission and ifs by rubber in compression, made in Paris by M. Sensaud de Lavaud, with an Alpax cast-alloy chassis and a steam-cooled 5475cc six-cylinder American engine. Few were built.

SERENISSIMA/*Italy 1965–1966*
Count Volpi's dream car, the Serenissima was offered with 3-litre and 3·5-litre dohc V-8 engines, but very few were built. The factory also produced various (not very successful) racing cars. Sasamotor of Modena was responsible for most Serenissima designs.

SERIN/*France 1899*
A light Bollée-like three-wheeler with a 4 hp horizontal engine.

SERPOLLET/*France 1889–1907*
Blacksmith's son Léon Serpollet, born in 1858, built his first steam car at the age of 18, but it produced 'more soot than motion'; he then devised a 'flash boiler' for the instantaneous generation of steam, set up shop in Montmartre and built a steam tricycle, which was the only self-propelled vehicle running in Paris in 1887.

1898 Serpollet cab

Two 1905 Serpollet 15hp tourers

Three Serpollet steam three-wheelers were built by Peugeot in 1889, but Peugeot's interest soon waned and Serpollet continued on his own, building twin-cylinder steam cars of 4/6 hp with coke-fired boilers and (from 1891) four wheels, though his backers insisted that he concentrate mainly on steam trams and railcars. In 1898, Serpollet met a wealthy American, Frank Gardner, who had dabbled in petrol car construction, and the two went into partnership. Gardner-Serpollet steam cars had a flat-twin engine with paraffin-fired boiler, and from 1900 became more and more like petrol vehicles in their styling. A light 5 hp model appeared that year; and from 1901, an 8 hp V-4 and flat-four engines of 6·9 and 12 hp were adopted. In 1902, a streamlined racing Serpollet, *Oeuf de Pâques*, was the first car to exceed 75 mph. The end of 1903 saw a 15 hp flat-four and the Serpollet Simplex, a 6 hp voiturette of uncomplicated design. In late 1904 came an improved 15 hp and a big 40 hp, both boasting a clutch and almost automatic engine control. There was, apparently, an eight-cylinder Serpollet for 1906, but Serpollet was already a very sick man. When he died of consumption in February 1907, the company quickly followed him to the grave.

SERVICE/*England 1902–1906*
Probably a French import, this 7/8 hp car had a twin-cylinder Gnôme engine and a pressed-steel chassis. Controls were 'simple, and carried out on top of the steering wheel'. A 6½ hp Aster-engined Service with tubular chassis, 'perfectly practical and very graceful', competed in the 1905 Small Car Trials.

SETA/*England 1976 to date*
An extremely futuristic looking glass-fibre sports-car kit based on the ubiquitous VW floorpan, the Seta is one of several latter-day machines to feature gull-wing doors.

SEVEN/*England 1973 to date*
Caterham Cars had long since marketed the Lotus Seven and thus logically took over full production of this front-engined, spartan sports

car when Chapman's company shed it on their way up market. The glass-fibre-bodied S4 ceased production in 1974. Now only the prettier, alloy-bodied S3 is made.

SEVERIN/*USA 1920–1922*
An assembled car, the Severin featured a six-cylinder Continental engine and 122-inch wheelbase, the five-passenger touring car selling for $2550.

SFA/*France 1912*
The Société Française d'Automobiles et d'Aviation, of Orléans, offered the BGV monobloc 12 hp four of 1544cc.

SGV/*USA 1910–1915*
Successor to the Acme, the 25 hp SGV had a monobloc four-cylinder engine of 3167cc.

SHAD-WYCK/*USA 1917–1923*
A good deal of mystery surrounds this marque, which was under the control of the Shadburne Brothers of Chicago, although it seems that the initial spate of cars marketed as Shad-Wycks between 1917 and 1919 were left over Bour-Davis cars with another emblem! The 1920–23 line claimed to have two different engines (depending on what chart one read)—Weidely or Rochester-Duesenberg—and it appears that some cars may have actually been made. The Shadburne Brothers were also involved in the final days of the National, Jackson and Dixie Flyer automobiles.

SHAMROCK/*England 1908*
A 12/14 hp four-cylinder model built by an associated company of Straker-Squire.

SHANGHAI/*China 1960 to date*
Appearing in prototype form in 1958, this car was originally produced as the Feng Huang (Phoenix). After the Cultural Revolution, it became the Shanghai SH 760. Only about 2000 Shanghais are built annually, using a 2·2 litre six-cylinder engine. A new prototype, SH 771, appeared in 1978.

SHAPECRAFT/*England 1963–1964*
Racing driver Barry Wood was the man who persuaded Shapecraft to make a fastback conversion for the Lotus Elan. Altogether some 20 were built, their aluminium roofs and tails being riveted to the glass-fibre bodywork. Peter Sellers and Tony Brandon were among the customers.

SHARON/*USA 1915*
A tandem-seated 12/15 cyclecar (sister marque to Ritz) with friction drive, built by Driggs-Seabury.

SHARP-ARROW/*USA 1908–1910*
William H. Sharp's sporting roadsters were similar in concept to the Mercer, also built in Trenton, NJ. In 1908 a Sharp-Arrow, driven by its designer, won the 188-mile Vanderbilt Motor Parkway Garden City Sweepstake Race at an average of over 60 mph.

SHAW/*USA 1920–1921*
The Shaw was a spin-off of the earlier Shaw taxicab interests, and the passenger car introduced for 1920, was a 136-inch wheelbase automobile using a Rochester-Duesenberg four-cylinder engine. The open touring car was priced at $5000, the closed cars commanding considerably higher prices. Later a Weidely 12-cylinder engine was used. For a time, the Shaw masqueraded under a different name 'Colonial'. It later reverted to 'Shaw'; shortly thereafter the company was sold to Yellow Cab, which marketed the existing chassis—but with a Continental six-cylinder engine—as the 'Ambassador'.

SHAWMUT/*USA 1905–1909*
These 6391cc four-cylinder tourers succeeded the Phelps.

SHEEN/*England 1964–1965*
The brainchild of Surrey wine merchant, Peter Sheen, the two aluminium-bodied, two-seater Sheen Imperators were based on the Hillman Imp floorpan. Production was planned with glass-fibre shells, but the project never got off the ground.

1920 Shad-Wyck Six

SHEFFIELD-SIMPLEX/*England 1906–1922*
One of the great Edwardian cars, the round-radiatored Sheffield-Simplex was sponsored by Earl Fitzwilliam and designed by Percy Richardson. It retained the two-pedal control of the Brotherhood-Crocker and from 1908 to 1913 the 45 hp six of 6982cc was available in 'gearboxless' form (with one normal speed and an 'emergency box'). One gearboxless 45 hp even went from Land's End to John O'Groats on its

1909/10 Sheffield-Simplex 45hp

single gear. The 1910 14/20 hp seemed to have an engine based closely on the Renault 14/20; the same year a three-speed 20/30 hp six appeared, and soon a re-designed 30 hp development of this was the company's leading model. But the post-war Sheffield-Simplex was the 45 hp; in its final version its bi-bloc engine was replaced by an anachronistic unit of 7777cc with individually-cast cylinders.

SHELBY/*USA 1962–1970*
Racing driver Carroll Shelby modified ACs and Mustangs in California. Ford V-8 engines of 4736cc or 6977cc were fitted in British ACs. These fast Shelby Cobras were so popular that 1100 were sold in three years. Even more successful were the Shelby GTs based on stock Mustang fastbacks. With reassembled bodies and modified suspension and engines (4736cc and 6997cc), over 14,000 were sold by selected Ford dealers. In 1968 FoMoCo took over the Shelby operation; the Cobra name later appeared on Ford's Torino fastback.

SHEPPEE/*England 1912*
A 25 hp steam car from a firm better known for steam commercials.

SHERIDAN/*USA 1920–1921*
Produced in the former Inter-State factory at Muncie, Indiana, the Sheridan was an early General Motors car. Its plans called for both a four and a V-8 (although the latter failed to materialize beyond the drawing board). Designed to fill the gap between the Chevrolet and Oakland, the car used a Northway engine and had a wheelbase of 116 inches. Price of the touring car was $1800. In 1922, the factory was acquired by William C. Durant, and the Sheridan car, with a longer wheelbase, Ansted engine and new emblem, was continued as the Durant Six.

SHORT-ASHBY/*England 1921–1923*
Designed by Victor Ashby and manufactured by Short Brothers, aircraft manufacturers, this light car was powered by a French Ruby engine of 970cc.

SHRIVE/*England 1969 to date*
The first of the production Mk6 Bentley Specials, the Shrive is distinguished by its neat, cast-aluminium footplates and enormous Lucas P100 headlamps. On the Shrive, the original grille is retained, as is the bonnet (though in modified form). The body is glass-fibre, the wings steel.

SHW/*Germany 1923–1926*
Designed by Professor Kamm of Stuttgart (famed for his work on car aerodynamics), the SHW was built by Schwabische Hütten-Werke at Boblingen. It had a sv 1030cc flat-twin engine and front-wheel-drive. There was not enough money for large-scale production.

SIATA/*Italy 1949–1970*
This small factory, having concentrated on tuning Fiat cars pre-war, built a wide range of very sporting cars with engines from 494cc to 1990cc from 1949. From 1960 onwards, there was close co-operation with Abarth. The most popular Siata models had 843cc, 1295cc, 1481cc and 1579cc engines; one of the last Siatas had a rear-mounted four-cylinder 843cc engine and a two-seater cabriolet body.

SIBLEY/*USA 1910–1911*
A two-passenger roadster with 30 hp four-cylinder 3622cc engine. The firm was still offering spare parts in 1918.

SICAM/*France 1919–1922*
Marcel Violet, engineer and pioneer of the two-stroke, created the Société Industrielle de Construction d'Automobiles et de Moteurs in Pantin, Seine, and built proprietary two-stroke engines. He also made some cyclecars powered with his twin-cylinder two-stroke 487cc engine.

SICO/*England 1905*
The Sandholme Iron Co. of Todmorden, Lancashire, built this 18 hp four-cylinder model with an Abbot constant-mesh gearbox.

SIDDELEY, WOLSELEY-SIDDELEY
England 1902–1910
Originally little more than modified 12 hp and 18 hp Peugeots assembled in Coventry, Siddeley soon launched a 6 hp single-cylinder model built for them in Wolseley's Crayford, Kent, factory. In May 1905 Wolseley absorbed the Siddeley Autocar Company and John Davenport Siddeley became manager of the new company, which marketed its cars as Wolseley-Siddeleys, Siddeley-Wolseleys or simply Siddeleys. New models were designed by Charles Rimmington, including a 40 hp which covered a 10,000-mile reliability trial and needed only 1s. 10d-worth of replacement parts.

SIDEA/*France 1921–1925*
The Société Industrielle des Etablissements Automobiles in Charleville-Mézières, Ardennes, made some cars with 1168cc and 1693cc SCAP engines. Taken over by Jouffret, they were renamed Sidea-Jouffret in 1923.

SIEGEL/*Germany 1908–1910*
A now forgotten 9 hp car with a vee-twin motorcycle engine, probably by Fafnir.

SIEMENS-SCHUCKERT
Germany 1907–1910
This big Berlin-based works bought Protos at almost the same time that they entered the market with their own car designs. Among these were a 1596cc four-cylinder and a 1501cc version, with sv engines made by Korting. Some carried the Protos trade mark on the radiator.

SIGMA/*Switzerland 1909–1914*
The Société Industrielle Genevoise de Mécanique et d'Automobiles, headed by a son of one of the founders of Piccard-Pictet, took over the old Lucia factory, and began production of four-cylinder 1470cc cars with round radiators. In 1911, the company became sole licensees for the Knight sleeve-valve engine in Switzerland, introducing two 'valveless' models — an 18 hp of 2614cc and a 28 hp of 4576cc. Sigma cars enjoyed a number of sporting successes, including second place in the 1910 Targa Florio.

1921 Sigma 10hp
four-seater

SIGMA/*France 1913–1928*
Made in Levallois, Seine, these were initially Ballot and Chapuis-Dornier-engined cars. After the war, they had various Ballot, SCAP and CIME engines from 894cc to 1614cc.

SILENT KNIGHT/*USA 1906–1909*
Built to promote Charles Yale Knight's sleeve-valve engine, the 40 hp Silent Knight was made in Chicago. Despite testimonials referring to it as 'the peer of all other types', the car was not a commercial success.

SILHOUETTE/*England 1971 to date*
A sleek glass-fibre-bodied two-seater sports car, designed to bolt on to the VW 'Beetle' floorpan.

SILVA-CORONER/*France 1927*
Made by M. Silva-Coroner, these were ohv straight-eight-engined cars of 2490cc.

SILVER HAWK/*England 1920–1921*
Noel Macklin, having cut his automotive teeth on the Eric-Campbell, decided to build a sports car based on that design, which he called the Silver Hawk, with a tuned sv 1373cc engine.

SILVER KNIGHT/*USA 1917*
Conover T. Silver of New York built this sporting model, using Willys-Knight chassis.

1917 Silver-Knight, built on a Willys-Knight chassis

SILVERTOWN/*England 1905–1910*
An electric car, with coachwork by
W. & F. Thorn; in 1908 a 4wd model was
available.

SILVER VOLT/*Puerto Rico 1979 to date*
An initial run of 300 electric station wagons was
to be given a one-year test by 'qualified residents' of Fort Lauderdale, Florida, before
production of these $14,500 models began. Up
to 7000 were to be built annually from 1980. Its
special battery enables the Silver Volt to take an
80 per cent charge in 45 minutes and to reach
70 mph. A $120,000 luxury version was planned.

SIMA-STANDARD/*France 1929–1932*
When M. Violet left the SIMA company, engineer Emile Dombret made some cars using
spares from other manufacturers. There were
two models, a 5 hp of 855cc and a 7 hp of 1307cc.

SIMA-VIOLET/*France 1924–1929*
The Société Industrielle de Materiel Automobile in Courbevoie was run by the prolific
Marcel Violet who made a 496cc twin-cylinder
two-stroke cyclecar and some two-stroke racing
cars, of which the best was a flat-four of 1484cc.

1923 Sima-Violet team for the Bol d'Or

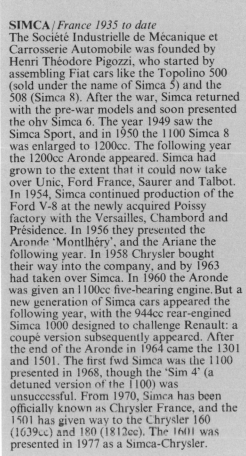

SIMA/*France 1935 to date*
The Société Industrielle de Mécanique et
Carrosserie Automobile was founded by
Henri Théodore Pigozzi, who started by
assembling Fiat cars like the Topolino 500
(sold under the name of Simca 5) and the
508 (Simca 8). After the war, Simca returned
with the pre-war models and soon presented
the ohv Simca 6. The year 1949 saw the
Simca Sport, and in 1950 the 1100 Simca 8
was enlarged to 1200cc. The following year
the 1200cc Aronde appeared. Simca had
grown to the extent that it could now take
over Unic, Ford France, Saurer and Talbot.
In 1954, Simca continued production of the
Ford V-8 at the newly acquired Poissy
factory with the Versailles, Chambord and
Présidence. In 1956 they presented the
Aronde 'Montlhéry', and the Ariane the
following year. In 1958 Chrysler bought
their way into the company, and by 1963
had taken over Simca. In 1960 the Aronde
was given an 1100cc five-bearing engine. But a
new generation of Simca cars appeared the
following year, with the 944cc rear-engined
Simca 1000 designed to challenge Renault: a
coupé version subsequently appeared. After
the end of the Aronde in 1964 came the 1301
and 1501. The first fwd Simca was the 1100
presented in 1968, though the 'Sim 4' (a
detuned version of the 1100) was
unsuccessful. From 1970, Simca has been
officially known as Chrysler France, and the
1501 has given way to the Chrysler 160
(1639cc) and 180 (1812cc). The 1601 was
presented in 1977 as a Simca-Chrysler.

1938 Simca-Huit Gordini two-seater

1957 Simca Aronde Montlhéry

1978 Simca 1100LX

1896 Simms light car

1927 Simson-Supra sports two-seater

SIMMS, SIMMS-WELBECK
England 1899–1908
Frederick R. Simms was the original importer of Daimler engines into Britain in 1893, and helped to found Daimler of Coventry. With Robert Bosch, he devised the low-tension magneto, and in 1899 he developed a motor quadricycle equipped with a quick-firing machine gun. An armoured 'war car' was also built to his design by Vickers, Sons & Maxim. His first private vehicle was the strange little 'Motor Wheel', steered by its single rear wheel and driven by two front ones; it was capable of 'turning turtle on the slightest provocation' (which it did several times in the 1900 1000-Miles Trial). Simms built his own engines, which were used in vacuum carpet cleaners and road rollers, as well as cars and motorcycles. An early project was an overhead camshaft '100 hp' power unit for a fire engine. In 1903 the Simms-Welbeck name was adopted, and two four-cylinder models, a 20/25 hp and a 30/35 hp introduced. The Simms-Welbeck was the first production car to be equipped with bumpers; sprung pneumatic devices of Simms's invention. There was a 12/14 hp four, as well, and in 1907 came a pair-cast six of 6494cc.

SIMMS / *USA 1920–1921*
Simms built five-passenger touring cars only — and very few of those. An own-make four-cylinder engine was used and the price was $1015. The Simms was succeeded by the Innes.

SIMPLEX / *Holland 1898–1915*
The Simplex Machine en Rijwielfabrieken of Amsterdam were engineers and cycle makers, whose first cars were based on the Benz. A front-engined Fafnir-powered voiturette appeared in 1902. Vivinus engines were also used.

SIMPLEX / *England 1902*
A car built by A. Ryall, Frome, Somerset.

SIMPLEX / *France 1920–1921*
A light car with a horizontal 735cc single-cylinder engine.

SIMPLIC / *England 1914*
A 5 hp two-seat cyclecar, selling for only £75.

SIMPLICIA / *France 1910*
This 10/12 hp light car had independent front suspension and a backbone chassis in unit with its Aster engine and gearbox.

SIMPLICITY / *USA 1906–1910*
'Without gears, therefore without trouble', this was a $3000 40 hp from Evansville, Indiana.

SIMPLO / *USA 1908–1909*
A $600 10/12 hp twin-cylinder friction-drive runabout built in St Louis. It had a detachable 'mother-in-law' seat.

SIMPSON / *Scotland 1897–1904*
John Simpson, an engineer from Stirling, built about 20 steam cars, of 6 hp, 10 hp and 12 hp.

SIMSON-SUPRA / *Germany 1911–1933*
These very sporting cars were built by a well-known armaments factory, Simson & Co. of Suhl in Thuringia. The cars designed by Paul Henze and built after 1924 were especially noteworthy. Earlier models had 1559cc and 2595cc four-cylinder ioe engines; Henze created ohc and dohc 1960cc four-cylinder cars. Single ohc versions developed 40 bhp at 3000 rpm, dohc cars 60–66 bhp at 4000 rpm. There was also an ohv 3108cc six-cylinder model in the production, which was always limited as every car was built by hand. The last Simson-Supra was a sv 4673cc straight-eight.

SINGER

SINGER / *England 1905–1970*
The first Singer car — the firm had been making motorcycles from 1900 — was made under licence from Lea-Francis; it was a 15 hp three-cylinder horizontal-engined device with connecting rods no less than 39 inches long! By 1907 this design had been dropped, and replaced by vertical two-, three- or four-cylinder White and Poppe engines, rated at 8 hp, 10 hp and 12 hp. Two larger models used Aster engines (12/14 hp and 22 hp), though Singer soon developed its own power unit; in 1912 the popular 10 hp was announced, with rear-axle-mounted gearbox. This was continued after the War, though in 1922 a conventional gearbox position was adopted. The car was re-designed the following year. A bewildering number of models followed, the ohc 848cc Junior of 1927 being very significant. The following year, Singer was third in the British car production stakes behind Morris and Austin. By the mid-1930s all models had ohc engines, a particularly appropriate layout for the A. G. Booth-designed Sports Nine. One of these was placed 13th at Le Mans in 1933 and 7th in 1934, resulting in the model being given the generic title of 'Le Mans'; 1100cc and 1½-litre engines were supplied to HRG for their sports car production. After World War Two, pre-war designs were continued until the SM 1500 of 1949, while the 1500 Roadster appeared two years later. The Hunter saloon of 1955 failed to save the company; in 1956 Singer was taken over by the Rootes Group. The Hunter was replaced by the Gazelle (of Hillman Minx lineage). From then on Singers were upmarket Hillmans, with the Chamois of 1965 being an Imp derivative. The 1496cc-engined Gazelle and the 1725cc Vogue also lasted until the marque ceased in 1970.

10hp Singer Junior tourer, 1926

SINGER/*USA 1915–1920*
Singer was the successor to Palmer-Singer; it featured a six-cylinder Herschell-Spillman engine and a distinctive vee-radiator. The last Singers had a V-12 Weidely engine; total production of this luxury marque seems to have been about 1100.

SINGLE CENTER/*USA 1907–1908*
'Not a buggy but a racy-looking automobile runabout', this friction-drive 12/15 hp flat-twin-engined high-wheeler came from Evansville, Indiana.

SINPAR/*France 1907–1914*
De Dion-engined voiturettes ('Sinpar' implying 'without equal') from Courbevoie, Siene, with 4½ hp and 8 hp power units. A 1912–14 8 hp four was identical to the 8 hp Demeester.

SINTZ/*USA 1899–1904*
The Sintz Gas Engine Company from Grand Rapids, Michigan, built all types of carriage, as well as rail cars and light trams, powered by a two-stroke engine of their own manufacture.

LA SIRENE/*France 1900–1902*
A 5 hp vee-twin with three-speed and reverse gear and tonneau body, built by Fernandez of Paris.

SIRRON/*England 1909–1916*
Mr Norris was one of the promoters of this light car (hence 'Sirron'), which first appeared, built from imported French components, as a 13·9 hp four-cylinder of 1767cc. This was given a longer stroke in 1910 (making it 1944cc) and joined by a short-lived 16/20 hp of 2723cc in 1911. The following year saw a new 16/20 hp (2554cc) and a 12/16 hp (2212cc). The sole 1913 Sirron was a 2412cc 14/20 hp, then in 1914 came the 10/12 hp light car with 'luxurious full-sized two-seated torpedo body'. It had a 1357cc four-cylinder engine and sold for 220 guineas, complete with Koh-i-Noor dynamo lighting set.

SIR VIVAL/*USA 1960*
This most extraordinary car was manufactured by the Hollow Boring Co., Worcester, Mass., and was billed as an experimental safety car. The Sir Vival was built in two sections, hinged in the middle, and both sections were completely surrounded by rubber bumpers. The driver sat in the rear section, higher than the passengers, and turned the car's front section by means of a swivel. Around him was a drum-shaped windshield which provided unobstructed vision and which could be rotated and cleaned at the touch of a switch.

SISCART/*France 1908–1909*
At the 1908 Paris Salon, this firm showed a two-seater 8 hp car, a 12 hp 'type course' and a side-entrance 12 hp phaeton.

SIVA/*Italy 1967–1969*
Equipped with Conrero-tuned German 1996cc Ford V-6 engines developing 130-bhp, the Siva Sirio was a beautiful two-seater 'Spider' coupé with a tubular chassis frame and a top speed of over 200 kph (125 mph).

SIVA/*England 1969 to date*
Neville Trickett's fertile brain has resulted in countless diverse vehicles over the years, many under the Siva banner. These include the futuristic, VW-based S160, the Saluki, the Aston Martin-powered S530, the go-anywhere Llama, and a variety of Edwardian replicas.

1913 10/12hp Sirron two-seater

SIX/*France 1923*
A little-known six-cylinder car of 1791cc.

SIXCYL/*France 1907–1908*
Built in the Bréguet aviation works in Paris under the supervision of Paul Chenu who also constructed cars under his own name from 1903. There were two Sixcyls, a 30/50 hp (6126cc) and a 50/80 hp (8822cc).

1974 Siva Llama

1972 Siva V-8 coupé

SIZAIRE-BERWICK
France/England 1913–1927
The 'poor man's Rolls' was a luxury car designed by Maurice Sizaire, and built pre-war at Courbevoie, Seine. It had a 20 hp engine of 4072cc. Its radiator copied the Rolls exactly, but Rolls-Royce sued them (and settled out of court when they discovered they had omitted to register their radiator design, Sizaire-Berwick thereafter adopting a handsome vee-fronted cooler). Post-war, the engine was uprated to 4·5 litres, and, from 1920, the Sizaire-Berwick was also built in England, at Park Royal. Austin gained a controlling share in the British operation in 1923, and, until production ceased in 1925, some depressing cars with 12 hp and 20 hp Austin engines were offered. The French operation lasted for two more years, ending with Lycoming-Six power units.

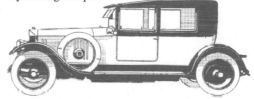

1920 Sizaire-Berwick 25hp coupé

1934 Singer Le Mans team

1925 Sizaire Frères tourer

SIZAIRE FRERES/*France 1923–1929*
Maurice and Georges Sizaire made some interesting cars with independent suspension all-round in their Courbevoie, Seine, works. The first model, an ohv 1996cc four, was made until the end, but they also tried Knight and Hotchkiss engines and experimented with a 3000cc Knight sleeve-valve six.

SIZAIRE-NAUDIN/*France 1905–1921*
There was little conventional about Maurice and Georges Sizaire's first car, which appeared at the Exposition des Petits Inventeurs in March 1905: it had a single-cylinder 6 hp engine in a wooden chassis with independent front suspension by a transverse spring and sliding pillars, as well as direct drive on all three forward speeds by a triple-ratio pinion engaged with the crown-wheel by a cam device. This design was progressively developed and became more conventional. By the outbreak of war, a four of 1593cc was available, and, post-war, a 2·3-litre.

M. Naudin at the wheel of a 1907 Sizaire-Naudin

SJR/*USA 1915–1916*
A small Boston-built four-seater roadster, powered by a four-cylinder Wisconsin engine.

SKELTON/*USA 1920–1922*
An assembled car, the Skelton used a four-cylinder Lycoming engine and other proven standard components. Skelton cars were built by the Standard Car Company of St Louis, Missouri, a tramcar and railway carriage company of high renown, which pre-1911 had built the American Mors and later the Standard six.

SKENE/*USA 1900–1901*
The twin-cylinder 5 hp Skene steamer, from Springfield, Mass., was undistinguished in design, despite its makers' claim of 'many points of superiority'.

SKEOCH/*England 1921*
This cyclecar used a 348cc single-cylinder Precision engine. A two-speed Burman gearbox was fitted, and final-drive was by chain.

SKIRROW/*England 1936–1939*
These midget racing cars produced by Harry Skirrow of London used a 1000cc JAP engine, with chain drive to all four wheels.

1907 Sizaire-Naudin 7hp two-seater

SKODA/*Czechoslovakia 1924 to date*
The first Skoda was a Marc Birkigt-designed French Hispano-Suiza, built under licence at Plzen by this big arms- and machine-works. Soon afterwards, Skoda took over the Laurin & Klement car factory at Mladá Boleslav, where they built the 1950cc four-cylinder models 110 and 120 and the 3495cc sleeve-valve six-cylinder models 350 and 360. There were also the 3880cc eight-cylinder 860 and the Type 645 with a 2490cc six-cylinder engine. The four-cylinder Type 430 was a best-seller. During the 1930s, the 995cc four-cylinder Popular and the 1380cc Rapid had excellent sales. Another good model was the six-cylinder 2480cc Superb. The last pre-war range included the sv 995cc Popular and the ohv 1089cc Popular. The Rapid now had a modern ohv 1560cc engine and the Superb an ohv 3140cc six-cylinder motor. After 1945, Skoda built mainly ohv 1089cc and 1221cc four-cylinder cars, including the Octavia and Felicia. From 1964 onwards, following the erection of a big modern works, Skoda has concentrated mainly on rear-engined cars. The first had a 988cc engine, while the four-cylinder 120 LS with an 1172cc engine was introduced in 1977.

1934 Skoda 420 Popular saloon

1976 Skoda Estelle

SKRIVA/*France 1922–1924*
Made in Paris, these were sleeve-valve Sergant-engined cars of 2402cc.

SK SIMPLEX/*England 1907–1910*
Smeddle & Kennedy, of Newcastle upon Tyne, offered ohc one- and two-cylinder light cars of 6 hp (1030cc) and 8/10 hp (1419cc), similar in appearance to the Sizaire Naudin.

SKY/*France 1919–1920*
Made in Levallois, Seine, by the Société Internationale de Mécanique et de Construction, these cars used 1693cc Ballot engines.

SLM/*Switzerland 1899, 1935*
This locomotive works at Winterthur built an opposed-piston voiturette in 1899 before turning to steam lorries. In 1935 they made three SLM-Pescara sports cars to the design of the Spanish Marquis de Pescara. A V-16 of 3·6 litres, the SLM-Pescara, was capable of 165 kph (103 mph).

SLR/*England 1963–1965*
'Sprinzel Lawrencetune Racing' brought together two keen racing protagonists of the 1960s for the purpose of beating Porsche at their own racing game. Though essentially competition machines, the three SLRs—one based on a

Triumph TR4 chassis, the others on Morgan hardware—did see road use and would undoubtedly have sold well, had they gone into production. Each was fitted with a beautiful alloy body styled by Rolls-Royce man Chris Spender and built by Williams and Pritchard.

SM/*England 1904–1905*
George J. Shave was formerly works manager of Locomobile's British works in Kensington, London, with Irving J. Morse, he devised a flash boiler with completely automatic control. The SM car, built by the successors to Locomobile, had a four-cylinder monobloc single-cylinder engine which developed 8½ hp, capable of 40 mph: a 20 hp model was also available.

SMB/*Italy 1906–1908*
A small-production 3140cc four-cylinder car built with a four-speed gearbox in unit with the engine.

SMITH/*USA 1905–1911*
Starting life as plain Smith, by 1907 this marque from Topeka, Kansas, had become the Great Smith, 'World's Greatest $2500 Car'. It was a conventional four-cylinder with full-elliptic springs and 'magnificent upholstery'.

SMITH & CO/*Denmark c1903*
No technical details are known about this car except that it had a single-cylinder engine in front and tiller steering. The prototype was built by one of the employees of Smith & Co A/S, Odense, but the directors decided not to go into car manufacturing.

SMITH & DOWSE/*England 1900*
Motor engineers and repairers at Isleworth, Middlesex, Smith and Dowse built cars to special order.

SMITH FLYER/*USA 1917–c1920*
Motoring at its most basic, the Milwaukee-built Smith Flyer consisted of four cycle wheels linked by planks, which served as both floor and suspension. Two bucket seats were the sole bodywork; power was supplied by a Smith Motor Wheel (a power-pack attachment for pedal cycles), mounted at the rear. A 'clutch' pedal merely lifted this fifth wheel off the road. In winter, the wheels could be replaced by ski-runners. From 1920 to 1923, the 'Flyer' was built by Briggs & Stratton; a 12v electric, the 'Auto Red Bug', lasted from 1923 to 1928.

SNA/*Switzerland 1903–1914*
Fritz Henriod designed the air-cooled cars of the Société Neuchâteloise d'Automobiles. First models had flat-twin engines of 6/8 cv, 10/12 cv and 18/20 cv at the front, under a bonnet shaped like an upturned boat. Some SNAs had electric headlamps. In 1907 came a 25/30 cv of 4942cc, with four cylinders in line, cooled by twin fans; it resembled the contemporary CGV in external appearance, and six chassis were fitted with Charles-Edouard Henriod's friction drive. The 25/30 cv lasted till the end of production.

SNYDER/*USA 1906–1908*
A flat-twin 10/12 hp engine powered this high-wheeled buggy from Dansville, Illinois.

SOAMES/*England 1903–1906*
One of the first cars to have a flexibly-mounted engine to minimize vibration, the Soames also had a three-speed constant-mesh gearbox.

1903 Soames

SOCIETE GENERALE DES VOITURES AUTOMOBILES/*France 1900*
Built by the Compagnie Française de Moteurs à Gaz, this was probably the first company to offer diesel engines in addition to two- and four-cylinder petrol-engined cars.

SODERBLOM/*Sweden 1903*
Söderbloms Gjuteri & Mekaniska Verkstad, of Eskilstuna, normally produced lorries, but one passenger car was built to special order. It had a water-cooled 10 hp twin-cylinder engine, a two-speed gearbox and chain drive. The body was a five-seater tourer.

SOLANET/*France 1921*
A rear-engined V-8 car made by Count Solanet. It seems that only one was built.

SOLIDOR/*Germany 1905–1907*
Berlin-assembled Passy-Thellier cars were marketed under this name.

SOLOMOBIL/*Germany 1921–1923*
Built at Chemnitz, the Hugo Mitzenheim-designed Solomobil was a three-wheeler; Solomobil later produced a cyclecar with four wheels and a sv 12 hp vee-twin engine.

SOMEA/*Belgium 1920–1921*
Paul Bastien, later of Metallurgique and Stutz, designed the 2-litre ohc SOMEA, launched at the 1920 Brussels Show. Only prototypes were built of this successor to the ALP.

SOMMER/*USA 1904–1907*
An offshoot of the 1902–1904 Hammer-Sommer, the Sommer had a 12 hp twin under the seat and, at first, a 'coalscuttle' bonnet.

SONCIN/*France 1900–1902*
A two-seated 4½ hp voiturette, forerunner of Grégoire.

SORIANO-PEDROSO/*France 1919–1924*
Made in Biarritz by two Spaniards, the Marques de Pedroso and Senor Soriano, these were initially Ballot-engined 1131cc and 1590cc cars. Then Soriano-Pedroso built a 902cc Ruby-engined cyclecar and a straight-eight prototype; however, their main product was marine engines.

SOUTHERN/*USA 1909*
Built in Jackson, Tennessee, the sporty Southern Roadster sold for $1500.

SOUTHERN/*USA 1921–1922*
Two Southern cars—both tourers—are known to have been built, one probably in 1920 and the other a year later. These cars had Herschell-Spillman engines and Rolls-Royce-shaped radiators. Prices were quoted as $2375 and $2995 respectively.

SOUTHERN CROSS/*Australia 1931–1935*
A most unusual car, financed by flying pioneer Sir Charles Kingsford Smith, the Southern Cross featured a monocoque chassis/body, made from laminated plywood. When rumours circulated that the body was a fire risk, the timber was sheathed in steel. The Southern Cross was powered by a locally-made flat-four engine of unknown capacity. It developed 55 bhp, giving a brisk performance for the day. Open and closed models were produced. Two cars were built using an Australian-developed torque-converter in place of the conventional clutch. The total number of production vehicles is uncertain, but is believed to have been about 10. None survives. Kingsford Smith was in the process of raising additional capital for the project when he was killed attempting a new England-Australia air record.

1934 Southern Cross saloon

SOVEREIGN/*USA 1906–1907*
Built on European lines, this was a chain-driven four-cylinder touring car of 7633cc, with an eight-seat aluminium Roi-des-Belges body.

SPA/*Italy 1906–1928*
Matteo Ceirano designed and constructed the SPA at Torino. Among the SPA cars were a 1526cc twin-cylinder and four-cylinder models from 2615cc to 7598cc. There were also two six-cylinder models of 5100cc and 11,536cc. After the war, the range of models included 2680cc four-cylinder and 4380cc six-cylinder models. A sporting version of the six had a dohc 24-valve head; even this advanced car could not prevent the end of SPA after the war. Fiat took over SPA in 1925, and production became centred on trucks. In pre-war days, Ciuppa won the 1909 Targa Florio on a SPA.

1912 15hp SPA tourer

SPAG/*France 1927–1928*
Made in Asnières, Seine, by MM. Simille and Pequignot, these were 1100cc Ruby and 1500cc SCAP-engined sports cars.

SPARKS/*USA 1899–1900*
This San Franciscan company offered a twin-cylinder 4hp car with belt-drive to all four wheels at 'less than $700'. A prospectus was issued, but it may have been just a stock promotion fraud.

SPARTAN/*USA 1911*
Built at the Motorette works in Hartford, Connecticut, by C. W. Kelsey, the Spartan never went into production. Conventional in most aspects, the Spartan featured front doors—a novelty in 1911.

SPARTAN/*England 1973 to date*
Jim McIntyre built the first Spartan after years of repairing sports cars. Traditional in approach and touch and resilient, Spartans have been powered by countless engines, from the Ford Mexico to the Rover V-8. Initially using a Triumph chassis, now with a purpose-built unit, production has topped 1000.

1978 Spartan sports two-seater

SPATZ/*Germany 1956–1958*
The red rear-engined Spatz was based on a design by racing driver Egon Brutsch and had first a 198cc Sachs two-stroke engine, then a 246cc Victoria two-stroke engine. Originally made by Friedrich of Traunreuth (Bavaria), the Spatz was later built by Victoria at Nuremberg. Total output was around 1500 cars. It was a small open two-seater with mini-wheels. The Nuremberg-built version bore the Victoria trade mark.

SPAULDING/*USA 1910–1916*
From Grinnell, Iowa, the Spaulding 30 was available with epicyclic or sliding gear-change.

SPEEDSPORT/*Belgium 1924–1927*
A sports car assembled in Brussels from Model T Ford components.

1908 Speedwell (GB) 24hp Roi-des-Belges

SPEEDWELL/*England 1900–1908*
Speedwell were chiefly motor agents but also marketed cars under their own name. In 1904, there were three Speedwells, single-cylinders of 6hp and 9hp and a 10hp twin. Four-cylinders of 14/16hp and 24/30hp appeared for 1905, and late in 1906 a 25hp four was available, with a handsome circular radiator and a double rear-axle, with separate load-carrying and driving members. For 1907, a 45hp six was listed, and in 1908, the last year of production, came a 45/50hp six.

SPEEDWELL/*USA 1907–1914*
'The surprise of the Automobile World', the first Speedwells—designed by George Loomis—were a 40/45hp four and a six, built next door to the Wright Brothers aircraft works at Dayton, Ohio. About 25 cars were built in the first year, after which the six was dropped, production rising to 100 in 1908, 400 in 1909. Later Speedwells had 6899cc six-cylinder engines; a double rotary-valve engine was offered from 1913 in addition to an engine with conventional valves.

SPEEDY/*England 1905–1906*
Jackson Brothers & Lord of Salford, Lancashire, built this 4hp tricar, which was unusual in having the passenger seated at the rear in a 'comfortable and cosy seat'.

SPEEDY/*England 1920–1921*
A cyclecar built in Peckham, South London, the Speedy used an 8hp air-cooled vee-twin engine. Drive was by chain and belt. It was hoped to mass-produce the Speedy, but these heady ambitions were never realized.

SPENCER/*USA 1921–1922*
A small car using a four-cylinder engine of the company's own make, the five-passenger touring car sold for $850 and rode on wood artillery wheels. Few of these 104-inch wheelbase Spencers were built.

SPERBER/*Germany 1911–1919*
The 500 man workforce of NAW of Hameln (builders of the Colibri) also built the small Sperber cars with sv 1330cc, 1545cc and 1592cc four-cylinder engines. Production was not resumed after the War, and Selve bought the NAW works for the production of Selve cars in 1919.

1913 Sperber 1545cc tourer

1974 SP Highwayman

SPERLING/*USA 1921–1923*
The Sperling was an export automobile and, thus, equipped with right-hand steering. It featured a four-cylinder Supreme engine and slightly pointed radiator. Both open and closed cars were available, the five-passenger touring model being listed at $980.

SP HIGHWAYMAN/*England 1974–1975*
Built by established restorers, Hooe Garage of Sussex, the SPs were the brainchild of Bugatti-man Jack Perkins. The first was open, the second closed in by a unique tinted glass roof. Both featured Rover power and clever negative-roll front suspension.

SPHINX/*France 1912–1925*
Made in Courbevoie, then in Asnières, Seine, by MM. Forster and Terrier, these were cyclecars with 1399cc twin Forster engines; they were also available with the 6 hp single-cylinder Aster. After the war they also made a four-cylinder 1327cc Altos-engined car.

SPHINX/*USA 1914–1915*
The Sphinx was built as a five-passenger touring car; an estimated 250 to 300 units were produced of this sole model. A four-cylinder Lycoming engine was employed, and wood or wire wheels were available. It has been stated that the advent of the 1916 Overland (a car similar to the Sphinx but giving better performance for less price) was responsible for the demise of this marque. The Sphinx Motor Car Co., of York, Pa., was succeeded by the DuPont Motor Car Co., which briefly continued the Sphinx under the DuPont name, an estimated 40 to 50 being sold later in 1915.

1914 Sphinx (US) 2932cc tourer

SPHINX/*Germany 1921–1925*
A more-or-less home-made small car with a sv four-cylinder engine of 1320cc.

SPIDOS/*France 1921–1925*
Made in Lyon, this was a 902cc Ruby-engined cyclecar.

SPINELL/*Germany 1924–1926*
Equipped with an ohv 496cc Kuhne single-cylinder motorcycle engine, the Spinell was just another chain-driven cyclecar.

SPITZ/*Austria 1901–1907*
Originally a car dealer, Spitz entered car manufacture (at the Gräf & Stift works in Vienna) with a four-wheel-driven design. Otto Hieronymus, famous as a designer and racing driver, later designed a 24 hp four-cylinder car, which won many races. Production versions included 16 hp, 20 hp and 24 hp models.

SPO/*France 1908–1911*
The Société Française du Petit Outillage was a manufacturer of engines and components at Clichy (Seine). They also built complete chassis.

SPORTS JUNIOR/*England 1920–1921*
This was a 10 hp two-seater with a four-cylinder Peters engine and detachable disc wheels.

SPRINGFIELD/*USA 1908–1911*
Springfield built in limited numbers — 1910 production was 100 cars — but for 1911 offered a 'made-to-order car for 300 exacting people', though the main choice offered seemed to be in the colour scheme. This shaft-drive car sold for $2500, with 'touring or torpedo body'.

SPRINGUEL/*Belgium 1907–1910*
Springuel of Liège, who merged with Impéria in 1910, built a 24 hp pair-cast four. It was manufactured in small numbers.

SPYKER/*Holland 1900–1925*
The Spijker brothers, carriage-builders based at Trompenburg, built a two-cylinder car in 1900. As early as 1903 they completed a one-off four-wheel-drive, four-wheel-brake, six-cylinder racer designed by the Belgian Laviolette, though a small number of 40 hp four-wheel-drive tourers were subsequently completed. That year a 16 hp twin and a 20/24 hp four were introduced. In 1904 they introduced the 'Dustless' chassis, with liberal undershielding to minimize dust-raising on unmade roads. The entire output of four-cylinder cars for 1904-06 was exported to England, where there were also many twin-cylinder Spyker taxis in London. An 80/100 hp Spyker won the Pekin-Paris race in 1907, the last year of Spijker family involvement, while from 1909 all models were fitted with worm-driven transverse camshafts, for smooth running. The post-war Spyker C4, with a 5741cc Maybach engine and French chassis, was designed by aero-engineer Fritz Koolhoven; a curious aeroplane-styled 'Aerocoque' sports, with vestigial tail surfaces, was listed. Over-expansion during the war proved Spyker's downfall. Attempts to market Mathis 1·2-litres as Spykers and to assemble American trucks failed to delay the inevitable demise.

1913 Spyker 20hp landaulette

SQUIRE/*England 1934–1936*
Adrian Squire built his visually exciting sports cars at a small garage at the top of Remenham Hill, near Henley-on-Thames. Powered by a potent supercharged 1½-litre R1 Anzani engine, the Squire had a preselector gearbox for good acceleration. Available in two chassis lengths, with bodywork by Vanden Plas or Ranalah, the Squire was one of the best-looking British sports cars of its day. Unfortunately there were snags. Prices began at £1195 and the engines proved unreliable unless regularly maintained. Even the announcement of a cheaper two-seater, with body by Markham of Reading, failed to attract buyers, and only seven cars were built during the two years of production. However, another two cars were subsequently built up by Val Zethrin, owner of one of the two long chassis examples. The Squire made brief appearances at Brooklands in 1935, driven by Luis Fontes, who only managed to finish once, being placed in a Mountain Handicap race at the track.

1935 Squire raced by Luis Fontes

305

1937 SS Jaguar 2½-litre coupé

SS / *England 1932–1945*

The forerunner of Jaguar Cars, this company was founded in 1934, though William Lyons and William Walmsley had been making motor-cycle sidecars from 1921. They graduated to producing distinctive bodies on Austin, Morris and Standard chassis. The SS1 of 1932 sprang from the Swallow-bodied Standard 16, having a low coupé body and long bonnet and cost just £310, the engine being a conventional 2054cc six-cylinder Standard unit. In addition, the SS11 used the 1052cc Standard Little Nine engine. The first sports car was the 2½-litre 90 of 1935, with stylish two-seater bodywork. A good-looking four-door sports saloon was named the Jaguar and, although the 2·7-litre engine had Standard origins, it had been much improved by Harry Weslake and W. M. Heynes. Particularly handsome was the two-seater SS100 of 1936, powered by a 2½-litre engine, also Standard-based. A new 3½-litre power unit was used not only in the saloon and drophead coupé for 1938 but — more significantly — in the 100. In this more powerful form, it cost only £445, yet was capable of the magic 100 mph. After World War Two the company was re-named Jaguar Cars, in view of the, by then, sinister associations of the original initials.

STABILIA / *France 1907–1930*

Vrard, the inventor of the Stabilia, worked with Léon Bollée from 1896, then with De Dion. He showed his first car at the 1904 Paris Salon, though serious production did not begin until 1907. The 'uncapsizable' Stabilia was under-slung at front and rear, giving a very low build. A pair-cast 2·2-litre four-cylinder engine was used initially and various small fours were subsequently offered. Though bizarre suspen-

1920 Stabilia 12-15 torpedo

1939 SS100 Sports two-seater

sion mediums like coil-springs in tension were adopted from time to time, the basic layout of the Stabilia remained constant.

STACK / *England 1921–1925*

A 766cc vee-twin engine was used in the Stack, made in East Croydon, Surrey. Transmission was by friction discs with chain final drive.

STAFFORD / *England 1920–1921*

An assembled car with an ohv 1790cc Dorman engine.

STAG / *England 1913–1914*

A 5/6hp cyclecar built in Sherwood, Nottinghamshire.

STAIGER / *Germany 1924–1926*

Made by Autostaiger of Stuttgart, this was yet another small 12 hp car with a sv four-cylinder engine.

STAINES-SIMPLEX / *England 1906*

With a Renault-style dashboard radiator and bonnet, the Staines-Simplex (or SSS) first ap-

peared as a 16/18 hp four. An 8/10 hp twin was introduced in September 1908. Production was spasmodic, apparently only taking place when the chauffeurs employed by the Staines Motor Company had nothing else to do.

STALLION / *USA 1979*

Silver Classic Coachcraft of California build this glass-fibre-bodied car based on the design of Shelby's AC Cobra. The Stallion is powered by 4949cc Ford V-8 engines.

STANDARD / *England 1903–1963*

Standard cars were so-called because they were assembled from standardized patterns and interchangeable parts. The company was founded by R. W. Maudslay (whose cousin designed the Maudslay car, also made in Coventry). The first production Standards were fitted with over-square single- and twin-cylinder engines, though by 1906 two six-cylinder models were listed. A 12 hp four appeared in about 1909 while a 9·5 hp Rhyl was marketed for 1913. The post-war era saw an enlarged version of the Rhyl, the SLS, appear — to become the 11·6 hp

SLO of 1921. A six-cylinder model, the 2·2-litre, was marketed for 1927; the following year the Popular Nine appeared, with a fabric body and worm-driven rear-axle. In 1929 Captain John Black became Standard's managing director, and two years later the company was offering a Big Nine and 16 hp and 20 hp sixes, while a Little Nine appeared in 1932. A Ten came in 1934 and in 1936 the Flying Standard range was

1929 Standard Nine Teignmouth fabric saloon

introduced in 12 hp, 16 hp and 20 hp variants. A short-lived 2·7-litre V-8 was a feature of the 1937 season. By contrast, the 1-litre Eight was popular in 1939. Standard bought the bankrupt Triumph company in 1945 and the first true new model of the post-war era was the Vanguard of 1948, with a 2·1-litre wet liner four-cylinder engine. The company's small car was the 803cc Eight of 1954, later joined by a larger Ten, the engine and independent front suspension being transferred to the Triumph Herald of 1959. A take-over of the company by Leyland Motors took place in 1961, the Triumph marque becoming the flagship of the group. The last Standards, which were phased out in May 1963, were the 2138cc Ensign and Vanguard Six, the engine of which was used in the Triumph 2000. As a marque name Standard ceased to exist; what once had been a complimentary title had become debased.

STANDARD/*USA 1904–c1908*
Successor to the 'US Long Distance', this was a 25 hp four with wooden side-entrance coachwork, retailing at $3500.

STANDARD/*Italy 1906–1908*
The Fabbrica Automobili Standard of Torino built a 10/14 hp four-cylinder car, also sold as FAS.

STANDARD/*Germany 1911–1912*
Equipped with unreliable and not fully-developed Henröid rotary-valve engines, the four-cylinder cars made at Berlin-Charlottenburg did not gain many friends or customers.

STANDARD/*USA 1912–1923*
The Standard Steel Company of Pittsburgh was among the first companies to offer a V-8, from 1916. Its 80 hp engine had a swept volume of 5217cc. Standard Steel, builders of railway carriages, also made World War One armoured cars.

1936 Flying Standard Sixteen

1957 Standard Vanguard III

STANDARD/*Germany 1933–1935, 1950–1954*
This famous motorcycle factory, owned by Wilhelm Gutbrod, first built the Josef Ganz-designed Standard-Superior with a 494cc twin-cylinder two-stroke vertical-engine in the back. A second version had a 396cc motor of similar design. Gutbrod-Superior cars with twin-cylinder two-stroke engines of 593cc and 663cc were made from 1950 to 1954.

1934 Standard (German) coupé

STANDARD/*India 1960s to date*
The Standard MkIII from Madras, based on the Triumph Herald, was superseded in 1973 by the Gazele.

STANDARD SIX/*USA 1909–1910*
After building Mors cars under licence as 'American Mors' from 1906, this St Louis company built an ohv 50 hp six of 6965cc under their own name.

STANDARD STEAM CAR/*USA 1920–1921*
The Standard, also known as the Scott-Newcomb, featured a Rolls-Royce-shaped condenser and closely resembled the Roamer gasoline car in appearance. The twin-cylinder horizontal steam engine used kerosene for fuel and, it was claimed, raised a full head of steam within one minute! One touring car is known to have been built; as many as five cars of this type have been reported, although this is unverified.

STANDISH/*USA 1924–1925*
Only two Standish cars were built by the Luxor Cab Mfg. Co. of Framingham, Mass., a division of the M. P. Moller Co. (builder of the Dagmar automobile). The Standish resembled both the Dagmar and the Luxor, and carried a pointed radiator which was later used by the Elysee truck, another Moller product. It had a Continental six and a 124-inch wheelbase.

307

STANGUELLINI/*Italy 1946–1965*
Known in pre-war days as a tuner of Fiats
(mainly the Ballila), Vittorio Stanguellini also
built after the war many sporting cars with
741cc and 1089cc Fiat engines, in most cases
with dohc. His bigger engines developed 90 bhp,
some even over 100 bhp. He also built rear-
engined Fiat-powered Formula Junior cars.

STANHOPE/*England 1919–1925*
This three-wheeler from Leeds was belt-driven,
power coming from an 8 hp JAP vee-twin.
Although the car was known as the Bramham
from 1922 to 1924, it re-emerged as the Stanhope in 1925.

1920 Stanhope fwd three-wheel two-seater

STANWOOD/*USA 1920–1922*
A typical assembled car with a Continental six-
cylinder engine, the Stanwood offered a line of
open and closed body styles.

STAR/*England 1897–1932*
Edward Lisle's Wolverhampton-based Star
Engineering Company built cycles from 1883,
and built its first 3½ hp Benz-based car in 1897. A
two-cylinder version appeared in 1900, followed
a year later by a Panhard-type 7 hp vertical twin.
Mercedes provided the inspiration for the 1903
12/16 hp four, joined by a 3261cc version in late
1905. Star's first six, the 6227cc 30 hp, was listed
from 1906 to 1911. A new 15 hp of 2862cc
appeared in 1909, and was replaced in 1912 by

1904 7hp Star three-seater

STANLEY
USA 1899–1927
Identical twins F. E. and F. O. Stanley sold
their photographic dry plate business to
Kodak and began building steam cars as a
hobby in 1897; they received so many orders
that they began building a batch of 200
steam buggies. But a consortium bought
them out for $250,000 to build their design
as the Locomobile, and they then developed
an improved model with twin-cylinder
engine geared direct to the back axle; this
went into production in 1901. The fire-tube
boiler was eventually shifted to the front
under the famous 'coffin nose' bonnet. In
1906, a racing Stanley Steamer, its body
developed in a wind tunnel, exceeded
127 mph at Ormond Beach, Daytona,
Florida. The production 1907 Gentleman's
Speedy Roadster could reach over 75 mph.
A foot-and-mouth disease epidemic in the
Stanley's New England home area in 1914
caused the removal of many roadside horse-
troughs, so the cars had to be fitted with
condensers in 1915. Development costs cut
production that year to 126, compared with
743 in 1914, though it rose to 500 in 1917,
the last year in which the Stanley brothers
were involved. Prescott Warren controlled
Stanley until 1924, but the marque never
recovered from the post-war slump. The
company was taken over by the Steam
Vehicle Corporation of America of
Allentown, Pa., but it is unlikely that they
built any further Stanleys before they ceased
trading in 1927.

1910 Stanley Model 71 20hp tourer

the famous 15·9 four of 3016cc; in 1914 this model and the 3817cc 20·1 hp were offered with streamline torpedo coachwork and bullnose radiators. The 15·9 hp and 20·1 hp survived until 1921, when they were supplanted by a sv 11·9 hp of 1795cc, which became a 1945cc 12/25 in 1924; the similar 12/40 hp Sports had front-wheel brakes and pushrod ohv. A six-cylinder version was known as the 18/40 hp. Two years later came two new models, the 2120cc ohv 14/40 hp four and the 3181cc 20/60 hp six. In 1928, Star was taken over by Guy, and the range cut to two sixes, the 18/50 hp and the 20/60 hp. These were totally redesigned in 1930 as the Comet and Planet, with four-wheel hydraulic jacking and servo brakes, offering '1941 motoring luxury and economy', but production was suspended in March 1932.

1931 Star Planet Coupé

1909 Star 12hp two-seater

STAR/*Italy 1905–1921*
Yet another enterprise belonging to the Giovanni Ceirano, Star had nothing in common with the British Star car, but was virtually identical with the Ceirano-designed and -built Rapid cars, except for minor differences in the shape of the bodywork, the radiator and other small items.

STAR/*USA 1908*
An ephemeral marque built by Model, of Peru, Indiana, who offered a chain-drive twin and a shaft-drive four.

STAR/*USA 1922–1928*
Billy Durant's Star, originally built in Elizabeth, NJ, was an assembled car with a 2137cc Continental monobloc four; selling at only $490, it was intended to rival the Model T Ford, and by 1923 the marque was seventh in popularity in America. A six was added to the range in 1926, with a sv 2774cc engine. During 1927, front-wheel brakes were added, and in 1928 the six was renamed 'Durant Model 55'. The marque—known as 'Rugby' outside the USA—was a casualty of the collapse of Durant's 'Second Empire'.

STARLING/*England 1905–1909*
Edward Lisle Jr ran the Star Cycle Company of Wolverhampton, which in 1905 produced the 6 hp single-cylinder Starling; it sold for only £110 in two seater form. In 1907 a 10 hp twin was introduced.

STARLITE/*USA 1959*
Kish Industries of Lansing, Michigan, designed the 148-inch long Starlite. The car had sports car styling and was powered by an electric motor. Two body styles were planned, but nothing came of the project.

START/*Czechoslovakia 1921–1931*
The first Petrášek-designed Start had an 1105cc twin-cylinder engine, another—four-seater—model a sv 1459cc four-cylinder engine. The last Start was an air-cooled twin cylinder of modern design, but few were built.

STATUS/*England 1970–1974*
The rear-engined Status Minipower, originally known as the Symbol, was the brainchild of ex-Lotus man Brian Luff (he was also involved in the Clan project). Featuring a glass-fibre-clad spaceframe chassis, it was light and manageable. Twenty chassis were built, but only eight complete kits sold before production ceased in 1974. One of several proposed body designs formed the basis for the 365, another Status product.

STAUNAU/*Germany 1950–1951*
The front-wheel-drive Staunau, powered by 398cc or 746cc Ilo two-stroke twin-cylinder engines, was probably one of the worst small cars ever made after World War Two.

STAVER/*USA 1907–1914*
The first Staver cars were 18/20 hp high-wheelers, but after two years the company was building conventional four-cylinder models, available with touring or torpedo coachwork. The 1914 Staver 65 was a 7413cc monobloc six.

STEAMOBILE/*USA 1900–1902*
A 7/9 hp twin-cylinder steam buggy from Keene, New Hampshire, designed by one Locke.

STEARNS/*USA 1898–1930*
The first cars built by Frank B. Stearns of Cleveland, Ohio, were single-cylinder gas buggies with tiller steering, replaced by wheel

steering on the 4083cc model of 1900. Plans in 1901 to build ten cars a day were greeted with press scepticism. A front-engined twin appeared in 1902, priced at $3000. A 36 hp four on Mercedes lines appeared in 1904, developing into the 1906 40/45 hp four with cast aluminium body panels. This was soon joined by the 45/90 hp six of 12,913cc, reckoned to be the fastest stock car of its day. In 1909 came a 15/30 hp, 'The Ultimate Car', and 1914 saw two Knight sleeve-valve-engined models, the 5·1-litre four and 6·8-litre six; a V-8 joined the range in 1917. Frank Stearns retired in 1919, and in 1925 Willys Overland took over (though they retained the Stearns hallmark of a white line round the inside edge of the radiator shell). The last Stearns Knights of 1929–30 were a 27·3 hp six and a 6·3-litre straight-eight.

1929 Stearns-Knight Model 8 Coupé

STEARNS/*USA 1900–1904*
A twin-cylinder steam carriage with side-tiller steering from Syracuse, NY.

STECO/*USA 1914*
A streamlined 10 hp tandem-seat cyclecar of aggressive appearance, from Chicago. Independent front suspension was featured.

STEEL/*France 1907*
An obscure marque built by Lochner, Willem, et Cie of Meudon (Seine et Oise), the Steel had a 2043cc four-cylinder 13/15 hp engine.

1925 Steiger sports two-seater

STEIGER / *Germany 1920–1926*
Superb Paul Henze-designed four-cylinder cars with ohc 2604cc (later 2824cc) long-stroke engines, which were also built as sports cars with neat two-seater bodywork, and gained many successes. Steigers were hand-made and expensive. Noll of Düsseldorf—known also as a Bugatti driver—supplied Steiger parts after the works (at Burgrieden, near Laupheim) closed.

STEINMETZ / *USA 1920–1927*
Said to be the only electric car produced south of the Mason-Dixon line, the Steinmetz from Baltimore, Maryland, was named after the crippled 'Electrical Wizard', Charles Steinmetz (who drove a Detroit Electric).

STELA / *France 1941–1948*
Electric cars made in Villeurbanne, Rhône, during World War Two; most of them were delivery vans.

STELKA / *Czechoslovakia 1920–1922*
A machine works at Přímbram, which started light car manufacture with very limited technical and commercial possibilities. The Stelka, designed by Rudolf Stelšovsky, the owner of the factory, was a 1080cc twin-cylinder with a high, narrow body.

STELLA / *Switzerland 1906–1913*
Successors to the CIEM, Stella cars were distinguished by a round radiator, and used a conventional transmission. Initially a 3-litre 10 cv was built, followed by other four-cylinder models of 14/16 cv, 18/20 cv and 24/30 cv.

1908 Stella 16/20hp – 'a perfect gem'

STELLITE / *England 1913–1919*
The 1100cc Stellite was built by Electric Ordnance and Accessories of Birmingham, a Wolseley offshoot. The chassis of this £157 car was of flitch-plated wood, and up to 1915 only two speeds were available.

STEPHENS / *England 1898–1900*
R. Stephens, a Clevedon, Somerset, cycle engineer, built about a dozen 8 hp twin-cylinder cars with belt and chain drive and independent suspension—the prototype still survives.

STEPHENS / *USA 1916–1924*
An offshoot of the Moline Plow Company, the Stephens was always built as a six-cylinder—the 'Salient Six'—of 3671cc, with ohv from 1918, after which the company switched from Continental engines to their own make power units.

STERLING / *USA 1908–1915*
Forerunner of the Elcar, these were fours of 30 hp (4185cc) and 40 hp (5808cc).

STERLING / *England 1913*
A belt-driven, JAP-engined cyclecar from Leeds.

STERLING/ *USA 1917–1923*
The Ams-Sterling of 1917 was a roadster with an ohv 2081cc LeRoi four-cylinder engine. Later models also used a Herschell-Spillman six.

1917 Ams-Sterling roadster

1924 Sterling-Knight

STERLING-KNIGHT / *USA 1921, 1923–1926*
Sterling-Knight started in Cleveland, Ohio, with 1921 models, but suspended production that year owing to lack of capital. After reorganization, with a factory in Warren, Ohio, production started anew in 1923 and continued until mid-1926. The cars featured a Knight-type six-cylinder engine and bodies by Phillips. Between 425 and 450 were built.

STEUDEL / *Germany 1903–1909*
Best known as producers of car and marine engines, Steudel in their early years built small two- and four-cylinder cars with proprietary engines made by De Dion, Aster and Fafnir, of up to 16 hp.

STEVENS / *England 1976–1978*
Already involved in the manufacture of custom-built delivery vans, Tony Stevens ventured into the realm of sports car manufacture with the two-seater Sienna in 1976. Based on the Reliant Kitten, the Sienna was capable of 60 mpg. Despite interest from Reliant, the project never got off the ground.

STEVENS-DURYEA / *USA 1900–1927*
J. Frank Duryea, having quarrelled with his brother Charles, joined Stevens Arms & Tools, of Chicopee Falls, Mass., who began production in the Overman factory of a 6 hp horizontal-twin Victoria Stanhope with tiller steering, joined in 1905 by a 20 hp four of conventional appearance. In 1905 came the 9·6-litre Big Six with three-point suspension of its engine/gearbox unit. From 1907, the company concentrated on big sixes. The last new model was the 1915 Model D 7·7-litre. Frank Duryea sold his share in the company that year, and production was suspended until 1920, when the Model D was revived—as Model E. Later, in 1923, the marque was taken over by Ray M. Owen (of Owen Magnetic), and the plant built Raulang electric cars and coachwork. Few Stevens-Duryeas were built after 1924.

STEWART / *USA 1915–1916*
The Stewart, like the Renault, sported a sloping hood and had its radiator mounted at the rear of the engine. Roadsters and touring cars were available, and a Continental six-cylinder engine was used. Price of the touring model was $1950. The Stewart Company is better known for its commercial vehicles, which were manufactured from 1912 to 1942.

The 'Distinctive' Stewart Six, 1913

STEWART / *USA 1922–1923*
The petrol-powered Stewart was successor to the Stewart-Coats Steamer, which itself was connected with the Coats Steam Car. Stewart offered three models, a four (using a Herschell-Spillman engine) and two sixes, the 'Royal Palm' which featured a Rutenber, and a larger model powered by what purported to be an engine of Stewart's own design. It is thought that no more than a single pilot model of each type—if that—made up the total production.

STEWART-COATS / *USA 1922*
An offshoot of the Coats Steam Car, operations were located in Columbus and Bowling Green, Ohio. Only a pilot model was made.

STEYR / *Austria 1920 to date*
Hans Ledwinka, famous creator of Nesselsdorf and Tatra cars, joined the Steyr armaments works in 1917. Their first car appeared on the

1936 Steyr 22PS streamline saloon

market in 1920 with a 12/40 hp six-cylinder ohc engine of 3325cc; a sv 1814cc four-cylinder model followed. The Six underwent much development until 1929, Ledwinka returning to Tatra in 1923. In 1926 a smaller six-cylinder model of 1560cc appeared, followed by yet another ohc version, this time of 4014cc. The first models had pointed radiators, later cars flat coolers; most engines used a single overhead-camshaft. The range of models also included ohv 2078cc sixes and also the ohv 1990cc Steyr 120S. In 1929-30, Ferdinand Porsche designed a new luxurious Steyr, the straight-eight 'Austria', which never went into production. In 1934 the factory merged with the Puch combine, of which Austro-Daimler was part — that was the end of Austro-Daimler cars. The first small Steyr was the Type 100 of 1934, with a sv 1385cc four-cylinder engine; in 1937 came the 1498cc Type 200, which was also available (as Type 220) with an ohv 2260cc power unit. The 1158cc Steyr 55 of 1938 was small and very streamlined. It had a sv flat-four engine, and was the successor to the Type 50 984cc of 1936. From 1949 onwards, Steyr assembled Fiat cars from Austria; from 1957 onwards they built the Fiat 500 as the Steyr-Puch 500 with an own-make flat twin-cylinder engine, built mainly at the Graz (Puch) factory. Steyr was also connected with the assembly of Opel cars in the mid-1930s. In 1979 they began manufacture of 4wd vehicles for Mercedes.

The Steyr-built Mercedes 4wd G

STILSON / USA 1907-1910
Stilson offered big Herschell-Spillman-engined sixes with an early form of hydraulically controlled clutch.

STIMSON / England 1972 to date
A six-wheeled, mini-powered, open-topped, go-anywhere vehicle with fully independent suspension. Available complete or in kit form.

STIMULA / France 1907-1914
This company, from St Chamond, Loire, offered an 8 hp single, as well as fours from 10/12 hp to 16/20 hp.

STIRLING / Scotland 1897-1903
Stirling, of Hamilton, Lanarkshire, were old-established coachbuilders who built their first 4 hp Stirling-Daimler in January 1897, on Coventy-Daimler lines. Until 1900 they built their own dog-cart and waggonette bodies on Coventry-Daimler chassis, and then imported the archaic Clément-Panhard voiturette, which they sold as the Clement-Stirling or Stirling-Panhard. After 1903 they only built lorries.

STIRLING / USA 1920-1921
An assembled car, the Newark, New Jersey-built Stirling featured a six-cylinder Continental engine; the five-passenger touring car was priced at $2350. Only six Stirling cars were built.

STODDARD-DAYTON / USA 1904-1913
The first examples of this highly-regarded marque from Dayton had 4605cc Rutenber engines; sixes were available from 1907. Stoddard-Dayton became part of the US Motor Company, and went down when that failed. The final range consisted of three fours — the 3707cc 'Savoy', the 4766cc 'Stratford' and the 5808cc 'Saybrook' — and a massive Knight sleeve-valve six of 8691cc.

STOEWER / Germany 1899-1939
Emil and Bernhard Stoewer were pioneers of the German car industry. They owned an iron-works at Stettin (now in Poland) and produced first De Dion-engined three-wheelers and then rear-engined 2080cc twin-cylinder cars. Other twin-cylinder models had 1526cc and 2280cc power units. The first four-cylinder Stoewer was of 3052cc; 1906 saw a new 5880cc four-cylinder and even an 8829cc six-cylinder. Four-cylinder models of 1501cc and 2544cc followed. In 1910, Stoewer cars were built under licence by Mathis of Strasbourg. An ohv 11,160cc six-cylinder, which had a modified Loutzky-designed aero-engine. This model was built soon after World War One in which Stoewer had produced these aeroengines under Argus licence to use up surplus parts. A racing version of this was successfully driven by works-driver Emil Kordewan. A smaller racing car of 2490cc had a four-cylinder ohc engine and streamlined body-work. Production after 1918 included 1570cc, 2120cc and 2292cc four-cylinder models and sv six-cylinder cars with 3107cc and 3383cc engines. The year 1928 saw the introduction of 1997cc and 2462cc straight-eight models. There was also the 3974cc eight-cylinder Gigant (also available in a 3633cc version), while the Marschall had eight cylinders displacing 2963cc. The last big Stoewer was the beautiful 4905cc 100 hp straight-eight Repräsentant. Stoewer was for many years a typical family business, with the founder-owners and their families taking an active part. Unfortunately

1930 Stoewer fwd saloon

the factory ran into financial difficulties and, after a reorganization in the early 1930s, the founders left the works. Economic reasons led to the manufacture of cheaper cars in the 1930s. The first, in 1931, was an 1188cc V-4 with front-wheel drive. The Greif-Junior was built under Tatra licence, with an ohv air-cooled 1474cc flat-four engine from 1936 to 1939. Own-design engines were used in 1354cc, 1460cc and 2390cc four-cylinder models, the ohv six-cylinder 3585cc Arcona and the 2488cc V-8 Greif. During World War Two, Stoewer supplied cars to the German forces, but the works were not rebuilt after extensive damage in an air raid.

STOKVIS / Holland c1913
Built by W. J. Stokvis of Arnhem, the Stokvis is believed to have been a prototype only.

1925 Stolle

STOLLE / Germany 1925
An advanced design, the ohc 1494cc four-cylinder Stolle sports car developed 40 bhp, and was the work of the famous motorcycle designer Martin Stolle (of BMW, Victoria and D-Rad fame). Only a few Stolle cars had been built when Hugo Stinnes, who was backing the venture, died suddenly; Vorster & Stolle, the Munich-based factory, had to close.

STONEBOW / England 1900-1902
Named after an ancient gateway near the premises of its begetter, R. M. Wright of Lincoln. The Stonebow dog-cart, available with 5 hp or 7 hp engine, was probably built by Payne & Bates of Coventry, makers of the Godiva.

1913 2016cc Knight-engined Stoneleigh torpedo

STONELEIGH / England 1912-1914, 1922-1924
A 12 hp four-cylinder model, the Stoneleigh had a conventionally-mounted radiator, unlike its sister marque, Siddeley-Deasy, which used a dashboard cooler. The post-war Stoneleigh light car had a vee-twin 1-litre power unit, reputedly designed to use up war-surplus aero-engine cylinders.

STORCK/*USA 1901–1903*
Selling at $725–800, this was a light steam runabout assembled by cycle agent Frank Storck of Red Bank, NJ.

STORERO/*Italy 1912–1919*
Storero of Turin produced a 4396cc 20/30 hp and a 6280cc 24/80 hp version. Designer was Cesare Scacchi.

STOREY/*England 1920–1930*
Although early examples of the marque used proprietary engines (Coventry-Simplex and Chapuis-Dornier), at the end of 1920 engines of Storey Motors' own manufacture were used in 10, 12, 15·9 and 20 hp forms. The earlier cars were fitted with rear-axle-mounted gearboxes, but the unit reverted to a more conventional position with these later power units. The company was reconstituted in 1921, with production being transferred from Tonbridge, Kent, to Clapham Park, London. Initially, Storey engines were fitted, though later on Meadows power units were featured. Another reconstruction in 1925 saw three models listed: 10/25 and 14/40 fours plus a 17/70 six-cylinder, though production by this stage had been reduced to a trickle.

STORK KAR/*USA 1919–1921*
A typical assembled car, with a four-cylinder Lycoming engine, the Stork Kar was identical to a number of others of its type, including the Norwalk and the Marshall (which is hardly surprising, as all of these were made by Piedmont). The Stork Kar differed only in featuring right-hand steering for the export market.

STOTT/*England 1903*
Made in Manchester, the Stott was built to individual order with either 9 hp single-cylinder or 12 hp twin-cylinder power units.

STOUT/*USA 1946*
William Bushnell Stout was once credited with 'more technical innovations than any man since Edison'. He designed a car which had neither axles nor chassis, the wheels simply being attached to the body. Suspension was by compressed air cylinders and the engine was rear-mounted. It was one of the earliest cars to use glass-fibre extensively. Mr. Stout built these 137-inch wheelbase cars as experimental exercises, but the Consolidated-Vultee Aircraft Corp. held the rights to manufacture.

STRADA/*England 1974–1975*
Though exhibited at the London motor show in 1974, the mid-engined Strada never went into serious production. Its striking mid-engined glass-fibre-bodied design nevertheless caused quite a stir.

STRAKER-SQUIRE/*England 1906–1926*
Starting with licence-production of the French Cornilleau St Beuve 25 hp, Sidney Straker & Squire of Bristol (builders of steam 'lurries' from 1901), progressed to the 16/20 hp 'Car for the Connoisseur' in 1907 (a sister company built the 12/14 hp Shamrock). Roy Fedden designed the 15 hp Straker-Squire of 1908, the marque's most successful model. During World War One,

1914 Straker-Squire 15/20hp Standard Limousine

1924 Straker-Squire 24/80hp

Straker Squire built Rolls-Royce Eagle aero-engines: the general lines of this power unit were used in the post-war model which appeared in prototype form in 1918. Produced at Edmonton, North London, this 24/80 hp Straker-Squire had an ohc 4-litre engine with six separately-cast cylinders — but this 'Aeroplane of the Road' didn't reach production until 1921, and the old 15 hp had to be revived as a stop-gap. A 1460cc Dorman-engined sports appeared in 1923, too late to save the company from receivership in 1924.

STRATHMORE/*USA 1899–1912*
In the optimistic tone of their day, this Boston, Mass., firm advertised 'motor vehicles built to order—carriages, coaches, runabouts'. These were illustrated by a dramatic picture of a nine-seated stagecoach-like vehicle, apparently steam-powered, careering along with no visible means of control.

STRATTON/*USA 1922–1923*
The Stratton (sometimes spelled 'Strattan') was absorbed by Premier before more than one or two prototypes were built. Because of its new parent company, the name occasionally crops up as 'Premier-Stratton' or 'Stratton-Premier' in automobile trade journals of the time. The car

had an own-make four-cylinder engine. Price of the touring car was $575.

STREATHAM/*England 1902*
These were 6 hp single- and 8 hp twin-cylinder cars, the brakes of which could be 'made to act backwards as well as forwards'.

STRINGER/*USA 1901*
A four-cylinder steamer from Marion, Ohio.

STRINGER-WINCO/*England 1921–1932*
The Stringer-Winco light car used a four-cylinder 1088cc Alpha engine. In 1922 they produced the Stringer Type S or Stringer-Smith using an 11·9 hp Meadows engine. Alpha engines of 9 hp and 11 hp featured in later models.

STRØMMEN/*Norway 1933–1940*
The Strømmen factory built advanced buses with unitary construction and assembled American Dodge cars. Some of the special long-wheelbase versions were known simply as Strømmen, though they were Dodge-based.

STUART/*England 1906–1907*
A *de luxe* version of the Starling, the Stuart was a 7 hp twin-cylinder shaft-drive car, available with two-, three- or four-seater bodywork.

STUDEBAKER / USA 1902–1964

Founded as wagon builders in 1854 in South Bend, Indiana, Studebaker were the 'largest vehicle house in the world' by 1875. Turn-of-the-century orders for automobile chassis led to the building of 20 Studebaker electrics in 1902, the first petrol Studebakers (actually built by Garford) appeared in 1904, joined by a cheaper range (built by EMF) in 1908. Studebaker and EMF merged in 1910 as the Studebaker Corporation, and the Garford, EMF and Flanders models were all phased out. A two-car line, the 3146cc four and 4736cc six, appeared in 1914, the four being replaced by a new 3392cc Light Six in 1920, when a Big Six of 5810cc was also available alongside the old Special Six. A straight-eight, the President, was launched in 1928, and the sixes renamed Dictator and Commander, acquiring smaller eights in 1929. From 1928 to 1933, when it was declared bankrupt, Studebaker owned Pierce-Arrow. The receivers sold this off, dropped the President 8 and launched new sixes using the engine from the discontinued

Rockne to put Studebaker back in business. Raymond Loewy was hired as styling consultant in 1936, the embarrassingly named 'Dictator' was toppled in 1938, and a new small six, the 2687cc Champion, appeared in the 1939 model year, pushing sales in both 1940 and 1941 over the 100,000 mark. Studebaker was one of the first companies to launch brand-new post-war models, in May 1946. Styling was by Loewy, with front fenders blending into the body and a full-width grille combining to earn this range — Champion and Commander, with 2786cc or 3704 sv sixes — the 'coming or going?' nickname. The 1950 models had a cyclops headlamp, and Studebaker's first V-8, a 3802cc unit, appeared in 1951. New Studebakers, the 2769cc Champion six, the V-8 Commander and the Land Cruiser, appeared in 1953, with classic styling by Robert E. Bourke, chief designer of the Loewy studios; chromium plate and a wraparound windscreen impaired its looks in 1955, after the Packard takeover. The Loewy studios produced a neat re-skinning of the

existing body to produce the 1956 Flight Hawk (3032cc six), Power Hawk (3671cc V-8), Sky Hawk (4244cc V-8) and Golden Hawk (5768cc Packard V-8). However, sales continued to fall, unchecked by the launch of the frugal Scotsman, powered by the old sv six. There was a disastrous facelift in 1958, with grafted-on dual headlamps and tailfins, though the compact Lark (readied for production by stylist Duncan McRae in just ten months) of 1959, reversed the slipping sales to some extent; the only other 1959 Studebaker was the 4736cc Silver Hawk V-8. A wider Lark range was available in 1962, and mid-way through the year the distinctive glass-fibre-bodied Avanti sport coupé was announced. Power was by the 4736cc V-8, with optional supercharger, in which form an Avanti took 29 stock car records. But the Avanti, the elegant Lark and the Hawk GT of 1962–64 came too late to avert new financial difficulties which resulted in production being transferred to Canada in 1964, where Studebaker struggled along fitfully until 1966.

1923 Studebaker Big Six Four-Seat Speedster

Studebaker 25/30hp six-cylinder tourer, c.1915

1956 Studebaker Silver Hawk

1963 Studebaker Lark convertible

STURGES/*USA 1895*
A crude four-seater electric carriage, built in Chicago.

STURTEVANT/*USA 1904–1908*
From 1905, this 7800cc four-cylinder roadster from Boston used a primitive automatic transmission.

STUTZ/*USA 1911–1935*
Harry Stutz of Indianapolis built a racing car in five weeks, to prove the quality of his gearbox/rear-axle unit, and entered it in the first Indianapolis 500-mile race in 1900. It finished 11th, earning the slogan 'the car that made good in a day'. Production of Stutz cars, powered by 6·3-litre Wisconsin engines, began soon after. In 1914 came the archetypal Stutz, the stark Bearcat speedster, promoted by the racing successes of the 'White Squadron' Stutz team, with highly non-standard 16-valve 4851cc Wisconsin engines. A 1916 Bearcat broke the trans-America record, taking 11 days 7½ hours for the trip. In 1919 Harry Stutz left to build the HCS, and the company came under the control of steel tycoon Charles Schwab, whereupon Stutz

1928 Stutz Black Hawk Special, an attempt to take the World Land Speed Record

began building their own four- and six-cylinder engines. The last Bearcat was the 4·7-litre Speedway Six of 1924. Frederick E. Moscovics acquired Stutz in 1925 and brought in Belgian designer Paul Bastien, late of Métallurgique, whose ohc 4·7-litre Safety Stutz Vertical Eight was an extremely low-built car, boasting four-wheel hydraulic brakes and wire-mesh safety glass. A Stutz Black Hawk Speedster finished second in the 1928 Le Mans 24-hours race. The Black Hawk six of 1929 ranks as a separate marque. In 1931 came a revived Bearcat with the twin ohc DV 32 power unit and a guaranteed 100 mph top speed. From 1928 to 1938, Stutz offered a rear-engined light van, the Pak-Age-Car; but car production ceased in 1935.

1933 Stutz Super Bearcat

STUTZ/*USA 1970 to date*
The Stutz Blackhawk is not a facsimile of the original classic, but a modern luxury car styled by Virgil Exner. The Stutz Motor Company of America took the Stutz name because it epitomized the best money could buy. The new Stutz is hand-assembled in Italy by Carrozzeria of Modena, utilizing a Pontiac V-8 and modified Pontiac chassis.

STUYVESANT/*USA 1911–1912*
A big, costly ($4200) 9·4-litre six from Sandusky, Ohio.

SUBARU/*Japan 1958 to date*
Part of the former Nakajima Aircraft Company, Fuji Sangyo was organized in 1945, then reformed in 1950 by order of the occupying Allied forces into 12 smaller companies, of which five became Fuji Heavy Industries in 1953, building scooters, railway rolling stock and aircraft power units. They joined Nissan in 1968. Their first car, the 360, with a rear-mounted two-stroke engine, appeared in 1958. The Subaru 1000 appeared in 1966, and in 1968 came the 997cc front-engined, front-wheel-drive FE, with all-round independent suspension. A 1088cc version appeared in 1970, followed a year later by a 1300cc model. The current Leone series dates back to that year; the 1978 models used 1361cc and 1595cc engines and the Complex range included two 4wd models. The Rex minicar range now has a low-emission 544cc four-stroke engine.

SUBURBAN/*USA 1911–1912*
A De Schaum venture, the Suburban Limited was a 4261cc six, available in three styles.

SUCCESS/*USA 1906–1909*
A crude high-wheeler buggy with the single-cylinder two-stroke engine mounted on the side of the body, the Success, from St Louis, Missouri, was claimed to cover 100 miles per gallon. With iron-tyred wheels it sold for $250. John C. Higdon, head of the Success Auto-Buggy Manufacturing Co., had built his first horseless carriage in 1896.

SUERE/*France 1905–1931*
Established in Paris, Suère started with a 763cc single-cylinder car, replaced by a four-cylinder 1592cc Ballot-powered model in 1913. After the war they presented a 1413cc sv V-8. In 1921 there was an 1874cc four-cylinder Ballot-engined car, followed in 1925 by an Altos-engined 1990cc six. After that, Suère made cars with SCAP and CIME proprietary engines from 1500cc to 2000cc.

SULTAN/*France/USA 1903–1910*
Sultan cars were built by Martin & Lethimonnier of Paris. Martin, who had experience of American manufacturing methods, was the designer; he also designed an 'excellent hydraulic clutch'. Robust and elegant, Sultan cars had the cylinders cast separately, with brass water-jackets. The 1907 range consisted of 6/9 hp, 9/12 hp, 13/18 hp and 20/30 hp models; that year, too, a 7897cc car was built for — and failed to start in — the Kaiserpreis. In August 1907, Martin drove one of his cars — they were also

Martin, the designer, driving his 1907 Sultan a few moments before the crash in which he died

known as Martin-Lethimonniers — in the Criterium de France. On the outskirts of Bordeaux he collided with another competitor in a Peugeot and was killed, together with his works driver, Villemain. It was doubtless Martin's American connections which brought about the creation of the Sultan Motors Corporation of Springfield, Mass. — a branch of the Otis Elevator Company — which began building Sultans for the American market in 1906. Like the French company, it went out of business in 1910.

SUMINOE/*Japan 1954–1955*
A Tokyo bodybuilder made this spindly 'Flying Feather' two-seater powered by a rear-mounted 350cc twin-cylinder engine.

SUMMIT/*Australia 1922–1926*
Advertised as a 'New Wonder Car' the conventionally designed Summit tourer was unusual in several ways. It was very well equipped, down to a radio and electric stop lights (in 1922), and came with a full 12 months' warranty. The power unit was a four-cylinder Lycoming engine of 3·4 litres. An unusual mechanical feature was the use of triplex combination springs running the full length of the chassis frame. It is not known how many cars were built, but only one survives.

SUN/*Germany 1906–1908*
Founded in Berlin by Paul and Emil Jeannin, Sun produced big and expensive cars with four-cylinder engines from 22 hp to 75 hp. Paul Jeannin was a designer with Argus in earlier years. Most cars had shaft-drive, some models retained chain-drive.

SUN/*USA 1915–1918*
A 22 hp six, built by former Haynes staffmen.

SUN/*USA 1921–1924*
The Sun Runabout, from Toledo, had a 22 i.- ohv Cameron air-cooled engine.

SUNBEAM, SUNBEAM-TALBOT
England 1899–1976

Like many of their contemporaries, Sunbeam were bicycle manufacturers who went into the motor business. Their first car, the Sunbeam-Mabley, was a strange device, looking rather like a Victorian sofa on wheels, powered by a single-cylinder 326cc engine. More conventional were the Thomas Pullinger-designed models based on the French Berliet car. These 12 hp Sunbeams were solidly-made fours, produced between 1902 and 1905. Six-cylinder engines put in a brief appearance between 1904 and 1907. In 1909 the Breton designer, Louis Coatalen, joined the Wolverhampton company; he was responsible for the cars which achieved a sensational 1–2–3 victory for the marque in the Coupe de *l'Auto* race of 1912. This was with a modified version of the sv 3-litre 12/16 hp model which remained in production until 1921. The Sunbeam, Talbot, Darracq combine was created in 1920. The 16 hp and 24 hp Sunbeam models received ohv in 1922, while a six-cylinder car, the 16/50 hp, joined the range in 1924. A magnificent dohc 3-litre six-cylinder was announced for 1924 and made in small numbers until 1930. The company's racing programme was maintained, the marque's outstanding victory being Segrave's win in the 1923 French Grand Prix, the first British GP victory. He repeated his success at the following year's San Sebastian event. Sunbeams maintained their careful, well-engineered designs into the 1930s, a new model being the 2·9-litre Speed model of 1933 (though the Dawn of the following year, with its ohv 1·6-litre four-cylinder engine, was hardly in the Coatalen traditions). The collapse of the unwieldy STD combine in 1935 saw a takeover by the Rootes Group. Consequently there were no Sunbeams in 1938 and the name was combined with Talbot to create the Sunbeam-Talbot of 1939. Sunbeam-Talbots were merely luxury versions of Hillman and Humber models. The Sunbeam name did not re-appear in its own right until 1953 with the announcement of the Sunbeam Alpine, a two-seater variant of the Sunbeam Talbot 90. Three years later came the Hillman Minx-based Rapier, starting with a 1·4-litre engine, later increased to 1·5 litres. On the sports car front, further versions of the Alpine theme followed; in 1964 came the Tiger, basically an Alpine fitted with a 4·3-litre Ford V-8. An exercise in badge engineering was the Sunbeam Stiletto, a coupé version of the Hillman Imp, though the fastback Rapier of 1968 was a distinctive offering. 'Sunbeam' was used as a model name for the front-engined Chrysler of 1977, a far cry from its Grand Prix ancestry.

1925 Sunbeam 20/60hp six-cylinder tourer

1906 Sunbeam 16hp six-cylinder tourer

1913 12/16hp Sunbeam tourer

1955 Sunbeam Alpine

1963 Sunbeam Alpine GT Coupé

SUP/*France 1919–1922*
The Société Usines de Paquis, from Mézières (Ardennes) showed 10 hp cars at the 1919 Paris Salon. The marque was closely linked with Hinstin.

SUPER/*France 1912–1914*
Levêque of Ruby built this belt-drive tandem-seat cyclecar, with single- or twin-cylinder motorcycle engines.

SUPERIOR/*Germany 1905–1906*
This bicycle manufacturer assembled Fafnir-built Omnimobil components, fitted 6 hp twin-cylinder 704cc engines, and called the result 'Superior'.

SUPERIOR/*Canada 1911–1912*
A four-cylinder 25 hp engine powered this assembled car from the Ontario oil town of Petrolia.

SURREY/*England 1921–1930*
This assembled light car from Putney, London, used some Model T Ford parts and a Coventry-Climax engine. Later, Meadows engines of 9·8 hp and 11·8 hp were available.

SURRIDGE/*England 1912–1913*
The Surridge Cyclar was a cyclecar produced by a firm of accessory factors from Camberwell. It had a twin-cylinder 978cc Fafnir engine and a five-speed friction transmission.

SUZUKI/*Japan 1955 to date*
Founded in 1909 as Suzuki Shokkuki Seisakusho, this famous Hamamatsu motorcycle firm did not enter the car field until 1955, with the Suzulite 360 utility car. The fwd Fronte 360 appeared in 1967, followed a year later by the Fronte 500. As well as an updated version of the Fronte, Suzuki now also offers the Jimny, a light (539cc, three-cylinder) 4wd utility model.

SVELTE/*France 1906–1907*
A range of cars from 16 hp to 50 hp built by a well-known small-arms and bicycle works from St Etienne (Loire).

SVP/*France 1905–1906*
An 8 hp two-seater with belt intermediate transmission.

SWALLOW/*England 1922*
Two models of Swallow were built. One had a twin-cylinder Blackburne engine and the other a four-cylinder Dorman. A two-speed epicyclic gearbox featured in both instances.

SWALLOW DORETTI
England 1954–1955
Built by a Walsall coachbuilding company descended from Swallow Sidecars (parent of SS cars), this sports car used Triumph TR2 engine and drive-train in a tubular chassis with elegant two-seat bodywork.

SWAN/*France 1922–1923*
'Four cylinders, four speeds, four seats' was the slogan promoting M. Bloch's Altos-engined light cars, of 1328cc, 1359cc and 1779cc, from Neuilly (Seine).

SWEANY/*USA 1895*
Dr F. L. Sweany's steam carriage, built by the Chas. S. Caffrey Company of Camden, NJ, was driven by four 3 hp motors, one for each wheel. It failed to reach production.

1903 Swift 6hp two-seater

c.1919 Swift 12hp coupé

SWIFT/*England 1900–1931*
Swift of Coventry had made sewing machines and bicycles long before they went into the car business; their first car used the famous De Dion Bouton engine. Although early examples were probably made from assembled French parts, in 1904 a Swift-designed voiturette was announced, though it still had a 4½ hp De Dion engine. Other proprietary engines by Simms and Aster featured on some later models, though the 1906 10 hp was significant in having a Swift-designed engine. Although this was a twin, a four-cylinder 10 hp car appeared in 1912. After the War the company unfortunately became embroiled in the ill-fated Harper Bean combine, which did little to aid their finances. Post-war models included the aforementioned Ten and a new Twelve which appeared in 1920. The Ten was modernized in 1923 with a detachable cylinder head and unit construction engine and gearbox, the Twelve later receiving a similar facelift. A 17·9 hp 18/50 hp arrived in 1925. A new Ten appeared later in 1930 and in 1931, the last year of production, the cheap 8 hp Cadet at £149 did not sell in large enough numbers to save the old-established concern.

SYLPHE/*France 1921–1922*
The Société d'Etude et de Realisations des Automobiles Sylphe made these little-known light cars with 6 hp four-cylinder engines in Neuilly, Seine.

1929 10hp Swift Migrant Sun or Shade Saloon

SYRENA/*Poland 1956 to date*
The Syrena is a three-cylinder two-stroke of 842cc built by Fabryka Samochodow Osobowych in Warsaw. It has changed little since its introduction.

SZAWE/*Germany 1921–1924*
Szawes were expensively-built luxury cars designed by Georg Bergmann for Szabo & Wechselmann, Berlin coachbuilders. The range included a sv 2536cc four-cylinder with an engine and chassis built for Szawe by NAG. Szawe's masterpiece was the ohc 2570cc six-cylinder with fully-enclosed valve-gear. Szawe production was limited; the last cars were made by the Ehrhardt works until production came to an end in 1924.

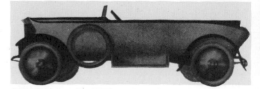
1921 Szawe ohc 2570cc six-cylinder sports tourer

TAG / *Switzerland 1978*

Shown at the 1978 Paris Salon, the TAG 'Function Car' was a Cadillac-based six-wheeler incorporating a telecommunications centre. The price was around £120,000, depending whether or not the car was bullet-proofed.

TAGA / *France 1921*

A Model T Ford-based car from Courbevoie, Seine, with Rolls-Royce-like radiator.

TAGA (La Ford Francisée) Torpédo Sport Luxe

TAINE / *France 1907–1909*

An obscure four-cylinder light car from Asnières (Seine), also sold as 'La Joyeuse'.

TAKURI / *Japan 1907–1909*

Japan's first production petrol car, the Takura was built in Tokyo to the design of Komanosuke Uchiyama. About a dozen of these 1875cc flat-twins were built.

TALBOT (TALBOT-LAGO)

France 1920–1959, 1979 to date

Known as Darracq to 1920, Talbot of Suresnes, Seine, was acquired that year by the British Sunbeam-Talbot combine. For some years cars were made on both sides of the Channel under the joint names of Talbot Darracq: this led to some confusion, for they were sold from France as Talbot and from England as Darracq. The same confusion happened with the firm's racing cars. The first models to leave the Suresnes factory after the merger were the 18/20, the four-cylinder ohv 10 cv (1505cc) and 12/14 cv (2950cc) as well as the 4594cc V-8, discontinued in 1923. The four-cylinder models were built until 1926. In 1927 came the excellent six-cylinder Talbots, available in three versions—

TALBOT

England 1903–1938, 1979 to date

The origins of the Talbot go back to 1903, when a syndicate, financed by the Earl of Shrewsbury and Talbot, was formed to build French Cléments for the English market. They were initially known as Clement-Talbots, though the French connection was gradually dropped and the Talbot slowly emerged as a marque in its own right. As befitted the times, a variety of models was offered, from an 11 hp twin to a mighty 50 hp four-cylinder. The year 1906 saw the first of the truly British Talbots, a 3·8-litre 20 hp car. This and the 12/16 were fairly fleet of foot and established a competitive reputation for themselves. By 1914 the range included a six-cylinder model and a 4½-litre 25 hp car, later known as the 25/50. Although the company became enmeshed in the Sunbeam-Talbot-Darracq combine after World War One, Georges Roesch, an outstanding Swiss engineer who had joined Talbot in 1916, was responsible for the 10/23 of 1923 which complemented some of the models of the pre-war range. Roesch's next car was the pushrod ohv 1666cc 14/45, a refined and well-engineered six with significantly light valve gear, offered alongside the older 20/60 model in 1927 and 1928, though it was the company's sole model for the following two years. From this sprang the 75 and 90 variants for 1931, while the following year the 3-litre 105 with new six-cylinder engine appeared, remaining in production until 1937. The ultimate development of this theme came with the 110 of 1935, having a larger bore than the 105, giving 3½ litres. These fast, quiet and reliable cars lent themselves naturally to sporting activities, 3rd and 4th places being attained at the Le Mans 24 Hour race in 1930, with class wins at the Irish Grand Prix, the Ulster Tourist Trophy race and the Brooklands 500 Mile event. The 105 similarly lent itself to the racing circuits, chalking up a 3rd place at Le Mans in 1932. Unfortunately, at the end of 1932, the factory association with the Tolworth concern of Fox and Nicholl (who prepared these splendid machines for the circuits) came to an end, though this did not prevent a team of 105s from attaining a joint win (with the Adler team) in the 1934 Alpine Rally, an event they had also won in 1932. Tragically, in 1935 the Rootes Group took control of Clement-Talbot. A concern with a background of sales, rather than engineering, was hardly likely to look sympathetically on Roesch and his intelligently created cars, and in 1936 a Rootes Talbot Ten, with Hillman Minx ancestry, appeared. In 1938 the marque was re-named Sunbeam-Talbot. In 1979 Peugeot-Citroën announced it would use the Talbot name on all its European products.

1913 25hp Talbot (London) sports two-seater

1914 publicity for the London-built Talbot

1919 Talbot 25/50hp limousine-landaulette

1930 Talbot (London) six-cylinder 75 saloon

2687cc, 2915cc and the 3027cc sport model. In 1930 Talbot presented a straight-eight of 3800cc, of which very few were made. In 1935, the old French factory saw the arrival of the brilliant engineer Anthony Lago, who modified the six to create the Talbot-Lago Special engine of 4000cc. After the war Talbot-Lago had a great racing history with the wonderful 4483cc ohv six-cylinders. Their 'Record' models sold very well. In 1955 Talbot-Lago presented a 2500cc coupé with Maserati engine, and a 'Baby' 2·7-litre. BMW 2·6-litre engines were then used, and the last of the line had Simca power. In 1979 the Talbot name was resurrected by Peugeot-Citroën but used with the Simca name for the French market.

TAM / France 1914–1926
The Société des Travaux Automobiles et Mécaniques started in Boulogne, Seine, with a 12 hp 1874cc car. In 1920 they presented 8/10 hp Altos-engined 1328cc cars and 12 hp Decolange-engined cars of 2001cc.

TAMM / Germany 1922
A friction-driven light car with an air-cooled 678cc vee-twin motorcycle engine.

TAMPLIN / England 1919–1927
Captain Carden, who had also been responsible for the Carden of pre-war days, also created the Tamplin, which used a JAP vee-twin engine, drive being by chain and belt. Independent front suspension was a progressive feature although tandem seating, à la Bédelia, must have had its drawbacks. A conventional two-seater layout

came in 1922; later examples were fitted with Blackburne engines.

TANKETTE / England 1920
The Tankette was a strange device, a diminutive three-wheeler driven by a 2¼ hp single-cylinder two-stroke Union engine.

TARKINGTON / USA 1923
Reputedly designed by the brother of American novelist Booth Tarkington (as was the abortive Canadian Brock automobile), this was a relatively expensive car which never reached the market. Featuring a 126-inch wheelbase and a six-cylinder engine of its own make, the first pilot models were built in 1923, although the company had been organized three years earlier.

A Tamplin cyclecar taking part in a 1922 trial

c. 1904 Tarrant tonneau

TARRANT / Australia 1897–1907
Colonel Harley Tarrant made the first serious attempt to produce petrol-driven cars for general sale in Australia. His first model had a 6 hp Benz engine, but the later cars were fitted with locally made two- and four-cylinder units. Despite success in local motor sport, Tarrant cars failed to sell well, as the limited production made them very expensive. It is doubtful if Tarrant sold more than 16 cars. Two survive.

TATE / Canada 1912–1914
The Windsor-built 'aristocrat of electrics' used Tate's powerful 'Bifunctional' batteries: a full range, from roadsters to coupés, was offered.

TATIN / France 1898–1899
A steam-driven tricycle of simple design was Tatin's first offering, followed by a gawky tiller-steered, three-wheeled steam carriage, built by the Société Européenne d'Automobile of Paris.

TATRA / Czechoslovakia 1923 to date
Tatra succeeded Nesselsdorfer in 1923 and designer Hans Ledwinka revolutionized existing design principles by creating a frameless car with a large diameter backbone tube, in place of a conventional chassis. The air-cooled engine was a 1056cc flat-twin, mounted transversely above the front axle. This Tatra 11 was succeeded by the improved model 12, which was built until 1930. They were very sturdy cars, and were also successful in races. A water-cooled 2-litre six appeared in 1926. The 1·72-litre Type 30 flat-four superseded the two-cylinder versions in 1930. It, too, was air-cooled and had the engine transversely mounted. The water-cooled 2·3-litre Type 31 followed the earlier 2-litre six-cylinder in 1927, while the 1160cc Type 57 of the early 1930s was a new small air-cooled four-cylinder: the 1690cc Type 75 was similar in layout. In the early 1930s two water-cooled ohv luxury models appeared, one with a 3850cc six-cylinder engine, the other a

5990cc V-12. Few of these expensive models were built. In 1934, designer Hans Ledwinka, never short of unorthodox ideas, created another interesting car, the Tatra 77. It had an air-cooled V-8 engine of 2970cc mounted in the rear. The body was aerodynamic, with a central box-type frame. Only air-cooled cars were being made by Tatra when the war broke out. These were all four-cylinder models, the 52 (1910cc), the 57 (1260cc) and the 97 (1760cc), the latter being rear-engined, the others having flat-four engines in front. The rear-engined 2960cc model 87 was the successor to the Tatra 77. All now had ohv engines, except the model 52. After the war, Tatra first produced improved versions of the rear-engined cars with 2472cc V-8 engines, but concentrated more and more on big lorries. From 1949–51 they built successful sports cars and racing monoposti with rear air-cooled engines which, driven by Veřmirovsky, Soyka and Pavlíček, proved successful. From 1955 different versions of

the rear-engined Tatra 603 appeared, followed by the improved 613; most of these cars were supplied only to Governments in Eastern Europe. Production is now on a small scale. The present 613 has a dohc V-8 engine of 3495cc, mounted above the rear axle and giving 165 bhp at 5200 rpm. It can attain 120 mph.

Tatra 613

TAUNTON/*Belgium 1914–1922*
Backed by British capital, this Liège company does not seem to have started production until 1921, when an 1800cc four-cylinder was introduced.

TAUNUS/*Germany 1907–1909*
Ex-Adler employees founded this small company to manufacture a small 12 hp car with a twin-cylinder engine.

TAURINIA/*Italy 1902–c1908*
Named after the ancient tribe who founded Torino, this factory offered a 12 hp and a 14/20 hp, both four-cylinders.

TAUZIN/*France 1898*
A twin-cylinder voiturette with direct drive on all three speeds, by triple crown-wheels and pinions controlled by levers on the steering column.

1898 Tauzin twin-cylinder

TAYLOR, GUE/*England 1904*
A three-wheeled chassis sold complete, apart from the power unit, which was left to the buyer's discretion. This company later made Veloce motorcycles (the origin of Velocette).

TAYLOR/*England 1923–1924*
Built by Taylor Motors of Newcastle upon Tyne, the Taylor was an assembled car fitted with a 14 hp Meadows engine and gearbox.

1920 TB three-wheeled cyclecar

TB/*England 1920–1924*
One of the more attractive three-wheelers, the TB (Thomson Brothers) had an air-cooled 980cc twin-cylinder engine and Bugatti-style dummy radiator.

TECO/*Germany 1924–1925*
A motorcycle producer at Stettin (now Poland), which also built an ohv Selve-engined 1501cc four-cylinder car of sporting appearance and advanced design.

1911 10/12cv Terrot 1593cc four-cylinder bodied by Py-Laroche of Dijon (M. Py-Laroche seated at the rear)

TEMPERINO/*Italy 1919–1925*
The Temperino was a small car with a rotund body and a sv vee-twin 746cc engine, which was later superseded by an ohv 1096cc version. Production was on a small scale.

TEMPLAR/*USA 1918–1925*
Billed as the 'Superfine Small Car', the Cleveland-built Templar was a four-cylinder ohv sports model capable of some 45 mph. Its price of $2685 included a gradient meter, compass . . . and a 1-A Junior Autographic Kodak camera.

TEMPLE-CROWSLEY/*England 1906–1907*
A tricar built in London with wheel-steering. bucket seats and 5 hp Peugeot engine.

TEMPLE-WESTCOTT/*USA 1921–1922*
Virtually nothing has been discovered about this elusive make, other than the fact that a six-cylinder engine was used and an estimated 10 to 20 cars were built. The car is frequently erroneously listed as 'Temple-Woodgate'.

TEMPO/*Germany 1933–1935*
Tempo, after building commercial three-wheelers for many years, introduced a small car, the Pony, with a 198cc Ilo two-stroke engine in the 1930s. There was also the Tempo-Front T 6 and a Combi, which could be used as a delivery van as well as a private car. There were 596cc twin-cylinder versions as well, but few were built or sold.

TENTING/*France 1896–1899*
M. Tenting was an early protagonist of the infinitely variable friction drive. His opposed twin-cylinder engine used a primitive form of fuel injection.

TERRAPLANE/*USA 1932–1937*
This 2·6-litre sv six replaced the Essex; it was joined in 1933 by a straight-eight of 4 litres, which was the basis for the original Railtons. A swept-back grille and ifs characterized the 1934 models, which had the 3·5-litre Hudson six (export models retained the 2·6-litre engine). Hydraulic brakes were added in 1936.

TERROT/*France 1912–1914*
Better known as cycle and motorcycle builders, Terrot of Dijon also built 10 hp light cars with 1460cc four-cylinder monobloc engines.

T ET M/*France 1920–1922*
Pushbike makers Tremblay et Malençon made some single-cylinder 500cc cyclecars with belt drive.

TEXAN/*USA 1918–1922*
The Texan was as assembled a car as one could imagine, even the prototype being an Elcar with a new emblem. Texans featured Lycoming four-cylinder engines and were built as open models only, the five-passenger touring car selling for $1495. Although standard components were featured, oversize tyres were provided, ostensibly to make the car suitable for service in the Texas oil fields. An estimated 2000 cars and 1000 trucks were manufactured.

TEXMOBILE/*USA 1920–1922*
Centred in Dallas, Texas, where it was built by Little Motors Kar Co., the Texmobile was also billed as the 'Little Kar'. With a wheelbase of 102 inches, the four-cylinder Texmobile sold in touring car form for $750. Very few were marketed.

TH/*Spain 1915–1922*
Talleres Hereter of Barcelona, founded in 1905 to make spares and accessories for motor cars, began building light cars to the designs of the brothers Claudio and Carlos Baradat in 1915, initially under the name 'Ideal'. In 1918 an improved design, the 15 cv 'TH', with a four-cylinder 2121cc monobloc engine in unit with its gearbox, appeared. The company also built aero and marine power units.

THAMES/*England 1906–1911*
The Thames Ironworks, Shipbuilding and Engineering Company of Greenwich built commercials before launching a 45 hp six and a 40/45 hp four at the 1906 Olympia Show. Few cars seem to have been built until 1908, when a worm-drive twin of 1961cc and a tour of 3922cc were offered alongside sixes of 6981cc, 7778cc,

9653cc and a monstrous 80 hp of 12,931cc. By the end of 1910 (after an apparent pause in production in 1909) more modest cars—an 8 hp single of 1296cc and a 15 hp four of 2413cc—were the staple offerings. The 15 hp was available with four-wheel brakes.

THEOPHILE SCHNEIDER/*France 1910-1931*
Leaving Rochet-Schneider, Théophile Schneider formed Automobiles Théophile Schneider in Besançon, Doubs, in 1910. He made four-cylinders of 12 cv (1693cc), 18 cv (3685cc) and 25 cv (5195cc) as well as a six-cylinder 15 cv of 3180cc. For a long time, Théophile Schneiders remained old-fashioned, with the radiator behind the engine '*à la* Renault'. In 1912, a new model, the 14/16 cv of 2993cc, was added, and all these cars were made until the war. When the factory resumed production post-war, it was still building these pre-war models but with the radiator at the front. Most of the post-war production was based on the 14/16 cv, of which a six-cylinder version, the 4489cc 20 cv, was also built. In 1926 came a smaller car, the 7 cv with a 1172cc engine. This was the last new model to be made by this firm, which also built lorries.

THIEULIN/*France 1907–1908*
A light four-cylinder from Besançon (Doubs). Seven were built: one survives.

THOLOME/*France 1920–1922*
A cyclecar made in St. Ouen, Seine, by M. Tholomé, with a wooden chassis and 902cc Ruby engine. Tholomé moved to Levallois, Seine, and later fitted a 1093cc Ruby engine. A cheaper version with a vee-twin Train engine of 748cc was also available.

THOMAS/*USA 1902–c1919*
Edwin Ross Thomas bought the moribund Globe Cycle Company of Buffalo, New York, in 1900, producing his first cars, light single- and twin-cylinders, in 1902. A crocodile-bonneted 24 hp three-cylinder appeared in 1903, acquiring a conventional bonnet and the name Thomas-Flyer the next year. The 1905 range

1913 5501cc Théophile Schneider Type Sport

consisted of fours of 40 hp and 50 hp and a 60 hp six: the following year the Thomas-Flyer range was on European lines, reputedly a carbon copy of the contemporary Richard-Brasier. In 1907, a total of 700 cars and 400 taxicabs were built: a 1907 Thomas-Flyer 60 hp four won the 20,000-mile New York-Paris race in 1908. Sales peaked at 1908 cars in 1909, but the poor reliability record of the company's first shaft-drive model, the Model L Flyabout, caused a sales downturn to 913 in 1910, in which year E. R. Thomas (who had never learned to drive) sold the company to a New York banking company. Even so it went into receivership in August 1912, and its assets were auctioned off in 1913. Theoretically, Thomas-Flyers were available to special order until 1919.

THOMAS/*England 1903*
A weird two-seater three-wheeler on cycle lines, with a single-cylinder engine slung between the front wheels.

THOMAS/*USA 1906–1908*
A joint venture by employees of Olds and the E. R. Thomas Company of Buffalo, the Thomas-Detroit was a shaft-driven 40 hp four designed by Howard Coffin and available as a runabout or touring car. It was succeeded by the Chalmers-Detroit.

THOMOND/*Ireland 1925–1926*
Only prototypes of this ohv 1750cc four-cylinder from Dublin were built.

THOMPSON/*USA 1901–1902*
An electric runabout from Plainfield, NJ.

1898 Thomson (Australia)

THOMSON/*Australia 1896–1905*
Herbert Thomson built one of Australia's first cars, a lightweight 5 hp steamer. Work commenced in 1896; two years later the car was being driven extensively, with Thomson undertaking the longest car journeys of the day. He took orders for 150 cars but delivered only 12. One is known to survive. The four-wheeled phaeton seated six people. Its frame was built mainly of timber, with large-diameter wheels fitted with Dunlop pneumatic tyres. Steering was by side-lever. The vertical compound engine had tandem cylinders and ran at speeds up to 1000 rpm.

THOMSON/*USA 1898–1902*
Professor Elihu Thomson devised a four-cylinder steam carriage with a hydraulic steering lock incorporated in the tiller.

THOMSON/*France 1913–1928*
Thomas of Bordeaux assembled these cars from bought-in components. They had a distinctive vee-shaped radiator.

THOR/*England 1904–c1906*
The Simms-engined 6/8 hp Thor, built in Leicester, had a special cross-spring suspension, 'rendering pneumatic tyres, with all their troubles, unnecessary'.

The 1907 Thomas-Flyer which won the 1908 New York-Paris Race

1919 Thor landaulette

THOR/*England 1906–1923*
Simpson Taylor, of Buckingham Palace Road, London, claimed to have built cars from 1906, fitting American engines from 1913. In 1920 they stated that they were building three 2255cc four-cylinder cars a week.

THORN ET HOGAN/*France 1901–1902*
This Anglo-French concern offered cars on Panhard lines: a 12 hp started in the Paris-Berlin race of 1901.

THORNYCROFT/*England 1903–1913*
Thornycroft, builders of steam launches and lorries, entered the private car market in 1903 with petrol models of 1814cc (twin-cylinder) and 3626cc (four), the larger model having a dynamo fitted. The 1905 range was of more modern appearance, and new models of 18 hp and 30 hp (four-cylinder) and a 45 hp six were announced in 1907. The six was discontinued by 1911, and in 1912–13 only the 18 hp was available.

THRIGE/*Denmark 1909–1918*
Thomas B. Thrige AS, of Odense, built the first petrol-engined Thrige car in 1910, but an electric lorry had been built in 1909. In 1911 production started with cars using Ballot or Daimler sleeve-valve engines. Fifty cars of a very light type (so they could be used on the minor roads in Denmark, where cars over 450 kg (990 lb) were forbidden) were built, with four-cylinder 4/12 hp Ballot engines. The gearbox had three speeds, but there was no differential. Most parts came from France, including frame, axles, engine and steering. Other models in 1914 were the 8/22 hp, also with a four-cylinder Ballot engine, and the 13/35 with a four-cylinder Daimler Knight engine. Main production was lorries, taxis and buses.

THRUPP & MABERLY/*England 1896*
Another famous carriage builder who produced electric vehicles. An electric Victoria was built for the Queen of Spain to the design of a Spanish engineer named Julien.

THULIN/*Sweden 1920–1928*
After World War One, Thulinverken (of Landskrona) felt that the future for their aeroplanes and aeroplane engines might not be too good, and decided to start building cars. They bought the licence rights for the German AGA car – but AGA had bought *their* licence rights from FN in Belgium. The engine was a water-cooled four-cylinder of 20 hp. The radiator was sharply

pointed in the German fashion, and the body was also in typically German style. All parts were made in Sweden, except carburettor, instruments, tyres and electrical system. There were plans for 1000 cars, but only 300 were built before production stopped in 1924. A few years later, the Weiertz brothers (see Self) were engaged to produce an entirely new and advanced car, the low-built Type B. The engine was an ohv 1·7-litre four-cylinder unit, and the car had four-wheel brakes. In 1927, a few pilot cars were built. Unfortunately, American cars were cheap in Sweden at that time and Volvo had just started production, so the promising Type B was killed in its infancy. Around 10 cars were built, one presumably with a six-cylinder Hupmobile engine.

THURLOW/*England 1920–1921*
The Thurlow three-wheeler was built in Wimbledon, London, and used a 10 hp vee-twin Precision engine and three-speed Sturmey Archer gearbox.

TICI/*England 1972*
Stylist William Towns's idea of the city car, the diminutive Tici had its track equal to the wheelbase. The car was powered by a rear-mounted Mini engine.

1907 Thornycroft 45hp tourer

TIDAHOLM/*Sweden 1906–1913*
Lorries were built by Tidaholms Bruks AB from 1903, and a few of these were apparently converted to some very crude kind of passenger car. Three or four ordinary passenger cars were built, probably in 1911–12. One was exported to St. Petersburg in Russia. Tidaholm then concentrated on lorries and buses until 1933 when production ceased.

LE TIGRE/*France 1920*
Made in Asnières, Seine, Tigres were 10/12 hp Altos-engined cars of 1327cc.

TIMEIRE/*Ireland 1970*
Tim Conroy's Mini Special never reached its scheduled production. With an aluminium alloy fastback body, the prototype spent much of its time in competition before being pensioned off in 1973.

TINCHER/*USA 1903–1909*
Big, powerful cars (up to 90 hp, six-cylinder) initially from Chicago, latterly from South Bend, Indiana.

TINY/*England 1913–1915*
A substantially made cyclecar with an 8 hp vee-

twin JAP engine, tubular chassis and shaft drive, the 'torpedo'-bodied Tiny was built in Esholt, Yorkshire, by Nanson, Barker & Company, who later produced the Airedale.

TISSANDIER/*France 1896*
A two-seater car which ran in the 1896 Paris-Marseille Race.

TJORVEN/*Sweden 1969*
In 1964 Kalmar Verkstad and the Swedish Post Office started planning together for a small vehicle suited to local post distribution. The result was a small DAF-engined van with a sliding door on the driver's side. Production began in 1967: 1000 were ordered, using DAF 44 parts and glass-fibre bodies. In 1969 the 'Tjorven' (a name derived from a popular children's book) was presented. It was supposed to be a combination of passenger car and van, and had removable seats. The engine was a Renault R8, and most parts came from the DAF 55. Due to a financial crisis, no cars were produced.

TOKYO/*Japan 1911–1912*
A 3656cc four-cylinder model built in conjunction with Kunisue, Tokyo, in a small series.

TOLEDO/*USA 1900–1904*
A steam carriage powered by a vertical-twin engine with generally robust construction, built by one of Colonel Pope's companies.

TOLOSA/*France 1919–1927*
Made in Toulouse, Tolosas were assembled from US Army surplus Model T Ford parts.

TOM POUCE/*France 1920–1924*
MM. Blanc and Guillon started to make cyclecars in Puteaux, Seine, after the war with twin-cylinder two-stroke SICAM engines of 731cc and four-cylinder 1093cc Ruby and 1592cc Ballot power units. The marque moved to Dommartin, Somme, in 1923 with a new owner, M. Ernault, who built the last Tom Pouces with 723cc Lemaitre & Gerard engines.

TONY/*France 1920–1921*
Tony Bouley, maker of sidecars in Paris, built some cyclecars with various motorcycle and proprietary engines.

TONY HUBER/*France 1902–1906*
From Billancourt, Seine, the Tony Huber Company sold engines as well as complete cars. In 1906 they listed an 8 hp two-cylinder, a 16 hp four and a 25 hp four with copper water jackets.

TORBENSON/*USA 1902–1908*
In 1906 this Bloomfield, NJ, company was offering air-cooled three- and six-cylinder cars of 14 hp and 28 hp.

TORNADO/*England 1957–1963*
The ugly Typhoon, some 400 of which were sold, was replaced by the short-lived Tempest which in turn was superseded by the Talisman, without doubt Tornado's most important model. Now collectors' items, nearly 200 of these Ford-powered glass-fibre-bodied four-seaters were made.

1935 Tornax Sportwagen

TORNAX/*Germany 1934–1937*
Built by a well-known motorcycle factory at Wuppertal-Langerfeld, the Karpe-designed Tornax was one of the better little German sports cars. It had fwd and was powered by a mildly tuned 684cc DKW Meisterklasse twin-cylinder two-stroke engine.

TORO/*Philippines 1974 to date*
A 1300cc VW engine powers this sporty 2+2 coupé from Manilla.

TORPEDO/*England 1909*
Cycle maker F. Hopper of Barton-on-Humber offered this range—the 6 hp single and 10 hp twins were based on the contemporary Starling, and there was also a 10 hp four—for one year only.

TORPILLE/*France 1913–1924*
Made in Saumur, the first Torpilles were 1328cc Altos-engined cars. After the war production was resumed, along with new 1592cc Ballot-engined and 1693cc SCAP-engined models.

TOURAINE/*USA 1912–1915*
Forerunner of the Vim Motor Truck Company, Touraine followed a one-model policy with a T-head engine of 4343cc and two-, five- and seven-seat touring coachwork.

TOURAND/*France 1900–1908*
Originally built with a 6 hp twin-cylinder engine, the Tourand was produced spasmodically. The Suresnes, Seine, factory offered cars of up to 80 hp. The first Tourands had 6 hp twin-cylinder Crozet engines.

TOUREY/*France 1898*
Jules Tourey's 4 hp 'Petit Duc' was built very much on Benz lines.

TOURIST/*USA 1902–1909*
Built in Los Angeles, the Tourist Range consisted of friction-drive twins and fours with conventional gearboxes.

TOWARD & PHILIPSON/*England 1897*
A coke-fired six-seater steam wagonette with a three-stage tubular boiler.

TOYOTA/*Japan 1935 to date*
The Toyota Loom Company built their first car, the Chrysler Airflow-like A-1 45 hp six, in May 1935. Developments of this, available in tourer and sedan variants, were offered up to the war. The first post-war model, the 27 bhp SA two-door Toyopet sedan, appeared in 1947. In 1954 came the 1453cc ohv Crown, and in 1957 the Corona 1000cc was introduced, succeeded in 1965 by the New Corona two-door hardtop,

designed to fill a gap in the US market. In 1959 Toyota opened their Motomachi plant, producing Crown and Corona models, and in 1961 came the 700cc Publica: the next year Toyota built their millionth vehicle and began exporting to Europe. The two millionth vehicle came in 1965. In 1967, the Century model appeared, the Corona gained 1·5- and 1·6-litre engines, and the Crown acquired six-cylinder and V-8 power units. The Corona MkII was launched in 1968, and in 1969 the Corolla model became the first Toyota to reach a million units. Celica and Carina models were launched from the new Tsutsumi plant in December 1970, while two new Toyotas, the Starlet and a redesigned Corona, appeared in 1973. The 1979 range included the 993cc and 1166cc Starlet, the 1588cc Carina saloon and estate, the Celica, available in 1588cc and 1968cc models, and the 1968cc Cressida; the biggest Toyota was the 2563cc Crown luxury model.

1979 Toyota Corona

TRABANT/*Germany (East) 1958 to date*
A product of the nationalized East German car industry, all Trabants have front-wheel drive and two-stroke twin-cylinder in-line engines. Introduced with 499cc engines from 1963, they have used 594cc power-units. They are air-cooled, have a rotary inlet-valve and are built at Zwickau in Saxony. Bodywork is in resin-reinforced papier maché!

1961 Trabant saloon

TRACFORD/*France 1934–1936*
Made in Gennevilliers, Seine, this was an attempt by Louis Carle, a Ford-France director, to convert the Model Y Ford into a fwd model.

1935 8hp Tracford fwd saloon

1932 Tracta 3-litre saloon

TRACTA/*France 1926–1934*
Pioneer of front-wheel drive, engineer J. A. Grégoire made some excellent sports and touring cars in Asnières, Seine. He used such proprietary engines as the SCAP 1100cc and 1600cc (sometimes supercharged) and a 2·7-litre Continental; later a 3000cc Hotchkiss engine was used. Grégoire often raced the Tractas in endurance events.

TRACTION AERIENNE/*France 1921–c1926*
Another propeller-driven car like the Layat, this Neuilly, Seine, marque offered a saloon steered by the front wheels. It was also sold as the Eolia.

TRACTOBILE/*USA 1900–1902*
A steam *avant-train* attachment for horse-carriages, with a 'Battery of Patent Unit Boilers' and small two-cylinder engines acting on each front wheel. It was a venture apparently promoted by the egregious Mr. Pennington.

TRAEGER/*Germany 1922–1923*
Small producer of a 980cc four-cylinder 18 hp car, of which only a few reached the market.

TRAIN/*France 1924*
Famous maker of proprietary engines for the motorcycle and automobile industry, the Train factory of Courbevoie, Seine, made 350cc single-cylinder cyclecars, with friction transmission.

TRAVAUX MECANIQUES ET AUTOMOBILES/*France 1912*
Worm-drive monobloc 10/12 hp and 14 hp models from Courbevoie, Seine.

TRAVELER/*USA 1914–1915*
There were two models of this Detroit marque—a 3622cc four and a 5670cc six.

TRESKOW/*Germany 1905–1908*
A small car with a 1020cc twin-cylinder engine.

TRIBELHORN/*Switzerland 1899–1919*
Production of Tribelhorn electrics began in earnest in 1902. Three- and four-wheeled cars were offered. After 1919 only light utility vans were built.

TRIBET/*France 1909–1914*
The first cars built by Tribet, of Villeneuve-la-Garenne (Seine), were an 8/10 hp and a 12/16 hp: at Olympia in 1910 a 12 hp Cabriolette of 1539cc, selling for £325, was shown.

1965 TVR Trident

TRIBUNE/*USA 1913–1914*
An open tourer powered by a 4-litre Buda engine.

TRIDENT/*England/France 1919–1920*
A fwd tandem-seated three-wheeler of odd design, with the 8 hp engine on one side of the single front wheel. Prototypes were built in France, but production was planned to take place in England (though it probably never got under way).

TRIDENT/*England 1966–1978*
Once a TVR prototype based on the Healey 3000 chassis, the Trident was another of Fiore's striking designs. Available with 4·7-litre V-8, Ford V-6 and Triumph 2·5-litre engines, during its life the Trident notched up over 200 sales, some 50 per cent of which went abroad.

TRIOULEYRE/*France 1896–1898*
A horizontal-engined car on Benz lines. Two Triouleyres started in the 1896 Paris-Marseille.

TRIPPEL/*Germany 1934–1965*
During the war Hanns Trippel built amphibious cars in the occupied Bugatti works at Molsheim. These cars were similar to those he had produced in pre-war days with Adler and Opel engines at his small Homburg/Saar workshops. His post-war amphibians had 1147cc Triumph Herald four-cylinder engines. Trippel also designed the Amphicar.

TRITON/*England 1963*
A Surrey businessman planned to produce the Triton in quantity. As it turned out, the original David Johnson-Webb road-racer remains unique. Its round-tube space-frame chassis was topped by a two-seater body and powered by the evergreen BMC 'B' Series engine.

TRIUMPH/*USA 1906–c1910*
'The self-starting car — you merely push a lever and the motor responds', the Chicago-built Triumph sold for $2250–$2500.

TRIUMPH/*England 1923 to date*
Although Triumph had been making motorcycles since 1903, they did not build their first car until 1923, this being the 10/20, a 1·4-litre model. Two years later it was replaced by the 1900cc 13/30 (best remembered for being fitted with Lockheed external contracting hydraulic brakes). The year 1928 saw the appearance of the 832cc Super Seven, while 1931 marked the arrival of the Scorpion, powered by a fashionably small six-cylinder engine of 1·2 litres. A Coventry-Climax overhead inlet/side exhaust engine was featured in the Super Nine of 1932, joined the following year by the Ten. The sporting front was not neglected, and in 1934 came the Gloria, available with either 1100cc four-cylinder, or 1500cc six-cylinder engines, again by Coventry-Climax. A fabulous extravagance was the supercharged dohc 2-litre Dolomite, an unashamed copy of a contemporary Alfa Romeo: it found few buyers. By 1937 Triumph-made ohv engines were supplementing the Coventry-Climax units, the range by this time embracing the 1½-litre Gloria and four- and six-cylinder versions of the Dolomite, the name of the twin-cam eight thus being perpetuated. But financial solvency had been a constant problem, and the company was placed under receivership in 1939: it was not until 1945 that Triumph was snapped up by Sir John Black's Standard Motor Company. For Triumph's first post-war model, an 1800cc ohv engine made for the 1½-litre Jaguar was fitted to the razor-edge 1800 saloon and Roadster, the latter being the last series-production car to be fitted with a dickey seat. However, it was not long before a new engine appeared, this being Standard's wet-liner four, fitted to the range from 1949. In 2·1-litre form it powered the TR2 sports car

of 1953, the first model of a long and distinguished line. It was used in all the TR variants until the TR5 of 1967, being replaced by a 2·5-litre six. By contrast, saloon car production did not get into its stride until the 948cc Herald of 1959, the razor-edge Renown (the renamed 1800 saloon) having been phased out in 1955. In 1962 a six-cylinder version of the Herald, the Vitesse, was announced, while the Spitfire sports two-seater was another derivative. The sporting theme was further perpetuated by the 2-litre GT6 of 1967. Standard-Triumph had been taken over by Leyland

1936 Triumph Gloria Southern Cross Sports

Triumph Herald saloon

Motors in 1961, resulting in a rapid expansion of the range: the 2000 saloon came in 1964 followed by a 2·5 PI derivative, and the front-wheel-drive 1300 in 1966, while sporting laurels were upheld by the TR6 of 1969, replaced by the wedge-shaped TR7 of 1976. The 3-litre Stag of 1970 lasted until 1977, while the Dolomite of 1972 and the ohc 2-litre Dolomite Sprint offered sports car performance in the guise of a family saloon. In 1979 a convertible version of the TR7 was launched, and negotiations were begun whereby BL planned to build the Honda Accord as a 'Triumph' (see Honda).

1978 Triumph TR7

TROIKA/*France 1897–c1901*
Daniel Augé's Troïka voiturette had a 7hp twin-cylinder horizontal Cyclope engine with hot-tube ignition, and was 'remarkable for the power and simplicity of its mechanism'. A more conventional car was subsequently marketed under the Augé or Cyclope names.

TROJAN/*England 1922–1936, 1961–1965*
The Trojan was an ingenious utility car designed by Leslie Hounsfield. It was powered by a 1½-litre horizontal two-stroke twin-cylinder engine, while transmission was by two-speed epicyclic gearbox and double chains to a solid rear axle. A punt-type chassis was used, and long cantilever springs were fitted. Solid tyres were another unusual feature for the day. Although originally built by Leyland, the manufacture was taken over by Trojan Ltd. in 1928. An outcome of this change of manufacture resulted in the new RE model, which retained the same clever engine and transmission layout, but mounted at the rear of the car. Production was reduced to a trickle in the 1930s, though commercial versions of the design continued to sell well. The Mastra was announced for the 1936 season, with a 2·2-litre six-cylinder two-stroke engine: it did not go into production. Passenger cars did not feature again until 1962, when the company manufactured the Heinkel 'bubble car' under licence, after production had ceased in Germany.

1926 Trojan tourer

TROLL/*Norway 1956*
Although Troll Plastik & Bilindustri, of Lunde, planned a first series of 15 small cars with glass-fibre two-seater coupé bodies, only five were built. Twin-cylinder two-stroke engines and drive line were bought from the German Gutbrod company.

TUAR/*France 1914–1925*
M. Morin of Thouars, Deux-Sèvres, made cars using such proprietary engines as CIME, Fivet, Chapuis-Dornier, and Ruby.

Chassis of the 1907 Truffault voiturette

TRUFFAULT/*France 1907–1908*
A belt-driven single-cylinder voiturette with combined chassis/body frame and weird coil-spring suspension, built in Paris.

TRUMBULL/*USA 1913–1915*
This was a friction-drive four-cylinder light car, built by the American Cyclecar Company of Bridgeport, Connecticut.

TRUNER/*England 1913*
A vee-twin JAP engine powered this chain-driven cyclecar.

TUCKER/*USA 1946–1948*
Preston Tucker's 122mph dream car, designed with the aid of Alex Tremulis, was truly ahead of its time. It was powered by a rear-mounted Franklin flat-six helicopter engine converted to sealed-system water-cooling and had many safety features — all-round disc brakes, pop-out windscreen and padded dash. Suspension was independent all-round, and transmission was normally four-speed manual with preselector or electric shift, though some cars had 'Tucker-matic' transmissions with only 30 basic parts. Tucker had produced 51 cars in a former Dodge aircraft plant in Chicago before he was taken to court by the Securities Exchange Commission on allegations of stock fraud. Though he was exonerated in 1950, it was too late to resurrect the Tucker car, and Preston Tucker died in 1956 while negotiating to build a small car in Brazil. Of the 51 Tuckers built, 49 still survive.

TUDHOPE/*Canada 1906–1913*
Originally a high-wheeler, based on the McIntyre from Indianapolis: after a 1909 fire destroyed the firm's Orillia, Ontario, factory, a new start was made with an EMF-based four-cylinder. New four- and six-cylinder models appeared in 1912 — but the company failed a year later. Reorganized, it built a similar design under the name 'Fisher' until war work halted car production in 1914.

TULSA/*USA 1917–1923*
One of the few cars to be built in Oklahoma, the Tulsa was a strictly assembled product using Herschell-Spillman four- and six-cylinder engines. Only open cars were made: advertising emphasised the ruggedness of the cars and their suitability for working in the vicinity of Oklahoma oil wells.

TURBO/*Switzerland 1921*
With a five-cylinder radial engine of 1546cc and a triangulated girder chassis, the Turbo, from Zurich-Oerlikon, was a short-lived venture.

TURBO/*Germany 1923–1924*
S. W. Müller had little luck with his advanced five-cylinder radial-engined Turbo cars, with ohv 1546cc and 1980cc engines. After he failed at Oerlikon in Switzerland, he fared no better in Stuttgart, Germany. The Turbo had a tubular frame with coil-spring suspension, but was never fully developed. A 1980cc racing version had a special 75 bhp engine.

1949 Tucker sedan

1924 Turcat-Méry 15cv

TURCAT-MERY/*France 1896–1928*
Automobiles Turcat-Méry of Marseille made their first cars in 1896, using Panhard and Daimler engines until 1901, when their designs were taken up by De Diétrich. In 1907, Turcat-Méry offered a big six-cylinder of 10,200cc. In 1908, they listed a 28 cv (6333cc), 18 cv (3053cc) and 14 cv (2412cc) among many other models. After the war they made a 3015cc 15 cv in 1922, followed in 1923 by the 2978cc 15 cv. The following year a 2993cc 15 cv was added. In 1925 Turcat-Méry presented an ohc 12 cv of 2388cc. After 1926, the firm was forced to fit proprietary engines to survive. These included the SCAP and CIME 1500cc and 1700cc and some SCAP eight-cylinders, of which very few were made.

TURGAN-FOY/*France 1899–1910*
Powered by a vertical-crank 4½ hp twin-cylinder Filtz engine, the original Turgan-Foy had four-speed belt-and-pinion drive. From 1902, conventional engines of 16 hp, 24 hp and even 60 hp were used.

TURICUM/*Switzerland 1904–c1918*
Martin Fischer's first voiturettes, built in a former skittle-alley in Zürich, were single-seaters with pedal-operated steering and friction drive, but production vehicles, from a new factory in Uster, had wheel-steering and two seats. The name 'Turicum' is the Latin form of Zürich. The first four-cylinder Turicums appeared in 1908, still with friction drive. About a thousand cars had been built when production ceased.

TURINELLI & PEZZA/*Italy 1899*
A front-wheel-drive electric carriage from Milano.

TURNER/*England 1906–1907,1911–1930*
This Wolverhampton company concentrated on the Turner-Miesse steam car until 1906, when they produced the Seymour-Turner for Seymours of London. This had a 4·1-litre four-cylinder engine and shaft drive. Steam took over again, however, and it was not until 1911 that the Turner cyclecar appeared, having an 1100cc vee-twin engine. A Ten also appeared the following year, and at the same time a 2·1-litre Fifteen was announced. The company did not get into its post-war stride until 1922,

1913 10hp four-cylinder Turner

offering 1·8-litre and 2·3-litre models, though for 1923 a 1½-litre Dorman engine was adopted. In the latter half of the 1920s only the 12 hp car was made, production ceasing in 1930.

TURNER/*England 1954–1966*
A simple ladder-frame chassis and attractive lightweight glass-fibre body were the key to the success of the early Turners. Although remembered best as competition cars, subsequent Turners continued to offer excellent performance from modest power outputs.

TVR/*England 1954 to date*
TVR have survived the car kit era, countless management upheavals and a major fire to become a respected manufacturer. The MkI lasted until 1960, followed by the MkII (1960–62) and MkIII (1960–63). Then came the Griffith 200 (1964) and 400 (1965), followed by the 200V8 (1966), Tuscan SE and Vixen 1600 (1967), Vixen S2 (1968), Tuscan V6 (1969), 1600M (1972–73), 2500 (1970–73), and 2500 M and 3000 M (1972). The Turbo appeared in 1975, the Taimar in 1976. Beautifully finished glass-fibre-bodied two-seaters, today's TVRs are elegant, fast and reliable. Ford V-6 versions are available, with or without turbocharger; the 1979 Turbo Convertible could attain 130 mph.

TWOMBLY/*USA 1910–1911*
W. Irving Twombly spent six years and $250,000 in developing a car with a flat-four engine with no connecting rods and only two double-ended pistons: engine and transmission could be exchanged inside five minutes, and the bodywork could be altered from 'completely enclosed, heated and ventilated limousine, to open car in less time than it took to open the hood of a landaulette'.

TWOMBLY/*USA 1913–1915*
An underslung tandem-seated cyclecar with a four-cylinder 15 hp water-cooled engine, built by Driggs-Seabury.

TYNE/*England 1904*
A 12 hp two-cylinder model, sold by W. Galloway & Co. of Gateshead-on-Tyne, who were British agents for the Stanley Steamer.

TYSELEY/*England 1913*
The Bowden Brake Company of Birmingham marketed this 8 hp twin-cylinder shaft-drive cyclecar, which sold for 160 guineas.

1977 TVR Turbo coupé

U

ULMANN/*Germany 1903–1904*
Berlin-based Oldsmobile importer Edmund Ulmann also produced a few De Dion-engined 12 hp cars.

ULTIMA/*France 1912–1914*
This Lavallois-Perret, Seine, manufacturer offered single- and four-cylinder voiturettes of 954cc and 2121cc, with six-speed friction drive, built under Turicum licence.

ULTRAMOBIL/*Germany 1904–1908*
A single-cylinder 1590cc runabout, produced by outside companies under Olds licence for the Deutsche Ultramobil GmbH at Berlin-Halensee.

UNDERBERG/*France 1899–1909*
Built in Nantes, Loire-Atlantique, this was a belt-driven voiturette with a single-cylinder 3hp

1899 Underberg voiturette with Gaillardet engine

Gaillardet engine until 1901, when a 6/8 hp twin and 12/16 hp and 24/80 hp fours were available. They were sometimes known as the 'Salvator'.

UNIC
France 1904–1939
When Georges Richard left the Richard-Brasier concern in 1904, he founded Unic in Puteaux, Seine, starting with a twin-cylinder engined 10 cv of 1797cc. He added another model, the 2615cc 14 cv four, the following year. The 1943cc 12 cv (later enlarged to 2120cc) was sold mainly as a taxi and survived in production for nearly 20 years. Also notable were the 1909 4085cc six-cylinder and the 1914 4523cc. After the war Unic's 'bread and butter' model was the 1847cc four, along with the 12 cv taxis. Unic also specialized in building lorries of all sizes. A 1997cc sports model was presented in 1923, and the firm also offered sleeve-valve-engined cars — but without great success. In the 1930s, Unic marketed two eight-cylinder models and an ohv 3-litre six-cylinder. Unic was eventually taken over by Simca, who wanted a commercial vehicle department: it still survives in this guise.

1905 Georges-Richard Unic 10cv tourer

1924 Unic 12hp Type L saloon

c.1905 publicity for the Unic

UNICAR/*England 1956–1959*
A glass-fibre coupé powered by rear-mounted twin-cylinder two-stroke Excelsior engines of 225cc and 328cc, the Opperman Unicar sold for under £400.

1958 Opperman Unicar 328cc twin-cylinder

UNION/*Germany 1920–1922*
A small 1151cc two-cylinder car, built by Union-Werke AG in Mannheim. After the marque's demise (it was also known as Bravo) the works were taken over by Rabag, for licence production of Bugattis.

UNION/*USA 1921*
An assembled make, the Union only reached the prototype stage. It was mounted on a 118-inch wheelbase and used a Continental six-cylinder engine and other standard components. The touring car was to have sold for $2850. Headquarters of the Union were at Eaton, Ohio.

UNIPOWER/*England 1966–1970*
Undoubtedly one of the best of the Mini-based specials, the Unipower GT featured a very strong two-seater glass-fibre body, bonded to a complex space-frame powered from the rear by any suitable Mini engine. About 75 GTs were built, over half of which were exported.

UNIQUE/*England 1915–1916*
A twin-cylinder own-make engine of 1034cc powered this cyclecar from Clapham.

1920 Unit No 1 two-seater

UNIT/*England 1920–1923*
A rear-mounted flat-twin 1100cc engine powered the Unit No 1, a friction-drive light car promoted by Grice, late of GWK. In 1923 a front-mounted Coventry-Climax four was used.

UNITED/*USA 1920*
Built by the United Engine Co., of Greensburg, Indiana, the United failed to materialize beyond the prototype stage. A touring car of 121-inch wheelbase was announced for $1850. A Herschell-Spillman four-cylinder engine was used.

1919 Utilis cyclecar

UNITED STATES/*USA 1899*
The United States Automobile Company of Attleboro, Mass., built an electric car in which both the field and armature of the motor, which was mounted on the rear axle, revolved.

UPTON/*USA 1900–1907*
From a 3½ hp De Dion-powered runabout, this firm progressed to the big 1904 Beverly four, whose headlamps turned with the steering.

URECAR/*England 1923*
An 8·9 hp four-cylinder Dorman engine powered the Urecar; it seems possible that only one was made.

URRIC/*France 1905–1906*
A 'well-conceived' voiturette, shown at the 1905 Paris Salon.

US/*USA 1907–1908*
A '12 hp and over' four-cylinder air-cooled engine of 1767cc powered this two-seater runabout from Upper Sandusky, Ohio.

US AUTOMOBILE/*USA 1899–1901*
A 3 hp electric carriage with three speeds forward and two back.

US LONG DISTANCE/*USA 1901–1905*
The US Long Distance car was similar in appearance to the Curved-Dash Olds, but had left-hand steering by side tiller. In 1903 a conventional 25 hp four-cylinder five-seater 'Standard Tourist' appeared, and by 1905 the marque name had been changed to 'Standard'.

UTERMOHLE/*Germany 1903–1905*
This Cologne coachbuilder and car-importer also constructed a 16 hp Peugeot-engined four-cylinder car which was imported into England by Corben and Sons of London.

UTILE-SIMPLEX/*England 1904*
A single-cylinder two-speed four-seat car from Kew, which cost £150 complete.

UTILIS/*France 1923–1925*
M. Lafarge made this tiny cyclecar in Courbevoie, Seine, using a wooden chassis and two-stroke Train engine of 350cc.

UTILITAS/*Germany 1920–1922*
Only 200 kg (440 lb) in weight, this little car had a sv 785cc four-cylinder engine of advanced design. The Berlin factory also built cyclecars with one- and two-cylinder engines.

UTILITAIRE/*France 1907–1909*
An 8 hp belt-driven light car built in Paris and shown at the 1907 Salon. In 1908, two-stroke one- and three-cylinder models were listed.

UTILITY/*USA 1921–1922*
The Utility Four was built by Major Victor W. Pagé as a companion car to his 'Aero-Type Four' cars, which were displayed at the New York Auto Show in 1922. The Utility boasted a four-cylinder air-cooled engine, similar in design to the Aero-Type line, and four prototypes were made—a touring car, a roadster, a small pickup truck and a station wagon. Price for all models was planned at $1450.

1922 Utility Four range – and entire production

VABIS / *Sweden 1897–1911*

Vagnfabriksaktiebolaget i Södertälje, Södertälje, was a subsidiary of Surahammars Bruk, makers of railway rolling stock. In 1896 Gustaf Eriksson was employed by Surahammars Bruk to find out if car production was worthwhile. He built two experimental cars in 1897 and 1898, but they were not very successful. In 1903 the company exhibited cars in Stockholm and a 12 hp tonneau in Paris. Cars with four-cylinder (probably also twin-cylinder) engines were built until 1911, when Vabis merged with Scania.

La Va Bon Train two-seater, 1905

LA VA BON TRAIN / *France 1904–1914*

Larroumet and Lagarde, of Agen, Lot-et-Garonne, built this three-wheeler, whose name means 'goes like blazes'. With an iron chassis, wheel-steering and a 6 hp De Dion engine, between 50 and 100 La Va Bon Train cars are thought to have been built.

VAGHI / *Italy 1920–1924*

Originally a three-wheeler, the last Vaghis had a 546cc twin-cylinder engine and four wheels. There was a close connection with the SAM.

VAILLANT / *France 1922–1924*

A cyclecar made in Lyon with a Chapuis-Dornier engine of 961cc or 1350cc.

VAJA / *Czechoslovakia 1929–1930*

A sporting cyclecar, driven by a sv 746cc air-cooled flat-twin Itar engine. Weighing 360 kg (792 lb), it could reach 40 mph, but with the optional sv 996cc JAP vee-twin engine, could attain a heady 48 mph.

VAL / *England 1913–1914*

An 8 hp cyclecar with friction drive from Birmingham.

VALE / *England 1932–1936*

Built in London's Maida Vale, the Vale Special was initially powered by an 832cc Triumph engine. These cars were nearly all two-seaters, though the Tourette, a four-seater, was offered in 1933. In 1934 it was announced that larger engines would be fitted: these were Coventry-Climax fours and sixes of 1098cc and 1476cc respectively. A supercharged six-cylinder racing car was built in 1935 for Ian Connell, though production of all cars ceased the following year.

VALENTIA / *France 1907–1908*

'Tricars of all powers' built by Saunier of Vernon (Eure).

1897 Vallée racer 'La Pantoufle'

VALLEE / *France 1895–1901*

A Le Mans, Sarthe, cycle builder, Vallée first constructed a 4 hp flat-twin car on cycle lines; by 1898, twins of up to 7 hp were available. His oddest offering was the 1899 'Pantoufle' ('Slipper') racing car which had a 7603cc horizontal four-cylinder engine and a wide driving belt: it took its name from its streamlined nose, shaped like a Turkish slipper.

VALVELESS / *England 1908–1915*

The Valveless was the successor to the Ralph Lucas Valveless, and marked the entry of the David Brown group into motor manufacture. It had a 25 hp duplex two-stroke engine with 'only six working parts' (two pistons, two conrods and two crankshafts, which were geared together and counter-rotated).

VAN / *USA 1910–1911*

A 22 hp ohv four-cylinder engine powered this roadster from Grand Haven, Michigan.

VANDEN PLAS / *England 1960 to date*

Founded as the British branch of the famous Belgian coachbuilding firm, Vanden Plas was acquired by Austin after World War Two, and provided custom coachwork on the bigger Austin chassis. It became a separate marque in 1960 with the de luxe Austin Princess. In 1964 there was also the Vanden Plas 1100. The 1965

Princess R used a Rolls-Royce military engine of 3·9 litres. The latest Vanden Plas, the 1500, is a de luxe Austin Allegro. Vanden Plas also carried out coachwork for Daimler and Jaguar at their Park Royal, London, factory, but early in 1979 it was announced that the works were to be closed and activities transferred to Jaguar in Coventry.

VANDY / *England 1920–1921*

Built by members of the Vandervell family (of CAV motor accessories), the 23·5 hp Vandy was assembled from American components, including a 3772cc Rutenber engine.

VAN GINK / *Holland 1899–c1903*

With two separate rear-mounted 2½ hp engines, the Van Gink was a tubular-framed voiturette from an Amsterdam cycle maker.

VAN WAGONER / *USA 1899–1900*

'Built on a simple plan that does away with several levers and push-buttons', the Van Wagoner, from Syracuse, NY, could be 'controlled with one hand'. From 1900–03 it was built as the 'Syracuse'.

VAPOMOBILE / *England 1902–1904*

This Nottingham-based manufacturer made — or assembled — steam cars of various designs.

1902 Vapomobile steam car rotund phaeton

VAR / *Austria 1923–1926*

Gianni Varrone, half-Swiss, half-Viennese, worked with Nesselsdorf and Austro-Daimler before setting up his own factory at Hard (Voralberg). His voiturette had a wooden chassis/body and a curious flat-twin two-stroke engine with double-ended pistons and external connecting rods acting on the ends of the gudgeon pins, which protruded through a slot in the cylinder walls. Only prototypes were built.

VARLEY-WOODS / *England 1918–1921*

The Varley-Woods was so called because of the involvement of Ernest Vernon Varley Grossmith and John Robert Woods in the project. The former had been concerned with canned soups and mouth organ manufacture, while the latter was a Near East river trader. Built by Turners of Wolverhampton, the Varley-Woods was a good-looking car with a Rolls-Royce-type radiator and polished aluminium bonnet. A 1795cc Dorman engine was used, this interesting power unit having an aluminium block and ohc. But from mid-1920 a more conventional 14·3 hp Tylor was fitted.

VATE / *France 1908–1909*

Three models — an 8 hp single-cylinder, a 10 hp twin and a 15 hp four — were built by this firm from Puteaux, all with electric transmissions.

Vauxhall

VAUXHALL
England 1903 to date

The first Vauxhall of 1903 was an American-inspired 5½ cwt (616 lb) runabout with a transverse 5 hp horizontal engine, chain drive and tiller steering. A 6 hp version came out the next year, boasting the luxury of a reverse gear! In 1905 the company moved from London's Vauxhall to Luton, Bedfordshire, bringing out no less than three models of three-cylinder cars (though this time with vertical engines). These cars were successfully used in trials and hillclimbs, but an entry in the 1905 Tourist Trophy proved abortive, despite the use of a *six*-speed gearbox. Although demand continued, a more conventional shaft-driven car, the 18/20 four-cylinder model, proved extremely successful, leading to the demise of the earlier types. A 3-litre Vauxhall put up a sterling performance in the German Prince Henry Trials in 1910 and 1911. The engine capacity was increased to 4 litres and the car called the Prince Henry in recognition of the achievement. From this emerged the most famous of all Vauxhalls, the 30/98. For this, works manager L. H. Pomeroy increased the engine capacity to 4½ litres in 1913. A few examples were made before World War One, though it was again available in 1919. Designated the E-Type, it received a new ohv 4·2-litre engine and front-wheel brakes in 1922, thereafter being known as the OE. The company had been one of the few firms to continue manufacture throughout World War One, the D-Type being made for the services. In 1922 the cheaper 14/40 appeared and the D-Type was granted overhead valves. In December 1925 the American General Motors took over, though it was not until three years later that the first GM-inspired Vauxhalls appeared, the 20/60 with overhead valves, coil ignition and central gear-change. The 2-litre Cadet of 1931 was a cheap six announced the following year, offering a synchromesh gearbox and beating Rolls-Royce to the post. Two other lighter sixes, the 12 and 14, were introduced in 1933, though at the other end of the range the company offered a 3·2-litre six in 1934, this 'Big Six' surviving until 1937, when it was replaced by the independent suspension 25 hp model. Unitary construction on the four-cylinder 10 of 1938 gave Vauxhall another technical first in Britain. Priced at £158, though only having a three-speed gearbox, it offered 40 mpg. The following year all models were fitted with hydraulic brakes, one being the newly introduced J model, a 14 hp car with a 1781cc six-cylinder engine, costing a competitive £220. The post-war era saw the four-cylinder 10 and 12 and the six-cylinder 14 offered, though by 1948 all had been phased out, and replaced by the

1442cc Wyvern and the 2275cc Velox, using four- and six-cylinder engines respectively. These L-Type models featured completely new styling, with a markedly trans-Atlantic front end and faired-in headlights. A steering-column gear-change was another feature imported from America. In 1952 both models were re-styled, with short-stroke engines replacing the original power units. Three years later, a luxury version of the six, the Cresta, appeared costing £844. These E-Type models remained in production until 1957, a year that saw the introduction of the four-cylinder 1½-litre Victor with its distinctive wrap-around windscreen, the six being similarly adorned in 1958. By 1962 the Victor had been re-styled, the Velox and Cresta receiving similar treatment the following year. In 1964 more powerful engines were introduced, the Victor now displacing 1·6 litres, while the six was increased to 3·3 litres. Vauxhall made a major departure from previous practice in 1964 by announcing a new small car, the 1057cc Viva. It was re-styled for 1967 and again in 1970, this HC variant being offered in 1159cc and 1256cc forms. A completely new Victor appeared for 1968 in 1·6- and 2-

litre variants, having inclined ohc engines, the camshaft being driven by a neoprene belt, the first occasion that the feature was offered on a production car in Britain. The faithful 3·3-litre six was fitted into a similar bodyshell, and named the Ventora. It was 'all change' again in 1971, the Victors being upped to 1800cc and 2300cc and sporting chunkier bodywork also shared with the Ventora. The Victor engine, though of 1600cc, was also offered in the Viva bodyshell. A coupé version, the Firenza, appeared in 1971, with a choice of 1256cc, 1600cc and 2300cc engines. However, in 1973 the entire Viva/Firenza range was overhauled, the Viva being retained for the smallest capacity engines, the 1800 and 2300 being called Magnums. In 1975 a new model, the Chevette, was launched, a good-looking coupé with hatchback tailgate, powered by the 1256cc Viva engine, and available in 10 variants in 1979. Early in 1979 new Opel-based luxury models, the Carlton and Royale, were announced. The Cavalier, a 1300/1600/1900cc mid-sized saloon originally imported from Belgium, was by that time made in Britain. The last Viva was built in mid-1979.

1913 Vauxhall 25hp Prince Henry tourer

1961 Vauxhall Velox PA 2¼-litre six-cylinder saloon

1978 Vauxhall Royale

VAUZELLE/*France 1902–1908*
Emile Vauzelle originally marketed an Aster-engined 5 hp voiturette under the name Vauzelle-Morel, though in the marque's latter days its cars and voiturettes were known simply as 'Vauzelle'. A 12 hp 1815cc four was offered in 1907–08.

VECHET/*Czechoslovakia 1911–1914*
Small cars of sporting appearance: the first model was a water-cooled twin-cylinder of 1004cc, the second (and last) a 2111cc four-cylinder with a three-seater body. The production of these neat cars was on a small scale.

VEDOVELLI & PRIESTLEY/*France 1899*
A three-wheeled electric carriage which was steered by slowing the speed of rotation of the wheel on the inside of the curve.

VEDRINE/*France 1904–1910*
A. Védrine of Neuilly-sur-Seine was a coachbuilder who also made electric cars. The company won the 1905 French Town Car Trials.

VEE GEE/*England 1913*
An 8 hp cyclecar built by Vernon Gash, of Leeds.

VEERAC/*USA 1913*
'Valveless, Explosion Every Revolution, Air Cooled' summed up this two-cylinder 1655cc two-stroke from Anoka, Minnesota.

VEHEL/*France 1899–1901*
Available with 6 hp single or 8 hp twin power units, the Véhel was built by M. & A. Dulac of Paris.

VELIE/*USA 1909–1928*
W. L. Velie, of Moline, Illinois, had built up to 25,000 carriages annually for over 40 years, before producing the Velie '30' early in 1909. It had a four-cylinder 3295cc American & British engine, and its price of $1750 was based on projected sales of 10,000 in 1910. The 1915 season saw the 40 hp 'Biltwell Model 22' Continental-engined six at $1065, and for 1917 the 'Greater Velie Biltwell' was launched. Marque popularity in Shreveport, Louisiana, was such that a suburb of the town was named 'Velie' in 1916. The four-seat 'Sport Car' of 1918 had a long-stroke 4966cc six with triple external exhausts and a Victoria hood of impractical but elegant design. For the 1920s, Velies became cheaper and more angular, the company making its own 3335cc ohv six-cylinder power unit from 1922. Some 1927–28 models had a Lycoming straight-eight.

1918 Velie Sport Car

1903 Miniature Velox

VELOX/*England 1902–1904*
Velox of Coventry claimed to be 'one of the pioneers of the English motor trade'; their 1903 12 hp was a tubular-framed four-cylinder shaft-drive car. They also made the curious low-slung Baby Velox voiturette, of which one example survives.

VELOX/*Austria 1906–1910*
A single-cylinder 10 hp car with the engine mounted below the driver's seat. Many of these cars were used as taxicabs, while others were exported (mainly to Russia). Velox operated these cabs on many routes in and around Prague, which was then still in the Austro-Hungarian Empire. After car production ceased, Velox imported cars and parts and for some time operated the biggest garage in town.

1950 Veritas sports saloon

VERITAS/*Germany 1946–1952*
Founded by ex-German motorcycle racing champion Ernst Loof and some ex-BMW employees, Veritas first built sports and racing cars with the pre-war 1971cc BMW 328 six-cylinder engines. They also produced a few coupés and cabriolets with this engine, as well as with ohc 1899cc six-cylinder Heinkel motors. In conjunction with the French Panhard factory, Dyna-Veritas cars with ohv 744cc flat-twin Panhard engines were also built in small numbers. Lack of sufficient funds eventually led to the demise of this make, which also produced Meteor 2-litre FII racing cars. Successful Veritas racing drivers included Kling, Pietsch, Ulmen, Helfrich, Lang and Hirt.

VERMOREL/*France 1904–1930*
The first Vermorel cars, designed by Pilain, were horizontal twins of 2598cc, but serious production did not begin until 1908 with a pair-cast four of 1874cc, soon uprated to 2064cc. In 1912 a 3308cc four appeared, and a 1642cc light car was added at the end of the year. Though various sporting models were produced in the 1920s, the post-war mainstay of this Villefranche-sur-Saône, Rhône, factory was a four-cylinder 12 cv with dual rear springing.

1904 twin-cylinder 2597cc Vermorel

VERNON/*USA 1920–1921*
The Vernon succeeded the Able, which had been in business since 1917. With its own make of engine, the Vernon line featured a V-8 and a four: touring car prices were reported as being $1695 and $845 respectively. Production was limited.

VESPA/*France 1958–1961*
The Ateliers de Construction de Motos et Accessoires, established in Fourchambault, Nièvre, made the twin-cylinder two-stroke 400cc Vespa car under licence.

VESTA/*England 1903*
A 7 hp 'car set' for home assembly, sold by Danny Citröen of Holborn Viaduct.

VICEROY/*England 1915*
An 1162cc light car built in Nottingham.

VICI/*England 1906–1907*
A 12/16 hp four-cylinder engine powered this assembled car from NW London.

VICKSTOW/*England 1913*
Vickers and Bristow of London assembled the chassis of this £125 two-seater from bought-in components, mostly American. It had a 1968cc monobloc engine and a 'particularly smart' bullnose radiator.

*c.*1899 Victor steam Stanhope

VICTOR/*USA 1899–1904*
A. H. Overman, of Chicopee Falls, Mass., built the Victor steam and petrol cars. The 1899 Victor had a vertical twin-cylinder engine, and incorporated a curious anti-theft device — a spring lever under the seat locked the throttle when the driver rose to leave the car.

VICTOR/*England 1915–1921*
The Tyler Apparatus Company of London built this vee-radiatored cyclecar with 965cc Precision engine and belt drive.

VICTORIA/*Germany 1900–1909, 1956–1958*
Well known as a motorcycle manufacturer, Victoria of Nürnburg built single-, twin- and four-cylinder cars, using De Dion, Aster and Fafnir proprietary engines with capacities ranging from 482cc to 2680cc. From 1909 to 1956 they concentrated on two-wheelers, and entered car manufacture again with the Spatz.

VICTORIA/*Spain 1904–1905, 1917–1923*
Named after Queen Victoria Eugenie, the 1904 Madrid-built Victoria was available as a twin-cylinder 4 cv or a four-cylinder 18 cv. In 1917 the same company, the Garage Franco-Espagñol, began production of a neat ohv 950cc four-cylinder light car. About 100 were built before the London-based Gwynne company took over the design.

VICTORIA/*England 1907*
A 10/12 hp four-cylinder side-entrance phaeton from Godalming, Surrey.

VICTORIA COMBINATION
France 1899–1901
The Société Parisienne produced this curious tiller-steered two-seater, which used what amounted to the rear end of a De Dion tricycle as a front-wheel-drive unit. It was also known as the 'Eureka' ('with the little friction clutch'). More conventional Duc-Spider and Duc-Tonneau cars followed with Aster engines.

VICTORIAN/*Canada 1900*
A flat-twin prototype built by a Nova Scotian furniture manufacturer.

VICTRIX/*France 1903*
Successors to the 1902 Farman, Victrix cars were 6 hp single-cylinder voiturettes. Victrix engines of 12 hp and 24 hp were also made, but the cars in which they were used were sold as 'FAC'.

VICTRIX/*France 1919–c1924*
A 15hp, from Paris, 'of entirely French construction'.

VIKING/*USA 1929–1930*
Built by Olds, this was a lower-priced version of the La Salle, distinguished by a 4244cc V-8 with chain-driven camshaft between the blocks.

VIKING/*Isle of Man/England 1965–1967*
Some 20 Viking Minisprints were built. The car featured a square-tube chassis to which the fastback glass-fibre bodies were attached. All mechanical parts were from the Mini.

VILAIN/*France 1900–1905*
The Vilain, from Paris 16e, had an underfloor horizontal single-cylinder engine and two-speed chain drive.

VILLARD/*France 1925–1935*
When the Colombe cyclecar ceased production, the design was taken over by M. Villard in Janville, Eure et Loir, who made it under his own name. These small three-wheelers had a two-stroke Harissard engine of 346cc.

VINCKE/*Belgium 1894–c1905*
Belgium's first car manufacturer, Vincke, built heavy, Panhard-like vehicles at their Malines factory. In 1903, a model known as the Vincke-Halcrow was sold in England.

VINCO/*England 1904–1905*
A 3½ hp Fafnir-engined tricar made in Peterborough.

VINDELICA/*Germany 1899*
This make, sold in England as the PTS, showed a four-wheeled motor carriage at the 1899 National Cycle Show in London. The car cost £160; the hood was an extra £20. The company also made tricycles, including an expensive (£950) 'Tricycle and Goods Lorry'.

VINET/*France 1900–1904*
Aimed especially at 'doctors, architects, businessmen and commercial travellers', these low-built crocodile-bonneted voiturettes had Aster engines and 'combined every desire of the most exacting sportsmen'.

VINEX/*England 1903*
An obscure marque sold by Robert Ramsbottom of Manchester.

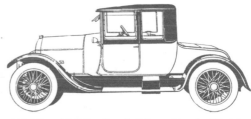

1923 Vinot 12/25hp Special Three-Quarter Coupé

VINOT-DEGUINGAND/*France 1901–1925*
Vinot-Deguingand of Puteaux and Nanterre, Seine, started with 1500cc twin-cylinders, then made four-cylinder models of 12 cv (2211cc) and 18 cv (3685cc). In 1911 they added a 50 cv six of 8101cc to their range. Vinot took over Gladiator in 1909, and their cars were often sold under that name — and *vice versa*. The 1912 9 cv of 1693cc was continued after the war alongside new models like the 12 cv of 2613cc and the 10 cv (1847cc). When Vinot failed, their works were bought by Donnet: the Deguingand name was resurrected in 1928 for the limited production of a Violet-designed cyclecar.

The 1900 fwd Victoria Combination (2¼hp De Dion engine), sold in Britain as the 'Eureka Voiturette'

1914 Violet-Bogey 10hp two-seater

VIOLET-BOGEY/*France 1912–1914*
Marcel Violet, prolific designer of curious two-strokes, also designed this lively twin-cylinder four-stroke cyclecar of 1·1 litres, with friction transmission and overhead inlet valves.

VIOLETTE/*France 1909–1914*
Built by Franc & Cie of Levallois-Perret, Seine, La Violette was a crude cyclecar designed by Marcel Violet. It had friction transmission, chain final drive and an armoured-wood chassis. Single and twin-cylinder engines were initially available, though a more conventional four-cylinder light car appeared in 1914.

VIPEN/*England 1898–c1904*
Probably Continental imports, the early cars offered by this Hull cycle manufacturer resembled the contemporary Panhards.

VIQUEOT/*USA/France 1905*
Chassis of 28/32 hp and 40/45 hp were built at Puteaux (Seine) for this marque and shipped to Long Island City for bodies to be fitted for the American market.

VIRATELLE/*France 1922–1926*
Made in Lyon by the Société Anonyme des Motocyclettes et Automobiles Viratelle, these were small 350cc-engined cyclecars.

VIRGINIA/*USA 1923*
The Virginia automobile was the result of a corporation change in what had been formerly Piedmont: any automobiles bearing the Virginia nameplate were simply Piedmont cars with the new name.

VIRUS/*France 1930–1935*
The Virus, made in Paris by the Garage Renouvier, was a fwd cyclecar with a 350cc two-stroke engine.

VIVINUS/*Belgium 1899–1912*
The original Vivinus was a single-cylinder belt-driven voiturette, also built under licence by New Orleans in England, Georges Richard in France and De Dietrich in Alsace-Lorraine. A twin-cylinder derivative appeared in 1900. Vivinus, whose factory was at Schaerbeek, Brussels, brought out a shaft-drive 15/18 hp

four, later offering twins and sixes on similar lines. The final range consisted of three fours — a 10/12 hp, a 16/20 hp and a 24/30 hp.

VOGTLAND/*Germany 1910–1912*
Small 12 hp and 20 hp cars with proprietary engines and many other bought-in parts.

VOGUE/*USA 1920–1923*
The Vogue was an assembled car closely affiliated with the Economy and built in Tiffin, Ohio. Two six-cylinder models were marketed throughout the Vogue's four years of production, the 6-55 (powered by a Herschell-Spillman engine) and the Continental-powered 6-66, touring models of which sold for $2285 and $2485 respectively. Several hundred cars were probably built.

VOISIN/*France 1919–1939*
Aviation pioneer Gabriel Voisin was forced to convert his Issy-les-Moulineaux, Seine, works after the war because there were no more orders for aeroplanes. He decided to build cars but, being a strong individualist, his cars were far from conventional, and all used sleeve-valve engines. The first car built by Voisin was a 18/23 cv of 3969cc, which was continued for nearly ten years. A 7238cc V-12 was exhibited as early as 1921; that year saw the launch of the 1244cc C4 four-cylinder model. In 1927, Voisin presented some attractive six-cylinder models, the best of which was the 13 cv of 2300cc. In 1930 came the 4800cc Diane and the Simoun 5·8-litre six. There was also the Sirocco V-12. In the 1930s, some Minerva models were built

VOLKSWAGEN/*Germany 1938 to date*
Ferdinand Porsche designed the prototypes of his 'Volkswagen' (people's car) at the behest of the Nazi party in 1934–36, and a series of 30 pilot cars was constructed in 1937 by Daimler-Benz. In 1938, Adolf Hitler laid the corner-stone of the Volkswagen factory at Wolfsburg, but though the cars were known as the 'KdF'-Wagen ('*Kraft durch Freude*' — 'Strength through Joy') and theoretically available on subscription, no cars were released to the public before the war. Various military VWs appeared, with a rear air-cooled flat-four engine of 1131cc, this power unit being used on the post-war models which began to be produced by loyal employees in the bomb-flattened ruins of the Wolfsburg factory. Both an Allied investigation team and Henry Ford II dismissed the VW (nicknamed '*Käfer*' — 'Beetle') as having no commercial future, but it went on to become the most successful car in motoring history, outselling even the Model T Ford. At Wolfsburg alone, 11,916,519 Beetles were built between 1945 and 1974, with millions more being built in other VW plants all over the world, especially in Brazil (where the Beetle was still in production in 1979) and in Australia, where an ambitious plan to build this model largely from locally sourced components, including the engine, during the boom years of the 1960s only lasted from 1960–68. Over the years, the Beetle acquired more powerful engines, of 1192cc (1954), 1285cc (1965), 1493cc (1966) and 1584cc (1970). The first

break with tradition was the VW 1500 of 1961: engines of up to 1795cc were subsequently adopted on this model. Then VW acquired NSU, and with it the new K70, with a front-mounted ohc water-cooled vertical four of 1594cc or 1795cc; this was produced as a VW from 1970 to 1974. In 1973, VW introduced the Passat, with engines of 1297cc to 1471cc, followed a year later by the Scirocco of 1093cc to 1457cc, and the Golf, with a 1093cc engine. In 1975 came the highly successful Polo minicar, with an 895cc engine; 1093cc and 1272cc versions were subsequently offered, and a version with a conventional boot instead of the hatchback was introduced under the name Derby. The Golf is now available with engines up to 1588cc, and is built (as the Rabbit) in Pennsylvania, with such success that US-built VW sales actually outstripped American Motors in the sales league in December 1978, only a few months after the factory had gone into operation. The Golf is also offered with a 1471cc ohc diesel engine. At the 1979 Geneva Show, a Cabriolet version was launched. At the beginning of 1979, VW announced a joint venture in which the Beetle was to be built in Egypt.

1978 VW 1303 Convertible

under licence without great success. The year 1936 saw a strange 6-litre straight-twelve, which remained a prototype. At the very end, Voisin was forced to use the American Graham 3500cc engine, the sole exception to the sleeve-valves. Gabriel Voisin made many of the bodies for his cars—it is said that he was helped in their design by architect Le Corbusier. These controversial bodies may not have been fashionable, but they certainly attracted a good deal of attention. Voisin's engineering drew heavily on aircraft practice, and he always made great use of light alloy. After the war, Voisin made the tiny Biscooter for Spain.

VOITUCAR/*England 1900*
With a 4½hp MMC-De Dion engine, the Voitucar was a two-seater ('best English carriage building') with an additional 'Emergency Seat for two more'.

VOLKSROD/*England 1967 to date*
Along with the various GP models, the Volksrod VW-based glass-fibre buggies were by far the best of an otherwise indifferent breed. Again, like GP, they still exist, short and long wheelbase versions selling for a little over £300 in early 1979.

Rudolf Valentino in his 1924 Voisin C5 tourer

1978 VW Golf, available with petrol or diesel engines

1978 VW Passat

VOLPE/*Italy 1947–1949*
An ambitious mini-car with a rear-mounted 123cc flat-twin two-stroke engine and a sporting open two-seater body, the Volpe was not a bestseller: the former aircraft factory at Piacenza soon ceased production of this little car.

VOLVO/*Sweden 1927 to date*
The first Volvo left the Göteborg factory on the morning of April 14, 1927. But planning had started in 1924 when Assar Gabrielsson and Gustaf Larson discussed assembling a car suited to Swedish roads from components commissioned from Swedish firms. The SKF ball-bearing company provided backing, and 10 prototypes were built and tested in 1926. The car had a 1·9-litre sv four-cylinder engine and was American-inspired—no wonder, as at least two of the designers had worked in the USA and the car was tested by a Swedish-born Hupmobile employee, later employed by Volvo to develop their six-cylinder cars. The OV4 tourer and the PV4 closed sedan sold around 1000 cars in two years. In 1929 a 3·1-litre six (PV651) on American lines appeared. The PV652 came in 1930, almost the same car, but with hydraulic brakes, and was developed until 1936. The PV36 Carioca of 1935 looked like a Chrysler Airflow and had ifs and an all-steel body. It was not a success, and was followed by the more conventional PV51/52 at the end of 1936. Volvo

1935 Volvo TR703 saloon

1960 Volvo P1800 sports coupé

1913 Vulcan 15.9hp coupé

produced nearly 2000 cars in 1937, although only 56 were exported. Commercial vehicles were still much more important. In 1938 the more streamlined PV53–56 appeared, a development of the earlier model. It was produced in small numbers during the war, often sold with a wood-burning gas-producer unit on a small trailer. The PV60 went into production in 1947, though prototypes were tested in 1942. It was to be the last six-cylinder Volvo for many years. The experimental PV40 developed just before the war was a small rear-engined car with an eight-cylinder radial engine and unit body construction, but production problems caused it to be abandoned. Planning started for the more conventional PV444, with a four-cylinder 1·4-litre ohv engine, ifs, rear coil-suspension and unit body construction. The car was shown in 1944 but lack of body steel meant that production only started in 1947. The car was redesigned in 1958 and called the PV544. The five-bearing 1·8-litre B18-engine appeared on the 1962 model. Altogether around half a million were built. In 1956 the 120 or 122 (there were many variations, and in Sweden the model was called Amazon) appeared, with a totally new body, but many mechanical components shared with the older model. Before it was dropped in 1970, 600,000 had been built. A sports car with glass-fibre body, the P1900, was built in 1956/57 but it was underpowered and unsuccessful. Its successor was the P1800, a two-seater coupé with the B18 engine. Pressed Steel in Scotland built the bodies and the cars were assembled by Jensen — the first cars came from England in 1961, three years after the car had been exhibited in New York, which caused some embarrassment in Göteborg. Production

was slow and assembly was moved to Göteborg in 1963. The Swedish-built cars were called P1800S, and in 1966 and 1969 the engine output was increased. The 1800E had electronic fuel injection and 130 bhp, enough for 110 mph. In 1971 a 2 + 2 (1800ES) was produced: 39,414 cars of various types of this sports car were built before production ended in 1973. The 100-series (first model was the 144, which meant 1 = 100-series, 4 = four-cylinder and 4 = four-door) was introduced in 1966 and had many safety features. The B18 engine was used, but in 1969 came the 2-litre B20 engine with fuel injection on one model in 1971. The line was redesigned in 1973 and given new ohc engines. In 1968 came the six-cylinder 164 with 3-litre B30 engine; later, cooperation with Renault and Peugeot resulted in a new V-6 engine. In 1974 Volvo bought the Dutch DAF factory and introduced the Volvo 66 in 1975, a DAF with safety features added. 1976 saw the Volvo 343, a new car with De Dion rear axle, four-cylinder engine and belt transmission. It is now available with an ordinary gearbox.

VOODOO / England 1971–1975
Started as a private venture, the Voodoo first appeared on the *Daily Telegraph* stand at the 1971 Motor Show. The centre of the sleek, glass-fibre body was bonded to the purpose-built chassis, while the nose and rear sections were bolted in place. Power came from a rear-mounted Hillman Imp unit.

VORAN / Germany 1926–1929
Belonging to NAG, Voran's Berlin factory first built motorcycles, then small sv 1076cc four-cylinder cars with Amilcar engines licence-built by Pluto. A 30 hp model had a 1461cc four-cylinder motor. These front-wheel-drive cars were designed by Richard Bussien.

VOUSEMOI / France 1904
Vousémoi ('*vous et moi*' — 'you and I') cars were available with either 10 hp twin or 16/20 hp four-cylinder Gnôme engines.

VOX / England 1912–1915
From the same makers as the L & P, this was a two-stroke 6/9 hp cyclecar of flimsy appearance.

VULCAN / England 1902–1928
The first Vulcan was a belt-driven single-cylinder model, the result of two years' experimentation by the Hampson brothers, Thomas and Joseph. A 10 hp twin followed, with 12 hp and 16 hp cars appearing in 1905. By the outbreak of World War One, a wide range of models had been built, most between 2- and 3-litres capacity. The post-war years were plagued by financial difficulties, caused to some extent by the firm's involvement with the Harper Bean combine. A 3½-litre V-8 appeared briefly in 1919; by 1922 Howard sleeve-valve engines were being considered but failed to materialize. Dorman engines were fitted to the 1·8-litre 12 and 2·6-litre 16/20, though the 20 hp used Vulcan's own 3·3-litre engine. From 1923 the company established a link with Lea-Francis, with Vulcan being responsible for some Lea-Francis engines and L-F making parts for Vulcan. Dealer resources were also pooled. But the Vulcan 12 of 1925 had a Dorman engine, even though it looked like a Lea-Francis! Private car production was gradually run down and from 1928 only commercial vehicles were produced.

VULCAN / USA 1913–1914
'Like a thunderbolt from a clear sky', the $750 Vulcan Speedster was a light car from Painesville, Ohio. Ambitious production plans for this 'truly remarkable car' — an $850 five-seater was also offered — came to nothing.

1907 Coupe des Voiturettes Vulpès racer

VULPES / France 1908–1910
Vulpes of Paris built an 8 hp single as well as fours up to 30/40 hp. In 1906 they listed a 12/15 hp and 20/24 hp featuring the circular radiator with raised header tank that distinguished the Vulpès. De Dion single- and Janus four-cylinder engines were used: the marque even had Grand Prix aspirations.

Volvo 264 GLE saloon

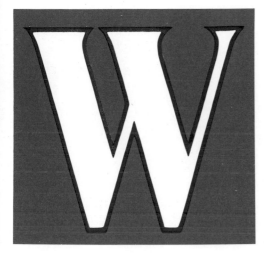

WADDINGTON/*England 1903*
A 6½ hp voiturette built in Middlesbrough with De Dion or Aster power unit.

WAF/*Austria 1910–1927*
Owned by Dr. Zachariades, WAF built cars on a limited scale in the former Bock & Hollander works. They offered four-, six- and, eventually, eight-cylinder models as well, which, driven by Zachariades, also competed in sporting events. Among smaller models, the 2·8-litre four-cylinder was a very good car for connoisseurs, as it was—like all WAF models—very expensive.

WAGGENHALS/*USA 1913–1915*
A 24 hp three-wheeler with chain drive to the rear wheel: a van version was built for the US Post Office.

WAHL/*USA 1913–1914*
This Chicago firm (whose name means 'choice' in German) offered 3261cc cars without name-plates for enterprising 'manufacturers' to sell as their own creation.

WALKER/*USA 1900–1901*
A two/four-seater steam carriage named after Orrin P. Walker, president of the Marlboro (Mass) Automobile & Carriage Co.

WALL/*England 1911*
Built by the makers of the Roc motorcycle, this curious machine resembled a wide sidecar mounted on a three-wheeled chassis, the single front wheel being controlled by a long tiller.

WALTER/*Czechoslovakia 1913–1937*
Founded by Josef Walter, this Jinonice-based factory built motorcycles and three-wheelers before they commenced production of cars of the highest calibre. Aeroengine manufacture was introduced in the 1920s. Walter originally built 18 hp, 25 hp and 30 hp four-cylinder cars: in the 1920s they offered 1540cc light cars with sv and ohv engines and a sv 2120cc four-cylinder model. Later versions had ohv engines of 1945cc and 1540cc. A beautiful 2990cc six-cylinder was added in 1929, soon followed by a 3·3-litre version. Many bodies were made by such

famous coachbuilders as Sodomka, Jech, Bro-žik, Aero (Weymann), Uhlik and others. A 5879cc V-12 Walter, the 'Royal', was the most expensive and luxurious car made by the factory: it was built between 1931 and 1934 in small numbers . . . even a bus with a 7354cc V-12 engine appeared on the market in 1931. More popular was the 1438cc four-cylinder Bijou; the six-cylinder Standard 3-litre and Super 3·3-litre touring cars also sold well. From 1933, Walter built 995cc and 1089cc Fiats with ohv four-cylinder engines under licence. During the 1920s racing cars were made for Walter works-driver Jindrich Knapp. Walter cars also won many big trials and rallies, often driven by the then owners, the Kumpera family. The factory, now nationalized, still produces aeroengines.

1931 5879cc Walter Royal 12-cylinder cabriolet

WALTHAM/*USA 1898–1901*
A typical tiller-steered steam runabout. Though the prototype was built in the Waltham Manufacturing Company's Orient cycle factory, there was no other connection.

WALTHAM/*USA 1922*
Successor to the friction-drive Metz, the Waltham had a conventional transmission. Featuring a Rutenber six-cylinder engine, the Waltham offered a full line of body types with prices beginning at $2450 for the touring car. Relatively few cars were built, and most of those were open models.

WALTON/*England 1904*
Built at Great Sankey, Warrington, Lancashire, this was a 5 hp twin-cylinder forecarriage with a water-cooled power unit.

WANDERER/*Germany 1911–1939*
Wanderer built superb tools, bicycles, motor-cycles and cars. Their first Wanderer cars had ioe 1145cc and ohv 1220cc four-cylinder engines with two- and three-seater bodywork. Improved versions of the 1220cc car were built until 1925. New in 1924 was an ohv 1550cc four-cylinder,

followed in 1926 by a 1940cc version. The first six-cylinder Wanderer, displacing 2540cc, appeared in 1928, and 1930 brought a 2995cc sports car into the Wanderer range. Together with DKW, Horch and Audi, Wanderer became a member of the newly founded Auto-Union in 1932. This brought a new shape to these excellent cars, and the 1692cc four-cylinder of 1933–34 resembled the DKW. The Wanderer works at Siegmar and Schonau in Saxony later built a range of six-cylinder models, with the W 50 of 1936–39 as one of the top versions. Its ohv 2257cc engine developed 50 bhp at 3500 rpm. Other models were the sv four-cylinder 1767cc W 24 and the sv six-cylinder 2632cc W 23.

WARE STEAM WAGON/*USA 1861–1867*
Although not an automobile in the true sense, the Ware Steam Wagon was not a 'one-off' but a make in its own right, several having been built by Elijah Ware of Bayonne, New Jersey. In addition, a Ware was probably the first self-propelled vehicle made in the United States to be exported. In 1866, a Ware Steam Wagon was exported to Rustico, Prince Edward Island (now a province of Canada but then a British Crown Colony), where it had been ordered by the local Catholic priest, a Father Belcourt.

WARFIELD/*England 1903*
A paraffin-fired four-cylinder steam car with a flash boiler.

WARNE/*England 1913–1915*
An 8 hp JAP-engined cyclecar from Letchworth, Hertfordshire.

WARP 8/*Wales c1976*
Masterminded by Welsh school teacher Owen Williams, the exotic-looking Warp 8 had a glass-fibre body bonded to a VW floorpan. Power came from a modified Porsche 1600 unit.

WARREN-DETROIT/*USA 1909–1914*
A monobloc 3707cc four-cylinder engine powered the Warren-Detroit 30: the '12-40' had a 4416cc power unit.

WARREN-LAMBERT/*England 1913–1922*
A twin-cylinder Warren-Lambert light car, built in Richmond, Surrey, climbed the 1:2½ gradient of Nailsworth Ladder four up in 1914, a feat repeated by the post-war four-cylinder model in 1920. Touring 1920 Warren-Lamberts had a 1330cc engine: the Sports model had a 1498cc power unit.

1926 Wanderer

1914 Warren-Lambert

WARTBURG/*Germany 1898–1904*

The Fahrzeugfabrik Eisenach was founded by Henrich Ehrhardt's arms factory to build Wartburg cars at Eisenach in Thuringia (now East Germany) under French Decauville licence. From 1903 onwards, the works became an independent car factory. The first cars had air- or water-cooled ioe 479cc twin-cylinder engines of 4 hp, 5 hp, 8½ hp and 10 hp. Later four-cylinder models were up to 3140cc. Former Scheibler and Cudell designer Willi Seck joined Eisenach in 1903 and created new cars, which became known as Dixi. BMW took over the Dixi works in 1928, and produced the Austin Seven under licence in 1929–31, calling it the BMW 'Wartburg'.

WARTBURG/*Germany 1956 to date*

This three-cylinder two-stroke car, built by the nationalized (former Wartburg, Dixi and BMW) works at Eisenach in Thuringia (East Germany), has front-wheel drive. Originally with a 900cc engine, from 1957 on power output was increased from 37 bhp to 50 bhp. In 1962, a 991cc engine was specified. The 1979 version of the Wartburg still used this three-cylinder unit.

WARWICK/*England 1960–1962*

Bernie Rodgers left Peerless to produce this Triumph TR development of his design: a 3·5-litre Buick V-8 was also offered in 1961.

WASHINGTON/*USA 1909–1911*

Built by the Carter Motor Car Corporation, of Washington, DC, (former maker of the Carter Twin Engine) the Washington car was guaranteed for five years. Embarrassingly, it only survived in production for two.

WASHINGTON/*USA 1921–1924*

Built in Eaton, Ohio, the Washington was a typical assembled car of its time, featuring two six-cylinder models in 1921 and 1922, using Falls and Continental engines. The Falls engine was dropped for 1923; the last gasoline Washingtons were built that year and used the Continental power plant. For 1924, a steam car was announced and one pilot model was built. An estimated 65 units constituted the entire production of this make.

1964 Wartburg saloon

1972 Wartburg Knight

WASHINGTON/*USA 1923*

This car was announced but never built. Operations were centred on Washington, Penn. This car had no connection with the contemporary Washington from Eaton, Ohio.

WASP/*England 1907–1908*

The Wasp was a 3064cc shaft-driven six-cylinder model selling at £500 complete.

WASP/*USA 1920–1925*

Built by Karl H. Martin of Bennington, Vermont, formerly the designer of the Roamer, Deering Magnetic and Kenworthy auto-mobiles, the Wasp appeared as a four-cylinder car between 1920 and 1924 and as a six afterward, using Wisconsin and Continental engines exclusively. Relatively high-priced (the fours selling for $5500 each), the entire output of 18 Wasp cars carried Victoria coachwork. Elaborate plans for a complete line of other open styles as well as a complete line of formal closed cars did not materialize. Mr Martin, a devout Episcopalian (Anglican), had designed and cast a handsome St. Christopher Medal during World War One which had proved popular with US Armed Forces: all Wasp automobiles carried one of these medals on the dashboard as standard equipment.

1924 Wasp Victoria

1960 Warwick GT

WASSE/*England 1903*
Wasse cars in 8 hp and 16 hp forms were shown at the 1903 Crystal Palace Show.

WATROUS/*USA 1905–1907*
Better known for their fire-engines, this Elmira (NY) firm also built 12 hp two-cylinder light cars, priced from $400.

WATTEL & MORTIER/*France 1921–1923*
A six-cylinder car made in Paris with a sleeve-valve engine of 2655cc.

WAVERLEY/*England 1910–1931*
The first Waverleys used a 9 hp vee-twin JAP engine with a rear-mounted gearbox. This was later joined by a 10 hp four-cylinder and 15 hp car, with engines by Chapuis-Dornier. After World War One the 12 was the staple model. From 1922 a 10 hp Coventry-Climax-engined 1½-litre was announced, and re-named the 11 hp two years later. A new 12 with a sleeve-valve engine was marketed in 1924, while a 16 hp model with Coventry-Climax engine appeared in 1925. A £100 car was an offering in 1925 with a water-cooled flat-twin 900cc engine, but there appears to have been few takers.

1913 Waverley 15hp all-weather coupé

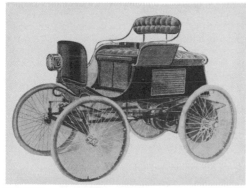

1899 Waverly electric runabout

WAVERLY/*USA 1898–1916*
Waverly Electrics were built by the Indiana Bicycle Company (a Pope firm) of Indianapolis. Among the vehicles offered was a 2½ hp brougham fitted with an electric heater. The marque survived until 1916, building shaft-drive electrics.

WAYLAND/*England 1901*
A tricar whose manufacturer is unknown.

WAYNE/*USA 1904–1908*
The 'Reliable Wayne', from Detroit, was available with either a 16 hp flat-twin engine or a vertical four-cylinder 24/28 hp power unit. The company's final offering was a 30 hp four selling for $2500 fully equipped — 'nothing to buy but the licence'.

WEARWELL/*England 1899–1900*
Two separate mid-mounted 4½ hp De Dion engines powered this Wolverhampton-built voiturette with a triangulated tubular chassis.

WEBB/*England 1922–1923*
A stylish 9 hp Alpha-engined 1088cc four-seater from Stourport, Worcestershire.

WEBER/*Switzerland 1899–1906*
J. Weber & Cie of Uster (Zürich) were textile machinery manufacturers who built Rapid tri-voiturettes under licence, before turning to 2642cc single-cylinder cars with infinitely variable belt drive by expanding pulleys.

WEGMANN/*Germany 1925–1926*
A small car with a 1016cc four-cylinder Steudel engine, built by a railway carriage producer at Kassel.

WEIDMANN/*Switzerland 1905–1908*
Also known as 'Brunau', this Zürich marque had its unit engine/gearbox mounted on a sub-frame. Monobloc fours of 14/18 hp and 20/24 hp were offered.

WEIGEL/*England 1906–1910*
Danny Weigel was an ebullient motor agent and one of the prime movers in the establishment of the Clement-Talbot company in 1903: the cars he brought out under his own name in 1906 were suspiciously similar to the contemporary Itala. At first a 7433cc 40 hp was offered, followed in 1907 by a 60 hp six of 11,150cc and a 4562cc 25 hp. That same year, Weigel built the first British straight-eight Grand Prix car, using two 40 hp engines coupled end-to-end. The company was re-formed in 1907, moving in London from Islington to Notting Hill, where a 2850cc 20 hp was announced for 1910, but Weigel was taken over by Crowdy soon after.

WEISS/*Germany 1902–1906*
'Every speed without gears' was the slogan of Weiss cars, made in Berlin. They had friction drive and own-make two- and four-cylinder engines from 6 hp to 14 hp. Otto Weiss & Co. also supplied engines to other manufacturers.

WEISS-MANFRED/*Hungary 1927–1931*
A sv 875cc four-cylinder car, which gained fame when its creator, Ing. Victor Szmick, finished second in the 1929 Monte-Carlo Rally behind a 4718cc Graham Paige. Early Weiss-Manfred models — from a big machine and arms factory at Budapest — had 746cc engines.

WELCH/*USA 1903–1911*
Former cycle builders from Chelsea, Michigan, the Welch brothers began serious production in 1904 in Pontiac. Their first car, a twin-cylinder 20 hp, had ohv in hemispherical heads. A 36 hp four appeared around 1906, with an overhead camshaft and an odd three-speed constant-mesh transmission with a separate hand clutch for each speed. A six was built in 1907–08. In 1911, General Motors took over Welch, merged it with Rainier and created the Marquette.

WELDOER/*Canada 1913*
A twin-cylinder friction-drive cyclecar from Kitchener, Ontario, built by the Welker-Doerr Company.

WELER/*France 1920–1923*
Another cyclecar made by M. Violet in Levallois, Seine, with a twin-cylinder 1060cc two-stroke engine with rotary valves. It was also available with 500cc and 1380cc engines.

1920 Weler cyclecar

1902 Weller 20hp tonneau

WELLER/*England 1902–1904*
The Weller brothers of West Norwood, London, built a 20 hp four-cylinder with inlet valves whose time and degree of opening could be controlled by the driver. A 10 hp two-cylinder and a 1¾ hp motorcycle were also offered. Weller was the founder of AC.

WELLINGTON/*England 1900–1901*
Motor agent Frank Wellington built this rear-engined 2½ hp single-cylinder voiturette.

WENDAX/*Germany 1950–1951*
One of the really bad cars, built soon after World War Two, with insufficient technical and financial facilities. It had a 746cc two-cylinder Ilo two-stroke engine and was hand-built in limited numbers. Production ceased after the reputation of this primitive car worsened.

WENKELMOBIL/*Germany 1904–1907*
Early Wenkel-designed cars with one- and two-cylinder proprietary engines, supplied by De Dion, Fafnir and other producers.

WERNER/*France 1906–1914*
One of the great names in motorcycle manufacture, Werner Frères also built a 5 hp twin-cylinder tricar and a 7/9 hp based on the Sizaire-Naudin. A 10/14 hp four was added for 1908, and in 1912 four-cylinder models of 1833cc, 3016cc and 4072cc were listed, with attractive sloping radiators.

WEST, WEST-ASTER/*England 1904–1912*
West of Coventry built a range of cars, all with Aster engines. In 1906 they offered a 15 hp, 16/20 hp, and 20/22 hp, all with four-cylinders; the following year a six was announced, with separate cylinders and a lubrication system worked by exhaust pressure. It had a curious gear-change, in which the lever had only two fore-and-aft positions, yet managed to control a three-speed and reverse gearbox (noisily, one imagines . . .). From 1908, chassis were made for other firms.

WESTCAR/*England 1922–1926*
The Westcar was the brainchild of Major Charles Prescott-Westcar and was built by the Strode Engineering Works of Herne, Kent. The Westcar used an 11·9 hp four-cylinder engine by Dorman: the same company also built the Heron.

WESTCOTT/*USA 1910–1925*
The first Westcotts had 45/50 hp Rutenber four-cylinder engines and sold for $2000–$2250. For 1915, the range consisted of three fours and a Northway-engined six. The 1917 Springfield Touring Sedan had foldaway window glasses so that it became a 'hard-top' tourer: by 1920 Westcotts were being exported to Europe, despite their limited production. The 1921 range consisted of two monobloc sixes, the 3670cc 'C-38' and the 4966cc 'C-48'. The last production Westcott had a 4078cc six; hydraulic four-wheeled brakes were offered in 1925.

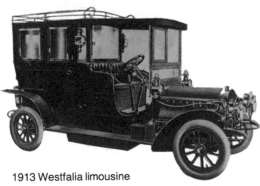

1913 Westfalia limousine

WESTFALIA/*Germany 1907–1914*
A still extant producer of dairy apparatus, Ramesohl & Schmidt at Oelde—and for some time also at Bielefeld—built excellent cars with De Dion and Fafnir one- and two-cylinder engines. A 1570cc four-cylinder was made from 1909 to 1914; two other contemporary models had 1945cc and 2125cc engines. The biggest Westfalia car had a sv 2536cc four-cylinder engine. The four-cylinder engines were of Westfalia's own design and manufacture.

WESTFIELD/*USA 1902–1903*
These were 'complete automobiles ready for power', though the company did also build some steam- and petrol-engined cars.

WESTINGHOUSE/*France 1904–1912*
The Le Havre factory of the American Westinghouse Electric company produced these cars. The 1908 range consisted of a 20/30 hp shaft-driven four of 4084cc and a 35/40 hp chain-driven four of 6333cc, with hydraulic shock absorbers of surprisingly modern appearance.

WESTLAKE/*England 1907*
Sold by Hubert Bowes Lyon, of Dorney Peach, Taplow, Maidenhead, the Westlake was a two-seater six-cylinder voiturette with a 'generally racy appearance'. It sold for 190 guineas in air-cooled form, 225 guineas with water-cooling. A two-speed epicyclic gear and a two-throw crankshaft were features of its design.

WESTLAND/*England 1906–1907*
A 10/12 hp Aster-engined model 'built to order' by Fred W. Baker's Stourbridge Motor and Carriage Works.

WESTMINSTER/*England 1906–1908*
The 20 hp Westminster, with a four-cylinder (3402cc) engine, was available with either shaft drive ('for high-class town work') or chain drive ('for country work and touring purposes').

WESTWOOD/*England 1920–1926*
An 11·9 hp Dorman-engined light car was this Wigan company's first model, followed in 1924 by a similar car with 14 hp Meadows power.

WEYHER ET RICHEMOND
France 1905–1910
Two 'well-known Austrian engineers', Friedmann and Knoller, designed the 15 cv Weyher et Richemond steam car, built at Pantin, near Paris. It had a flash boiler fired by paraffin, and was styled on petrol car lines, with the boiler at the front under a well-ventilated bonnet. The chassis price was 15,000 francs, and there were internal-expanding brakes on all four wheels, almost certainly the first time this feature had been offered on a production car. Petrol cars were this firm's later products and a six-cylinder model—as well as 16/20 hp and 28/32 hp fours—was shown at the 1907 Paris Salon.

WHARTON/*USA 1921–1922*
An ambitious enterprise which achieved very little, Wharton, of Dallas, Texas, announced three different models, a four, six and an eight. Whether any of the fours or sixes were actually built is speculative, although at least one of the large eight-cylinder cars—a roadster—is known to have been built. This was powered by a converted Curtiss aircraft OX-5 engine with an 8226cc displacement, developing 104 bhp at 1900 rpm. Wharton was better known as a manufacturer of tractors.

WHERWELL/*England 1920–1921*
A 7 hp flat-twin Coventry-Victor engine was used in the Wherwell, which had friction transmission and chain drive. Only three examples were built.

1907 Westinghouse in the Coupe de la Presse

WHITE

WHITE / *USA 1900–1918*

The 'Incomparable' White steam car was designed by Rollin H. White of the White Sewing Machine Company of Cleveland, Ohio: it first appeared as a typical steam buggy, distinguished only by its 'semi-flash' boiler, which ensured virtually automatic control. In the first full year of production, 1901, White sold 193 runabouts, and in 1903 they introduced a 10 hp wheel-steered tonneau with a double-acting compound engine under a bonnet with frontal condenser. Chassis was of armoured wood. A 15 hp model of more substantial construction appeared in late 1904, capable of 50 mph, and in 1907 came the more powerful Model L 20 hp and 30 hp Model K. All these models had a two-speed back axle and clutch mechanism, but improved design meant that these features were omitted from the 1909 20 hp Model O and 40 hp Model M, which had Joy valve gear

of simpler design than the Stevenson Link motion used on the earlier cars. But the contracting market for steam cars led White to introduce a Delahaye-based petrol model in 1910, production of steamers ceasing in 1911. From 1912, a 60 hp six was available, and White listed 12 models, becoming the third biggest American luxury car manufacturer. A 32-valve four appeared in 1917, but White relinquished car production for commercials the next year. There were, however, some notable exceptions to the rule, including a large special sedan built in 1920 for a Philadelphia sportsman and a series of special coupés, constructed on the taxicab chassis, for salesmen of the Coca-Cola Company. Two special sedans were made to special order for a Boston physician in 1924 and 1935. The latter of these was mounted on White's light truck chassis and carried custom coachwork by Bender of Cleveland, Ohio.

1905 15hp White steamer

1904 10hp White steam car

1924 White sedan

WHITEHEAD / *England 1921*
The Whitehead, which had a wooden chassis, used a 1498cc Coventry-Simplex engine and Moss gearbox. Only about 16 examples were built.

WHITEHEAD-THANET
England 1920–1921
This company planned to assemble 100,000 cars a year, using a British 16/20 hp engine in an American chassis, but probably did not build even one of them.

WHITEHURST-HOMER
England 1905–1906
A 3½ hp tricar built in Longsight, Manchester.

WHITGIFT / *England 1913*
An 8 hp vee-twin JAP engine powered this chain-drive cyclecar from Croydon, Surrey, named after a famous Elizabethan inhabitant of the town.

WHITING / *USA 1910–1912*
Built in Flint, Michigan, the Whiting 40 hp had overhead exhaust valves, while the 20 hp had an L-head engine.

WHITLOCK / *England 1903–c1930*
Royal coachbuilders Henry Whitlock & Company dated from 1778, and were motor agents by 1903, when they offered a range of Whitlock-Century cars. Their first genuine production models were the 1904 Whitlock-Asters, twins of 10 hp and 12 hp, with armoured-wood chassis, and fours of 14 hp and 20 hp, with pressed-steel frames. At the 1906 Olympia Show, Whitlock exhibited fours of 12/14 hp (chain drive) and 18/22 hp (shaft drive), but production ceased soon after. In 1914, Whitlock was taken over by motor agent J. A. Lawton, who announced two new four-cylinder models, a 2413cc 12/16 hp and a 4398cc 20/30 hp: these were sold as Lawtons in 1914, Whitlocks in 1915. Post-war, the firm was known as Lawton-Goodman, but did not reintroduce the Whitlock car until 1922 in the guise of a light car with a 1496 Coventry-Climax engine. This proved, at £375 in two-seater form, too expensive to compete with cars like the Morris-Cowley, so in 1923 came the 14 hp, a Bentley-like car with a 1753cc ohv Coventry-Climax six (bored out in late 1925 to create the 1911cc 16/50 hp) moderately priced at £495 with sports bodywork. In 1926 came an ohv twin-carburettor Meadows-engined six, the 2972cc 20/70 hp, increased in late 1927 to 3301cc. Production probably ended late in 1930, though the marque was listed for some years after. Lawton-Goodman continue as commercial bodybuilders.

WHITNEY / *USA 1895–1899*
George E. Whitney of Boston, Mass., built a number of experimental steamers (a horizontal-engined 1896 twin-cylinder model survives) and founded the Whitney Motor Wagon Company. After the Stanley brothers sold their design to John Brisben Walker for $250,000, they built Whitney steamers under the name Stanley-Whitney (or McKay, from a sewing machine company owned by Francis E. Stanley) until 1902.

WHITNEY/*USA 1898–1905*
R. S. Whitney, of Brunswick, Maine, built three twin-cylinder steam cars in 1898–1905, after having made bicycles at nearby Lisbon Falls for some years. The first two, completed in 1899 and 1902, resembled the contemporary Locomobile: the third was built of riveted $\frac{1}{16}$-inch steel plates cut out with a cold chisel.

WHITWOOD/*England 1934–1936*
The Whitwood was a tandem two-seater two-wheeler, complete with stabilizing wheels! A variety of engines was available, from a 150cc two-stroke to a 1000cc vee-twin JAP.

WIGAN-BARLOW/*England 1922–1923*
Made — surprisingly — in Coventry, this was an unsuccessful assembled light car with 1368cc Coventry-Climax or 1496cc Meadows engines.

WIKOV/*Czechoslovakia 1927–1936*
Made by an agricultural machine factory at Prostějov, the Richter-designed Wikov had an ohc 1490cc four-cylinder engine, originally de-

1931 Wikov seven-passenger saloon

signed by Ansaldo in Italy. Most cars had four-seater bodies, but a few two-seater sports-racing cars were built, too. Driven by Szyzycki, Konečnik, Václavik, Kreml and E. Wichterle (one of the factory owners), Wikov cars gained many sporting successes. A streamlined prototype, built under Jaray Patents, appeared in 1931. Some of the last models had ohc 1740cc and 1960cc engines. A 3480cc eight-cylinder never saw production.

WILBROOK/*England 1913*
A 9 hp JAP-engined four-seat cyclecar with four-wheel brakes.

WILBURY/*England 1900*
The 5 hp 'Vibrationless' Wilbury could attain a top speed of 20 mph, claimed its makers, Motor Fittings & Engineering Co., of Redhill, Surrey. It was sold either as a complete vehicle or in component form for assembly by enterprising cycle traders.

WILCOX/*USA 1910–1911*
Designed by Claude E. Cox, the 30/40 hp Wilcox had engine, clutch and gearbox incorporated in the same casing.

WILFORD/*Belgium 1897–c1901*
Though it was powered by a single-cylinder heavy-oil engine, the lumpish Wilford was capable of rapid progress: one achieved 60 mph in 1899.

WILKINS/*USA 1899*
Mr Wilkins, of San Francisco, built a massive 12 hp car whose infinitely variable belt drive and steering were operated electrically by push-buttons. The prototype, fitted out as a primitive

WILLYS (WILLYS-OVERLAND)
USA 1908–1956
Salesman John North Willys took over the Overland company, which had been producing gas buggies since 1903, to save it from receivership, and reformed it as the Willys-Overland Company in 1908. Initially, a four-cylinder runabout with epicyclic gearing was produced, and the profits from the first year's sales of 465 cars enabled two new models, the Overland Six and the 45 hp Willys Six, to go into production. By 1910, Willys-Overland had outgrown its 300 ft-long tin shed works, and moved into the old Pope-Toledo factory in Toledo, Ohio. Sales in 1914 reached 80,000, due mainly to the 3949cc Overland Model 79 four-cylinder; electric lighting and starting were adopted in 1914, in which year the first Willys-Knight was built. This 4529cc sleeve-valve four was based on the 1912–14 Edwards-Knight, and the Willys-Knight marque survived until 1932–33. In 1920, a British venture, Willys-Overland-Crossley, was established, to assemble Overland Fours for the UK market, including a 1924 version of this model (distinguished by U-shaped transverse suspension) with a Morris-Oxford engine. The US company survived a major financial crisis in 1921–23, and by April 1925 was building 250 Overland Sixes and 600 Overland Fours daily, plus 5200 Willys-Knights a month. In 1926 came a new low-priced model, the Whippet, aimed at competing with the Ford and Chevrolet; it was eventually the cheapest car on the US market, priced at $495, but never secured the hoped-for market success. In 1929 John

c.1924 Overland (Willys) in 'colonial' conditions

c. 1925 Wills Sainte Claire Grey Goose two-seater roadster

motor caravan, was scheduled by its optimistic inventor for a transcontinental tour 'once it was proved roadworthy'.

WILKINSON/*England 1903–1907, 1912–1913*

This famous London swordsmith sold the Belgian De Cosmo 24 hp under its own name in 1903–04. The 1906 14 hp four had the 'Tacchi' patent gear-change: in 1912 came a light car powered by the 7 hp water-cooled four-cylinder engine of the Wilkinson-TMC motorcycle. A development of this became the first Deemster.

WILLIS/*England 1913*

An 8 hp cyclecar 'embodying many novel features'.

WILLIS/*USA 1928*

Designed by D. E. Willis, this car featured a nine-cylinder engine. The pilot model was based on a Gardner chassis, but the Willis never got into production. Willis also built a prototype three-cylinder car, and designed the DEW.

WILLS SAINTE CLAIRE/*USA 1921–1927*

Childe Harold Wills, an expert metallurgist, was the engineer behind the early Ford cars, including the Model T: he broke with Ford in 1919 and spent his $1,592,128 severance pay in developing 4400 acres at Marysville, Michigan, into a model industrial community, aiming to build a car ten years ahead of its time. Named after local beauty spot Lake Ste Claire, the Wills Sainte Claire, appearing in 1921, was a metallurgical masterpiece, the first car to use molybdenum steel. Its ohc 60 degree V-8 engine reflected the latest European thinking and bristled with refinements, such as a cooling fan which automatically cut out at speeds of more than 40 mph. But the Wills Sainte Claire Grey Goose was an ugly duckling as far as styling went: sales peaked at 1500 in 1923, and then tailed off. An ohc 4·5-litre straight-six replaced the V-8 in 1925, succeeded by a pushrod unit in 1926, just before the marque's demise.

WILSON/*England 1935–1936*

This conventional looking electric car was built by Partridge Wilson & Co. Ltd., of Leicester. About 40 cars were made in the two years of production, making it the top selling British electric car of the inter-war years!

Willys unloaded his share in the company for $21 million and became US Ambassador to Poland. The company collapsed in the slump, and went into receivership again. Willys hurried back, but could not save the situation; he died in 1933, in which year the ugly aerodynamic Willys 77 was introduced. With more acceptable styling, it survived until 1942 as the 'Willys-Americar'. During the war, Willys produced 361,349 Jeeps, and continued producing them for civilian use when hostilities ceased. An enclosed 'Jeep Station Wagon' appeared in July 1946, and the 1948 range was extended to include several commercial models and the Brook Stevens-designed Jeepster Phaeton, current for four years, powered by sv Willys fours and sixes of 2196cc and 2425cc respectively. A brand-new range of passenger cars appeared in 1952, the Aero-Lark powered by the sv six, and the Aero-Wing, Aero-Ace and Aero-Eagle with a 2638cc ohv six. A total of 31,363 Aero Willys was built in 1952, and 41,735 in 1953, when a gold 'W' on the grille commemorated the 50th anniversary of Overland. That year, the ailing Kaiser group bought Willys-Overland, but 1954 models were little changed, except for the option of Kaiser's 3703cc sv six. A supercharger was fitted to some Aero Willys, boosting output to 140 bhp. The 1955 models were mildly face-lifted, and the Aero name dropped in favour of Custom (sedans) and Bermuda (hardtops). After only 6564 of the 1955 models had been sold, the decision was taken to end US passenger-car production, though the Aero resurfaced in the Willys-Overland factory in Brazil, where it was built until 1962.

1923 'British Built' Overland (Willys)

Julia Faye with her 1930 Willys-Knight coupé

1962 'Aero' Willys sedan

10/12hp Windsor tourer, c.1926

1904 Wilson-Pilcher

WILSON-PILCHER/*England 1901–1907*
Fitted with an early form of preselector gear, the Wilson-Pilcher had an 8 hp four-cylinder horizontal engine. Latterly it was built by Sir W. G. Armstrong, Whitworth & Co.

WILTON/*England 1913–1924*
Wilton's first cars were an 8 hp JAP-engined twin which sold at £160 and a 1093cc own-make four, which continued into 1914. The post-1919 Wiltons had a 1490cc four-cylinder engine and worm final drive. The firm built their own bodywork in their Tooting factory.

WINDHAM/*England 1906*
King's Messenger Captain W. G. Windham's 'Sliding Detachable Motor Bodies' were normally fitted to Renault and Mercedes chassis, but in 1906 he offered a 20/30 hp car under his own name.

WINDHOFF/*Germany 1907–1914*
A manufacturer of engines and components who entered car production at their Rheine/Westfalen works with 2012cc and 4960cc four-cylinder and 3018cc and 6125cc six-cylinder models. Fours of 1540cc, with ohc engine, and 2612cc, with ioe, appeared in 1912. The last Windhoff car was the C 15/40, with a 3920cc six-cylinder engine.

WINDSOR/*England 1924–1927*
The Windsor was a well-made light car, with a 10·4 hp 1353cc pushrod ohv engine of the company's own manufacture. A four-speed gearbox was another agreeable feature. Not surprisingly, the cars were not cheap and at £400 each only a few were made, manufacturers J. Bartle & Co, of London W11, ceasing production in 1927.

WINDSOR/*USA 1929–1930*
The Windsor 'White Prince' was a Moon model, introduced as an eight in 1929. A Continental engine was employed and the price of the five-passenger sedan was $1995. In 1930, the Windsor name superseded that of Moon: subsequent cars carried the Windsor insignia.

WINDSOR STEAM CAR
USA/Canada 1922–1923
The Windsor Steam Car was to have been the Canadian version of the Trask-Detroit Steam Car — later the Detroit Steam Car.

WINGFIELD/*England 1909–1920*
The 1913 15 hp Wingfield was a conventional four-cylinder shaft-driven car selling at £320 in chassis form.

WING MIDGET/*USA 1922*
A one-passenger car, the Wing Midget resembled a racing car, was mounted on a 60-inch wheelbase and powered by a four-cylinder air-cooled Cameron engine. It featured double chain drive. Several Wing Midgets were built: some were featured in an early silent film.

1913 Windhoff tourer

WINNER/*USA 1900*
This 5 hp gasolene runabout was built by the Elgin Automobile Company, who also made the Elgin electric.

WINNIPEG/*Canada 1921,1923*
The Winnipeg was a bid by a Manitoba-based company to market an automobile to sell in the prairie provinces of Canada. The radiator emblem featured a sheaf of Manitoba's primary product, with the legend 'Good as the Wheat'. The one and only 1921 Winnipeg was a four, actually nothing more than a Hatfield car with changed badge. The company floundered for a while, but was back in business in 1923, this time with a six, of which between five and ten were shown for promotional purposes. The six, in truth, was the Davis car with the ubiquitous 'wheat-sheaf' emblem: again, the venture failed.

WINSON/*England 1920*
Precision or Blackburne 8 hp engines powered the Winson cyclecar from Rochdale, Lancashire. Friction drive was employed.

1915 Winter cyclecar

WINTER/*England 1915*
A sporting belt-drive cyclecar from Wandsworth with an own-make 988cc four-cylinder air-cooled engine.

WINTERS/*USA 1909*
Twin-cylinder air-cooled engines of 10 hp and 14 hp powered these high-wheelers from Coffeyville, Kansas.

WINTHER/*USA 1920–1923*
A subsidiary of the Winther Truck Company, the Winther Motors Division built a creditable, if not exciting, assembled car in its four years of production. A Herschell-Spillman six-cylinder engine was used exclusively. Wheelbase was 120 inches and prices of the five-passenger touring model were $2650 for 1920 and 1921 and $400 less in 1922 and 1923. An estimated 500 cars were produced. The basic Winther design was also used for the 1923 Harris Six.

1920 Winther six tourer

WINTON

WINTON / *USA 1896–1924*

Scottish engineer Alexander Winton jumped ship in America, and founded a cycle company in Cleveland, Ohio. In 1896 he built a two-cylinder car, and went into production with light phaetons in 1897. Twenty-five were built in the first year, the twelfth being bought by James Ward Packard. A 3·8-litre Winton single-cylinder took part in the 1900 Gordon Bennett race. In 1901 a twin-cylinder phaeton was introduced, and in 1903 Dr H. Nelson made the first successful trans-America drive in one of these cars. Winton built two racers for the 1903 Gordon Bennett, low-profiled 'Bullets', one with a 17,028cc straight-eight and only one speed. A flat-four, the Winton Quad, appeared in 1904; at the end of that year the twin was discontinued. Vertical

1907 Winton 18/24hp with detachable canopy

fours of 16/20 hp, 24/30 hp and 50/100 hp were standardized in 1905: they still had the pneumatic speed governor characteristic of the marque. They introduced a new type of suspension — two superimposed semi-elliptic springs so shackled that on smooth roads only one spring was used, and on rough going both were called into play. In 1906, production was concentrated on the 5801cc Model K 30 hp: a 40 hp appeared in 1907. The Six-Teen-Six of 1908 boasted 7817cc, and in 1909 a 9505cc six incorporated a pneumatic starter; by 1911 it had a built-in tyre pump also. Conventional pair-cast sixes were built thereafter, acquiring electric lighting and starting in 1915. Car production ceased in 1924, when the company decided to concentrate on marine diesel engines.

The four- and eight-cylinder Winton Bullet racers for the 1903 Gordon Bennett race in Ireland

WITHERS / *England 1907–1915*

The 1907 Withers was a 24/30 hp model built in Paddington, London. In 1913 20 hp, 25 hp, 30 hp and 35/40 hp fours were offered, at chassis prices ranging from £430 to £600.

WITTEKIND / *Germany 1921–1925*

Wittekind of Berlin concentrated on small cars with 780cc, 896cc and 1280cc four-cylinder engines, but not many were made.

WIZARD / *USA 1921–1923*

Whether the Wizard was something of a hoax or not is a matter of guesswork today, as the

company's only brochure hailed from 'Wizard, North Carolina', a non-existent place on the map of America! The announcement called for a 'Junior' and a 'Senior' car featuring vee-twin and four-cylinder engines respectively; one 'Junior' chassis is known to have been built, the two-passenger roadster being listed at $395. Wizard may have had some connection with Schuler, but this has not been proven.

WM / *Poland 1927–1928*

A flat-twin four-stroke engine powered this light car from Warsaw; mass-production plans eventually came to nothing.

WOLF / *England 1904–1905*

A 5½/6 hp three-wheeler with a two-speed constant-mesh gearbox from Wolverhampton.

WOLF / *France 1913*

An imported French 12/14 hp four-cylinder, sold by Seale & De Becker of London.

WOLFE / *USA 1907–1909*

Built in Minneapolis, the Wolfe was a conventional tourer with a choice of air-cooled 3294cc Carrico or 30 hp water-cooled Continental engines. From 1909–12, the cars were known as 'Wilcox'.

WOLSELEY / *England 1899–1976*

In 1895 the Wolseley Sheep Shearing Company asked Herbert Austin, who had worked for them in Australia, to design a car with which they could enter the motor business. The result was a tricar fitted with a flat-twin engine, inspired by the French Léon Bollée. Four-wheeled prototypes appeared in 1899, and a 3½ hp single-cylinder example competed in the 1000 Mile Trial of 1900. A horizontal engine was a feature of all Wolseleys until 1905. But Colonel Siddeley, a Wolseley director and importer of French cars, insisted that vertical-engined Siddeleys or Wolseley-Siddeleys appear alongside the old horizontal engined models, a compromise that probably hastened Austin's departure, when he started building vertical-engined cars under his own name. After he left in 1906, models were known variously as Siddeleys, Wolseley-Siddeleys or Wolseley/Siddeley liaison lasted until 1910 with large four- and six-cylinder cars prevailing. During World War One Wolseley built the ohc Hispano-Suiza V-8 aeroengine under licence, so it was no surprise to find this camshaft layout on their 1·3-litre 10 hp model after the war. Other variations on the same theme were the 12 hp and 15 hp models; in 1925 the 10 developed into the 11/22, while the ohc layout was replaced by a cheaper side-valve layout for the 16/35, which superseded the 15 in the same year. Although a new ohc six, the 16/45, appeared in 1927, the company had gone bankrupt in the meantime, being snapped up by William Morris in the face of opposition from Herbert Austin. It was not long before the Wolseley-inspired ohc began appearing in the contemporary MG and Morris models, the 1928 Wolseleys being a 2·7-litre straight-eight and a four-cylinder 12/32. The 21/60, a six, followed, being a Wolseley edition of the Morris Isis. A significant event of 1930 was the appearance of the ohc 1·3-litre Hornet, while larger six- and eight-cylinder cars were also available. Although the Hornet was later increased to 1·4 litres, 1936 was the last year of the ohc Wolseleys. Pushrod-engined replacements included the Super Six and 1·8-litre 14/56. The post-war era saw the Morris-inspired ohv 8 and 10, while the four-cylinder ohc 4/50 and the six-cylinder 6/80 reverted to the old Wolseley tradition, the latter power unit being shared with Morris. However, the 4/44 of 1953 used a detuned MG TD engine, though rationalization was reflected in the 1500 of 1958, in effect an expanded Morris Minor. A variant of the Mini, the Hornet, appeared in 1962, while plusher versions of the fwd 1100 and 1800 models displayed the famous illuminated radiator badge, a feature of the marque since 1933.

1904 Wolseley 10hp tourer

1912 Wolseley Roi des Belges 16hp tourer

WOLSIT / *Italy 1907–c1908*
Licence-built Wolseleys — 10/20 hp twin, 16/24 and 30/40 hp fours and 45/60 hp six — from Legnano.

WOLVERINE / *USA 1904–1906*
Built by the Reid Manufacturing Company of Detroit, Michigan, the Wolverine was a 20 hp live-axle model.

WOLVERINE / *USA 1927–1928*
This is actually a small Reo, but as it carried its own advertising, specification listing and badge, it should be classified as a separate make. The Wolverine was introduced in April 1927. Engine was a six by Continental and wheelbase was 114 inches. Body styles included both a two-door and four-door sedan and a 2/4 seat cabriolet-roadster. It was readily distinguished by two groups of horizontal hood louvres.

WOLVERINE SPECIAL / *USA 1917–1920*
A sporty two-seater roadster, the Wolverine Special was powered by a Wisconsin four-cylinder engine, this being replaced in 1918 by a Rochester-Duesenberg four. The car featured a vee-type radiator, the motif being carried on into the wings. Door steps replaced running-boards and wire wheels were standard. Only three cars were completed.

WOODILL / *USA 1958–1959*
The Woodill Wildfire was created by Woody Woodill, a Willys/Dodge dealer. The glass-fibre sports car body on an own-make frame utilized many Willys components including their 90 hp F-head six-cylinder engine. Priced at $1200 in kit form or from $2900 as an assembled car, it was said to be the first glass-fibre car to be produced in volume. Approximately 300 Woodills were made.

WOODROW / *England 1913–1915*
This cyclecar used initially an 8 hp air-cooled Jap vee-twin, subsequently a water-cooled 9 hp Precision. A sharp-nosed sports model was offered.

WOODS / *USA 1899–1919*
For the first 18 years of their existence, Woods of Chicago built conventional, expensive elec-

c.1920 Wolseley

1957 Wolseley 15/50 saloon

1974 Wolseley Six

tric cars. Then, in 1917, came the $2650 Woods Dual Power, with a 12 hp Continental petrol engine supplementing its electric motor, which was mounted where the gearbox would normally go. With both engines running, the Dual Power could reach 35 mph.

WOODS MOBILETTE/USA 1913–1916
A soap box cart reputedly inspired Francis A. Woods to build 'America's first cyclecar', a narrow tandem or staggered two seater with a four-cylinder engine and underslung front suspension. Ease of storage was emphasized: 'It will even climb the stairs to a second, a third, or any storey, if the turns of the stairs are not too sharp . . . it will go anywhere that you can put an upright piano.'

WOOLER/England 1920–1921
The Wooler had a flat-twin engine with rotary valves. The whole device was rather crude, with belt drive to a worm-gear rear axle, but coil-sprung independent front suspension was featured.

WORLDMOBILE
USA 1928
Although seven prototypes were announced, only one may have actually been built. The Worldmobile used an eight-cylinder Lycoming engine and disc wheels, many other components being taken from other makes of car. The Lima, Ohio-based Worldmobile announced that a sedan would be priced at $1700, but production was not forthcoming.

WORTH/USA 1899–1901
A Chicago-built motor buggy which won five gold medals at the 1900 Chicago Auto Meet.

WSM/England 1961–1967
About 25 of the pretty WSM alloy-bodied Sprites were made, half of which were exported to the USA. The originator, Douglas Wilson-Spratt, also built one-off specials based on a Healey 3000, an MGB and even an MG 1100.

WYNER/Austria 1903–1905
A Vienna agent for Belgian Miesse steam cars, Wyner also built petrol cars with one-, two- and four-cylinder engines of 9 hp to 40 hp. Wyner also sold De Dion and Darracq cars; his own used De Dion engines.

345

X/*France 1908–1909*
An 'unknown quantity' built at Kremlin-Bicêtre (Seine) and shown at the 1908 Paris Salon.

XENIA/*USA 1914*
Designed by P. E. Hawkins, the Xenia cyclecar had an 1164cc vee-twin Deluxe engine and the odd combination of epicyclic gearbox and belt final drive.

YALE/*USA 1903*
'A car with the doubt and the jar left out', the 12 hp Yale from Toledo, Ohio, was claimed to have been 'selected for export purposes by English experts . . . as the safest, simplest and most economical car made in America'. One-, two- and four-cylinder engines were used, in conjunction with epicyclic gearing.

1917 Yale two-seater

YALE/*USA 1916–1918*
The Yale was built in Saginaw, Michigan, and used its own-make V-8 engine. Available both as a touring car and 2/4 passenger speedster, this car featured the 'Neutralock', a theft-deterring device as standard equipment. Wire wheels and rakish lines made the Yale one of the sportier cars of the time, although production was small.

YAMABA/*Japan 1904*
Thought to be the first Japanese-built car, this was a heavy two-cylinder steam waggonette of crude appearance.

YAXA/*Switzerland 1912–1914*
'*Y a que ça*' ('It's the only one there is') was the phonetic rendering of this marque from Genève, built by Charles Baehni, an early collaborator of Charles-Edouard Henriod. The Yaxa was a 1692cc light car with a four-cylinder Zedel engine. Central gear and brake levers were an advanced touch. Baehni drove a Yaxa to victory in the 1913 Coupe de la Gruyère.

YEOVIL/*England 1895–1897*
Petters of Yeovil were gas engine manufacturers who collaborated with local coachbuilders Hill & Boll to build approximately 12 cars powered by Petter paraffin engines.

YLN/*Taiwan 1953 to date*
Founded as the Yue Loong Engineering Company, YLN adopted its present title in 1960. It builds sedans and jeeps under American Motors and Nissan licence at its Taipei factory, including the 1567cc 707 De Luxe and the diesel-engined 2164cc 803 DL.

1930 Z limousine

Z (ZBROJOVKA)/*Czechoslovakia 1927–1936*
A big arms factory, Zbrojovka of Brno-Židenice was part of the Skoda Group, but had — as far as car manufacture was concerned — no connection with Skoda cars. All Z cars were two-strokes, even their first model, the 'Disk', a B. Novotny-designed 660cc twin-cylinder, which never went into quantity manufacture. The first production Z had a 1004cc twin-cylinder engine, followed by an improved version with a rotary inlet valve. In 1933, more two-strokes with rotary inlet-valves, a fwd 900cc twin-cylinder and a 1490cc four-cylinder model, also with fwd, appeared on the market. They sold well. Z works racing cars included 1100cc two-, four- and six-cylinder and 1490cc eight-cylinder two-strokes, most of which had superchargers.

ZAGATO/*Italy 1966–1968*
Made by the famous coachbuilder, who created many very sporting Alfa Romeo cars between the wars, the 'new' Zagato was a modern version of the 1750cc Alfa Romeos of the late 1920s. It was a 100 mph 'Gran Sport' open two-seater, with a 1600cc Giulia TI engine.

ZAPOROZHETS/*Russia 1965 to date*
Exported to Austria as the Eliette, and to other markets as the Yalta, this NSU Prinz-like rear-engined car from the Ukraine had its 881cc V-4 power unit replaced with a 1200cc unit in 1968.

1919 Le Zebre Type D 10hp Torpedo

LE ZEBRE/*France 1910–1931*
The small Zèbre was a popular car made at Suresnes, Seine, at first with a single-cylinder four-stroke 5 hp engine of 636cc. In 1913, Zèbre presented two more models, a 6 hp of 785cc and a 10 hp of 1743cc, both four-cylinders. After the war, Zèbre resumed production with an 8 hp sv 997cc, the forerunner of the famous 5 hp Citroën (designed by Jules Salomon after he left Le Zèbre). The last production model was a 10 hp of 1974cc with a Ricardo head. The year Zèbre closed, they presented a prototype with a single-cylinder CLM diesel engine.

ZEDEL/*France/Switzerland 1906–1921*
Zurcher-Luthi were well-known Swiss motor-cycle makers whose first voiturette — an 1128cc four-cylinder — was built in 1906 in the factory at Pontarlier, France, which they opened to avoid customs duties. But production was really centred in a new factory at St Aubin, Switzerland. A 10 cv four of 1791cc appeared in 1908. In 1921 Zedel merged with the French marque Donnet to form Donnet-Zedel.

ZEILLER & FOURNIER/*France 1920–1924*
Made in Levallois, Seine, by MM. Zeiller & Fournier, these were light 1130cc Ballot-engined cyclecars with friction drive.

ZENDIK/*England 1913–1914*
An 8 hp Chater-Lea-engined cyclecar with two-speed chain-and-dog transmission.

ZENIA/*France 1913–1920*
This Paris-based marque made a 2998cc car before the war. In 1919 they resumed production, offering three Altos-engined models of 1779cc, 2297cc and 2950cc.

1913 Coupe de l'Auto Zénia

ZENITH, ZENITH-POPULAR
England 1905–1906
Zenith were better known for their motorcycles with infinitely variable Gradua belt drive than for their cars. The two-seater Zenith-Popular of 1906 was a light four-wheeler with a 6 hp twin-cylinder Stevens engine and underslung suspension.

ZENT / *USA 1902–1907*
Zent offered epicyclic-geared cars with two, three and four cylinders. In 1908 their products were renamed 'Bellefontaine' after the town in which they were built.

ZEPHYR / *England 1914–1921*
A 12 hp four-cylinder of 1944cc built by a Lowestoft (Suffolk) firm more famous for their lightweight pistons.

A Zeta coupé

ZETA / *Australia 1963–1966*
The highly original Zeta was another example of a locally designed car using a mixture of local and imported components. It came from Lightburn Industries, major producers of car jacks, concrete mixers, industrial products and power tools. The glass-fibre body was an ungainly but ingenious design with huge doors. The seats could be laid flat, or quickly removed to provide a large carrying area. The seats could also be placed on the roof to provide a grandstand view for sporting events. Total weight was 960 lb. Power came from a Villiers 324cc two-stroke engine driving the front wheels, with a Burman gearbox and Girling brakes. Despite plans to build 50 a week, only 363 were sold over a three-year period. The company also tried to build a Michelotti-styled rear-engined sports car, a diminutive design with a 500cc German FMR two-stroke engine developing 25 bhp. It, too, had a glass-fibre body, built on a tubular chassis. Some 48 were made.

ZEVACO / *France 1923–1925*
M. Zevaco of Eaubonne, Val d'Oise, made some light cars with 995cc Train vee-twin, and 950cc and 1350cc Chapuis-Dornier engines.

ZIL / *Russia 1956 to date*
Rivalling the Chaika as prestige transport for Soviet officials, the ZIL (Zavod Imieni Likhatchev) succeeded the ZIS (Zavod Imieni Stalina) of 1936–56, originally inspired by the Buick straight-eight and since 1945 built with Packard body dies. Still Packard-inspired until 1963, the ZIL then acquired more modern US-type styling as the 111G. The 114 seven-seater appeared in 1967 and the current Zil-117, a 7-litre V-8, dates from 1971.

ZIM / *France 1922–1924*
M. Zimmermann of Epernay, Marne, made some cyclecars with a sv 344cc single-cylinder engine and chain drive.

ZIMMERMAN / *USA 1908–1914*
Starting life as a wheel-steered high-wheeler with dummy bonnet, this marque from Auburn, Indiana, began building conventional four-cylinder cars in 1910, with a six appearing in 1912.

ZIP / *USA 1914*
A water-cooled four-cylinder 1287cc cyclecar from Davenport, Iowa.

ZITA / *England 1971–1972*
A very shapely two-seater based on VW mechanicals, the Zita ZS was intended to sell as a kit. However, the project was stillborn and only two cars were ever made.

ZUNDAPP / *Germany 1957–1958*
Still a leading manufacturer of mopeds and motorcycles, Zündapp of München built the unconventional Dornier-designed Janus mini-car, a four-seater in which the two rear-passengers sat with their backs to those in front, looking through the rear window. Power was by a 248cc single-cylinder Zündapp two-stroke engine! Total production of the Janus was 6900 cars.

ZUST / *Italy 1905–1914*
Excellent cars, designed and produced by Swiss-born Ing. Roberto Züst, whose first prototypes dated from the turn of the century. The range of models included a 10/15 hp three-cylinder of 1722cc, as well as 12 hp (2296cc), 18/24 hp (4082cc), 20/35 hp (4982cc), 28/40 hp (7429cc) and 50/70 hp (9889cc) four-cylinder models. After the war OM cars were made at this Brescia works.

ZWICKAU / *Germany 1955–1959*
Built at the former Audi works at Zwickau in Saxony (East Germany) this was the successor to the 684cc IFA F 8 model. It had the same twin-cylinder two-stroke engine and front-wheel drive: it was supplied as a coupé and a kombi.

1908 Targa Bologna Züst

1908 New York–Paris Züst

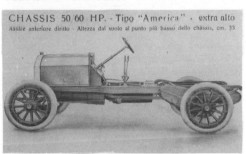

50/60hp Züst Tipo America chassis, 1909

Cross-references

ABAM   German licence-built Kriéger.
ACCARY   *see* Hédéa.
ADEX   *see* Excelsior.
AERO MINOR   *see* Minor.
AERO TYPE   *see* Pagé.
AFG   *see* Gorm.
AIGLE   *see* AER.
AIGLON   *see* Alliance 1905–1908.
AILSA CRAIG   *see* Craig-Dörwald.
AIRETTE   *see* Rex 1901–1914.
AIREX   *see* Rex 1901–1914.
AKD   *see* Abingdon 1922–1923.
ALBANY (1902–1905)   *see* Lamplough-Albany.
ALBRUÑA   *see* Brown 1899–1911.
ALLREIT   *see* Allright 1908–1913.
ALVECHURCH   *see* Dunkley.
AMEDEE BOLLEE   *see* Bollée.
AMERICAINE   *see* Cohendet.
AMERICAN MORS   *see* Standard (USA) 1909–1910, Skelton.
AMERICAN MOTOR   *see* Automobile Company of America.
AMERICAN TOURIST   *see* American Underslung.
AMERICAN VOITURETTE   Alternative name for Car-Nation (*see* Keeton).
AMPLEX   *see* American Simplex.
ANGLIAN   British importer's name for Ariès.
AQUILA   *see* Maillard.
ARIEL (USA)   *see* Maryland.
AROP   *see* Seidel-Arop.
AST-REX   *see* Rex 1901–1914.
ATOM   *see* Fairthorpe.
ATTICA   Greek-built Fuldamobil.
AUGE   *see* Troïka.
AUTHI   British Motor Corporation models licence-built in Spain.
AUTOAR (ARGENTINA)   *see* Cisitalia.
AUTO-FORE-CARRIAGE   USA licence-built Kuhlstein-Vollmer.
AUTO RED BUG   *see* Smith Flyer.
AWE   *see* EMW.

BABY FRISWELL   British importer's name for 1906 6½ hp Delage.
BAILEY & LAMBERT   *see* Pelham.
BAMBI   Chile-built Fuldamobil.
BANTAM   *see* American Austin.
BARCAR   *see* Phoenix 1903–1908.
BAUDOUIN   *see* Déchamps.
BAYARD-CLEMENT   *see* Clément.
BECKETT & FARLOW   *see* Mathieu.
BEDFORD   British importer's name for 1910–1914 Buick.
BELGA RISE   Sizaire Frères car built in Belgium from 1929.
BELLEFONTAINE   *see* Zent.
BENOVA   *see* Benjamin.
BERNARDI   *see* Miari e Giusti.
BEVERLY   *see* Upton.
BGS   *see* Bouquet, Garcin & Schivre.
BIADA-ELIZALDE   *see* Elizalde.
BINGHAMPTON   Incorrect form of 'Binghamton'.
BLACK CROW   *see* Crow-Elkhart.
BRAMHAM   *see* Stanhope.
BRENNA   *see* Brennabor.
BRIGGS & STRATTON   *see* Smith Flyer.
BRITISH IDEAL   6 & 8 hp Schaudels licence-built in Birmingham.
BRITISH MERCEDES   *see* Daimler-Mercedes.
BRITISH PEERLESS   *see* Peerless 1902–1904.
BRIXIA-ZUST   *see* Züst.
BROWN-WHITNEY   *see* Brown.
BRUNAU   *see* Weidmann.
BUAT   *see* Léon Buat.

BUGGYAUT   *see* Duryea.
BURLINGTON   British importer's name for De Dietrich-Bugatti.

CAB   *see* Automobilette.
CAESAR   English importer's name for Schacchi.
CALEDONIAN   *see* Argyl 1976 to date.
CANADIAN CROW   *see* Crow-Elkhart.
CANELLO-DURKOPP   *see* Durkopp.
CAR   *see* Cosmos.
CAR-NATION   *see* Keeton.
CATALONIA   *see* Rebour.
CDS   *see* Cognet de Seynes.
CELER   An undocumented Nottingham make, possibly connected with Binks (Leader).
CHAIKA   *see* GAZ.
CHAMPROBERT   *see* Electrogenia.
CHARETTE   *see* International 1898–1904.
CHARRON   *see* CGV.
CHAVANET   *see* Automoto.
CHENU   *see* Sixcyl.
LA CICOGNE   *see* Bignan.
CID   *see* Cottereau.
CLARKSON   *see* Chelmsford.
CLEMENT-STIRLING   *see* Stirling.
CLEMENT-TALBOT   *see* Talbot (England).
CLEVELAND SIX   *see* Chandler.
COBRA   *see* Shelby.
COCHOT   *see* Lutèce.
COLOMBES   *see* Villard.
COLONIAL (USA/Canada 1922)   *see* Canadian.
COLT   *see* Mitsubishi.
COLUMBIA (steam)   *see* Crouch 1899–1900.
CONTAL   *see* Mototri Contal.
CORONET   *see* Powerdrive.
CROWN MAGNETIC   *see* Owen Magnetic.
CSB   *see* Cornilleau Ste Beuve.
CUMMIKAR   *see* Ronteix.

DACIA   Renault 12 licence-built in Bucarest (Romania) since 1969.
DALGLEISH-GULLANE   Scottish-modified 1907 De Dion Bouton.
DART (USA 1912)   *see* Martin.
D'AUX   *see* Causan.
DA VINCI   *see* Scripps-Booth.
DAWFIELD, PHILIPS   *see* DPL.
DE DIETRICH   *see* Lorraine-Dietrich.
DE LUCA   Coventry Daimlers licence-built in Naples, Italy (1906–1911).
DE LUXE   *see* Car De Luxe.
DEMEESTER   *see* Jouffret.
DEW (1913–1914)   Forerunner of Victor Cyclecar.
DICKINSON   *see* Morette.
DLG   *see* Dyke.
DONG-FENG   *see* Hong-Ki.
DONINGTON   *see* Johnard.
DOUGILL   *see* Frick.
DOWNSHIRE   *see* Chambers.
DREXEL   *see* Farmack.
DUNAMIS   *see* Miesse.
DUREY-SOHEY   *see* Hanzer.
DUX   *see* Damazin & Pujos.
DyG   *see* Diaz y Grillo.

EB DEBONAIR   *see* LMB.
L'ECLAIR (1897)   *see* Maison Parisienne.
EHV, EISENHUTH   *see* Compound.
L'ELASTES   c1907 name for Motobloc.
ELBURN   *see* Ruby.
ELECTROBAT   *see* Morris & Salom.
ELECTROCYCLETTE   *see* AEM.
EL-FAY   *see* Elcar.
ELIETTE   *see* Zaphorozhets.
ELKHART   *see* Elcar.
ELMO   *see* Electromobile.

ENGLISH MECHANIC, EM   *see* Hyler-White.
EOLIA   *see* Traction Aérienne.
ERCO   *see* Eos.
ESPERANTO   USA importer's name for Prunel.
ETOILE DE FRANCE   *see* Darmont.
EUREKA   *see* Victoria Combination.
EUSKALDUNA   1928 successor to CEYC (Spain).

FAC   *see* Victrix.
FACILE   *see* Britannia.
FAIF   *see* Isotta Fraschini.
FAS   *see* Standard (Italy 1906–1908).
FASA   Spanish-built Renault models.
FAVORIT   *see* Kroboth.
FEG   *see* Erdmann.
FERNA   *see* HH.
FIAT-HISPANIA   *see* Seat.
FIDES   Italian-built Brasier.
FJTA   *see* Junior.
FRAM   *see* Cantono.
LA FRANCAISE   *see* Diamant.
FRISKY   *see* Meadows.
FRONTENAC (Canada)   1931–1932 *see* De Vaux, Durant; 1933–1934 *see* Continental.
F-S   *see* Petrel.

GAILLARDET   *see* Doctoresse.
GARDNER-SERPOLLET   *see* Serpollet.
GATSO   *see* Gatford.
GEORGIA KNAP   *see* Knap.
GLOBE (1906)   *see* Kitchon-Weller.
GOGGOMOBIL (Germany)   *see* Glas.
GORHAM   *see* Lilla.
GRAFFORD   *see* Graf & Stift.
GREAT SMITH   *see* Smith.
GTM   *see* Cox.
GWYNNE-ALBERT   *see* Albert.
GYROSCOPE   *see* Blomstrom.

HAG   *see* Hansa.
HAINSSELLIN   *see* HL.
HANS VAHAAR   Indian-built Fuldamobil.
HARDINGE   *see* Pullman.
HARLE   *see* Sautter-Harlé.
HARRIS-LEON LAISNE   *see* Léon Laisne.
HERCULES   *see* Ducroiset.
HEWBENZ   1901 English importer's name for Benz.
HISA   *see* Hermes (Italy).
HMC (1903)   *see* Highgate.
HOFFMANN & CZERNY   *see* Continental (Austria).
HURMID   *see* Hurst.
HYLANDER   *see* Highlander.

IDEAL   *see* TH (Spain).
IMPERIAL (USA 1903–1904)   *see* Columbus.
INDUCO   *see* Marguerite.
ISETTA   *see* ISO.
ITALIANA   *see* Owen (England).
IZZER   *see* Model.

JACK ENDERS   *see* Mourre.
JACK MULLER   *see* BNC.
JACKSON-BUCKMOBILE   *see* Buckmobile.
JACKSON-COVERT   *see* Covert.
JANUS   *see* Zündapp.
JC   *see* Corre.
JDS   *see* Deasy.
LA JOYEUSE   *see* Taine.
JUSTICIALISTA   *see* Graciela.

KAISER CARABELA   Original name for IKA-Renault.
KANE-PENNINGTON   *see* Pennington.
KAUTZ   *see* Ansbach.
KIBLINGER   *see* McIntyre.

KNIGHT & KILBOURNE   *see* Silent
  Knight.
KNIPPERDOLLING   Small Dürkopp from
  1908.

LACROIX ET DE LAVILLE   *see* La Nef.
LAFAYETTE (USA 1934–1939)   Nash
  model designation.
L & K   *see* Laurin & Klement.
LEANDER   *see* Cadogan.
LEONARD   *see* Medici.
LEON BOLLEE   *see* Bollée.
LEPRECHAUN   Irish-assembled Stanhope.
LETHIMONNIER   *see* Sultane.
LA LICORNE   *see* Corre-LaLicorne.
LIEGEOIS   Proposed Belgian licence-built
  Duryea (1900).
LITTLE GREG   *see* Grégoire.
LITTLE KAR   *see* Texmobile.
LLOYD & PLAISTER   *see* L & P.
LM   *see* Little Midland.
LOCKE   *see* Puritan (steam).
LA LOCOMOTRICE   1905 24/30 hp
  Rochet-Schneider licence-built by Nagant.
LORELEY   *see* Ley.
LPC   *see* Lewis (1913–1916).
LUC (Germany)   *see* Dinos.
LUCAS   *see* Ralph Lucas.
LUXOR   *see* Dagmar, Standish.
LYNX (1898)   *see* Le Blon.

MA   *see* Alvarez.
MAGIC   Fischer sleeve-valve car sold by
  Withers.
MARCHAND-DUFAUX   *see* Dufaux.
MARSHALL   *see* Belsize.
MARTIN & LETHIMONNIER   *see* Sultane.
MASS-PAIGE   English importer's name for
  Paige.
MAYA GT   *see* Camber.
McKAY   *see* Whitney.
MENDELSSOHN   *see* Passy-Thellier.
MERCEDES-ELECTRIQUE-MIXTE   *see*
  Austro-Daimler.
METEOR (USA 1900–1904)   *see*
  Automotor.
METEOR (USA 1902–1905)   *see* Berg.
METROPOLITAINE   *see* Cadix.
MGP   1912 name for Margaria.
MILDE-GAILLARDET   *see* Mildé.
MINIATURE VELOX   *see* Velox.
MLB   *see* Landry & Beyroux.
MO-CAR   *see* Arrol-Johnston.
MOHAWK-MANON   *see* Manon.
MORANO-MARGUERITE   *see* Marguerite.
MORRIS-LEON-BOLLEE   *see* Bollée.
MOTOCAR   *see* Micron.
MOTORMOBILE   English importer's name
  for 1902–1904 Vilain.
MOYEA   *see* Sampson.

NEW EAGLE   *see* Eagle.
NEW KYMA   *see* Kyma.
NEW LEADER   *see* Leader.
NEW PARRY   *see* Parry.
NEW PICK   *see* Pick.
NEWTON-CEIRANO   *see* Ceirano.
NEW TURRELL   *see* Accles-Turrell.
NISSAN   *see* Datsun.
NOBEL   British-built Fuldamobil.
NO-NAME   *see* Horley.
NUOVA INNOCENTI   *see* Innocenti.

OAKMAN   *see* Hertel.
OCTOAUTO   *see* Reeves.
OLYMPIC   *see* Gearless.
ONFRAY   *see* Compagnie Française.
OP   *see* Phrixus.
OPELIT-MOPETTA   *see* Brutsch.
OPPERMAN   *see* Unicar.

ORIO & MARCHAND   *see* Decauville.
ORLEANS   *see* New Orleans.
OVERLAND   *see* Willys.

PALM   Modified 1918–1919 Model T Ford
  sold by E. W. Brown of Melbourne,
  Australia.
PALM (England)   *see* Palmerston.
PAQUIS   *see* SUP.
PARISIA   *see* Owen (England).
PASSE-PARTOUT   *see* Reyrol.
PEGASUS   British importer's name for Ader
  and Cottereau.
PENNANT   *see* Bailey.
PETELECTA   *see* Owen (England).
PETTER   *see* Seaton-Petter, Yeovil.
PIERRON   *see* Mass.
PLM   Belgian-built Keller station wagon.
LA PLUS SIMPLE   *see* Legros.
PMC   *see* Premier (England).
POBIEDA   *see* GAZ.
LA POLAIRE   *see* Leon Buat.
POLONEZ   *see* Polski-Fiat.
PORTLAND (1903)   *see* International.
POWERFUL   British importer's name for
  Kriéger electric.
PREMIER-STRATTON   *see* Stratton.
PRINCESS   British Leyland marque
  succeeding Wolseley from 1976.
PROPULCYCLE   *see* Madoz.
PTS   *see* Vindelica.
PURITAN (1914)   *see* Scripps-Booth.

QED   *see* Marshall-Arter.

R & L   *see* Rauch & Lang.
RAULANG   *see* Rauch & Lang.
REGENT   *see* Bock & Hollender.
REISSIG   *see* RAW.
RELIABLE WAYNE   *see* Wayne.
REMO   *see* Rex (England 1901–1914).
RENAUX   *see* l'Energie.
RENNSTEIG   *see* Schilling.
RENOWN   1920 successor to Palm.
REPLICAR   *see* Glassic.
RGS-ATALANTA   *see* Atalanta
  (1937–1939).
RICHARD-BRASIER   *see* Georges-Richard.
RIGS THAT RUN   *see* St Louis.
RLC   *see* Rubury Lindsay.
ROLLING   *see* Dupressoir.
ROYAL CORONET   *see* Cope-Bohemian.
ROYAL DETROITER   *see* Detroiter.
ROYAL INTERNATIONAL   *see*
  International (England).
RUBAY   *see* Leon Rubay.
RUGBY   *see* Star (USA).
RUTHERFORD   *see* EJYR.

SABRA   *see* Rom Carmel.
SAG   *see* Pic-Pic.
SALVATOR   *see* Underberg.
SARACEN   *see* Reading.
SARATOGA TOURIST   *see* Elite (1901).
SASCHA   *see* Austro-Daimler.
SAVENTHEM   *see* Excelsior (Belgium).
SCOOTACAR   *see* Rytecraft.
SCOOTMOBILE   *see* Martin 1920–1922.
SCORPION   *see* Innes Lee.
SCOTT-NEWCOMB   *see* Standard Steam
  Car.
SEIGFRIED   *see* RAW.
SEM   *see* Morisse.
SEVEN LITTLE BUFFALOES   *see* De
  Schaum.
SEXTOAUTO   *see* Reeves.
SEYMOUR   *see* Turner.
SFA   *see* Automotrice.
SHAVE-MORSE   *see* SM.
SHERET   *see* Carden.

SHOEMAKER   *see* St Joe.
SIDDELEY-DEASY   *see* Deasy.
SIENNA   *see* Stevens.
LA SILENCIEUSE   English importer's
  name for Vinot-Deguingand.
SINCLAIR   *see* Clift.
SLIM-PILAIN   *see* Pilain.
SMEDDLE-KENNEDY   *see* SK Simplex.
SNOEK   Bolide licence-built in Belgium c1900.
SOCIETE CONTINENTAL
  D'AUTOMOBILES   *see* Gautier Wehrlé.
SOCIETE PARISIENNE   *see* Victoria
  Combination.
SPERRY   1900–1901 name for Cleveland
  Electric.
SRC   *see* Matas.
SSS   *see* Staines-Simplex.
STANLEY-WHITNEY   *see* Whitney.
STAUGHTON   English importer's name for
  Prosper-Lambert.
STORERO   *see* Schacchi.
STRATTAN   *see* Stratton.
SYMBOL   *see* Status.
SYRACUSE   *see* Van Wagoner.

TALBOT-DARRACQ   *see* Darracq, Talbot
  (France).
TAMA   *see* Prince.
TEMPLE-WOODGATE   *see* Temple-
  Westcott.
TESTE ET MORET   *see* La Mouche.
TH (England 1906)   *see* Farnell.
TOBOGGAN   *see* Armadale.
TOULOUSE   *see* Able.
TRASK-DETROIT   *see* Detroit Steam Car.
TRIPLEX   *see* Chicagoan.
TWEENIE   *see* Ruby.
TWENTIETH CENTURY   *see* Owen
  (England).

UNION   *see* Lambert.
URSUS   *see* Menegault-Basset.
UTILITY   *see* Page.

VCS   *see* Schilling.
VELOCAR MOCHET   *see* CM.
VELOMOBILE   *see* Eastmead-Biggs.
VERNON-DERBY   English importer's name
  for French Derby sports car.
VERTEX   *see* James & Browne.
VESTA (1898)   *see* Bamber & Lewis. Also
  English name for La Minerve (1899–1906).
VICTOR   English importer's name for
  Créanche.
VICTOR PAGE   *see* Page.
VINDEC   *see* Allright.
VOLGA   *see* GAZ.
VOX   *see* L & P.

WARD-LEONARD   *see* Knickerbocker.
WATSONIA   *see* Dürkopp.
WESTON   *see* Grout.
WHIPPET   *see* Willys.
WHITING-GRANT   *see* Grant.
WILLYS-VIASA   Jeeps built for Spanish
  market.
WINCO   1913–1914 twin cylinder
  predecessor of Stringer-Winco.
WINDORA   Ariès imported into England by
  S. A. Marples, whose aunts were named
  Winifred and Dora.
WOLSELEY-SIDDELEY   *see* Wolseley.
WORTHINGTON   *see* Berg.

YALTA   *see* Zaphorozhets.
YORK   *see* Pullman.
YUE LOONG   *see* YLN.

ZEBRA   English name for Le Zèbre.
ZHIGULI   *see* Lada.

Glossary

Air cooled: An engine in which the heat generated by combustion in the cylinders is dispersed by convection, either by radiating fins or by forced draught.

ALAM horsepower rating: A formula used by the Association of Licenced Automobile Manufacturers in the early days of the US motor industry (and known as the SAE rating after their demise). ALAM hp equals cylinder bore (in inches) squared times number of cylinders plus 2.5, at a speed of 1000rpm.

Annular gear: A toothed wheel with the teeth formed on the inner circumference.

Armoured chassis: A frame basically made of wood, but strengthened by steel flitch plates bolted on.

Artillery wheel: A road wheel with wooden or steel spokes, of greater strength than the conventional cart wheel.

Assembled car: A car whose engine, gearbox, axles and other components were supplied by various proprietary makers, the factory merely assembling this kit of parts.

Axle, Dead: An axle on which the wheels revolve, but which itself does not revolve.

Axle, Floating: A live axle in which the half-shafts carry none of the car weight, but just carry the wheels. There are also 'semi-floating' and 'three-quarter-floating' axles.

Axle, Live: An axle containing the shafts which drive the wheels.

Axle, Swing: A form of independent rear suspension in which the outer axle casings pivot around a fixed differential unit.

Beau de Rochas cycle: An obsolete term for the four-stroke cycle.

Belt drive: A transmission system using leather or rubber belts and pulleys to transmit power to the driving wheels.

bhp: Short for 'brake horse power' – though a visitor to the 1902 Crystal Palace Motor Show assured his girlfriend that it meant 'British horse power' ('When an Englishman says "10hp" he means 10; when a Frenchman says "10hp" he means 8').

Bi-block: An engine with its cylinders cast in two blocks (of two, three or four cylinders each).

Blower: A slang term for a supercharger (or a fan used to assist air cooling).

Boiler, Fire-tube: A tubular steel boiler with end plates connected by open-ended thin tubes through which the hot gases pass, heating the water surrounding the tubes to boiling point.

Boiler, Flash: A steam boiler in which steam is generated almost instantaneously, the boiler carrying only a minimum of water.

Boiler, Water-tube: A steam boiler with the water carried in tubes around which the hot gases circulate.

Brake, Band: A brake contracting on the outside of a drum.

Brake, Disc: The most efficient form of car brake; callipers grip the faces of a revolving disc.

Brake, Drum: Commonly used, this type of brake has shoes expanding inside a drum.

Brakes, Mechanical: Little used since the 1950s except to operate parking brake mechanisms, this once-universal braking system uses metal rods or cables to actuate the brakes instead of hydraulic fluid operating in flexible pipes as in all modern cars.

Cam: A shaped piece of metal revolving on a shaft and imparting a regular motion to a rod or lever. Most importantly used to operate the engine valves.

Cardan: A universally jointed shaft driving the rear axle.

Chain drive: Linking gearbox to rear axle by chains and sprockets instead of shaft, this transmission system was mostly obsolete by 1914.

Clincher tyre: An obsolete design which has beads formed on the tyre which engage in channels on the wheel rims, air pressure in the tyre locking it to the rim.

Clutch, Cone: Instead of flat discs of friction material, the driving and driven faces of this type of clutch are sections of a cone.

Clutch, Scroll: Used mostly by Mercedes in pre-1914 days, this type of clutch employs the gripping action of a powerful steel spring coiled round a shaft.

Coil, Trembler: In early ignition systems, trembler coils 'buzzed' like a doorbell to make-and-break the primary ignition circuit.

Compound engine: A multiple-expansion engine in which the steam (or, in at least one case, the exhaust gases of a petrol engine), after leaving the high-pressure cylinders, is exhausted into a low-pressure cylinder to make maximum use of its expansive energy.

Connecting rod: The rod which links piston to crankshaft.

Crypto gear: An epicyclic transmission using sun-and-planet gears.

cv: The French unit of horsepower (*cheval vapeur* = 'steam horse').

De Dion axle: Originally invented for De Dion Bouton steam carriages by Bouton's brother-in-law Trépardoux, this system uses a dead rear axle and independent universally jointed half-shafts to transmit power from a differential unit fixed to the frame.

Desaxé: A cylinder offset relative to the centre of the crankshaft, the theory being that the connecting rod gives a more direct thrust to the crankshaft on the working stroke, increasing mechanical efficiency and reducing wear.

Desmodromic: Valves which are both opened *and* closed mechanically. Normally only found in racing engines.

Diesel engine: An internal combustion engine in which the compression in the cylinders is so great that it ignites the fuel/air mixture.

dohc: Double overhead camshaft.

Dos-à-dos: A four-seater car with the passengers sitting back to back.

Drip feed: A primitive lubrication system in which oil was dripped through visible sight feeds on the dash before feeding the various engine bearings. Sometimes known as a 'total loss' (or to disgruntled owners, 'dead loss') system as the theory was that, if you increased the drip rate to the point where the exhaust was just tinged with oil smoke, then the engine was being adequately lubricated.

Dry-sump lubrication: Generally used on racing engines, this system uses a remote oil tank with a feed pump supplying oil to the engine bearings and a scavenge pump taking it from the engine and returning it to the tank.

eoi: Exhaust over inlet valves; *see* F-head.

Epicyclic gear: An internally toothed drum containing 'planetary' gears which revolve around the main shaft, which carries a 'sun' gear wheel with which they mesh.

F-head: An engine with (normally) overhead inlet and side exhaust valves, though the alternative configuration of side inlet, overhead exhaust has been used.

Flat-twin (or -four): An engine with opposed horizontal cylinders.

Four-stroke engine: An engine operating on the four cycles (in two crankshaft revolutions) of induction, compression, ignition, exhaust (or, vulgarly, 'suck, squeeze, bang, blow').

4wd: Four-wheel drive.

Friction drive: Formerly used on light cars of feeble performance, this transmission system dispensed with gearing, using instead a friction wheel at right angles to the flywheel, and capable of being moved across its face so that varying drive ratios (and reverse) could be obtained.

fwb: Front-wheel brakes.

fwd: Front-wheel drive.

Gravity feed: A system for supplying fuel to the carburettor by mounting the tank above the level of the jet so that it flowed naturally without the need for a fuel pump. If the tank was mounted too low (as on the Model T Ford, where it was under the driver's seat), the car would have to be reversed up hills when the fuel level was low, to maintain sufficient head of fuel at the jet.

Horsepower: The rate of energy expended in a given time by a motor. One horsepower represents the energy expended in raising 33,000lb by 1 foot in 60 seconds. Some early cars were advertised with two horsepower figures (e.g. 20/24hp), representing power at 1000rpm, and a (usually optimistic) maximum power output.

Hot-tube ignition: An ignition system used on some primitive engines instead of electric ignition (or, where electric ignition was fitted and mistrusted, as an emergency ignition), in which a closed metal (usually platinum) tube projecting into the combustion chamber was heated outside the cylinder by a Bunsen burner fed by the petrol supply. When the compressed gas/air mixture came into contact with this tube, ignition took place.

ifs: Independent front suspension.

ioe: Inlet over exhaust valves; *see* F-head.

irs: Independent rear suspension.

Jackshaft: In chain-drive transmission, a shaft running across the frame with a sprocket at either end from which the drive to the rear wheels by chain is taken.

Junk ring: The equivalent of a piston ring used to seal the sleeves in a sleeve-valve engine.

Knight engine: A sleeve-valve engine with two sleeves per cylinder.

Landaulette: A formal car whose rear portion may be opened.

L-head: A side-valve engine with inlet and exhaust valves on one side of the block, actuated by a single camshaft.

Low-tension ignition: A magneto which initially generates a low voltage current.

Magneto: Once the most common form of ignition, a magneto is an electric generator which produces the ignition current independently of any batteries. A low-tension magneto uses a coil to amplify the current, whereas a high-tension magneto produces sufficient current on its own.

Monobloc: An engine with all its cylinders cast in one piece.

ohc: Overhead camshaft.

ohv: Overhead valves.

Otto cycle: The four-stroke cycle of internal combustion, named after Dr. Nikolas August Otto who introduced it in his 'silent gas engine' of 1876. (There was also a curious pedal-propelled two-wheeler called the Otto dicycle.)

Pair-cast: An engine with its cylinders cast in blocks of two cylinders.

Petrol: Known as 'gasoline' in the USA, this colourless, inflammable and increasingly costly liquid distilled from crude petroleum is the most commonly used motor fuel. The word 'Petrol', however, is strictly speaking a trade name belonging to Carless, Capel & Leonard, of London, dating from the end of the nineteenth century.

Petrol-electric: A transmission system in which an internal-combustion engine, running at more or less constant speed, drives a dynamo supplying current to electric motors, sometimes mounted in the wheel hubs, sometimes in the final drive. Because an internal-combustion engine running at a constant speed is most economical, this obsolete transmission system is being re-examined.

Phaeton: An open touring car.

Planetary gear: Another name for Epicyclic gear.

Poppet valve: The conventional type of valve used in four-stroke engines.

Port: An aperture through which gases enter or leave the cylinder.

PS: The German unit of horsepower (*pferde stärke*).

Pushrods: Steel rods actuating overhead valves through the medium of rockers; pushrods are operated by cams low down in the crankcase.

RAC rating: Used mostly to determine taxation liability, this method of calculation of power output ignores the engine stroke. RAC rating is the bore in millimetres squared, multiplied by the number of cylinders and divided by 1613.

Roi-des-Belges: An open car with elaborately contoured seat backs based, it is said, on the armchairs in the boudoir of Cléo de Mérode, dancer and *petite amie* of King Leopold II of Belgium, for whom the first body of this type was made (1902).

Rotary engine: Early rotary engines had cylinders which rotated around a stationary crankshaft, the misapprehension under which their promotors laboured being that the gyroscopic effect steadied the engine, while the revolving cylinders were better cooled than static cylinders. Modern rotary engines – the Wankel is the most successful, but has found only limited application – have rotating 'pistons' running inside a specially shaped combustion chamber and geared to an output shaft.

Rotary valve: Driven by chain or gearing, rotary valves incorporated ports which communicated with inlet or exhaust ports. Supposedly more silent than poppet valves, they were very difficult to lubricate properly and therefore tended to seize.

rpm: Revolutions per minute.

Rumble seat: American equivalent of 'dickey seat'.

Runabout: A low-powered two-seater car.

Sleeve valve: The double sleeve-valve engine invented by C. Y. Knight has two concentric sliding sleeves surrounding the piston, operated by a shaft revolving at half engine speed; on the inlet stroke slots formed in the two sleeves coincide in register with the inlet port, on the exhaust stroke slots in both sleeves reveal the exhaust port, and on the compression and firing strokes the ports are out of line. Single sleeve-valve engines have one sleeve incorporating slots, which is twisted to and fro as it goes up and down to uncover the ports.

Slide valve: A relation of the sleeve valve, only the slide valves form just part of the cylinder wall, sliding up and down to reveal inlet and exhaust ports.

Splash lubrication: A system by which the big-end bearings are lubricated by the revolving crankshaft dipping into troughs, which are replenished by a pump or by scoops on the flywheel.

Supercharger: A device for forcing fuel/air into the cylinder for extra power.

Surface carburettor: The most primitive form of carburettor, consisting of a container in which petrol, agitated by the motion of the car, gives off inflammable vapour, which is drawn into the cylinder and ignited.

sv: Side valve.

T-head: An early type of side-valve engine layout with the inlet valves on one side of the cylinder head and the exhaust valves on the other, necessitating the use of two camshafts.

Tonneau: An early form of four-seat car with back seats entered through a rear door.

Tourer: An open car, normally with four/five seats.

Town car: A formal car with an open driver's seat and the rear seats enclosed.

Two-stroke: An engine cycle with a power impulse every other stroke. The fuel/air mixture is sucked into the crankcase and compressed beneath the piston before passing into the combustion chamber through ports in the cylinder wall uncovered by the piston. This system eliminates valves and timing gear, but is less efficient than the four-stroke cycle.

Vis-à-vis: A four-seater car with the passengers facing each other.

Walking beam: A long rocker arm which operates overhead valves from a camshaft set low down in the crankcase.

Worm drive: A form of final drive using helical worm screw gears instead of bevel gears.

Conversion factors

Table of cylinder bores and strokes in millimetres and inches

The following figures are approximate, and intended only as a rough guide for comparison.

Millimetres		Inches
62 × 100	...	$2^7/_{16}$ × $3^{15}/_{16}$
65 × 120	...	$2^9/_{16}$ × 4¾
66 × 70	...	$2^9/_{16}$ × 2¾
67 × 70	...	2⅝ × 2¾
67 × 73	...	2⅝ × 2⅞
67 × 77	...	2⅝ × 3
70 × 70	...	2¾ × 2¾
70 × 73	...	2¾ × 2⅞
70 × 77	...	2¾ × 3
72 × 77	...	$2^{13}/_{16}$ × 3
73 × 73	...	2⅞ × 2⅞
73 × 80	...	2⅞ × 3⅛
77 × 77	...	3 × 3
77 × 80	...	3 × 3⅛
77 × 83	...	3 × 3¼
78 × 78	...	$3^1/_{16}$ × $3^1/_{16}$
80 × 80	...	3⅛ × 3⅛
80 × 86	...	3⅛ × 3⅜
83 × 83	...	3¼ × 3¼
83 × 86	...	3¼ × 3⅜
86 × 86	...	3⅜ × 3⅜
84 × 90	...	$3^5/_{16}$ × $3^9/_{16}$
90 × 90	...	$3^9/_{16}$ × $3^9/_{16}$
90 × 110	...	$3^9/_{16}$ × $4^5/_{16}$
95 × 115	...	3¾ × $4^9/_{16}$
100 × 115	...	$3^{15}/_{16}$ × $4^9/_{16}$
105 × 118	...	4⅛ × 4⅝
108 × 120	...	4¼ × 4¾
110 × 125	...	$4^5/_{16}$ × $4^{15}/_{16}$
112 × 128	...	$4^7/_{16}$ × $5^1/_{16}$
114 × 130	...	4½ × 5⅛
116 × 134	...	$4^9/_{16}$ × $5^5/_{16}$
118 × 138	...	4⅝ × $5^7/_{16}$
120 × 140	...	4¾ × 5½
122 × 143	...	$4^{13}/_{16}$ × 5⅝
124 × 146	...	4⅞ × 5¾
126 × 148	...	$4^{15}/_{16}$ × $5^{13}/_{16}$
128 × 150	...	$5^1/_{16}$ × $5^{15}/_{16}$
130 × 152	...	5⅛ × 6
140 × 160	...	5½ × 6⅜

1 in	=	2.54cm
1 cu in	=	16.3871cc
1 metre	=	3.28ft
1 gallon (Imp)	=	4.546 litres
1 pint	=	0.568 litres
1 gallon (Imp)	=	1.2 gallon (US)
1 lb	=	0.454kg
1 ton	=	1016kg
1 litre	=	61.02cu in
1 mkg	=	7.233lb ft
10 psi	=	0.703kg/sq cm
1 bhp	=	745.7 watts

$$\text{Litres}/100\text{km} = \frac{282.5}{\text{mpg}}$$

$$\text{Mph}/1{,}000\text{rpm} = \frac{60{,}000}{\text{gear ratio} \times \text{rev/mile}}$$

$$\text{RAC hp} = \frac{D^2 \times N}{2.5} \quad (D=\text{bore dia.}) \quad (N=\text{no. of cyl.})$$

$$\text{B.m.e.p.} = \frac{2.47 \times \text{torque (lb ft)}}{\text{displacement (cc)}}$$

Mean piston speed = 0.0656 × stroke (cm) × rpm

1bhp = 1.014CV

To find the cubic capacity of an engine, square the bore diameter (in centimetres or inches), multiply by .7854, and multiply the result by the stroke. Then multiply by number of cylinders.

1 volume of petrol yields 276 volumes of petrol vapour.
1lb of petrol requires 200 volumes of air for complete combustion.

Gradients

A grade of 1 in 5 equals 20 per cent or angle of 11° 19′

	per cent	angle
1 in 6	17	9° 26′
1 in 7	14	8° 09′
1 in 8	12½	7° 08′
1 in 9	11	6° 17′
1 in 10	10	5° 43′
1 in 11	9	5° 11′
1 in 12	8	4° 46′
1 in 13	7¾	4° 24′
1 in 14	7	4° 05′

Acknowledgements

The publishers would like to thank the following for providing the photographs used in this book: Alfa Romeo (GB) Ltd.; Associated Press Ltd.; James O. Barron; David Burgess Wise; Citroën Cars Ltd.; Daimler-Benz AG Bildarchiv; Pedr Davis; Mirco Decet; Mary Evans Picture Library; Michael Fear; Fiat Motor Company; Ford Motor Company; General Motors; Geoffrey Goddard; Nancy Hoffman Gallery, New York; Robert Lamplough; Mark Lawrence; Mansell Collection; Keith Marvin; Michelin Tyre Co.; Motor Magazine; Musée National des Techniques, Paris; National Motor Museum, Beaulieu; Orbis Publishing; Pininfarina; Jacques Potherat; Hervé Poulain; Renault Ltd.; Saab (GB) Ltd.; Jasper Spencer Smith; Erwin Tragatsch; D. B. Tubbs; Waddington and Tooth Galleries Ltd, London; Nicky Wright.